1900s

- **1906** Nichrome wire used as an element in electric fires for the first time.
- **1906** Women aged over 24 get the vote in Finland.
- **1906** San Francisco, California, is razed to the ground by a violent earthquake and fire.
- **1907** New Zealand becomes independent from British rule.

- **1907** More than 1 million immigrants enter US.
- **1907** First circus is set up by the Ringling brothers.
- **1908** The first international soccer match is played in Austria.
- **1908** The first Model T Ford goes on sale in the US.

- **1909** The SOS danger signal is first used at sea for a wreck off the Azores.
- **1909** Curtis Model-D pusher flies in first speed contest.

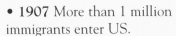

1910s

- **1916** Irish nationalists stage an Easter uprising in Dublin.
- **1916** One million Allied and German soldiers die in the Somme offensive in France.
- **1916** The Russian monk Gregory Rasputin is murdered by two relatives of the czar.
- **1917** Czar Nicholas II abdicates.

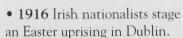

World War I on the side of the Allies.
- **1917** The Bolsheviks, led by Lenin, seize power in Russia.
- **1917** Mata Hari, the exotic dancer, is executed by the French for spying.
- **1918** In the Urals, the Russian royal family is murdered in a cellar.

- **1918** Led by Faisal and T. E. Lawrence, Arab forces capture Damascus, Syria.
- **1918** The Great War ends and peace comes to Europe.

1920s

- **1927** Duke Ellington begins playing at the Cotton Club.
- **1927** US pilot Charles Lindbergh flies nonstop across the Atlantic.
- **1927** The first "talkie," US film *The Jazz Singer*, stars Al Jolson.
- **1927** Tomb of Genghis Khan found.

- **1927** In China, Chiang Kai-shek crushes attempted coup by communists.
- **1927** Model A Ford is released on the market with a choice of four colors.
- **1928** Flying doctor service begins in Australia.
- **1929** Valentine Day's massacre in Chicago, Illinois.

- **1929** Benito Mussolini's Fascist Party rigs an election in Italy and forms a government.
- **1929** US Wall Street crash leads to world financial crisis.

1930s

- **1936** 200 out-of-work UK men go on the Jarrow hunger march.
- **1936** German troops march into the cities of the Rhineland.
- **1936** Edward VIII of the UK abdicates to marry a divorcee.
- **1936** France abandons the Gold Standard and prints money freely.

- **1937** *Marie Claire* magazine is launched in Paris, France.
- **1938** Austria is made a German province.
- **1938** Action Comics, with Superman, is launched.
- **1939** After the invasion of Poland, Britain and France declare war on Germany.

- **1939** Soviet Igor Sikorsky designs the first helicopter with rotor arms for lift.

1940s

- **1944** Starving Dutch resort to eating tulip bulbs.
- **1945** Hitler and Eva Braun commit suicide in Berlin.
- **1945** Germany surrenders and Europe celebrates VE Day.
- **1945** After two atom bombs are dropped, Japan surrenders.
- **1946** The United Nations holds its first session.

- **1947** Marshall Plan offers aid to countries in western Europe.
- **1947** Dutch Jewish girl Anne Frank's war diary is published.
- **1947** US pilot Chuck Yeager flies faster than the speed of sound.
- **1948** Mahatma Gandhi is assassinated at prayers in India.
- **1948** Jewish leaders declare the new Jewish state of Israel.

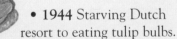
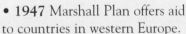

- **1948** Birth-rate soars in a postwar baby boom.
- **1949** NATO (the North Atlantic Treaty Organization) is formed.

CHILDREN'S HISTORY OF THE
20th
CENTURY

CHILDREN'S
HISTORY OF THE
20th
CENTURY

A DK Publishing Book
www.dk.com

A DK Publishing Book
www.dk.com

Senior editors Bridget Hopkinson, Miranda Smith
Senior art editor Andrew Nash
Editors Susila Baybars, Laura Buller,
Julie Ferris, Melanie Halton, Helena Spiteri
US editor Camela Decaire
Art editors Diane Klein, Sharon Spencer
Designers Goldberry Broad, Carlton Hibbert,
Joseph Hoyle, Susan St. Louis
Managing editors Gillian Denton, Linda Martin
Managing art editor Julia Harris
Production Charlotte Traill
Picture research Melissa Albany, Jo Carlill,
James Clarke, Kathy Lockley
Research Prue Grice, Sean Stancioff
DTP designer Nicola Studdart

Written by Simon Adams, Robin Cross,
Ann Kramer, Haydn Middleton, Sally Tagholm

First American Edition, 1999
6 8 10 9 7 5

Published in the United States by DK Publishing, Inc.
95 Madison Avenue
New York, New York 10016
Copyright © 1999 Dorling Kindersley Limited, London

Material from this book originally published as
Junior Chronicle of the 20th Century in 1997

Published in Great Britain by Dorling Kindersley Limited.

A catalog record for this book is available from the Library of Congress.

ISBN 0 7894 4722 3

Color reproduction by Colourscan, Singapore
Printed and bound in China by L.Rex Printing Co., Ltd.

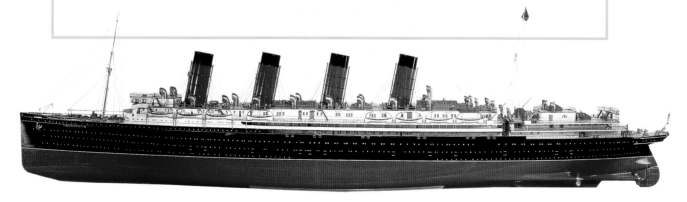

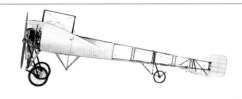

FOREWORD

The 20th century has been a time of unique change, exploration, discovery, and invention. CHILDREN'S HISTORY OF THE 20TH CENTURY first looks at the best and the worst of the past 100 years and voices children's hopes for the future. It then proceeds to tell the story of an extraordinary century month by month, year by year. Lively news stories and dramatic images bring to life the historic events that have transformed the world, as well as lesser events of particular interest to younger readers.

The Wright brothers' first flight, Neil Armstrong's historic steps on the Moon, the splitting of the atom, the creation of antimatter, television, satellites, two world wars, AIDS, and the struggle for democracy have all played a major part in defining the 20th century. Disney cartoons, trend-setting fashions, musical innovations, and the microchip have also left their mark.

Throughout the book, special pages examine in depth topics such as life in the trenches in World War I, the "Roaring Twenties," the Spanish Civil War, movies, the "Swinging Sixties," the Vietnam War, the end of the Cold War, space exploration, the impact of information technology, and prospects for the new millennium. The world leaders, sports and movie stars, musicians, inventors and scientists, and even lawbreakers who have made this century memorable have their own section in the back of the book. With its groundbreaking news stories, CHILDREN'S HISTORY OF THE 20TH CENTURY is a detailed diary of world events, presenting all the changes of this incredible century as they happened.

CONTENTS

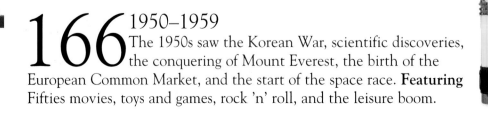

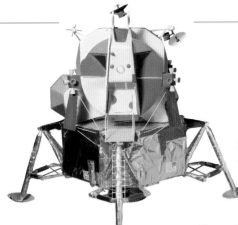

190 1960–1969
The "Swinging Sixties" was a decade of miniskirts, flower power, pop music, the US civil rights movement, and China's cultural revolution. **Featuring** the race to the Moon, Sixties culture, television, and peace and protest.

220 1970–1979
A decade of international terrorism, protest, political scandal, platform shoes, and punk music. **Featuring** the war in Vietnam, the feminist fight, sounds of the Seventies, and the microchip revolution.

250 1980–1989
Yuppies, AIDS, power dressing, gender bending, superpowers, and conservative politics defined the Eighties. **Featuring** Live Aid, minimalism, the "green" movement, and the end of the Cold War.

280 1990–1999
The Nineties saw the Gulf War, ethnic conflicts, international cooperation, and the rise of the Internet. **Featuring** the technological "global village," Nineties music, the end of apartheid, space exploration, and hopes for the future.

Century at a Glance

THE 21ST CENTURY

JANUARY 1, 1900, WAS WELCOMED around the world with fireworks and celebrations. People were excited about the new century, but no one could have imagined the immense changes the 20th century would bring. Now we are on the brink of another era – the 21st century. The world in the last 100 years has changed almost beyond recognition, and as we look forward to the millennium celebrations, we asked today's young people how they will remember the past and what their hopes are for the future.

THE PAST 100 YEARS, THE WORST

AS THE 20TH CENTURY MOVES into the 21st, what do you think you will remember of the last 100 years? It has been a time of amazing contrasts, bringing both positive and negative changes. Technological advances have revolutionized the way we live, but not without cost – industrial pollution has seriously damaged the environment, and millions of people have died as the result of improved military technology.

SOLDIERS IN WORLD WAR I, 1914–1918

"Millions of people were killed in the World Wars and countless families suffered from losses. Countries were destroyed. Imagine bombs bombarding your town at night, a bomb tearing through your house, and destroying every possession you own."
Lindsey Anderson, aged 13, South Dakota

"World War II is something that should never be repeated."
Jessica Alatorre, aged 13, Florida

"Nuclear weapons are extremely dangerous. This was proved during the bombing of Hiroshima and Nagasaki during World War II. People suffered severe aftereffects for many years. If nuclear weapons are not restricted they will eventually destroy the whole world."
Philip Conheady, aged 14, Norway

THE ATOM BOMB, FIRST DROPPED IN 1945

INDUSTRIAL POLLUTION

"Large amounts of pollution have caused a hole in the ozone layer. The pollution is harming humans and animals by making them breathe hazardous chemicals. It is also harming our environment by killing trees and plants."
Jason Harmon, aged 14, Tennessee

...AND THE BEST

The 20th century has also seen some of the greatest innovations in history. In particular, faster communications have changed the way we view the world and given us a new sense of global citizenship.

ALEXANDER FLEMING DISCOVERED PENICILLIN IN 1928

THE MICROCHIP, INVENTED IN 1971

"The invention of computers
and the Internet is one of the positive things that has happened in the 20th century. Computers support many businesses and run numerous things that people take for granted, such as traffic lights and elevators. The Internet is a great way to access information, buy items, and communicate with people around the world."
Maud Holma, aged 13, Finland

"The discovery of penicillin was very important.
Until its discovery, countless people died from infections that can now be cured by the use of the antibiotic."
Josh Golden, aged 14, Texas

INTERNATIONAL PASSENGER JET

HOMER SIMPSON, ONE OF THE 20TH CENTURY'S POPULAR TV CHARACTERS

"Television is one of the best inventions of the
past 100 years. It is an easy method of communication used throughout the world which makes people aware of what is happening in different places."
Kristina Madsen, aged 13, New York

"Improved methods of transportation have been a positive development.
Instead of traveling by ship to another country, you can take a jet plane."
Kristina Madsen, aged 13, New York

NELSON MANDELA, ELECTED PRESIDENT OF SOUTH AFRICA IN 1994

"The end of apartheid proves that there is still hope for decency."
Rachel Greenes, aged 13, Alaska

"The ending of apartheid
in South Africa was one of the most significant events of this century. The laws of apartheid determined where black people would be able to live, what jobs they could have, and what kind of an education they would receive. Racial tension between blacks and whites, as well as the intervention of the rest of the world, resulted in the first democratic vote in 1994 when the great leader Nelson Mandela came to power."
Angie van der Merwe, aged 13, South Africa

HOW WOULD YOU CHANGE THE WORLD?

HARVESTING RICE
IN THE HIMALAYAS

HOW CAN WE CREATE a peaceful world for people to live in? What can we do to protect the environment? Can we provide enough food for everyone on our planet? These are just some of the questions facing us in the 21st century. What would you do to make the world a better place?

"To ensure that there was enough food for everyone in the world, I would try to provide both the means and the money for everyone to grow their own food or trade for things they can't grow themselves. In times of need other countries would lend supplies."
Rory McCann,
aged 14,
Great Britain

THE TIGER IS ONE OF THE WORLD'S ENDANGERED ANIMALS

"I would do everything I could to try and give everyone an equal chance in life."
Lucy Dunn, aged 12,
Great Britain

"I would make more animal sanctuaries for endangered species such as tigers, gorillas, pandas, and whales. I would make sure that the nature reserves were protected."
Nanna Krebs, aged 14, Denmark

"Wind turbines could be put into places where wind is naturally channeled – on the slopes of hills and in open, flat areas, and mini-turbines could be put along the sides of high buildings in city streets to generate power."
Finn McCann, aged 12,
Great Britain

WIND TURBINES
GENERATE ELECTRICITY
WITHOUT POLLUTION

PEACE RALLY IN
NORTHERN IRELAND

"I would like it if countries
found a peaceful solution to their
differences of opinion."
*Jason Shonibone, aged 12,
Great Britain*

"I would stop all wars and
make peace in the world."
Akkan Adil, aged 12, Great Britain

"I would make policies to counteract the
effects of global warming. I would plant
a tree to replace every tree that is cut down. In this
way, I would be able to keep the levels of our vital
gas, oxygen, up. I would also keep carbon dioxide
levels down."
Joss Garman, aged 13, Great Britain

TREE SEEDLING READY
FOR PLANTING

HUMPBACK
WHALE

"There are some
beautiful creatures
in the world and it is our
duty to protect them."
*Zuzi Feltham, aged 11,
Great Britain*

THE NEXT 100 YEARS

THE LAST 100 YEARS have seen amazing inventions such as the computer and the space rocket. In the next 100 years, technological advances will continue to affect the way we live. By 2100, people may live longer, have robot servants, and be able to take vacations in space. What do you think life will be like in the 21st century?

"I think that we will probably land on Mars and other planets in our solar system. Maybe people will be going into space on a regular basis. Other planets could be used as an alternative place to live for humans."
Alicyn Farren, aged 14, Massachusetts

"Our knowledge of space will expand into new dimensions."
Nick Christiansen, aged 13, Maryland

"Children will be taught at home by computers."
Nicole Hawksby, aged 13, Massachusetts

"Pupils of the 21st century will be linked to virtual schools which will offer individualized learning programs designed to suit their individual needs and learning styles. Going to school will mean logging on to a computer.
Mark Henry, aged 12, Northern Ireland

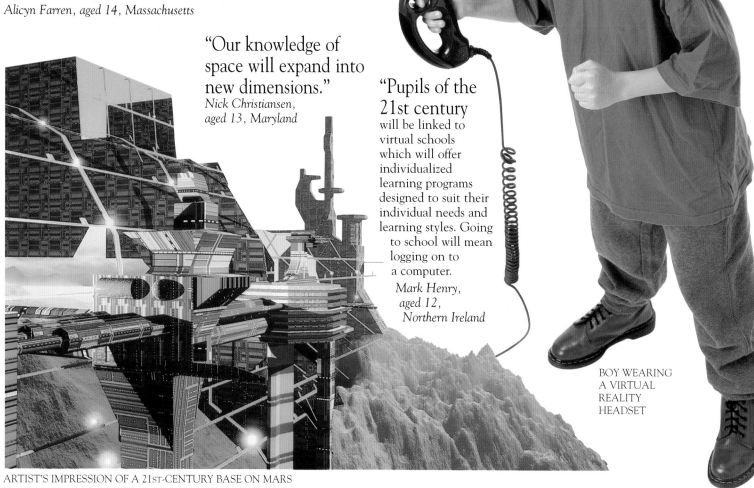

ARTIST'S IMPRESSION OF A 21ST-CENTURY BASE ON MARS

BOY WEARING A VIRTUAL REALITY HEADSET

"I believe that in 100 years' time we will have flying cars."
Anna Rhodes, aged 14, Australia

"You will be able to fly a car and you will no longer have to drive, because you will tell the car where to go and it will take you there."
Whitney Davidson, aged 13, Indiana

FLYING CARS FROM THE FILM *FIFTH ELEMENT* (1997)

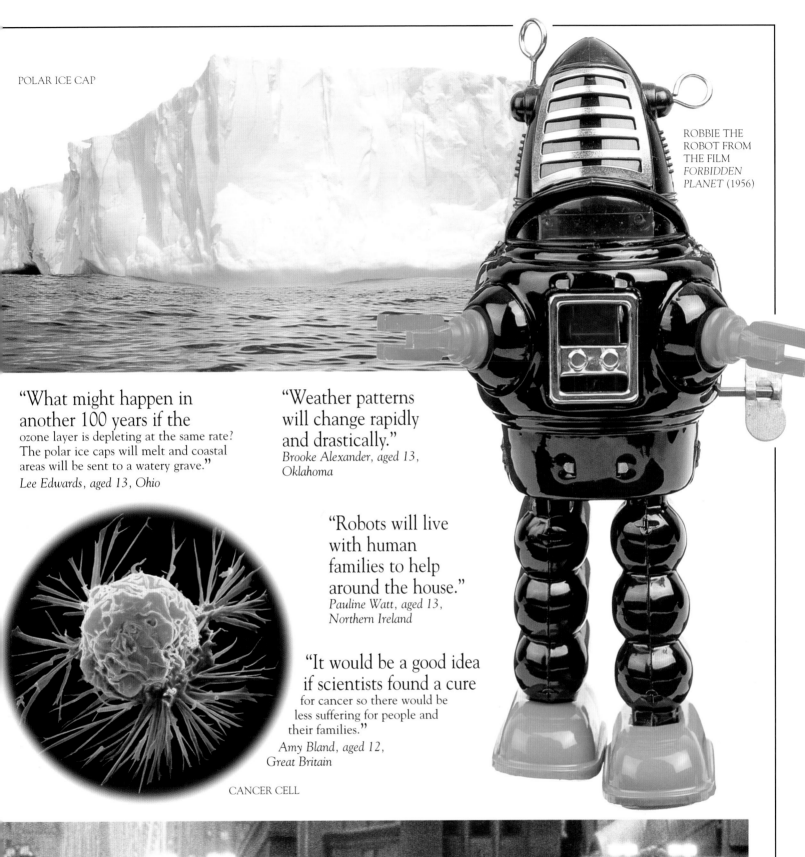

POLAR ICE CAP

ROBBIE THE
ROBOT FROM
THE FILM
*FORBIDDEN
PLANET* (1956)

"What might happen in another 100 years if the ozone layer is depleting at the same rate? The polar ice caps will melt and coastal areas will be sent to a watery grave."
Lee Edwards, aged 13, Ohio

"Weather patterns will change rapidly and drastically."
Brooke Alexander, aged 13, Oklahoma

"Robots will live with human families to help around the house."
Pauline Watt, aged 13, Northern Ireland

"It would be a good idea if scientists found a cure for cancer so there would be less suffering for people and their families."
Amy Bland, aged 12, Great Britain

CANCER CELL

1900

Dawn of the century

JANUARY 1

After celebrating wildly into the early hours of the morning, people woke up today to the dawn of a new century. In spite of concerns over the course of events in the South African War and the actions of Boxer rebels in China, the general feeling is one of optimism since the state of world affairs is far rosier than it was at the start of the 19th century. During the last 100 years there have been remarkable developments in communications and industry. Today there is every hope that along with further progress in these and other important fields, the years that follow will bring worldwide peace and prosperity.

Detail from a poster to celebrate the start of the 20th century

World Exhibition opens in Paris

APRIL 14

The president of France Émile Loubet today opened the World Exhibition in Paris, the biggest of its kind ever staged in Europe. The exhibition site covers 547 acres (221 hectares) along the Rue des Nations and the Quai d'Orsay. Among the sights on display are electrical illuminations in the Palace of Electricity (above) and the Hall of Illusions. In a pavilion dedicated to his sculpture, a new work by Auguste Rodin, *The Kiss*, is attracting great attention from art critics.

THE MAGIC OF OZ
The Wonderful Wizard of Oz, written by US author Frank Baum, is a new tale certain to enchant children. It tells of Dorothy, who is whisked away by a tornado to the magical land of Oz.

JANUARY–JUNE

World Events	**JAN** The British army is defeated by Boers at the Battle of Spion Kop in the South African, or Boer, War.	**MAR** In India, millions of famine victims appeal for help from the British government as their meager food supplies run out.	**MAY** The South African town of Mafeking is relieved by British forces after a seven-month siege by Boer troops.	**JUN** Chinese rebels, the "Fists of Righteous Harmony," known as the Boxers, try to expel all Europeans from China.
Entertainment	**FEB** US college tennis star Dwight F. Davis puts up a trophy for an international contest.	**MAR** New York University becomes the site for the Hall of Fame, set up for notable Americans.	**MAY** UK actress Lillie Langtry is a hit in the US with the play *The Degenerates*.	**MAY** The second Olympic Games opens in Paris and will run until the end of July.
Innovations	**FEB** Eastman Kodak Co. launches the Brownie Box camera in the US, priced $1. WALL PAINTING, KNOSSOS	**MAR** UK archaeologist Arthur Evans begins to unearth an ancient civilization at Knossos, Crete.	**APR** The world's first tape recorder, which uses magnetic wire, is demonstrated at the Paris Exhibition. BOX OF PLASTICINE	**MAY** Commercial production of Plasticine modeling clay begins in an old flour mill at Bathampton, UK.

HARBUTT'S PLASTICINE
For Home Modelling
A Game! A Toy! An Occupation!

1900

The final whistle

Casey Jones in Engine 638

APRIL 29

Casey Jones, a Kansas-born train driver, died today in an act of great heroism. Late in starting out from Memphis, Tennessee, Jones was pushing the *Cannon Ball Express* to its limits on the dangerous route to Canton, Mississippi. As he entered Vaughan, Mississippi, a stationary train forced him to slam on the brakes. Seeing that a collision was about to happen, he made his fireman jump out, but stayed himself to slow down the train and save many passengers' lives.

Paris Métro opens

JULY 10

Paris today celebrates the opening of the Chemin-de-Fer Métropolitain de Paris, the underground railroad Parisians have nicknamed "le Métro." Construction of the 6.25-mile (10-km) long railroad began in 1898. Many of the stations are designed by the architect Hector Guimard, whose ornate wrought-iron designs are winning praise across the city.

Métro entrance of Guimard design

Liftoff for Zeppelin

JULY 1

Count Ferdinand von Zeppelin's huge airship moved forward, backward, and sideways before it rose off the ground and finally proved it could fly. The maiden flight took place over Lake Constance, Switzerland, and lasted for more than an hour. The airship contains 16 cells filled with hydrogen gas and is powered by two 16 hp engines.

The latest tennis racket has a grooved grip and fishtail handle

Airship LZ1 rises above Lake Constance

US victory in first Davis Cup

AUGUST 10

The US tennis team today won the first International Lawn Tennis Trophy, the Davis Cup, at the Longwood Cricket Club, Boston, Mass. The US team was leading Britain 3–0 in a five-match series when rain forced an early end to the contest.

JULY–DECEMBER

JUL Umberto I, the king of Italy, is shot four times by an anarchist at Monza, near Milan, and dies almost immediately.

AUG German philosopher Friedrich Nietzsche, noted for his concept of the "superman," dies at the age of 56.

AUG The first long-distance bus service is introduced on the 200-mile (320-km) journey from London to Leeds in the UK.

COCA-COLA

AUG Allied European forces, 10,000 strong, storm Peking in China to end the 56-day siege by Boxer rebels.

AUG Coca-Cola, in the form of a syrup, is first brought to Europe from the US and is an immediate success.

SEP Italian explorer the Duke of Abruzzi comes closer to the north pole than anyone before him.

NOV British forces step up hostilities in South Africa by opening concentration camps and setting fire to Boer farms.

OCT Austrian psychiatrist Sigmund Freud publishes a groundbreaking book, *The Interpretation of Dreams*.

NOV Viennese scientist Dr. Karl Landsteiner discovers and classifies three different blood types.

SIGMUND FREUD

NOV Republican William McKinley wins a second term in the White House as US president.

NOV Oscar Wilde, the notorious Irish playwright and wit, dies in exile in Paris at the age of 44.

DEC German Max Planck proposes his Quantum Theory of energy in atom-sized units.

1901

Australia gains its independence

JANUARY 1

A new country was born this morning when the six British colonies in Australia joined together as an independent nation. The Commonwealth of Australia, as the new country is formally known, is holding celebrations in Sydney today that will draw an estimated 50,000 people. A new government, led by Edmund Barton, has already been formed. One of its first tasks will be to agree on a site for the new capital city.

End of an era

Queen Victoria

JANUARY 22

After a short illness, Victoria, Queen of Britain and Empress of India, died today at Osborne, her seaside home on the Isle of Wight, surrounded by close members of her family. She was 81. Victoria's reign lasted nearly 64 years, longer than any monarch before her. It was an age of expansion in which trade and industry flourished and the British Empire stretched to all four corners of the world.

New Mercedes made

MARCH 31

The German auto manufacturer Gottlieb Daimler today delivered a remarkable new car to Émil Jellinek, consul-general of the Austro-Hungarian Empire, in Nice, France. The high-performance car, especially made for the consul-general and named Mercedes after his daughter (above left), is an improved version of a model designed by Daimler two years ago. The Mercedes is unlike the horse-drawn carriages that are still a common sight on our roads. The car has a 4-cylinder, 5.9-liter engine, giving it a top speed of 50 mph (80 km/h).

The new high-performance Mercedes

JANUARY–JUNE

World Events	**FEB** Leaders from around the world come to London, UK, to attend the funeral of Queen Victoria.	**MAR** Students and workers stage riots in major Russian cities to protest against the new government regulations.	**MAY** In a confidential memorandum, the UK votes to uphold its policy of "splendid isolation" from events in Europe.	**JUN** A new constitution for Cuba is agreed upon that gives the US government almost total control over the island.
Entertainment	**JAN** Russian playwright Anton Chekhov's *Three Sisters* premieres in Moscow.	**JAN** Italian opera composer Giuseppe Verdi, best known for *Rigoletto*, dies at the age of 88.	**APR** French sculptor Auguste Rodin's new sculpture of Victor Hugo attracts criticism from art critics and patrons.	**MAY** French film producer Claude Grivolas invents a projector that makes three-dimensional pictures.
Innovations	**JAN** UK toy maker Frank Hornby introduces Meccano, a self-assembly engineering toy.	**MAR** The first diesel engine goes on exhibit, demonstrated by the Diesel Motor Co., Manchester, UK.	**MAY** The world's first multistory parking lot, made up of seven levels, opens off Piccadilly, London, UK.	**JUN** French physicist Henri Becquerel discovers small particles inside atoms known as electrons.

MECCANO

AUGUSTE RODIN

1901

Harlequin and His Companion *by Pablo Picasso*

Great art talent spotted in Paris

JUNE 24

An exhibition by a Spanish artist is receiving much praise in Paris. Nineteen-year-old Pablo Picasso from Malaga set up a studio in Montmartre earlier this year, and has become known as "Le Petit Goya" because of his native Andalusian hat. Picasso's paintings show a remarkable range of subjects. Dancers of the Moulin Rouge, children, courtesans, and race meetings are among the subjects that fill the canvases of this talented painter, who seems destined for future greatness.

US president dies

SEPTEMBER 14

US president William McKinley died early this morning, eight days after he was shot by Polish anarchist Leon Czolgosz while opening an exhibition in Buffalo, New York. At first the president's wounds were not thought to be serious, but in the last few days his medical condition has deteriorated rapidly.

Vice-President Theodore Roosevelt was tracked down in the Adirondack Mountains and brought back hastily to Buffalo, but he arrived a few hours after McKinley's death. Roosevelt took the oath of office as the new president this afternoon. At 42, he is the youngest ever United States president to come to power.

PING PONG IS THE LATEST CRAZE

Ping Pong fever is sweeping Europe and the United States this year as families convert their tables into indoor tennis courts. The game, originally known as Gossima, failed to catch on until its manufacturer changed its name to Ping Pong. The first tournament was held in December this year.

JULY–DECEMBER

SEP A peace protocol is signed in Peking, China, formally ending the Boxer Rebellion.

AUG Irish athlete Peter O' Connor sets a new world long-jump record of 24 ft 11 in (7.6 m).

JUL German doctor Robert Koch proposes that the bubonic plague may have been due solely to rats.

LITHOGRAPH BY TOULOUSE-LAUTREC

SEP The Ashanti kingdom in Africa is annexed by the UK to the Gold Coast Colony.

SEP French painter Henri de Toulouse-Lautrec dies in Malrome, southern France, at the age of 36.

AUG A new US car manufacturer is founded in Detroit, Michigan. It will produce Cadillac cars.

OCT Booker T. Washington is the first black American to be invited to dine at the White House in Washington, D.C.

OCT US yacht *Columbia* beats the UK *Shamrock II* in a very close finish to retain the America's Cup.

DEC US businessman King C. Gillette invents the disposable razor, revolutionizing home grooming.

REVERSE OF NOBEL PRIZE MEDAL

DEC The first Nobel Prizes are awarded in Norway and Sweden to those who have been of great benefit to humankind.

DEC Intrigue continues over the mystery author of *Claudine à Paris*, who is thought to be a woman.

DEC Italian inventor Guglielmo Marconi transmits the first radio signal across the Atlantic Ocean.

1902

Louis Tiffany's lamps are all the rage in modern homes

Major art show opens in Paris

APRIL 20

An exciting new exhibition of "modern style" art, or "Art Nouveau" as it is known in France, opened today at the Société Nationale des Beaux-Arts in Paris. This decorative arts style has been developing all over Europe for the past few years and is characterized by sinuous lines and patterns of organic forms. It can be seen in many places: from the posters of Alphonse Mucha and the jewelry of René Lalique, to the design of the Métro stations in Paris and the furnishings for our homes.

Méliès excels

MAY 1

A *Voyage to the Moon*, the latest film from French director Georges Méliès, has been made using sophisticated new techniques. Audiences will be spellbound at the special effects that run throughout this 13-minute production, which took three months and cost a record 10,000 francs to make. The plot, loosely based on a novel by Jules Verne, tells the story of six scientists who visit the Moon and are captured by the strange Sélénites.

The spacecraft lands in the eye of the Moon

Mount Pelée erupts

MAY 8

Of the 30,000 inhabitants of St. Pierre, the capital of the Caribbean island of Martinique, a drunk in jail was the only survivor when Mount Pelée erupted this morning. Shortly before 8 a.m. the volcano threw out a cloud of glowing gas that engulfed the port within minutes. An eyewitness on a ship in the harbor stated that a "wave of fire was on us and over us like a lightning flash." Latest reports confirm that all the buildings in the town have been destroyed.

JANUARY–JUNE

World Events	**JAN** After crushing the Boxer Rebellion, the Chinese imperial court returns to Peking.	**JAN** The UK signs an alliance with Japan to safeguard both countries' interests in China and Korea.	**APR** Russian and Chinese officials sign an agreement in Peking to restore Manchuria to Chinese control.	**JUN** Congress authorizes President Roosevelt to negotiate up to $40 million to build a canal across the Panama isthmus.
Entertainment	**JAN** Michigan beats Stanford in the first college Rose Bowl football game.	**MAR** UK author Conan Doyle publishes a new Holmes mystery, *The Hound of the Baskervilles*.	**APR** French film producer Charles Pathé opens a new film studio at Vincennes in Paris.	**JUN** Renault, the French car manufacturer, wins every prize in the first Paris–Vienna auto race.
Innovations	**FEB** US doctors prove that yellow fever is spread by a species of mosquito.	**FEB** *Motor Cycling*, a magazine for motorcycle enthusiasts, goes on sale in the UK.	**APR** Cecil Rhodes's will provides funds for US, German, and UK citizens to study at Oxford University.	**MAY** US inventor Thomas Edison develops a new longer-lasting and lightweight type of electric battery.

THE HOUND OF THE BASKERVILLES

THOMAS EDISON

1902

Boer War ends in South Africa

JUNE 1

Last night, in the Transvaal border town of Vereeniging, Boer leaders signed a peace treaty with Britain, finally ending the bitter conflict that has lasted for two years and seven months. The war started when the Boer states of the South African Republic, seeking to keep control of their rich goldfields, refused to give resident foreigners political rights. In signing the treaty, the Boers have agreed to meet the British terms: to lay down their weapons and recognize the British monarch as their sovereign. This bitter pill was made easier to swallow by the fact that the Boers will receive

£3 million from the British government to assist with the restocking and repairing of their farmlands. The treaty also promises that self-government will follow at a later date. These are such favorable terms that it is questionable who is in fact the real winner of the war.

Birth of the "teddy"

NOVEMBER 18

A cartoon by Clifford Berryman in the *Washington Post* has sparked the idea for a new children's toy. The cartoon shows US President Theodore "Teddy" Roosevelt refusing to shoot a captive bear cub while on an unsuccessful bear hunt in Mississippi. Toy makers are now eager to transform the cartoon bear into a toy made of brown plush with movable arms and legs. The "teddy" bear, as it is affectionately being called, is certain to be popular as a mascot for the well-respected president and future sales predictions are high.

The new toy bear is called "teddy" after President Roosevelt's nickname

PETER RABBIT DEBUTS

A charming character appeared in children's literature this year in Britain. Written and illustrated with watercolors by Beatrix Potter, *The Tale of Peter Rabbit* tells of mischievous Peter's adventure in Mr. McGregor's garden and introduces us to his sisters, Flopsy, Mopsy, and Cottontail.

JULY–DECEMBER

JUL The celebrated 1,000-year-old Gothic belltower of St. Mark's Cathedral in Venice, Italy, collapses during a safety inspection.

AUG French film director George Méliès reenacts the coronation of Edward VII in his film studio.

JUL German scientists patent the formula for barbituric acid, which is used to produce sleeping pills.

ST. MARK'S BELLTOWER

AUG At the age of 60 and despite concerns of ill health, Edward VII is crowned king of Britain in Westminster Abbey, London, UK.

SEP Émile Zola, French author of *Germinal* and *L'Assommoir*, dies from suffocation at the age of 62.

AUG The first parcel mail is sent from the UK to the US on the White Star ocean liner *Teutonic*.

OCT Russian exile Leon Trotsky escapes from Siberia and makes his way to London, UK, arriving at comrade Lenin's door.

OCT British writer Rudyard Kipling publishes a collection of *Just So Stories* for children.

NOV J. M. Bacon becomes the first person to cross the Irish Sea in a hot-air balloon.

JUST SO STORIES

DEC The Aswan Dam, a great engineering feat, officially opens in Egypt.

NOV Sales of Italian tenor Enrico Caruso's first record reach one million copies.

DEC Major Ronald Ross is given the Nobel Prize for his work on malaria.

1900 GERMAN ZEPPELIN
AIRSHIP *LZ1* FIRST LIFTS OFF

1909 FRENCH DEPERDUSSIN
MAKES SLEEK MONOPLANES

1909 MODEL-D PUSHER
WINS AIRSPEED CONTEST

Twelve seconds of glory

Soon after 10:30 a.m. on December 17, 1903, Orville Wright took to the air above the beach at Kitty Hawk, North Carolina. His first flight in *Flyer* lasted 12 seconds and covered 120 ft (36 m). By the fourth and final flight of the day, his brother Wilbur had covered 853 ft (260 m) in a flight lasting 59 seconds.

PIONEERS OF AVIATION

FOR HUNDREDS OF YEARS inventors had been devising ways of flying through the air with the ease of a bird. Although balloons and airships had taken to the skies, it was not until a cold December day in 1903 that the Wright brothers made the first powered, sustained, and heavier-than-air flight. After that, aircraft technology progressed at a rapid rate and aviators crossed first the English Channel and then the Atlantic and Pacific oceans. In 1914 the onset of World War I created a demand for fast, agile fighter planes, and by 1918 the airplane had become a relatively sophisticated and reliable machine. The introduction of passenger flights between major cities in the 1920s confirmed that a new age of travel had arrived.

Blériot crosses the Channel

In July 1909, French aviator Louis Blériot became the first person to fly across the English Channel. He took off from Sangatte, France, and flew northwest to land at Dover Castle in England after a flight lasting 43 minutes. His Type XI monoplane, which he designed, had control wires to warp the wings and was made of strong, flexible woods. After his flight, Blériot became a celebrity. More than 100 of his planes were ordered and he became the first large-scale aircraft manufacturer.

LOUIS
BLÉRIOT

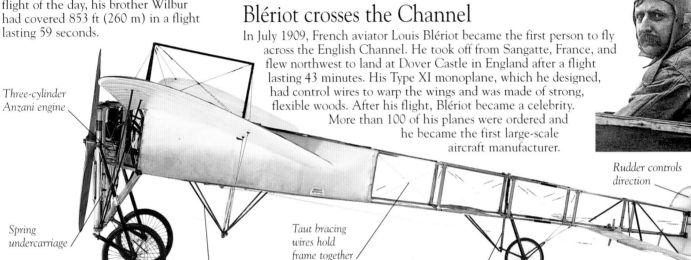

Three-cylinder Anzani engine

Spring undercarriage

Wing-warp control wires

Taut bracing wires hold frame together

Frame made of ash, hickory, and spruce

Rudder controls direction

BLÉRIOT TYPE XI 1909

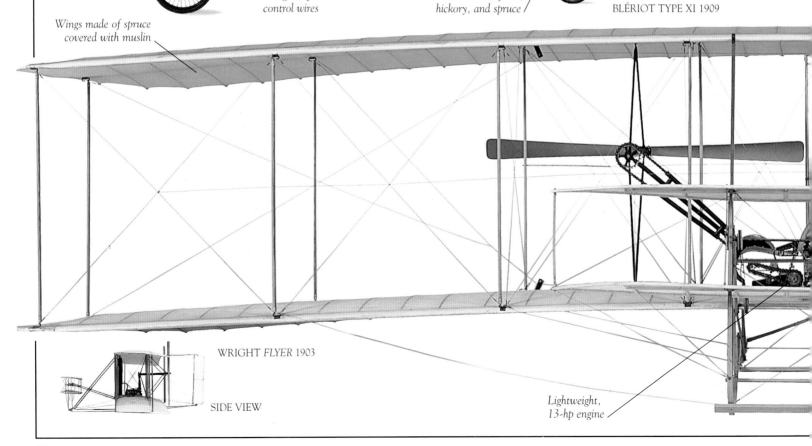

Wings made of spruce covered with muslin

WRIGHT *FLYER* 1903

SIDE VIEW

Lightweight, 13-hp engine

1915 FOKKER TRIPLANE
IS MADE BY THE DUTCH

1917 GERMAN LVG CVI
IS DEVELOPED FOR WAR

1917 AGILE SOPWITH PUP TAKES
PART IN DRAMATIC "DOGFIGHTS"

Air shows

Displays of flying skills quickly became popular as bold young aviators demonstrated incredible feats above the heads of adoring crowds. Many became superstars – Louis Paulham earned more than one million francs from his flying exploits.

GOGGLES

Cuffs with buttons to keep out the wind

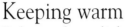

FUR-LINED
BOOTS

LEATHER
FLIGHT JACKET

Keeping warm

Early aircraft gave little protection to the pilots, who sat in uncomfortable seats that were open to the elements. Wool-lined leather jackets, sheepskin-lined gloves and boots, windproof leather helmets, and goggles were all needed to keep out the cold.

GLOVES

Women pilots

Women also put themselves in the record books. In 1930, Amy Johnson became the first woman to fly solo from Britain to Australia. Two years later, Amelia Earhart flew solo across the Atlantic Ocean.

Across the Atlantic

Piloting a Vickers-Vimy biplane, Captain John Alcock from Britain and US navigator Lieutenant Arthur Brown became the first people to fly nonstop across the Atlantic Ocean. They left Newfoundland on June 15, 1919, flying through fog and sleet storms to crash-land in an Irish bog 16 hours 12 minutes later. They covered the 1,900 miles (3,040 km) at an average speed of 120 mph (192 km/h).

Twin propellers were handmade by the Wright brothers

Interplane strut

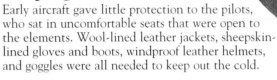

Harness supported the pilot

Twisting the wings

Flyer was able to achieve controlled flight because the Wright brothers developed a way to warp, or twist, the wings. A taut cable connected the wings and allowed either side of the craft to be lifted so that it could fly level or make banked turns.

1903

Slaughtered Jewish victims

Western film a smash success

MAY 15

A ten-minute film from US director Edwin S. Porter is breaking new ground in film production. *The Great Train Robbery* is set in the American West and the plot features cowboys and outlaws. The film is packed with action and suspense: a robbery, a horseback escape, and a chase by the local posse are punctuated with fist-fights and gunplay. The filming was done largely on location and clever editing gives the movie a realistic atmosphere that has not previously been achieved. The highlight of the film is when the head outlaw turns toward the camera and fires his Colt revolver at point-blank range. The screen then turns red, prompting screams from the audience! This formula is such a success that it is certain we will be seeing more films like this.

George Barnes, who plays the role of a gun-wielding outlaw

Pogroms in Russia

APRIL 16

In a pogrom, or organized attack, that began two days ago on Easter Monday, Russian peasants have murdered hundreds of Jews in Kishinev, southwestern Russia. The slaughter is an act of revenge for the killing of a Christian boy. Local people suspect that both he and a girl that was missing last week were killed by Jews. Police are turning a blind eye while the Jewish population, which makes up almost half of the 100,000 inhabitants of the town, is brutally attacked, and its homes and businesses are set on fire and destroyed.

NEW LONDON NOVEL

The Call of the Wild is the story of a tame dog that returns to the wild after his master dies and ends up leading a wolf pack. It is earning praise for its US author Jack London, who has based the tale on his experiences in Alaska.

JANUARY–JUNE

World Events

JAN A coronation reception is held on the great plains at Delhi to crown Edward VII emperor of India.

MAR In an attempt to keep undesirables out, the US imposes a $2 head tax on all immigrants entering the country.

APR In Holland, the Dutch government forces an end to the strike of railroad and dock workers by calling in troops.

JUN The Serbian king and queen are murdered by rebellious army officers who burst into the Royal Palace in Belgrade.

Entertainment

JAN A musical production of *The Wonderful Wizard of Oz* opens on Broadway, New York City.

MAR An exhibition of modern art, including works by Matisse and Derain, opens in Paris, France.

MAY French painter Paul Gauguin, known for his Tahiti paintings, dies in the South Pacific at the age of 54.

MAY The first Paris–Madrid road race is abandoned when six die at Bordeaux on the first day.

Innovations

JAN UK doctor Henry Smith perfects the operation for curing eye cataracts.

AN IMMIGRANT FAMILY

FEB US dentists propose that porcelain can replace gold or silver for filling teeth or making crowns.

MAY The first outdoor telephone kiosk, installed in High Holborn, London, UK, goes into operation.

DETAIL FROM A GAUGUIN PAINTING

JUN The year-old Pepsi-Cola company registers its trade name "Pepsi-Cola" in the US.

1903

Cyclist sweeps to victory

JULY 19

After 19 grueling days in the saddle, Maurice Garin, a 32-year-old chimney sweep from France, today won the first Tour de France cycle race. Cyclists started the six-stage race in Paris on July 1 and covered a distance of 1,509 miles (2,428 km), with stops at Lyons, Marseilles, Toulouse, Bordeaux, and Nantes. Garin finished in fine style, 2 hours 49 minutes ahead of his nearest rival, the unknown Louis Pothier, "the butcher of Sens." Of the original 60 entrants, only 21 finished the race, which was the brainchild of *Le Vélo* journalist Henri Desgrange. Over the past weeks, crowds have flocked to watch and cheer the cyclists on, and the Tour has been the talk of France. Organizers hope to make it an annual event in the future.

Maurice Garin speeds his way to victory on the latest make of racing bicycle

Baseball battle

OCTOBER 13

Boston beat Pittsburgh 5–3 in the first World Series baseball competition in the United States. The new contest pits the winners of the National League against those of the American League in an end-of-season showdown. Favored to win, Pittsburgh was outplayed by Boston, and Patrick Dougherty hit two homers to ensure victory.

Woman wins the Nobel

DECEMBER 10

French scientist Marie Curie became the first woman to win a Nobel Prize when she was given the award for physics today. She shares the prize with her husband Pierre and colleague Henri Becquerel, in recognition of the work they have done to investigate the scientific mystery of what they are calling "radioactivity." Polish-born Marie proved several years ago that it is always present in uranium atoms, and has been working on the phenomenon ever since.

Marie and Pierre Curie in their laboratory

JULY–DECEMBER

AUG At its congress in the UK, the Russian Social Democratic Party splits into Mensheviks and Bolsheviks.	**SEP** Turks massacre 50,000 Bulgarian men, women, and children in an attempt to suppress the uprising in Macedonia.	**OCT** In the UK Emmeline Pankhurst founds the Women's Social and Political Union to campaign for women's right to vote.	**DEC** Japanese marines at Mok-Pho in Korea, an act that will increase brewing tension in the area.
JUL The world's first powerboat race takes place in Cork Harbour, Ireland.	**SEP** *Kit Carson*, a Western film, opens in Hollywood after *The Great Train Robbery's* success.	**NOV** French impressionist landscape painter Camille Pissarro dies in Paris at the age of 73.	**DEC** UK cricketer R. E. Foster scores a record test innings of 287 runs against Australia.
JUL President Roosevelt inaugurates a Pacific communications cable by sending a message around the world.	**MODEL A FORD** **JUL** The US Ford Motor Co. sells the first two-cylinder Model A to a physician in Michigan, for $850.	**NOV** Dutch physiologist Willem Einthoven invents the electro-cardiograph to monitor heart contractions.	**WRIGHT FLYER PROPELLER** **DEC** Orville and Wilbur Wright make the first powered flight at Kitty Hawk, North Carolina.

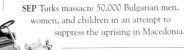

1904

Night raid stuns Russian fleet

FEBRUARY 10

Last night at Port Arthur, off the coast of Korea, Japanese torpedo boats carried out a surprise attack on the Russian fleet. A cruiser and two battleships have been severely damaged and there are claims by the Japanese that seven other warships in the area have been captured. Today in Tokyo, with the success of the raid confirmed, the emperor of Japan officially declared war on Russia. In the Russian capital of St. Petersburg, the Czar, unprepared for such a turn of events, was enjoying an evening at the opera. His officials waited until the end of the performance before telling him the news so as not to spoil his evening. The outbreak of war comes after months of tension in the Far East caused by Russian and Japanese rivalry over control of the Chinese province of Manchuria and over Korea. Within hours of the raid, 8,000 Japanese forces landed unopposed in Korea and began to march toward the capital, Seoul.

FANTASY OF ETERNAL YOUTH
Scottish dramatist J. M. Barrie has written a new play. In *Peter Pan*, Peter Pan and Tinkerbell take three children to Never-Never Land, where they meet Captain Hook.

Celebrations in St. Louis

APRIL 30
One hundred years after President Thomas Jefferson purchased much of the US Midwest from France, a world fair has opened in St. Louis, Missouri, to mark the event.

The world's largest ferris wheel

JANUARY–JUNE

World Events	**JAN** Russia sends warships to Korea, an indication that war with Japan is imminent.	**FEB** The British consul Roger Casement publishes an account of Belgian atrocities in the Congo.	**APR** UK and French governments sign the Entente Cordiale, resolving all their former disagreements.	**MAY** The steerage fare on ocean liners is cut to $10, increasing the number of immigrants entering the US.
Entertainment	**FEB** Popular Italian tenor Enrico Caruso makes his first recording in the US.	**FEB** Italian composer Giacomo Puccini's opera *Madame Butterfly* flops at its Milan premiere.	**MAY** Czech composer Antonin Dvorák, much of whose work has folk influences, dies at the age of 62.	**JUN** Jack White wins the Open Golf Championship in the UK with a record low score of 296.
Innovations	**MAR** US *Daily Illustrated Mirror* is the first newspaper to carry color photographs.	**MAR** Lucien Bull makes a major breakthrough in developing slow-motion photography in France.	**MAY** UK explorer Henry Morton Stanley, leader of many African expeditions, dies at the age of 63.	**JUN** The excavation of a remarkable Viking burial ship begins at Oseberg, Norway.

MADAME BUTTERFLY

ENTENTE CORDIALE

1904

The huge fair is attracting large crowds, despite the sweltering heat. Sales of ice cream have soared after at least three vendors came up with the idea of selling their wares in cone-shaped holders made of waffle pastry. Richard Blechtynden has also started a new craze, putting ice in his tea and selling it as a cold drink.

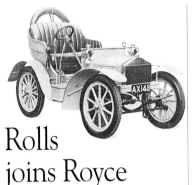

Rolls joins Royce

MAY 4

Charles Rolls and Henry Royce are all set to go into partnership. A provisional agreement has been made today in which Rolls, a London car dealer, will sell the cars made by Royce, a self-made engineer based in Manchester. The luxury cars will be sold under the name of Rolls-Royce, with the partnership aiming to build on the reputation for perfection already established by Royce over the past year.

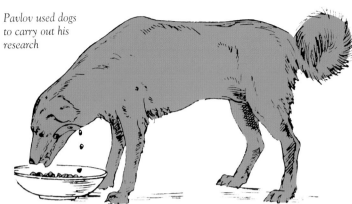

Pavlov used dogs to carry out his research

Behavior can be learned!

DECEMBER 10

Russian physiologist Ivan Pavlov today received the Nobel Prize for his research into how the digestive system works. His experiments, which he carried out on dogs, have shown that nerve messages transmitted from the brain play a part in the digestion of the food we eat. Scientists, however, are more excited by what Pavlov calls his "conditioned reflex" experiments, which may be of major importance in understanding how we learn. Pavlov has found that if a bell is rung each time a dog is fed, it will eventually salivate when it hears the sound of a bell alone, even if no food is visible. If the same is true of humans, it suggests that kinds of behavior can be learned, just like any other skill.

Railroad crosses Siberia

SEPTEMBER 25

Thirteen years after plans were laid to build a railroad across Russia to the Pacific coast, the Great Siberian Railway, a landmark in railroad engineering, is finally complete. The 4,580-mile (7,371-km) track stretches from the Ural mountains in the west to Vladivostock in the east. The Russian government hopes it will open up Siberia and boost trade with China and the Far East.

The railroad has more than 1,000 stations along the route

JULY–DECEMBER

SEP Helen Keller, who has been blind, deaf, and dumb since the age of two, graduates with honors in the US.

JUL The third Olympic Games open in St. Louis, Missouri, and will run until the end of August.

JUL A Gobron-Brillié is the first car to travel over 100 mph (160 km/h) at Ostend, Belgium.

HELEN KELLER

SEP British troops enter Lhasa and force a treaty on Tibet, preventing the Dalai Lama from making foreign deals.

JUL Russian dramatist and story-writer Anton Chekhov, known for *Uncle Vanya*, dies at the age of 44.

AUG SS *Victorian*, the first ocean-going turbine steamer, is launched in Belfast for the Irish Allan Line.

OCT The Russian fleet, on its way to fight Japan, fires on UK trawlers in the North Sea.

NOV Irish dramatist George Bernard Shaw's controversial new play *John Bull's Other Island* opens in London.

OCT UK inventor John Fleming creates a new electric diode valve, a breakthrough for radio technology.

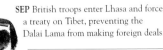

PRESIDENT ROOSEVELT

NOV Theodore Roosevelt wins a four-year term as US president in his own right, after taking over from McKinley.

DEC French film pioneer Georges Méliès shoots a new special effects movie, *Voyage Beyond the Possible*.

OCT Germany is the first country to produce postcards that have pictures in natural color.

1905

CONSERVATION

In 1889 ruthless hunting had reduced the 60 million bison roaming the Great Plains to 85. The American Bison Society has helped increase numbers to 1,000.

Bloody Sunday riots in St. Petersburg

JANUARY 22

More than 100 men, women, and children were shot dead and many more wounded when Russian troops opened fire on demonstrators outside the Winter Palace in St. Petersburg this afternoon. The demonstration of 300,000 workers, led by the radical priest Father Georgy Gapon, had marched through the Russian capital to petition Czar Nicholas II for better working conditions. It was stopped outside the Winter Palace by lines of infantry backed by Cossack troops. As the demonstration attempted to move forward, the troops opened fire without warning on the unarmed crowd. The attack, which is already being called "Bloody Sunday," is likely to kindle the growing unrest against the Russian government and "Little Father" Czar Nicholas II.

Sherlock Holmes returns

MARCH 31

If you thought that Sherlock Holmes had died falling off a precipice at the Reichenbach Falls with his arch-enemy Moriarty, be prepared for a surprise, for Sherlock Holmes is alive and back at work again. Holmes's many fans refused to accept his death,

Holmes, wearing a deerstalker cap, is accompanied by Watson

so British author Sir Arthur Conan Doyle brought his detective-hero back to life. Today the new stories from the *Strand* magazine are published in a single volume, *The Return of Sherlock Holmes*. However, as the London *Daily Telegraph* reports, perhaps "realization is not up to expectation."

JANUARY–JUNE

World Events

JAN The Russian garrison at Port Arthur falls to the Japanese after a seven-month siege.

MAR The 200,000-strong Russian army is defeated by the Japanese at Mukden, a key point for control of Manchuria.

APR More than 10,000 people die in an earthquake that hits the province of Lahore in northeastern India.

JUN The Norwegian parliament refuses to recognize the Swedish king and declares its independence.

Entertainment

JAN Baroness Emmuska Orczy's *The Scarlet Pimpernel* is published in the UK.

MAR Jules Verne, French science fiction writer of *20,000 Leagues Under The Sea*, dies at the age of 77.

MAY Dutch-born oriental dancer Mata Hari wins much praise after her debut appearance in Paris, France.

JUN A group of Expressionist artists forms in Dresden, Germany, taking the name "Die Brücke" (The Bridge).

Innovations

JAN Belgian Henri Oedenkoven founds the first vegetarian organization.

20,000 LEAGUES UNDER THE SEA

FEB The first Rotary Club is founded in Chicago to promote high standards in business practice.

APR French psychologist Alfred Binet develops an intelligence test to test the brain on its ability to reason.

EARTHQUAKE IN INDIA

APR The world's first mobile public library service is set up in Washington County, Maryland.

1905

Japan set for victory

MAY 28

The Russian fleet suffered a devastating defeat today in the Straits of Tsushima between Korea and Japan. This, following losses at Port Arthur and Mukden earlier this year, finally dashes all Russian hopes of defeating Japan in the year-long war for control of Manchuria and Korea. The 38-strong Russian fleet entered the strait at 1:30 p.m., but within hours their formation was wrecked and all but three ships had been sunk, disabled, or captured. The victorious Japanese, on the other hand, lost only three of their boats.

Potemkin crew stage mutiny

JUNE 27

Anchored off the Black Sea port of Odessa, sailors on the Russian battleship *Potemkin* staged a mutiny after a sailor complained about bad food and was shot by a lieutenant. The crew promptly set upon its superiors; members threw the commander and several officers overboard and raised the red flag of revolution. In

Odessa the authorities, already suffering from civil unrest, must now cope with an all-out strike in sympathy.

The Open Window *by Henri Matisse*

"Les Fauves" shock Paris

OCTOBER 1

The annual exhibition at the Salon d'Automne in Paris features a new group of artists who have turned their backs on traditional techniques and use primary colors straight from the tube. The result: bold, bright canvases that are so startling that art critic Louis Vauxcelles has called the group "Les Fauves" – the wild beasts – a name they have readily adopted. Henri Matisse from northern France is the originator of this group of brash young artists, which includes Georges Braque, André Derain, Maurice de Vlaminck, and Raoul Dufy.

JULY–DECEMBER

SEP France, assured of UK support, agrees to call a conference with Germany to discuss its intentions in Morocco.

SEP US President Roosevelt organizes the signing of a treaty in New Hampshire to end the Russo-Japanese war.

OCT In a new manifesto Czar Nicholas II promises Russians limited civil rights and an elected parliament, the Duma.

OCT In the UK, suffragettes Emmeline Pankhurst and Annie Kenney prefer to go to prison than pay fines for assault.

JUL US tennis player May Sutton becomes the first non-Briton to win the Wimbledon ladies' singles title.

NOV The first nickelodeon, a theater showing several short films for 5 cents, opens in Pittsburgh, Pennsylvania.

DEC Russian choreographer Michael Fokine writes a dance, *The Dying Swan*, for ballerina Anna Pavlova.

DEC Hungarian composer Franz Lehár's operetta *The Merry Widow* premieres in Vienna, Austria.

JUL The world's first artificial textile yarn – rayon – starts commercial production in Europe.

ALBERT EINSTEIN

JUL German-born physicist Albert Einstein proposes the idea that time and motion are relative.

DEC The recently produced one-arm bandit slot machines are a great success in San Francisco, CA.

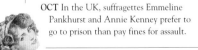

FRANZ LEHÁR'S MERRY WIDOW

DEC German doctor Robert Koch receives the Nobel Prize for identifying the tuberculosis germ.

LIFE IN THE NEW CENTURY

DURING THE EARLY YEARS OF THIS CENTURY, life in the home was remarkably changed by one phenomenon – electricity. Although it was known about in the 1700s, it was nearly 200 years before electricity made its impact on everyday life. The application of a power source to appliances such as washing machines and vacuum cleaners removed much of the hard work from domestic labor and led to cleaner, warmer, and brighter houses. Electricity also saved time, releasing people from housework so that they could enjoy their leisure hours. The invention of the gramophone meant that musicians were no longer needed to play music in the home and introduced a new form of entertainment for people who had previously spent time sewing, reading, and drawing. People in the new century were certainly in for a change.

All lit up

Electricity was supplied to many houses in Europe in the early 1900s, enabling homeowners to replace their oil lamps and candles with electric lights.

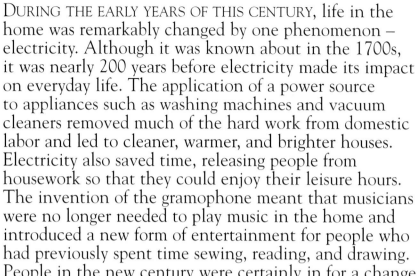

WASHING MACHINE 1907

Fisher washer

No invention eased the burden of housework more than Alva Fisher's electric washing machine of 1907. Clothes were washed in a drum driven by an electric motor. The drum's rotation reversed occasionally so that the clothes did not tangle up in a big knot.

Tea's made

The first automatic tea maker was a bizarre-looking contraption, operated by a number of levers and springs. It is doubtful whether it actually saved any time!

Steam from kettle activates tea maker

Bell sounds when tea is ready

AUTOMATIC TEA MAKER 1904

ELECTRIC OVEN & STOVE 1912

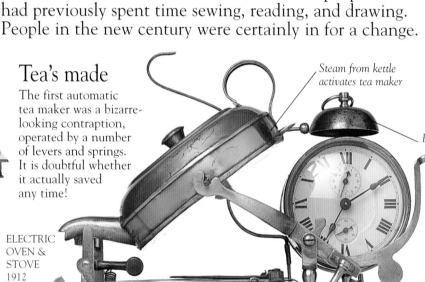

Bellow power

This early vacuum cleaner needed two people to operate it – one to work the bellows, and another to move the device around. In 1908 mass-produced electric vacuums, designed by William Hoover, made their appearance in the United States.

Cooking electric

Gas ovens were already in use when the first electric-powered oven was produced, so the manufacturers advertised the safety and economy of the new stove.

A pressing business

The first electric arc irons were highly dangerous since they required an electric spark to leap between two carbon rods to generate heat. Safer irons, which worked by heating up an element within the iron, appeared a few years later.

DAISY VACUUM CLEANER 1901

Insulated wooden handle

Hand-powered bellows create a vacuum to suck up dirt

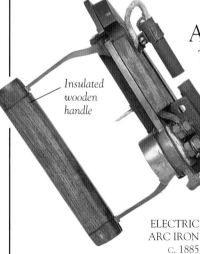

Heavy cast-iron base to press fabric

ELECTRIC ARC IRON C. 1885

BROWNIE BOX CAMERA 1900

Snap happy

Photography came within the reach of the entire population with the introduction of the Brownie Box camera. The camera, which went on sale in the United States in 1900, only cost $1, encouraging amateur photographers to record everything from family portraits to sports events.

Connecting

Early telephone exchanges were manual. An operator answered your call, took your number and the number you wanted to be connected to, and plugged in your line wire to complete the appropriate electrical circuit.

Mouthpiece

Earpiece

CANDLESTICK TELEPHONE 1912

Getting in touch

Scottish-born Alexander Graham Bell invented the telephone in 1876, revolutionizing communications. At the turn of the century most middle-class homes had a telephone.

Horn amplifies sound

GRAMOPHONE EARLY 1900s

Music in the home

Thomas Edison invented a phonograph in 1877 that could both record and play back sounds stored on a piece of tinfoil wrapped around a rotating drum, but its sound quality was poor. Emile Berliner improved on this system by developing a flat-disk record player, or gramophone, in 1888. By the early 1900s pieces of music up to four minutes long could be played in homes for the first time without any musicians being present!

Needle rests in groove and vibrates from side to side as disk revolves

The development of radio

Italian Guglielmo Marconi sent the first radio message across the Atlantic Ocean in 1901. Regular daily broadcasts started in the United States in 1907, but it was not until the 1920s that national broadcasting companies began to make an impact on popular entertainment.

Flat disk made of shellac sits on turntable

1906

San Francisco razed to the ground

APRIL 19

At 5:16 yesterday morning, the city of San Francisco was shaken to its very roots when a violent earthquake struck. Five more shocks followed. Stone buildings shook and their foundations split, roads buckled, and the wharfs in the port warped and shattered. At least 1,000 people are feared dead, but this number is sure to rise as rescue teams begin to sift through the piles of rubble. Those who could fled the city on trains and ferry boats. Last night, parks and squares were full as people slept outdoors, afraid to go back to their houses in case another quake struck. Most of the severe damage, however, was caused by the fire that followed the quake.

Temporary business establishments on Market Street

Dreadnought outclasses all rivals

FEBRUARY 10

The biggest and fastest battleship in the world, HMS *Dreadnought*, was launched in Britain by King Edward VII today. The revolutionary ship, which took just four months to build, surpasses its rivals in naval firepower – it has ten 12-inch (30-cm) guns on each side, eight of which can fire at the same time. Experts believe that *Dreadnought* will make all competitors obsolete.

JANUARY–JUNE

World Events	**JAN** The Liberal Party achieves a landslide victory in the British general elections.	**FEB** The Japanese government announces its intention to double the size of its navy within three years.	**MAR** At the Spanish seaport of Algeciras, a conference decides to give Spain and France joint control over Morocco.	**MAY** The first Duma, an elected parliament that was formed to advise the Czar and his ministers, meets in St. Petersburg, Russia.
Entertainment	**JAN** US dancer Isadora Duncan is banned from performing in Germany.	**MAR** England beats France 35–8 in the first international rugby competition, held in Paris.	**APR** An interim Olympic Games is held in Athens, Greece, to rekindle enthusiasm for the Olympic ideal.	**MAY** Norwegian playwright Henrik Ibsen, author of *Ghosts* and *Hedda Gabler*, dies at the age of 78.
Innovations	**JAN** A car sets a new speed record for 1 mile (1.6 km) of 28.2 seconds in Florida.	**FEB** US businessman William K. Kellogg forms a company to market his corn flake breakfast cereal.	**APR** French physicist Pierre Curie, winner of the Nobel Prize in 1903, dies in a road accident at the age of 46.	**JUN** The world's largest and fastest ocean liner, Cunard's *Lusitania*, is launched in Glasgow, Scotland.

THE LATEST RUGBY BALL

HENRIK IBSEN

1906

Looking east on Sacramento Street

Swept along by strong winds, it raged from the business to the residential districts, engulfing the flimsy wooden buildings in its path. It will cost an estimated $250 million to rebuild the city.

UP IN HOT AIR

Hot-air ballooning has grown in popularity this year, with many races being held. The first international contest, held in Paris, France, was won by US Army lieutenant Frank Lahm.

Cézanne dies

OCTOBER 22

The world's greatest living painter, Paul Cézanne, died today at his family house in Aix-en-Provence, France. He was 67. As a young artist Cézanne was identified with the Impressionists, but in his later work he was more interested in portraying the solidity and permanence of objects. Through his still lifes and landscape paintings, he has greatly influenced the new generation of artists, including Pablo Picasso.

Self-portrait of Paul Cézanne

Grand Prix held in Le Mans

JUNE 27

The world's first Grand Prix auto race finished today at Le Mans, France. The 780-mile (1250-km) race was organized by the Automobile Club of France and took place over two days. The competitors raced around 12 laps of a 65-mile (104-km) triangular course. The winner, Hungarian driver Ferenc Szisz, drove his 90 hp, 13-liter Renault at an average speed of 63 mph (100 km/h). His winning time of 12 hours 14 minutes started from when he got behind the wheel and included stops for tire changes, which he handled himself. The Le Mans race attracted crowds of spectators and will almost certainly become an annual event.

The winner Szisz at full speed

Pictures move!

OCTOBER 31

The first animated cartoon, *Humorous Phases of Funny Faces*, has been produced by British designer John Stuart Blackton. The film, made using stop-frame photography, shows a man blowing cigar smoke on a woman, which makes her vanish (above).

JULY–DECEMBER

JUL Major Dreyfus is declared innocent of treason by the French government after an 11-year fight to clear his name.

JUL The Duma, dissolved by the Russian government, meets in Finland and calls on Russians to refuse to pay their taxes.

SEP Following the resignation of Cuba's president, the US imposes a provisional government there until order is restored.

DEC The UK grants self-government to the Transvaal and Orange River Colonies in southern Africa.

JUL UK tennis ace H. L. Doherty wins the Wimbledon men's singles title for the fifth year running.

AUG Film companies worldwide set up studios in New York, establishing it as the undisputed US film center.

NOV George Bernard Shaw's *The Doctor's Dilemma*, containing the Irish playwright's first death scene, premieres in London, UK.

DEC Gabel's "Automatic Entertainer," the world's first jukebox, is a great success after its launch in the US.

LAWRENCE DOHERTY

AUG Canadian surgeons perform kidney operations on animals to prove that transplants are possible for people.

OCT The permanent wave (perm), a costly and time-consuming process, is shown to UK hairdressers.

OCT German professor Arthur Korn transmits the first picture by telegraph, the culmination of several years' work.

A RADIO DIODE

DEC The first known radio broadcast is made in the US by R. A. Fessenden, who transmits a poem and a talk.

TOWARD A NEW LIFE

ONE OF THE GREATEST MIGRATIONS in human history took place during the 19th and early 20th centuries, when millions of people fled poverty and persecution in their homelands and traveled to the United States. The immigrants came from South and Central America, Europe, and eastern Asia, attracted by the opportunity to begin a new life in a new country. At first they were welcomed with open arms, but as their numbers grew, many US citizens feared that the huge influx would reduce the country to anarchy. Restrictions were gradually placed on immigrants until, in 1921, a Quota Law was passed restricting the numbers allowed to enter. Between 1892 and 1954, the immigration center on Ellis Island processed more than 12 million immigrants. Today, half of the 255 million people in the United States can trace their roots back to Ellis Island.

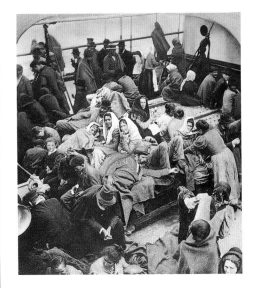

Across the Atlantic Ocean

Immigrants came to the United States by passenger liner. Because many were poor, they could afford to travel only by steerage, or third, class. Conditions on board were cramped – hundreds of families lived below deck in dormitories with only bunks to sleep on. In 1904 the reduction of the steerage class fare to $10 made the journey affordable for even the poorest immigrants.

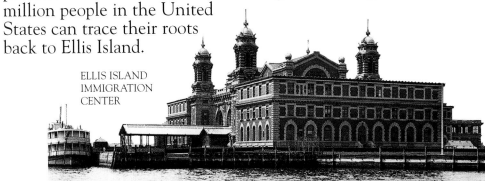

ELLIS ISLAND IMMIGRATION CENTER

Arrival at Ellis Island

On arrival in the United States, immigrants were processed on Ellis Island in New York Harbor. The immigration center contained dormitories, a medical examination room, and the Great Hall, where immigrants waited to receive their entrance papers. The center finally closed in 1954. After years of neglect, it has now been restored. It is regarded as a national monument.

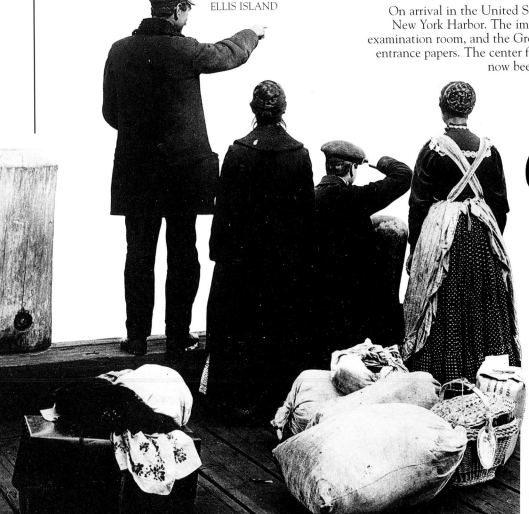

AN IMMIGRANT FAMILY LOOKS ASHORE FROM ELLIS ISLAND

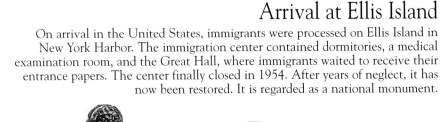

A new life

Many immigrants found fame and fortune in the United States. In 1912, London-born actor Charlie Chaplin arrived on tour as part of a music hall revue. Within a few years he became the most famous film actor in the world.

The melting pot

Until 1890 most immigrants came from northwestern Europe, particularly Germany, Ireland, and Britain. After 1890 a new wave of people arrived from Italy, Austro-Hungary, and Russia. At first, the immigrant groups lived and mixed only with their friends and families, but gradually they mingled together, creating a melting pot of cultures and religions.

1914 IMMIGRATION DECLINES AT
THE OUTBREAK OF WORLD WAR I

1917 LITERACY TEST ENSURES THAT ALL
IMMIGRANTS CAN READ AND WRITE

1921 UNITED STATES RESTRICTS
THE NUMBERS OF IMMIGRANTS

Waiting to be let in

In the Great Hall, immigrants stood in long lines waiting for an interview with officials in the Registry Room. Providing they were of sound mind and body and were not criminals or anarchists, they were then given papers allowing them to settle in the United States. Only two out of every 100 people were refused admittance.

PEOPLE LINE UP IN THE GREAT HALL

DOCTOR EXAMINES
IMMIGRANT CHILDREN

Open wide!

All immigrants were given a health check-up to make sure they were not carrying any contagious diseases. If they were healthy, they received a card signifying a clean bill of health; unhealthy immigrants could be sent back to their homeland.

A warm welcome

The Statue of Liberty, which stands on an island neighboring Ellis Island, was the first thing many immigrants would have seen. On the base of the statue are the words of a poem by Emma Lazarus: "Give me your tired, your poor, Your huddled masses yearning to breathe free." It is recognized as a symbol of freedom throughout the world.

THE STATUE
OF LIBERTY

Seven rays represent seven seas and seven continents

Ticket to ride

On Ellis Island immigrants could buy railroad tickets at a special discount to enable them to travel to their new homes in the United States. From New York they took the train to cities as far away as Chicago, and some even made it to the West Coast, to San Francisco.

IMMIGRANTS WAIT FOR A TRAIN TO A NEW LIFE

A SPECIAL
DISCOUNT RAIL
TICKET FOR
IMMIGRANTS

1907

Civil rights protest by Gandhi

MARCH 22

In South Africa Indian-born lawyer Mohandas Gandhi has said he will start a campaign of "Satyagraha," or civil non-violent disobedience, against the Transvaal government. He is protesting against the recently passed Asiatic Law Amendment Ordinance bill, the effects of which will come into force on July 1. The new law will require all Indian residents in South Africa to have their fingerprints taken, after which they will receive a certificate of registration, which they will be obliged to carry with them at all times. If they fail to do this, the

Mohandas Gandhi

Indians could face loss of residence, a fine, or even deportation. Mr. Gandhi, who qualified as a barrister in London, has been resident in South Africa since 1893. He is objecting to the bill on the grounds that it constitutes racial discrimination against the large Indian community living in the country.

ANIMALS ON DISPLAY

A new type of zoo opened in Hamburg this year, inspired by the vision of German animal trainer Carl Hagenbeck. Angry at the caged conditions most animals were kept in, he purchased a 67-acre (27-hectare) site on the outskirts of Hamburg and created a zoo that gave the animals freedom to wander while still protecting spectators' safety.

Picasso's new style causes uproar

MARCH 31

A startling new painting by Spanish-born artist Pablo Picasso has shocked the art world. Opinions are divided on the bizarre canvas, entitled *Les Demoiselles d'Avignon*, which is on show at his studio in Montmartre. The picture is vast – almost 8 ft (2.5 m) square – and features five naked women. Rumor has it that they are prostitutes. Whoever they are, their portraits are far from flattering, with savage, masklike heads and dislocated bodies. Fellow artist Georges Braque is horrified, accusing Picasso of "drinking turpentine and spitting fire." But some critics are excited by this bold new approach to portraiture, finding in it influences of the work of the late Cézanne.

Les Demoiselles d'Avignon by Pablo Picasso

JANUARY–JUNE

World Events	JAN A huge earthquake devastates the Jamaican capital of Kingston and kills 700–800 people.	JAN At a lavish ceremony Mohammad Ali Mirza is crowned Shah of Persia in the Royal Palace of Tehran.	APR Plans to construct a tunnel under the English Channel are withdrawn due to fears about defense.	JUN In Russia, Czar Nicholas II dissolves the second Duma, or parliament, accusing some deputies of treason.
Entertainment	JAN UK music halls are quiet as artists strike for better pay.	JAN The premiere of *The Playboy of the Western World* in Dublin, Ireland, provokes riots.	MAR The world's first model-aircraft competition takes place at Crystal Palace, London, UK.	MAY The world's first 24-hour car race, the Endurance Derby, is held in Philadelphia, Pennsylvania.
Innovations	JAN The Hurley Machine Corp. of Chicago, IL, announces the first electric washing machine. **RADIO RECEIVER**	FEB The De Forest Radio Telephone Co. makes the first regular experimental radio broadcasts in New York.	APR In Paris, French doctors announce the discovery of a serum that can cure dysentery. **AUGUSTE AND HENRI LUMIÈRE**	JUN The pioneering Lumière brothers claim a breakthrough in developing color photography.

1907

Brooklands opens for racing

JULY 6

The world's first track specially built for car racing is now open at Brooklands, southern England. The track, which is 2.77 miles (4.45 km) long, is covered with a thin layer of concrete. It is oval in shape like a horse racing track, and the corners bank steeply at each end, enabling the cars to take them at speed. At today's opening meeting, British driver J. E. Hutton won the Montague Cup in a Mercedes.

British boys learn outdoor skills

JULY 29

Four days ago Sir Robert Baden-Powell, the Boer war hero, took 20 boys to camp on Brownsea Island in Poole Harbour, southern England. While there, the boys learned outdoor skills and basic first aid. Baden-Powell's purpose was to introduce British boys to the discipline and duty he had seen in the army scouts. The camp was a great success, and today Baden-Powell officially set up the Boy Scout organization in London.

The Boy Scouts wear a distinctive uniform

New Zealand gains its independence

SEPTEMBER 26

The British colony of New Zealand, situated in the southwestern Pacific Ocean, became independent today after 67 years of British rule. New Zealand has had self-government for several years now, and has a long tradition of equal rights for its citizens. In 1893 it was the first country in the world to give women the vote, and it was among the first countries to introduce social security benefits and pensions. It also has an excellent public health service. Starting today it will become an independent Dominion within the British Empire.

Government buildings in the capital of Wellington

Vertical takeoff a reality at last

NOVEMBER 13

French bicycle-maker Paul Cornu flew straight into the record books today as his motor-driven helicopter rose vertically into the air above a field near Lisieux, Normandy. Cornu's craft is powered by two motor-driven propellers, or rotors, which push the craft vertically up off the ground.

Although the craft rose just 1 ft (0.3 m) today, Cornu hopes to win the 50,000-franc prize on offer to the first Frenchman who completes an aerial circuit of 0.6 miles (1 km).

Cornu's helicopter

JULY–DECEMBER

JUL Riots start in the Korean capital of Seoul after the Japanese insist on the abdication of the Korean emperor.

JUL The first of the *Zeigfeld Follies*, a spectacular music and dancing show, is performed in New York City.

AUG The Singer Building in New York City, although incomplete, is the tallest building in the world.

EDVARD GRIEG

JUL Germany, Austria, and Italy renew the Triple Alliance for another six years, despite reservations from Italy.

SEP Norwegian composer Edvard Grieg, famous for his *Peer Gynt* suite, dies at the age of 64.

SEP USS *Virginia* and *Connecticut* are the first naval vessels to be equipped with radio-telephones.

AUG French gunships stage a two-day bombardment on Casablanca, Morocco, following anti-European hostilities.

NOV *The Count of Monte Cristo* is shot in Los Angeles, establishing the city as a major US film location.

OCT The *Lusitania* breaks the record for crossing the North Atlantic and takes the prestigious Blue Riband.

THE LUSITANIA

DEC The US's "Great White Fleet" of 16 battleships leaves on a world tour to show off US strength.

DEC Rudyard Kipling, UK author of *The Jungle Book*, wins the Nobel Prize for Literature.

DEC The world's first circus, set up by the Ringling Brothers, has a successful year in the US.

1908

Gold medalist disqualified

Stewards help Pietri, with his legs folding beneath him, to cross the finishing line

JULY 30

Italian athlete Dorando Pietri today received a gold cup from Queen Alexandra of Britain as an acknowledgment for his valiant failure to win the Olympic marathon. Pietri had dominated the race from its start at Windsor and led throughout the 26-mile (41-km) course. As he entered the White City stadium in London for the final leg of the race, he tripped, stumbled four or five times, and fell. He received medical attention and a helping hand from race stewards as, half-conscious, he crossed the finish line. Sadly he was disqualified for receiving assistance and first prize was awarded to runner-up John Hayes of the United States.

JUMPING JUKEBOX

An advanced version of the jukebox invented in 1906, the hexaphone plays a selection of tunes recorded on cylinders.

New automobile for the masses

The Model T is the sturdiest car on the market

AUGUST 12

The first Model T Ford went on sale in the US today for $850, the fulfillment of Henry Ford's promise to "build a car for the multitude." The car is made of a tough but lightweight steel alloy, and is built using the revolutionary assembly line technique that the Ford Motor Co. hopes will mass-produce 18,000 cars a year.

JANUARY–JUNE

World Events

FEB King Carlos I of Portugal and his heir are assassinated in Lisbon in the wake of the failed revolution.

FEB Emmeline Pankhurst, leading campaigner in the UK suffrage movement, complains about the conditions of prison life.

MAY The Franco-British exhibition opens in London, with the White City stadium as its centerpiece.

JUN 200,000 people gather in Hyde Park, London, UK, in support of the women's suffrage movement.

Entertainment

JAN Austrian composer and conductor Gustav Mahler makes his US debut in New York City.

FEB The US film industry heads west, attracted by cheap labor and the climate and scenery of southern California.

MAY French artist Claude Monet destroys many of his paintings, believing them to be unsatisfactory.

JUN Russian composer Nikolai Rimsky-Korsakov, noted for *Scheherazade*, dies at the age of 64.

Innovations

FEB Dutch scientists succeed in producing a form of solid helium for the first time.

BELL OF THE MAURETANIA

MAR The UK Cunard liner the *Mauretania* sets a record Atlantic crossing time of 5 days 5 mins.

MAY Commercial quantities of crude oil are first struck in Persia, in the Middle East, at Masjid-i-Sulaiman.

DEMONSTRATION IN HYDE PARK

JUN The first international soccer game is played in Vienna, with England beating Austria 6–1.

1908

Badger's cache, stored for winter

Fantasy written for children

OCTOBER 31

Kenneth Grahame, a secretary in the Bank of England, has proved to be one of this year's most unlikely authors. *The Wind in the Willows*, published earlier this month, tells a story about the exciting adventures of Badger, Ratty, Toad, Mole, and other creatures who live around the riverbank. This enchanting tale is certain to entertain children and adults alike for many years to come.

Two-year-old Emperor Pu Yi stands next to his father Prince Chun and his younger brother

Toddler ascends Chinese throne

DECEMBER 2

Following the death of Emperor Kuang-Hsu, Hsuan T'ung, or Pu Yi, has ascended to the imperial throne of China. It will be many years before he is able to rule the country himself, so in the meantime his father, Prince Chun, will control the nation as regent. This is the will of Tsu-Hsi, the former dowager empress, who in recent years has exercised considerable influence in China. After her suspicious death there were rumors that the royal dynasty might be on the verge of collapse, to be replaced by a republican government.

Street scene in Messina showing earthquake wreckage

Earthquake in Italy

DECEMBER 28

Messina, the second largest city in Sicily, was struck early this morning by the most violent earthquake ever recorded in Europe. Of the city's 150,000 inhabitants, it is estimated that more than half have died in the explosion, with many more still trapped under the debris. The damage that it has caused is widespread. Not only the city of Messina but also its surrounding villages and the towns in Calabria, the toe of mainland Italy, have suffered from the devastating effects of its force. A fine collection of ancient Italian architecture has been reduced to rubble. Eyewitness reports say that the earthquake caused a tidal wave that surged across the Straits of Messina, engulfing the city of Reggio and other nearby ports. An international rescue operation is being organized, but it will be days before the precise damage and death toll are known and the process of rebuilding can begin.

JULY–DECEMBER

JUL A revolt staged by the Young Turk movement forces Sultan Abdul Hamid II to restore Turkey's constitution.

JUL US author Joel Chandler Harris, creator of Uncle Remus and Br'er Rabbit, dies at the age of 60.

SEP German scientist Hermann Minkowski is the first person to define time as the fourth dimension.

BR'ER RABBIT

AUG The Belgian parliament votes to take the control of the Belgian Congo from its king, Leopold II.

AUG UK cricketer W. G. Grace plays his final first-class game at the end of an eminent 43-year career.

SEP US aircraft pioneer Orville Wright establishes a new flight time record, staying airborne for 70 mins.

OCT Austria-Hungary annexes the Balkan states of Bosnia and Herzegovina by decree and with the approval of Russia.

DEC Texan boxer Jack Johnson becomes the first black American to win the world heavyweight boxing championship.

NOV German physicist Albert Einstein presents his quantum theory of light at a Switzerland conference.

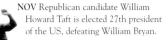

JACK JOHNSON

NOV Republican candidate William Howard Taft is elected 27th president of the US, defeating William Bryan.

DEC Léon Gaumont's Cité Elgé, advertized as the world's largest film studio, is completed in Paris, France.

DEC Ernest Rutherford from the UK wins the Nobel Prize for his work on radioactivity and the atom.

THE GREAT OCEAN LINERS

FLAG OF THE WHITE STAR SHIPPING LINE

BETWEEN THE AGES of the slow but beautiful sailing ships of the 1800s and the sleek, fast jet planes of the 1950s, the only way to travel was by ocean liner. Driven by powerful steam turbines, these floating palaces carried thousands of passengers across the seas. They were called liners because they worked regular routes, or lines. Competition between the different shipping companies was fierce, as each tried to carry more passengers more quickly across the ocean and earn the prestigious "Blue Riband" for the fastest North Atlantic crossing. Throughout the heyday of liner travel, the Cunard Line, based in Liverpool, England, led the way in building record-breaking ships, including the *Mauretania* in 1907 and the *Queen Mary* in 1936.

ADVERTISING POSTER FOR THE CUNARD LINE

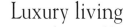

Battling for supremacy

Cunard, White Star, the North German Lloyd Line, Hamburg-Amerika, and the smaller lines all battled for supremacy on the all-important North Atlantic route. They built liners that were bigger, faster, and more luxurious than their competitors in order to attract customers.

Luxury living

For first-class passengers, life on board an ocean liner was like being in a luxury hotel. There were many ballrooms, dining rooms, smoking rooms, and lounges, which were lavishly furnished and decorated with gilt mirrors and wood paneling.

DINING ROOM OF WHITE STAR'S *BRITANNIC*

Cunard's leading lady

The *Mauretania*, nicknamed "The Grand Old Lady of the Atlantic," made 538 crossings in a career lasting 28 years. She had accommodations for 560 first-class, 475 second-class, and 1,300 third-class passengers. They were looked after by 376 staff, while a crew of 366 ran the ship.

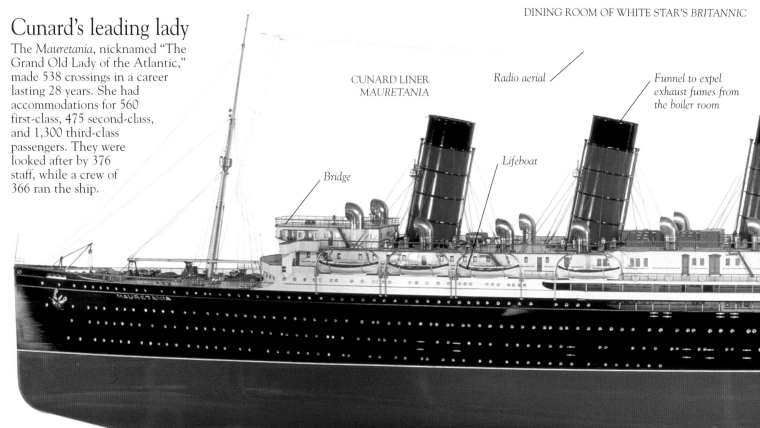

CUNARD LINER MAURETANIA

Radio aerial

Funnel to expel exhaust fumes from the boiler room

Lifeboat

Bridge

Swimming at sea

In 1911, the *Olympic*, sister ship of the *Titanic*, became the first liner to have an outside swimming pool. Also on board were indoor pools, saunas, and deck games such as shuffleboard and quoits, a ring-tossing game. The liners of later years had at least one movie theater.

BY THE 1930s OUTDOOR POOLS WERE A COMMON FEATURE ON OCEAN LINERS

CUNARD FLAG

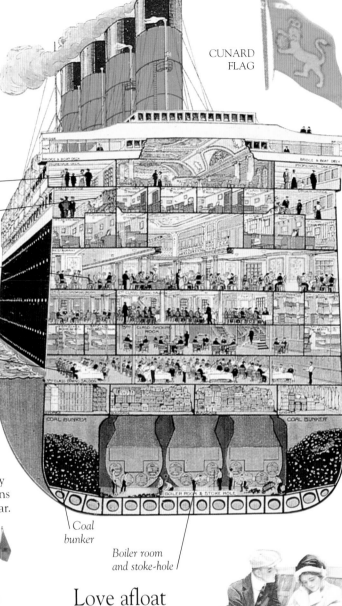

Promenade deck

Garden lounge

First-class restaurant

CROSS SECTION OF THE *AQUITANIA*

Third-class restaurant

The loss of the *Titanic*

The *Titanic*, the pride of the White Star Line, departed on her maiden voyage on April 10, 1912. Tragedy struck after four days when she hit an iceberg and sank. The wreck was discovered 73 years later in 1985, and divers began salvage work.

The super-liner

Cunard launched the impressive *Aquitania* in 1914, some years after the new generation of super-liners in 1907. Although she was no record-breaker, she offered a superb degree of luxury in her first-class accommodations and immediately became popular.

Coal bunker

Boiler room and stoke-hole

First-class music and lounge room

First-class smoking room

Love afloat

A long voyage provided the perfect opportunity for couples to get to know each other better, and many a romance blossomed on board.

Baggage crane

Second-class lounge

Bridge for docking

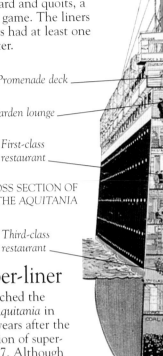

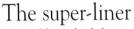

1909

Souvenir postcard featuring Charles Pathé holding a newsreel camera

News is broadcast to film audiences

MARCH 31

The pioneering French film producers Émile and Charles Pathé have now started to film the news. Beginning this week, the latest events from around the world will be shown once a week as part of the film program at their theater in Paris. Entitled *Pathé Faits Divers* and edited by Albert Gaveau, the newsreel will act as a witness to current events. To achieve this, the Pathé brothers have sent an army of cameramen to every continent of the globe to search out the week's important and sensational stories. The newsreel, which is intended for general distribution, will soon be shown in other countries.

Ballets Russes captivates Paris

MAY 20

A new dance company, the Ballets Russes, headed by Russian impresario Sergei Diaghilev, has caused a sensation in Paris. Last night's premiere in the Théâtre Châtelet was met with rapturous applause. Performing Polovtsian Dances from *Prince Igor* and *Les Sylphides*, the troupe, led by Vaslav Nijinsky and Anna Pavlova, electrified audiences by displaying Mikhail Fokine's daring choreography that combines music, drama, and painting. But it was Nijinsky who stole the limelight as he defied gravity in his leaps across the stage. One critic has described him as having "the power of youth, drunk with rhythm, terrifying in his muscular energy." During its stay in Paris, the company will aim to show a full repertoire of its talents.

A star is born

JUNE 10

All eyes in Hollywood are on a 16-year-old Canadian girl. Toronto-born Mary Pickford had been performing on Broadway in New York for two years when her acting talent was spotted by film director D. W. Griffith. Following her screen debut in *The Violin Maker of Cremona* at the beginning of the year, he has now offered her a part in his next film, *Her First Biscuits*. It is expected that her career will go from one hit film to the next.

JANUARY–JUNE

World Events	**MAR** Handpicked by Roosevelt, William Howard Taft is inaugurated 27th president of the US.	**MAR** The "Great Powers" urge Serbia to cease waging war with Austria-Hungary over control of Bosnia and Herzegovina.	**APR** Young Turks overthrow the sultan of Turkey and replace him with his brother, who assumes the title Mohammed V.	**APR** UK chancellor David Lloyd George raises taxes on the rich to pay for pensions in the "People's Budget".
Entertainment	**FEB** Italian poet Filippo Tommaso Marinetti publishes *The Futurist Manifesto* in Paris.	**MAR** J. M. Synge, Irish playwright of the notorious *The Playboy of the Western World*, dies at the age of 37.	**APR** A memorial to the UK poets Keats and Shelley is opened by the Spanish Steps in Rome, Italy.	**JUN** King Edward VII opens the Victoria and Albert Museum in South Kensington, London, UK.
Innovations	**JAN** UK astronomers report that they might have sighted a ninth new planet. **SOUTH POLE EXPLORERS**	**JAN** Ernest Shackleton leads a British expedition nearer to the south pole than ever before.	**MAY** Bacteriologist Paul Ehrlich produces the world's first successful anti-syphilis drug in Germany. **DAVID LLOYD GEORGE**	**JUN** The SOS danger signal is first used at sea when SS *Slavonia* is wrecked off the Azores.

1909

Claim for north pole conquest confirmed

DECEMBER 21
US naval commander Robert Peary has been officially declared the first person to reach the north pole. A committee appointed by Copenhagen University in Denmark made the decision today after rejecting evidence supplied by Dr. Frederick Cook from New York, who has also made this claim. The controversy that started earlier this year after Peary claimed that he reached the pole first on April 6 should now end. Peary set sail from the US on board *Theodore Roosevelt* in July 1908 and established a base camp at Cape Columbia. He left the camp the following March and crossed 90 miles (145 km) of mountainous terrain before making the 36-day trek across the frozen Arctic Ocean to the pole itself. On this, his third attempt to reach the north pole, Peary was accompanied by four Eskimos and Matthew Henson, his chief assistant since his first expedition to the Arctic in 1891.

Near the north pole, Henson (centre) and the team of Eskimos

Peary with the husky dogs he used to pull the sleds carrying his supplies

BUILDING IN STEEL
"Steel is the epic of this age," pronounced US architect Frank Lloyd Wright this year, and new buildings across the world are proving him right. In Barcelona, Spain, Antonio Gaudí has designed the Casa Milá apartment building. It looks as if it is quarried from solid stone, but in fact it is supported by a hidden steel structure.

JULY–DECEMBER

JUL The shah of Persia Mohammed Ali is deposed in favor of his 12-year-old brother, Ahmed Mirza.

JUL UK tennis player Arthur Gore is the oldest man, at 41, to win the singles title at Wimbledon.

JUL French aviator Louis Blériot is the first person to fly across the English Channel, taking 37 minutes.

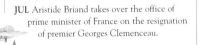

BLÉRIOT ARRIVES AT DOVER, UK

JUL Aristide Briand takes over the office of prime minister of France on the resignation of premier Georges Clemenceau.

AUG The US Simplified Spelling Board publishes a dictionary of 3,261 words to be altered.

SEP German psychologists Sigmund Freud and Carl Jung tour the US, lecturing on psychoanalysis.

NOV The "People's Budget" is defeated in the House of Lords, creating a major constitutional crisis in the UK.

NOV Russian composer Sergei Rachmaninov premieres his third piano concerto in New York.

DEC US chemist Leo Baekeland prepares to market his newly invented synthetic plastic – "Bakelite."

LOUIS BOTHA

DEC The Union of South Africa is proclaimed independent, with Louis Botha as its first prime minister.

DEC US architect Frank Lloyd Wright completes the acclaimed Robie House in Chicago.

DEC Italian Guglielmo Marconi shares the Nobel Prize for physics with K. F. Braun from Germany.

1910

Second death

APRIL 21

The well-loved US novelist and humorist Mark Twain died today at the age of 74. Twain was reported to have died once before, and he was

Huckleberry Finn catches a rabbit

forced to send a cable to the Associated Press stating that "the report of my death was an exaggeration." This time there is no mistake. Born Samuel Langhorne Clemens, Twain began life as a river pilot. He took his pen name "mark twain" from a river call meaning "two fathoms." His novels *Tom Sawyer* and *The Adventures of Huckleberry Finn* will almost certainly become children's classics.

Black rights group founded

MAY 1

The National Association for the Advancement of Colored People (NAACP) officially came into being in the United States today. It is formed from a group of liberals and radicals who came together last year after the anti-black riots. The new group hopes to bring an end to racial discrimination, using education and litigation to get its message across. It will distribute informational pamphlets and is planning to publish a journal containing the work of black authors and artists later this year.

NAACP co-founder W. E. B. Du Bois

The sight of the comet in the night sky causes amazement and alarm

Fear greets comet's arrival

MAY 16

Halley's Comet is very close to approaching Earth Some people are terrified, convinced that the comet will release poisonous gases into the atmosphere. Others are planning comet parties to celebrate. The comet is of particular interest to scientists, who will use the event, which occurs only once every 75 years, to increase their astronomical knowledge.

South Africa unites

MAY 31

The Union of South Africa, declared independent by a royal proclamation last December, became a self-governing dominion of the British Empire today. The new country unites the British colonies of the Cape and Natal with the former Boer countries of Transvaal and the Orange River. The new government will be headed by Louis Botha, who led the defeated Boer army nine years ago. But it hopes to put memories of the Boer War behind it, as Botha strives to achieve unification.

Map showing the united provinces of South Africa

Transvaal

Orange River

Natal

Cape Colony

INDIAN OCEAN

☐ British   ☐ Boer

JANUARY– JUNE

World Events	**FEB** Greece, led by Cretan-born Eleutherios Venizélos, clashes with Turkey over control of Crete.	**FEB** The Chinese army occupies Lhasa, Tibet, forcing the Tibetan spiritual leader, the Dalai Lama, to flee Tibet for India.	**FEB** Boutros Pasha Gahli, the first Egyptian prime minister under UK rule, is shot dead by a nationalist fanatic.	**MAY** The UK king Edward VII dies at the age of 68 after a nine-year reign; he is succeeded by his son George .
Entertainment	**MAR** *In Old California* is the first film to be made in the Hollywood area.	**MAR** A US banker pays £103,000 for a Franz Hal painting, the largest sum ever paid for any piece of art.	**MAR** The first *Frankenstein* film, starring Charles Ogle, is made by the Edison studio in New York.	**JUN** A new season of the popular Ballets Russes opens in France with Igor Stravinsky's *The Firebird*.
Innovations	**FEB** An X-ray machine guides a surgeon to remove a nail from the lung of a boy in the US.	**BARONESS DE LAROCHE** **MAR** French aristocrat Baroness de Laroche becomes the first woman to be granted a pilot's license.	**JUN** UK explorer Captain Robert Scott sets out from England for the South Pole on board the *Terra Nova*. **TERRA NOVA**	**JUN** The first aerial reconnaissance mission is made by two pilots from the French army around Vincennes.

1910

Ethel Le Neve is led down the ship's gangway, with Crippen following

IT TAKES TWO TO TANGO

Tango fever has swept across the United States and Europe this year as couples take to the dance floor to perform the latest complicated steps. The original, intimate and sexy dance came from the slums and backstreets of Argentina during the 19th century. Today, in a more restrained form, it is all the rage among fashionable young people on both sides of the Atlantic.

Radio used to catch criminal

JULY 31

Dr. Hawley Harvey Crippen, wanted for the brutal murder of his wife in Camden Town, London, was arrested at sea today thanks to the use of ship-to-shore radio. Crippen disappeared from his home in London on July 9. He fled to Belgium with his mistress, the 27-year-old Ethel Le Neve, and then, posing as Mr. Robinson and son, they boarded the SS *Montrose*, bound for Quebec. The ship's captain, noticing the couple's odd behavior – he spotted the "men" holding hands, as well as other things that did not add up – radioed back to Britain with his suspicions. Crippen will be brought back to Britain, where he will have to face trial for murder.

Portugal overthrows its king

OCTOBER 4

In a well-planned coup, republican revolutionaries have overthrown the Portuguese monarchy. The 20-year-old king, Manuel II, who came to the throne after the assassination of his father and brother, has fled to Gibraltar. The revolution comes after a decade of discontent against royal extravagance in the face of widespread poverty. Last night, hostilities broke out in the capital of Lisbon. Sailors joined in and shelled strategic points from ships on the Tagus River. This morning most of the fighting had ceased and cries of "long live the Republic" were heard as victorious soldiers and sailors marched through the city.

JULY–DECEMBER

AUG UK founder of nursing Florence Nightingale, also known as the "Lady of the Lamp," dies at the age of 90.

JUL Former US heavyweight boxing champion Jack Johnson takes the title from current holder Jim Jeffries.

AUG The first 8-mile (13-km) stretch of the Panama Canal is opened at its eastern end near the Caribbean.

FLORENCE NIGHTINGALE

AUG Following its victory over Russia in Manchuria, Japan formally annexes the strategically important Korea.

SEP Self-taught French painter Henri Rousseau, who created bold, dream-like canvases, dies at age 66.

SEP The first flights are made across the French Alps and the Pyrenees as aviation continues to progress.

SEP Louis Botha loses his seat in South Africa's first parliamentary elections, but his Nationalist Party wins by a safe majority.

NOV The work of Post-impressionist painters, including Picasso, Matisse, and Gauguin, is shown in the UK.

SEP Pioneering French physicist and Nobel Prize winner Marie Curie isolates pure radium for the first time.

OCT Dr. Hawley Crippen, brought back to the UK from Canada to face trial for murder, is sentenced to death.

NOV Russian novelist Leo Tolstoy, author of *War and Peace* and *Anna Karenina*, dies at the age of 82.

LEO TOLSTOY

DEC The first neon lighting, developed by Georges Claude, is used at the Paris Auto Show.

1911

Mexican dictator surrenders

MAY 25

The Mexican dictator Porfirio Díaz was forced to resign from office today after almost 31 years in power. He has carried out his brutal rule by ruthlessly eliminating any opposition. His bold efforts to transform Mexico's economy were unfortunately achieved at the expense of the peasants, who have become serfs to a few rich landowners. Such actions have bred discontent. But the real trouble started last year when Francisco Madero stood against him for the position of president. Rather than risk a contest, Díaz swiftly had him arrested and imprisoned. However, Madero was released on bail and escaped to Texas. From

Former president Porfirio Díaz

there, aided by rebel forces led by Zapata in the north and Pancho Villa in the south, he organized the uprising to oust the dictator. As provisional president, Madero now has the difficult task of governing this unruly and unhappy country.

THE SECRET GARDEN

British author Frances Hodgson Burnett has written one of the most popular children's novels of the year. *The Secret Garden* tells the story of Mary, an orphan who is sent to live in the gloomy mansion of her uncle. She is wretched and disagreeable until she discovers a garden hidden behind a wall that opens her eyes to the world around her.

Inca city discovered

JULY 24

High in the Andes, US archaeologist Hiram Bingham today discovered the ruins of Machu Picchu, the last capital of the ancient Inca civilization. Bingham was on an expedition near Cuzco in Peru. He followed an Indian guide through the jungle and up sheer cliffs before he came upon the city on a flat piece of land nestled between two towering peaks. The site has long been known to Peruvians, but its camouflaged location has kept it a secret from Europeans for centuries. The discovery of the ruined city is of great importance to knowledge of Peruvian history. Archaeologists will be able to find out more about the Inca civilization, which disappeared soon after the Spanish conquest of South America in the mid-16th century.

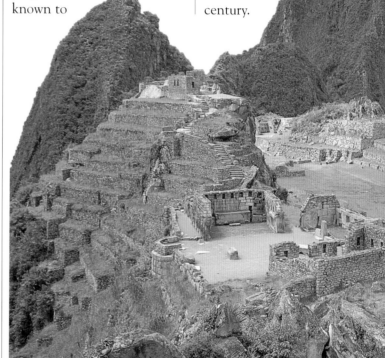

JANUARY– JUNE

World Events	**MAR** As trouble brews in Mexico, President Taft sends 30,000 US troops to guard the border territory.	**MAR** The UK announces plans to build five more *Dreadnought* battleships for the Royal Navy in response to German naval expansion.	**APR** Following an appeal from the sultan of Morocco, France sends troops to protect Europeans in both Casablanca and Fez.	**APR** US troops intervene in the Mexican civil war, crossing the Rio Grande and fighting the rebel forces led by Francisco Madero.
Entertainment	**JAN** Richard Strauss's opera *Der Rosenkavalier* debuts in Dresden, Germany.	**FEB** *A Tale of Two Cities*, based on the novel by Charles Dickens, is produced as a film in the US.	**MAY** Austrian composer and conductor Gustav Mahler dies at the age of 50.	**MAY** The first Indianapolis 500 road race is won by US race car driver Ray Harroun.
Innovations	**JAN** The Academie des Sciences in Paris refuses membership to Marie Curie. **STRAUSS'S DER ROSENKAVALIER**	**MAR** Clocks in France are put back 9 mins 21 secs to join the world on Greenwich Mean Time.	**MAY** The White Star shipping line launches the SS *Titanic*, the largest vessel afloat, in Belfast, Ireland. **RAY HARROUN IN MARMON WASP**	**MAY** White Star's SS *Olympic* is the world's first ocean liner to have an outside swimming pool.

1911

Painting stolen

AUGUST 22

Last night the *Mona Lisa* was stolen from the Louvre, the premier art gallery in Paris, France. Today astonished curators are wondering why any thief would be foolish enough to steal the painting, reasoning that the world-famous picture could never be resold. However, now that it has vanished, police must solve a crime as enigmatic as the *Mona Lisa*'s smile itself.

The Mona Lisa, painted 400 years ago by Leonardo da Vinci, is today viewed as a masterpiece

The hidden city of Machu Picchu, situated high up in the Andes mountains

Imperial regime abolished in China

DECEMBER 29

Dr. Sun Yat-sen was elected president of a newly declared republic of China today, so bringing to an end more than 2,000 years of Chinese imperial history. This turn of events comes as a result of the nationalist uprising that started in central China in October. Sun Yat-sen, the leader of the revolution, has been an active reformer for many years. As leader of the nationalist Kuomintang Party, he has campaigned to bring an end to the 300-year rule of the corrupt Manchu dynasty and to establish a stable government in China. His support has grown rapidly in recent years, as imperial rule has become increasingly dictatorial and of a conservative nature. It is still too early to know what the future government of China will be like, but one thing is sure: China has seen its last emperor.

Sun Yat-sen and his wife stand in a regal pose

JULY–DECEMBER

JUL Germany sends the gunboat *Panther* to the Moroccan port of Agadir, provoking a crisis with France.

SEP The first Channel swim for 36 years is made by Thomas Burgess from Yorkshire, UK.

JUL The first windshield wipers, a rubber device operated by a piece of string, are fitted to a Benz.

AIRMAIL ARRIVES AT WINDSOR

SEP Peter Stolypin, the hard-line Russian prime minister, dies after he is shot while attending the opera at Kiev.

SEP French poet and art critic Guillaume Apollinaire is arrested for stealing the *Mona Lisa*.

SEP A two-week experimental airmail service is set up between Hendon and Windsor in the UK.

OCT Pu Yi, the five-year-old emperor of China, surrenders his power and agrees to grant a constitution.

DEC "The Blue Rider" group of artists, led by Kandinsky and Franz Marc, has its first show in Munich, Germany.

DEC French physicist Marie Curie wins an unprecedented second Nobel Prize for her scientific research.

ALEXANDER'S RAGTIME BAND

NOV The crisis at Agadir in North Africa ends as Germany accepts French control in Morocco.

DEC *Alexander's Ragtime Band*, a tune by US songwriter Irving Berlin, is the hit of the year.

DEC Norwegian explorer Roald Amundsen becomes the first man to reach the South Pole.

OCTOBER 19, 1911 AMUNDSEN
LEAVES BASE AT FRAMHEIM

NOVEMBER 1, 1911 SCOTT
LEAVES BASE AT CAPE EVANS

DECEMBER 14, 1911 AMUNE
REACHES SOUTH POLE

THE RACE TO THE SOUTH POLE

IN 1911, THE CONQUEST OF THE SOUTH POLE was the one of the few remaining challenges left for explorers. Two years before, Robert Peary of the United States reached the north pole, and the race was now on to penetrate the frozen continent of Antarctica. Late in 1911, two teams of explorers set out across the ice and snow in search of this ultimate goal. One team, led by Norwegian Arctic explorer Roald Amundsen, was well organized and properly equipped for the extreme conditions. The other, a British team led by Captain Robert Scott, concentrated on scientific research and underestimated the physical difficulties of reaching the pole. Their different approaches decided the victors.

MODEL OF THE *FRAM*

Amundsen sails south

Amundsen's ship, the *Fram*, was specially built to resist the crushing pressure of ice, a danger when sailing in Antarctic waters. He set off from Norway in June 1910 and sailed south across the Atlantic Ocean, arriving at the Antarctic in January 1911. He anchored at the Bay of Whales in the Ross Sea, where he wintered with eight companions and 116 dogs.

The route to the pole

The closest Amundsen and Scott could get to the pole by boat was via the Ross Sea. They set up base camps on opposite sides of the Ross Ice Shelf at Framheim and Cape Evans. From there they went on foot across the Ross Ice Shelf and over the Transantarctic Mountains to the Antarctic plateau and the mythical 90° S of the pole.

90° South

Amundsen's route

Scott's route

Scott's last camp

Framheim

Cape Evans

Ross Sea

ANTARCTICA

WISTING

HASSEL

AMUNDSEN

BJAALAND

HANSEN

A team of experts

In addition to being experienced navigators, the four men who accompanied Amundsen were chosen for their expertise in various fields: dog handling, sled-driving, skiing, and whale harpooning. The team was used to the bitter climate of Norway and were prepared for the snow and cold encountered in the Antarctic.

Winter at Framheim

Amundsen spent the Antarctic winter at base camp, where he prepared for the grueling final stage of the expedition. He arranged several trips along the planned route and established depots in which to store supplies of food and fuel. He trained the dog teams, and reduced the sled loads to a minimum.

Scientific exploration

Scott and his team placed great emphasis on scientific discovery. They attached a milometer to the back of one of their sleds to record the distance they traveled, and took daily weather readings. Their return journey was severely hindered by more than 35 lb (15 kg) of geological specimens, which they had collected en route.

JANUARY 17, 1912 SCOTT
REACHES SOUTH POLE

JANUARY 1912 AMUNDSEN
RETURNS FROM POLE A HERO

MARCH 1912 SCOTT'S TEAM
PERISHES BEFORE REACHING SAFETY

HORSES PULL THE SLEDS ON
SCOTT'S EXPEDITION

Scott's expedition

Scott used motorized sleds and horses as well as huskies for transportation – not a wise decision. The powered sleds broke down, and the horses died of exposure as frozen sweat encrusted on their bodies, leaving the men to pull the sleds. Scott arranged for some of his team to turn back as they progressed, so that he was only accompanied by four – Wilson, Oates, Bowers, and Evans – at the Pole itself.

SNOWSHOE
WORN BY OATES

SNOWSHOE
USED BY A HORSE

First to the pole

After crossing more than 2,000 miles (3,200 km) of snow and ice, Amundsen and his team reached the south pole in fine, sunny weather on December 14, 1911. There they raised the Norwegian flag and rested for a few days, returning safely to base camp after just 96 days.

SCOTT'S TEAM

A disappointing second

Scott and his team reached the south pole on January 17, 1912, only to discover evidence that their Norwegian rivals had beaten them to it. Sadly, they began the long trek home. The party was suffering from frostbite, fatigue, and lack of food. The onset of severe blizzards was the ultimate blow and all five men died, three of them just a short distance from a food dump.

Amundsen relied entirely on huskies to pull his sleds

Huskies sweat through their noses

Thick coat makes huskies suitable for bitter conditions

AMUNDSEN PLACES
THE NORWEGIAN FLAG
AT THE SOUTH POLE

41

1912

Leap into the unknown

MARCH 1

Albert Berry made history today when he parachuted to the ground after jumping out of a biplane. The dramatic event took place at 1,500 ft (457 m) over Jefferson Barracks in central Missouri. Berry plummeted some 400 ft (122 m) before his parachute opened, but his jump went without a hitch, and he landed safely on the parade ground as planned.

Sarah makes screen breakthrough

MARCH 9

After the flop of *Tosca* a few years ago, Sarah Bernhardt is

Leading lady Sarah Bernhardt

once again winning critical acclaim for her "golden bell" voice and superb acting. The French tragic actress is already established as a great stage performer on both sides of the Atlantic. Now, at the age of 68, she is also a screen success. Bernhardt plays the leading role in *La Dame aux Camélias*, made last year in Paris by Henri Pouctal and Paul Capellani. She is currently filming in another title role, *Queen Elizabeth*, due for release later this year.

Titanic sinks in worst sea disaster

A few survivors watch the great ship go down

APRIL 15

Early this morning White Star's great SS *Titanic* hit an iceberg and sank, causing one of the greatest disasters ever to happen at sea. Over 1,500 of its 2,224 passengers and crew are thought to have perished in the icy waters of the North Atlantic. The *Titanic* was launched last year in Belfast, Ireland. It was the biggest and most luxurious ship in the world, and the pride of the White Star fleet. It was also believed to be unsinkable, as the hull was fitted with 16 watertight compartments, enabling it to stay afloat even if two flooded. But its maiden voyage was also to be its last. Four days into its journey from Southampton, Britain, to New York, the ship was speeding through an

JANUARY– JUNE

World Events	**FEB** China is officially declared a Republic, with Yuan Shi-kai as its leader.	**MAY** In the House of Commons, the British government passes a bill to grant Home Rule to Ireland.	**MAY** Italy bombards the entrance to the Turkish Dardanelles and occupies the Greek island of Rhodes.	**MAY** The first issue of the Bolshevik newspaper *Pravda*, meaning "truth", is published in St. Petersburg, Russia.
Entertainment	**FEB** England beats Australia 4–1 in a five-match cricket series to regain the Ashes.  **ROBERT FALCON SCOTT**	**MAR** In the UK, the boat race between Oxford and Cambridge has to be re-rowed as both boats sink.	**MAY** *Prélude à l'Après Midi d'un Faune*, a ballet danced by Nijinsky, causes controversy in France.	**MAY** The expressionist "Blue Rider Group" puts on a second exhibition of paintings in Munich, Germany.
Innovations	**JAN** In France, Professor Dastre pioneers a cornea graft to restore lost eyesight.	**MAR** Captain Scott and his British team finally reach the south pole, but perish on their return journey.	**APR** Major new discoveries are made at the Roman town of Pompeii, Italy, as more excavations are carried out.  **NIJINSKY'S NEW BALLET**	**JUN** Races are timed electronically for the first time at the 5th Olympic Games in Stockholm, Sweden.

1912

ice field near Newfoundland, hoping to win the "Blue Riband" for the fastest Atlantic crossing. It collided with an iceberg that ripped through the starboard side, breaking open a 300-ft (91-m) gash. The ship tilted forward and slowly slid beneath the waves. Within three hours it had completely disappeared. Passengers made a frantic attempt to get on deck and board the lifeboats, but few were successful. It has been suggested that there were, in fact, not enough lifeboats to accommodate all the people on board and that in the confusion some went off only half full. The first ship on the scene, the *Carpathia*, took the 700 survivors to Halifax, Nova Scotia, where they are recovering. There will be a full inquiry into this tragic affair.

A lifeboat heads for the Carpathia, *the first ship on the scene*

Royal Pavlova

JULY 3

The first Royal Command Performance was held last night in London, UK. Russian ballet dancer Anna Pavlova topped the bill and performed her "Dying Swan" routine to great applause.

Pavlova simulates the beating of a swan's wings with her arms

The Keystone Kops on the beat

Keystone hits the funny bone

SEPTEMBER 23

The newly formed Keystone Pictures Corporation releases its first two pictures today in Hollywood, California. *Cohen Collects a Debt* and *The Water Nymph* are the first productions of Mack Sennett's company of "popular fun-makers," most notable of whom is the stunning Mabel Normand. Future weekly releases will feature a team of accident-prone policemen known as the Keystone Kops.

DOUBLE GOLD

US athlete Jim Thorpe was the star of this year's Olympic Games in Stockholm, Sweden, winning two gold medals. He won the pentathlon, but caused a sensation in the decathlon with a world-record score of 8,412.955 points. The Swedish king, expressing his admiration, said "Sir, you are the greatest athlete in the world." Thorpe replied "Thanks, King."

JULY–DECEMBER

SEP In Ireland 471,414 Ulster Protestants sign a "Solemn Covenant" pledging themselves to resist the imposition of Irish Home Rule.

SEP French Cubist artist George Braque creates his first picture using a paper collage technique, entitled *Fruit Dish and Glass*.

AUG French doctor Gaston Odin claims that he has isolated and cultivated a microbe of cancer.

OLIVER TWIST

SEP A conflict between Bulgaria and Turkey heats up in the Balkans, causing Greece, Serbia, and Bulgaria to mobilize troops.

DEC The first UK feature film, *Oliver Twist*, which is directed by Cecil Hepworth, opens in London.

SEP Electrical loudspeakers are used for the first time in public at the Olympic Theater in Chicago, IL.

OCT The Balkan league – Greece, Serbia, Bulgaria, and Montenegro – launches a major offensive against Turkey.

DEC The first ice show, *Flirting at St. Moritz*, starring Charlotte Oelschlagel, opens in Germany.

DEC German geologist Alfred Wegener outlines his theory on how today's continents have formed.

PILTDOWN MAN

OCT Turkey, preoccupied with the Balkan threat, signs a peace treaty at Ouchy, Switzerland, to end its war with Italy.

DEC *It's a Long Way to Tipperary*, a song by UK duo Jack Judge and Harry Williams, is a smash hit.

DEC The skull of the Piltdown Man, believed to be 50,000 years old, is found in Sussex, UK.

VOTES FOR WOMEN

WSPU EMBLEM SHOWS A YOUNG WOMAN CARRYING THE BANNER OF FREEDOM

THE ISSUE OF WOMEN'S SUFFRAGE was not new. By the beginning of the 20th century, women all over the world had been campaigning for the right to vote for many years. Although women in New Zealand achieved their goal in 1893, in most countries campaigning continued for much longer. In Britain the Women's Social and Political Union (WSPU), founded by Emmeline Pankhurst in 1903, staged a notorious and influential campaign that attracted thousands of supporters. They fought for the vote with "Deeds, not Words" in a war against the government that became increasingly fierce and bitter in the years leading up to World War I. The women, nicknamed "suffragettes," adopted militant direct action tactics that included heckling, mass demonstrations, and bold stunts. They finally achieved their goal in 1918.

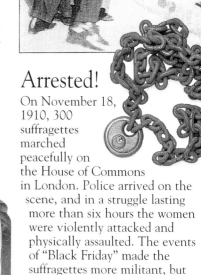

Arrested!

On November 18, 1910, 300 suffragettes marched peacefully on the House of Commons in London. Police arrived on the scene, and in a struggle lasting more than six hours the women were violently attacked and physically assaulted. The events of "Black Friday" made the suffragettes more militant, but more wary of encountering police.

Quite at ease

In 1906, Finnish women became the first in Europe to receive the vote. The following year, 19 had seats in parliament. *The Times* in London reported that all "appeared quite at ease."

Military precision

The WSPU was organized along military lines. Emmeline Pankhurst inspired the "troops," while her eldest daughter, Christabel, led them. Like soldiers, suffragettes followed orders without question and were prepared to go to any lengths, even to die, for their cause.

CHRISTABEL (LEFT) AND EMMELINE PANKHURST

US WOMEN DEMONSTRATE FOR THE RIGHT TO VOTE

"Votes for women" sash in suffragette colors

US women's fight for the vote had support in every state

KANSAS IDAHO WASHINGTON WYOMING COLOR

DETAIL FROM A VOTES FOR WOMEN COVER

Women's suffrage in Asia

Women all over Asia campaigned for the right to vote. The Women's Indian Association raised the issue in 1917, but the vote was not given universally until 1949, two years after Indian independence. Japanese women started campaigning in the 1920s, but had to wait until 1945 before they could vote. In China, women's right to vote came as part of the new communist regime.

Spreading the word

The WSPU knew how to get its message across. It set up a publishing company, The Woman's Press, and produced its own newspapers, *Votes for Women* and the more militant *Suffragette*. On street corners suffragettes gave pamphlets to passersby.

Behind bars

FORCE-FEEDING EQUIPMENT

Between 1906 and 1914, thousands of suffragettes were arrested in Britain and many were imprisoned. Some went on hunger strike. The government, worried that women would die and become martyrs, introduced force feeding, a brutal torture that caused a public outcry.

Women often wore white dresses on demonstrations

OREGON   ILLINOIS

SUFFRAGETTES WORE COARSE CALICO CLOTHING IN PRISON

Playing cat and mouse

In 1913, the British government introduced what became known as the "Cat and Mouse Act." Like a cat that plays with a mouse rather than kills it, the authorities released seriously ill hunger strikers from prison, but rearrested them as they recovered.

BUTTONS DECORATED WITH WHITE, GREEN, AND PURPLE

TRICOLOR ROSETTE WAS WORN ON EVERY MARCH

Suffrage in the States

As elsewhere, women's suffrage in the United States was a long, hard struggle, made more difficult by some who saw it as a diversion to achieving black rights. At first campaigning was on a state-by-state basis, but in 1890 it began to be fought on a federal level. Tactics varied from gentle persuasion to militancy, until the campaign achieved victory across the country in 1920.

Colors of suffrage

Green for life, purple for honor, and white for purity were the colors of the WSPU, and supporters wore them with pride. Fashion houses and department stores were quick to design appropriately colored clothing and merchandise.

1913

The riot of spring

MAY 30

The premiere of Russian composer Igor Stravinsky's ballet *The Rite of Spring* was met with boos and whistles last night in Paris. The audience was unprepared for the dissonant and pounding rhythms of the music and Vaslav Nijinsky's fierce choreography, performed by the Ballets Russes.

Stravinsky with leading dancer Nijinsky

World's biggest train station opens

FEBRUARY 2

Grand Central Station, New York City's impressive new railroad terminal, opened for business today. Situated in central Manhattan, it is the largest railroad station in the world, with 48 tracks. The steel-framed building, which is covered with granite and marble, was designed by US architects Warren and Wetmore. It is a fine example of the Beaux Arts style, which dominates many of today's public buildings. Sculptures of the Roman gods Mercury, Hercules, and Minerva crown the entrance, and the interior is dominated by a high-vaulted ceiling painted with more than 2,500 stars.

THE ZIPPER

Swedish inventor Gideon Sundback has made a new kind of fastener – the zipper – for clothing. His idea of mounting metal teeth onto parallel strips of cloth was patented this April. It will be ready for manufacture next year.

Martyr at the Derby

JUNE 4

High drama occurred today at the Derby, an annual horse race held in Britain at Epsom, Surrey. In the middle of the race a woman rushed onto the track and grabbed at the reins of Anmer, the king's horse. Both horse and rider were brought down by her action. The jockey suffered slight injuries; the woman, who has been identified as Emily Davison, was knocked out and is unlikely to regain consciousness. Miss Davison is a suffragette and is now being hailed as a martyr by fellow campaigners.

Emily Davison brings down the king's horse

JANUARY–JUNE

World Events	**JAN** In France, Aristide Briand succeeds Raymond Poincaré as prime minister and forms a new cabinet.	**FEB** In Mexico, right-wing army commander Victoriano Huerta seizes power from President Madero and has him killed.	**MAY** A peace treaty is signed in London, UK, bringing an end to the first Balkan War between Turkey and the Balkan States.	**JUN** The second Balkan War begins as Bulgaria turns on its former allies, and attacks Serbia and Greece.
Entertainment	**JAN** US athlete Jim Thorpe is stripped of his Olympic medals for once competing as a professional.	**FEB** The first international exhibition of modern art, featuring Van Gogh and Cézanne, opens in New York City.	**JUN** US comic actor Roscoe "Fatty" Arbuckle makes his film debut in two of the new Keystone comedies.	**JUN** Ladies and Mixed Doubles matches are first held at the British Wimbledon Tennis Championship.
Innovations	**FEB** A relief party recovers the bodies of the unsuccessful British South Pole expedition team. **JIM THORPE**	**MAR** The first bull-nosed Morris Oxford is made at the Oxford car factory in Cowley, UK.	**APR** Professor Behring announces the development of a new serum for diphtheria in Berlin, Germany. **WOOLWORTH BUILDING**	**APR** The 791-ft (241-m) Woolworth Building, the world's tallest building, is completed in New York City.

1913

Ford's revolutionary assembly line rolls

Blast links two oceans

If all goes well, 250,000 Model T cars will be built next year

OCTOBER 7

US car manufacturer Henry Ford today started an industrial revolution at his Highland Park factory in Michigan by introducing the assembly line. Each car will no longer be assembled from scratch in one place by skilled workers. Now, a 249-ft (76-m) long conveyer belt will move the partly assembled cars along the factory floor, allowing teams of unskilled men to work on one particular part before it moves on to the next team. Ford estimates that this new process will reduce the assembly time of a car to no more than six hours, resulting in a huge increase in output and, most importantly for the consumer, a big drop in price.

OCTOBER 10

With a push of a button, the last remaining piece of rock between the Atlantic and Pacific oceans was removed. More than 4,000 miles (6,437 km) away in Washington, D.C., President Woodrow Wilson set off the blast of dynamite. This dramatic gesture brings the long-running Panama Canal project in Central America near to completion. Hero of the day was Colonel George Goethals, chief engineer on the project since 1907. After some final building work, the canal will be ready to receive the first ships next year.

JULY–DECEMBER

AUG In the Balkans, Bulgaria agrees to a peace settlement, although it is forced to give up most of its newly gained land.

SEP The recently renovated and refurbished Gaumont Picture Palace reopens for business in Paris, France.

AUG Russian aviator Lt. Peter Nesterov performs the first loop-the-loop, a spectacular airplane stunt.

GAUMONT PICTURE PALACE

SEP The Irish Home Rule Bill is passed by the British parliament, but Irish Ulster Unionists prepare to oppose it.

NOV British comic actor Charlie Chaplin makes his film debut in the US in *Making a Living*.

AUG Stainless steel, an alloy of steel and chromium that does not rust, is cast in Sheffield, UK.

NOV Yuan Shi-kai, elected president of the Chinese Republic last month, dismisses the parliament and sets up a dictatorship.

DEC The first crossword puzzle is printed in the *New York World* weekend supplement in the US.

SEP German inventor Rudolf Diesel, who created the revolutionary diesel engine, dies at the age of 55.

THE FIRST CROSSWORD

NOV Mexican rebels led by Pancho Villa prepare to move on Mexico City and besiege right-wing President Huerta.

DEC The *Mona Lisa*, stolen from the Louvre in 1911, is recovered in Florence, Italy.

OCT The world's first oil-driven battleship, HMS *Queen Elizabeth*, is launched in Portsmouth, UK.

1914

Austrian Archduke assassinated

JUNE 28

The heir to the Austrian throne Archduke Franz Ferdinand and his wife were assassinated today during their official visit to the Bosnian capital of Sarajevo. The assassin, Gavrilo Princip, who is a Bosnian Serb, ran out from the crowd and fired two shots at the couple with a Browning pistol. Both victims died almost immediately from their wounds. It appears that the assassination was part of a carefully laid plot. Earlier in the day the couple had had a narrow escape when a bomb was thrown at their car, but the Archduke knocked it away, injuring people in the following car. It is unclear who might be responsible for the attack, but there are suspicions that it may be Serbia, which opposes Austrian rule in Bosnia. If this is true, it can be expected that Austria will take the strongest action.

War breaks out in Europe

AUGUST 4

Europe is at war! After two weeks of high tension across the Continent, all the major powers are now embroiled in conflict. France, Russia, and Britain stand on one side, facing Germany and Austria-Hungary on the other. The headlong rush into war was triggered by the assassination of Franz Ferdinand in June. On July 23, Austria issued Serbia an ultimatum, requesting that it collaborate to find those responsible for the plot.

Kitchener summons British volunteers

Archduke Franz Ferdinand at the start of his fateful journey

Serbia refused, and five days later Austria declared war and invaded. Russia rushed to defend its ally Serbia, while Germany came to the aid of its ally Austria. On August 3 Germany declared war on France and invaded Belgium. Britain, pledged to defend Belgian neutrality, entered the conflict today, declaring war on Germany. Opinion is divided on how long the war might last. The commander of the British Expeditionary Force, Sir John French, thinks it will be over by Christmas, but Secretary of State for War Lord Kitchener believes that it could be much longer.

World Events	**FEB** Northern Ireland appears on the brink of civil war as Protestants violently resist home rule.	**MAR** The editor of *Le Figaro* is shot dead by the French finance minister's wife for planning to slur her husband's name.	**APR** A 3,000-strong force of US marines intervenes in the Mexican civil war and seizes the port of Vera Cruz.	**JUN** The assassination of Archduke Franz Ferdinand leads to growing tension between Austria and Serbia.
Entertainment	**FEB** *The Word, the Flesh, and the Devil* is the world's first feature film to be shot in color.	**MAR** Seven US newspapers, including the *New York Times*, issue the world's first newspaper color supplement.	**APR** The bad language in Irish playwright George Bernard Shaw's *Pygmalion* causes much controversy.	**JUN** Wyndham Lewis publishes *Blast*, the manifesto of the futurist Vorticist art movement, in London, UK.
Innovations	**JAN** The US Ford Motor Co. introduces the $5 work day for all its employees.	**FEB** UK explorer Campbell Beasley discovers the remains of three Inca cities hidden in the jungles of Peru.	**MAY** UK explorer Ernest Shackleton leaves the UK on a major three-year exploration of Antarctica.	**JUN** At Hamburg, Kaiser Wilhelm II launches the German-built *Bismarck*, the world's largest ship.

INCA VASE

PYGMALION

1914

Russian prisoners of war

Russians routed on Eastern Front

AUGUST 31

After four days of heavy fighting at Tannenberg on the Polish-German border, the Russian Second Army, led by General Samsonov, has suffered a terrible defeat at the hands of the Germans. According to eyewitness accounts, the battle was very one-sided, with the Russian cavalry proving no match for the heavily armed and well-organized German infantry. It is estimated that more than 100,000 Russian soldiers have been taken prisoner. The defeat is being taken well by Russian authorities, who have already achieved a chain of successes and made inroads into German territory. However, it will change the shape of the campaign on the Eastern Front.

THE TRAMP
Dressed in a baggy suit with a battered hat and holding a cane, British-born actor Charlie Chaplin has launched a new star. His first appearance dressed as the Tramp in the film *Kid Auto Races at Venice* has captured the hearts of US audiences.

Paris saved from German attack

SEPTEMBER 10

The German attempt to knock France quickly out of the war ground to a halt today after six days of fighting on the Marne River in northeastern France. The German plan, devised by General von Schlieffen, was to make a headlong sweep through Belgium and around the north of Paris, avoiding the heavily armed forts along the common Franco-German border. At first the bold attempt at a knockout blow against the French capital seemed to be succeeding. Within days of occupying Luxembourg and invading Belgium, the German army was moving quickly through France, but a decisive French counteroffensive of fresh troops has finally halted the advance. The German army is now in retreat and is digging itself in in deep trenches along the Aisne River, 25 miles (40 km) to the north. The fighting – the first major engagement in western Europe between the warring sides – is thought to have resulted in as many as 500,000 casualties.

French soldiers in action

Truce halts war for Christmas

DECEMBER 25

Along a small section of the Western Front south of Messines, Belgium, soldiers on both sides of the war celebrated Christmas together. They exchanged gifts of cigars and jam and some are rumored to have played a game of soccer.

JULY–DECEMBER

JUL Austria delivers an ultimatum to Serbia containing such humiliating demands that it makes war almost inevitable.

AUG 72-year-old Sam Lucas becomes the first black actor to star in a feature film – *Uncle Tom's Cabin*.

AUG Electrically controlled lights for directing traffic are introduced in Cleveland, Ohio.

PETROGRAD

SEP The Russian government changes the name of its capital city to Petrograd because St. Petersburg sounded too German.

SEP German painter Auguste Macke and French novelist Henri Alain-Fournier are both killed in battle.

AUG The Panama Canal, joining the north Atlantic and south Pacific oceans, is finally completed.

OCT In the "Race to the Sea" Germany and the Allies wage battles through northern France in an attempt to outflank each other.

DEC US cartoonist John Gruelle paints a face on his daughter's faceless rag doll – and invents the Raggedy Ann Doll.

OCT Russian manufacturer Sikorsky experiments with the design of a multi-engined heavy bomber.

TRENCH SPADE

NOV Stalemate is reached: a line of trenches now stretches from the English Channel to the border of Switzerland.

DEC Among the new books published this year is *Dubliners*, a collection of short stories by Irish writer James Joyce.

OCT The US Eastman Kodak Co. announces the invention of a color photographic process.

TRENCH WARFARE

WHEN WAR BROKE OUT IN 1914, the battles between German and Allied soldiers were fought using heavy artillery and machine guns. It soon became clear that the best means of defense in such attacks was to pick up a spade and dig a hole. Lines of trenches evolved; complex webs made up of front line, communication, support, and reserve trenches, gunpits, and listening posts. At the rear were dugouts used as living quarters and storage. The front was fortified with barbed wire and watched over by armed sentries. Many men spent the entire war in these cramped, muddy ditches. In addition to suffering from the cold and rain, the horrors the men had to deal with included rats, lice, and lack of hygiene.

Front line of trenches

Eyeholes were situated about 1 ft (0.3 m) below the line of vision

GERMAN ARTILLERY OBSERVATION INSTRUMENT

The Western Front

Within three months of war starting, the front line between the German and Allied armies in western Europe became fixed. A line of trenches stretched from the English Channel to the Swiss border. Over the next four years many battles (starred right) were fought to try to break the deadlock, but the front line held, shifting no more than 10 miles (16 km) in either direction, until the final months of the war in 1918.

Look out

Snipers would ruthlessly gun down any soldiers who put their heads over the top or climbed out of their trenches. During attacks, observation instruments were used to get a 3-D vision of fire over the battle ground. At other times soldiers used trench periscopes, nicknamed "donkeys' ears" due to their shape, to observe what was happening in relative safety.

Poison gas

In an attempt to break the stalemate, German armies first used chlorine gas at Ypres in April 1915. A swirling cloud of thick greenish-yellow vapor drifted over the Allied lines, blinding the soldiers and causing the loss of 5,000 lives. Both sides swiftly developed the use of phosgene and mustard gas, causing choking, vomiting, and gut rot. Gas attacks became hated and feared by all soldiers in the war.

BRITISH TROOPS SUFFERING FROM THE BLINDING EFFECTS OF GAS

Communications

Troops in the trenches needed to be able to communicate quickly with their officers and each other. In order to relate what was going on in different sections of the line, field telephones, like this German "feld fernsprecher," were located both in the dugouts and at the observation posts, and connected up by a telephone wire. Radios, runners, dogs, and even pigeons were also used to convey messages.

Rats spread disease through the trenches

NOVEMBER 1916 ONE MILLION DIE
AFTER FOUR-MONTH SOMME OFFENSIVE

APRIL 1917 US TROOPS ENTER THE
WAR ON THE SIDE OF THE ALLIES

NOVEMBER 1918 END OF THE
GREAT WAR, ALLIES VICTORIOUS

BRITISH SOLDIERS

Weaponry

The main weapons used at the front were machine guns, artillery shells, and, after 1916, tanks. Individual soldiers were equipped with a rifle, grenades for knocking out the enemy at close quarters, and clubs and knives for one-to-one combat. During an assault soldiers used wire-cutters to cut through any wire that had not been destroyed in the initial artillery barrage.

GERMAN CLUB

BRITISH MILLS BOMB

FRENCH TRENCH KNIFE

GERMAN STICK GRENADE

BRITISH WIRE-CUTTERS

Waiting for action

Fighting did not take place every day on the Western Front, and some sections of line could often be quiet for months at a time. The biggest enemy the soldiers then encountered was boredom. The men would sit for hours in cramped, unhygienic conditions, with little to look forward to except the next meal. While they waited for their next orders, writing or receiving letters from home were favored activities.

LETTERS HOME FROM A BRITISH SOLDIER

Illustrations helped convey what war was like

1915

Outrage at epic movie premiere

MARCH 3

There were demonstrations outside the Liberty Theater in New York today at the premiere of *The Birth of a Nation*, the new film by US filmmaker D. W. Griffith. Black activists, angry at the film's distorted view of black history and the Civil War, are trying to have the film banned. The activists are offended in particular by the scenes of black-faced white actors committing racial atrocities and the idealized portrayal of the Ku Klux Klan. The 180-minute-long film was also shown to President Wilson at a private viewing held at the White House. "It is like writing history with lightning," he said. "And my only regret is that it is all so terribly true."

SS *Lusitania* sunk

MAY 8

The sinking of the British liner SS *Lusitania* by German torpedoes off the coast of Ireland yesterday afternoon was met with outrage by the US public. The *Lusitania* had almost completed its North Atlantic crossing from New York to Liverpool when a German submarine struck without warning at 2:12 pm. The ship was hit by two torpedoes and sank within 21 minutes. Of the 1,198 passengers, more than 500 have survived the ordeal. Among the 1,400 passengers who drowned are 128 US citizens, including prominent people and close friends of President Wilson. The US State Department said it viewed the sinking "most seriously," and the former President Theodore Roosevelt condemned it as an "act of piracy." Commentators are wondering what effect the sinking of the *Lusitania* will have on the US's policy of neutrality.

Nurse executed on spy charge

OCTOBER 12

British nurse Edith Cavell was shot for treason today by a German firing squad in the Belgian capital of Brussels. Cavell, who had run a school for nurses in the city since 1906, continued to work when war broke out last year and treated the sick and injured of all nations in the conflict. Despite the respect she had gained for her work from both warring sides, she was arrested on August 5 and charged with harboring Belgians who were eligible to fight, and with helping British and French soldiers escape to safety across the Dutch border.

Nurse Edith Cavell and her dogs

JANUARY– JUNE

World Events	**JAN** German Zeppelin airships begin a bombing campaign against the UK by attacking ports on the east coast.	**FEB** Germany begins submarine warfare against the UK to try to frighten away neutral shipping and destroy the UK's economy.	**APR** Allied forces land on the Gallipoli Peninsula in Turkey in an attempt to force an entrance through to the Black Sea.	**MAY** Italy leaves the Triple Alliance with Germany and Austria and enters the war on the side of the Allies.
Entertainment	**FEB** In Berlin, it is decided to abandon plans to stage next year's Olympic Games in Germany.	**FEB** French actress Sarah Bernhardt has her right leg amputated following a fall during a performance of *La Tosca*.	**APR** Jess Willard, the US "Great White Hope," wins the World Heavyweight boxing title, defeating Jack Johnson.	**APR** British war poet and romantic hero Rupert Brooke dies in Greece at the age of 28 from blood poisoning.
Innovations	**JAN** The first transcontinental telephone call is made between New York and San Francisco.	**JAN** Germans carry out the first-ever gas attack in warfare against Russian troops at Bolimov on the Eastern Front.	**APR** The first antichlorine gas masks are issued to British troops in the second Battle of Ypres, France.	**JUN** The first 3-D films, developed by E. S. Porter and W. E. Wadell, are shown in New York City.

ZEPPELIN BOMB

GAS MASK

1915

Women's work boosts war effort

NOVEMBER 10

Last March the British government appealed for women to sign up for work in factories in order to free men to fight. The thousands of women who volunteered are now achieving excellent results. One survey suggests that productivity has risen two and a half times. The initially wary factory foremen acknowledge that women's energy, punctuality, and willingness make them more than ideal substitutes for their male counterparts. Most women are involved in producing vital munitions, working up to 12 hours a day 7 days a week to ensure that the troops have enough arms.

Women workers in a shell factory

SHELL-SHOCKED

Long-range shells filled with gas or pieces of shrapnel have introduced a terrifying new dimension to warfare this year. Fired from behind the safety of enemy lines, the shells can inflict great damage on frontline troops sheltering in their trenches.

Allies retreat from Gallipoli shore

DECEMBER 20

After eight months of futile fighting, Allied forces retreated from the Gallipoli Peninsula in western Turkey last night. Under cover of darkness, troops from Britain, New Zealand, and Australia slipped away, leaving the peninsula in the hands of its Turkish rulers. More than 25,000 troops have been killed in the fighting, with more than 76,000 wounded, 96,000 taken to the hospital, and at least 13,000 missing. Commentators are calling the Allied withdrawal the biggest setback of the war so far.

Medal given to Turkish troops

The ill-fated expedition to Gallipoli was originally designed to force a passage through the Dardanelles strait into the Black Sea, and so open up a route to supply Russia with much-needed weapons. It was intended that this would knock Turkey out of the war and, by threatening Austria and Germany from the east through the Balkans, would break the deadlock in western Europe. The strategic peninsula that overlooks the Dardanelles was first bombarded in February this year, but then an Allied naval assault in March failed when six ships were sunk in an unidentified minefield. The troops finally went ashore on April 25, but by then the element of surprise was lost and the Turks had reinforced their positions. Despite some successes, the Allies remained pinned down on the beaches and were unable to capture the peninsula. The Australian and New Zealand troops have displayed great acts of heroism, but the cost of the fighting has proved to be too great, hence the instruction to withdraw. No lives were lost in this final retreat.

JULY–DECEMBER

SEP The fall offensive opens on the Western Front, with French troops under the command of General Joffre.

JUL The first tourist car is admitted into Yellowstone National Park in northwestern Wyoming.

OCT British ships begin to tow a torpedo-shaped device from their bows in order to disarm mines.

GENERAL JOFFRE

SEP Following the fall of the key Russian stronghold at Brest-Livosk, Czar Nicholas II takes personal control of the army.

OCT The Boston Red Sox buy pitcher Babe Ruth's contract from the Baltimore Orioles.

NOV An AB-2 flying boat of the US Navy is the first plane to be launched by catapult from a ship.

SEP Bulgaria enters the war on the side of Germany and Austria and moves its forces eastward toward Serbia.

OCT William G. Grace, the figurehead and greatest player to date in British test cricket, dies at the age of 67.

DEC As the production line continues to roll, the US Ford Motor Co. produces its one-millionth automobile.

W. G. GRACE

DEC Sir John French is replaced as commander in chief of the British forces by Sir Douglas Haig.

DEC Among the best-selling novels published this year was *The 39 Steps* by Scottish writer John Buchan.

DEC During the year German-born physicist Albert Einstein publishes his general theory of relativity.

1916

Major assault opens at Verdun

FEBRUARY 21
At exactly 7:15 this morning, German guns opened fire without warning at French positions around the fort of Verdun. During the course of the day more than a million shells fell as the Germans began their push at French defenses in this key sector of the Western Front. As the German infantry advanced behind their artillery, the French retaliated with machine gun fire. As yet it is unclear whether the German goal is to engage a large part of the French army in a lengthy battle of attrition, or to break through their lines.

For now the bulk of French troops are being kept away from the front line to minimize losses. However, they are suffering from an earlier decision by General Joffre who, thinking that the Germans would strike farther north at Champagne, had reduced defenses at Verdun.

Pancho Villa and some of his bandits

US troops sent to pursue Villa

MARCH 15
A force of 4,000 US soldiers, led by Brigadier-General John Pershing, crossed the border into Mexico today in pursuit of Mexican rebel leader Pancho Villa. They will join 5,000 men who are already looking for the bandit. Villa is responsible for the deaths of 18 US mining engineers who were removed from a train near Chihuahua and shot on January 16. He also cold-bloodedly killed 19 inhabitants of Columbus, New Mexico, on March 9. The reasons for these attacks are open to debate, but some reports say that Villa is hoping to draw the United States into the Mexican civil war and expose the weakness of the Mexican government.

JANUARY– MARCH

World Events

JAN Austro-Hungarian forces attack Montenegro and quickly overrun the small Balkan country.

JAN The last Allied troops leave the Gallipoli Peninsula in Turkey after they fail in their attempt to take it over.

FEB For the fifth time, the Italian army tries to break through the Austro-Hungarian lines at the Isonzo River.

MAR The first president of the Chinese Republic, Yuan Shi-kai, dies, leaving China without a clear political leader.

Entertainment

FEB US author Henry James, who wrote *The Portrait of a Lady*, dies at the age of 72.

DADA POSTER BY
KURT SCHWITTERS

FEB A group of artists, creators of a new art form called "Dada," meet in Zurich, Switzerland.

FEB The first in a new cartoon series, *Krazy Kat and Ignatz Mouse Discuss the Letter G*, is shown in New York City.

MAR Handsome US actor Douglas Fairbanks Senior makes his film debut in *The Habit of Happiness*.

Innovations

JAN As war continues, sugar rationing is introduced in the London area, UK.

FEB The first British fighter squadron goes into operation in St. Omer, northern France.

FEB Air-to-ground radio is first demonstrated by a British military pilot to Lord Kitchener in France.

DOUGLAS
FAIRBANKS

MAR The Austrian War Dog Institute begins to train dogs to be used to guide blind people.

1916

WOMEN AT WAR

As men are drafted into armies to fight in the front lines, women all over Europe are playing an increasingly important part in the war. Factories, farms, and even public transportation are now being run by women workers, without whose contribution many vital services would otherwise grind to a halt.

Devastated corner of Sackville Street, Dublin

Rebels stage Easter Rising in Dublin

APRIL 24

In what appears to be a prearranged uprising, Irish nationalists in Dublin started a full-scale rebellion against British rule this morning, Easter Monday. The rebels, led by Patrick Pearse of the Irish Republican Brotherhood and trade union leader James Connolly of Sinn Féin, seized the General Post Office on Sackville Street in the center of the city, and declared Ireland to be an independent republic. Other buildings across Dublin have been occupied, but attempts to seize Dublin Castle, the headquarters of British rule in Ireland, and an arsenal in Phoenix Park have failed. Fighting has broken out between republicans and British troops as both sides struggle to take control of key positions in the city. To cope with the worsening situation, Britain has called in reinforcements from other parts of Ireland.

Sea battle at Jutland

MAY 31

In what is being dubbed "the greatest naval battle ever waged," British and German *Dreadnought* battleships clashed at Jutland off the coast of Denmark today. A conflict between the fleets has been brewing for some time, with the Germans eager to break the long-standing Allied blockade off their coast. The outcome of who won however, is not clear, with both sides claiming victory. Although the German fleet is the first to have retreated, the British fleet suffered greater losses in both ships and men. The test will be whether the German High Seas Fleet will venture out of port again to face the firepower of the British Grand Fleet. Meanwhile, the Allied blockade remains.

APRIL–JUNE

APR President Wilson threatens to break US diplomatic relations with Germany if it continues submarine warfare.

APR The International Olympic Committee cancels the Olympic Games until the war is over.

APR The first major airlift of supplies is conducted by British pilots to a besieged garrison at Kut al-Imara, Iraq.

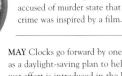

DAYLIGHT SAVING

MAY British general Sir John Maxwell orders the execution of the rebels involved in the Easter Rising.

APR Two French girls who are accused of murder state that their crime was inspired by a film.

MAY Clocks go forward by one hour as a daylight-saving plan to help the war effort is introduced in the UK.

JUN Russian armies commanded by General Alexei Brusilov make huge advances into Austria-Hungary on the Eastern Front.

MAY Norman Rockwell designs the cover for the first edition of the Philadelphia *Saturday Evening Post*.

JUN US timber magnate William Boeing tests his newly designed airplane in Washington, D.C.

RUSSIAN GENERAL ALEXEI BRUSILOV

JUN British war minister Lord Kitchener dies when the HMS *Hampshire* is sunk by a German mine off the Orkney Islands.

JUN The final episode of *The Vampires* series is shown in Paris, starring the beautiful Musidora.

JUN The US Bell Telephone Co. demonstrates an open-air public-address system on Staten Island.

1916

Carnage as Somme campaign opens

British Pals battalion badge

JULY 1 At 7:30 this morning, the artillery barrage against German lines that has lasted for seven days came to an end. Five minutes later, thousands of Allied troops advanced, only to be mowed down by enemy gunfire. This evening, 57,470 Allied and 8,000 German soldiers lie dead or injured in no-man's land. The attack on German lines near the Somme River in northern France has temporarily ground to a halt amid the worst scenes of slaughter the war has seen. In this long-prepared-for offensive, the troops attacked on a 20-mile (32-km) front, but the army was not at its full strength. The 25 British divisions were mostly made up of Pals battalions, who are enthusiastic but inexperienced volunteers, and the French army only provided 11, rather than the 40 divisions it had promised, because most of its men were tied up fighting at Verdun. The problem was that the Germans held the high ground surrounding the river, so much of the advance was uphill. In addition, the heavily fortified German lines were left relatively unscathed by the initial bombardment. The battle plan, devised by British Field Marshal Haig, called for a massive push against the German front line that would break the stalemate and lead to a speedy victory in the war.

He calculated that the Allies would advance about 2.5 miles (4 km) by the end of the first day. He had not reckoned on the strength of the German fortifications, nor that they would retreat into second-line bunkers and ride out the bombardment. As the unwitting Allied soldiers climbed out of their trenches this morning, they were not met with the light resistance they had expected, but with a savage hail of gunfire. Loaded down with more than 65 lb (30 kg) of equipment, the soldiers could only progress at a slow walk, making each one an easy target for the German gunners. A truce at midday allowed some of the dead and wounded to be carried away from the battlefield. Tonight the British army must reflect on this most terrible result.

German machine gun on trench mount

JULY–SEPTEMBER

World Events	**AUG** Former British diplomat Roger Casement is executed for trying to smuggle arms to Irish rebels.	**AUG** Kaiser Wilhelm II appoints Paul von Hindenburg, victor of the Battle of Tannenburg, his chief of general staff.	**AUG** Romania joins the Allies and invades Austria-Hungary; Germany declares war on Romania; Turkey declares war on Russia.	**SEP** The Owen-Keating Labor Law, to diminish the appalling conditions of child labor, is passed in the US.
Entertainment	**JUL** French symbolist painter of dreamlike images Odilon Redon dies at the age of 76.	**AUG** *Chu Chin Chow* premieres at Her Majesty's Theatre in London and is popular with British troops.	**AUG** Spanish artist Picasso begins designing scenery for *Parade*, a new ballet for Diaghilev's Ballets Russes.	**SEP** The New York premiere of D. W. Griffith's film *Intolerance*, starring Lillian Gish, receives rave reviews.
Innovations	**JUL** The US Coca-Cola Co. introduces a contoured bottle to make imitations difficult.	**JUL** The German U-boat *UC7* becomes the first submarine to be sunk by depth charges.	**AUG** The US Ford Motor Co. announces the launch of a touring car at the incredibly low price of $250.	**SEP** False eyelashes are worn for the first time by US actress Seena Owen in D. W. Griffith's *Intolerance*.

PAUL VON HINDENBURG

US ACTRESS LILLIAN GISH

1916

NURSES AT THE FRONT

The unsung heroes of the war are the nurses who tend the injured. Often operating in extreme danger, they venture into no-man's land, the ground between the front lines, to rescue the wounded. Sometimes they carry out minor surgery on the spot before the casualty is moved to safety.

Tanks set to revolutionize war

SEPTEMBER 15

The British army revealed its latest weapon today: the tank. Built in the strictest secrecy, this armored vehicle can roll over difficult terrain and withstand all but the most powerful artillery. This morning a fleet of 32 tanks was deployed on the Somme and within two hours they had pushed back the front line 7 miles (11 km). German machine gunners scattered in their path and more than 2,000 were taken prisoner.

British Mark I tank

"Miracle worker" murdered

DECEMBER 30

The Russian monk Gregory Rasputin was murdered today by two relatives of Czar Nicholas II. Rasputin was lured to the home of Prince Yussupov, where he was shot and bludgeoned to death before being dumped in the Neva River. The monk first came to St. Petersburg in 1905. He became a confident of the Czarina since he was able to stop the bleeding of her hemophiliac son. Now the Czar is at the Eastern Front, and Rasputin took advantage of his position to influence the Czarina in political decisions. He has been made to pay heavily for his ambition.

Rasputin, the so-called "miracle worker"

OCTOBER–DECEMBER

NOV On the Western Front the Battle of the Somme ends, having caused more than one million deaths on both sides.

NOV US author and adventurer Jack London, who wrote *Call of the Wild*, dies of alcoholism at the age of 40.

NOV US-born inventor of the machine gun Hiram Mixam dies at the age of 76.

NOV Franz Josef, who ruled the 17 nationalities of the Austro-Hungarian Empire for 68 years, dies at the age of 86.

DEC French Impressionist artist Claude Monet began work this year on *Waterlilies*, a series of murals.

DEC US Earth scientist Albert Michelson determines that the Earth has a molten core.

EMPEROR FRANZ JOSEF

DEC David Lloyd George becomes British prime minister in place of Herbert Asquith and forms a new war cabinet of five men.

DEC The Nobel Prize for literature is awarded to Swedish poet Carl Gustav; no other prizes are awarded.

DEC Fortune cookies, produced this year by the Hong Kong Noodle Co. in Los Angeles, prove popular.

DAVID LLOYD GEORGE

DEC Continuing stalemate in the trenches on the Western Front makes for the third and bleakest Christmas of the war.

DEC *The Planets* orchestral suite is completed this year by British composer Gustav Holst.

DEC Cutex, the first liquid nail polish, is introduced this year in the US by Notham Warren.

1917

US counters submarine threat

FEBRUARY 26

Congress agreed today that US ships could be armed so that they will be able to counter attacks by German submarines. This latest move follows the announcement by Germany on February 1 that any ships found trading in Allied waters would be sunk without warning. Two days later the United States broke off diplomatic relations with Germany. Despite these events, US congressmen are still reluctant to sanction war.

MESSENGER PIGEONS

In an ingenious attempt to communicate with troops in the front line, the Allies are using messenger pigeons. More than half a million specially trained birds are being parachuted into France. They then fly back to England carrying vital messages. Some even work as spies – reconnaissance pigeons carry tiny cameras to photograph enemy defenses.

US "doughboys" land in France

JUNE 27

Following the US's declaration of war against Germany on April 6, the first US troopships arrived off the French coast at dawn today. The landing site had been kept a secret, but by the time the troops, nicknamed "doughboys," lined up on parade on French soil, a huge crowd had gathered to welcome them ashore. Commanded by Major General John "Black Jack" Pershing, a veteran of wars in the Philippines and Mexico, these troops are the first of many thousands that will soon be pouring into France to help the Allied war effort. The deployment of US troops on the Western Front will give a huge boost to the war-weary Allies. With the help of US resources, there is new hope that the fortunes of war will turn in their favor.

Recruitment poster for the US Navy

JANUARY–JUNE

World Events			
MAR As discontent grows among the Russian peoples, Czar Nicholas II abdicates.	**APR** Bolshevik leader Lenin returns from exile in Switzerland to Petrograd, traveling with German assistance.	**APR** US president Woodrow Wilson declares war on Germany in order "to save democracy," and prepares to send troops to Europe.	**JUN** German planes make the first bombing raid on London, UK; a 15-minute attack on the East End kills 100 and injures 400 people.

Entertainment			
FEB The musical *Oh, Boy!* premieres at the Princess Theater, New York City.	**MAR** New Orleans group the Original Dixieland Jazz Band makes the first jazz recording.	**APR** *The Butcher Boy* is filmed in New York, featuring talented new actor Buster Keaton.	**MAY** French poet G. Apollinaire describes Picasso's costumes for the ballet *Parade* as "surrealist."

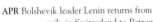

FIRST JAZZ RECORD

Innovations			
JAN German scientists Hahn and Meitner discover the element proactium.	**MAY** The first international airmail service begins operating between Italy and Albania.	**MAY** The world's first airmail stamps are issued in Italy for use on the air service between Rome and Turin.	**JUN** US communications company AT & T introduces the world's first telex service for United Press.

GERMAN LVG CV1 BOMBER PLANE

1917

Chaim Weizmann

Jews promised new homeland

NOVEMBER 9

A week ago British foreign secretary Arthur Balfour promised the Jewish people full support in establishing a homeland in Palestine. The British war cabinet is now hoping that the declaration will encourage members of the Zionist movement, led by Dr. Chaim Weizmann, to fully support the Allied war effort.

Allies capture Passchendaele

NOVEMBER 6

After months of fighting, the bomb-blasted remains of the village of Passchendaele, Belgium, are finally in Allied hands. The third Battle of Ypres began over three months ago on July 31, when British and French troops began bombarding the nearby ridge. In the initial offensive more than four million rounds were fired by 3,000 British guns – the heaviest of the bombardments made yet – in an attempt to break through German lines. However, as

was the case at the Somme last year, more attention was paid to the initial artillery bombardment than to the land over which the soldiers were required to fight. The front line at Ypres was a disastrous place from which to attack as it was surrounded on three sides by the German army. In addition, bad weather has plagued the attack from the start, turning the battlefield into a sea of mud. Today's small victory has been achieved once again at a terrible price – more

than 400,000 Allied lives have been lost and very little land has been gained in return. It is expected that British generals will call a halt to the attack in the next few days.

British stretcher-bearers struggle against the mud near the Belgian village of Passchendaele

---

JULY–DECEMBER

JUL Lenin flees Russia after a Bolshevik uprising is crushed by the new Russian government led by Alexander Kerensky.

JUL A group of Dutch artists led by Piet Mondrian get together to publish *De Stijl*, a small modern art magazine.

AUG British commander Edwin Dunning is the first pilot to land his plane on a moving ship, HMS *Furious*.

MATA HARI

OCT Italian troops are heavily defeated by German and Austro-Hungarian troops at Caporetto in northeastern Italy.

OCT Mata Hari, the Dutch dancer sentenced to death for spying for the Germans, is executed in Paris, France.

NOV At the Battle of Cambrai, the Germans use mustard gas for the first time, causing heavy Allied casualties.

NOV Having returned to Petrograd in October, Lenin leads a Bolshevik coup and seizes power from Kerensky.

NOV French sculptor August Rodin, best known for his controversial work *The Kiss*, dies at the age of 77.

DEC British physicist Charles Glover Barkla wins the Nobel Prize for physics for his work on X rays.

VLADIMIR ILYICH LENIN

DEC The fall of Jerusalem in Palestine to British forces marks the climax of a 14-month offensive against the Turks.

DEC The first Pulitzer Prizes for literature, journalism, and music are awarded in New York.

DEC Argentinean Don Frederico Valle produces the world's first full-length cartoon feature film.

THE RUSSIAN REVOLUTION

IN 1917 A REVOLUTION TOOK PLACE in Russia that was to affect the entire world. The old order, led by Czar Nicholas II, was overthrown, to be replaced first by the provisional government and then by a Bolshevik government. Led by Lenin, this government set about changing Russian society along communist lines. It took all private property into state control and gave the land to the peasants to farm. The country also gained a new name – the USSR (Union of Soviet Socialist Republics). The world's first communist nation had to fight for its life as opponents inside the country, armed by foreign governments, tried to overthrow it. After three years of vicious civil war, the communists gained complete control of the country. The revolution had succeeded.

On the boil

There was a dramatic rise in revolutionary feeling throughout Russia in the early 1900s. Many political parties campaigned to get rid of the powerful Russian nobility in order to construct a fairer society.

The royal family

Czar Nicholas II lived in great luxury in Petrograd and ruled over a vast empire. However, he was a weak leader who stifled all attempts at reforming the government of Russia.

The first revolution

When food riots broke out in March 1917, the Russian army, disillusioned with the czar, took the side of the people. Without the support of the army, Nicholas II had no choice but to abdicate and the provisional government, run by members of the middle class, took control. Unfortunately it, too, failed to tackle the country's social and economic problems.

KERENSKY, LEADER OF THE PROVISIONAL GOVERNMENT FROM JULY 1917

Russia at war

In 1914 Russia sided with France and Britain in World War I. After initial successes, poor organization, bad leadership, and food shortages led to a series of defeats. By 1917 the army was on the point of collapse.

The power of Rasputin

Grigori Rasputin exercised considerable control over the royal family. When Nicholas II took control of the armed forces in 1915, Rasputin dominated the civil government. He was assassinated in 1916 by jealous rivals.

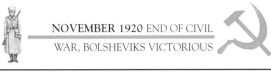

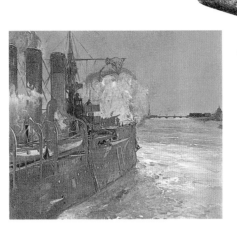

THE AURORA FIRES FROM THE NEVA RIVER

LEON TROTSKY, A KEY PLAYER IN THE RUSSIAN REVOLUTION

STATUES OF LENIN WERE ERECTED IN EVERY TOWN AND CITY OF THE SOVIET UNION

The Bolshevik Revolution

On the night of November 7, 1917, the Bolsheviks, led by Lenin, staged an armed coup in Petrograd. In a many pronged attack, they captured all the bridges and public buildings, and surrounded, shelled, and seized control of the Winter Palace. Two days later, Lenin officially announced the end of the provisional government.

Military organizer

Exiled twice to Siberia for revolutionary activity, Trotsky worked alongside Lenin toward communism. A brilliant military organizer, he trained the workers and set up the Red Army to defend the revolution in the civil war.

The new order

Following the revolution, the Bolsheviks began to transform Russia into the world's first communist state. They set about fulfilling their promise of "Peace, Bread, and Land," but opposition to the new regime put the country into civil war. The Red Army fought against the opposing "White" armies for three years before a victory was achieved and communism was finally allowed to flourish.

HAMMER AND SICKLE, EMBLEM OF THE SOVIET UNION

Power for the people

Lenin's communist party, the Bolsheviks, wanted a people's revolution in which the masses at the bottom of the social order would rise up against the middle classes and the nobility.

The man behind the revolution

The driving force behind the Russian Revolution, Lenin spent much of his youth in exile in Europe. He studied the work of Karl Marx, who believed that a government should be based on equality, and planned a revolutionary takeover of Russia. In March 1917, Lenin was living in Switzerland, but after the uprising he returned to Petrograd in April. He rallied support among the peasants with rousing speeches, and demanded the overthrow of the provisional government. Despite opposition from some members of his own Bolshevik Party, he organized the successful Revolution and took over as leader of the Soviet Union.

1918

Cartoon drawing of US president Woodrow Wilson

Germans attack Western Front

Wilson outlines terms for peace

JANUARY 8

In a speech to Congress today, President Wilson outlined US war goals and put forward 14 points for a post-war peace. These include ensuring absolute freedom of navigation on the seas, the removal of all trade barriers, and a reduction in arms to the lowest point "consistent with domestic safety." Among the various territorial details listed in the proposal are that Germany should evacuate the territory it has occupied, the people of Austria-Hungary should gain their independence, and that Poland should finally be recognized as an independent state with access to the sea.

MARCH 31

Ten days ago the German army launched a huge offensive on the Allied front line between Arras and La Fère in France. Now its soldiers, reinforced by troops from the Eastern Front, who have come to France following the Russian withdrawal from the war, have advanced more than 40 miles (64 km) and have taken 80,000 Allied prisoners. Commanded by General von Ludendorff, the attack has used entirely new tactics. The German artillery first launched a short, powerful bombardment of high explosives and gas and smoke shells. Then shock troops were sent to probe for weak spots in the Allied front line rather than making the usual infantry charge. The plan is to achieve a speedy victory before the bulk of US troops reaches the front line. The operation has been successful so far, with the Allies hastily retreating toward the city of Paris in confusion.

German submachine gun

JANUARY–MARCH

World Events	**JAN** The Bolsheviks establish the Red Army in Russia to defend the revolution.	**MAR** Russia signs the peace treaty of Brest-Livosk with Germany and Austria-Hungary, and leaves WWI.	**MAR** Following the terms of the peace treaty Germany and Turkey gain large regions of western and southern Russia.	**MAR** The Russian government moves its capital city from Petrograd to Moscow to keep away from the war zones.
Entertainment	**JAN** A major new exhibition of paintings by Matisse and Picasso opens in Paris, France.	**FEB** Austrian artist Gustav Klimt, who painted in the Art Nouveau style, dies at the age of 55.	**FEB** US composer George Gershwin's new song *Swanee* is sung in public for the first time in New York City.	**MAR** French composer Claude Debussy, who wrote *Prélude à l'après midi d'un faune*, dies at the age of 55.
Innovations	**JAN** German engineers begin construction of the first all-metal airplane.	**MAR** Trials for the new Browning light machine gun are conducted successfully in New Jersey.	**MAR** The world's first regular airmail service is set up between cities in Austria-Hungary.	**MAR** US manufacturer Henry Ford turns out the first mass-produced tractors at the rate of 80 per day.

THE KISS BY GUSTAV KLIMT

CLAUDE DEBUSSY

1918

PLAYING SOLDIERS

While the adults fight a real war in the trenches of Europe, their children are enacting battles in the safety of their homes. Playing with tin soldiers is a popular game, but the difference is that unlike real soldiers, the tin ones will fight another day.

"Red Baron" shot down in flames

German fighter pilot the "Red Baron"

APRIL 22

The "Red Baron" is dead! Germany's most famous fighter pilot, Baron Manfred von Richthofen, was shot down and killed over the battlefields of northern France yesterday. The "Red Baron," nicknamed after his red Fokker triplane, is said to have destroyed an astonishing 80 Allied aircraft in less than two years. His successes were matched by the deadly marksmen in his squadron, Richthofen's Circus, who carried out his tactics of waiting for the enemy plane to fly toward them before returning fire. His flying skills have earned him great respect, and his funeral today, held at the site of his death, was conducted with full military honors.

Long-range weapon "Big Bertha" bombs Paris

JUNE 26

Despite its huge range and crude targeting, "Big Bertha" is once again raining down destruction on the people of Paris. More than 800 people have already been killed by this vast howitzer, which is thought to be located nearly 63 miles (100 km) away behind German lines. "Big Bertha," named after the wife of its manufacturer Gustave Krupp, fires 1,764-lb (800-kg) shells from its 16.5-in (420-mm) muzzle. The heavy bombardment of the French capital began over three months ago on March 23, but it took some time to find out from where the gun was being fired. The task was difficult as the Germans moved "Big Bertha", around at night on railroad tracks so that it could easily be hidden from Allied reconnaissance. The gun was eventually located by means of aerial photography.

"Big Bertha," also known as the Paris gun

APRIL–JUNE

APR The Allies agree that US troops will fight as a single army under the command of US General Pershing.

APR Charlie Chaplin's new film A Dog's Life, the first under his million-dollar contract, opens in the US.

APR The UK sets up the Royal Air Force (RAF) in order to fight an effective air war against Germany.

ELMO LINCOLN AS TARZAN

APR Romania signs a peace treaty with Germany and Austria-Hungary in exchange for land in Russia.

APR US actor Elmo Lincoln stars in a screen version of Edgar Rice Burroughs's novel Tarzan of the Apes.

APR The first battle fought by opposing tanks takes place at Villers Bretonneaux in France.

JUN Austro-Hungarian forces make a further attack on Italian lines in northeastern Italy, but are repelled.

MAY Vera Kholodnaya, the "queen of the Russian screen," stars in two films that premiere in Moscow.

MAY The first US airmail service is established between New York City and Washington, D.C.

RUSSIAN ACTRESS VERA KHOLODNAYA

JUN Civil war rages in Russia as the Red Army struggles against opposing "White" Russians.

MAY D. W. Griffith leads the US film industry's effort to help the war by selling bonds.

JUN A playing speed for records of 78 revolutions per minute is becoming standardized.

1918

Czar murdered

JULY 16

Nicholas II, the former czar of Russia, was murdered with his family in the Urals mountain town of Ekaterinburg today. Approaching White armies had frightened the Bolshevik locals, who shot the royal family in the cellar of the house where they were being detained.

Decisive conflict at Amiens

AUGUST 8

In the words of German general Erich von Ludendorff, it has been "a black day for the German army." This morning 20 Allied divisions, including British, Canadian, Australian, US, and French troops, went into action on the Western Front near Amiens, France. Increasing numbers of tanks and planes were used in the attack, as the face of warfare continues to change. By the end of the day the Germans had been pushed back 5 miles (8 km) to the lines they occupied before their successful offensive last spring. The beleaguered German soldiers surrendered without a struggle, many only too relieved to get out of the front line of fire.

Allied forces go over the top in the momentous thrust against the German army

---

JULY–SEPTEMBER

World Events	**JUL** Fighting under one supreme command, the Allies halt the German advance in the second Battle of Marne.	**JUL** French commander General Foch leads the Allies in a major offensive on the Western Front using a new tactic of elastic defense.	**SEP** Allied forces capture the Hindenburg Line, the most fortified German trenches, and begin their advance into Belgium.	**SEP** Spanish flu sweeps through Europe, causing millions of deaths and crippling the war effort on both sides.
Entertainment	**JUL** Baseball is declared nonessential under the US "Work or Fight" law.	**SEP** US stage actress Mae West wows Broadway in *Sometime*, in which she introduces the "shimmy" dance.	**SEP** The work of Gerard Manley Hopkins, a celebrated British poet and Jesuit priest, is published posthumously.	**SEP** Russian composer Igor Stravinsky's ballet *A Soldier's Tale* is first performed in Lausanne, Switzerland.
Innovations	**JUL** In the US Henry Ford launches the first *Eagle* boat, a type of fast submarine-chaser.	**HELMET WORN BY GERMANS** — **AUG** "Par Avion" ("by air") airmail stickers are first used in the transport of mail by the French civil air service.	**AUG** The German army uses the 0.5-in (13-mm) *T-Gewehr 18* antitank weapon for the first time.	**RED CROSS NURSE** — **SEP** The world's largest reflecting telescope, housed at Mount Wilson in California, comes into use.

1918

Lawrence of Arabia

Arab triumph

OCTOBER 1

Arab forces are celebrating today after capturing the ancient city of Damascus in Syria. Led by the Arab prince Feisal and advised by Major Lawrence, a young British officer known as Lawrence of Arabia, Arab armies have been in open revolt against Turkish rule since June 1916. The opposing forces used guerrilla tactics as they fought their way through the barren wastes of the Arabian desert on camels. Today's victory, following the British capture of Jerusalem last December, confirms the Arab liberation from the Ottoman Empire.

Peace in Europe: war is over

Jubilant soldiers celebrate the end of the war

NOVEMBER 11

At 11 a.m. on the eleventh day of the eleventh month of the year, the guns of war have fallen silent across Europe. After four-and-a-quarter years of bitter fighting, German leaders have admitted defeat and signed an armistice with the Allies. The truce, signed at dawn in a railroad car in the forest of Compiègne in northern France, brings to an end one of the most bitter conflicts in European history.

WAR ART
Artists on both sides of the conflict have drawn on their experiences to produce some controversial and disturbing paintings. The young British artist Paul Nash has painted the devastated Flanders landscape (above) entitled, ironically, *We Are Making a New World*.

Deaths count the real cost of war

NOVEMBER 30

As the year draws to a close, the world is beginning to count the cost of the Great War, which ended earlier this month. No one will ever know exactly how many people lost their lives in the fighting, but it is thought to be in excess of ten million, a number greater than in any other single conflict in history. A whole generation of young men from all classes and walks of life has been lost to many nations.

OCTOBER–DECEMBER

OCT Italian forces achieve a major victory against Austro-Hungarian forces at Vittorio Veneto; Austria-Hungary sues for peace.

OCT The Austro-Hungarian Empire, led by Emperor Karl, begins to break up as Czechoslovakia declares itself a republic.

OCT In the shadow of defeat, and with many of its allies already withdrawn from the conflict, Germany appeals for an armistice.

NOV The kingdom of the Serbs, Croats, and Slovenes is created out of former Austrian and independent nations.

OCT Following the success of the film *Tarzan of the Ape: The Romance of Tarzan* is released in New York City.

NOV British war poet Wilfred Owen is killed in action at the age of 25, just a week before the war ends.

NOV French Surrealist poet and art critic Guillaume Apollinaire dies at the age of 38.

DEC A film version of the opera *Carmen* starring Pola Negri is released in Germany.

OCT The world's first propaganda broadcast incites German civilians to remove their government.

WILFRED OWEN

DEC The world's first three-color traffic lights are introduced in New York City.

DEC Two German scientists win Nobel Prizes, Max Planck for physics and Fritz Haber for chemistry.

FILM VERSION OF CARMEN

DEC Electric clocks are sold commercially by Henry Ellis Warren in Massachussetts.

1919

Revolutionaries murdered

JANUARY 15

Four days ago an uprising by communist "Spartacists" in Berlin was crushed by the German government. Today Karl Liebknecht and "Red Rosa" Luxemburg, the leaders of the revolt, were murdered and their bodies thrown into a canal. Their calls for the formation of a socialist republic had stood little chance of success, but they are still being hailed as martyrs.

Rosa Luxemburg

Bauhaus reforms art education

APRIL 12

A revolutionary new school of art has been founded by the German architect Walter Gropius in the city of Weimar. The goal of the Bauhaus school is to combine the visual arts with architecture, and to teach the students design and craft skills that are suited to the modern industrial age. Tutors include the notable artists Wassily Kandinsky and Paul Klee.

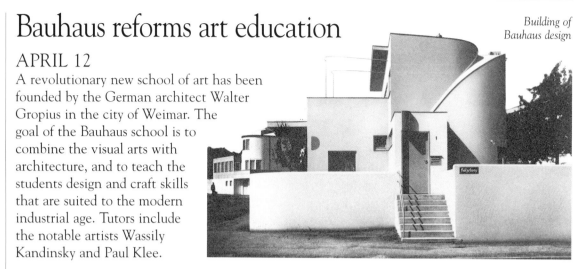
Building of Bauhaus design

Crowds massacred in Amritsar

APRIL 13

At least 500 people were killed and 1,500 injured when British troops opened fire on demonstrators in the northern Indian city of Amritsar today. All over the country Indian people have been protesting the new security laws, but events came to a head when Brigadier General Dyer called out his troops to restore peace. He gave the order to fire into the crowd without warning, an act that resulted in chaos. Today's massacre will do little to reduce the current strong anti-British feeling.

Amritsar's Golden Temple, most sacred to Indian Sikhs

JANUARY–JUNE

World Events	**JAN** The Sinn Féin politicians elected to the British parliament meet at an unofficial Irish parliament in Dublin.	**FEB** At the Paris peace conference in Versailles, 27 nations agree to US president Wilson's proposal for a League of Nations.	**MAR** Italian socialist Benito Mussolini founds a new political party, the "Fasci d'Italiani di Combattimento," in Italy.	**APR** Éamon de Valera, known as "Dev" to his followers, is elected president of the Irish parliament, the Dáil.
Entertainment	**MAR** The antiwar film *J'accuse*, by French director Abel Gance, premieres in Paris, France.	**APR** Jazz arrives in Europe when the Original Dixieland Jazz Band makes its debut in London, UK.	**JUN** US actress Lillian Gish stars in *True Heart Susie*, in which she plays a naïve country girl.	**JUN** The first photomontage is begun by artists George Grosz and John Heartfield in Germany.
Innovations	**JAN** British scientist Ernest Rutherford is the first to split the atom, the smallest particle. **ERNEST RUTHERFORD**	**MAR** British scientists, watching the eclipse of the sun, confirm Einstein's theory of relativity.	**MAY** Charles Strite of Minnesota patents his latest invention, the pop-up electric toaster. **JOHN ALCOCK AND ARTHUR BROWN**	**JUN** British John Alcock and US Arthur Brown are the first pilots to fly nonstop across the Atlantic.

1919

Stars form own film company

APRIL 17

Four of Hollywood's biggest stars, Douglas Fairbanks, Charlie Chaplin, Mary Pickford, and D. W. Griffith, have formed a company, United Artists in America. They hope to control more of the profits from their work, and share in its distribution.

Tide turns for Red Army in Russian civil war

OCTOBER 21

After nearly two years of civil war in Russia, the Bolshevik Red Army is making gains on its "White" opponents for the first time. White armies, led by Alexander Kolchak and Anton Deniken, have been progressing rapidly on both eastern and southern fronts, but this has stretched them too far. Leon Trotsky, leader of the disciplined and highly motivated Red Army, seized his chance. In the past weeks he has taken the upper hand, and his troops are now on the offensive on all fronts.

Peace agreement at Versailles

JUNE 28

At ten minutes to four this afternoon two grim-faced German delegates signed a peace treaty in the Palace of Versailles outside Paris, France. The Great War has officially come to an end. The treaty has been drawn up by the Allies following six months of negotiations. The terms it proposes are so harsh that the German chancellor and his cabinet at first resigned rather than agree to sign it. But the Allied threat of military occupation forced their National Assembly to meekly concede. The French are protesting that the terms are too lenient, but British prime minister Lloyd George fears that the stage has been set for another world war.

FELIX THE CAT A new cartoon character made his appearance this year. Felix the Cat, a perky and indestructible character devised by the Australian cartoonist Pat Sullivan, is delighting everyone who sees his antics on the screen.

JULY–DECEMBER

AUG Following the death of Louis Botha, General Jan Smuts becomes the new prime minister of South Africa at the age of 49.

NOV The US Senate rejects the Versailles peace treaty, a setback for President Wilson who has been campaigning strongly for it.

DEC US-born Nancy Astor is the first female member of Parliament in London's House of Commons.

DEC British prime minister Lloyd George puts forward a proposal to divide Ireland into two states.

JUL US boxer Jack Dempsey beats Jess Willard in three rounds in the World Heavyweight Championship.

JUL French tennis player Suzanne Lenglen wins the Ladies Singles at the first post-war Wimbledon, UK.

SEP The world's first film school, the State School of Cinematography, opens in Moscow, Russia.

DEC French Impressionist painter Auguste Renoir dies in Cannes, France, at the age of 78.

SEP The first intercontinental airline service begins regular flights between Europe and North Africa.

GENERAL JAN SMUTS

SEP US aviator Roland Rohlfs sets a flight altitude record of 34,610 ft (10,550 m) in a Curtiss *Wasp*.

DEC Trailer caravans make their first appearance at the annual motor show at Olympia in London, UK.

LES PARAPLUIES **BY RENOIR**

DEC Belgian doctor Jules Bordet wins the Nobel Prize for medicine for his work on immunology.

1920

Yankees scoop baseball "Babe" for $125,000

JANUARY 5

Baseball history was made today when the New York Yankees signed Babe Ruth for $125,000 – the largest signing fee that has ever been paid. Twenty-four-year-old Babe Ruth, whose real name is George Herman Ruth, was born in Baltimore. He began his professional baseball career in 1914, playing for the Baltimore Orioles, but transferred soon after to the Boston Red Sox. A left-handed pitcher, Babe quickly made a name for himself as a remarkable player. Out of 158 games for Boston, he achieved a pitching record of 89 victories and 46 losses. He has recently become known

Babe Ruth in action

for regularly scoring home runs and will join the New York Yankees as a hitter. His great batting ability and colorful personality are sure to attract many supporters.

Alcohol banned in United States

JANUARY 16

The US goes dry today as Prohibition officially comes into force. To mark the start of an alcohol-free new year, last night the longtime antialcohol campaigner, evangelist William "Billy" Sunday, along with 10,000 followers, held a mock funeral for John Barleycorn, the spirit of malt liquor. No doubt "mourners" marked his passing with glasses of fizzy soda rather than whiskey.

"Mourners" dance around John Barleycorn's coffin

Garvey calls for black rights

AUGUST 1

A national conference of the Universal Negro Improvement Association (UNIA), initiated by black nationalist leader Marcus Garvey, opened in Harlem, New York, today. Jamaican-born Garvey founded the UNIA in 1914 "to promote race pride" among black people. His goal is to create a black empire in Africa, free of white interference because he believes black Americans cannot achieve full rights in the US. Inspiring speeches made in his "back to Africa" campaign and his newspaper, *Negro World*, have already earned him considerable support.

DADAISTS SHOCK ART WORLD

Art and protest are coming together in a new movement called Dadaism. Taking the motto "Destruction is also creation," the Dadaists have set out to shock the conventional art world. In New York, Marcel Duchamp has exhibited a urinal signed R. Mutt; in Cologne, Max Ernst and Jean Arp invited visitors to smash their paintings.

JANUARY–JUNE

World Events	**JAN** The newly formed League of Nations, consisting of 29 countries, holds its first meeting in Paris, France.	**MAR** The "Kapp Putsch," a coup to seize Berlin, Germany, fails because conspirators do not secure support of the army.	**APR** The newly formed extremist National Socialist (Nazi) Party in Germany adopts the swastika as its symbol.	**JUN** The Treaty of Trianon, which reduces the size of Hungary and ends the Austro-Hungarian empire, is signed.
Entertainment	**JAN** Controversial Italian artist Amadeo Modigliani dies in Paris at the age of only 35.	**MAR** A screen adaptation of Robert Louis Stevenson's novel *Treasure Island* is released in Hollywood.	**MAR** US screen stars Mary Pickford and Douglas Fairbanks marry in Los Angeles.	**JUN** In the UK, opera singer Nellie Melba broadcasts a concert of songs that includes *Home Sweet Home*.
Innovations	**JAN** The Good Humor bar, chocolate-covered ice cream on a stick, is made in the US.	**FEB** The first color cartoon film, *The Debut of Thomas Kat*, uses paintings on transparent celluloid.	**FEB** US explorer Robert Peary, who was the first person to reach the North Pole, dies at the age of 64.	**APR** KLM, the national airline of the Netherlands, operates a scheduled service from Amsterdam to London.

TREASURE ISLAND

NAZI PARTY SYMBOL

1920

Election results heard on radio

NOVEMBER 2

Several hundred US families tuned in on homemade radio receivers today to hear that Republican W. G. Harding has won the presidential election. The announcement marks the start of regular broadcasts by Westinghouse from their Pittsburgh radio station. It is expected that interest in radio sets will now soar.

Headphones are used for listening to today's radio broadcasts

Dublin suffers "Bloody Sunday"

NOVEMBER 21

Violence in Ireland reached new levels today as 14 British army officers and officials were killed in Dublin after dawn raids by the Irish Republican Army (IRA). In the afternoon the notoriously brutal British special force the Black and Tans retaliated by firing into a crowd of ordinary people at the Croke Park soccer ground. 12 people were killed, and 60 others were injured. The shocking events of today's "Bloody Sunday" come as the culmination of several months of increasing violence in Ireland. Last December the British government declared its intention to divide the country into two regions. The decision was met with outrage by the nationalist Sinn Féin party. Since then a battle using guerilla tactics has been waged between British troops and the IRA, led by Michael Collins. As more British troops enter Ireland in an attempt to impose order, the situation will be increasingly difficult to resolve.

Black and Tan auxiliaries, named after the color of their uniforms, stop and search a member of the Sinn Féin

---

JULY–DECEMBER

AUG After more than 50 years of campaigning, US women gain the vote as Congress passes the 19th amendment to the constitution.

AUG The seventh Olympic Games opens in Antwerp, Belgium, after a gap of eight years due to World War I.

JUL The Southern California Telephone Co. sets up a public radio telephone service in the US.

US SUFFRAGETTE

SEP Indian nationalist Mohandas Gandhi launches a peaceful noncooperation movement against the UK.

SEP Margaret Gorman is crowned the first Miss America in Atlantic City, New Jersey.

OCT The Ministry of Transport in the UK instructs motorists to raise their right arm to indicate stopping.

NOV Civil war ends in Russia as the Red Army, led by Leon Trotsky, achieves victory for the communist Bolsheviks.

DEC African-American singer Mamie Smith records the first blues record, *Crazy Blues*, which is a US smash hit.

NOV The first electrical recording is made by British inventors L. Guest and H. Merriman in Westminster, London.

LEON TROTSKY

DEC The British parliament passes an act to set up separate parliaments in Northern and Southern Ireland.

DEC British author Agatha Christie introduces detective Hercule Poirot in *The Mysterious Affair at Styles*.

DEC Retired US army officer John T. Thompson patents his submachine gun – the "Tommy" gun.

1921

New child star

FEBRUARY 6

Charlie Chaplin

Tears and laughter greeted Charlie Chaplin's first full-length film, *The Kid*, which opened in New York today. A clever blend of humor and pathos, the film stars British actor Chaplin in his famous tramp role. He befriends an endearing little waif, played by talented child actor five-year-old Jackie Coogan.

Jackie Coogan

Communist Party forms in China

JULY 1

Only four years after the Russian Revolution, a Communist Party has formed in China. As yet it has only 57 members, most of whom are students who have studied Karl Marx and believe that China's problems can only be solved by revolution. Their first meeting was held last month at a girls' school in Shanghai where, amid lively debate, they called for the overthrow of the wealthy "capitalist class." They believe that this is the only way to overcome China's poverty and unwanted foreign interference. Among those who attended was a young primary school teacher named Mao Zedong. He believes that

Young radicals Lin Bao and Mao (right)

Russian communism can be adapted to the needs of China, and prove influential in the future. Whether the Communists succeed in their aims remains to be seen.

SCREEN HEARTTHROB

Women everywhere are swooning over Rudolph Valentino. He first appeared as an Argentinian gigolo turned war hero in *The Four Horsemen of the Apocalypse* (right). But his smoldering-eyed performance in the title role of *The Sheik* will confirm his status as a sex symbol.

JANUARY–JUNE

World Events	**JAN** Wartime Allies fix German war debts at 132 million gold marks, to be paid over 42 years.	**JAN** Greece defies the League of Nations and declares war on Turkey, launching an offensive into Anatolia.	**MAR** Bolsheviks under Trotsky put down a mutiny of Russian sailors at Kronstadt as the Russian economy collapses.	**JUN** British king George V opens the new parliament in Belfast, Northern Ireland; James Craig is prime minister.
Entertainment	**JAN** *This Side of Paradise* by US writer F. Scott Fitzgerald continues to sell strongly.	**APR** The world's first radio sports commentary is made on Johnny Ray's fight with Johnny Dundee.	**MAY** Amid concerns over morality, a $10 fine for women who wear short skirts is issued in Chicago.	**MAY** The first international track and field meet for women opens in Monte Carlo, France.
Innovations	**MAR** Marie Stopes opens the first birth control clinic in London, despite much opposition.	**MAY** "Coco" Chanel launches her Chanel No. 5 perfume in Paris on the 5th day of the 5th month.	**MAY** The prospering Ford Motor Co. in Detroit mass produces a record 4,072 cars in one day.	**JUN** The world's largest airship, the R-38, built in the UK for the US navy, makes its maiden flight.

CHANEL N0. 5 PERFUME

A MODERN WOMAN

1921

Fight packs in heads and bucks

JULY 2

Boxing proved to be lucrative show business today. In a specially built stadium in New Jersey, US heavyweight champion Jack Dempsey took on French challenger Georges Carpentier, and defeated him in just ten minutes. Advance publicity attracted more than 80,000 spectators, and drew $1.7 million in gate money.

Dempsey and Carpentier slug it out in front of huge crowds

Sacco and Vanzetti – not guilty?

JULY 14

Amid a sea of controversy, a US jury today found two Italians – Nicola Sacco and Bartolomeo Vanzetti – guilty of a crime that took place last year. The pair allegedly murdered two men at a Massachusetts shoe factory and stole the $16,000 payroll. Vague accounts from witnesses led to their arrest. Although they were armed at the time and admitted to lying in their early statements to the police, they flatly deny that they carried out the robbery.

In fact, none of the stolen money can be traced to them. However, the fact that they are self-confessed anarchists, opposed to all forms of government, weighed heavily against them in the trial.

Sacco (left) and Vanzetti in handcuffs

Famine in Russia

AUGUST 4

Famine is devastating Russia. At least 18 million Russians are said to be starving, with the situation made worse by outbreaks of cholera and typhus. The immediate cause was a severe drought that destroyed the harvest. But a combination of the revolution and subsequent civil war has had a disastrous effect on the country's economy. Last March, in an attempt to combat this, Soviet leader Lenin brought in the New Economic Policy, which reintroduced limited private enterprise in place of state planning. A retreat from the communist way of thought, the policy has brought much criticism, and has not helped the famine. Now Lenin has appealed to the international community for aid.

Russian peasants line up for soup

JULY–DECEMBER

JUL Muslim Berbers under Abdel Krim attack and destroy the Spanish army at Anual in northern Morocco.

AUG In Italy 50,000 mourners attend the funeral of opera singer Enrico Caruso, who died at the age of 48.

JUL Canadians F. Banting and C. Best extract insulin from the pancreas, which they hope can be used to cure diabetes.

BOTTLE OF INSULIN

NOV Indians in Bombay burn clothing on a massive bonfire to campaign against the import of foreign cloth.

SEP Fans mob Charlie Chaplin as he arrives in London on his first visit to his native country in nine years.

SEP The world's first highway, the Avus Autobahn in Berlin, Germany, opens exclusively to motor traffic.

NOV Italian blackshirt Benito Mussolini declares himself "Il Duce," or leader, of the National Fascist Party.

NOV US dancer Isadora Duncan opens a dance school in Moscow, and dances for the communist Internationale.

NOV The British Legion holds a memorial day for those who died in WWI; paper poppies are sold.

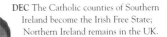

BENITO MUSSOLINI

DEC The Catholic counties of Southern Ireland become the Irish Free State; Northern Ireland remains in the UK.

DEC A male nude wrestling scene in UK novelist D. H. Lawrence's *Women in Love* causes controversy.

DEC Sales of fried potato slices, introduced as a snack food by E. Wise, continue to rise in the US.

1922

Vampire movie terrifies crowds

MARCH 5

Blood curdled at the Berlin premiere of *Nosferatu* as Bram Stoker's 1897 novel *Dracula* hits the screen. The film stars Max Schreck as a sinister Count Orlock (Dracula) complete with long fingernails and cavernous eyes. Strange camera angles and eerie images are used to terrifying effect by German director Fredrich Murnau.

Nosferatu – a masterpiece of German Expressionism

ISADORA BANNED
Isadora Duncan is not only renowned for her dancing. Her outrageous actions have gotten her booed offstage and banned from appearing in Boston, Massachusetts.

Minute broken

JULY 9

A staggering new world record was set today when 18-year-old Johnny Weissmuller swam 100 m (328 ft) in a remarkable 58.6 seconds. Austrian-born Weissmuller from Chicago is the first man to break the elusive one-minute barrier.

Michael Collins in Free State Army uniform

Irish leader shot dead

AUGUST 22

Irish nationalist Michael Collins was killed today by a ricocheting bullet from a Republican ambush in his native town of Cork. Collins, who was prime minister and co-founder of the Dáil Eireann, Ireland's provisional government, came to prominence in the Easter Rising of 1916. He went on to lead the Republicans in the guerilla campaign that forced the British to sue for peace in 1921. Although a convinced Republican, Collins supported the treaty that set up the Irish Free State in 1921, a move that angered his colleage Éamon de Valera. In January, de Valera rejected the treaty and resigned from the Dáil. Collins's shooting follows the untimely death of Arthur Griffith, president of the Dàil. With only two of its four original supporters now remaining, the treaty is now in jeopardy. General Richard Mulcahy, chief of staff for the Free State Army, referring to Collins's "strength, bravery, and unfinished work," has called for calm.

JANUARY–JUNE

World Events	Entertainment	Innovations
JAN In Russia, an estimated 33 million people face starvation as famine spreads through the Volga.	**FEB** A new magazine, *The Reader's Digest*, is launched in New York.	**JAN** In Canada, Leonard Thompson is the first diabetic to be treated with insulin.

MAR Indian nationalist Mahatma Gandhi is sentenced to six years' imprisonment following anti-British demonstrations.

FEB *Ulysses*, the controversial new novel by Irish writer James Joyce, is published in Paris, France.

FEB French physicist Marie Curie, co-discoverer of radium, is elected to the Académie des Sciences in Paris.

READER'S DIGEST EMBLEM

APR In the Irish Free State, Republicans seize Kilmainham jail in Dublin in a new wave of anti-Treaty insurrection.

APR *Robin Hood*, the latest film starring Douglas Fairbanks, astounds US audiences with its exciting technical innovations.

MAY A US teenager named George Frost installs a wireless in his Model T Ford, so creating the first car radio.

JUN British mountaineers climb to within 3, 200 ft (975 m) of the top of Everest, the world's highest mountain.

MAY The US magazine *Vanity Fair* coins the term "flapper" to describe brazen young women in society.

A FLAPPER

JUN US scientists claim that the sun produces a vitamin "D" in the body, which prevents the disease rickets.

1922

Fascists march on Rome

Mussolini is summoned to Rome after the success of the Facists' march

OCTOBER 30

The leader of the Facist Party Benito Mussolini – "Il Duce" to his followers – became the undisputed leader of Italy today. This follows a symbolic march on Rome two days ago by some 30,000 of his followers, who all wore the distinctive black shirts of the Fascist movement. Mussolini himself, who has built up a large following through his nationalism and strong anticommunist stand, did not actually take part in the march, but stayed in Milan awaiting its outcome. When the Fascists arrived in Rome, their presence was so strong that King Victor Emmanuel, fearing all-out civil war, sent for Mussolini and asked him to take up the post of prime minister. There can be little doubt now that the stage is set for Mussolini to take up dictatorial powers.

Airwaves receive regular news

NOVEMBER 15

This is the news. Yesterday evening at 6 p.m., and again at 9 p.m., news was broadcast from a room in Marconi House on the Strand in London. The material was provided by Reuters News Agency and it was read by Arthur Burrows. Most listeners heard the broadcast through personal headphones, but some fixed loudspeakers to their radio sets. Listeners can now expect a mixture of news, music, and talks to be available every day.

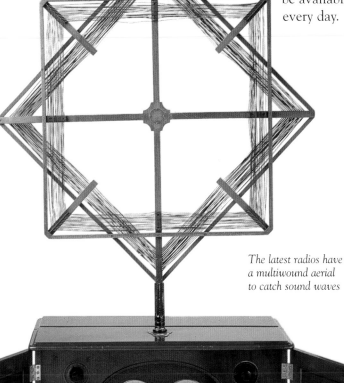

The latest radios have a multiwound aerial to catch sound waves

---

JULY–DECEMBER

AUG Turkey launches an offensive against Greece at the Battle of Afyon to recover land lost in World War I.

JUL Walter Hagen is the first US golfer to win the British Open at Sandwich, UK.

AUG Alexander Graham Bell, the Scottish inventor of the telephone, dies at the age of 75.

A GERMAN BANK NOTE

AUG The German mark goes into free fall, with its value dropping from 162 to 7,000 against the US dollar.

SEP The first 3-D feature film, *The Power of Love*, premieres in Los Angeles.

AUG US pilot James Doolittle makes the first coast-to-coast flight, taking less than 24 hours.

NOV After a 30-year search, British archaeologists uncover the tomb of Tutankhamen near Luxor, Egypt.

OCT Marie Lloyd, a popular singer and dancer in British music halls, dies at the age of 52.

OCT British social reformer George Cadbury, who made his fortune from chocolate, dies at the age of 83.

TUTANKHAMEN'S TREASURE

NOV The Italian Chamber of Deputies grants Benito Mussolini absolute power for one year.

DEC Huge acclaim greets US explorer Robert Flaherty's *Nanook of the North*, the first film documentary.

DEC Danish physicist Niels Bohr is awarded the Nobel Prize for his work on the structure of the atom.

THE TOMB OF TUTANKHAMEN

ON THE AFTERNOON OF NOVEMBER 26, 1922, in a remote Egyptian valley, one of the most amazing archaeological discoveries of the 20th century was made. Egyptologist Howard Carter, having cleared a passageway of debris, came to a sealed doorway covered with oval insignia bearing the name of Tutankhamen. He carefully removed some of the stones and peered inside. "Can you see anything?" asked his patron, Lord Carnarvon. "Yes, wonderful things," he replied. In front of him were thousands of objects, glinting with gold. Although robbers had stolen a large amount of the jewelry from the tomb soon after the pharaoh was buried, the majority of its contents, and most importantly the coffins containing the mummy, remained untouched. The splendor of the discovery, aided by extensive press coverage, created an international sensation. Tutankhamen, who had been forgotten for centuries, overnight became a household name, and his tomb a yardstick by which all archaeological finds became measured.

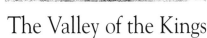

The Valley of the Kings

Situated in hills on the west bank of the Nile River, the valley was the final resting-place for many of the Egyptian pharaohs. For this reason it was a popular hunting-ground for archaeologists and by the 1920s, most of the tombs had been plundered. The tomb of Tutankhamen remained undisturbed until the 1920s since all record of his existence had been lost.

Carnarvon

Carter

The lordly patron

The British Lord Carnarvon had been fascinated by Egypt ever since he spent a winter there recovering from a car accident. He was rich enough to pursue his interest by employing Howard Carter as his personal archaeologist.

Annex

Sealed doorway

Burial chamber

Antechamber

Sealed doorway

Passage

PLAN OF TUTANKHAMEN'S TOMB

Treasury

Sealed doorway

Steps leading down

Painstaking work

Carter and his small team of archaeologists carried out their work inside the tomb with extreme care. Each object was recorded and photographed before it was removed, and many individual pieces were carefully treated to protect them from decay. It was three years before the mummy was unwrapped, and took ten years to clear the tomb.

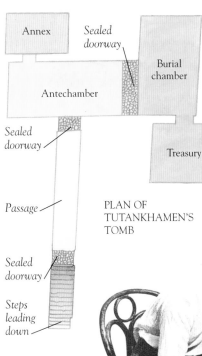

CARTER REMOVES BLACK RESIN COVERING THE INNERMOST COFFIN

The mummy lay in a nest of three coffins

STATUE OF ISIS, MADE OF WOOD OVERLAID WITH GOLD LEAF, ADORNS THE CANOPIC SHRINE

1923 THE ENTRANCE TO THE
BURIAL CHAMBER IS UNBLOCKED

1924 THE LID OF TUTANKHAMEN'S
SARCOPHAGUS IS FINALLY RAISED

1925 THE WRAPPINGS ARE REMOVED
FROM TUTANKHAMEN'S MUMMY

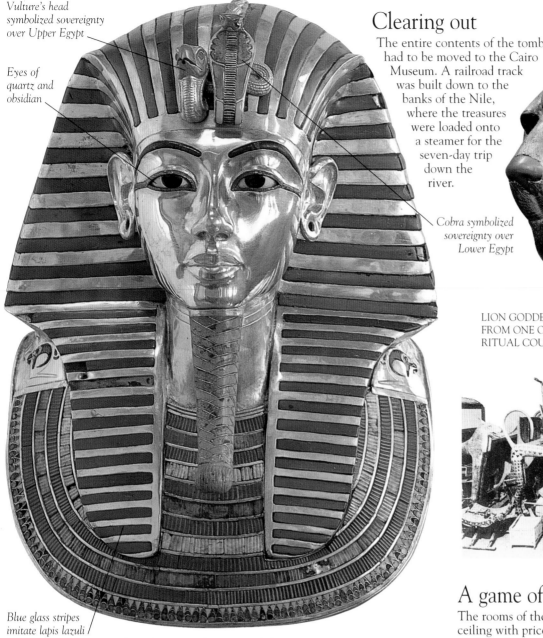

Vulture's head symbolized sovereignty over Upper Egypt

Eyes of quartz and obsidian

Clearing out

The entire contents of the tomb had to be moved to the Cairo Museum. A railroad track was built down to the banks of the Nile, where the treasures were loaded onto a steamer for the seven-day trip down the river.

Cobra symbolized sovereignty over Lower Egypt

LION GODDESS FROM ONE OF THE RITUAL COUCHES

FIRST VIEW OF THE ANTECHAMBER

Blue glass stripes imitate lapis lazuli

The face of Tutankhamen

Inside a quartzite sarcophagus, covered with a heavy lid of granite, were three coffins, each one fitting snugly inside the other. The smallest coffin was made of solid gold and contained the mummy of Tutankhamen, his face and shoulders covered with a mask of solid gold, semiprecious stones, and blue glass. An outstanding example of metalwork, this is one of the greatest treasures found in the tomb.

A game of Pick-Up Sticks

The rooms of the tomb were piled high from floor to ceiling with priceless objects. Ritual couches, statues, clothes, thrones, a large bed, jewelry, weapons, alabaster caskets, and musical instruments all lay in a jumbled heap, having been put there to accompany the pharaoh in his afterlife. It was a difficult task to remove one object without risking damage to others.

LORD CARNARVON

The boy king

Tutankhamen was only seven years old when he ascended the throne of Egypt in about 1333 BC. It is probable that he was the son of the pharaoh Akhenaten and his wife Kiya. The young pharaoh died suddenly at the age of 17 in 1323 BC.

The death curse

On one of the walls of the tomb an inscription stated that uncovering the tomb of the pharaoh would cause death. Four months after discovering the tomb, Lord Carnarvon died from pneumonia. A mosquito bite that he had cut while shaving had caused an untimely blood infection.

Death certificate

Cutthroat razor for shaving

1923

Bessie not blue

FEBRUARY 16

Bessie Smith, a talented new singer on the US jazz scene, made her first recording, *Downhearted Blues*, in New York today. Originally from Chattanooga, Tennessee, 29-year-old Bessie has been making a name for herself as the "empress of jazz" in honky tonk bars. Today she transfers her rich blues voice and impeccable rhythm into a recording that is sure to be a smash success.

Lenglen makes it five in a row

JULY 6

The crowds roared with delight when popular French tennis star Suzanne Lenglen defeated Kathleen McKane to win the Ladies Singles at Wimbledon today – for the fifth consecutive year. Miss Lenglen, who is coached by her father, started playing tennis at the age of 12. She won the women's hard-court championship at the age of 15, and, five years later, in 1919, won the Ladies Singles for the first time. An Olympic gold medalist, Miss Lenglen not only plays tennis brilliantly but also sets new fashions with her daring styles of tennis dress.

Lenglen sporting her new loose-fitting dress

Bessie Smith, the hot new talent on the music scene

Quake razes Tokyo

SEPTEMBER 6

The worst earthquake ever to have rocked Japan destroyed the cities of Tokyo and Yokohama nearly a week ago. Relief workers estimate that 300,000 people have died, thousands from the initial impact. The raging fires and flooding that followed the quake have made a further 2.5 million homeless. Today the scene is one of total chaos. More than one million refugees are trying to make their way out of Tokyo, while those who remain behind face severe food shortages and must survive on a handful of rice a day. Cholera is spreading as ditch-water is used for drinking. Despite all this, the work of reconstruction has begun.

MODEL RAILROAD

Any child can now be "chief engineer of their own railway" with a Hornby or Lionel train set. These miniature trains can be powered by electricity or steam. Extra cars, stations, and signals are also available.

JANUARY–JUNE

World Events	**MAR** The salt tax is restored in India, a move that will affect many families already living in an impoverished state.	**APR** Prince Albert, Duke of York, marries fashionable commoner Lady Elizabeth Bowes-Lyon at Westminster Abbey, UK.	**APR** Lord Carnarvon dies of an insect bite at the Tutankhamen dig in Egypt, causing rumors that the tomb is cursed.	**JUN** The Ku Klux Klan, the racist US secret society founded after the civil war, claims that it now has one million members.
Entertainment	**FEB** French designer "Coco" Chanel says even sweaters can be chic.	**MAR** The first issue of *Time*, a weekly news magazine, goes on sale in the US.	**APR** More than 600,000 attend the opening of the Yankee Stadium in New York.	**MAY** Frenchmen R. Leonard and A. Lagache win the first 24-hour Le Mans auto race.
Innovations	**FEB** German physicist Wilhelm Roentgen, who invented X rays, dies.	**ROYAL WEDDING SOUVENIR TIN** **MAR** The first special shopping center opens in the US with 150 stores and parking for 5,500 cars.	**APR** US World War I veteran Colonel Jacob Schick patents the first practical electric shaver.	**1923 RACING CAR** **MAY** US astronomer E. P. Hubble demonstrates that there are other star systems outside the Milky Way.

1923 RACING CAR

1923

Republic of Turkey formed

OCTOBER 29

General Mustapha Kemal today declared Turkey a republic, with himself as its president. Kemal has already proved himself a brilliant soldier and diplomat as leader of the Turkish nationalist movement. With military

expertise, he successfully drove out the Greek forces occupying Anatolia and helped secure the Treaty of Lausanne, which ended the conflict and guaranteed Turkey's border. Kemal, moving the capital city from Constantinople to Ankara, ends the centuries-old power of the sultans. He is aiming to turn the new Republic of Turkey into a modern state.

Conspirators Ludendorff and Hitler

Hitler fails with Beer-hall Putsch

NOVEMBER 12

Politics and farce came together in Germany when Adolf Hitler and General Erich von Ludendorff were arrested for attempting to overthrow the Bavarian government. Their so-called Beer Hall Putsch took place four days ago in Munich when Hitler, who is head of the extreme Nazi Party, burst into a beer hall with armed supporters, declaring that "the national revolution has begun." With help from Ludendorff, Hitler seized the city government, but failed to follow up his success. The next day he fled the city after being fired on by local police.

The mark collapses

NOVEMBER 20

The German mark is not worth the paper it is printed on as inflation spirals out of control. A loaf of bread now costs more than 200 billion marks. The collapse of the economy began in August 1922 when the Allies, at a conference in London, did not agree to allow Germany to postpone payment of war debts. It worsened in January when French and Belgian troops entered the Ruhr, the center of German industry, to pressurize repayment. The country is now in financial chaos as savings are wiped out and public discontent grows. In an attempt to restore financial order, the Reichsbank has today introduced a new currency, the Rentenmark.

German children use bundles of the worthless currency as building bricks

---

JULY–DECEMBER

JUL The USSR formally comes into being, consisting of Russia, Ukraine, White Russia, and Transcausia.

AUG US boxer Jack Dempsey retains the world heavyweight title in a dramatic 15-round bout.

JUL Russian airline Aeroflot begins operations with a six-passenger flight from Moscow to Nizhny Novgorod.

NEW EMBLEM OF THE USSR

SEP After a bloodless coup, Miguel Primo de Rivera assumes control in Spain and suspends the Spanish parliament.

SEP US film actor Lon Chaney gains acclaim as Quasimodo in *The Hunchback of Notre Dame.*

OCT A planetarium, for viewing the Solar System, opens at the Deutsche Museum in Munich, Germany.

OCT The UK agrees to make the African country of Southern Rhodesia a self-governing British colony.

OCT *Running Wild* opens in New York; its catchy song, *Charleston,* launches a new US dance craze.

NOV Further treasures from the tomb of Tutankhamen are found in the recently unblocked burial chamber.

TUTANKHAMEN'S SARCOPHAGUS

DEC In Mexico, Adolfo de la Huerta leads an unsuccessful revolt against the government.

DEC US film producer Cecil B. De Mille finishes his biblical epic *The Ten Commandments.*

DEC Vladimir Zworykin from Russia introduces his iconoscope, a device to transmit pictures.

1924

Father of USSR dies

JANUARY 21

Soviet leader Vladimir Ilyich Ulyanov, better known as Lenin, died today at the age of 54. Born into a politically active middle-class family in Simbirsk – his older brother was executed for attempting to assassinate Czar Alexander III – Lenin, too, followed this path. He received a law degree, but gave it up to work toward establishing communism in his native

Russia. He spent many years in forced exile, but returned to Petrograd in 1917 to lead his Bolshevik Party to victory in a dramatic coup, earning the title "father of the Russian Revolution." Lenin's death today leaves a serious power vacuum in the Soviet Union. His possible successors include Leon Trotsky, leader of the Red Army, and Joseph Stalin, general secretary of the Communist Party.

TABLE SOCCER

If the thought of running up and down a full-sized soccer field is far too exhausting, why not try it on a table? The new game from France, otherwise known as *match de foot*, is played on a green piece of cloth with players made of lead.

Fun and games in the snow

FEBRUARY 4

The first winter "Olympics" finished today at Chamonix in the French Alps. With the beautiful Mount Blanc as a backdrop, this new festival of winter sports lasted for a week and attracted competitors (mostly men, as only figure-skating was open to women) from 18 nations. There have been several top performers, among them the 29-year-old Norwegian Thorleif Haug, who won the 11-mile (18-km) and 31-mile (50-km) cross-country races as well as a bronze medal in ski-jumping, and the Finn Clas Thunberg who skated off with three gold medals, a silver, and a bronze. The idea of a winter games was controversial. Although the International Olympic Committee finally gave its approval to hold the event, they still denied use of the "Olympic" name.

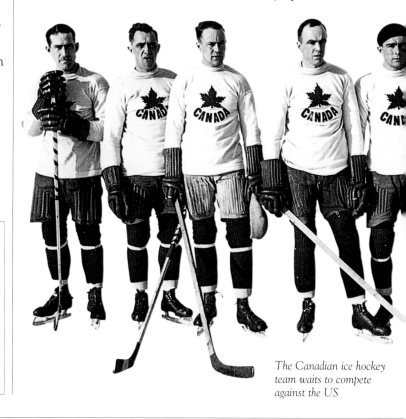

The Canadian ice hockey team waits to compete against the US

JANUARY–JUNE

World Events	JAN The first Labor government comes to power in the UK; Ramsay MacDonald is prime minister.	FEB British archaeologist Howard Carter lifts the lid on Tutankhamen's stone coffin, revealing a golden effigy.	APR Nazi leader Adolf Hitler is jailed for his part in the failed Beer Hall Putsch last November in Munich.	JUN British climber George Mallory, who climbed Mount Everest because "it is there," dies in the attempt.
Entertainment	MAR A beautiful Swedish actress, 18-year-old Greta Garbo, makes her film debut.	MAR Walt Disney makes *Alice's Wonderland*, the first in a series of cartoons, in Hollywood.	MAY British author E. Nesbit, who wrote *The Railway Children* and other popular stories, dies at the age of 85.	JUN Sales soar of *A Passage to India*, by UK author E. M. Forster, which explores Anglo-Indian tensions.
Innovations	FEB Countdown beeps precede the broadcast of a new regular time signal by the BBC in London.	**IMPERIAL AIRWAYS** MAR Based in Croydon, Imperial Airways, the UK's first national airline, takes to the air with a fleet of 13 planes.	APR Crossword mania hits the US after Simon and Schuster publishes the first book of crossword puzzles.	 **ADOLF HITLER BEHIND BARS** JUN The UK and Australia are the first countries to communicate by wireless as opposed to the telegraph.

1924

Studios merge

MARCH 16

A massive new film studio is formed in Hollywood. Metro-Goldwyn-Mayer (MGM) brings together three smaller US studios: Goldwyn Pictures, Metro Pictures, and Louis B. Mayer's company.

In cold blood

MAY 31

In a crime that has shocked the US, two 19-year-old boys from millionaire families have confessed to murdering a young neighbor for "thrills." Nathan Leopold and Richard Loeb, both successful university students, have described how they cold-bloodedly kidnapped and strangled 14-year-old Bobby Franks ten days ago and then demanded a $2,000 ransom from his parents. The two students have told police that they had wanted to murder someone for a long time. Their shocked parents have hired leading lawyer Clarence Darrow to defend them, and have said that the pair will plead not guilty on account of emotional illness.

Rinty is a natural performer in front of the camera and capable of all kinds of stunts

Nathan Leopold (left) and Richard Loeb

New canine star hits the screen

SEPTEMBER 1

Film audiences are applauding an unlikely new film star – a German Shepherd named Rin Tin Tin. The dog was discovered as a puppy by US army lieutenant Lee Duncan, who found him in a trench during World War I. Duncan took the dog, affectionately known as Rinty, back to the US and trained him for the screen. Rinty's first appearance was in the movie *The Man from Hell's River*, and he is currently starring in *Find Your Man*. Already as popular as some human stars, Rinty's future screen career is assured.

JULY–DECEMBER

AUG France and Belgium agree to withdraw their troops from the Ruhr within a year as Germany promises to pay off war debts.

SEP Indian nationalist Mahatma Gandhi goes on hunger strike in protest against the rioting between Muslims and Hindus.

OCT The League of Nations adopts the Geneva Protocol for settling international disputes peacefully rather than by war.

OCT The "Zinoviev Letter" is published, in which Moscow supposedly urges the UK to start a revolution.

JUL Distance runner Paavo Nurmi, the "Flying Finn," wins a record five gold medals at the Paris Olympic Games.

AUG A comic strip featuring little orphan Annie, her dog, and her doll appears in the *New York Daily News*.

OCT Deadpan US comedian Buster Keaton scores an immediate hit with his latest film, *The Navigator*.

NOV Italian opera composer Giacomo Puccini dies at the age of 66, leaving *Turandot* incomplete.

AUG US pilots L. Smith and E. Nelson complete the first round-the-world flight, starting and finishing in Seattle.

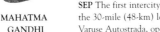

MAHATMA GANDHI

SEP The first intercity highway, the 30-mile (48-km) long Milano–Varuse Autostrada, opens in Italy.

NOV The new "fonofilm" process of creating sound on film is used to film a speech by US President Coolidge.

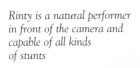

BUSTER KEATON

DEC People in the US can now blow their noses on disposable paper tissues made by Kleenex.

1920 COCKTAILS ARE POPULAR WITH
FASHIONABLE YOUNG CROWDS

1922 WIDE-LEGGED "OXFORD BAGS"
ARE ALL THE RAGE FOR MEN

1924 NEW SWIMSUITS
EXPOSE ARMS AND LEGS

THE ROARING TWENTIES

THE 1920S BEGAN WITH A BANG, as a war-weary world turned to enjoyment with a vengeance. The United States, which had emerged as a leading power after World War I, set the trend, influencing fashion, music, and even food. A new leisure industry sprang up and there were major breakthroughs in recording, film, and radio. Social attitudes were more relaxed, and young people rejected convention to follow free and daring lifestyles. Women in particular embraced a new freedom. They wore shorter skirts, cropped their hair, and danced brazenly in public. Jazz, too, had arrived; its syncopated sounds and rhythms permeated the clubs and dance halls of Chicago, New York, Paris, and London and gave the name "Jazz Age" to the era. However, as the Twenties roared on, the economy began to weaken. In 1929, the Wall Street Crash in New York brought days of carefree living to an abrupt end.

Jazz-age icons

Zelda and F. Scott Fitzgerald enjoyed a life of drinking and partying. A US writer, Fitzgerald called the era the "Jazz Age," and his novels *This Side of Paradise* and *The Great Gatsby* describe what it was like to be young and fashionable in the 1920s.

Jumpin' jazz

Black musicians had been playing jazz in the southern US states for many years, but as the recording industry grew, jazz musicians went north to Chicago and New York to make money. From there the exciting African-style rhythms moved across to Europe, in particular to Paris and London.

Give me five

One of the greatest and most influential jazz musicians in the 1920s was Louis Armstrong. In 1922 he teamed up with Joe "King" Oliver and together they created imaginative music that came to define New Orleans jazz. Later, with his band the Hot Fives, Armstrong thrilled audiences with his brilliant trumpet solos and virtuoso "scat" singing.

Rhapsody in Blue

In 1924 George Gershwin made his name as a composer with *Rhapsody in Blue*, "an experiment in modern music." Gershwin called it "a musical kaleidoscope of America," and its popularity swept the world. Gershwin's brilliant career, which included scores for *An American in Paris* and *Porgy and Bess*, lasted well into the 1930s.

THE RAW SOUND OF THE SAXOPHONE WAS A FEATURE OF JAZZ MUSIC

Strapped shoes

Going to the movies

Movies came of age in the 1920s. Great directors continued to produce silent masterpieces until, in 1927, *The Jazz Singer* synchronized pictures with sound. Movie-going became a weekly habit, and stars such as Mary Pickford, Greta Garbo, and sultry-eyed Rudolph·Valentino became heartthrobs and fashion leaders for a new mass audience.

RUDOLPH VALENTINO IN *THE SHEIK*

FRENCH FASHION DESIGNER "COCO" CHANEL IN TYPICAL CHANEL SUIT

The new woman

The role women had played in World War I, and the fact that many could now vote, shattered the concept of frail femininity. The 1920s saw the emergence of the liberated "New Woman," who favored an active lifestyle. This attitude was reflected in the clothing of the time. "Coco" Chanel created a new style of clothes for these women: stark, yet stylish outlines, and knitted jackets and sweaters influenced a generation and beyond.

Cloche hat to cover bobbed or shingled hair

Powder and rouge

Cupid-bow mouth painted with scarlet lipstick

Lowered waistline

Short skirt for freedom of movement

Silk stockings

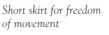

Doing the "Charleston"

Many new dances, such as the "lindy hop" and the "black bottom," began in the United States. They had their roots in the off-beat rhythms of African music, which had traveled through the black communities. Among them, the "Charleston" was the leading craze. The dancers moved frenetically, turning in their toes, kicking out their legs, and swinging their arms.

Flappers

Freedom was the theme of the 1920s and it was reflected in the new fashions, which were highly daring and much criticized by the establishment. This was the age of the flapper – the young woman who wore makeup, smoked in public, and danced and drank unchaperoned at cocktail parties and nightclubs.

STYLISH HEELED SHOES FOR EVENING WEAR

1925

Theory of evolution on trial

MAY 25
US biology teacher John Scopes has been arrested – for teaching evolution. His hearing will start in July in Dayton, Tennessee. Scopes, in teaching Darwin's theory that humans have evolved from apes, has gone against the Bible's account of the Creation. Christian fundamentalists in the state have recently introduced a law that makes this illegal. The case, already nicknamed the "Monkey Trial," is attracting media attention. Civil rights lawyer Clarence Darrow will conduct the defense and William Bryan, who has crusaded against evolution, will act for the prosecution. The judge is not allowing anyone to put forward scientific evidence.

John Scopes – the teacher at the center of the evolution argument

Art Deco tea set by potter Clarice Cliff

Home Cubism

APRIL 30
There are millions of visitors flocking to the Exposition Internationale des Arts Décoratifs in Paris, France. Architecture, interior design, and high fashion all appear in the distinctive bold coloring and geometrical shapes of Art Deco – a style that some people have described as Cubism domesticated. Among the exhibits are brilliant textiles by painter Raoul Dufy and beautiful gowns by "Coco" Chanel.

Ban on skilled jobs for blacks

JUNE 29
Racial segregation at work has officially come into force in South Africa. Today a bill was passed that bans black South Africans from doing skilled jobs in all industries. The first law along these lines, the Mines and Works Act, was passed in 1911 and blacks were forced to do badly paid, unskilled work. Demand for the policy increased and in 1922 white mine workers in the Witwatersrand gold fields staged a strike against the use of black workers. In a violent conflict more than 200 lives were lost. The law passed today will finally make the widely practiced color ban legal. It is one of the first measures introduced by the pact government, the recent coalition between the Afrikaaner National Party, which does not want to maintain ties with Britain or share power with blacks, and the Labor Party, which consists mainly of white urban workers. At the same time, Afrikaans, the Dutch-based dialect, has been made the official language of South Africa to help ensure white supremacy in the country.

World Events	**JAN** Following Lenin's death, Joseph Stalin makes moves to become the supreme head of the USSR.	**MAR** Chiang Kai-shek becomes leader of the nationalist Kuomintang, following the death of Chinese premier Sun Yat-sen.	**APR** The Australian government promises low-interest loans for settlers to encourage Britons to emigrate.	**MAY** In Italy, Catholic bishops condemn the "scandalous" women's fashions and ban bare-legged women from churches.
Entertainment	**FEB** The *New Yorker*, a weekly magazine containing stories and social commentary, goes on sale.	**MAR** As the US crossword craze grows, the Chicago Health Department says that crosswords are good for your health.	**JUN** Charlie Chaplin's *The Gold Rush*, which has taken longer than a year to make, premieres in Hollywood.	**JUN** UK playwright Noel Coward's *Hay Fever* opens in London's West End. It is his third play to be staged this year.
Innovations	**JAN** Canadian Arthur Sicard develops the snowblower, a machine for clearing snow. **CHIANG KAI-SHEK**	**FEB** London zoo announces it will install lighting to cheer up the animals during thick UK fogs.	**APR** In-flight movies get off the ground when UK Imperial Airways shows *The Lost World* during a flight. **UK EMIGRANT**	**JUN** The Chrysler motor company is founded in Detroit, Michigan, and produces a $1,500 luxury car.

1925

Klan marches on Washington, but rain stops demonstration

AUGUST 8

More than 40,000 members of the United States' most notorious secret society, the racist Ku Klux Klan, staged a major demonstration in the capital city of Washington today. The Klansmen wore their sinister attire of white robes and conical hoods, and waved US flags. The march ended at the foot of the Washington Memorial, where the planned ceremony and cross-burning was canceled due to heavy rain. The Klan, which today boasts a large membership of some four million, was founded in 1866 in Tennessee. It conducted a reign of terror against freed black slaves, with strange rituals, midnight rites, lynchings, and whippings that struck fear into the southern states, until the society was outlawed in 1871. However, in 1915, the Klan re-formed, and today actively crusades against black Americans, Jews, Catholics, and evolutionary Darwinism in its campaign for an all-white Protestant United States. The Klan has entered politics, and last year helped to prevent Catholic Democrat Al Smith from holding office. Today, even the fearsome Klan was powerless against the driving rain.

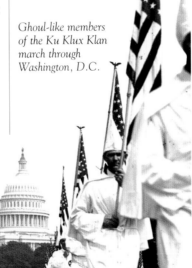

Ghoul-like members of the Ku Klux Klan march through Washington, D.C.

Great *Potemkin*

DECEMBER 21

Battleship Potemkin, the creation of Soviet director Sergei Eisenstein, premiered tonight in Moscow. The film, made to commemorate the 1905 Russian Revolution, tells of the mutiny that took place at the port of Odessa. Critics are raving about the film's stunning ten-minute sequence on the Odessa steps, in which clever editing and camera angles are used to show soldiers carrying out a seemingly endless massacre of innocent civilians.

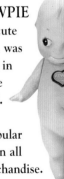

CUTE KEWPIE
Kewpie, the cute celluloid doll, was first patented in 1909 by Rose Cecil O'Neill. The doll has proved so popular she appears on all kinds of merchandise.

JULY–DECEMBER

JUL US teacher John Scopes, on trial for teaching Darwin's theory of evolution, is found guilty and fined $100.

SEP "Big Bill" Tilden, the US's most popular tennis player, leads his country to a sixth Davis Cup win.

JUL The first successful insulin treatment is performed in Europe at Guys Hospital in London, UK.

CHARLESTON DANCERS

JUL While in prison, German dictator Adolf Hitler publishes *Mein Kampf*, promoting Nazism and attacking Jews.

SEP The latest US dance craze the outrageous "Charleston" takes Europe by storm.

SEP In the Italian capital of Rome, the city's first subway line opens for business.

DEC The Locarno Conference finalizes post-World War I treaties and defines Franco-German and Belgo-German borders.

OCT Black US dancer Josephine Baker enchants Paris, France, with her performance in *La Revue Nègre*.

DEC The 35-mm miniature Leica camera, developed in Germany by E. Leitz, revolutionizes photography.

JOSEPHINE BAKER

DEC Reza Khan, who has ruled Persia since 1921, is declared shah and vows to modernize his country.

DEC *The Great Gatsby*, published this year by US author F. Scott Fitzgerald, receives great acclaim.

DEC The first-ever motel opens in San Luis Obispo, California, with room for 160 guests.

1926

Pictures sent by airwaves

JANUARY 27

Scottish inventor John Logie Baird has created a system for transmitting moving images via airwaves called a televisor. Members of the Royal Society in London applauded at its first public demonstration today. Later, a similar display was given to members of the scientific press. Baird scanned the faces of two dolls with a beam of light and, using a photo-electric cell, changed the light into electricity. The electric signals were sent to a receiver that reversed the process. The images flicker and are not as good as those in the movies, but Baird has proved that the concept of television is possible. It may become as popular as radio.

Baird's televisor

General strike hits Britain

MAY 12

The first general strike in Britain's history is over. It began when mine owners, threatened by foreign competition, proposed to cut the miners' wages and lengthen the working day. The miners refused, and went on strike, adopting the slogan "Not a penny off the pay, not a minute on the day." The Trades Union Congress (TUC) called for a general strike in their support and some three million workers – dockers, printers, railroadmen, construction workers, and iron and steel workers – responded. On May 4, nearly half of Britain's workforce stayed at home. But the government retaliated. It used soldiers and middle-class volunteers to keep food supplies moving and to provide some public transportation. On the radio and in its newspaper, *The British Gazette*, it put its case to the public. Seeing that the strike was not only failing in its goal to paralyze the country, but that it could also be seen as illegal, the TUC called it off today, leaving the miners to fight on alone.

JANUARY–JUNE

World Events

JAN Abdul Aziz ibn Saud becomes king of Hejaz, changing the name of the region to Saudi Arabia.

MAR Irish republican Éamon de Valera resigns as leader of the Sinn Féin, and founds the Fianna Fáil (Soldiers of Destiny).

APR At least 100 die in savage riots as fighting breaks out again between Muslims and Hindus in Calcutta, India.

MAY Polish nationalist and soldier Jozef Pilsudski marches on Warsaw with army troops and seizes power in Poland.

Entertainment

FEB French tennis champion Suzanne Lenglen announces her retirement from singles play.

MAR In the US, Douglas Fairbanks stars in *The Black Pirate*, the first full-length film to use two-tone color.

MAY US comic star Buster Keaton's latest film, *The General*, the story of a runaway train, thrills audiences across the world.

JUN US golfer Bobby Jones wins the prestigious US Open golf tournament, the first amateur to do so since 1897.

Innovations

JAN The Pasteur Institute in Paris announces the discovery of an antitetanus serum.

GODDARD'S LIQUID ROCKET

MAR US physicist Robert Goddard launches the first liquid fuel-propelled rocket in Massachusetts.

MAY Two US aviators, Richard Byrd and Floyd Bennett, make the first ever airplane flight over the North Pole.

BOBBY JONES

JUN The first electric pop-up toaster is produced by the McGraw Electric Co in the US and goes on sale for $13.50.

1926

Record swim

AUGUST 6

Nineteen-year-old Gertrude Ederle from the United States today became the first woman to swim the English Channel. She battled against currents, winds, and cold to swim the 35 miles (56 km) from France to Britain in 14 hours and 31 minutes – 2 hours faster than the current record held by a man. On arrival Ederle said, "It had to be done, and I did it."

THE COTTON CLUB

New York is the center for the flowering of US black music, art, and literature. Young white audiences are flocking to Harlem's Cotton Club, a new nightspot, to see African-style revues and hear the latest jazz sounds.

The bear with little brain

OCTOBER 14

A delightful little bear has entered children's literature – Winnie-the-Pooh, or Pooh for short. Created by British author A. A. Milne and beautifully drawn by E. H. Shepard, Pooh appears today in his first full-length book. Other characters in the stories include Christopher Robin (Milne's son) and a host of the boy's nursery friends – Piglet, Tigger, Eeyore, Kanga, and Roo.

Christopher Robin pulls on his boots, helped by Winnie-the-Pooh

New emperor for Japan

Hirohito ascends the throne of Japan on the death of his father, Emperor Yoshihito

DECEMBER 25

Japan has a new emperor, a position in the country that is considered divine. Twenty-five-year-old Hirohito will take over from his father, Yoshihito, who died today after a long illness. Yoshihito had ruled Japan for 14 years. Being in the position of the new head of state will not be totally unfamiliar to Hirohito, for he has been carrying out imperial duties for the past five years. In 1921, although still young, he was proclaimed regent because his father was seriously ill and incapable of "paying further attention to his state duties." At this time Hirohito successfully completed an important world tour, the first member of the Japanese imperial family to do so. However, despite coming to the throne today, his coronation, when he will take his place on the "August Heavenly Throne" and become a living god, will not take place for a few years.

JULY–DECEMBER

SEP Germany is finally admitted to the League of Nations; Brazil resigns in protest and Spain threatens to leave.

AUG Thousands of devoted women fans mourn the death of US screen heartthrob Rudolph Valentino, who was only 31.

AUG In the US, Warner Bros. develops "Vitaphone," a movie sound system that synchronizes all kinds of sounds.

HARRY HOUDINI

SEP Nationalist Kuomintang forces under Chiang Kai-shek capture Hangkow and begin the unification of China.

OCT US escape artist Harry Houdini dies from a burst appendix following a stomach injury sustained in a stunt.

SEP The pioneering Ford Motor Co. introduces a 5-day week and an 8-hour day for its workers in Detroit.

NOV In Italy the Pope says Mussolini must have divine protection to survive four assassination attempts in one year.

DEC The Bauhaus school of design moves to a site especially designed by Gropius at Dessau, Germany.

DEC US natural historians discover traces of what could be the earliest human ancestors in Outer Mongolia.

WATERLILY POND BY MONET

NOV Hunger and poverty force British miners to accept wage cuts and to return to work after their seven-month strike.

DEC French artist Claude Monet, a leader of the Impressionist movement, dies at the age of 66.

DEC Wireless popularity grows; now more than 2 million homes in the UK have radios.

FAMILY OUTING TO THE BEACH

NEW TRANSPORTATION

THE 1920S SAW HUGE GROWTH IN TRANSPORTATION and more people than ever before were on the move. In Europe and the United States railroad networks expanded and passenger airlines introduced scheduled flights, but the most remarkable developments were in automobiles. For the rich there were stunningly beautiful, handcrafted touring cars such as Lagondas or Bentleys. For those who were less well off, the decade saw the rise of the cheap, mass-produced car. Private car ownership became widespread, particularly in the United States, but by the end of the 1920s Britain and France were also producing affordable cars. The age of automobiles had arrived. Low-cost cars not only brought a new freedom to their owners, they also affected the infrastructure of the country. There was a demand for new roads and the building of new houses began on the outskirts of main cities.

FIAT WAS ITALY'S LEADING CAR PRODUCER

Finding the way

Driving became a major leisure activity during the 1920s. People took drives in the countryside, but lack of road signs often caused problems. Sales of road maps and other essential accessories soared.

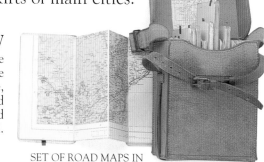

SET OF ROAD MAPS IN LEATHER INDEX CASE

Makes and marques

In 1920 there were hundreds of small producers making handcrafted cars. Each one had a unique marque, or badge. However, as mass production made cars cheaper, the smaller companies were taken over, or put out of business, by the large-scale manufacturers.

BUGATTI MADE SUPERB STYLISH CARS

BUGATTIS ON THE RACE TRACK

Built for speed

Although speed on the road was discouraged, speed on the track was a different matter. In May 1923 the first Le Mans 24-hour car race took place in France and ushered in an era of fast cars and a new sport – auto racing. The powerful new sports cars, which included the Duesenberg, Bentley, Alfa Romeo, and Bugatti, were fitted with huge engines and could exceed 100 mph (160 km/h), but they were expensive. Only the wealthy could afford to compete in auto races, but for others it was a sensational spectator sport.

Running board

1927 1ST- OR 2ND-CLASS
SEATS OFFERED ON PLANES

1928 A LONG-DISTANCE BUS
SERVICE OPERATES IN THE US

1930 STEAM TRAINS GIVE
WAY TO DIESEL AND ELECTRIC

FLIGHT ATTENDANTS ON UNITED AIRLINES

Taking to the air

After World War I pilots were employed in civil aviation, and the 1920s saw a steady growth in scheduled air services. Flying was surprisingly safe, but it was expensive and often uncomfortable. French airlines tried to ease the discomfort of flying by providing elaborate five-course meals and wine. In 1931 United Airlines recruited flight attendants to serve meals and assist passengers.

A quick hop

In 1933, as increasing numbers of people began to travel by air, the twin-engined Boeing 247 was launched. It could carry up to ten passengers over a distance of 600 miles (965 km) in four hours. Its advanced features included an all-metal skin, and wheels that could be pulled up once airborne.

Great Scot!

Although local rail lines were being electrified, the great mainline trains were largely still pulled by steam engines. Far from being an outdated mode of transportation, they were constantly being improved and were capable of traveling at terrific speeds. One of the great trains of the decade was the coal-burning "Flying Scotsman." In 1928, equipped with a walk-through tender so that crews could be changed at high speed, it began regular service between London and Edinburgh, taking about eight hours to cover the 400 miles (640 km).

THE FLYING SCOTSMAN

Windshield

Cars for all

The cheap, popular car began with US manufacturer Henry Ford. In 1908 he applied mass-production techniques in his factories and launched the Model T. With its simple design, four-cylinder engine, push-pedal gear, four seats, and cape hood, it was the first "family" car. It was cheap, and the US public rushed to buy it. Car owners had the freedom to travel wherever they wanted, whenever they wanted. Family outings became part of everyday life, and people could live some distance from their workplace.

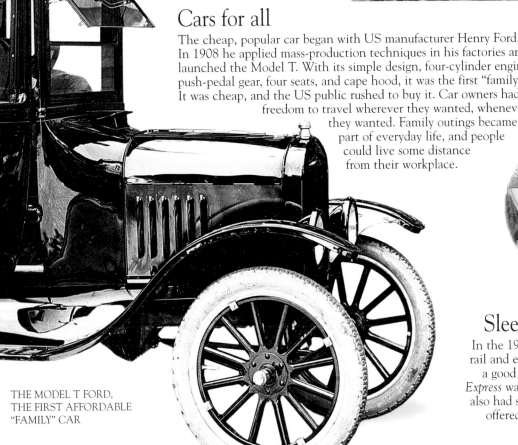

THE MODEL T FORD,
THE FIRST AFFORDABLE
"FAMILY" CAR

SLEEPING COMPARTMENT
OF AN EXPRESS TRAIN

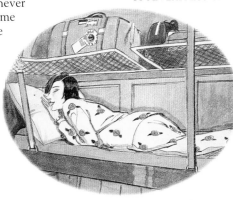
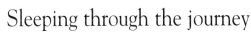

Sleeping through the journey

In the 1920s most people traveled long distances by rail and even the moderately wealthy could travel in a good degree of comfort. The glamorous *Orient Express* was the height of luxury, but the smaller trains also had sleeping compartments and dining cars that offered excellent food in elegant surroundings.

1927

Land speed record smashed

MARCH 29

British racing driver Major Henry Segrave achieved a land speed record today of 203.841 mph (328.041 km/h) in his Sunbeam *Mystery*. Only six weeks ago Malcolm Campbell set what seemed to be an unbeatable record –

174.883 mph (281.439 km/h) – in the British-made *Bluebird*, but Segrave has convincingly smashed it. Campbell praised his rival on an "excellent

feat," but says he already has a new, faster car and is confident that he can regain the record. It seems that the speed race is set to continue.

Future vision

JANUARY 10

Austrian director Fritz Lang's latest film, *Metropolis*, has been hailed as a masterpiece after its premiere in Berlin. Set in the year 2000, it uses special effects to re-create a gigantic city that is ruled by machines. The plot focuses on the exploited workers, who stage a rebellion incited by a beautiful, but evil, robot that is ultimately destroyed.

Lindbergh first to fly Atlantic solo

MAY 21

Waiting crowds of over 100,000 people at St. Bourget near Paris, France, cheered as US pilot Charles Lindbergh completed his nonstop Atlantic flight. Lindbergh is not the first pilot to achieve this feat, but he will go down in history as he is the

Charles Lindbergh – dashing in his flying gear

first to do it solo. The 26-year-old departed from Roosevelt Field in New York yesterday. His single-engined monoplane, *Spirit of St. Louis*, was so laden with fuel it barely cleared the runway. Buffeted by wind and rain, the little craft at times came within 10 ft (3 m) of the waves. Lindbergh, weary from lack of sleep, kept going by munching on sandwiches. He finally landed at 10:24 this evening, having flown the 3,600 miles (5,793 km) in 33 1/2 hours. The handsome Midwesterner is already being hailed as a national hero.

JANUARY–JUNE

World Events	**FEB** An uprising against the military dictatorship of Antonio Carmona is crushed in Lisbon, Portugal.	**MAR** In China, nationalist troops led by Chiang Kai-shek defeat the warlords and capture the rich port of Shanghai.	**APR** Chiang Kai-shek sets his troops against the communist trade unions and prepares to set up a new government.	**MAY** The UK and Russia sever diplomatic relations as the British accuse Russian trade delegates of spying.
Entertainment	**FEB** Clara Bow becomes known as the "It" girl after playing a flapper in the US film *It*.	**FEB** Paris audiences are stunned by a recital by 10-year-old US violinist Yehudi Menuhin.	**MAY** In the UK, the number of hairdressers soars as women flock to have their hair fashionably bobbed.	**MAY** In the UK, British snooker player Joe Davis wins the first ever World Professional Snooker Championship.
Innovations	**JAN** A telephone service is set up between London and New York.	**JAN** The first underwater color photograph is published in US *National Geographic* magazine.	**MAR** Archaeologists in Iraq find what they claim is a 5,000-year-old manicure set on the site of the ancient city of Ur.	**MAY** Wireless radio listeners around the world hear the latest news and cricket scores live from London UK.

YEHUDI MENUHIN

THE "BOB" HAIRCUT

1927

Vienna burns as riots rock the city

JULY 16

Vienna burned today as riots spread through the Austrian capital. Economic hardship and post-war difficulties have caused tension to build up between the supporters of the socialist government and those who want to make Austria part of Germany. Problems came to a head yesterday when charges against three Nazis, for the murder of two communists, were dropped. The socialist press called for retribution, labor leaders called for a general strike, and workers took to the streets. When soldiers mutinied in their support, the opposition called for chancellor Ignaz Seipel's resignation. However, Seipel appealed to right-wing provinces for help, and troops entered Vienna, where they clashed violently with rioters. At present, 12,000 troops and police are patrolling the debris-strewn streets of the city and order is being restored. However, demands for unity with Germany are now expected to begin again.

Troops set up a blockade using whatever material is at hand

Crowds stunned as pictures "talk"

OCTOBER 6

US movie audiences went wild as they heard the first live speech in a feature-length movie – and not only words, but songs as well. *The Jazz Singer* has been produced by Warner Bros., which last year developed the Vitaphone, a new system that records synchronized music and speech. The film stars the talented Al Jolson, who plays the son of a Jewish cantor torn between a life in the synagogue and one singing on Broadway. Although the sound is slightly indistinct, it does

Al Jolson in The Jazz Singer

appear that Jolson is speaking directly to the audience. He performs four sequences of dialogue and song in what is, for the most part, a silent movie. At today's premiere in New York, the atmosphere in the theater was electric when he began singing *Toot, Toot, Tootsie Goodbye*, and as he uttered the prophetic words "you ain't heard nothin' yet," the audience stood up and cheered, some people even climbed onto their seats with excitement. It is clear that the "talkies" have arrived; actors with squeaky voices had better watch out!

TARKA THE OTTER

Children everywhere will love the new book by British author Henry Williamson. Entitled *Tarka the Otter*, it narrates in faithfully observed detail the life of a Devon otter, describing all the events and the landscape of the surrounding countryside through the eyes of the otter itself.

JULY–DECEMBER

JUL Kevin O'Higgins, vice-president of the Irish Free State, is shot dead, fueling fears of further civil war in Ireland.

JUL The love affair between John Gilbert and Swedish film star Greta Garbo boosts box office takings.

JUL Christopher Stone from the UK is the first ever radio DJ to broadcast a program of selected records.

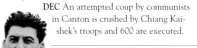

GARBO AND GILBERT

AUG In the US, Italian-born anarchists Sacco and Vanzetti die in the electric chair, despite worldwide protests.

SEP US dancer Isadora Duncan dies at the age of 49 when she is accidentally strangled by her scarf.

AUG Vets in France say they have developed a vaccine for distemper, a life-threatening disease among dogs.

NOV In Russia, Joseph Stalin continues to remove opposition, and expels rival Leon Trotsky from the Communist Party.

DEC US jazz composer and pianist Duke Ellington opens at the Cotton Club, the famous Harlem nightclub.

OCT Russian archaeologist Peter Koslov discovers the 700-year-old tomb of Genghis Khan in China.

JOSEPH STALIN

DEC An attempted coup by communists in Canton is crushed by Chiang Kai-shek's troops and 600 are executed.

DEC *Show Boat*, a musical by US composers Hammerstein and Kern, opens in New York City.

DEC The new Model A Ford, a successor to the Model T, rolls off the production line in the US.

1928

Woman claims to be a Romanov

FEBRUARY 6

Ten years ago the Russian royal family was murdered during the country's turbulent civil war. Now a woman has arrived in the United States claiming to be Anastasia Romanov, the youngest daughter of Czar Nicholas II. Mrs. Chaikovsky, as she is now called, says she managed to survive the massacre of her family because she was shielded from the bullets by one of her sisters. Mr. Gleb Botkin, son of the former Czar's doctor, has confirmed her identity and says they were childhood friends. Mrs.

Mrs. Anastasia Chaikovsky

Chaikovsky is not the first to claim to be a Romanov, but whether or not her story is true remains to be seen.

Australian doctors take to the air

MAY 15

A flying doctor service has been set up in Queensland, Australia, where there are only ten local doctors for an area of 250,000 square miles (647,450 square km). The doctors, who can be contacted by Morse radio, will be flown to patients in a de-Havilland airplane provided by the Queensland and Northern Territory Aerial Service (QANTAS).

Chinese nationalist army enters Peking

JUNE 8

Nationalist forces, led by General Chiang Kai-shek, entered the Chinese capital city of Peking yesterday. In the streets, student supporters cheered and waved flags. The arrival of Chiang's troops marks the end of the civil war. It also brings hope that China may be unified under one government for the first

In 1926, his Kuomintang army, which included communists, set out on the "Northern Expedition" to drive out the warlords. By March last year, after a series of successes, Chiang's army was in control of the key port of Shanghai and the whole of China south of the Yangtze River. In December, after an attempted coup by the

time since 1916, when power passed to the warlords. Chiang Kai-shek, a former military commander, took control of the Nationalist Party three years ago on the death of Sun Yat-sen.

communists, Chiang turned on them, brutally expelling them from the Kuomintang. Now that he has successfully taken control of Peking, Chiang may be regarded as the effective ruler of China.

JANUARY–JUNE

World Events	**JAN** In Russia, Joseph Stalin exiles all key opposition figures, including Leon Trotsky, Lenin's right-hand man.	**APR** In China, nationalist troops launch a major offensive, with the ultimate goal of capturing the capital of Peking.	**MAY** The long struggle of British suffragettes comes to an end as the voting age for women drops to 21, the same as for men.		**MAY** In the US, stock market prices plummet on Wall Street as more shares than ever before change hands in a day.
Entertainment	**JAN** Thomas Hardy, British author of *Tess* and *Jude the Obscure*, dies at the age of 87.	**MAR** Cloche hats are the latest headgear fashion for flappers on both sides of the Atlantic Ocean.	**MAY** The 9th Olympic Games, held in Amsterdam, Holland, attracts competitors from 46 countries.		**JUN** *The Jazz Singer*, the first "talkie," is shown in Paris, France, and creates a stir in the European film industry.
Innovations	**FEB** The world's first fully air-conditioned office building opens in San Antonio, Texas.	**CLOCHE HAT** 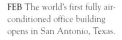 **MAY** The *Flying Scotsman*, the rail service from London to Edinburgh, UK, reaches 70mph (112 km/h).	**JUN** Norwegian explorer Roald Amundsen, who was first to reach the South Pole, is missing in the Arctic.	**ROALD AMUNDSEN**	**JUN** US aviator Amelia Earhart, as a passenger, is the first woman to cross the Atlantic Ocean by air.

1928

Penicillin discovered

SEPTEMBER 30

Scottish doctor and bacteriologist Alexander Fleming has made one of the most remarkable medical discoveries – completely by chance. While he was on vacation he left a dish of the *staphylococcus* bacteria, which causes infection in humans, lying around in his laboratory. When he returned three weeks later, he noticed a *penicillium notatum* mold, which often grows on stale bread, had contaminated the dish. The area around the mold however, was free of bacteria, suggesting that its presence had stopped bacterial growth. Fleming's next task is to isolate the active chemical present in *penicillium*, which may take some years. But he has discovered that it does not harm human white blood cells, so is hopeful that it may eventually be used to treat human bacterial infections.

Alexander Fleming in his laboratory at St. Mary's Hospital, London

Mouse set for stardom

NOVEMBER 18

The first animated cartoon with sound, *Steamboat Willie*, opened at New York's Colony Theater today, and launched a new star – Mickey Mouse. The joint creation of US animators Walt Disney and Ub Iwerks, Mickey has previously appeared in two silent films, but with little success. Disney's masterstroke was to give the mouse a voice (his own) and use sound as part of the humor. Today, the comical mouse was an instant success. No doubt he will win many fans.

New star Mickey Mouse at the helm in Steamboat Willie

JULY–DECEMBER

AUG The Kellogg-Briand pact, officially abolishing all war, is signed by 15 nations at the French Foreign Ministry in Paris.

JUL The jazz term "boogie woogie" is coined when Clarence "Pine Top" records *Pine Top Boogie Woogie*.

JUL The first commercially available TV set, made by the Daven Co., goes on sale in the US, priced at $75.

BERTOLT BRECHT

SEP The regent of Ethiopia, Ras Tafari, stages a palace coup, forces the empress Zauditu to abdicate, and seizes power.

AUG German playwright Bertolt Brecht's *The Threepenny Opera* opens in Berlin, with music by Kurt Weill.

AUG British car manufacturer Morris Motors launches a new model, the Morris Minor, in the UK.

OCT Russian leader Joseph Stalin introduces his first economic Five-Year Plan to industrialize the Soviet Union.

NOV French composer Joseph Ravel's *Boléro*, which is inspired by a Spanish folk tune, premieres in Paris.

SEP The iron lung, developed last year by US physicist Philip Drinker, is used for the first time in the US.

HERBERT HOOVER

NOV Republican Herbert Hoover is elected US president with a landslide victory over Democrat Al Smith.

DEC US composer George Gershwin's *An American in Paris* opens in New York, with Gershwin at the piano.

DEC Hungarian biochemist Albert Szent-Györgyi isolates vitamin C.

1929

Bonjour Tintin

JANUARY 10
Belgian cartoonist George Remi, also known as Hergé, has created a new cartoon character – Tintin, the boy detective. His adventures appear in *Le Petit Vingtième*, the children's section of the newspaper *Vingtième Siècle*.

Massacre of the mob

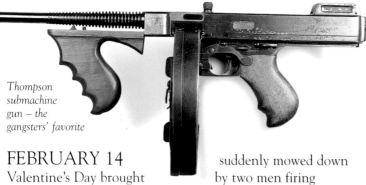

Thompson submachine gun – the gangsters' favorite

FEBRUARY 14
Valentine's Day brought bullets, not roses, to seven gangsters who were gunned down in Chicago this morning. The men, who were all members of George "Bugs" Moran's North Side gang, were lured to a warehouse by the prospect of a first-rate liquor deal. Shortly after they arrived, a Cadillac disguised as a police car pulled up for what appeared to be a routine inspection. Lined up against the wall, the men were suddenly mowed down by two men firing submachine guns and finished off by another two with pistols. The police believe the killing is the work of Al "Scarface" Capone, king of the Chicago underworld and deadly rival of Moran. Gang warfare for control of the lucrative trade in illegal alcohol has been common in Chicago since 1920, when Prohibition was introduced. A massacre on today's scale, however, is unprecedented.

Hollywood awards its best

The Academy Award – a figure on a reel of film

Clara Bow with Richard Arlen and Charles "Buddy" Rogers in Wings

MAY 17
A banquet was held in Hollywood last night for the first awards ceremony of the movie industry. The Academy of Motion Picture Arts and Sciences, founded by Louis B. Mayer of MGM, voted William Wellman's war film, *Wings*, best picture of 1927–28. A special award was given to Warner Brothers for the pioneering talkie *The Jazz Singer*. The gold-plated statuettes were presented by popular actor Douglas Fairbanks, the president of the Academy. A total of 13 awards were given to various films, actors, and technicians.

THE DAWN OF THE TELEVISION AGE
As the decade is ending, a new medium – television – has begun to appear. After a period of experimentation, in October this year the British Broadcasting Company began to televise a daily program of shows. But as yet few people have TV sets on which to watch them!

JANUARY–JUNE

World Events

JAN Wyatt Earp, former US peace officer of Dodge City, Kansas, dies at the age of 80 – with his boots off.

MAR Benito Mussolini's Fascist Party wins a rigged election and forms Italy's first fascist government.

MAY In Berlin, Germany, 15 people die when street fighting breaks out between communist demonstrators and police.

JUN Allied forces put forward the Young Plan, a concessionary deal that reworks and reduces German war repayments.

Entertainment

FEB British society beauty Lillie Langtry, the "Jersey Lily," dies in her Riviera home at the age of 74.

FEB MGM's *Broadway Melody*, the world's first all-singing, all-dancing musical, breaks US box office records.

APR *Un Chien Andalou*, the first Surrealist film, is made by Spanish director Louis Buñuel.

MAY The four Marx Brothers make their hilarious and zany US film debut in *The Cocoanuts*.

A REHEARSAL FOR BROADWAY MELODY

Innovations

FEB The first individually packaged frozen food goes on sale in Toronto, Canada.

MAR The UK introduces a long-distance airmail service, delivering to India, Egypt, Pakistan, and Iraq.

MAY German scientist Hans Berger develops a new device to measure the brain's electrical activity.

UN CHIEN ANDALOU

JUN The first color television image is demonstrated in the Bell Laboratories in New York.

1929

Popeye makes his debut

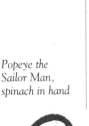

Popeye the Sailor Man, spinach in hand

Crowds gather in Lakehurst for the arrival of the Graf Zeppelin

JULY 1

The newest cartoon character to appear in a comic strip is one-eyed, spinach-eating Popeye the Sailor Man. Popeye is the creation of US strip cartoonist Elzie Crisler Segar. The son of a housepainter, Segar took a course in cartoon design and went to Chicago to work on *Charlie Chaplin's Comic Capers*. His first creation was Barry the Boob for the *Chicago Herald*. Moving to New York, he started up his own comic strip, *Thimble Theater*. Today it features big-hearted Popeye, together with his corncob pipe – and several cans of spinach.

Zeppelin airship circles the world

AUGUST 29

The German-built airship *Graf Zeppelin* landed in Lakehurst, New Jersey, today, having circled the world. Its creator, Dr. Hugo Eckener, piloted the airship, which carried a crew of 37 and 16 passengers. The giant airship made just three stops during its 19,500-mile (31,200-km) journey – in Germany, Japan, and Los Angeles. The historic trip, which is another first for aviation, took 21 days, seven hours, and 26 minutes.

Wall Street crashes

US stockbrokers struggle with a tangled mass of ticker tape

OCTOBER 24

The New York Stock Exchange has collapsed, with terrified investors selling more than 13 million shares in one day. Today's crash started last Saturday when a wave of panic caused share prices to plummet.

Intervention by some major banks restored confidence, but it was only temporary. Prices continued to slide, and today the crash was complete. The causes are complex, but much has to do with the US's post-war boom. The economy has grown rapidly, and millions of people have invested to make quick profits. During the last two or three years however, the economy has slowed down, and experts have indicated that some stocks were vastly overpriced. This created a crisis of confidence. Banks called in loans, and those who borrowed to buy shares started to sell rapidly. After today's events, millions face financial ruin, not only in the United States, but in countries all over the world.

JULY–DECEMBER

JUL Border clashes between Chinese and Soviet troops, following the rupture of trade relations, bring fresh fears of war.

AUG Great Russian impresario Sergei Diaghilev, founder of the Ballets Russes, dies suddenly in Italy at the age of 57.

JUL The German liner SS *Bremen* crosses the Atlantic Ocean in a record time of 4 days, 14 hrs, and 30 mins.

SERGEI DIAGHILEV

AUG In Jerusalem, Palestine, fighting breaks out between Arabs and Jews over access to the Wailing Wall; 113 Jews are killed.

AUG German novelist Erich Marie Remarque's *All Quiet on the Western Front* evokes the horrors of trench warfare.

SEP In the UK, traffic lights are standardized: red for stop, green for go, and amber to warn of change.

OCT The kingdom of the Serbs, Croats, and Slovenes is renamed Yugoslavia under the 'dictatorship of King Alexander.

NOV The first exhibition by Spanish Surrealist artist Salvador Dali opens in Paris.

OCT London crowds stared upward as the UK's R 101, the world's biggest airship, flew over the capital.

AIRSHIP R 101

NOV Following New York's stock market crash last month, economic depression deepens in the US and the UK.

DEC German author Thomas Mann wins the Nobel Prize for *The Magic Mountain*.

NOV US navy commander Richard Byrd makes the first flight over the Antarctic continent.

THE GANGSTER ERA

THE ARRIVAL OF PROHIBITION in 1920 sparked off an unprecedented wave of crime, making it as much a feature of 1920s America as the Charleston. Bootlegging – the making, selling, and transportation of illegal alcohol – was highly profitable, and Chicago, nicknamed "the wickedest city in the world," became the center of its trade. Rival gangs battled it out for control of this multimillion-dollar industry, while police were bought off and corruption spread upward through city hall. Speakeasies, illegal bars where respectable citizens rubbed shoulders with gangsters, and stills for producing illegal alcohol were widely available. But by 1933, the public, sick of violence and rotgut alcohol, demanded change; Prohibition was repealed and gangsters were forced to look elsewhere for easy money.

Illegal drinking

Alcohol was carried in hip flasks and consumed in speakeasies, illegal bars that sprang up everywhere. In New York, where there had been 15,000 legal bars, there were soon 32,000 speakeasies, with names like "Chez Florence" or "Frankie and Johnny's." Some were disguised as ice-cream parlors, others were jazz-filled basement dives where customers needed passwords to enter.

REBELLIOUS WOMEN DRINK FROM HIP FLASKS

A new era of clean living

Prohibition – banning the manufacture, sale, and drinking of alcohol – was enforced through the Volstead Act on January 17, 1920. It was hailed as the start of an era of clear thinking and clean living. In fact, it created big business for corrupt gangsters.

Fedora hat

Flamboyant suit

Double-barreled shotgun

ARMED HENCHMEN STAND BESIDE THEIR SPECIALLY ADAPTED CAR

Spats

Bonnie and Clyde

Bonnie Parker and Clyde Barrow had a short but bloody criminal career. They robbed banks and gas stations, and committed some 12 murders in the southwestern United States. They were gunned down by Texas Rangers in 1934.

The kings of vice

Prohibition created ideal conditions for crime to flourish. In 1920 "Diamond" Jim Colosimo was boss of the Chicago underworld, but Johnny Torrio had Colosimo shot, and took over his position. He split Chicago into sections and set about organizing the city's criminals into an efficient force of professional bootleggers. They smuggled alcohol from abroad, took over breweries, and produced rotgut alcohol, which they sold at huge profits. The gangsters ruled the city like feudal overlords, bribing police and city officials, and living like millionaires. Gang warfare was common; rivals were blasted to death or "taken for a ride." Their murders were usually followed by lavish funerals.

1929 VALENTINE'S DAY
MASSACRE IN CHICAGO

1931 CAPONE IS ARRESTED AND
IMPRISONED FOR TAX EVASION

1933 VOLSTEAD ACT IS REPEALED;
PROHIBITION COMES TO AN END

C28169

"Scarface" Capone

Al "Scarface" Capone was the undisputed head of the Chicago gangsters. Brought up in New York, Capone went to Chicago in 1920 to work for gang leader Johnny Torrio. Capone learned quickly, and by 1925 Torrio had faded into the background, and Capone controlled the city's crime his own way. Ruthlessly brutal, he was said to have been responsible for over 400 murders. His dealings secured him an annual income of more than $20 million and allowed him to lead a flamboyant lifestyle. He drove a $30,000 bullet-proof armored Cadillac and wore expensive clothes.

*Violin case
hides gun*

Sawed-off shotgun

Gun power

Gunfire was a commonplace sound on the street, as gangsters used firepower to defend their profits. The Thompson "tommy" submachine gun was favored for mass executions, otherwise gangsters used sawed-off shotguns or bombs. At least 2,500 gangsters and federal agents were killed during Prohibition.

Celluloid gangsters

Gangsterism became something of a cult. Small boys mimicked mobsters and there was a spate of gangster films. *Little Caesar*, starring Edward G. Robinson, set the pattern in 1930, and *The Public Enemy*, which launched James Cagney as a screen gangster, was released a year later.

JAMES CAGNEY AND
JEAN HARLOW STAR
IN *THE PUBLIC ENEMY*

*Slots for
gun barrels*

*Getaway
driver*

A CRATE OF
CAPTURED LIQUOR
IS UNLOADED

*Steel-armored
body*

422-000

Law and order

In 1924 J. Edgar Hoover became director of the Federal Bureau of Investigation and began to wage war against the bootleggers. Federal agents raided speakeasies and intercepted illegal alcohol, but were powerless against the unruly lawlessness. Many "feds" were poorly paid and easy to bribe.

1930

Stalin's new state farms

Soviet propaganda poster promoting Stalin's new collective farms

New planet

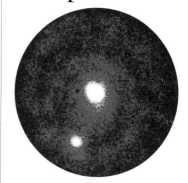

FEBRUARY 18
US astronomer Clyde Tombaugh has spotted a new planet in our Solar System. It is named Pluto after the Greek god of the underworld.

JANUARY 5
Soviet leader Joseph Stalin today declared that all farmland in the Soviet Union will be "collectively owned" by the people. Commentators believe there will be chaos throughout the countryside as plans are made to combine millions of small farms into large, state-owned units. Stalin has sent thousands of special agents to oversee the operation and has threatened to seize land if people refuse to cooperate. The peasants will now be expected to work on the vast new state farms for a wage instead of farming their own land. Stalin believes his new measures will soon double the Soviet Union's agricultural output and strengthen party control.

ON TIME
With its sleek, curved shape, this elegant Zephyr clock epitomizes the style of Art Deco that is currently at the forefront of modern design.

Garbo talks

MARCH 15
Fans of silent screen star Greta Garbo have finally heard her speak. In her new film *Anna Christie*, Garbo's first words are uttered in a deep, husky voice, "Gif me a visky – and don't be stingy, baby."
It seems that Garbo will be successful in making the transition from silent films to "talkies."

JANUARY–JUNE

World Events	**FEB** In Spain, riots follow the fall of military dictator General Primo de Rivera.	**MAR** US gangster Al Capone is released from prison after serving nine months for tax evasion.	**APR** The US, Britain, France, Italy, and Japan agree to cut naval fleets to control the arms race.	**MAY** French troops leave the Rhineland five years before the date set in the Versailles Treaty.
Entertainment	**JAN** In Sydney, Australian cricketer Donald Bradman scores a record 452 runs.	**FEB** *The Maltese Falcon* by US crime writer Dashiell Hammett is published to wide acclaim.	**MAY** The US antiwar film *All Quiet on the Western Front*, directed by Lewis Milestone, opens in the US.	**JUN** The first newsreel theater opens on Shaftesbury Avenue in London, UK.
Innovations	**JAN** Opening of first picture telegraphy service between the UK and Germany.	**MAR** Nylon is discovered by Wallace Carrothers of the Du Pont Company in the US.	**APR** UK actress Peggy O'Neil is the first person ever to be interviewed on television.	**JUN** The world's first flight attendant, Ellen Church, starts work for United Airlines.

DONALD BRADMAN

ALL QUIET ON THE WESTERN FRONT

1930

Gandhi's salt march

Mahatma Gandhi on his great march across India

APRIL 6

Mahatma Gandhi reached the coast at Dandi today after a 240-mile (320-km) march across India. He is protesting the tax on salt production imposed on Indians by their British rulers – a tax that he believes is unfair. At Dandi, he symbolically picked up a small piece of natural salt from the mud flats as the crowds called out, "Hail deliverer." Gandhi still defies the British authorities to arrest him.

The champ retires

NOVEMBER 17

US golfer Bobby Jones today retired from competition. He has run out of golfers to beat! In a single year, 28-year-old Jones has completed the supposedly impossible grand slam – the United States Open and Amateur, and the British Open and Amateur.

Grand slam golf champion Bobby Jones

Solo flight feat

Amy Johnson waves to the crowds

APRIL 24

Amy Johnson arrived in Darwin today after flying solo from Britain to Australia. She is the first woman ever to do so. Her epic 10,000-mile (16,000-km) flight began 19 days ago. At one stage she was forced to make an emergency landing in Java in order to mend the wings of her *Gipsy Moth* aircraft with adhesive plaster. Twenty-seven-year-old Amy made her intrepid journey after only 100 hours of flying experience. She left Britain almost unnoticed, but is now an international heroine.

JULY–DECEMBER

JUL Mackenzie King resigns as Canadian prime minister and is succeeded by Richard B. Bennet.		**JUL** Following a liberal revolt in Brazil, Dr. Getulio Vargas is installed as temporary president.	**NOV** In East Africa, Ras Tafari is crowned "king of kings" and becomes Emperor Haile Selassie of Abyssinia.	**DEC** US President Herbert Hoover asks Congress for $150 million to help the unemployed.
JUL Uruguay wins soccer's first World Cup in Montevideo, beating Argentina 4–2.		**SEP** William Van Alen's Art Deco skyscraper, the Chrysler Building, is completed in New York.	**OCT** US studio MGM releases the film *Billy the Kid* in the new "Realife" widescreen process.	**DEC** The Youth Hostel Association (YHA) is formed in England and Wales.
JUL The skull of a man who lived a million years ago has been found in China.	**FIRST WORLD CUP**	**SEP** Dutch chemist P. J. W. Debye uses X rays to investigate the structure of molecules.	**OCT** US company Birdseye perfects its quick-freezing method and frozen peas go on sale.	**DEC** Acrylic plastics (Perspex) are invented in the UK and the US.

EMPEROR HAILE SELASSIE

1931

New republic for Spain

APRIL 14

After seven years of authoritarian rule, King Alfonso XIII has abdicated and Spain has declared itself a republic. King Alfonso's abdication was inevitable after the victory of the Republican Party in the recent elections as well as the resignation of Spain's military dictator, General Miguel Primo de Rivera. It was made clear that if the king did not step down, civil war would erupt. While the republicans celebrate in Madrid, the Spanish royal family is on its way to live in exile in Britain.

Stratospheric record

Piccard and Kipfer land their balloon in the Austrian Tyrol

MAY 27

The Swiss physicist Auguste Piccard and fellow scientist Paul Kipfer have become the first men to reach the Earth's stratosphere. They took off in a huge hydrogen-filled balloon from the town of Augsburg in Germany, and rose a staggering 50,135 ft (15,281 m) into the stratosphere. Their adventure ended when they landed safely on a glacier in the high Austrian Tyrol. An airtight gondola (passenger compartment), designed by Piccard, enabled them to survive the low air density and intense cold at such extreme height. The purpose of the journey was to study the sun's cosmic rays.

Al Capone

"Scarface" jailed again

OCTOBER 17

Al "Scarface" Capone has been jailed again, this time for income tax fraud. The gangster, whose crime empire has dominated Chicago since the 1920s, has been given a stiff 11-year sentence. He must also pay a staggering $137,328 in back taxes. The investigation was led by Eliot Ness, a 28-year-old justice department agent.

A monster hit

NOVEMBER 21

Hollywood is certainly enjoying a horror boom at the moment. *Dracula* was an immediate success earlier this year, and today's release of James Whale's horror film *Frankenstein* is certain to pull in massive audiences. Boris Karloff stars as the poor, bewildered monster in this tragic fantasy horror.

JANUARY–DECEMBER

World Events	**JAN** Pierre Laval becomes the new prime minister of France.	**MAY** President Herbert Hoover opens the 1,250-ft (381-m) high Empire State Building in New York City.	**MAY** Soviet leader Stalin announces the second five-year plan for the introduction of state-owned farms.	**JUL** The Benguella Katanga, the first trans-African railroad, opens in southern Africa, spanning the continent from east to west.
Entertainment	**JAN** Soviet ballerina Anna Pavlova, famous for her "Dying Swan," dies at age 49.	**FEB** Hungarian-born Béla Lugosi stars as the vampire in Tod Browning's US film *Dracula*.	**MAY** *Public Enemy*, a tough gangster movie starring James Cagney, causes a sensation in Hollywood, Calif.	**SEP** The children's book *The Story of Babar* by Cécile de Brunhoff is an instant best-seller in Europe.
Innovations	**MAR** Electric razors are manufactured by Schick Inc. in Connecticut.	**MAR** US engineer Harold Edgerton invents the first electronic reusable camera flash.	**MAY** Thousands of people flock to visit the world's first open zoo at Whipsnade in the UK.	**JUL** Central Ice Co. installs the first ice-vending machine in Los Angeles, California.

PRIMA BALLERINA ANNA PAVLOVA

BABAR

1932

Broadcasting House in London

BBC finds a new home

MAY 1

The British Broadcasting Corporation, known as the BBC, has moved to new London headquarters. The spectacular new home of radio and television looms like a liner under its radio masts. A plaque inside the entrance to this national institution bears the motto "Nation Shall Speak Peace Unto Nation."

Troops maneuver their guns

Bolivia and Paraguay at war

JUNE 15

Full-scale war has erupted between the Latin American countries of Bolivia and Paraguay over the Gran Chaco, which is a large, densely forested, low-lying plain bordering the two countries. Paraguay has invested millions of dollars in the Gran Chaco to raise cattle and "quebracho," a hardwood that is used for tanning leather. Income from these goods has become a vital ingredient in the survival of Paraguay's weak economy. Landlocked Bolivia, on the other hand, needs access to the Gran Chaco in order to trade overseas. Bolivia, with a population that is three times the size of Paraguay and an army trained by German mercenaries, seems set to win the war.

ELECTRIC GUITAR

American musician Adolph Rickenbacker has introduced a new guitar that amplifies sound electronically. Popular music may never sound the same again.

Roosevelt's "New Deal"

NOVEMBER 8

Franklin D. Roosevelt, the Democratic candidate for the US presidency, has won a landslide victory over the Republican president Herbert Hoover. Roosevelt scooped all but six of the 48 states and gained a majority of over seven million in the popular vote. The campaign has been full of optimism. He has promised a "New Deal," a complete program of reforms scheduled to be put into effect over the next few years. Above all, he has promised that when he becomes president "No American will starve."

Roosevelt wins landslide victory

JANUARY–DECEMBER

FEB Japanese troops create the puppet state of Manchuko, securing their control over Manchuria.

MAY US film producer Walt Disney releases *Flowers and Trees*, the first film in three-strip Technicolor.

JAN The Sukkur Dam, the largest irrigation project in the world, opens in India.

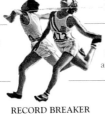

**RECORD BREAKER
MILDRED "BABE" DIDRIKSON**

MAR After nine years of construction, the Sydney Harbour Bridge opens in Australia.

AUG US Mildred Didrikson is the most successful track-and-field athlete at the Olympic Games.

MAR US scientists announce the development of the first vaccine against yellow fever.

MAY US aviator Amelia Earhart becomes the first woman to fly solo across the Atlantic Ocean.

OCT US Jean Harlow and Clark Gable star in the film *Red Dust*, a romance set in a rubber plantation.

MAR The UK's *Times Weekly Edition* is the first newspaper to feature color photographs.

**THE EARTH
IS DATED**

OCT German physicist Albert Einstein dates the age of the Earth at an amazing ten billion years.

NOV UK author John Galsworthy wins the Nobel Prize for his Forsyte novels.

AUG US food manufacturer Forrest Mars launches a nougat, caramel, and chocolate Mars Bar.

THE GREAT DEPRESSION

By 1925 IT SEEMED THAT THE UPHEAVALS of World War I were over and that a new era of peace and economic stability had arrived. This illusion was shattered in 1929 with the crash of the New York Stock Exchange. It was the beginning of an economic depression that, throughout the following decade, was to affect the whole world. For several years the prices of staple products such as wheat, rubber, and sugar had been falling. This made it very difficult for countries exporting these commodities. Their national incomes dropped and they could not afford to buy goods manufactured in Europe and the United States. All over the world exports fell, factory production slowed down, and, before long, millions of jobs disappeared. In industrialized countries up to a quarter of the workforce was out of work. Full recovery did not come about until the buildup to World War II, when the world's major economies employed all their resources to meet the needs of the war effort.

COFFEE

SUGAR BEET

Falling prices

Sugar beets and coffee were just two staple products that suffered steeply falling prices from the mid-1920s. The effect on the countries that exported them was disastrous. Coffee made up 75 percent of Brazil's exports. The collapse of the market led to a three-month civil war and the dictatorship of the unpopular president Getulio Vargas.

PROPAGANDA POSTER URGES GERMANS TO FOLLOW HITLER

Our last hope

Recession and unemployment led many people to support extreme right-wing parties such as Hitler's Nationalist Socialist Workers' (Nazi) Party in Germany, which they hoped would pull them out of poverty.

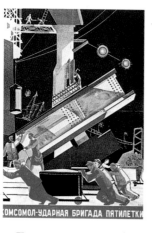

Economic miracle

In the 1930s Stalin introduced a series of five-year plans to boost the production of coal and steel. They transformed the Soviet Union from a backward agricultural society into a major industrial power. But many workers were used as slave labor, with little reward for their efforts.

Living on the breadline

Long lines of unemployed people waiting for food were a common sight in large cities. With little or no public welfare provisions, hundreds of starving people had no alternative but to wait in line for free soup provided by private charities. Millions found themselves in absolute poverty, often having to choose between fuel to keep them from freezing, and food to keep from them starving. Families lost their homes and were forced onto the streets. Young people delayed marriage until prospects improved, which led to a massive drop in the birthrate.

Apples for sale

Professional people were hit just as badly by the Depression as everyone else. It was a common sight to see ex-businessmen lining the streets of large cities selling apples or farm produce to make a little money for other food and clothing.

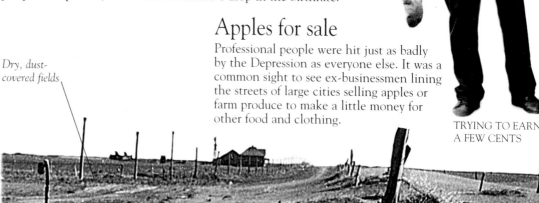

Dry, dust-covered fields

TRYING TO EARN A FEW CENTS

FRENCH STRIKERS DEMAND WORK OR BREAD

PRESIDENT ROOSEVELT MEETS THE FARMERS

New Deal

When Franklin D. Roosevelt was elected president in 1932 he offered the American people a New Deal – a series of rescue programs to stimulate the economy and to bring work to the unemployed. Among them was the Agricultural Adjustment Act of 1933, which gave farmers government subsidies in return for limiting the output of their produce.

In protest

Strikes, hunger marches, and riots occurred frequently during the Depression. In France, widespread strikes paralyzed industrial production. This resulted in a period of great political unrest, which led to the 1936 election of France's first socialist prime minister, Léon Blum, at the head of the Popular Front. His government made many promises to striking workers, including a 40-hour week and a minimum wage. But these reforms proved too expensive and Blum was forced to resign the following year.

A POVERTY-STRICKEN MIGRANT WORKER WITH HER SMALL CHILDREN

Midwest dust bowl

In 1935 a series of catastrophic dust storms swept across the American Midwest, leaving a terrible trail of destruction. High winds blew clouds of dust over fields and farms, destroying millions of dollars' worth of crops and suffocating herds of cattle. Thousands of farmers were ruined and forced to leave their homes behind them in search of work and a new life. Many went west to find work fruit-picking in the orchards of California.

Abandoned farmhouse in the Midwest

1933

Hitler is chancellor

Adolf Hitler, the new German chancellor

JANUARY 30

Adolf Hitler has been appointed chancellor of Germany by President von Hindenburg. The 44-year-old leader of the Nazi Party has come to power at a time when Germany's democratic system faces virtual collapse. In recent weeks, the country has come to the brink of civil war, with members of the Nazi Party and the German communists fighting vicious street battles. Although support for the Nazis seemed to be fading, a series of backroom intrigues has led to Hitler being awarded the chancellorship. Aside from Hitler himself, the 11-strong German cabinet has only two other Nazis in it. The rest are right-wing nationalists.

AIR FRANCE

The airline industry is continuing to grow. The latest major international airline to emerge is Air France. It formed in August after the merger of four airline companies and the purchase of Compagnie Générale Aéropostale.

Reichstag on fire

Flames lick the dome of the Reichstag

FEBRUARY 28

A mysterious fire has gutted Berlin's Reichstag, the building that houses the German parliament. The new chancellor, Adolf Hitler, has accused the communists of starting the fire and has used this to persuade President von Hindenburg to sign a decree suspending all freedom of speech and assembly.

King Kong brings the latest in special-effects technology to the screen

Monkey trouble

MARCH 2

Fay Wray's new leading man is tall, dark, and menacing – he is a giant gorilla called King Kong. Captured on Skull Island, Kong is taken to New York, where he escapes. Although he seems huge on the screen, in real life Kong is a tiny, jointed model, given life by Willis O'Brien's clever "stop-go" animation.

JANUARY–JUNE

World Events	**JAN** The Spanish government authorizes martial law as revolutionary forces grow.	**MAR** F. D. Roosevelt is sworn in as the 32nd US president, declaring "The only thing we have to fear is fear itself."	**MAR** In Germany, the Enabling Act allows Hitler rather than the president to rule by decree.	**MAY** Women vote for the first time in South Africa; the results lead to a coalition between Hertzog and Smuts.
Entertainment	**JAN** René Clair's latest film *Quatorze Juillet (July 14)* is released in Paris, France.	**MAR** Lloyd Bacon's US musical film *42nd Street*, starring Ginger Rogers and Warner Baxter, is released.	**JUN** Hollywood star Charlie Chaplin marries actress Paulette Goddard in a secret ceremony in Los Angeles, CA.	**JUN** Italian Primo Carnera defeats Jack Sharkey to win the world heavyweight boxing title in New York.
Innovations	**FEB** The first "correct time" service opens in the Paris telephone area.	**APR** Four Britons make the first flight over Mount Everest in a Westland Wallace biplane.	**APR** Sir Frederick Henry Royce, co-founder of the UK motor-car company Rolls-Royce, dies.	**JUN** The first drive-in movie theater, the Camden Automobile Theater, opens in New Jersey.

QUATORZE JUILLET

PRIMO CARNERA

1933

Dictator rules

MARCH 22

Portugal's new constitution, passed today, gives António de Oliveira Salazar's single-party government the right to suspend all individual civil liberties.

Champ again

JULY 8

In a thrilling final at the tennis championships at Wimbledon, in the UK, the reigning women's champion, American Helen Wills Moody, has beaten the popular British challenger Dorothy Round 6–4, 6–8, 6–3. For the crowd watching on a blazing hot summer day, the tension on Centre Court was almost unbearable. It is the sixth time in the last seven years that Helen Wills Moody has won this sought-after title.

Dietrich sets trend for menswear

MAY 21

German film star Marlene Dietrich, who moved to Hollywood in 1931, has created a fashion sensation. She appears in a scene in the new Paramount movie *Morocco* wearing a man's top hat and tails. Even off the set the languid Marlene is frequently seen in men's pants and suits, and arrived in France today wearing a brown suit, coat, beret, and red necktie. "I am at heart a gentleman," the film star said when interviewed. The Dietrich look – "Dietrickery" – has caught on, and women are flocking to buy similar outfits.

Hollywood star Marlene Dietrich

JULY–DECEMBER

AUG Indian activist Mahatma Gandhi is released from a prison hospital in Poona, emaciated after a five-day hunger strike.

SEP The Shroud of Turin, a linen cloth believed to be the burial shroud of Jesus, is shown to a crowd of 25,000 people in Italy.

OCT Hitler announces in Berlin that Germany is withdrawing from the League of Nations.

DEC The US finally toasts farewell to Prohibition, as Utah is the last state to ratify the 21st Amendment.

JUL The opera *Arabella* by Richard Strauss premieres in Germany.

RICHARD STRAUSS'S OPERA ARABELLA

SEP Fred Perry is the first UK tennis player to win the US Open since 1903.

NOV In the US, a film version of Louisa May Alcott's novel *Little Women* is released.

LITTLE WOMEN

DEC Fred Astaire and Ginger Rogers star together in the US film *Flying Down to Rio*.

JUL US pilot Roscoe Turner flies from New York to Los Angeles in a record time of 11 hours 30 mins.

OCT The German post office opens the first "telex" service between Berlin and Hamburg.

OCT More than 9,000 Arabs riot in protest against Jewish emigration to Palestine.

DEC Imperial Airways and Indian Trans-Continental start the first London-Singapore service.

1934

Japan appoints Pu-Yi as puppet emperor

MARCH 1

Pu-Yi, once known as the boy emperor of China, has been installed as the puppet emperor, with no actual power, of the conquered Chinese province of Manchuria. The young emperor is the apparent ruler but the Japanese are actually in control of Manchuria and have renamed the Chinese province Manchukuo. Some spectacular celebrations took place in the capital city of Hsinking to mark the grand occasion. Lama priests and painted geishas mingled with medal-wearing soldiers and members of the Mongol cavalry, while delegations of Chinese nobles in ornate and splendid robes paid homage to their new emperor.

Pu-Yi, puppet emperor of Manchukuo

Italy triumphs

JUNE 10

In front of a beaming Benito Mussolini, the Italian soccer team snatched a late goal to beat Czechoslovakia 2–1 in the World Cup Final. The team was guided by its brilliant manager, Victorio Pozzo.

"Nessie" rises

AUGUST 8

Public excitement at reported sightings of a monster in Loch Ness, Scotland, has increased since the publication of a remarkable photograph taken by a British surgeon. Can this really be "Nessie?"

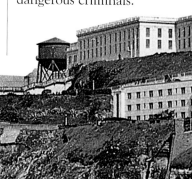

The elusive monster

Prison on Alcatraz

AUGUST 18

Alcatraz prison, built on a large rock in the middle of San Francisco Bay, off the coast of California, opened as a federal penitentiary today. In the past the island has housed a giant fortress and lighthouse that was specially built to guard San Francisco. Raised on the fortress foundations, the "escape-proof" prison will house only the most dangerous criminals.

JANUARY–JUNE

World Events

FEB French prime minister Edouard Daladier is forced to resign following two days of major riots in Paris.

MAY In Canada, Oliva and Elzire Dionne become the proud parents of the first set of quintuplets to survive birth.

MAY Gangster couple Bonnie Parker and Clyde Barrow are shot dead by police in an ambush in Louisiana.

JUN Hitler arrests and executes the leaders of the German Storm Troopers (SA) in the "Night of the Long Knives."

Entertainment

FEB Noel Coward's play *Conversation Piece* opens in London, UK.

FEB *It Happened One Night*, a comedy starring Clark Gable, is a box-office hit.

JUN Walt Disney's Donald Duck makes his first appearance in the cartoon *The Little Wise Hen*.

JUN US film thriller *The Thin Man*, based on Dashiel Hammett's best-selling novel, is released.

Innovations

FEB In Germany, Deutsche Lufthansa introduces the first transatlantic airmail service.

DRIVING TESTS INTRODUCED

MAR The UK Automobile Association introduces the first voluntary driving tests.

MAR The first practical radar test is carried out by Dr. Rudolph Kuhold in Germany.

CAT'S-EYE ROAD STUDS

APR UK inventor Percy Shaw revolutionizes road safety with his cat's-eye road studs.

1934

MARY POPPINS
British author P. L. Travers has just published her novel about a "perfect" nanny who delights her young charges with her special brand of magic.

Anything Goes opens on Broadway

NOVEMBER 21
Anything Goes, a new musical comedy, opened at New York's Alvin Theater on Broadway today. The story, by P. G. Wodehouse and Guy Bolton, follows the romantic adventures of a group of passengers on board a luxury transatlantic liner. Ethel Merman and William Caxton star in the leading roles. The show features a wealth of irresistible lyrics and melodies composed by that maestro of US popular music Cole Porter. The show includes the catchy hit songs *You're the Top*, *All Through the Night*, and *I Get a Kick out of You*.

US federal prison on Alcatraz Island in San Francisco Bay

JULY–DECEMBER

JUL Chancellor Englebert Dollfuss is assassinated in an attempted Nazi coup in Austria.

JUL UK tennis players Fred Perry and Dorothy Round win the singles titles at Wimbledon.

AUG In the UK, Elizabeth Cowell is the first woman to make a live television broadcast for the BBC.

CHANCELLOR DOLLFUSS

OCT In China, the Red Army begins its legendary "Long March" after breaking out of a nationalist blockade.

SEP German actress Marlene Dietrich plays Russia's Catherine the Great in the US film *The Scarlet Empress*.

AUG US explorers Barton and Beebe navigate a bathyscaphe a record 3,028 ft (922 m) below sea level.

OCT King Alexander of Yugoslavia and French foreign minister Louis Barthou are assassinated by a Croatian nationalist in France.

NOV In Germany, Leni Rienfenstahl causes a sensation with her film-documentary *Triumph of the Will*.

AUG In the US, Chrysler introduces the first car with a curved one-piece windshield.

FRENCH AVIATOR RAYMOND DELOTTE

DEC Secret trials begin in the Soviet Union after the assassination of Josef Stalin's chief aide Sergei Kirov.

NOV Italian playwright Luigi Pirandello is awarded the Nobel Prize for Literature.

DEC Delotte's record is broken by Francesco Agello who flies at 440 mph (708 km/h).

1935

Oscar for Shirley

FEBRUARY 27

A miniature Oscar has been awarded to seven-year-old actress Shirley Temple at the Academy Awards ceremony in Hollywood for her "outstanding contribution" to the movies. The singing and dancing

child star made her film debut three years ago in *Red-Haired Alibi*. Following her recent success in *Little Miss Marker*, this curly haired, dimple-cheeked cherub is now Hollywood's favorite star. "It is a splendid thing," commented President Roosevelt. "For 15 cents an American can go to a movie and look at the smiling face of a baby and forget his troubles."

Shirley Temple curtsies to her fans

Lavish decor in station

Moscow metro

MAY 15

The Moscow metro began a regular service at 7 a.m. today. This new rail network is certainly the most impressive underground system in the world. Each of the 104 stations in the network is decorated in a different style, many of them resembling palace halls with amazing marble panels, chandeliers, stained glass, and a wealth of fine paintings. The building of the stations was carried out under the direction of Nikita Khrushchev, the Communist Party chief.

TWIN DOLLS

Rag dolls are enjoying a new wave of popularity at the moment. These felt and velvet twins are manufactured by the Chad Valley toy company in the United Kingdom.

German Jews deprived

SEPTEMBER 15

Hitler's Nuremberg decrees have deprived 600,000 Jews of their German citizenship and banned them from a long list of jobs including teaching and journalism. Existing marriages between Jews and non-Jews have been rendered illegal and couples who will not divorce are subject to imprisonment.

Star symbolizes hatred of Jews

JANUARY–JUNE

World Events

FEB Turkish women win the vote and participate in a parliamentary election for the first time.

MAR King Prajadhipok of Siam gives up the throne to his nine-year-old nephew Ananda Mahidol.

MAY British soldier and writer T. E. Lawrence (Lawrence of Arabia) dies after five days in a coma following a motorcycle crash.

JUN Bolivia and Paraguay sign an armistice to end their three-year dispute over the Chaco region.

Entertainment

JAN The Soviet Union holds its first annual international film festival in Moscow.

MAR *Becky Sharpe* is the first film to use the trichrome Technicolor method perfected by Herbert Kalmus.

APR The film *Les Misérables*, based on Victor Hugo's successful novel about the French Revolution, premieres in the US.

JUN Alfred Hitchcock's new thriller, *The 39 Steps*, set in the Scottish Highlands, premieres in London.

PHYSICIST ROBERT WATSON-WATT

Innovations

JAN The first canned beer is introduced by Kreuger beer in New Jersey.

FEB Physicist Robert Watson-Watt builds the first practical radar equipment for detecting aircraft.

FEB Y-fronts manufactured by Cooper underwear go on sale in Chicago, Illinois.

THE NORMANDIE

MAY France's most luxurious liner, the *Normandie*, travels from Le Havre to New York on her maiden voyage.

1935

LAVORO PER L'EUROPA
RESA DALL'ASSE
PADRONA DEI SUOI DESTINI

Poster depicting Italy plowing its way through the African continent

Mao's march ends

OCTOBER 20
After 12 long months of marching, fighting, and terrible suffering, the Chinese Communist First Front Army, led by Mao Zedong, has reached relative safety in the Shaanxi province. The communists began their 6,000-mile (9,600-km) journey across southwestern China when the nationalist government launched a fierce campaign against their bases in the Kiangsi province. Although pursued by Kuomintang troops, the marchers' worst battles were with nature. Only 10,000 of the original 100,000 who set off survived the ordeal.

Mao Zedong, founder of the Chinese Communist Party

Italy invades Abyssinia

OCTOBER 3
The long-expected Italian invasion of the North African kingdom of Abyssinia has begun. After months of border clashes, two armies from the Italian colonies of Eritrea and Italian Somaliland have advanced into Abyssinia. Emperor Haile Selassie's army of Abyssinian tribesmen, armed with spears and ancient muskets, stands no chance against the might of the Italian troops supported by heavy tanks and bombers.

First flight of Hawker Hurricane

NOVEMBER 6
A British fighter aircraft has made its maiden flight. It will be the first Royal Air Force (RAF) fighter with a top speed of over 300 mph (480 km/h) and the first to be armed with eight machine guns.

The Hawker Hurricane on its maiden flight

JULY–DECEMBER

AUG In the US, the Social Security Bill is passed, introducing welfare for the sick, old, and unemployed.

OCT George Gershwin's *Porgy and Bess*, the first all-black stage musical, opens in New York City.

JUL In the UK, the first-ever paperback novel, *Ariel* by André Maurois, is published by Penguin Books.

PARKING METER

AUG Riots break out in the French cities of Paris, Le Havre, and Brest in protest over unemployment.

NOV Clark Gable stars as the dashing Fletcher Christian in the US film adventure *Mutiny on the Bounty*.

JUL The world's first 150 parking meters are installed in the streets of Oklahoma City.

NOV Mackenzie King is appointed prime minister of Canada following the victory of the Liberal Party.

NOV The Marx Brothers star in their first comedy film for MGM, *A Night at the Opera*.

JUL The first modern opinion poll, conducted on car ownership, is published in the US.

MONOPOLY GAME

NOV King George II of Greece is returned to the throne after spending 12 years in exile.

DEC Monopoly, a new board game, goes on sale in the US, priced at $2.50.

NOV The *New York Times* is the first newspaper to store back issues on microfilm.

1931 GENERAL ELECTRIC
BUILDING, NEW YORK CITY

1932 ARNOS GROVE UNDERGROUND
STATION, LONDON, UK

1932 DAILY EXPRESS
BUILDING, NAPIER, NZ

ARCHITECTURE OF THE THIRTIES

THE BAUHAUS

THE 1930S WAS A DECADE of exciting changes in building design. Steel, glass, and reinforced concrete were used in new ways to create some remarkable constructions. Two distinct styles emerged. Art Deco, influenced by Egyptian, Aztec, and Chinese architecture featured striking geometric motifs, creating a heightened sense of drama. Some of New York's most elaborate skyscrapers, such as the Chrysler Building and the Empire State, were designed in the Art Deco style. The International Style was much less ornate. It emerged from the German Bauhaus movement and relied upon clean, simple lines. The goal of the International Style architects was to create "machines for living" – buildings that were spacious, functional, and economical.

Le Corbusier
Charles-Édouard Jeanneret, known as Le Corbusier (French slang for "the crow"), was one of the greatest architects of the International Style.

International villa
Designed by Le Corbusier in 1931, the Villa Savoye in Poissy, France, is a perfect example of the International Style. It has a geometric shape, white concrete walls, a flat roof, and a long line of windows to give a sense of light and space inside. The whole building is supported by stilts, creating the impression that the villa is growing out of the landscape. Inside, concrete screens divide the living quarters and a ramp rises through the center of the house to the terraces on the upper floor.

OVERHEAD VIEW, VILLA SAVOYE

Ramp

Curved wall

Flat roof

HILVERSUM TOWN HALL

Clock tower

Town hall
Willem Dudok designed this town hall in the Netherlands. Its plain walls and elegant windows show the influence of the De Stijl (The Style) artists.

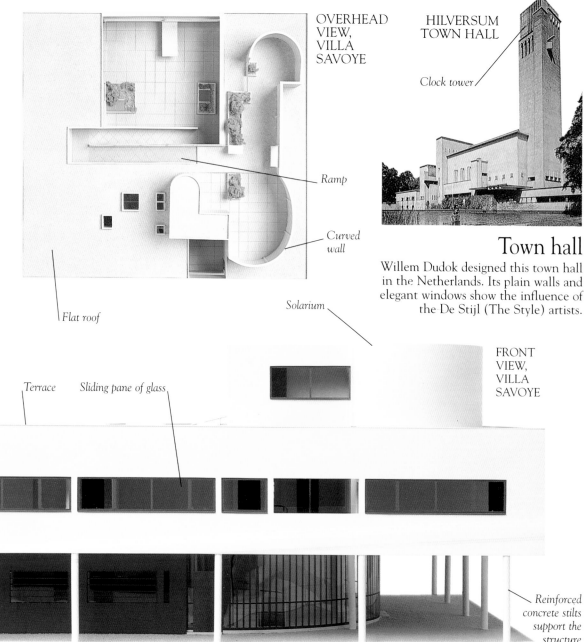

Solarium

FRONT VIEW, VILLA SAVOYE

Cement rendered wall of lightweight slabs

Terrace

Sliding pane of glass

Garages on the ground floor

Reinforced concrete stilts support the structure

1934 BATTERSEA POWER
STATION, LONDON, UK

1936 MIAMI BEACH MOVIE
THEATER, FLORIDA

1937 CHRIST THE KING CHURCH,
CORK, IRELAND

Ornate tower

The Chrysler building in New York has been described as "a jewel" of the Art Deco period. Designed by the architect William Van Alen, it stands 1,047 ft (319 m) tall. Its elegant cathedral-like exterior is ornately decorated with bold features such as the eagle gargoyles on each corner of the sixty-first floor. The interior has lavish details, such as elevator doors inlaid with cherry wood and brass.

Sparkling stainless steel spire

Semicircular sunbursts, a typical feature of Art Deco

Tower is made of white glazed brick

CHRYSLER BUILDING

CHRYSLER BUILDING SPIRE

Clean living

In contrast to the cluttered rooms of the 1900s, interiors in the 1930s emphasized clean lines and new materials, such as Bakelite.

Skyscraper

By the 1930s, construction techniques had greatly improved. Higher-grade steel girders, and safer passenger elevators, allowed architects to build higher and higher. When the 1,250-ft (381-m) Empire State Building was erected in New York in 1931 it was the tallest building in the world, with 102 stories, 73 elevators, and 1,860 steps. Its construction was so well planned that it only took 15 months to complete.

Projecting eagle gargoyle

CHRYSLER BUILDING DETAIL

HOOVER BUILDING

Scalloped masthead

Circular lantern

Observation tower

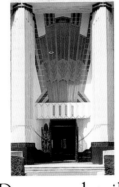

Windows are trimmed with aluminum and nickel

Limestone and granite facing

Fanlike decoration

Light industry

The Hoover building in London, UK, was designed by the firm Wallis, Gilbert, and Partners. With its white walls, metal-framed windows, and stripped corners and cornices, it is considered to be one of the most distinguished examples of British Art Deco.

Doorway detail

Elaborate tiling above the doorway of the Hoover building is influenced by the buildings of ancient Egypt.

SYDNEY HARBOUR BRIDGE

Masterpiece in design

Sydney Harbour Bridge, known for its characteristic shape on the Sydney skyline, is Australia's greatest engineering feat. At 5,413 ft (1,650 m) it is the longest single-span bridge in the world. It opened in March 1932, after nine years of construction.

Flat roof

Stepped cornice

Ground floor entrance

EMPIRE STATE BUILDING

1936

Machine mania

FEBRUARY 5

The film *Modern Times* throws Charlie Chaplin's famous tramp character into the modern world. The Tramp gets a job on an assembly line, causes chaos, and ends up in jail. The film pokes fun at the manic nature of factory life, but it also has a serious side, exposing the hardships encountered by factory workers. Chaplin intended to make *Modern Times* his first film with sound, but could not decide what voice to give the Tramp. In the end, all we hear is a strange little nonsense song.

A PEOPLE'S CAR

The first "people's car" is in the early stages of design in Germany and Volkswagen expects to go into production soon. Hitler hopes that the car will put the nation on wheels and do for Germany what Ford did for the United States.

Germans enter the Rhineland

Local crowds salute the German troops as they march into the cities of the Rhineland

MARCH 7

At dawn today, in defiance of the Treaty of Versailles and on the orders of Adolf Hitler, German troops marched into the cities of the Rhineland. The region was lost by Germany to France at the end of World War I. Hitler's move was a gamble because no one knew how the French were going to react. Hitler's own generals advised him against taking such a risk and General Werner von Blomberg, minister of war, gave orders for the troops to be withdrawn the minute the French and British showed signs of response. French politicians want to take military action, but the generals are pleading for restraint. The British have told the French to do nothing until Hitler's action has been given "full consideration." No one is calling Hitler's bluff. He has proposed a new treaty that guarantees peace for the next 25 years, and the British are taking this as evidence of peaceful intent. According to one newspaper, he has "merely reoccupied his own backyard."

JANUARY–JUNE

World Events

JAN The UK mourns the death of King George V, who is succeeded to the throne by Edward Prince of Wales.

MAY Sixteen-year-old Crown Prince Farouk, the eldest son of King Fuad, is proclaimed king of Egypt after his father's death.

MAY Italian fascist leader Mussolini claims the rebirth of an empire with the annexation of Abyssinia.

JUN Léon Blum, leader of the Socialist Party, wins the election to become prime minister of France.

Entertainment

JAN UK author and poet Rudyard Kipling dies at the age of 70.

MAYERLING

FEB Charles Boyer and Danielle Darrieux star in the French film *Mayerling*, a tragic love story.

APR In the US, baseball player Joe Di Maggio plays his first competitive game with the New York Yankees.

MAY US film stars Gary Cooper and Jean Arthur star in Frank Capra's thought-provoking comedy *Mr. Deeds Goes to Town*.

Innovations

JAN German scientists Dr. Jaeger and Dr. Espig produce the first synthetic emerald.

APR In the UK, *Supermarine Spitfire I*, the RAF's new weapon, has its maiden flight.

MAY In Germany, Rudolph Opitz flies the twin-engined Messerschmitt *Bf 110* fighter for the first time.

JOE DI MAGGIO

MAY Gatwick, the first airport with covered walkways leading to the aircraft, opens in the UK.

1936

The official poster of the Olympics

Sour Olympics

AUGUST 16

The Berlin Olympic Games closed today with a host of outstanding records set by athletes from 49 competing nations. However, this great sports occasion has left a bitter taste in many people's mouths. Although the games were organized by Germany to a high standard, Hitler transformed the event into a gigantic propaganda exercise to glorify the Nazi regime. The games were awarded to Berlin before Hitler came to power. Once his dictatorial and racist policies became known, there were a number of moves, particularly in the United States, to organize a boycott. The Nazi regime actively promotes the Aryan race – white people of non-Jewish descent. So, when the undisputed star of the Games was the US black athlete Jesse Owens, Hitler was so angry that he refused publicly to congratulate this fine young man. Owens won gold medals in two sprint events, the long jump – setting a staggering Olympic record of 26.4 ft (8.06 m) – and the relay. When the crowds rose to salute Owens on his final victory, Hitler could contain himself no longer and stormed out of the Olympic stadium in a furious rage.

Jesse Owens shatters the long jump world record

King quits for love

DECEMBER 11

King Edward VIII of England has abdicated the throne of Britain. He is going to marry Wallis Simpson, the twice-divorced American, against the advice of the government and the church. The king made his abdication speech from Windsor Castle in a radio broadcast that sent shock waves across a stunned nation. Although the king has many supporters in parliament and among the press barons, there is an overwhelming feeling that the British people will not accept Mrs. Simpson as their queen. The king will be succeeded by his younger brother, Albert George.

The king and Mrs. Simpson on holiday last summer in Yugoslavia

---

JULY–DECEMBER

JUL Civil war erupts in Spain when General Franco heads an army rebellion against the republican government.

JUL UK film tycoon J. Arthur Rank establishes a Hollywood-style studio at Pinewood in London, UK.

JUL The giant German airship *Hindenburg* crosses the Atlantic in a record time of 46 hours.

CIVIL WAR IN SPAIN

AUG Soviet premier Stalin has 16 political opponents, two of them his former comrades, executed for treason.

AUG The BBC makes its first television broadcast from Alexandra Palace, London, in the UK.

SEP UK aviator Beryl Markham is the first woman to fly solo across the Atlantic from east to west.

OCT In the UK, 200 unemployed men "march against starvation" on the Jarrow Crusade across England.

NOV Nadia Boulanger is the first woman to conduct the London Philharmonic Orchestra in the UK.

OCT The $120-million Hoover Dam opens on the Colorado River between Nevada and Arizona.

LIFE MAGAZINE

NOV In the US, Roosevelt becomes the first president to win a second four-year-term since 1914.

NOV *Life*, a new photo-magazine featuring news and human interest stories, is launched in the US.

OCT US airline Pan Am starts the first transpacific service from San Francisco to the Philippines.

1937

Margot's debut

Margot Fonteyn with stage mask

JANUARY 19

British ballerina Margot Fonteyn, at age 18, has made a sensational debut in *Giselle* at Sadler's Wells theater in London. Fonteyn, whose real name is Peggy Hookham, will become the prima ballerina at Sadler's Wells, a post left vacant since the departure of Alicia Markova two years ago.

Fonteyn steps into Markova's shoes

Pride of Germany in flames

MAY 6

In the United States, the German airship *Hindenburg* exploded in a ball of flames today as it approached Lakehurst Field, New Jersey, after a routine transatlantic flight from Frankfurt. The ship was destroyed in less than a minute, and 35 of the 97 passengers and crew on board are dead. Since its maiden flight in 1936, the *Hindenburg* has become a symbol of Nazi Germany. It was the world's largest airship, longer than any battleship and capable of carrying 70 passengers across the Atlantic in luxury. The Hindenburg's arrival at Lakehurst was delayed by a thunderstorm, and when it approached the landing tower, eyewitnesses saw a sudden flash on top of the *Hindenburg*. Within ten seconds the airship was ablaze. Sabotage is suspected, but a more likely explanation is that, following the storm, static electricity in the air ignited hydrogen leaking from the craft's gasbags.

The cover of a German magazine shows the horror of the explosion

George VI crowned

MAY 12

On the day that had originally been chosen for the coronation of Edward VIII, George VI and Queen Elizabeth were crowned in Westminster Abbey in London, England. A million well-wishers lined the streets to watch the procession, and millions more listened to the ceremony on their radios.

The new royal family

JANUARY–JUNE

World Events

JAN Major floods in the US Midwest leave millions of families homeless and destitute.

JAN 13 former Bolshevik leaders are sentenced to death for conspiring with Trotsky to overthrow Stalin.

APR The German air force, fighting for Franco in the Spanish Civil War, carries out a massive air raid on the Basque town of Guernica.

JUN Former king of England, Edward, Duke of Windsor, marries Wallis Simpson at the Château de Candé in France.

Entertainment

APR Rodgers and Hart's musical *Babes in Arms* opens in the US.

APR Sabu, a former stable boy in India, stars in the film *Elephant Boy*.

APR US film studio Warner Bros. releases the cartoon *Porky's Duck Hunt*, with Daffy Duck.

MAY US writer Margaret Mitchell wins the Pulitzer Prize for her best-selling novel *Gone With the Wind*.

Innovations

JAN Turk Sabiha Gokchen is the first woman to fly on a combat mission.

ELEPHANT BOY

JAN UK aviator Jean Batten wins the Britannia Trophy following her solo flight from London to New Zealand.

APR UK engineer and ex-pilot Frank Whittle builds the first prototype jet engine.

FRANK WHITTLE'S JET ENGINE

JUN The first color news photograph, published in the US, shows the Hindenburg in flames.

1937

Golden span

MAY 27

Some 200,000 people have crossed the Golden Gate Bridge today in celebration of one of the greatest engineering marvels to be built this century. The longest suspension bridge in the world spans 7 miles (11 km) across San Francisco Bay in California.

PARIS
1937
MAI-NOVEMBRE
EXPOSITION INTERNATIONALE

PARIS EXPOSITION

Funfairs, pavilions, and arcades are attracting millions of visitors to the Paris Expo. The monumental stone towers of Germany and the Soviet Union are proving to be the most popular structures.

Japan attacks China

JULY 7

War has broken out between China and Japan after Japanese troops on a military exercise in the state of Manchukuo opened fire on a Chinese patrol just outside the Chinese capital, Peking. The Japanese claim they were provoked, but it is probable that they set up the incident as an excuse to attack China.

A fairy-tale success

Snow White sings to the woodland animals

DECEMBER 21

Today is the premiere of Walt Disney's *Snow White and the Seven Dwarfs*. Disney hit the road to fame and fortune back in 1928 with his Silly Symphony cartoons starring the lovable Mickey Mouse. *Snow White and the Seven Dwarfs* is the first feature-length animation in three-strip Technicolor. The film is an enormous financial and artistic gamble for Disney. It cost a staggering $1.5 million to produce and took a large team of artists and animators over four years to complete. It is a musical fantasy based on the popular brothers Grimm fairy tale about Snow White, her friends the seven dwarfs, and an evil queen. In addition to the new and extraordinary visual techniques, the film features some unforgettable songs, including *Some Day My Prince Will Come*, *Whistle While You Work*, and *Hi-Ho, Hi-Ho, It's Off To Work We Go*, which are certain to be big hits with both young and old. Walt Disney plans to follow *Snow White* with more feature-length animations, which he will base on popular children's stories.

JULY–DECEMBER

JUL The UK government announces proposals to partition Palestine to end the conflict between Jews and Arabs.

JUL George Gershwin, celebrated US composer, dies tragically from a brain tumor at the age of 39.

JUL Nestlé introduces the "milky bar," a white chocolate bar made from cocoa butter, milk, and sugar.

US COMPOSER GEORGE GERSHWIN

JUL US aviator Amelia Earhart disappears on the last half of her round-the-world flight attempt.

SEPT US singer Bessie Smith, known as the "empress of blues," dies in a car accident in Memphis, aged 43.

SEPT In Germany, the first national prizes are awarded to Nazi artists and scientists.

OCT Duke and Duchess of Windsor meet Hitler when in Berlin, Germany, to "study social conditions and housing problems."

NOV John Steinbeck's play *Of Mice and Men*, a moving tale of two farm workers, opens in New York City.

OCT The first major car show opens at the new Earls Court Exhibition Center in London, UK.

AVIATOR AMELIA EARHART

NOV In northern Spain, 6,000 republican forces surrender to General Franco's nationalist army at Gijon.

DEC The musical comedy *Me and My Girl* opens at the Victoria Palace theater in London, UK.

NOV J. Armand Bombardier designs the first snowmobile in Quebec, Canada.

THE SPANISH CIVIL WAR

IN 1931 THE SPANISH MONARCHY was overthrown and King Alfonso XIII went into exile. A republican government was elected and introduced socialist policies to limit the power of the wealthy ruling elite, the church, and the army. In 1936 the army rose up against the new government. General Francisco Franco emerged as the leader of the army rebels, who became known as the nationalists. In the bloody civil war that followed Franco received military aid from Germany and Italy. The republicans were supported by the Soviet Union and an International Brigade of volunteers from various countries. By the end of 1936 Franco's nationalists had seized almost half of Spain, but the war dragged on for another three years before the republican resistance finally collapsed.

General Franco

The nationalist leader General Franco was declared Chief of the Spanish State in 1936. Although not a brilliant general, Franco was extremely ruthless and, supported by the fascists in Spain, Germany, and Italy, he eventually led the nationalists to victory.

Franco's nationalist forces in July 1936

Rebels with a cause

The republican forces were less well trained and equipped than the nationalists, who were mostly professional soldiers. The republican ranks were swelled by regiments of the International Brigade, an army of idealistic young Europeans and Americans who saw the Spanish Civil War as the first great struggle of democracy against fascism.

REPUBLICAN SOLDIERS

Nationalist-held territory

In the summer of 1936 the nationalists took most of western Spain. They gradually overcame the republicans by gaining control of most of Spain's coastline and cutting off their supply lines.

REPUBLICAN POLITICAL CARTOON

Taunting the enemy

This republican propaganda poster shows caricatures of Franco's main supporters. A fat bishop represents the church, and one of the generals who supported the nationalists is seen armed with a toy cannon. The monocled banker in the stern wears a swastika badge, symbol of Nazi Germany. He holds a bag of money, which represents aid from Germany.

OCT 1936 SOVIET UNION
SENDS AID TO REPUBLICANS

NOV 1936 GERMAN JUNKERS
AIRCRAFT BOMB MADRID

MAR 1939 VICTORY FOR
THE NATIONALISTS

GERMAN JUNKERS AIRCRAFT OVER MADRID

Raid on Madrid

Germany and Italy supplied Franco with most of his air force. The German contingent was called the Condor Legion and operated from the nationalist-held island of Majorca, attacking republican strongholds like Madrid and Barcelona.

A country in ruins

After three years of bitter fighting, and the massacre of thousands of civilians by both sides, Spain was a devastated land. Industry and agriculture were in ruins and millions were on the verge of starvation. About 750,000 people died in the Spanish Civil War.

CHILDREN SIT IN THE
RUINS OF MADRID

PISTOL USED BY
REPUBLICAN FORCES

Detachable butt

Pistol can deliver a short burst of automatic fire

A writer's war

Many poets and writers were drawn to the struggle in Spain. The British writer George Orwell fought as a volunteer on the Republican side. He wrote about his experiences in *Homage to Catalonia*, which paints a vivid picture of the grim conditions in the front line.

GEORGE ORWELL

Call to arms

This pistol is the kind of weapon that was used by the republican forces. They were never as well equipped as their nationalist opponents and were always short of ammunition. For them it was a war of ancient rifles and jamming machine guns. In one battle, artillery shells had to be rushed to the republican front line straight from the factory that made them. Their fighter aircraft were often too slow to catch the nationalist bombers carrying out air raids on republican-held cities.

Hollywood's heroes

This scene from the movie *For Whom the Bell Tolls* (1943) shows a motley band of republican soldiers. The film was adapted from the best-selling novel by US writer Ernest Hemingway, who covered the war as a journalist. His sympathies were strongly on the side of the republicans.

Picasso painting protests against war

On April 26, 1937, the German Condor Legion carried out a heavy bombing raid on the town of Guernica in the Basque region of Spain. The center of the town was completely destroyed and nearly 1,700 people were killed. In his painting *Guernica*, Spanish artist Pablo Picasso depicted the agony and terror of the helpless citizens as the bombs fell around them.

1938

A celebration of French history

FEBRUARY 9

Director Jean Renoir has just released *La Marseillaise*, a remarkable documentary-style film telling the story of the French Revolution. There must have been a tremendous temptation to deal with the leading figures of the period. Instead, Renoir has chosen to contrast the lives of ordinary people and the aristocracy. The film follows the fortunes of a group of revolutionary volunteers who leave their humble homes in the city of Marseilles and march to Paris in protest over the corrupt monarchy of Louis XVI.

Lise Delamare (center) plays the French queen Marie Antoinette

Propaganda poster depicts Hitler as ruler of Austria

Hitler claims Austria

MARCH 14

Adolf Hitler has made Austria a province of Germany. The Austrian-born dictator drove through the streets of Vienna, capital city of his native land, in a spectacular procession led by tanks and field guns. In the brown uniform of his storm troopers, Hitler stood upright in his open car and gave the fascist salute to the ecstatic crowds that had come to greet him. Later in the evening Hitler appeared on his hotel balcony and proudly told the Austrian people, "The German nation will never again be rent apart."

New hero of Sherwood

MAY 12

Warner Bros. has just released *The Adventures of Robin Hood*, starring Errol Flynn as the legendary hero of Sherwood Forest. The swashbuckling adventure has a superb cast, including Olivia de Havilland as the beautiful Maid Marian. The film is shot in three-strip Technicolor and cost $2 million to produce. It features some superb sets and boasts a record number of action stunts, including Robin Hood's duel to death with the hissable villain Sir Guy of Gisbourne.

JANUARY–MARCH

World Events	**JAN** Austrian psychiatrist Sigmund Freud moves to the UK after being persecuted by the Nazis.	**JAN** Mikhail Kalinin is elected president of the Soviet Union Supreme Praesidium.	**JAN** The Dominion of Australia celebrates the 150th anniversary of European settlement.	**FEB** King Carol of Romania ousts Premier Octavian Goga from Romania and becomes dictator.
Entertainment	**JAN** US jazz musician Benny Goodman plays to a sell-out audience at Carnegie Hall.	**FEB** US child star Tommy Kelly stars in the film version of Mark Twain's novel *The Adventures of Tom Sawyer*.	**MAR** In the UK, BBC radio broadcasts the first comedy series *Bandwagon*, starring Arthur Askey.	**MAR** Cary Grant and Katherine Hepburn star in the US screwball film comedy *Bringing Up Baby*.
Innovations	**FEB** US chemical company E. I. du Pont produces, the first nylon product, toothbrush bristles.	**FEB** The first purpose-built air-raid shelter for the general public to use is opened in central London, UK.	**FEB** UK engineer John Logie Baird demonstrates the first high-definition color TV in the UK.	**MAR** Low-voltage fluorescent lights go on sale in major department stores in the US, priced at $1.50 and $2.00.

SIGMUND FREUD

AUSTRALIAN KOALA BEARS

1938

Chinese bombed

JUNE 8

For ten days and nights Japanese bombers have been mercilessly bombing the defenseless Chinese city of Canton. Thousands of people are dead and countless injured. Entire areas of the city have been reduced to piles of rubble. Air-raid warnings no longer work, and when the sound of a fresh swarm of Japanese bombers is heard, soldiers and police run through the streets shouting "They are coming." There are so many false alarms that the city is being kept in a state of agonizing suspense. Power stations have been destroyed and there is no electricity, not even in the hospitals. The only light people have is from the blazing oil refineries and the many fires burning all over the city. The Japanese have made it perfectly clear that they are determined to bomb Canton into submission. Nationalist leader General Chiang Kai-shek has no more fighters left to defend the city. Japan has control of most of China's coastline, as well as most of the major cities, railroads, and large parts of China's interior, making it very difficult for China to receive weapons and ammunition. But still the brave people of Canton refuse to surrender.

HITLER YOUTH

The spectacular Nuremberg Rally is held every September in Germany. It is the high point of the year for members of the Hitler Youth, who proudly show off their military-style training in front of their leader, the Führer.

Authorities search for survivors after a bombing raid

Knockout

JUNE 22

Joe Louis, the brilliant 24-year-old US boxer, has wreaked revenge on Max Schmeling, the reigning German champion. Schmeling knocked out the young Louis two years ago, but at Yankee Stadium in New York City, Louis's amazing punching power demolished his challenger in the fourth round.

APRIL–JUNE

APR France's first socialist prime minister Leon Blum is forced to resign following the defeat of his radical budget.

APR *The Adventures of Marco Polo* is released in Hollywood, with Gary Cooper in the title role.

APR US chemist Roy J. Plunkett accidentally discovers a new non-stick substance and calls it Teflon.

POSTER TO CELEBRATE HITLER'S ROME VISIT

MAY Adolf Hitler and Benito Mussolini meet in Rome, Italy, and pledge lasting friendship in a grand ceremony.

JUN US writer John P. Marquand wins the Pulitzer Prize for fiction for his novel *The Late George Apley*.

APR New York is the first US state to pass a law requiring medical tests for marriage licenses.

JUN US President Franklin D. Roosevelt signs the Labor Standards Act, introducing a minimum wage of 25 cents an hour.

JUN Italy wins its second consecutive World Cup, beating the Hungarians 4–2 in Paris, France.

APR Two US companies begin production of fluorescent lamps, available in seven colors.

CHANCELLOR KURT VON SCHUSCHNIGG

JUN Kurt von Schuschnigg, the last chancellor of pre-Nazi Austria, is tried for treason.

JUN *Action Comics*, featuring a new action-hero called Superman, is launched in New York.

JUN The first television serial, a comedy called *Vine Street*, is broadcast in Los Angeles.

1938

Mallard sets new world speed record

JULY 3

A British locomotive has set a new world speed record for steam engines of 127 mph (203 km/h). Mallard, a streamlined Gresley A4 Pacific, achieved the record while pulling a special train, including a speed-recording car, down a gradient on the main line between Grantham and Peterborough. British engineer Sir Nigel Gresley, who designed Mallard, was on board to record the speed. The locomotive maintained a speed of 120 mph (193 km/h) for over 5 miles (8 km), beating the previous British record of 114 mph (183 km/h) set by Coronation Scot.

Around the world in three days

JULY 14

The dashing multimillionaire Howard Hughes has flown around the world in his specially built Lockheed 14 Electra. By keeping his stopovers to a minimum, the heroic pilot circulated the northern hemisphere in the remarkable time of 3 days, 19 hours, and 8 minutes –

almost half the time it took his fellow US pilot Wiley Post four years ago. After landing the plane in front of 25,000 screaming fans at New York's Floyd Bennet Field, Hughes declared, "Any one of the airline pilots of this nation could have done the same thing."

Chamberlain promises peace

SEPTEMBER 30

There will be no war in Czechoslovakia. Germany, Britain, and France have agreed to give Hitler Czech Sudetenland at a conference held in Munich. They hope that by appeasing the Nazis war will be averted. Back in London today, Prime Minister Neville Chamberlain proudly told the nation, "I believe it is peace for our time."

Chamberlain displays new peace accord

Mallard, the fastest locomotive in the world

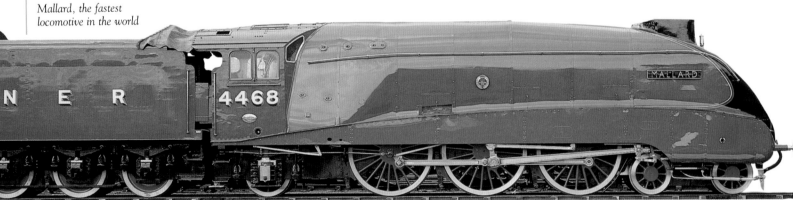

JULY–SEPTEMBER

	World Events	Entertainment	Innovations
	JUL A peace treaty is agreed by Paraguay and Bolivia, ending the dispute over the Chaco region.	**AUG** Celebrations are held in the Netherlands to mark the 40th anniversary of Queen Wilhelmina's accession to the throne.	**AUG** Germans living in the Czech territory of the Sudetenland hold mass rallies demanding union with Germany.	**AUG** German pilot Kurt Henke flies nonstop from Berlin, Germany, to New York in a record time of 24 hours 36 minutes.
	JUL US tennis player Helen Wills Moody wins her eighth Wimbledon singles victory.	**JUL** French actress Danielle Darrieux stars in her first US film, *The Rage of Hollywood*, with Douglas Fairbanks, Jr.	**AUG** British cricketer Len Hutton scores a record 363 runs in a test match against Australia in the UK.	**SEP** Alfred Hitchcock's latest mystery thriller, *The Lady Vanishes*, is released in the UK.
	JUL The first children's zoo opens in Regents Park, London, in the UK.	**JUL** The first experimental television transmissions begin in the Soviet Union.	**AUG** The BBC transmits the first feature-length film on TV, *The Student of Prague*, a German film with subtitles.	**SEP** Long-lasting nylon-bristled toothbrushes are marketed for the first time in the US.

QUEEN WILHELMINA'S DAUGHTER JULIANA

KURT HENKE

1938

Awesome Orson causes hysteria

OCTOBER 30

Orson Welles, the talented 23-year-old actor and producer, has thrown the population of the United States into mass hysteria with his sensational radio broadcast of H. G. Wells's science fiction thriller *The War of the Worlds*. The radio play simulated a news broadcast, with bulletins and on-the-spot coverage of Martians "as high as skyscrapers" landing in New Jersey. It sounded so realistic that about one million listeners actually believed there was a Martian invasion. Welles claims to be astounded by the uproar, but he has certainly demonstrated the power of broadcasting.

Orson Wells broadcasts War of the Worlds *to the public*

Local residents laugh at the damage caused to Jewish stores in Germany

The night of broken glass

NOVEMBER 10

Last night, the German Jewish community was subjected to unprecedented violence. More than 7,000 Jewish-owned stores were broken into and looted, synagogues were burned to the ground, and hundreds of Jews were beaten in the streets. German propaganda minister Dr. Josef Goebbels claims the violence was sparked by the assassination of a German diplomat by a Jewish student in Paris. But it is clear that the rampage of destruction was organized by the Nazi Party itself. Because of the piles of broken glass left lying in the streets after the looting of the stores, this event will be known by everyone as "Kristallnacht," or "Crystal Night."

Fisherman discovers a "living fossil"

NOVEMBER 22

A fisherman made an extraordinary catch today. While fishing from his boat near the Comoro Islands off the coast of South Africa, he reeled in a living coelacanth fish. Many fossil coelacanths have been known to have existed, dating back some 400 million years, but scientific experts were convinced the fish became extinct about 70 million years ago. The species has remained virtually unchanged from its original form. It is a bony fish with a distinctive, fleshy, three-lobed tail and flipperlike fins. It was Professor Smith, an ichthyologist from South Africa, who first identified the living coelacanth, and is offering a generous reward of £100 to anyone who can find a second living specimen.

Fossil coelacanth

The living coelacanth

OCTOBER–DECEMBER

OCT Czech president Edward Bënes resigns in protest over the German occupation of the Sudetenland.

SEP *The Corn Is Green*, a moving play about a Welsh boy who wins a place at university, opens in the UK.

OCT The first successful flexible drinking straw is designed by US entrepreneur Joseph Friedman.

PICTURE POST

NOV Eighteen synagogues are destroyed by firebomb attacks in Vienna, the capital city of Austria.

OCT *Picture Post*, a new illustrated news magazine, is launched by Edward Hulton in the UK.

OCT US physicist and lawyer Chester Carlson makes the first successful Xerox copy with his Xerox machine.

NOV Adolf Hitler decorates US aviator Charles Lindbergh with the German Service Cross.

DEC Russian film director Sergei Eisenstein produces *Alexander Nevsky*, his first film with sound.

DEC First drunk-driving test, the Drunkometer, is used by a police department in Indianapolis.

ALEXANDER NEVSKY

DEC The British government unveils the "National Register," stating what people will do in time of war.

DEC UK actor Leslie Howard stars in the film *Pygmalion*, based on Bernard Shaw's play.

DEC Boeing's *Stratoliner*, the first pressurized airliner, makes its maiden flight in the US.

1930 NEWLY RELEASED SUNTAN
PRODUCTS IN DEMAND IN STORES

1931 THE HEMLINE ON LADIES' DRESSES
LENGTHENS TO JUST ABOVE THE ANKLE

1932 SUNGLASSES BECOME
A FASHION ACCESSORY

HIGH LIFE IN THE THIRTIES

IT IS EASY TO SEE THE 1930s as the decade of the Depression, with sweeping unemployment, the rise of dictators, and the drift toward war, poverty, and homelessness. But for the more fortunate sectors of society, such as those born into money, and film and radio stars, it was an age of glamor, beauty, and style. Fashion changed dramatically, and new feminine styles were celebrated by challenging young designers such as Elsa Schiaparelli and Mainbocher (the favorite designer of the Duchess of Windsor). Hollywood, too, became enormously influential in setting styles – not only for women but also for men. Stage and movie theaters sprang up everywhere and people flocked to see musicals. If you could not live the lives of the rich and famous, you could read about them in one of the many new celebrity magazines that were becoming increasingly popular. Or you could read in a newspaper about the leisurely pursuits of wealthy society, and royalty and aristocracy in Britain.

An evening at the theater

Theater thrived in the 1930s. British stars Noel Coward and Gertrude Lawrence starred in several sparkling comedies, such as *Cavalcade* and *Private Lives*, which had a high-society setting. Coward wrote the plays and the pencil-thin Lawrence dazzled audiences in her elegant costumes.

The golden age of the musical

Musicals experienced a golden age in the Thirties. US composers such as Irving Berlin, George Gershwin, and Cole Porter wrote the songs for a number of successful shows. Popular shows of the day, including the synchronized dance group the Rockettes, were staged at New York City's lavish Radio City Music Hall. Situated in Rockefeller Center, Radio City was the largest theater in the world.

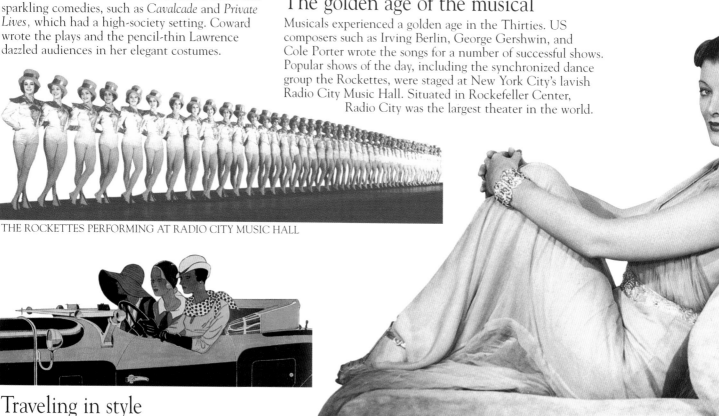

THE ROCKETTES PERFORMING AT RADIO CITY MUSIC HALL

Traveling in style

For the rich and famous the 1930s was the era of "grand routier," or "grand touring." In Europe, the wealthy drove their luxury cars to fashionable bathing spots such as Nice in the French Riviera. Magnificent cars including Mercedes, Lagondas, and Bentleys were often exclusively designed to meet their owners' particular requirements, with special fittings such as drinks cabinets. Wealthy female celebrities, including actress Marlene Dietrich, even went as far as to have their cars painted to match the colors of their favorite outfits.

1934 AUBURN UNVEILS NEW
SPORTS CAR IN THE US

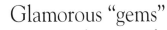

1935 FRED AND GINGER DANCE THEIR
WAY TO FAME IN THE FILM *TOP HAT*

1937 *MARIE CLAIRE* MAGAZINE
IS LAUNCHED IN PARIS, FRANCE

A new look

Commercial art and design flourished in the 1930s. Vast sums of money were spent on colorful and sophisticated advertisements to promote all kinds of products. This innovative poster by A. M. Cassandre is designed to promote a popular French alcoholic drink.

Glamorous "gems"

Costume jewelry was considered a cheap imitation before French designer Coco Chanel transformed it into an art form. She poured scorn on people who bought gems simply to flaunt their wealth, and set about designing her own "fake" jewelry. Chanel made her fakes as stunning and sought-after as the real thing. Alongside slinky evening bags, costume jewelry became an essential fashion accessory to complement the elegant evening gowns of the 1930s.

Beaded flowers and embroidery

Garden path design

EVENING BAG

CHANEL GLASS NECKLACE

Glass beads

EVENING COAT WITH FUR TRIM

Celebrity couple

Nowhere seemed more glamorous in the Thirties than Hollywood, the American film capital of the world. The sophisticated costumes worn by screen idols set fashion trends for women all over the world. The acting couple William Powell and Myrna Loy were considered to be among the most stylish in the business.

Haute couture

High fashion gradually changed from the boyish designs of the 1920s to a more feminine and elegant look in the 1930s. French designer Coco Chanel remained a popular choice, but she was challenged by Italian designer Elsa Schiaparelli. Famous for introducing "shocking pink" evening wear, Schiaparelli was influenced by the artist Salvador Dali.

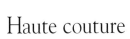

EVENING DRESS BY ELSA SCHIAPARELLI

1939

Uranium atom split in half

German physicist Otto Hahn

JANUARY 28

German physicist Otto Hahn and his colleague Fritz Strassmann have made a discovery of great scientific potential. Through their experiments, the two men have discovered that when uranium atoms are bombarded with neutrons, they split in half, releasing more neutrons, and producing huge amounts of energy. The released neutrons cause other uranium atoms to split, releasing more energy and more neutrons. Otto Hahn has called this continual process "nuclear fission." His work raises the possibility of harnessing energy to build a bomb of colossal destructive power.

Hitler's troops march into Prague

Prague is invaded

MARCH 15

Adolf Hitler took the Czech Sudetenland six months ago – now he has swallowed up the rest of Czechoslovakia. Hitler entered Prague, the Czech capital, today and installed himself in Hradzin Castle, the ancient palace of the Bohemian kings. The reception the German army has received is, however, in striking contrast to the tremendous welcome given to them in the Sudetenland and in Austria. In Prague, the crowds wept and courageously sang the national anthem as they were forced to salute the invading Nazi soldiers.

ANGLO-SAXON FIND

An Anglo-Saxon burial boat has been discovered during an archaeological dig at Sutton Hoo in Britain. The boat was filled with gold, silver, and weapons, and is the most significant find this century.

Western hero

MARCH 22

Since its release on March 2, *Stagecoach* has attracted so many people to the box office that John Wayne, who has only appeared in low-budget films until now, has become an instant success.

	World Events	Entertainment	Innovations
JAN	JAN The Irish Republican Army begins a major bombing campaign aimed at English cities.	JAN W. B. Yeats, Irish poet, dramatist, and Nobel prize-winner, dies at age 73.	JAN Anderson air-raid shelters are erected by the inhabitants of Islington, London, UK.
FEB	FEB The UK government decides that Palestine should not become a Jewish state, but an independent Arab-Jewish state.	FEB US actor Spencer Tracy wins an Academy Award for Best Actor for his role as Father Flanagan in *Boys' Town*.	FEB The first washing machine is demonstrated at the British Industry Fair in London in the UK.
MAR	MAR In the Vatican City in Rome, Italy, Cardinal Eugenio Pacella is elected Pope Pius XII on his 63rd birthday.	MAR In Durban, South Africa, a cricket test match against England is declared a draw after ten days.	MAR The launch of instant coffee in the UK by Swiss company Nestlé is a huge hit with the public.
MAR	MAR The Spanish Civil War ends as nationalist leader General Franco takes control of Madrid.	MAR Hollywood film stars Clark Gable and Carole Lombard marry in Kingman, Arizona.	MAR The UK Interplanetary Society conclude a two-year study for landing men on the Moon.

IRISH POET W. B. YEATS

POPE PIUS XII

1939

Three-year-old inherits throne

APRIL 4

Iraq is in mourning following the sudden death of King Ghazi in a car crash. Officials suspect a plot by the British, who still maintain important air bases in Iraq. King Ghazi has been succeeded by his son, three-year-old Amir Faisal. The boy's uncle, Amir Abdul Ilah, has been appointed regent, but the real power in Iraq lies in the hands of the reforming prime minister General Nuri.

Amir Faisal, the new king of Iraq

New York views the future

APRIL 30

At 3:12 p.m. today, President Frankin D. Roosevelt opened the World's Fair in Queens, New York, where 60 nations and 1,300 businesses are exhibiting the latest technological wonders. The most impressive structures are the Trylon, a 700-ft- (213-m-) tall tower, and the Perisphere, a 200-ft (60-m) giant sphere showing a futuristic film set in the year 2036.

Aerial view of the Trylon and Perisphere

Across the Atlantic in style

The Boeing 314A Dixie Clipper flying boat

JUNE 28

The world's first scheduled transatlantic passenger flights began today when Pan America's Boeing 314A *Dixie Clipper* flying boat took off from Manhasset Bay at Port Washington in New York. It is carrying 22 passengers to the city of Marseilles in southern France.

The first passengers have paid an amazing $675 for a roundtrip ticket on the 45-hour 52-minute flight, which includes a 22-hour stopover in the Azores in Spain. They are traveling in the lap of luxury – the flying boat is equipped with dining rooms and staterooms that are worthy of an ocean liner. This is the first air service to cross the Atlantic since the 1937 *Hindenberg* disaster killed 35 people and halted Germany's airship flights.

APRIL–JUNE

APR King Zog of Albania flees his country when Italian troops capture Tiranë, the capital city.

APR UK actor Laurence Olivier stars in the film *Wuthering Heights*, based on Emily Brontë's classic novel.

APR German aviator Fritz Wendel sets an air.speed record of 480 mph (768 km/h) in the first Messerschmitt jet.

KING ZOG OF ALBANIA

APR At the New York World's Fair in Queen's, Frankin D. Roosevelt becomes the first president to be televised.

APR US black contralto Marian Anderson sings in front of 75,000 people at the Lincoln Memorial, Washington, D.C.

APR Swiss chemist Paul Hermann Müller confirms the bug-killing properties of the chemical DDT.

APR Adolf Hitler tears up the 1934 Anglo-German naval treaty and denounces the mutual assistance pact with Poland.

MAY Batman, created by 18-year-old US artist Bob Kane, makes his first appearance in *Detective Comics*.

APR The Kodak company introduces the first color film at the New York World Fair in the USA.

ROBERT MENZIES

MAY Robert Menzies, at only age 44, succeeds Joseph Lyons as the new prime minister of Australia.

MAY US baseball star Lou Gehrig retires after 2,130 consecutive games with the New York Yankees.

MAY First regular North Atlantic airmail service is inaugurated between New York and Lisbon or Marseilles.

1939

Jazz king is *In the Mood*

AUGUST 1

The rich saxophone sound of the Glenn Miller Band has scored a huge hit in the United States with its latest recording, the swinging riff tune *In the Mood*. Thirty-five-year-old Miller is now established as one of the country's most popular band leaders. He began his career in 1926 playing the trombone with Ben Pollack's band, before organizing other people's bands, most notably those of Tommy Dorsey and Ray Noble. The Glenn Miller Band is famous for its popular orchestrated dance music. Its leader achieves the band's distinctive sound by blending the playing of a clarinet with a quartet of saxophones.

17-year-old Judy goes to Oz

AUGUST 17

Tonight is the Hollywood premiere of a new film, *The Wizard of Oz*, a magical $3 million Technicolor musical fantasy starring a bright new actress, 17-year-old Judy Garland. The story follows the dream adventures of Dorothy (played by Garland), who is carried away by a twister to the magical land of the Munchkins, where she meets a scarecrow, a tin man, and a cowardly lion.

Dorothy meets the scarecrow on the yellow brick road

British children evacuate cities

Young evacuees arrive in the countryside

AUGUST 31

As the prospect of war with Germany draws nearer, one-and-a-half million British children are being evacuated out of large cities and into safer areas in the countryside or small towns that are less likely to be targets of air raids. The children, who are being accompanied by their schoolteachers, are only allowed to carry one spare set of clothes and a gas mask. Buses have been taken off their usual routes to carry the children to train stations. Billeting officers are receiving the "townie" children and intoducing them to their new host families. But there are already some problems. Often, the evacuees are bewildered and unprepared for such new experiences. Many of them have never seen cows, sheep, or even fields before. Some have never slept in a bed, or learned how to use a knife and fork. Some middle-class hosts, shocked by the filthy condition of some of the children from city slums, do not seem to know how to handle their young charges.

JULY–SEPTEMBER

World Events JUL UK prime minister Winston Churchill urges the UK to make a military alliance with the Soviet Union.	AUG The Soviet Union shocks the rest of Europe by signing a nonaggression pact with Germany.	SEP US president Frankin D. Roosevelt announces that the US will remain neutral in the European war.	SEP Stained-glass windows are removed from Notre Dame Cathedral for fear of air raids in Paris, France.
Entertainment SEPT In the UK, the BBC TV service is suspended at the outbreak of war.	SEP UK actor Basil Rathbone stars as Sherlock Holmes in the film *The Hound of the Baskervilles*.	SEP In the UK, ENSA, an entertainment organization for the armed forces, is formed.	SEP US author John Steinbeck's outstanding novel *The Grapes of Wrath* is published in the US.
Innovations AUG British aircraft are the first to be installed with airborne interception radar. **NAZI SOVIET PACT**	AUG The first airplane powered by a jet engine, the *Heinkel He-178*, is demonstrated in Germany.	SEP UK company ICI starts the regular production of a new chemical material called polyethylene. **NORTH ROSE WINDOW**	SEP The first football game is televized by NBC-TV from Randall's Island, New York.

1939

German tanks advance into Poland

Poland is invaded

SEPTEMBER 1

Hitler has invaded Poland. The invasion began when the Luftwaffe, the German air force, led by state-of-the art dive-bombers, launched a massive attack on Polish airfields, communication centers, and the entire railroad system. Columns of fast-moving German tanks raced ahead of the Polish infantry cutting supply lines and spreading mass panic and terror. It is the first time the Germans have used their revolutionary "Blitzkrieg," or "lightning war," tactics, which are aimed at taking the enemy by surprise.

War is declared

SEPTEMBER 3

At 11:15 this morning, the British prime minister Neville Chamberlain informed an anxious nation that Britain is at war with Germany. Yesterday the British government had issued Adolf Hitler with an ultimatum demanding he withdraw all German forces from Poland. Hitler failed to reply, and consequently Britain declared war. Some hours later, the French ultimatum ran out, and at 5 pm France, too, declared war. The Allies of 1914 find themselves once again united in a war against oppression. Only a few minutes after the prime minister's radio broadcast the first air-raid sirens wailed in London. It proved a false alarm, but it is a warning of the terrible destruction that may follow.

Finnish troops camouflaged in the snow

Winter war in Finland

NOVEMBER 30

The Soviet Union has invaded Finland after the Finns refused to surrender Karelia, an area of land bordering the outskirts of the Soviet city of Leningrad. Over a million soldiers of the Red Army have launched a massive attack across the frozen waters that divide Finland from Russia. The Finns have only a handful of tanks and aircraft, but their ski patrols are very well trained for conducting warfare in the snow. In contrast, the Red Army does not have the correct equipment to be able to function in the freezing Arctic temperatures.

OCTOBER–DECEMBER

OCT Over 150,000 British troops are moved to France to strengthen the French troops against any German attack.

DEC *The Black Swan,* a new pirate film starring Tyrone Power, premieres in Hollywood, Calif.

SEP In the US, Birds Eye introduces first pre-cooked frozen meals, chicken fricassée and steak.

GONE WITH THE WIND

NOV In Munich, Germany, Adolf Hitler narrowly escapes a bomb explosion that kills seven high-ranking Nazis.

DEC *Gone with the Wind,* the most eagerly awaited film of the year, is released in the US.

DEC In the US General Electric launches the first refrigerator with a freezer compartment.

NOV Magnetic mines laid by German submarines sink 60,000 tons of British shipping off the east coast of England.

DEC In London, UK, the Royal Opera House is turned into a dance-hall to entertain the public during blackouts.

DEC The first propeller torpedo boats are manufactured for the Finnish navy by Higgins Industries Inc. in the US.

NYLON STOCKINGS

DEC The German battleship *The Graf Spee* is sunk in Montevideo, Uruguay, after a fierce battle with British cruisers.

DEC *We'll Hang Out the Washing on the Siegfield Line* is the biggest popular hit song of the year in the UK.

DEC In the US, nylon stockings go on sale for the first time, at a price of $1.15 a pair.

1940

An Oscar for Hattie

FEBRUARY 29

Producer David O. Selznick's spectacular Civil War epic *Gone with the Wind* has swept the Academy Awards at the Academy's ceremony in Los Angeles. The film won nine Oscars, including best picture and best director. The warmest welcome of the night went to actress Hattie McDaniel, who won the Oscar for best supporting actress for her performance as Scarlett's faithful servant. She is the first black person to win an Academy Award. However, racial prejudice is still so strong in Hollywood that permission was needed for McDaniel to sit at David O. Selznick's table during the Awards ceremony.

Hattie McDaniel with her Oscar for best supporting actress

Holland and Belgium invaded

MAY 10

Hitler's foreign minister Joachim von Ribbentrop today informed Dutch and Belgian envoys that German armed forces had crossed the borders of their countries. Holland and Belgium have been taken by surprise by the German invasion and are expected to surrender any day, in spite of requests to the Allies for support. Already the vital Belgian fortress of Eben Emael has fallen to a daring assault by German airborne troops, and German tanks are pouring through the forests of the Ardennes on France's border with Belgium. Following the Nazi invasion of Denmark and Norway on April 9, 1940, Hitler now appears intent on taking the Blitzkrieg, or "lightning war," to the Low Countries.

Devastation left by the German forces as they traveled through France

WURLITZER
In US cafés, bars, and restaurants, jukeboxes like this ornate Wurlitzer are becoming increasingly popular. A coin in the slot will play any song the user selects.

JANUARY–APRIL

World Events	JAN Seventy people are dying every day, mainly from starvation, in the Warsaw Jewish ghetto, Poland.	JAN For the first time since 1918, Britain introduces food rationing. Butter, sugar, ham, and bacon are now in short supply.	FEB The new five-year-old Dalai Lama is installed as the fourteenth spiritual leader of the Tibetan Buddhists.	APR Six people are killed by the explosion of an IRA land mine at Dublin Castle in the city of Dublin, Ireland.
Entertainment	JAN The US film version of John Steinbeck's novel *The Grapes of Wrath* is a triumph.	FEB US cartoonists Joe Barbera and William Hanna create a new cat and mouse team, *Tom and Jerry*.	FEB Walt Disney releases *Pinnochio*, his second full-length feature film, based on the classic Italian story by Collodi.	FEB US film stars Mae West and W. C. Fields star in the Hollywood comedy *My Little Chickadee*.
Innovations	JAN A UK company makes an electrical cable that can detonate magnetic mines. **THE GRAPES OF WRATH**	MAR The UK passenger liner *Queen Elizabeth* completes her secret maiden voyage.	MAR A new census puts the population of the US at 131 million. The average age is 28. **THE DALAI LAMA, SPIRITUAL LEADER**	APR US explorer Richard Byrd's current expedition to Antarctica charts previously unknown areas.

1940

British forces flee Dunkirk

JUNE 4

The evacuation of Dunkirk, codenamed Operation Dynamo, is now complete. The operation, launched on May 26, was an emergency measure to rescue Allied soldiers retreating from a powerful German advance. Following their invasion of Holland last month, the unstoppable German troops crossed the Meuse River and swept northward to the Channel, cutting off the British Expeditionary Force from their French allies. A week later the Germans had reached the Channel coast, and the British fled to the port of Dunkirk. There, under constant bombardment from German guns and aircraft, the warships of the Royal Navy and an armada of "little ships" sailed by civilians have rescued nearly 300,000 British, French, and Belgian soldiers from the beaches. However, many men have been left behind to a dismal fate, and some 200 ships and their crews, including naval warships, have been lost.

Soldiers struggle to reach safety off the beach at Dunkirk

French forces surrender

JUNE 22

France has surrendered to Germany. Today, at Compiègne, the French delegation has agreed to cease fighting. Adolf Hitler forced them to sign the armistice in the same railroad car in which the Germans surrendered in November 1918 at the end of World War I. In front of news cameras, the German dictator danced a jig. After the guns had fallen silent around Dunkirk, French resistance quickly collapsed, and on June 14, German troops marched into Paris. Only days later the French government fled south to Bordeaux. Now the northern half of France faces an uncertain future under German occupation, and the Nazi swastika flag flies from the Eiffel Tower in the capital city of Paris.

MAY–AUGUST

MAY Following Neville Chamberlain's resignation, Winston Churchill becomes the UK's prime minister.

MAY UK fascist leader Sir Oswald Mosley is interned under a new law allowing for the arrest of "suspected persons."

JUN General Charles de Gaulle says to his countrymen over the BBC, "The flame of the French Resistance must not go out."

AUG Exiled Bolshevik leader Leon Trotsky is assassinated with an ice pick by Ramon Mercader in Mexico City.

JUN Paul Klee, German artist and teacher at the influential Bauhaus school, dies at age 61.

JUL In the UK, artists Stanley Spencer and Paul Nash are officially appointed to record the events of the war.

JUL The British government advises women to conserve wood by choosing flat-heeled shoes instead of high heels.

AUG US star Bing Crosby's new country-and-western record, *San Antonio Rose*, is a massive hit.

MAY The first automatic swing doors are installed in a New York restaurant in the US.

WINSTON CHURCHILL

JUN UK scientists discover that German bombers are guided to their targets by following radio beams.

JUL Scientist Albert Einstein states that there is no theory that can provide a logical basis for physics.

CHARLES DE GAULLE

AUG Penicillin is developed for medical use at Radcliffe Infirmary, Oxford, in the UK.

1940

German air raids in Battle of Britain

SEPTEMBER 7

The city of London has experienced its first major air raid since the Battle of Britain began on July 10. Hundreds of the German bombers, escorted by deadly swarms of fighters, left their French bases and arrived over London very early this morning. The heaviest attacks were suffered by the docklands of London's East End and the fighter airfields in the Thames Valley. Unknown to the Germans, the Royal Air Force (RAF) had advance warning that the Luftwaffe, or German airforce, were fast approaching because of the radar system that has been in operation throughout the war. According to a spokesperson at London's Air Ministry, the Luftwaffe has lost 99 planes in this raid, and the RAF lost 22. In July, Hermann Goering, commander of the Luftwaffe, sent German planes to attack British ports and shipping in the Channel, the narrow band of sea between England and France. In August, Goering switched his strategy and sent 1,000 planes across the Channel daily to bomb RAF bases and British radar installations. The attacks today are an example of Goering's shifts in tactics, suggesting that, for all his boasts, he has failed to soften British defenses and bring the country to its knees.

German fighter plane approaches the white cliffs of Dover on the southern coast of Britain

Boys find ancient treasure trove

SEPTEMBER 12

Four French schoolboys have discovered a cave full of prehistoric paintings. While out hunting rabbits near a village in the Dordogne their dog disappeared down a hole. Climbing down after it, the boys found a cave with walls covered by magnificent paintings of animal hunting scenes. One wall showed a bison and a rhinoceros, another showed a beautiful unicornlike creature. Some of the animals pictured are now extinct or no longer native to Europe. Archaeologists have dated the paintings to around 15,000–13,000 BC.

SEPTEMBER–DECEMBER

World Events	**SEP** Japan signs a ten-year military pact, in which it allies itself with Germany and Italy.	**SEP** The "Dig for Victory" campaign is introduced in the UK to encourage families to grow their own vegetables.	**NOV** US president Franklin D. Roosevelt is reelected for a third term in a landslide victory.		**NOV** The Germans bomb the UK city of Coventry, destroying the cathedral and killing 568 people.
Entertainment	**OCT** Princess Elizabeth makes her first radio broadcast to child evacuees in the UK.	**OCT** The first "Smellie" feature film with flower and food odors is shown in New York, USA.	**NOV** Walt Disney's new musical animation film *Fantasia* is released in Hollywood, California.		**DEC** Charlie Chaplin's satirical comedy about Hitler, *The Great Dictator*, is released in the US.
Innovations	**OCT** The US army carries out its first experiments with night photography.	**OCT** Motorized bicycles are used for the first time by women in the British forces.	**OCT** Engineer Karl Pabst designs the first lightweight military-style Jeep for use by the US army.		**DEC** In the US, Colonel Sanders formulates his special recipe for Kentucky Fried Chicken.

PRINCESS ELIZABETH AND PRINCESS MARGARET

THE GREAT DICTATOR

1941

Balkans surrender

APRIL 27

The Nazi swastika flag is flying on the Parthenon, the famous ancient temple that overlooks the Greek capital, Athens. Greece was forced to surrender to the German army on April 21. The British soldiers who were garrisoned around Athens fought a slow retreat, covered by Greek infantry, to a point on the coast south of Athens where the troops were able to evacuate by sea. Yugoslavia has also surrendered to the German Blitzkrieg. The German invasion of Yugoslavia followed the overthrow of the pro-Nazi government of Prince Paul of Yugoslavia on March 27. The Yugoslav armed forces were poorly armed and bitterly divided, so they were able to offer little resistance to the far superior force of the German army.

AIR RAID SAFETY

It is the job of British air-raid wardens to make sure that people are safe during an air raid. They wear a special uniform with a blue helmet so that they can be easily recognized. The wardens help rescue teams and firefighters.

General Erwin Rommel

Rommel arrives in Tripoli

FEBRUARY 12

The British army in north Africa has a new force to reckon with. German troops have arrived in Tripoli, Libya, to reinforce their Italian allies, who have suffered a series of defeats at the hands of the British. In command of the German force, known as the Afrika Korps, is General Erwin Rommel, a formidable leader who made a name for himself last year at the head of a superior tank division in the occupation of France.

Artist's impression of German dive bombers flying over the city of Athens

---

JAN The Italian-held port of Tobruk in Libya falls to triumphant British and Australian troops.

JAN Irish writer James Joyce, author of *Ulysses* and *Finnegan's Wake*, dies in Switzerland at age 58.

JAN The first airplane ejection seat is tested in the German Heinkel *He 280* jet fighter.

JAMES JOYCE

MAR US president Franklin D. Roosevelt signs the Lend Lease Act, a program promising aid to the Allies.

JAN Tamara Lobora of the USSR becomes the first woman camera operator to shoot a feature film.

FEB The Royal Air Force (RAF) establishes the first air-sea rescue team to operate in the UK.

MAR War work becomes compulsory for all women aged 16 to 49 without young children in the UK.

FEB *Mother Courage and her Children*, by German playwright Bertolt Brecht, opens in Switzerland.

FEB In the UK, a policeman suffering from septicemia is cured by the new drug penicillin.

PRIME MINISTER BOGDAN PHILOFF

MAR Bulgarian prime minister Bogdan Philoff signs the Tripartite Pact, allying Bulgaria with Germany and Italy.

MAR US film *The Thief of Baghdad*, an Arabian Nights story with amazing special effects, is released.

APR The first playgroup for preschool children is opened in Wellington, New Zealand.

1941

London blitzed by German bombers

St. Paul's Cathedral has survived the raid

MAY 10

Bombers of the German air force last night launched a massive raid on London. In just a few hours, 550 German planes dropped hundreds of high explosive bombs, starting more than 2,000 fires and killing 1,436 civilians.

Many streets are impassable in the center of the city and much of historic London has been destroyed. Other British cities have been heavily bombed in recent months, but none have suffered such extensive damage and loss of life as London did last night.

"Unsinkable" ship is sunk

MAY 27

Germany claimed that her newest and fastest battleship, the *Bismarck*, was unsinkable. But the ship now lies at the bottom of the Atlantic after a merciless pounding by the British Royal Navy. The attack was prompted by the *Bismarck's* sinking of British ship HMS *Hood*.

Germans invade

JUNE 22

Hitler has broken Germany's nonaggression pact with Stalin and invaded the Soviet Union. In an operation named "Barbarossa," a massive onslaught by the German army began at dawn this morning. It has caught the Soviets unaware. On this first day of fighting, more than 1,800 Soviet aircraft have been destroyed. It seems that the Germans are trying to achieve another Blitzkrieg victory, but the sheer size of the Soviet Union may make this impossible.

MAY–AUGUST

World Events	MAY Hitler's deputy Rudolph Hess crash lands in Scotland with an "important message."	MAY Major fascist strongholds in Italian East Africa surrender to British troops.	AUG Churchill and Roosevelt agree on the Atlantic Charter, an alliance between the UK and the US.	AUG Soviet leader Joseph Stalin orders the destruction of a giant dam in order to hinder the Nazi advance.
Entertainment	MAY US premiere of Orson Welles's cinematic masterpiece *Citizen Kane*.	MAY US boxer Joe Louis successfully defends his title for the seventeenth time.	JUL The BBC launches Britain's "V for Victory" campaign throughout Europe.	AUG Rabindranath Tagore, Nobel Prize-winning Indian writer, dies at age 80.
Innovations	MAY Scientists in the UK develop the synthetic polyester fabric Terylene.	MAY The Gloster E28/39, a British top secret jet-powered aircraft, makes its first flight.	JUL The first commercial TV broadcasting begins in the US, with NBC and CBS competing.	AUG Clipboards, portable writing boards, are manufactured by a company in Bremen, Germany.

CITIZEN KANE

ROOSEVELT AND CHURCHILL

1941

Winter slows Nazi advance

NOVEMBER 21

The German advance in the Soviet Union is starting to slow down. After many easy victories, the German army is now approaching the Soviet capital of Moscow. But the Germans have found a new enemy – the savage Russian winter. Most of their soldiers are without winter clothing, and the engines in their trucks and tanks are freezing up. Meanwhile, the Soviets are receiving reinforcements of fresh troops from Siberia, better equipped to fight in the Arctic conditions.

German soldiers

Japanese attack Pearl Harbor

DECEMBER 7

Japan has made a devastating and unprovoked attack on the United States. Just before eight o'clock this morning, 360 Japanese aircraft burst through low cloud over the US Pacific Fleet base at Pearl Harbor in Hawaii. It was the deadly beginning of a surprise strike that has crippled the US Pacific Fleet. The Japanese fighters, dive-bombers, and torpedo-bombers were launched from a task force of aircraft carriers that had sailed in great secrecy to within 300 miles (483 km) of Pearl Harbor. The base was defenseless, its battleships riding at anchor, its aircraft parked wingtip to wingtip on the runways, and ammunition locked away. In less than two hours, eight of the US Pacific Fleet's battleships had been either sunk or disabled and more than 2,400 people had been killed. Luckily for the United States, however, two aircraft carriers were not in the harbor at the time of the attack, and escaped damage.

SEPTEMBER–DECEMBER

SEP Mohammed Reza Pavlevi is the new 21-year-old shah of Iran. He promises to be a "completely constitutional monarch."

SEP US director John Huston makes an impressive debut with *The Maltese Falcon*, starring Humphrey Bogart.

OCT The first British commerical flying-boat service begins to operate from the UK to Cairo, Egypt.

AEROSOL CAN

SEP All Jews in Germany over the age of six are required to wear the Star of David in public as a "mark of shame."

OCT *Dumbo*, Walt Disney's lively animated movie about a flying elephant, premieres in New York City.

OCT The world's first aerosol can, containing insect spray, is patented in the US by Goodhue and Sullivan.

DEC Following the Japanese attack on Pearl Harbor, the US and Britain both declare war on Japan.

NOV Repairs to the US's famous presidents at Mount Rushmore are completed.

DEC A United States Navy submarine sinks the first Japanese merchant ship of the war.

RUSHMORE FACELIFT

DEC Italy and Germany declare war on the US. President Roosevelt responds by declaring war on Italy and Germany.

NOV UK director Alfred Hitchcock's latest film, *Suspicion*, premieres.

DEC New Japanese fighter plane with a liquid-cooled engine makes its first flight.

HOME FRONTS

WORLD WAR II was fought not only on the battlefields but also on the home front. By 1943 a walk down any European city street was full of the reminders of war: men and women in their uniforms, bomb damage from air raids, gas masks, food shortages, and long lines. Posters urged the young and old to help in the war effort. Everything, from scraps of iron for planes to leftover bones for glue, was saved and recycled. Thousands of children were evacuated from cities to the countryside. Their teachers went with them so that the children's education would not be interrupted.

FIRE SERVICE BADGE

Fire in the sky

The incendiary bomb was designed to set buildings ablaze during an air raid by generating intense heat. During a big attack, thousands of these bombs were dropped on cities, causing furious fires. It was vital that incendiary bombs were dealt with as quickly as possible. This was the job of firefighters and wardens.

KILO MAGNESIUM (ELECTRON) INCENDIARY BOMB

Inflatable shelter

This cigarette card depicts a French-designed inflatable balloon shelter for protection in poison-gas raids. This was one of many ingenious precautions that never actually went into mass production.

FAMILY LISTENING TO RADIO

Wartime radio

Radio audiences reached a peak in the war years. Listening to the news kept families in touch with the daily progress of the war, but they also relied on the radio for entertainment. Comedy, drama, and children's programs all helped keep up people's spirits.

HARVESTING VEGETABLES IN A CATHEDRAL SQUARE, LENINGRAD

Harvesting food

During the war, blockades all over Europe and the rest of the world resulted in major food shortages. Everyone with a garden or an allotment was encouraged to grow vegetables and other crops. Fields and parks were dug up and turned into vegetable gardens to help supplement daily diets.

Eggs in cans

Eggs, and other foodstuffs, were rationed, or distributed sparingly. Some people kept a chicken coop in their garden, but most had to use dried eggs, which had the same nutritional value as fresh eggs, but did not taste as good.

1942 CHOCOLATE IN THE US IS
SENT TO ARMED FORCES

1944 RICE RATION IN JAPAN
IS CUT BY TWO THIRDS

1944/5 STARVING DUTCH
ARE EATING TULIP BULBS

Business as usual

Between 1940 and 1941, Hitler carried out a sustained bombing campaign against Britain known as the Blitz. Despite severe bomb damage, most people continued their normal daily routine.

DELIVERING
MILK DURING
THE BLITZ

Head strap

WAR GAMES

There were many war-related toys manufactured during the war to pass long evenings in the blackout, when windows were covered to stop enemy aircraft from spotting a light. The goal of this game is to be the first to reach Berlin to assassinate Adolf Hitler.

Gas mask is made of rubber

Eye piece

"MICKEY MOUSE"
GAS MASK

Label states evacuee's destination

Masked

Over 38 million gas masks, some of them Mickey Mouse ones for children, were issued to the British public before war broke out. But the expected gas attacks never happened.

SCHOOL
GAS MASK
DRILL

Air filter

Living in fear

All over Europe, families were broken up by the war. In England, two million children were sent to the countryside, and some were sent overseas to Canada and Australia. In Germany, many children were evacuated in 1942 when Allied bombing increased. Some children enjoyed being in the countryside, but most wanted to return home, preferring the bombs to being away from their families.

1942

Yanks in UK

JANUARY 26

The first US GIs (so-called because their equipment is labeled Government Issue) have arrived in Britain. They came ashore at Belfast in Northern Ireland, where they received a warm welcome from the local residents.

Japanese tanks advance through Singapore

Singapore falls swiftly to Japan

FEBRUARY 15

The great naval base of Singapore has fallen to Japan. The island, which lies off the southern tip of the British colony of Malaya, was heavily fortified against a naval attack. But the Japanese bombarded the island from the land. The fall of Singapore has deprived the Allies of their only major dry dock between Durban in South Africa and Pearl Harbor in Hawaii. In a radio broadcast to the British nation last night, Prime Minister Winston Churchill described the loss as "a heavy and far-reaching military defeat." Around 138,000 Allied troops were captured by the Japanese.

Japanese-Americans detained

MAY 31

Following the Japanese attack on Pearl Harbor, the US government has rounded up all citizens of Japanese descent living in the United States, and sent them to detention camps in the deserts of the West. There are no criminal charges against these people, but their guards have strict instructions to shoot anybody who tries to escape.

Battle of Midway

JUNE 6

The Japanese have suffered their first major defeat in a naval battle off Midway Island in the Pacific. The US fleet used a special code-breaking machine to decode an intercepted top secret Japanese message. This decrypted message gave them advance warning of a plan to bomb Midway Island. As the Japanese attacked the island with dive-bombers, the US fleet in turn launched a surprise naval attack on the Japanese fleet and sank four of its aircraft carriers.

JANUARY–JUNE

World Events	APR The people of Malta are awarded the George Cross for their endurance of German bombing.	JUN SS deputy chief Reinhard Heydrich, "the butcher of Moravia," is assassinated in Czechoslovakia by Resistance agents.	JUN Major General Dwight Eisenhower is given command from headquarters in London of all US forces in Europe.	JUN In France, all Jews over the age of six are ordered to wear the Star of David on their clothes at all times.
Entertainment	JAN US film star Carole Lombard is killed in a TWA airliner crash near Las Vegas, Nevada.	FEB US bandleader Glenn Miller sells one million copies of "Chatanooga Choo Choo," and wins a gold record.	APR Spencer Tracy and Katharine Hepburn star in the US film comedy *Woman of the Year*.	MAY US athlete Cornelius Warmerdam sets record for pole vault of 15.7 ft (4.78 m).
Innovations	MAR The BBC broadcasts a daily Morse code news bulletin to the French Resistance.	THE BRITISH GEORGE CROSS — APR The first T-shirts are manufactured for sailors serving in the US Navy.	JUN Nylon parachutes are used for the first time in Hertford in the UK.	**MAJOR GENERAL EISENHOWER** — JUN The Cooperative Society of Romford launches the first UK self-service grocery store.

1942

Dieppe disaster

AUGUST 19

A reconnaissance raid on the German-held seaport of Dieppe in northern France has ended in disaster for the Allies. Several thousand UK, US, Canadian, and Free French troops landed on the beaches, but the Germans were waiting for them. Over 3,000 soldiers, mostly Canadians, lost their lives.

Victory for Monty at El Alamein

NOVEMBER 4

General Montgomery, the flamboyant commander of the British Eighth Army, has halted the German Afrika Corps at El Alamein outside Cairo, Egypt. Throughout the summer Montgomery has assembled 230,000 soldiers and equipped them with the latest US tanks. On October 23, the British artillery opened fire with the heaviest barrage the African continent has ever known, bringing Italian and German troops to a standstill. Erwin Rommel, commander of the Afrika Corps, was absent on sick leave when the battle broke out. He rushed back to North Africa to find the Eighth Army smashing defenses, destroying tanks, and taking prisoners.

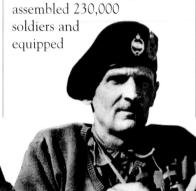

Sinatra's debut

DECEMBER 30

New York's Paramount Theater has witnessed the birth of a new singing sensation – the young star Frank Sinatra. The 27-year-old has the potential to become one of the US's most popular crooners.

WAR DOLL

Vogue Dolls in the US have issued this figure to mark the formation of Women Accepted for Volunteer Emergency Services (WAVES). They will perform noncombat duties!

JULY–DECEMBER

JUL The German Sixth Army launches an assault on the city of Stalingrad in the Soviet Union.

JUL US actor James Cagney stars in the musical film comedy *Yankee Doodle Dandy*.

JUL The first jet fighter, the German Messerschmitt Me 262, makes its maiden flight.

IRVING BERLIN

JUL A death camp at Treblinka in Poland, to be used for the mass murder of Jewish people, is opened by the Germans.

JUL Irving Berlin's musical *This is the Army* opens at the Broadway Theater in New York City.

JUL The Oxford Committee for Famine Relief (OXFAM) is founded by Gilbert Murray in the UK.

NOV Operation Torch gets underway as General Eisenhower leads the Allied landings in Morocco and Algeria.

NOV *Stars and Stripes*, a daily paper for US GIs in Europe, is published in the UK.

OCT The XP-59 turbojet aircraft is successfully tested in the air for the first time in the US.

WILLIAM BEVERIDGE

DEC A blueprint for UK post-war social security by Sir William Beveridge, the Beveridge Report, is made public.

DEC US singer Bing Crosby has a big hit with the timely song "White Christmas."

DEC Physicist Enrico Fermi conducts first sustained nuclear chain reaction in the US.

1943

Play it, Sam

JANUARY 14

As Allied leaders meet for a conference in the North African city of Casablanca, moviegoers are flocking to see *Casablanca*, Warner studio's romantic war drama starring Humphrey Bogart as Rick and Ingrid Bergman as the unforgettable Ilsa.

A LITTLE PRINCE

French pilot and author Antoine de Saint-Exupéry has written a delightful story called *The Little Prince*. It tells the tale of a pilot who accidentally lands in a desert, where he meets a charming little boy from outer space. The inspiration for the book came from the author's own experience when he crashed in the Libyan desert while attempting to set a new flying record.

German army surrenders at Stalingrad

JANUARY 31

Amid the savage snows of the Soviet winter, the German Sixth Army has suffered a shattering defeat at the hands of the Soviet Red Army at Stalingrad. Commanded by Field Marshal Paulus, the German army has been suffering heavy losses since fighting first broke out last August. The Germans reached Stalingrad in September, but by November the Soviets had closed in on them. Field Marshal Paulus twice rejected a surrender ultimatum from the Soviets although his position was hopeless. Finally, when he was on the point of giving way, Hitler himself refused to grant the order for evacuation and instead instructed his army to "hold their positions to the last man." This they tried to do, and it cost in total the lives of 300,000 German troops as well as 450,000 of their Italian and Romanian allies. A further 108,000 Germans have been captured and marched off to prison camps.

Captured German soldiers

JANUARY–MARCH

World Events	**JAN** Allied troops take Tripoli in Libya, the last remaining Italian-held city.	**JAN** British RAF Mosquito bombers launch the first two daylight raids on Berlin in Germany.	**FEB** Indian social reformer Mahatma Gandhi begins a 21-day hunger strike in protest over his imprisonment in Poona.	**MAR** In Frankfurt, Germany, several key bridges along the Oder River are destroyed by saboteurs.
Entertainment	**MAR** *Mrs. Miniver* wins an Academy Award for Best Film in Hollywood, California.	**MAR** The musical *Oklahoma!*, set in the American Midwest, opens at the St. James Theater in New York City.	**MAR** The fantasy adventure film *Baron Münchhausen* opens in Berlin, Germany, after three years in production.	**MAR** Soviet composer Sergei Rachmaninov dies at his Beverly Hills home in California at age 69.
Innovations	**JAN** An amphibian tank for military use, Thornycroft Terrapin I, is tested in UK.	**JAN** French naval engineer Jacques-Yves Cousteau successfully tests his "Aqua-Lung" breathing apparatus.	**FEB** The first telephone answering machine, able to give and receive messages, is developed in Switzerland.	**MAR** The first kidney machine is developed in secret for the Dutch resistance by Willem Kolff.

OKLAHOMA! PREMIERES

BARON MÜNCHHAUSEN

1943

Massacre of the Warsaw ghetto

APRIL 19

News is reaching the rest of the world of a bloodbath in Poland's Warsaw ghetto, with about 40,000 Jews murdered by German troops. After invading Poland in 1939, the Nazis forced 450,000 Jews into the ghetto, cutting them off from the rest of the city.

Since then, many have been sent to unknown destinations, while others have perished. Today German troops were ordered in to clear out the remaining 60,000 inhabitants, and were met with fierce resistance by armed Jews. However, the Jews' defiant gesture has proved futile.

Allies capture North Africa

MAY 12

The Italian and German armies in North Africa have surrendered. After a long, hard battle following the British victory at El Alamein in November 1942, the German Afrika Corps and its Italian allies have been pushed into a pocket of land inside Tunisia from which there is no escape. This afternoon, the British commander in Tunisia radioed the British prime minister Winston Churchill and told him, "All enemy resistance has ceased. We are the masters of the North African shores."

"Bouncing" bombs dropped

Aerial view of floods

MAY 16

In one of the most daring air raids of the war, a small number of British Lancaster heavy bombers, led by Wing Commander Guy Gibson, blasted three dams and caused flood waters to destroy much of the Ruhr, Germany's industrial heartland. The Lancasters dropped new "bouncing" bombs – huge depth charges designed to bounce across the water, hit the dam walls, and explode.

APRIL–JUNE

APR The German army discovers a mass grave of more than 4,000 Polish officers in the Katyn Forest, Poland.

MAY RKO releases the horror film *I Walked with a Zombie* in Hollywood, California.

APR In Maryland, Judy Johnson is the first female jockey to win a professional race.

BLETCHLEY PARK HEADQUARTERS

MAY The Allies begin a major bombing campaign aimed at Italian cities and military bases.

MAY French director Jean Renoir releases the film *This Land Is Mine* in the US.

JUN Code-breaking "bombes" decipher German Enigma messages at Bletchley Park, UK.

MAY Part-time war work becomes compulsory for all British women between the ages of 18 and 45.

JUN UK actor Charlie Chaplin marries Oona O'Neill, daughter of playwright Eugene O'Neill.

JUN In the UK, the General Post Office (GPO) introduces the first prestamped airmail stationery.

JUN The new French Committee of Liberation led by General de Gaulle pledges to liberate French territory.

JUN UK actor Leslie Howard disappears when his plane is shot down in the Bay of Biscay.

LESLIE HOWARD

JUN The SCUBA (self-contained underwater breathing apparatus) aqualung is designed in France.

1943

Ladislao Biro's perfect pen

JUNE 10

The Hungarian hypnotist and journalist Ladislao Biro has patented a revolutionary writing pen. Four years ago, when working as an editor on a magazine in Budapest, Biro first thought about using printer's quick-drying ink in a pen. Now, his remarkable pen has been perfected. It combines a rotating steel ball as its point with a tiny tube containing quick-drying ink.

Soviet tanks firing a barrage against Waffen SS and Wehrmacht opposition

German army smashed at Kursk

JULY 13

Today Adolf Hitler ordered a withdrawal in the greatest tank battle of the century. The German attack had begun seven days ago in the flat cornfields around Kursk in the Soviet Union. Hitler, who was desperate for a victory following his disaster at Stalingrad, had attached enormous importance to the offensive. The finest divisions of the Wehrmacht and Waffen SS, equipped with 3,000 armored vehicles including new Tigers, the most powerful tanks yet built, tried to batter their way through the heavily fortified Soviet defenses. The battle reached a climax on July 12, when 1,500 German and Soviet tanks fought at close range. The Soviet tanks proved superior, with greater firing power. They pushed their way through minefields, antitank guns, and mud with great efficiency. After a week of ferocious fighting, the Germans have been driven back. The Soviet army is now preparing to launch its own attack on the dispirited enemy, using fresh troops.

JULY–SEPTEMBER

World Events

JUL A severe famine grips the province of Bengal in northeastern India.

JUL In Italy, Mussolini is overthrown and Marshal Pietro Badoglio forms a new government.

JUL Jean Moulin, president of the French National Resistance Council, is captured and executed by the German Gestapo.

AUG British RAF bombers attack a top-secret Nazi rocket base at Peenemünde in northern Germany.

Entertainment

JUL Ingrid Bergman stars in the US film *For Whom the Bell Tolls*.

JUL Hollywood stars Rita Hayworth and Orson Welles are married in Santa Monica, CA.

JUL An Allied bombing raid on Rome, Italy, manages to avoid hitting major historic sites and buildings.

SEP US actor Paul Robeson is the first black American to star in the Broadway production of *Othello*.

Innovations

JUL The US uses the first amphibian supply craft for its Sicilian landings.

FAMINE IN BENGAL

AUG Allied intelligence reports that Germany is testing a new flying bomb in Blizna, Poland.

AUG The German Luftwaffe launches the Hs 293, the first guided missile, in an attack over the Bay of Biscay.

JEAN MOULIN

SEP A new tax scheme called PAYE, Pay As You Earn, is announced in the UK to reduce income tax evasion.

1943

Allies take Palermo

JULY 22

The race to capture the Sicilian capital of Palermo has been won by the United States. It began on July 9, when United States airborne troops touched down on the southern tip of the island of Sicily. In a rapid thrust to the north, US troops reached the city of Palermo yesterday, trapping an estimated 45,000 German and Italian troops. The US Army, commanded by the flamboyant General Patton, received a rapturous welcome from the local Sicilians, who frantically scrambled to acquire any US cigarettes and chocolate. The remaining German defenders of Sicily are now retreating toward the town of Messina, from which they plan to evacuate their forces to mainland Italy. The victory has given the Allies access to a new airfield, from which their planes can strike at the German and Italian positions.

Smoking ruins in the city of Hamburg

US soldiers drive through the streets of Palermo

Fierce bombing in Hamburg

AUGUST 2

The center of the German port of Hamburg has been devastated by a series of Allied air raids. Bombing day and night, the British RAF bombers and US air force created huge firestorms that killed at least 50,000 people and destroyed over 250,000 homes. The city's shipyards and factories have been reduced to rubble, with the Nazi propaganda chief Josef Goebbels declaring the air raids a "catastrophe."

Italy joins forces with Allies

OCTOBER 13

Italy has declared war on Germany. Marshal Pietro Badoglio, the successor of Benito Mussolini, opened talks with Allied troops that landed on the Italian mainland three weeks ago. German troops have moved in quickly to fill the vacuum left by their Italian allies.

Marshal Badoglio

OCTOBER–DECEMBER

OCT In Sweden, 4,200 British prisoners of war are exchanged for Germans in the first major exchange of the war.

OCT Austrian theater producer and director Max Reinhardt dies in the US at age 50.

OCT Penicillin is first used to treat wounds of Allied soldiers fighting in the Mediterranean.

PENICILLIN CULTURE

OCT Allied leaders meet China's Chiang Kai-shek in Cairo, Egypt, to discuss measures to defeat Japan.

NOV Leonard Bernstein makes his debut conducting the New York Philharmonic Orchestra in the US.

OCT First children's adventure playground opened in a suburb of Copenhagen in Denmark.

NOV Allied leaders Churchill, Roosevelt, and Stalin attend a summit in Tehran, Iran, to coordinate war strategies.

DEC The musical production of *Carmen Jones* opens on Broadway in New York City.

OCT Irish coffee is invented by an Irish chef to warm transatlantic flying-boat passengers.

TEHRAN CONFERENCE

DEC The Soviet army launches an offensive in the Ukraine after regaining two-thirds of Soviet territory from Germany.

DEC Beatrix Potter, creator of *Peter Rabbit*, dies in the UK at age 77.

DEC The first electronic computer, *Colossus I*, is built in the UK.

WOMEN AT WAR

CIVILIANS HAD A VITAL PART to play in World War II. Women were thrust into the front line of the war effort, taking the place of men who had joined the armed services. They worked in shipyards and factories, drove ambulances in air raids, and were called up to join the army, navy, and air force. In the Soviet Union some women flew fighter aircraft. By 1943 most unmarried women in Britain between the ages of 20 and 40 were working for the war effort. In Australia, Canada, and Britain, women joined the Women's Land Army, and in factories in the United States, they often made up the majority of the workforce.

Modest protection

At the beginning of the war the fear of attack by poison gas was very real. Civilians had to carry gas masks with them at all times. Some women used elegant bags like this one to conceal them.

Mothers of invention

This 1942 German poster urges women to give their old clothes for the war effort. From 1941 all new clothing and footwear in Germany went to the armed forces. When cotton thread ran out, women darned and repaired their clothes using string dyed with shoe polish.

SHOPPING WITH A RATION BOOK

UTILITY SILK STOCKINGS

Professional shoppers

In all the warring countries, the ration book was a vital item for every housewife. The food coupons ensured a dull but healthy diet. Although rationing promised fair shares for everyone, it also created a thriving black market. Women became expert at finding bargains, haggling, and swapping coupons for less available food.

Inventive wartime fashion

With strict rationing everywhere, the "Utility Look" became the wartime fashion for women. It cut out all unnecessary frills, and the material used and price charged were both closely controlled by governments. Silk stockings were a particularly rare item, but women were inventive and painted their legs with make-up instead. In France, women used flowers, feathers, and even wood shavings to decorate hats.

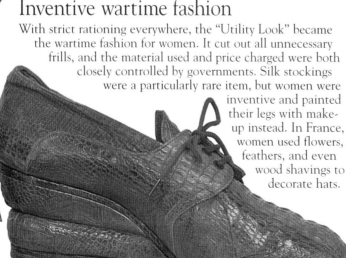

UTILITY WEDGE SHOES

A WOMAN OPERATING A SEARCHLIGHT

Antiaircraft command

During the war, thousands of women served alongside men in antiaircraft batteries. They handled searchlights, drove army trucks, and plotted the paths of enemy aircraft on radar. In some countries women were even allowed to operate the antiaircraft guns.

1942 NAVY DISPATCH RIDERS
DELIVER MESSAGES IN UK

1943 RUSSIAN WOMEN FLY
AIRCRAFT INTO WAR ZONES

1944 JAPANESE WOMEN ARE
EMPLOYED IN ARMS FACTORIES

Scarves became wartime fashion for working women

Women workers wore mens' uniforms, including heavy helmets

Women rarely wore pants in public before the war

WOMEN WELDERS FOR AN ARMAMENTS FACTORY

Role model "Rosie"

The fictional "Rosie the Riveter" poses on the cover of the US *Post* magazine in 1943. She was the symbol of thousands of real "Rosies" working in the US war industry. The money they made and the skills they acquired gave women workers a new confidence, as well as independence from their traditional responsibilities.

The land girls

Over 80,000 women served in the Women's Land Army in Britain. Many Australians and Canadians also chose to work in the fields to provide food for the war effort. Some worked in the timber industry felling trees and working in sawmills. Others were milkmaids, harvesters, or even ratcatchers.

"Doing your bit"

Many women became factory workers during the war, taking jobs in industry that had previously been done exclusively by men. There was a vital need for workers in munitions factories, but women also proved to be expert welders, crane operators, and truck drivers. They were paid less than the men, however, and when the war ended, most women had to leave their jobs for the men returning home from the forces.

1944

A Russian soldier surveys the city

Soviet Union smashes siege line

JANUARY 27

The long siege of Leningrad is finally over. For 900 days, the Nazis have been trying to starve the people of this Soviet city into submission. However, the advancing Red Army has succeeded in driving the Germans back beyond artillery range. The Nazi strategy had nearly succeeded. During the long, harsh winters, as many as 300 people a day died of hunger, illness, or the cold. In all, about one million people perished in the city. Despite this, the citizens of Leningrad fought back, managing to hold out until the Soviet armored forces attacked, driving the Nazis away.

Mondrian dies

FEBRUARY 1

The famous Dutch artist Piet Mondrian has died. Mondrian has been described as the painter of geometry, since his canvases are based entirely on straight-sided forms, like *Composition No. III with red, yellow, blue* c. 1935 (left).

Freedom for Rome

JUNE 4

Troops of the US Fifth Army have entered Rome. Their commander, the flamboyant general Mark Clark, had made the Italian capital his principal objective and was determined to beat all the other Allied armies to the prize, even if it meant ignoring the orders of the overall commander in Italy, the British general Sir Harold Alexander. Only three days ago, Hitler ordered the German commander, Field Marshal Albert Kesselring, to withdraw and declared Rome an "open city," sparing it from the destruction that is likely to be caused by street battles. Happily, the city's historic sites have been untouched by the ravages of war. Now the Germans are gone and the streets are flooded with excited Italian civilians who crowd around the US soldiers, welcoming them with open arms. Many of the US troops are utterly exhausted from the hard fighting in Italy and, after accepting gifts of wine, they slump down to sleep wherever they are in the streets. General Clark is the hero of the hour, but critics are suggesting that his well-known hunger for publicity has upset Allied plans.

JANUARY–MARCH

World Events	**JAN** Allied troops land on the beaches of Anzio in southern Italy to outflank German defense lines.	**FEB** US forces launch "Operation Brewer," an assault on the Japanese-occupied Admiralty Islands in the Pacific.	**FEB** UK RAF Mosquitoes stage a precision raid on Amiens, France, to free French Resistance leaders.	**MAR** A large Allied force is dropped into Burma by glider and strategically positioned, ready to attack the Japanese.
Entertainment	**JAN** French dramatist and war hero Jean Giraudoux dies at age 61.	**JAN** Eleven-year-old Elizabeth Taylor stars in *National Velvet*, made by the US MGM studio.	**JAN** Norwegian artist Edvard Munch, a founder of Expressionism, dies at age 80.	**FEB** The BBC plans to develop a school radio program to accompany the new UK education system.
Innovations	**JAN** Helicopters are used in warfare for the first time by the US army.	**JAN** The first printed circuit boards are used in electronic equipment for warfare.	**FEB** The first night reconnaissance photographs are taken by the US airforce over Italy.	**MAR** The first ballpoint pens are manufactured for use by the RAF in the UK.

ANZIO LANDINGS

ARTIST EDVARD MUNCH

1944

Allied troops storm Normandy beaches

JUNE 6

In an operation code-named "Overlord," two Allied armies, with over 100,000 US, British, and Canadian troops, landed at dawn today on the Normandy coast in northern France. The order to invade came from General Eisenhower, the supreme commander in Europe. First, airborne troops landed behind the German coastal defenses to provide cover for troops that stormed the beaches in amphibious tanks, fighting through Nazi defenses to liberate the first pieces of French soil. The most serious resistance from the Germans took place on a beach that was code-named "Omaha," where heavy fighting caused 3,000 Allied casualties. The preparations for the invasion of Normandy had been intense. An air offensive on German communication lines in northern France lasted several weeks and the Allies used an elaborate deception to convince the Nazis that the main attack would begin in the Pas de Calais rather than Normandy. More troops go ashore tomorrow.

APRIL–JUNE

APR Japanese forces are defeated by the UK Fourteenth Army at Kohima, in Assam, a state in northeast India.

APR The Allies achieve air superiority over the Nazis with a relentless and carefully planned bombing campaign.

APR The first of 500,000 pre-fabricated homes designed for bombed-out families are on display in London in the UK.

JUN Iceland, which has shared a royal family with Denmark since 1381, becomes the Republic of Iceland.

APR US actress Marlene Dietrich entertains the Allied troops in Italy and northern Africa.

MAY *Gaslight*, a suspense thriller starring Charles Boyer and Ingrid Bergman, premieres in the US.

MAY French existentialist writer Jean-Paul Sartre's new one-act play *No Exit* opens in Paris, France.

JUN US actor Gregory Peck makes his screen debut playing a resistance fighter in *Days of Glory*.

DR. LEAKEY

APR Quinine, used as a treatment for malaria, is synthesized by scientists at Harvard University in Massachusetts.

MAY UK anthropologist Dr. Leakey discovers fossils and tools used by people in the Old Stone Age.

MAY The first eye bank facility is opened by New York City hospitals in the US.

ICELAND'S FLAG

JUN For the first time, napalm, a highly flammable substance, is used in warfare by the UK army.

1944

V-1 launched

JUNE 13
Adolf Hitler has unleashed Germany's flying bomb on the south of England. This deadly, pilotless, sub-winged weapon flies at a speed of 352 mph (563 km/h) over a range of 161 miles (257 km). Launched from catapult ramps in the Pas de Calais in northern France, the V-1 is guided by a gyroscopic compass and driven by a pulse jet engine. Its warhead carries an incredible one ton of high explosives. When the V-1 reaches a measured distance, the engine stalls and the bomb falls to earth, exploding within 15 seconds of impact. The bombs have already scored direct hits on vulnerable places, including a convent, a church, and a hospital. The British public has been warned to take cover if the curious engine noise stops. The popular belief is that as long as you can still hear the engine, you are safe.

WAR GAMES
Toys are scarce in wartime, but British children are having plenty of fun collecting these miniature flags issued free with national newspapers. Children use them to chart the strategic positions of the Allied and opposing forces on a map of the world.

Hermann Goering and leading Nazis examine Hitler's wrecked headquarters

Hitler death attempt

JULY 20
Adolf Hitler has survived an assassination attempt at his Wolf's Lair headquarters in East Prussia. A suitcase bomb was planted under a table in Hitler's conference room. It caused a huge explosion, shattering the entire room and killing three senior Nazi officers. Hitler escaped with only minor cuts and burns. The assassination was led by Claus von Stauffenberg, a crippled war hero who fought in Russia in 1943. Von Stauffenberg and his band of plotters face execution. The Führer has taken his near escape as a sign that fate is preserving him to continue his important life's work.

JULY–SEPTEMBER

World Events	AUG The UK parliament passes an education act to provide all children with free education.	SEP V-2 rockets, more deadly successors of the V-1s, are launched on London, UK, from bases in Holland and Germany.	SEP In Germany, all males aged 16 to 60 are called up for compulsory service in the "Volkssturm" ("home guard").	SEP The Allies liberate Antwerp in Belgium and destroy the V-1 flying bomb site in the Pas de Calais in northern France.
Entertainment	JUL US comedian Bob Hope entertains Allied forces with his comedy show in the Solomon Islands.	SEP Warner Brothers releases the hilarious comedy *Arsenic and Old Lace*, starring US actor Cary Grant.	SEP Dancer and actor Fred Astaire puts on a private show for Allied forces stationed in France.	SEP Laurence Olivier and Ralph Richardson star in *Richard III* at the New Theatre in London, UK.
Innovations	JUL John Logie Baird attempts an "all-electronic" color television system in the UK.	AUG Germany introduces postcodes, a form of address coding that makes delivery of mail more efficient.	AUG The German Messerschmidt Me 262A-2 *Sturmvogel*, "Stormbird," is used in battle for the first time.	SEP The Swedish Volvo PV44 is the first car to be fitted with a laminated glass windshield.

BOB HOPE

GERMAN GUARD

1944

Paris liberated by the Allies

AUGUST 25

After four years of Nazi occupation, Paris has at last been liberated. Adolf Hitler planned to have the French capital demolished rather than allow it to fall into Allied hands, but General von Choltitz, the German commander in Paris, defied Hitler and surrendered the beautiful city intact. The first Allied forces to enter Paris, to the ecstatic jubilation of the Parisians, were the French Fourth Armored Division, led by General Jacques Leclerc. In the evening, the popular General de Gaulle marched through the crowds down the Champs Elysées.

Japanese navy crushed at Leyte

OCTOBER 26

This evening United States warships are in pursuit of the battered survivors of the Japanese navy after a three-day battle off the coast of the Philippines. General Douglas MacArthur, overall land commander in the Pacific, has landed on the central Philippine island of Leyte to congratulate his own troops on their successful invasion of the island. Commenting on the sea battle, he declared that "the Japanese navy has suffered its most crushing defeat of the war".

MacArthur addresses US troops

OCTOBER–DECEMBER

OCT Field-Marshal Rommel commits suicide rather than face the consequences of his participation in the plot to kill Hitler.

NOV Franklin D. Roosevelt wins a record fourth term as US president, with 432 votes over republican Thomas Dewey.

NOV Three RAF Lancaster bombers sink the German *Tirpitz* warship in the Tromso Fjord in northern Norway.

DEC Civil war erupts in Greece when the National People's Liberation Army seizes part of Athens.

OCT The Martha Graham Dance Company performs Aaron Copland's ballet *Appalachian Spring* in the US.

DEC The Green Bay Packers defeat the New York Giants in the National Football League championship.

DEC US film *National Velvet* is released in Hollywood, starring 11-year-old UK actress Elizabeth Taylor.

DEC Glenn Miller's plane is reported missing on a routine flight over the English Channel.

FIELD-MARSHAL ERWIN ROMMEL

OCT Two Messerschmidt Me 262A fighters beome the first jet aircraft to be shot down in aerial combat.

NOV US surgeon Alfred Blalock performs the first successful heart operation on a newborn baby.

DEC UK chemists develop chromatography, a technique used to separate mixtures of liquids or gases.

NATIONAL VELVET

DEC In the UK, Decca Records releases the first high-fidelity (hi-fi) recordings.

1940 SOE SET UP TO COORDINATE
RESISTANCE GROUPS IN EUROPE

1940 CHARLES DE GAULLE ESTABLISHES
FREE FRENCH NATIONAL COMMITTEE

1942 TITO ORGANIZES
YUGOSLAV UNDERGROUND

OCCUPATION AND RESISTANCE

BY THE SUMMER OF 1942 German conquests in Europe stretched from the Atlantic coast of France to the Caucasus mountains in the Soviet Union. The industry, agriculture, and workforces of these vast occupied territories became the property of Germany. The German treatment of the nations they occupied varied. In Poland, the population was used as a source of slave labor, and in Greece thousands of people starved to death when most of the country's food stocks were seized by the German army. Underground resistance groups were established in many places, but their success was often influenced by the geography of the region. In mountainous areas like Yugoslavia, resistance groups found it easier to operate undetected. In flat countries such as Holland and Denmark, passive resistance in the form of strikes, posters, and patriotic graffiti was more common.

Hidden map

Secret maps could be hidden beneath the surface of some seemingly ordinary playing cards for use by British agents working in Europe.

ODETTE SANSOM

Secret agent

Odette Sansom was recruited as a radio operator by the British Special Operations Executive (SOE). She worked in France with agent Peter Churchill until they were captured by the Germans. Released at the end of the war, Sansom was awarded the George Cross for her bravery.

German soldier choosing a postcard to send home

ILS DONNENT LEUR SANG

DONNEZ VOTRE TRAVAIL
pour sauver l'Europe du Bolchevisme

Nazi propaganda

This German propaganda poster urges French workers to join the fight against communism. Germany's war industry relied on volunteers from the occupied countries as well as slave labor from Eastern Europe and French prisoners-of-war. Enforced recruitment drove many young men into resistance groups.

Puppet prime minister

Vidkun Quisling led the Norwegian Nazi Party before the war, and when the Germans invaded in 1940, they installed him as head of the Norwegian government. Disliked by most Norwegians, he acted as a puppet for the Germans. After the war Quisling was tried for treason and executed in 1945. His name has been adopted as an international by-word for traitor.

Life in occupied Paris

Under occupation, Paris remained the playground city of Europe as German soldiers packed its cafes, theaters, and clubs. For most of the French, life went on as usual. Posters reminded them that if they offered no resistance, their families and property would be safe. However, many bars and restaurants were reserved exclusively for German soldiers, and the Nazi swastika hung from the Eiffel Tower.

Secret radios

SOE agents in occupied Europe used radios concealed in suitcases to send coded messages. Agents also carried a range of weapons, such as explosive pens, bicycle pumps that concealed a single-action shotgun, and silent pistols that could be hidden in clothing.

Headphones allowed agents to listen to broadcasts in silence

Transmitter works using electrical or battery power

Ever vigilant

"Keep quiet! The Germans have fled, but their spies remain!" Posters like this were produced by the Allies after the liberation of France in 1944 to remind the French people that Nazi Germany still posed a threat.

Apparatus packs into a suitcase, and weighs 32 lb (14.5 kg)

In disguise

There were more than 11,000 agents in the British Special Operations Executive (SOE). The SOE was set up in July 1940 to gather information in German-occupied Europe, carry out sabotage, and support resistance groups. In the words of Winston Churchill, the British prime minister, their goal was to "set Europe ablaze."

Voltage adjuster

FRENCH RESISTANCE FIGHTERS BEING BRIEFED

The Maquis

The French Maquis was set up in 1943, after the Germans demanded 400,000 men to work in German industry. To avoid forced labor, thousands formed resistance groups in remote countryside regions. By May 1944, the Maquis numbered 35,000 although only about 8,000 had enough ammunition for more than one day's serious fighting. After D-Day in 1944, thousands of tons of equipment was parachuted to the Maquis, who attacked the Germans in central and southern France.

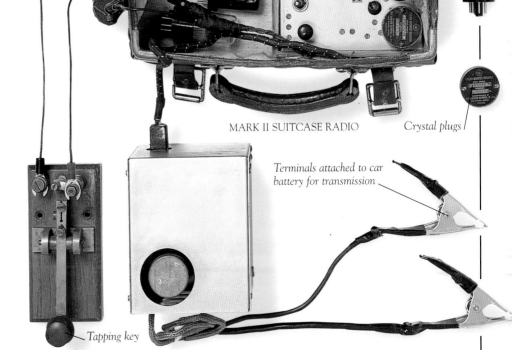

MARK II SUITCASE RADIO

Crystal plugs

Terminals attached to car battery for transmission

Tapping key

1945

Allies flatten Dresden in single night of bombing

US capture Iwo Jima

FEBRUARY 15

The beautiful and historic city of Dresden in Germany has been devastated by an Allied bombing raid. For three nights nearly 800 British Lancaster planes and 300 US Flying Fortresses have ruthlessly obliterated many of the grandest architectural monuments of this showpiece city. Dresden has suffered so few bombing raids that all its antiaircraft guns have been removed. The death toll is thought to be as high as 100,000, many of them refugees, with total casualties estimated at around 400,000.

The bombing has aroused widespread criticism. In Britain, some observers have accused the chief of the RAF Bomber Command, Air Marshal Sir Arthur Harris, of clinging despite everything to his controversial theory that terror bombing can by itself destroy the enemy's will to fight. Senior Allied military officers are in uproar about the need to attack such a strategically unimportant target. They would have preferred to see the bombers step up attacks on German communications and oil installations.

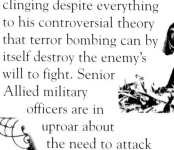

Dresden devastated after a night of bombing

US marines hoist the Stars and Stripes on Mount Suribachi

FEBRUARY 23

The US flag has been raised on the peak of Mount Suribachi, the highest point on the tiny Pacific island of Iwo Jima, where Japanese troops are firmly entrenched. An agressive attack on the heavily fortified island began four days ago when US battleships, cruisers, and aircraft carriers began relentlessly pounding the whole island. Taking control from the Japanese has cost the lives of 6,800 US servicemen and wounded 18,000 others. Many days of fighting still lie ahead before this speck in the ocean can be turned into an air base from which to bomb the neighboring islands of Japan.

JANUARY–FEBRUARY

World Events

JAN US president Franklin D. Roosevelt is inaugurated for a record fourth term in office.

JAN Seven thousand people are killed when the German *Wilhelm Gustloff* is sunk by a Soviet submarine in the Baltic.

JAN The Soviet Red Army discover the horrors of the Auschwitz concentration camp in Poland, where millions of Jews died.

FEB Winston Churchill, Joseph Stalin, and Franklin D. Roosevelt carve up the postwar world at Yalta, in the Ukraine.

Entertainment

JAN US singer Perry Como has a hit with *Till the End of Time.*

JAN Sergei Eisenstein's *Ivan the Terrible* is released in Moscow in the Soviet Union.

FEB Brazilian musician Villa Lobos composes the musical score for the film *The Green Mansions.*

FEB Walt Disney premieres his latest cartoon feature *The Three Caballeros* starring Donald Duck.

Innovations

JAN The world's first fluoridated water supply is available in Michigan.

WILHELM GUSTLOFF

JAN Soviet scientists start to develop high-thrust liquid-propellant rocket engines.

FEB A vertically launched rocket interceptor crashes on its first and only test flight in the USSR.

THE YALTA CONFERENCE

FEB The USSR begins flight trials of the *RD-100* rocket engine, a version of the German V2.

1945

Les Enfants du Paradis

MARCH 9
A remarkable new film, *Les Enfants du Paradis* ("The Children of Paradise"), has premiered in Paris, France.

This epic story, set in the theater world of Paris, has become a symbol of the rebirth of France after German occupation.

F. D. R. dies on eve of victory

APRIL 12
Franklin D. Roosevelt has died of a brain hemorrhage. While resting at the resort of Warm Springs in Georgia, the US president complained of a headache. A few hours later he was dead. When informed of her husband's death, Mrs. Roosevelt said, "I am more sorry for the people of this country and of the world than I am for ourselves."

Hitler suicide

APRIL 30
Adolf Hitler has committed suicide in his bunker beneath the Reich Chancellory garden in Berlin. Hitler refused pleas from his generals to escape from Berlin. Yesterday, as Russian shells and rockets were raging above him in the battle for Berlin, Hitler married Eva Braun, the woman who has been his mistress since 1932. Hitler and Braun withdrew to their private quarters, where they both bit into lethal cyanide capsules. Simultaneously, Hitler shot himself with a pistol. Their bodies were then carried upstairs by their aides and into the gardens where they were doused with gasoline and burned along with great piles of Nazi documents. Only ten days ago, Hitler celebrated his 56th birthday.

Hitler and Eva Braun

MARCH–APRIL

MAR Japanese schools and universities are shut down and everyone over the age of six is ordered to do war work.

APR In Germany, the Soviet army launches an offensive to capture Berlin from its bridgehead on the Oder River.

APR Mussolini and his mistress Clara Petacci are shot dead by Italian partisans and found in the Piazza Loretto in Milan, Italy.

APR The Soviet army takes Vienna in Austria, and installs Karl Renner as prime minister of the provisional government.

MAR *The Picture of Dorian Gray*, based on the novel by Oscar Wilde, is released in the US.

APR Oscar Hammerstein's musical *Carousel* opens at New York's City's Majestic Theater.

APR Sylvester the cat makes his first appearance in *Life with Feathers*, a new cartoon released by Warner Brothers.

APR US jazz-band leader Lionel Hampton releases his *All American Award Concert* album to great acclaim.

CAROUSEL OPENS ON BROADWAY

APR The Heinkel *He 162* is the first aircraft to go into service with a operational ejector seat.

APR Hungarian scientists succeed in reflecting radar signals from the Moon.

APR Hungarian scientist Lajos Jánossy investigates the effects of cosmic rays upon the Earth's atmosphere.

BENITO MUSSOLINI

APR Dr. Claus Maertens invents the comfortable Doc Marten shoe after he suffers a ski injury while on holiday.

1945

Truth revealed as death camps discovered

Slave laborers found by US troops at Buchenwald camp

Survivors tell their stories to their GI liberators

APRIL 30

Allied troops have uncovered the horrifying truth of the Nazi concentration camps. Hundreds of thousands of Jews had been rounded up by the Nazis and shipped to concentration camps across occupied Europe as part of Hitler's "final solution" to eliminate the Jewish race. Political, religious, and sexual "undesirables" faced a similar persecution. Soviet, British, and American soldiers liberating death camps such as Belsen, Treblinka, and Auschwitz were greeted by pits piled high with rotting corpses and survivors who were little more than walking skeletons. The survivors have described how the inmates were separated on arrival, most of them herded into the "shower rooms" where they were gassed to death. The rest were forced to work as slave labor until starvation and appalling living conditions weakened them and they too were gassed. Women and children were often forced into prostitution and, at some camps, the inmates were experimented on by Nazi scientists. Despite every effort being made to save the emaciated prisoners, hundreds are dying every day.

The Allies have known about the camps for years, but were so preoccupied by strategic campaigns that they did not select them for bombing.

MAY–JUNE

World Events	MAY UK broadcaster William Joyce, "Lord Haw-Haw," is arrested on a charge of treason.	MAY Heinrich Himmler, chief of Nazi Germany's SS and Gestapo, kills himself while in British custody.	JUN In the Battle of Okinawa, Japanese kamikaze pilots crash their aircraft into enemy targets, killing 5,000 US seamen.	JUN In Ottawa, the capital of Canada, MacKenzie King's Liberal Party is returned to power in a general election.
Entertainment	MAY The US actress Judy Garland stars in *The Clock*, a romantic war film.	MAY US singer Doris Day and the Les Brown Orchestra have a hit with the song *Sentimental Journey*.	MAY German director Max Ophüls releases his latest film, *From Mayerling to Sarajevo*, in Paris, France.	JUN Benjamin Britten's opera *Peter Grimes* premieres at London's recently opened Sadler's Wells Theater, in the UK.
Innovations	MAY Tridone is developed to treat postwar convulsive disorders such as epilepsy.	MAY UK scientist Arthur C. Clarke advocates geostationary orbit for global communications.	MAY Wernher von Braun and other German rocket scientists surrender to the US Seventh Army.	JUN The UK government introduces the Family Allowance, a weekly payment to help families.

THE CLOCK

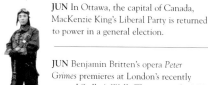

KAMIKAZE PILOT

1945

Montgomery accepts German surrender terms

MAY 4

In a tent on the desolate Luneburg Heath, south of Hamburg, Field Marshal Montgomery today received the first surrender of the German forces – all those in northwestern Germany, Holland, and Denmark. The Allies expect the final surrender of the German High Command to take place within the next few days. At last, peace has come to a war-torn Europe.

General Friedenburg signs the surrender terms

VE Day celebrated

MAY 8

Dull skies and drizzle have not dampened the British celebrations of Victory in Europe (VE) Day. In London, delirious crowds headed for Buckingham Palace to cheer the royal family. As darkness fell, the British capital was ablaze with floodlights and fireworks for the first time since war broke out in 1939. At street parties across the nation, bonfires topped with effigies of Adolf Hitler and his henchmen were lit to mark the end of Nazi Germany. There

have been similar scenes of celebration in Paris and Rome. In Moscow, in the Soviet Union, captured German flags were piled at the feet of Soviet leaders in Red Square.

Allied victory

MAY 7

Germany surrendered unconditionally to the Allies at 2:41 this morning. The German High Command made its final surrender in a little red schoolhouse in Reims, France. General Bedell Smith signed for the Western Allies and General Ivan Suslapatov was chief witness for the Soviet Union. Since then, German troops have been giving themselves up to the Allies in droves.

German troops surrender to the Allies

Children celebrating the end of the war at a street party

JULY–AUGUST

JUL At the Potsdam Conference in Germany, Allied leaders disagree over where Germany's postwar boundaries should be drawn.

AUG The US unleashes an atomic bomb on the city of Nagasaki, in Japan, killing more than 65,000 innocent Japanese civilians.

AUG Marshal Pétain, former premier of France, is sentenced to death, but reprieved by General De Gaulle because he is 89 years old.

AUG Following the defeat of Japan, conflict breaks out in that country between the nationalist government and the communists.

JUL The BBC broadcasts *The Robinson Family*, the first daily drama serial in the UK.

AUG US jazz musician Charlie Parker has a hit with the popular tune *Now's the Time*.

AUG The Czechoslovakian government nationalizes all the country's film companies.

AUG The Louvre art museum in Paris, France, is reopened to the general public.

JUL The first atomic explosion takes place in Almogordo in the New Mexico desert.

NAGASAKI OBLITERATED

JUL A vaccine against A and B influenza is used on the US army for the first time.

AUG Benadryl is developed in the US to treat common allergies such as hayfever and asthma.

THE LOUVRE

AUG Finnish scientist Arturri Virtanen develops a method for preserving cattle fodder.

1945

Devastating bomb dropped on Japan

AUGUST 6

At 8:15 a.m. this morning an American bomber plane called *Enola Gay* released its solitary bomb over the city of Hiroshima in Japan, and a new era in warfare began. As a result of a single atomic explosion, an estimated 80,000 people were killed instantly, and much of Hiroshima has simply ceased to exist. The people at the center of the blast have been completely vaporized, with charred shadows their only remains. Radiation levels in the area are dangerously high. A mushroom-shaped cloud of smoke and dust rising 5 miles (8 km) in the air above the city is all that can be seen. Relying on the explosive power of an atomic reaction, the atom bomb has been developed by an international team of scientists in the United States in a top-secret operation code-named the "Manhattan Project." The US launched the attack after Japan failed to surrender unconditionally, although rumors persist that this unprecedented use of nuclear weapons was unnecessary. What is clear now is that Japan will either have to surrender or face further nuclear attacks. The Allies believe the attack will lead to an end to the war.

CHILD VICTIMS

The young survivors of the Hiroshima bomb wear masks over their noses and mouths. The masks help combat the odor of death clinging to the city's ruins. People are living in makeshift shelters in the blasted wastelands of both Hiroshima and Nagasaki.

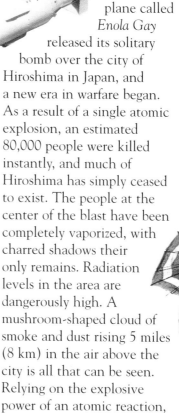

SEPTEMBER–OCTOBER

	World Events	Entertainment	Innovations
	SEP UK troops take control of the colony of Hong Kong as Japanese troops return to Japan.	**SEP** The Italian film *Rome, Open City* is unpopular as it reminds people of the war.	**SEP** The Universal Jeep, the first Jeep for civilian use, is produced in the US.
	OCT French traitor Pierre Laval is denied the right of appeal after being sentenced to death for collaborating with the Germans.	**SEP** Former child actress Shirley Temple marries John Agar in Hollywood, California.	**SEP** A helicopter crosses the English Channel between France and the UK for the first time.
	OCT Egypt, Iraq, Syria, and Lebanon form the Arab League and warn that the creation of a Jewish state will cause trouble.	**OCT** US star Joan Crawford returns to the screen in *Mildred Pierce*, the story of an overachieving woman.	**OCT** Fluorescent lighting is first used in Europe in an underground station in London, UK.
	OCT Colonel Juan Péron takes over the government of Argentina again, only eight days after being ousted by the army.	**OCT** The Moscow Dynamo soccer team leaves the USSR for a tour of the UK and wins every match.	**OCT** The first microwave oven is patented in the US by the Raytheon Company.

PIERRE LAVAL

JOAN CRAWFORD

1945

Victory celebrations

Crowds celebrate in the streets of New York

Official surrender

SEPTEMBER 2

This morning gray skies hung over Tokyo Bay as a formal Japanese delegation arrived on the deck of the US battleship *Missouri* to sign an unconditional surrender. The Japanese conceded defeat after a second atomic bomb killed over 65,000 people in the city of Nagasaki. Although the Allies celebrated victory last month, today's ceremony means that World War II is officially over.

Japanese delegation arrives to sign surrender

AUGUST 15

Last night's news that Japan has decided to surrender has sparked off celebrations in the United States and Australia. In San Francisco, the news was greeted with a wild wailing of air-raid sirens, the honking of car horns, and the hooting of ship's sirens. Traffic has been brought to a halt in cities across the United States as singing, cheering, and dancing crowds fill the streets. In the US capital Washington, D.C., the military police were called in to keep a huge and excited mob from invading the White House, and in New York an estimated two million people jammed Times Square. In Sydney, Australia, a million people let their hair down, mobbing army trucks and Jeeps, snatching off servicemen's hats, and swapping kisses. In stark contrast, the citizens of Tokyo, Japan, shuffled through their ruined city to the gates of the emperor's palace, where they stood and wept.

Ho Chi Minh's new republic

SEPTEMBER 2

After hearing news of the Japanese surrender, Ho Chi Minh, leader of Vietnam's communist-dominated Viet Minh Party, has declared the country a republic. The former French colony in Southeast Asia had been occupied by the Japanese since 1941. Armed by the Americans, the Viet Minh have today taken control.

NOVEMBER–DECEMBER

NOV Marshal Tito's National Front Party wins an overwhelming majority in a general election in Yugoslavia.

NOV The trial of 21 leading Nazis is opened in Nuremberg, Germany, before an Allied International Military Tribunal.

NOV General Charles de Gaulle is elected the president of the provisional government in France.

DEC Mussolini's daughter Edda Mussolini Ciano is jailed for two years in Italy for aiding fascism.

NOV Popular jazz artist Woody Herman releases a hit album called *The Thundering Herd*.

NOV "Bebop" is the new sound sweeping across the US. Small "combos" play loud, fast music.

NOV Jerome Kern, US composer of many well-loved hits including *Show Boat*, dies at age 60.

NOV Film critics warmly receive UK director Alfred Hitchcock's latest thriller, *Spellbound*.

NOV The first air-sea rescue by helicopter is carried out by the US army off Long Island Sound.

NUREMBERG TRIALS

NOV US chemist Earl W. Tupper develops airtight plastic boxes called "Tupperware."

DEC The first bumper-stickers are manufactured by Forest Gill at the Gill Studios, Kansas.

JEROME KERN

DEC Lurex, used to make metallic yarns, is first manufactured by Dobecknum Co.

1939 IGOR SIKORSKY
DESIGNS THE HELICOPTER

1939 THE GERMAN HEINKEL *178*
IS THE FIRST JET AIRCRAFT

1940 US ARMY INTRODUCES
THE ALL-PURPOSE JEEP

TECHNOLOGY OF WAR

SCIENTISTS AND TECHNICIANS played a vital role in World War II. Many of the most important battles were fought not on the front line but in laboratories and factories. Science was applied to every aspect of each country's war effort, from developing weapons to devising a healthy and tasty diet from the increasingly rationed food supplies. The demands of war also speeded up research on technologies that had been started in the 1930s, including radar, computer sciences, atomic fission, and the jet aircraft. War brought together the forces of science and industry as no peacetime event could have done. However, other scientific advances, such as the invention of the atom bomb, cast a shadow over the world that remained for years to come.

ALBERT
EINSTEIN

Intelligent advice

The brilliant physicist Albert Einstein fled Nazi Germany for the US in 1933. He warned President Roosevelt of the dangers if Germany became the first to develop an atom bomb.

Enigma variations

The signals from the German "Enigma" machine, which was used for secret military communications, baffled the enemy cipher experts for many years. When the operator pressed a letter key, rotors working under the keyboard made a different letter appear on the display board. The receiving Enigma machine reversed this process. The British breaking of the Enigma code was one of the great technical feats of the war.

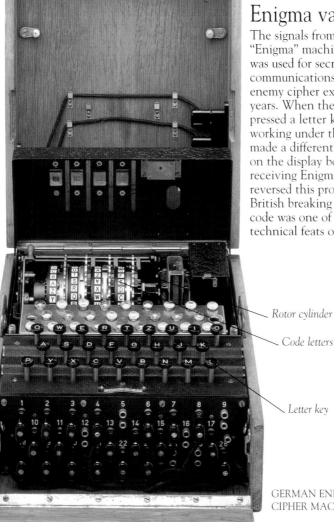

Rotor cylinder

Code letters

Letter key

GERMAN ENIGMA
CIPHER MACHINE

Front panel

MASS PRODUCTION OF MESSERSCHMITT AIRCRAFT

Air attack

Willy Messerschmitt began work on the German *Me109* in 1934, and by the outbreak of war it had become one of the most outstanding fighter planes in the world. It was built in greater numbers than any other German combat aircraft. The most common aircraft during WWII was the Soviet *Il-2 Stormovik*. Over 35,000 were built between 1941 and 1945 in three huge factories.

Exploding pigs

Nicknamed "Pigs," these Italian underwater torpedo craft had a detachable warhead in the nose. The two-man crew would attach the warhead to the hull of an enemy ship. A time fuse in the bomb allowed them to escape before it exploded. In December 1941, Italian "human torpedoes" badly damaged two British battleships in Alexandria Harbour in Egypt.

Warhead

1941 FIRST RADAR-
NIGHT FIGHTERS USED

1942 SELF-CONTAINED UNDERWATER
BREATHING APPARATUS PERFECTED

1944 LAUNCH OF THE V-1 "FLYING
BOMB," THE FIRST CRUISE MISSILE

A RADAR
DISPLAY

Rocket man

Wernher von Braun was the technical director
of the secret German rocket establishment at
Peenemünde from 1934, where he created deadly
missiles such as the V-1 and V-2 rockets. At the
end of the war, von Braun, together
with other German rocket scientists,
surrendered and were taken to
America. These scientists played
an important role in the creation
of the US space program.

OPPENHEIMER
INSPECTS THE
REMAINS OF
THE SITE

Bombsite

The atom bomb was
designed by scientist Robert
Openheimer as part of a
project overseen by US
General Leslie R Groves. The
two men tested the bomb in
New Mexico before it was
dropped over Japan.

Early warning

This radar display is
tracking enemy aircraft from
an American aircraft carrier in the
Pacific. The word "radar" stands for "radio
detecting and ranging," a phrase coined in 1942.
Developed in the 1930s, it was one of the key
technologies of the war. In the Battle of Britain,
the British used ground radar to detect enemy
bomber formations. Later, radar was carried in
German bombers to help find targets, and by the
Allies in the vast spaces of the Pacific to find the
enemy and to range the guns on their warships.

Mechanical mind

The first successful general-
purpose computer was called
ENIAC (short for Electronic
Numerical Integrator And
Calculator). It was designed
by American scientists John
Mauchley and John Eckert
and weighed 33 tons. The
computer increased processing
speeds a thousand times, but
had to be partially rewired each
time it was programmed.

ENIAC COMPUTER

Two-man cockpit

ITALIAN MAIALE
"HUMAN TORPEDO"

Rudder

Propeller

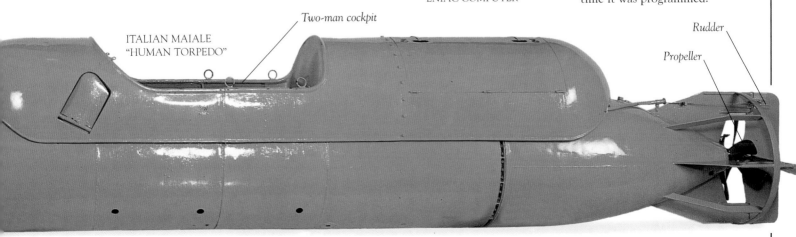

1946

Nations united

JANUARY 11

The general assembly of the United Nations has held its first session in London. British prime minister Clement Attlee told the gathered representatives of 51 nations, "Our aim is the creation of justice and security."

"Iron Curtain" division in Europe

MARCH 5

Britain's wartime leader Sir Winston Churchill has found a new enemy to fight – the threat of communism. In a speech he gave while touring the United States, he warned that "an Iron Curtain has descended across Europe." He believes that the differences between the capitalist and communist countries are irreconcilable, and the USSR is commited to expansionism. He urged an alliance between the United States and Britain to counter Soviet aggression.

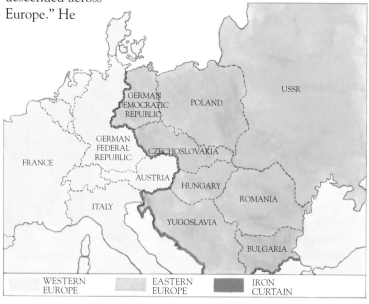

| WESTERN EUROPE | EASTERN EUROPE | IRON CURTAIN |

Palestine splits

MAY 1

A new plan for Palestine, drawn up by Britain and the United States, threatens to lead to bloodshed. It proposes to divide Palestine into separate Jewish and Arab states, but it seems certain that both groups will reject the plan. Jews all over the world consider that Palestine is their homeland, and thousands have traveled to settle there.

Jews climb aboard refugee ship

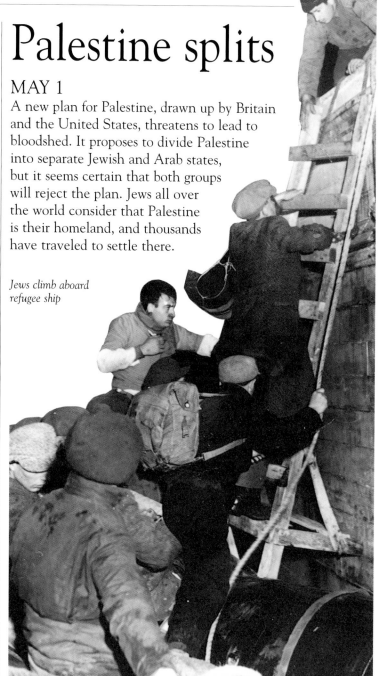

JANUARY–JUNE

World Events

JAN Emperor Hirohito of Japan declares his divinity a "false conception" founded in fiction.

FEB Colonel Juan D. Perón is elected as the president of Argentina for a six-year term, despite heavy opposition from the US.

FEB Anti-UK protestors and riot police clash in Bombay, India, and more than 60 Indians are killed and 500 injured.

JUN Italian women are able to vote in national elections for the first time. Enrico de Nicola is elected president.

Entertainment

JAN UK director David Lean's film of *Great Expectations* premieres.

MAY US film star Lana Turner heads the cast of the menacing film *The Postman Always Rings Twice*.

JUN Television licenses, to raise revenue to support the BBC, are introduced in the UK.

JUN The BBC revives TV broadcasts in the UK interrupted by the war.

Innovations

FEB US company IBM introduces a new electronic calculator using vacuum tubes.

PRESIDENT PERÓN OF ARGENTINA

MAY Dr. Spock's *Common Sense Book of Baby and Child Care* is published in the US.

MAY A huge 15 ton (14-tonne) German V-2 rocket climbs 75 miles (120 km) in a US missile test.

ITALIAN WOMEN GET THE VOTE

JUN Scotsman John Logie Baird, the man first to show TV pictures, dies at age 58.

1946

Two-piece shock

JULY 5

A sensation was caused in Paris today by the "bikini" bathing suit. This new bathing costume, named after Bikini Atoll in the Pacific, is a tiny two-piece affair and can be packed into a matchbox or pulled through a wedding ring. The world's tiniest bathing suit was worn by 19-year-old Micheline Bernardini, a nude dancer from the Casino de Paris, at a contest at the Molitor swimming pool to find the most beautiful bather of 1946.

Micheline Bernardini models the new bikini

The longest screen kiss

JULY 22

UK director Alfred Hitchcock has defied the censors with his new film *Notorious*. Cary Grant keeps Ingrid Bergman in his arms for the longest embrace in screen history, his kiss only interrupted by a telephone call.

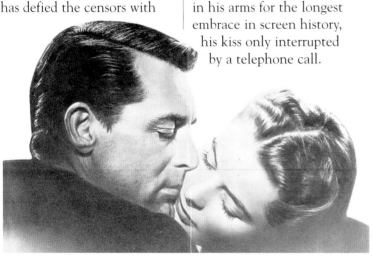

Top Nazis sentenced

OCTOBER 16

The war crimes trial being held at Nuremberg, Germany, is over and sentence has been passed by the panel of judges representing the Allies. Of the 21 Nazi leaders on trial, 11 have been sentenced to death and the rest received heavy prison sentences.

However, the biggest war criminals of all are absent from the trial. Adolf Hitler and SS Chief Heinrich Himmler both committed suicide at the end of the war and Hitler's secretary, Martin Bormann, is missing.

JITTERBUGGING

US armed forces stationed in Europe have started a Jitterbug dance craze. The dance was first seen in the United States in the 1930s and has now spread to many parts of the world. Dancers Jitterbug to swing and boogie-woogie music. Both partners need to be athletic in order to complete the Jitterbug's "underarm swing."

JULY–DECEMBER

JUL In the worst anti-Jewish pogrom since war ended, 39 Jews and four Poles are killed in Poland.

AUG H. G. Wells, UK author of *The Time Machine* and *The War of the Worlds*, dies at age 79.

JUL The US military conducts the first underwater atomic explosion off the Bikini Atoll in the Pacific.

BEAUTY AND THE BEAST

AUG Chinese communist leader Mao Zedong orders an all-out civil war against the Nationalists.

DEC French film director Jean Cocteau's *Beauty and the Beast* wins the Louis Delloc Prize.

SEP The first car with electrically operated windows, the Daimler DE36, is manufactured in the UK.

OCT Nazi Hermann Goering commits suicide by swallowing cyanide hours before he is due to be executed.

DEC US boxer Sugar Ray Robinson wins the welterweight championship in New York City.

NOV A nonsmudging ballpoint pen called the Biro after its Hungarian inventor goes on sale in the UK.

SUGAR RAY ROBINSON

NOV The National Health Service (NHS) is created in the UK by the Labor government.

DEC Swiss mystic author Herman Hesse wins the Nobel Prize for literature.

DEC UK scientists Donald Hay and Edward Appleton discover that sunspots emit radio waves.

1947

Dior unveils "New Look"

FEBRUARY 12

French designer Christian Dior has created a fashion sensation with his "New Look." The elegant, feminine designs are certain to be a big hit with women hungry for something new. The dresses feature a narrow waist, tight bodice, and padded hips.

"New-Look" style suit

Anne Frank's diary published

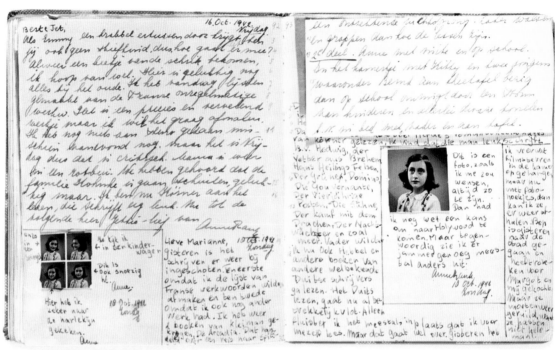

An entry made in Anne Frank's diary in October 1942

JUNE 15

"In spite of everything I still believe people are really good at heart." These moving words come from one of the pages of a diary kept by a young Jewish girl named Anne Frank during the war. When the Nazis overran Holland in 1940 the Frank family went into hiding. Day after day, in constant fear of being discovered, Anne took comfort from pouring out her thoughts in a diary. After two years, the family was betrayed by Dutch informers, arrested by the Gestapo (secret police), and sent to concentration camps. Anne died of typhus in March 1945. Her father has had his daughter's remarkable writings published and now millions of readers can gain some insight into the nightmare of living through the Holocaust.

DEAD SEA SCROLLS

A great archaeological find has been made in Palestine. A young herdsman stumbled upon some jars filled with ancient manuscripts in a cave by the Dead Sea. Some of them have been dated to 200 BC.

JANUARY–JUNE

World Events	FEB In Germany, UK and US agents round up hundreds of Nazis who have been in hiding.	MAR In the UK, Lord Mountbatten is appointed viceroy of India in order to oversee the transfer of government to India.	MAR Henry Ford, who changed the car industry with his mass-produced Model T, dies in the US at age 83.	JUN US secretary of state George Marshall reveals his plan for the reconstruction of postwar Europe.
Entertainment	FEB The lively musical *Brigadoon* opens at the Ziegfeld Theater in New York City.	APR In the US, Jackie Robinson is the first black American to play in major league baseball since 1884.	JUN The musical *Annie Get Your Gun* opens to rave reviews in the West End of London, UK.	JUN UK actor Laurence Olivier is awarded a knighthood for his contribution to the theater.
Innovations	JAN UK scientist J. A. Sargrove is the first to develop a printed circuit board.	MAR In the UK, Prime Minister Clement Attlee makes the first party political broadcast on BBC radio.	APR The first duty-free shop selling wine and spirits opens at Shannon Airport in Ireland.	APR The first microwave ovens go on sale in the US, but they fail to make an impact on the public.

JACKIE ROBINSON

THE MARSHALL PLAN

1947

Independent India

AUGUST 15

After 163 monumental years the sun has set on the British Raj. The British colony of India was today replaced by the independent countries of India and Pakistan. Lord Mountbatten has relinquished his title as viceroy and has become governor-general of the new dominion of India. Fearing the outbreak of civil war between the conflicting communities of Hindus and Muslims, Mountbatten had been negiotating partition plans since 1946. Last June, he held talks with Jawaharlal Nehru, leader of the Congress Party, and Mohammed Jinnah, leader of the Muslim League. Broad agreement was reached on plans for the partition, but Mahatma Gandhi, who worked closely with Nehru to achieve independence, adamantly opposed the division of India. He had hoped the country would remain united and urged that Hindus and Muslims live in peace.

Jawaharlal Nehru with Mahatma Gandhi

Yeager shatters sound barrier

OCTOBER 14

US daredevil pilot Chuck Yeager has become the first person to fly faster than the speed of sound. At Muroc Dry

Lake in California, Yeager piloted his bullet-shaped aerodynamic Bell *X-I* rocket plane smoothly through the sound barrier at a fantastic speed of 700 mph (1,120 km/h).

Witch hunt in Hollywood

NOVEMBER 26

In Hollywood, movie capital of the world, a hunt for undercover communists has wrecked the career of ten leading US writers and film directors. The so-called "Hollywood Ten" refused to appear before a congressional committee to answer questions about their political activities. Because of this, they have been cited for contempt of Congress, blacklisted, and given prison sentences. Edward Dmytryk (above), the director of the highly successful film *Crossfire*, has been dismissed by RKO. Several actors, including Humphrey Bogart, Gene Kelly, and Jane Wyatt, plan to protest against the running of the committee.

JULY–DECEMBER

SEP In the newly partitioned India, thousands are killed as riots break out between Hindus and Muslims.

AUG US actor Danny Kaye stars in the film comedy *The Secret Life of Walter Mitty*.

SEP The first frozen orange juice concentrate is manufactured by a citrus cooperative in the US.

THE ROYAL UK NEWLYWEDS

NOV Princess Elizabeth, daughter of King George VI, marries Lieutenant Philip Mountbatten in London, UK.

OCT Twelve-year-old Julie Andrews stars in the musical show *Starlight Roof* in the UK.

OCT President Truman makes the first presidential address to the US nation on the television.

NOV The UN general assembly votes in favor of the partition of Palestine and the emergence of a new Jewish state.

NOV The Edinburgh Festival of Music and Drama is founded in Scotland.

NOV In Romania, Anna Pauker becomes the first female foreign minister.

MIRACLE ON 34TH STREET

DEC The Greek government dissolves the communist-controlled National Liberation Front.

DEC The children's film *Miracle on 34th Street* opens to crowds in the US.

DEC The first transistor is patented by US physicist William Shockley.

AFTER THE WAR

WORLD WAR II was responsible for an estimated fifty-five million deaths, and many were innocent civilian victims. Huge areas of Europe and southwestern Asia had been bombed and devastated. Not only were military targets hit, but houses, schools, and road and rail networks lay in ruins. Famine loomed and the roads of Asia were clogged with thousands of refugees. Soldiers returning to their native countries found their homes destroyed and their families scattered. Yet amid the gloom there was a growing hope for a new world that would be free of tyranny.

Welcome home

As the guns of war fell silent in Europe and the Far East, millions of servicemen returned home and tried to settle back into family life. But many returned to find changed circumstances. They found the task of readjusting difficult, and this led to a soaring divorce rate in the first few years after the war.

Demobilization

After World War I soldiers had been promised "a land fit for heroes," but all they found was unemployment. At the end of World War II, governments were determined not to make the same mistake again. But it was an expensive task to return millions of men and women to civilian life. Some countries were bankrupt, while others were deeply in debt. In Britain, each demobilized soldier received a government gift of £199 and a complete set of new clothing.

EX-SERVICEMAN IS FITTED WITH A NEW SUIT

FEMALE CHAIN GANG IN BERLIN

Prefabrication

Britain had the worst housing shortage of any Allied country. The new Labour government set out to build 400,000 new houses a year, but fell short of the target. A stop-gap solution was the temporary, quick-to-assemble, pre-fabricated house. The "pre-fab" was intended to last ten years, but continuing shortages of accommodation meant that many of them had to be used for much longer.

The rebuilding of Europe

Bombing raids had frequently targeted civilian centers and there were many European cities in ruins. Public buildings, factories, and transportation were severely damaged, and food, fuel, and water were in desperately short supply. People were half-starved and forced to take refuge anywhere that they could. In postwar cities in Germany, women outnumbered men, and in Berlin it was a common sight to see "chain gangs" of women, who were paid a small sum of money to help in the painstaking task of clearing away the rubble from the bombed streets.

Miraculous recovery

Immediately after the war, most German citizens simply concentrated on survival. But, after ten years of foreign investment and efficient town planning, Germany became one of the first European nations to recover from the trauma of war. Unlike the Allies, Germany had no huge military loans to pay back. So the Germans were able to rebuild their factories and new businesses once again flourished.

A land of prosperity

By 1945 the US was the richest and most powerful nation in the world. It remained physically untouched by war; factories continued to make new goods and there was no food rationing. The postwar economy leaped ahead of the rest of the world bringing new prosperity to millions of people. Farmers' incomes quadrupled and the wages of industrial workers rose by 70 percent. To Europeans recovering from the harshness of war, the US seemed like the land of plenty.

JAPANESE ORPHAN

Label states destination of orphan

Candy rations

In Britain, food rationing increased after the war. In July 1946 even bread was rationed, a measure introduced to help feed people in the British-occupied zone of Germany. It was not until the 1950s that people could enjoy unlimited quantities of luxury items such as candies and chocolates.

The aftermath of the atomic bomb

The atomic bombing of the Japanese cities of Hiroshima and Nagasaki shocked the world. Both cities were devastated and most of the population died. For months after, those who had survived the blasts suffered from radiation sickness and developed cancers linked to radiation. In later years there were other consequences, such as birth defects. The final death toll in Hiroshima alone has been estimated at nearly 300,000. Countless refugees, many of them small children, were left homeless and without their families to care for them.

THE WASTELAND OF HIROSHIMA

161

1948

Gandhi's murder stuns world

JANUARY 31

In India, thousands of people have gathered on the banks of the Jumna River to mourn the death of their spiritual leader Mahatma Gandhi. The spiritual father of Indian independence was shot three times yesterday by one of his countrymen at a prayer meeting in New Delhi. The assassin, who was identified as Nathuram Godse, a fanatical Hindu, was immediately seized by police and led away from the hysterical crowd. Mahatma Gandhi's body has been cremated and his ashes cast into the river.

Czech communists stage coup

Clement Gottwald

FEBRUARY 25

A communist coup has toppled the fragile coalition government of President Eduard Benes in Prague, Czechoslovakia. The communist premier Clement Gottwald has seized power and President Benes has announced the resignation of all of the center and right-wing ministers of the previous government.

Israel proclaimed

MAY 14

The Jewish leaders Chaim Weizmann and David Ben-Gurion have declared the independence of the new Jewish state of Israel. The announcement, which was timed to coincide with the departure of British troops, seems certain to commit the new nation to a war with its neighboring Arab states. Egyptian troops are already massing on Israel's southern border. The Jews are greatly outnumbered but are still braced to defend themselves. However their 30,000-strong defense force has no aircraft, tanks, or heavy artillery. The troubles began when the UN general assembly would not affirm the boundaries for the new state's borders. The only hope for true peace lies in persuading Jews and Arabs to find common ground in some of the partition proposals that were put to the United Nations last November.

Prime Minister David Ben-Gurion

President Chaim Weizmann

JANUARY–JUNE

World Events

JAN The Union of Burma is proclaimed an independent republic in jubilant celebrations.

MAY In South Africa, David F. Malan of the segregationist Nationalist Party becomes the new prime minister.

MAY In Hungary, the Social Democrats and the Communists merge to form the Hungarian Workers' Party.

JUN In the US, the Selective Service Act requires all men aged 18 to 25 to register for military duty.

Entertainment

JAN UK actress Vivien Leigh stars in the romantic film drama *Anna Karenina*.

FEB The celebrated Soviet film director Sergei Eisenstein dies of a heart attack at the age of 50.

JUN World heavyweight champ Joe Louis knocks out Joe Walcott to retain his title in the US.

JUN US poet T. S. Eliot, who wrote *The Wasteland*, is awarded the Nobel Prize for literature.

Innovations

FEB The UK General Certificate of Education (GCE) comes into use.

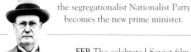

DAVID F. MALAN

JUN US scientist A. E. Mirsky discovers ribonucleic acid (RNA) in human chromosomes.

JUN Record producer Columbia introduces the first long-playing commercial vinyl records.

LONG-PLAYING RECORD

JUN Scrabble, the word game devised by architect Alfred Mosher Butts, is launched in the US.

1948

Blockade beaten

JUNE 30

An armada of aircraft is being assembled to feed the starving citizens of the Western-occupied zones of Berlin, the German capital. Since the end of the war Germany has been divided into four zones, each run by one of the victorious Allies. Berlin, which lies deep in the heart of the Soviet zone of Germany, is also divided into four zones. Since 1945, relations between the Soviet Union and the West have grown worse. On June 23 the Soviet army blocked all road and rail links. The first supply plane flew into the besieged city four days ago, and now 200 aircraft are flying in daily, delivering 2,500 tons of much-needed food.

ACTION PAINTING

US artist Jackson Pollock has shot to fame with "action" paintings such as *Alchemy*. This unique artist does not use a brush and palette. Instead, he fixes his canvas to the floor and drips paint all over the surface in huge, sweeping patterns.

A US plane carrying supplies lands in the German capital, Berlin

Tito breaks with Stalin

JULY 1

Marshal Tito is determined to prevent the Soviet Union from gaining control over Yugoslavia. Outraged, Soviet leader Josef Stalin expelled Yugoslavia from the Soviet-controlled Cominform (the international organization of communist parties) three days ago. The Yugoslavs have rallied around Tito to face the threat of an economic blockade and invasion.

Marshal Tito

JULY–DECEMBER

AUG The Republic of South Korea is proclaimed in Seoul with Syngham Rhee as president.

JUL King George VI of the UK opens the first post-war Olympic Games in London, UK.

JUL The world's first turbine-propeller aircraft, the UK Vickers *Viscount*, makes its maiden flight.

THE BICYCLE THIEF

SEP Communist leader Kim Il Sung proclaims the People's Republic of North Korea in Pyongyang.

NOV Vittorio de Sica's latest film, *The Bicycle Thief*, is praised by the film critics in Rome, Italy.

NOV Edwin Herbert Land's Polaroid camera proves very popular with the US public.

SEP Count Folke Bernadotte, the UN mediator in Israel, is assassinated there by Jewish terrorists.

NOV US actor Gene Kelly stars as D'Artagnan in the film *The Three Musketeers*.

DEC In the US, Richard and Maurice McDonald open a drive-in hamburger cafe.

McDONALD'S DRIVE-IN

DEC Seven Japanese officials are hanged in Tokyo following conviction as war criminals.

NOV Norman Mailer's war novel *The Naked and the Dead* is published.

DEC In Switzerland, Georges de Mestral invents Velcro, a new clothes fastener.

1949

Nato alliance forged

MARCH 18

Agreement has today been reached among western European countries and the United States to form a new military alliance to deter the threat of a Soviet attack. The alliance is to be called the North Atlantic Treaty Organization (NATO) and is being described by US officials as an "antidote to fear." The final agreement will be signed by leaders of the 12 countries next month. However, some commentators fear that it will polarize the world into two armed camps.

Hamlet takes five Oscars

MARCH 24

It was *Hamlet*'s night at the Academy Awards ceremony in Los Angeles, where the film scooped five Oscars. The British actor Laurence Olivier won Best Actor for his role of Hamlet in a film he also directed.

Italian champs perish in air crash

MAY 4

Italian soccer fans are in a state of shock tonight after hearing the tragic news that the whole Torino soccer team has been wiped out by a horrific plane crash. The team was on its way back from a tour of Portugal when the plane they were flying in crashed into the 2,631-ft (802-m) high Mount Superga on the outskirts of Turin in Italy. Thirty people are believed to have lost their lives in the disaster. The all-conquering Torino soccer team was on the verge of winning an amazing fifth successive league championship.

Remains of the plane carrying the Italian team

AUTOMATIC ROBOT

This amazing new Japanese robot is sure to appeal to children of all ages. It has a spring-and-gear motor that allows it to walk by itself. It is made of aluminum and has a humanoid appearance. Toy makers are predicting that robots will be one of the most popular toys this Christmas.

JANUARY– JUNE

World Events	JAN Race riots between Indians and Africans in South Africa result in 106 deaths.	FEB Army leaders in Argentina try to force Eva Perón out of public life, but Juan Perón threatens to resign as president.	APR The newly proclaimed independent Republic of Ireland leaves the UK Commonwealth.	JUN President Truman tries to calm anti-communist hysteria in the US, which was fueled by "loyalty" investigations.
Entertainment	JAN The first TV Emmy awards are presented in Los Angeles.	FEB German Jews protest at the Berlin premiere of hit film *Oliver*, accusing it of being antisemitic.	FEB Arthur Miller's provocative new play *Death of a Salesman* premieres in New York City.	MAR US boxer Joe Louis, nicknamed the "Brown Bomber," retires as the world heavyweight champion.
Innovations	JAN New "micro-groove" 45-rpm records are invented in the US.	MAR US air force pilots complete the first nonstop, round-the-world flight in *Lucky Lady II*.	APR The first Telethon is held in the US with Milton Berle staying on air for 14 hours to raise money for charity.	MAY The first heliport, a landing pad specially made for helicopters, is installed in New York.

SCENE FROM *OLIVER*

DEATH OF A SALESMAN

1949

Adenauer is new German chancellor

MAY 23

First results of the German election indicate that Dr. Konrad Adenauer has won the race to be first chancellor of the Federal Republic of Germany. The new state, made up of the American, French, and British zones of occupation, but not the Soviet zone, will come into being tomorrow. In recent months a constitution has been agreed that provides for a federal form of government and, remembering the recent atrocities of the Nazis, has built-in safeguards against the abuse of human rights.

Mao proclaims new republic

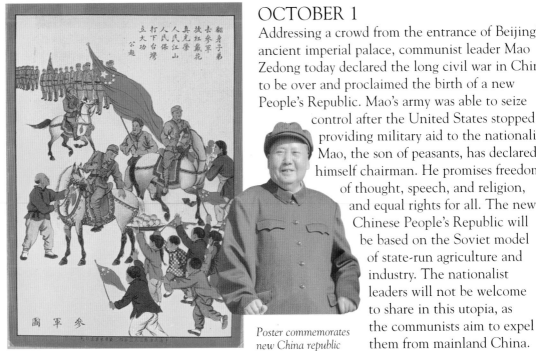

Poster commemorates new China republic

OCTOBER 1

Addressing a crowd from the entrance of Beijing's ancient imperial palace, communist leader Mao Zedong today declared the long civil war in China to be over and proclaimed the birth of a new People's Republic. Mao's army was able to seize control after the United States stopped providing military aid to the nationalists. Mao, the son of peasants, has declared himself chairman. He promises freedom of thought, speech, and religion, and equal rights for all. The new Chinese People's Republic will be based on the Soviet model of state-run agriculture and industry. The nationalist leaders will not be welcome to share in this utopia, as the communists aim to expel them from mainland China.

Peace in Greece

OCTOBER 16

For Greeks the horrors of war are finally over. The civil war that broke out when the Germans pulled out in 1944 has today ended. With aid from the United States, the Greek government has now defeated the communist-controlled guerrillas in their strongholds in the mountains. However, the many atrocities committed by both sides have left Greeks bitterly divided.

JULY–DECEMBER

JUL The Pope declares that any supporters of communism will be excommunicated from the faith.

SEP The USSR tests its first atomic bomb to the alarm of the US as well as that of western Europe.

OCT Soviet premier Joseph Stalin sets up a communist German state in the Soviet-controlled zone of that country.

DEC A total of 124,245 Germans are reported to have crossed over the border from East to West Germany this year.

JUL George Orwell's novel about the dangers of totalitarianism, *Nineteen Eighty-Four*, sells out in UK bookshops.

SEP Spy thriller *The Third Man*, starring Orson Welles, wins the Grand Prix at the Cannes Film Festival.

NOV A UK report shows that television is becoming more popular than movies.

DEC US film *On the Town*'s song *New York, New York* is a big hit.

JUL Silly Putty is accidentally discovered by a US chemist while working on silicon compounds.

NINETEEN EIGHTY-FOUR

JUL "Three-stripe" running shoes with molded rubber soles are launched in Germany by Adidas.

JUL UK engineers develop the De Havilland *Comet* jet airliner, the world's first jet airliner.

MAIDEN FLIGHT OF COMET JET

NOV The first disposable diapers, called Paddipads, go on sale in the UK.

1950

Atom spy jailed

MARCH 6

Scientist Klaus Fuchs, sentenced to 14 years in prison this month for passing vital atomic secrets to the USSR, has made further confessions about his Soviet contacts. Western intelligence services are now broadening their operation to uncover the spy network through which the secrets were betrayed.

Atomic secrets spy Klaus Fuchs

War breaks out in Korea

JUNE 25

At dawn today the communist People's Republic of North Korea launched a surprise invasion of the Republic of South Korea with the intention of unifying the Korean peninsula. It is expected that the United Nations security council will condemn the North Koreans and call for them to withdraw. Prior to the invasion, huge numbers of refugees had fled from the communist regime in the North across the 38th parallel of latitude. This marks the border between the two states and follows the line that divided the occupying forces of the Soviet Union and the United States at the end of World War II. The Soviet troops withdrew from the North only last year, and a US military government was in control of the South until 1948. It seems highly likely that both the Soviet Union and the US will become involved in this new conflict.

Korean refugees

US beats England 1–0

Soccer shocker

JUNE 28

The US beat the English at their own game – their national game, that is – in the first round of World Cup soccer in Brazil. The English put up a good fight, but the US bested them 1–0 at the Belo Horizonte stadium.

JANUARY–DECEMBER

World Events

JAN Under Jawaharlal Nehru's leadership, India becomes the world's largest democratic republic.

JUN In Canberra, Australia, Prime Minister Menzies promises a 3,000-strong force to support US troops in Korea.

SEP Jan Smuts, the former Boer guerrilla leader and renowned South African statesman, dies at the age of 80.

SEP A United Nations force led by General MacArthur lands at Inchon in South Korea in an attempt to recapture Seoul.

Entertainment

JAN Carol Reed's film *The Third Man* premieres in the UK.

FIRST CREDIT CARD

APR Soviet ballet dancer and choreographer Vaslav Nijinsky dies in London, UK, at age 60.

AUG US swimmer Florence Chadwick swims the Channel in 13 hours 23 mins, beating the women's record.

NOV Irish dramatist and critic George Bernard Shaw, author of the play *Pygmalion*, dies at the age of 94.

Innovations

FEB Diners' Club credit cards are launched in the US by Ralph Schneider.

JUN The first human kidney transplant is performed by US surgeon R. H. Lawler.

JUL The production of television sets in the UK has increased by 250% in a single year.

JAN SMUTS DIES

OCT In London, UK, the Bowler family celebrates the centennial of that UK institution, the bowler hat.

1951

Genius machine

JUNE 14

Two brilliant engineers from the US, John Eckert and John Mauchly, have invented the most advanced digital computer to date. It has been named UNIVAC (Universal Automatic Computer), and it can read 7,200 digits per second. UNIVAC uses in the US Census Bureau in Philadelphia where it will be used for processing vast amounts of data. It will completely change the business-machine industry.

magnetic tape to put in information (input) and take out information (output). Unlike its forerunners, this computer can handle both numbers and alphabetical characters equally well. UNIVAC has been installed

UNIVAC, the world's first commercial computer

The new United Nations headquarters in New York City are being made ready for the first session next year. Building work began in 1947 and was completed in 1950. The modern skyscraper was designed by an expert international committee of architects led by Wallace Kirkman Harrison.

Hero for a new generation

JULY 16

One of this season's most original books is *The Catcher in the Rye*, by US writer J. D. Salinger. The novel's hero is a troubled but funny prep-school drop-out who is called Holden Caulfield. He gives his own account of a series of events that led to him "cracking up." The story follows Holden on a two-day trip to New York where he observes the adult world around him with a mixture of innocence and irony. Holden's opinion of grown-ups – he thought they were all a bunch of "phonies" – and his behavior may prove controversial. But this is a book that speaks of teenage alienation with insight and understanding, and it seems certain to become a favorite with the younger generation.

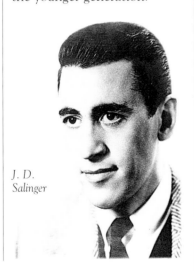

J. D. Salinger

JANUARY–DECEMBER

JAN United Nations forces repel a joint Chinese and North Korean offensive near the 38th parallel.

MAY Soviet Mikhail Botvinnik retains his world chess crown at the chess championships in Moscow.

JAN The celebrated German automobile engineer Ferdinand Porsche dies at the age of 76.

US TESTS A-BOMB

APR US President Truman fires commander of the UN forces General MacArthur after he threatened to invade China last month.

JUL Ace Argentine race car driver Juan Fangio wins the victor's laurels at the European grand prix in France.

APR The US Atomic Energy Commission begins A-bomb tests in the Nevada desert.

MAY People of color are removed from the electoral register in South Africa, and therefore cannot vote.

AUG New York's WCBS-TV broadcasts a baseball game in color for the first time.

AUG Deutsche Grammophon launches the first 33 rpm long-playing record.

PORSCHE AT UK MOTOR SHOW

NOV One million South Koreans are reported to have died since the onset of the Korean War in 1950.

DEC East Germany turns down an invitation to take part in the 1952 Olympics.

OCT The Porsche, the first German car exhibited in the UK since the war, is a huge success.

1952

Teenage tennis champion wows Wimbledon

JULY 5

A determined young Californian, Maureen Connolly, has won the prestigious Wimbledon women's singles tennis title in her first attempt, at the age of only 17. In the final, Connolly gradually wore down her opponent, fellow American Louise Brough, with her steady backhand and sure groundstrokes. She won in straight sets – 7–5, 6–3. With this victory "Little Mo," as she is known to her fans, becomes the youngest All-England champion since 15-year-old Lottie Dodd won in 1887. Having taken the US women's singles title at the age of 16, Little Mo seems certain to dominate the world of tennis for years to come.

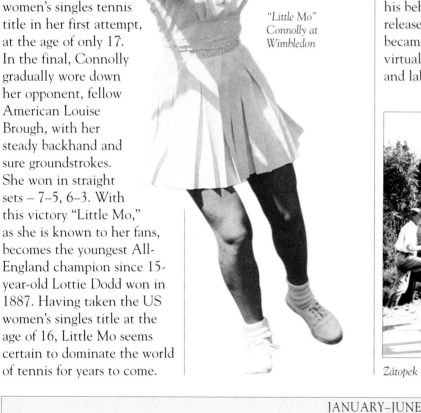

"Little Mo" Connolly at Wimbledon

Evita is dead

JULY 26

Eva Perón, the charismatic wife of Argentine president Juan Perón, has died of cancer at the age of 33. As Argentina's first lady, she provided a unique and glamorous figurehead. She was adored by the poverty-stricken "descamisados," or "the shirtless ones," whose rights she championed. To them, she was known simply as "Evita." Before she got married to labor minister Perón, Eva worked as an actress, and her dramatic talents proved a great asset. In 1945 when her husband was arrested for treason, she made an impassioned radio broadcast for the workers to rise up on his behalf. He was quickly released. When Juan Perón became president, Eva virtually ran the health and labor ministries and succeeded in winning the vote for women, legalizing divorce, and improving education. But Eva had her critics. Many held her at least partly to blame for the corruption and brutality of her husband's regime.

Eva Perón

Three Olympic golds for Czech

JULY 27

At the 15th Olympic Games in Helsinki, Finland, this week an amazing 29-year-old Czechoslovakian runner has stunned everyone. Emil Zátopek has won the 5,000 meters, the 10,000 meters, and the marathon in record times, earning the nickname the "Czech Express"!

Zátopek (left) during the marathon

JANUARY–JUNE

World Events	FEB King George VI of the UK dies at age 56 and Princess Elizabeth accedes to the throne.	MAR Dr. Kwame Nkrumah is elected as prime minister of the Gold Coast, the first African prime minister south of the Sahara.	APR US President Truman signs a peace treaty with Japan to mark the official end of World War II in the Pacific.	JUN In South Africa, blacks, Indians, and mixed race peoples begin a nonviolent campaign against apartheid.
Entertainment	JAN The Indian International Film Festival, the first festival of its kind in India, opens.	MAR A dazzling new musical, *Singin' in the Rain*, starring singer and dancer Gene Kelly, opens in Hollywood.	MAR UK actress Vivien Leigh wins an Oscar for her role in the hit film *A Streetcar Named Desire*.	MAY René Clément's moving film about the effects of war on two children, *Jeux Interdits*, opens in Paris, France.
Innovations	MAR An artificial heart valve is first used in an operation in Philadelphia.	MAR Two USAF *F-84 Thunderjets* make the longest sustained jet flights from the US to Germany.	MAY UK airline BOAC begins the first jet passenger service from the UK to South Africa.	JUN The USS *Nautilus*, the world's first nuclear-powered submarine, is launched in the US.

PRIME MINISTER NKRUMAH

OSCAR WINNER VIVIEN LEIGH

1952

US tests H-bomb

A vast mushroom cloud rises over Eniwetok Atoll in the South Pacific

NOVEMBER 1

According to eyewitness accounts, a small island off Eniwetok Atoll in the South Pacific Ocean has been obliterated in a US nuclear test explosion. Radioactive dust rose in a huge cloud 25 miles (40 km) high and 100 miles (160 km) wide over the test site. The blast is believed to have been caused by a new kind of weapon called a hydrogen bomb, or H-bomb. It is a thermonuclear device powered by a fusion reaction, rather than the fission reaction of the atom bomb.

This devastating superbomb explodes with a force that is an incredible 500 times greater than the atom bomb that destroyed the Japanese city of Hiroshima at the end of World War II. Many atomic scientists, such as Robert Oppenheimer and Enrico Fermi, are opposed to the idea of the H-bomb. It is believed that Soviet scientists will soon produce their own H-bomb. When both the superpowers, the United States and the Soviet Union, are equipped with such weapons, a war in the future will be a terrifying prospect.

Nobel Peace Prize for noble doctor

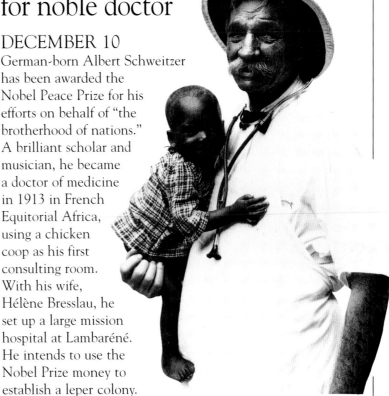

DECEMBER 10

German-born Albert Schweitzer has been awarded the Nobel Peace Prize for his efforts on behalf of "the brotherhood of nations." A brilliant scholar and musician, he became a doctor of medicine in 1913 in French Equitorial Africa, using a chicken coop as his first consulting room. With his wife, Hélène Bresslau, he set up a large mission hospital at Lambaréné. He intends to use the Nobel Prize money to establish a leper colony.

Albert Schweitzer in Africa

MONTESSORI EXPERIENCE

The pioneering educator Dr. Maria Montessori died this year at the age of 82. She opened her first school in 1907, and designed an educational system aimed at helping children develop their intelligence and independence. She wrote several books, including *The Montessori Method*, and her schools are now established all over Europe.

JULY – DECEMBER

JUL After his abdication, King Farouk of Egypt, the "playboy king," sails out of Alexandria in his luxury yacht.

JUL US film actor Gary Cooper stars in the popular moralistic Western *High Noon*.

SEP *This is Cinerama*, the first film in wide-angle Cinerama, is shown in New York City.

KING HUSSEIN OF JORDAN

AUG Still a schoolboy, Crown Prince Hussein becomes king of Jordan when his father is pronounced too ill to rule.

SEP In the US, actor Charlie Chaplin is investigated as a communist sympathizer.

NOV A Swedish Airways plane is the first passenger airliner to fly over the north pole.

OCT The UK declares a state of emergency in Kenya as Mau Mau terrorist attacks increase in the fight for independence.

NOV New Greek opera singer Maria Callas wins warm ovations in the UK for Bellini's *Norma*.

NOV In Cyprus, archaeologists discover a 2,000-year-old mosaic depicting Homer's tale *The Iliad*.

BRAZILIAN COFFEE BEANS

DEC In Brazil, the government forms a Coffee Institute to increase the national output of coffee.

NOV The *New Musical Express* publishes the first singles record chart in the UK.

NOV *Bwana Devil*, a 3-D film where lions "leap" from the screen, opens.

MOVIES OF THE FIFTIES

BEFORE THE 1950S movie theaters were the only places where people could watch moving pictures. Then television arrived. As more families bought television sets, film companies had to find bigger and better attractions to tempt viewers to leave their living rooms. TV programs were broadcast in black and white on small screens, so movie companies developed new "wide-screen" techniques like Cinerama and CinemaScope. In brilliant color, with stereophonic soundtracks, wide-screen movies promised "real-life" action. Perhaps the strangest movie device of all was Smell-o-vision, for which scents were pumped into the theater.

Drive-in movies
By the end of the 1950s there were 4,000 drive-in movie theaters in the open air throughout the United States. As many as 2,000 cars in curved rows could face the large screen, and small speakers were placed inside each car for sound.

Rockin' soundtrack
In 1955 *The Blackboard Jungle*, a film about rebellious teenagers, opened and closed with the song *Rock Around the Clock* by Bill Haley and the Comets. Young audiences went wild when it was played and soon many of the new "teen" genre movies were featuring rock 'n' roll soundtracks.

3-D movies
One of the craziest film gimmicks was 3-D movies. Audiences had to wear special glasses to get the 3-D effect, which made the action appear to burst from the screen. In 1952, the US adventure film *Bwana Devil* promised "a lion in your lap."

3-D VISION GLASSES

Childhood fantasy
The Red Balloon is a French fantasy film about a little boy who is followed through Paris by a friendly red balloon. When jealous schoolfriends pop his balloon, all the balloons of Paris converge upon the boy and lift him up to the sky. This charming tale won the Oscar for best original screenplay in 1956.

THE RED BALLOON

ROY ROGERS

Saturday matinees
Movie theaters put on special Saturday morning shows for children that were hugely popular in the days before most people had televisions. The programs featured animal characters such as Lassie the dog and Champion the Wonder Horse, and cowboy heroes like Roy Rogers and his horse Trigger. Many theaters also held child talent contests during the intermission.

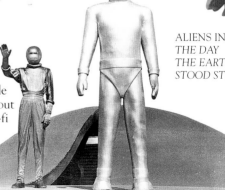

Science fiction
Although films about invaders from outer space and robots were popular, they were made with small budgets and without big-name actors. Some sci-fi films of the Fifties carried a serious message. The alien invaders in *The Day the Earth Stood Still* (1951) came to warn the Earth about the dangers of modern warfare.

ALIENS IN *THE DAY THE EARTH STOOD STILL*

GODZILLA

Big-budget epics

Wide-screen blockbusters were a feature of the 1950s, with their lavish sets, expensive all-star casts, and thousands of extras. *Ben Hur* (1959), a big-budget epic about a Roman gladiator, showed how successful they were when it won 11 Oscars.

CHARLTON HESTON STARS IN *BEN HUR*

Glassy eye

Special effects

Fantasy films like the Japanese feature *Godzilla* used special effects to create amazing screen monsters. They thrilled movie audiences in the Fifties, but today they look clumsy and almost comical alongside modern computer-generated images.

Fishlike mouth

Molded rubber mask

Webbed hands with sharp claws

Scaly suit made up of different sections

Fins

THE CREATURE FROM THE BLACK LAGOON

Marine monster

The Creature from the Black Lagoon (1954) featured a weird amphibious monster. The script was tacky, but the stunning underwater photography and convincing half-man, half-fish creature drew in large audiences.

171

1953

Death of a dictator

MARCH 5

Joseph Stalin, the leader of the Soviet Union for almost 30 years, has died from a brain hemorrhage at the age of 73. In 1917, Stalin was involved in the communist takeover of czarist Russia, led by Lenin and resulting in the creation of the Soviet Union. Although Lenin later found him "rude and uncomradely," Stalin swiftly rose to power when Lenin died in 1924.

Stalin's series of "five-year plans" helped modernize the vast country, and during World War II, he established the Soviet Union as a world power. He also created a totalitarian state, crushing all opposition. Stalin ("man of steel") was also nicknamed "Uncle Joe," showing that his people regarded him as both dictator and protector.

The body of Stalin lying in state in the Hall of Columns, Moscow

STEPPING OUT

Spike heels, or stilettoes, are all the rage with fashionable women. However, these elegant, ultra-high heels have their drawbacks – the wearer looks delightfully sophisticated until she gets them caught in a sidewalk grating!

Charlie Chaplin in exile

APRIL 17

Charlie Chaplin, the brilliant movie star and director, will never return to the US, his home for more than 40 years. Last fall, when he left his adopted country to promote the film *Limelight*, British-born Chaplin was banned from returning because he was suspected of supporting communism. Chaplin has surrendered his reentry permit, protesting bitterly that he has been the object of "vicious propaganda."

Scientists discover the key to life

The scientists with their DNA helix

APRIL 25

Francis Crick and James Watson, two scientists at Cambridge University in the UK, have unlocked one of the mysteries of life. They have discovered the structure of DNA, the chemical that makes the genes that pass on hereditary characteristics. The DNA molecule is made up of two intertwined strands – a double helix. Scientists can now figure out how living things reproduce themselves.

JANUARY–JUNE

World Events	JAN Yugoslav communist leader Josip Broz, known as Tito, is elected president of Yugoslavia.	FEB Flooding in Holland leaves more than 1,000 dead after dikes burst, and nearly 300 drown in the UK's east coast flood.	APR UN and communist prisoners-of-war are swapped at Panmunjon, Korea, but the war continues.	JUN Egypt is proclaimed a republic after army leaders depose King Fuad, infant son of ex-king Farouk.
Entertainment	JAN US country singer Hank Williams dies of a heart ailment at the age of 29.	FEB French actor Jacques Tati stars in *Monsieur Hulot's Holiday*, a film about an accident-prone bachelor.	MAR Soviet composer Sergei Prokofiev, whose works included *Peter and the Wolf*, dies at age 61.	MAY US writer Ernest Hemingway wins a Pulitzer Prize for his book *The Old Man and the Sea*.
Innovations	JAN The UK grounds all *Stratocruiser* aircraft after finding an engine defect.	FEB US film company Twentieth Century Fox announces the advent of wide-screen CinemaScope.	MAR US virologist Dr. Jonas Salk successfully tests a vaccine against the disease polio.	MAY US architect Frank Lloyd Wright receives a National Institute of Arts and Letters medal.

YUGOSLAV PRESIDENT TITO

COMPOSER SERGEI PROKOFIEV

1953

Peak pioneers

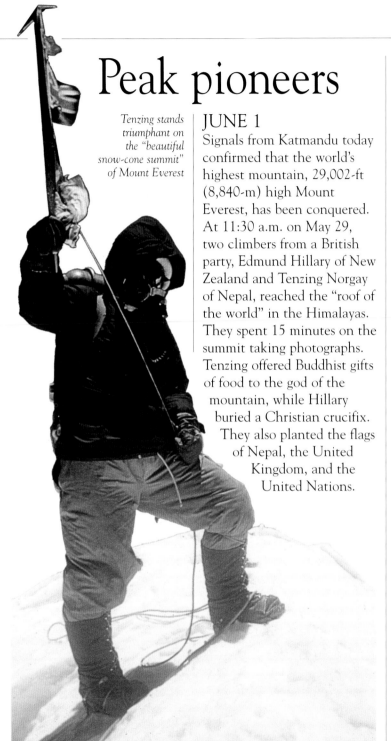

Tenzing stands triumphant on the "beautiful snow-cone summit" of Mount Everest

JUNE 1

Signals from Katmandu today confirmed that the world's highest mountain, 29,002-ft (8,840-m) high Mount Everest, has been conquered. At 11:30 a.m. on May 29, two climbers from a British party, Edmund Hillary of New Zealand and Tenzing Norgay of Nepal, reached the "roof of the world" in the Himalayas. They spent 15 minutes on the summit taking photographs. Tenzing offered Buddhist gifts of food to the god of the mountain, while Hillary buried a Christian crucifix. They also planted the flags of Nepal, the United Kingdom, and the United Nations.

A new Elizabethan era begins

JUNE 2

A new Elizabethan age began when Queen Elizabeth II of Great Britain was crowned today in Westminster Abbey, London. She succeeded to the throne last year on the death of her father King George VI. Millions of television viewers all over the world watched the coronation service as the new 27-year-old queen pledged herself to the service of her people in Great Britain and the Commonwealth.

Rebel leader

Marlon Brando in Laslo Benedek's The Wild One

DECEMBER 30

Rebel teenagers have a new hero – the leather-clad biker played by Marlon Brando in a new film *The Wild One*. The film follows the story of a motorcycle gang that descends on a small Californian town and wreaks havoc. Brando is the tough but sensitive gangleader Johnny, who when asked what he is rebelling against replies, "What've you got?"

JULY–DECEMBER

JUL The Korean armistice is signed at Panmunjom after three years of fighting and the loss of over two million lives.

JUL *Gentlemen Prefer Blondes*, a US film musical starring Jane Russell and Marilyn Monroe, opens.

SEP The first film in wide-screen CinemaScope, *The Robe*, premieres in Hollywood.

KOREAN ARMISTICE

AUG More than 1,000 are reported dead in Greece's Ionian islands after they are hit by earthquakes and huge tidal waves.

JUL US golfer Ben Hogan wins his third golf masters tournament in one year.

AUG Soviet prime minister Georgi Malenkov claims the USSR has the H-bomb.

AUG The shah flees Iran after a failed attempt to topple the nationalist leader Mohammad Mossadegh.

NOV Fiery Welsh poet Dylan Thomas dies at the Chelsea Hotel in New York at the age of 39.

NOV The US Bell *X-1A* rocket-powered plane flies at more than 1,600 mph (2,560 km/h).

NOV French soldiers capture Dien Bien Phu in Vietnam from the communist Viet Minh forces.

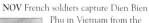

YETI FOOTPRINT

DEC UK PM Winston Churchill wins Nobel Prize for literature for his historical works.

DEC A UK-led expedition sets out to find the legendary yeti in the mountains of Nepal.

1954

New vaccine

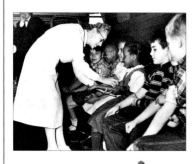

APRIL 12

The first vaccine against polio, a disease that affects thousands of children, is being tested on nearly one million children in the United States. Dr. Jonas Salk made the breakthrough after discovering that polio is caused by a virus. He hopes that the disease will now be wiped out.

SUPER-FAST FLYER

Mercedes has used race-track technology to make a new high-speed supercar, the 300SL *Gullwing*. With its roof-hinged "gullwing" doors open, it looks like a bird. It can fly along at a top speed of 140 mph (225 km/h).

Roger Bannister wins the battle to smash the four-minute mile barrier

Bannister breaks four-minute barrier

MAY 6

Just under one hundred years ago, the world record for running the mile stood at four minutes 55 seconds. No one thought it could be run in under four minutes. But today in Britain an athlete finally achieved the impossible. Roger Bannister, a 25-year-old medical student, ran a mile in three minutes 59.4 seconds at Oxford. Some experts had feared that the enormous exertion might kill him. Bannister survived, but said afterward that he was actually "prepared to die."

Beleaguered French troops at Dien Bien Phu

French defeated in Vietnam

MAY 7

The Vietnamese came closer to throwing off French rule today. Vietnam is a part of France's empire in Indochina but, since 1945, communist rebels known as the Viet Minh have been fighting to win back control of their own land. After a 55-day siege, they have now captured the strategically placed French fortress of Dien Bien Phu. This defeat may end French efforts to hold on to Indochina.

JANUARY–JUNE

World Events	JAN President Eisenhower of the US proposes that the vote be given to all 18-year-olds in the country.	APR UK security forces in Kenya mount the biggest round-up of Mau Mau terrorist suspects in the 18-month-old state of emergency.	MAY The government of Thailand offers bases to Western countries from which to fight communism in Southeast Asia.	JUN US President Eisenhower says he will prevent Senator McCarthy from investigating the CIA for communist infiltrators.
Entertainment	JAN Marilyn Monroe marries ex-baseball player Joe DiMaggio.	APR Frank Sinatra, star of the US film *From Here to Eternity*, wins an Oscar for best actor.	APR One of two famous brothers who pioneered film, Auguste Lumière dies in Lyon, France, at age 91.	JUN Mississippi-born singer Elvis Presley records his first single, *That's All Right Mama*.
Innovations	JAN The US launches the first nuclear-powered submarine, *Nautilus*. **FIRST NUCLEAR SUBMARINE**	JAN The first electronic computer is put into regular operation by a UK business.	MAR The Japanese crew of the *Lucky Dragon* suffers radiation sickness after US H-bomb tests at Bikini Atoll. **FILM PIONEER LUMIERE**	JUN The tomb of Pharaoh Sankhet, which dates from 2750 BC, is uncovered at Sakkara in Egypt.

1954

Segregation in the southern states – separate water fountains for blacks and whites

On the road to racial equality

MAY 17
A major step toward racial equality was made today in the United States. The Supreme Court overturned an 1846 law that stated that education could be "separate but equal." The new ruling means it is now illegal for black children to be barred from white schools. At present, 2.5 million black pupils in the southern United States are educated in poorly equipped schools, separated from white children.

Inside the Obninsk atomic power station

First atomic power station

JUNE 27
The world's first atomic power station opened today at Obninsk in the Soviet Union. The nuclear reactor can generate 5 megawatts of electricity, enough for a town of 5,000 people. It proves that nuclear energy can be used for beneficial purposes.

McCarthy's witch-hunts over

DECEMBER 2
US senator Joseph McCarthy was today condemned by the Senate for misconduct. For four years his opponents have been awaiting such a verdict, and they hope it will mean that McCarthy's spell over the American people has finally been broken. Since 1950 McCarthy has been waging a campaign to root out communist "spies and infiltrators" in the state department and, more recently, the army. Lacking hard evidence, McCarthy's committees have relied upon whispers and rumors to back up their accusations. This has led to an uncontrolled wave of anticommunist hysteria – "reds under the bed" have been suspected everywhere from Hollywood to the White House. Now it is possible that McCarthy's rule of terror may at last be over.

Senator McCarthy, left, challenges US army chiefs

JULY–DECEMBER

JUL In Geneva, it is agreed that Vietnam will be divided along the 17th parallel, with the communists controlling the north.

AUG The UN officially withdraws from Korea, one year after the ceasefire was signed at Panmunjon.

SEP Over 1,000 people are feared dead, and an estimated 36,000 are homeless, as a huge earthquake hits Algeria.

DEC In South Africa, the prime minister Johannes Strijdom calls for the imposition of stricter apartheid laws.

SEP World heavyweight boxer Rocky Marciano beats Ezzard Charles for his 47th consecutive victory in the US.

NOV French painter Henri Matisse, one of the leaders of the colorful Fauvist art movement, dies at age 84.

DEC US writer Ernest Hemingway, author of *A Farewell to Arms*, wins the Nobel Prize for literature.

DEC UK runner Roger Bannister retires from athletics to devote himself to his medical practice.

AUG UK firm Rolls-Royce announces it has developed a vertical takeoff jet, nicknamed the "Flying Bedstead."

HENRI MATISSE

NOV A Scandinavian airline begins the first passenger flights to the US over the north pole.

NOV The US National Cancer Institute claims a link between cancer and cigarette smoking.

AUTHOR ERNEST HEMINGWAY

DEC The USS *Forrestal* is the first aircraft carrier to be built that has an angled flight deck.

1953 MINIATURE "MATCHBOX"
CARS BECOME AN INSTANT HIT

1955 COLORFUL MODELING CLAY
FOR CHILDREN IS DEVELOPED

1957 THE "FLYING SAUCER"
FRISBEE IS RELEASED

FIFTIES TOYS AND GAMES

IN THE 1950S mass production and the introduction of plastic meant that children were able to choose from a wider range of toys than ever before. Alongside more traditional toys such as tin-plated cars and board games, cheap plastic novelty toys such as the hula hoop, the fluorescent yo-yo, and the Frisbee became runaway successes and developed into the latest fads. One of the most popular mass-produced toys was the Barbie® doll, the first ever "fashion model" doll, with a wardrobe of different outfits. At only $3, the fashion dolls were not expensive, and over 350,000 of them were sold in the first year alone. Once toy manufacturers realized the potential of this fast-growing market, the race was on to find the next worldwide craze.

To keep the hoop spinning, you have to swivel your hips

Hoop mania

Wooden hoops originated in Australia, but when a plastic version of them was launched in the United States in 1958, 25 million were sold in four months. Everyone wanted a plastic hoop and the craze soon spread worldwide.

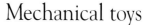
FRICTION-DRIVEN
TOY CAR

TIN-PLATE
MOTORCYCLIST

Mechanical toys

In the 20 years after World War II, Japanese toy manufacturers mass-produced imaginative and inexpensive toys for children that sold all over the world. They pioneered the use of plastic, but also made a wide range of tin-plate cars, trains, motorcycles, and space vehicles. Some of them had built-in battery-operated mechanisms that enabled them to perform noisy special effects.

The changing face of the Barbie® doll

FIRST EVER
BARBIE, 1959

ENCHANTED
EVENING BARBIE, 1961

LIVE ACTION
BARBIE, 1971

DAY TO NIGHT
BARBIE, 1985

ULTRA HAIR
BARBIE, 1993

Tiny trucks

Miniature motor vehicles that were inexpensive to make and buy became very popular in the 1950s. Japanese firms pioneered the use of plastic, but also manufactured a wide range of tinplate replicas of cars, semitrailers, pick-up trucks, and backhoes that were so desirable that even adults began collecting them!

1958 HOOP CRAZE TAKES OFF ON
BOTH SIDES OF THE ATLANTIC

1958 PLASTIC BUILDING BLOCKS BY
LEGO ARE HUGELY POPULAR

1959 NEON-COLORED PLASTIC
YO-YOS ARE ALL THE RAGE

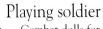

Playing soldier

Combat dolls for boys to play with became popular from the early 1950s onward. The US GI Joe came with a range of outfits and military accessories. He was closely related to Action Man (shown here) of Britain, Combat Joe of Japan, and Falcon of Brazil. These new toy soldiers soon became household names, and millions were sold each year throughout the world.

Stick-on insignia

Disk made of molded plastic

TOY
ROCKET
SHIP

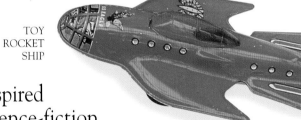

Inspired science-fiction

The real-life space race between the United States and the Soviet Union began in 1957, but even before that people were fascinated with outer space and UFOs. Fantasy toys like ray guns, rocket ships, and flying saucers were much in demand. Just like now, toys and other merchandise were often specially produced to tie in with popular cartoon characters and futuristic films and TV shows.

Acrylic plastic bubble

Flying objects

Flying disks became one of the biggest fads of the 1950s. These plastic toys were controlled with a flick of the wrist and became an instant success on beaches and in city parks. The first world champion was crowned in 1968.

Flashing light adds a new dimension

X-7

FLYING
SAUCER WITH
FLASHING LIGHTS

1955

Charlie Parker

Einstein's time is up

APRIL 18

One of the world's greatest scientists, Albert Einstein, died today in Princeton, NJ, his home since 1933. He was 76 years old. Einstein, born in Germany, was the founding father of modern physics. His revolutionary theory of relativity changed the way scientists thought about time and space, and his equation, $E = mc^2$, was the key to the development of nuclear energy. Einstein was a modest, philosophical man who loved classical music. Although his discoveries led to the creation of the atomic bomb, he was a leading campaigner for world peace.

Albert Einstein

Good-bye to all that jazz

MARCH 12

One of the leading talents of modern jazz, Charlie "Yardbird" Parker, has died in the US at the age of only 34. The self-taught alto saxophonist from Kansas City changed the way jazz is played. In the early 1940s he helped create a new music style called "bebop" with other young jazz musicians such as Dizzy Gillespie. Parker will be remembered for his inspired improvisations.

Keeping her cool?

JUNE 13

Publicity posters for Marilyn Monroe's new movie *The Seven-Year Itch*, which opened last week, have been creating quite a stir. The 29-year-old screen goddess is shown standing over a grating, her skirt billowing in an uprush of air from the subway. Pressure from the League of Decency forced Loew's State Theater in New York City, to remove its giant poster.

Marilyn "blows off steam" in New York City

JANUARY–JUNE

World Events	**FEB** Nikita Khrushchev emerges as the new leader of the USSR, replacing Georgi Malenkov.	**MAR** Floods in New South Wales, Australia, kill 200 people and 300,000 sheep, and leave 44,000 people homeless.	**MAY** The Warsaw Pact is signed by all the communist countries of eastern Europe to form a new military alliance.	**MAY** The Allied high commission, which has held sovereignty since the war, abolishes itself and gives sovereignty to West Germany.
Entertainment	**MAR** French fashion designer Christian Dior's spring collection introduces the A-line skirt.	**MAR** US actor Marlon Brando wins an Oscar for his performance as Terry Molloy in the film *On the Waterfront*.	**JUN** In France, three cars plow into the crowd at the Le Mans race track, killing 80.	**JUN** US high jumper Charles Dumas is the first person ever to clear 7 ft (2 m).
Innovations	**JAN** RCA demonstrates a new music "synthesizer" in New York City.	**JAN** The WHO (World Health Organization) says that atomic waste poses a serious health risk.	**JAN** In the UK, archaeologists confirm that fossilized "Piltdown Man" was a complete hoax.	**JUN** Kanchenjunga in the Himalayas, the highest unclimbed peak, is conquered by a UK team.

DIOR'S NEW A-LINE

CHARLES DUMAS

1955

Disney's wonderland

JULY 18

The world has never seen anything like it. Famous US filmmaker Walt Disney has fulfilled his dream of creating a "Never-Never Land" for children. His trail-blazing amusement park, called Disneyland, opened today in Anaheim, near Los Angeles. It is divided into three different realms called Fantasyland, Adventureland, and Frontierland. Visitors can take a ride on a Mississippi riverboat, experience the Wild West, sail in a pirate galleon, or fly through a Moonscape. Over five million people from around the world are expected to visit this magical kingdom every year.

THE SHARK
Citroën has launched its futuristic new car, the Citroën DS Décapotable. Nicknamed "the Shark" because of its sleek nose, the DS is stylish and practical, with semi-automatic gears.

Talented actor dies young

SEPTEMBER 30

James Dean, the US actor whose good looks and cool style quickly made him one of Hollywood's hottest stars, has died in a car crash outside Los Angeles. He was only 24. Dean's performance as a teenage rebel in his first film, *East of Eden*, was highly acclaimed. Two more movies, *Rebel Without a Cause* and *Giant*, have yet to be released.

James Dean, who lived too fast and died young

Flying saucers – no evidence

Photograph of an Unidentified Flying Object, or UFO, in Nevada

OCTOBER 25

Whatever science-fiction writers and filmmakers might say, there are no such things as flying saucers – and that's official. The US air force has just concluded an eight-year-long investigation into the UFO phenomenon and has found no evidence to suggest the existence of any alien spacecraft in our skies.

JULY–DECEMBER

JUL The first East-West heads of government meeting since 1945 takes place in Geneva, Switzerland.

JUL French cyclist Louison Bobet becomes the first man to win the Tour de France three times.

JUL The world's most eminent scientists sign a declaration condemning nuclear warfare.

LOUISON BOBET

SEP In Buenos Aires Juan Perón is overthrown and General Eduardo Lonardi becomes provisional president of Argentina.

JUL Turkish-born UK oil magnate Calouste Gulbenkian dies, leaving millions for art and charity.

JUL UK's Donald Campbell is the first to exceed 320 km/h (200 mph) in his turbo-jet hydroplane *Bluebird*.

NOV After terrorist attacks and the breakdown of talks between the UK, Greece, and Turkey, a state of emergency is declared in Cyprus.

JUL Canadian swimmer Marilyn Bell, aged 17, is the youngest person to swim the Channel.

SEP In the UK, MG Cars unveils a popular new sports model, the MG-A.

MARILYN BELL

DEC The United Nations admits 16 new countries as members, although it bars Mongolia and Japan.

AUG Nobel prize-winning German novelist Thomas Mann dies in Switzerland.

OCT In the UK the BBC demonstrates color TV at Alexandra Palace, London.

1956

US bus boycott

Mrs. Rosa Parks sits in the whites-only section of a bus in Montgomery, Alabama

FEBRUARY 29

In the state of Alabama, the fight for full civil rights for black people continues. Late last year the Interstate Commerce Commission ordered that black citizens should be able to sit wherever they choose on public transportation. However, Rosa Parks, a black woman living in Montgomery, Alabama, has been arrested for sitting at the front of a bus in a section still set aside for whites. After her arrest, black protesters in Montgomery organized a bus boycott and 115 of them were also jailed. Now huge crowds, supported by civil rights leader Dr. Martin Luther King, Jr., are demanding an end to any kind of "segregation."

Movie star Grace Kelly becomes a real-life princess

APRIL 19

Today on the French Riviera, a fairy-tale marriage was celebrated in front of more than 1,000 guests. The groom was Prince Rainier III, ruler of the tiny principality of Monaco. His bride was Grace Kelly, the US movie star famous across the world for her "iceberg beauty." Guests at the Catholic ceremony included dignitaries from 25 nations, and countless others watched the event on television. Grace Kelly, the young star from Philadelphia, has appeared in 11 films, and won an Academy Award for best actress in 1954 for her role in *The Country Girl*. As a real-life princess she intends to retire from her acting career. From now on her face will be appearing on postage stamps, not in publicity photographs.

Prince Rainier and Princess Grace marry

FROM THE HEART

Emil Nolde, the great German Expressionist painter, has died. Nolde was fascinated by primitive art and the use of rich colors to show emotion. This led him to paint many dramatic pictures.

JANUARY–JUNE

World Events

JAN The Sudan, Africa, is declared an independent republic, ending the joint Anglo-Egyptian administration.

FEB The US and UK governments sign a declaration warning developing countries against Soviet aid.

MAR Pakistan is proclaimed an Islamic republic, with Major-General Iskander Mirza its first president.

MAR Soviet leader Khrushchev denounces Stalin as a brutal and criminal murderer in a speech to the Communist Party elite.

Entertainment

JAN UK author A. A. Milne, famous for his stories about Winnie-the-Pooh, dies at age 74.

A. A. MILNE'S CHARACTER EEYORE

JAN The seventh winter Olympic Games open with a flourish in Cortina d'Ampezzo in Italy.

APR US world heavyweight boxing champion Rocky Marciano retires after 49 fights and 49 wins.

JUN Austrian conductor Herbert von Karajan becomes the artistic director of the Vienna State Opera.

Innovations

JAN The UK Astronomer Royal dismisses the idea of space travel as "ridiculous."

APR In Chicago, Illinois, a device that records TV programs onto tape is first demonstrated.

MAY The US drops an H-bomb from a plane for the first time, over Bikini Atoll in the Pacific.

ROCKY MARCIANO RETIRES

MAY In France, Teflon Co. markets a Teflon-coated frying pan as the first nonstick kitchenware.

1956

Suez Canal seized

JULY 26

Serious trouble is brewing in Egypt. The president, Colonel Gamal Abdel Nasser, has seized control of the Suez Canal, which runs through his country. Opened in 1869 and controlled by an Anglo-French company, the 103-mile (165-km) long waterway is vital for carrying Middle Eastern oil supplies through Egypt to Europe. Colonel Nasser aims to build a high dam at Aswan with the money the canal generates. His seizure of the canal comes after the United States and Britain refused to fund the project. The Egyptian people seem to have approved their president's actions. As for the outraged British and French, he says that they can "choke to death on their fury." The two countries will now have to decide what action to take.

The Egyptian sphinx whips the British lion and the French hen at Suez

Perfect pitching

OCTOBER 8

Sports history was made in the United States today, during the fifth game in the baseball World Series. Don Larsen, pitching for the New York Yankees against the Brooklyn Dodgers, tossed the first-ever perfect game, stopping every Dodger batter from reaching first base.

New York Yankees pitcher Don Larson, throwing the only perfect game in history

Uprising in Hungary

A captured Soviet tank flies the Hungarian flag in Budapest

OCTOBER 26

Since 1946 Hungary has been part of the Soviet Union's communist empire. Now, in the capital Budapest, rebels have destroyed the huge bronze statue of Stalin, and many thousands have died fighting with Soviet forces stationed in Hungary. Prime Minister Imre Nagy has sympathy for the rebels, but Soviet troops are said to be amassing on the Hungarian border with East Germany.

Screen goddess

NOVEMBER 28

French actress Brigitte Bardot is the beautiful star of the new film *And God Created Woman*, directed by her husband Roger Vadim. Her sensual character has shocked Hollywood, but Vadim says she is simply a liberated and beautiful young woman.

Bardot in And God Created Woman

JULY–DECEMBER

SEP The USSR and Japan agree to end their state of war, in place since World War II, and to restore full diplomatic relations.

AUG German dramatist Bertolt Brecht, whose work included *The Threepenny Opera*, dies in Berlin at age 58.

AUG The first large-scale atomic power station, at Calder Hall in England, begins generating.

ELVIS PERFORMS LIVE ON TV

OCT In Egypt, Anglo-French forces bomb the Suez Canal area after the UN calls for a ban on the use of force by its members.

SEP In the US, Elvis Presley performs live on the Ed Sullivan Show, viewed by 82% of the potential audience.

SEP US air force pilot Kincheloe flies a Bell X-2 rocket airplane to an altitude of 125,907 ft (38,376 m).

NOV Anglo-French forces move into Egypt and seize control of the Suez Canal zone from the Egyptians.

SEP The Bill Haley film *Rock Around the Clock* causes rebellious British teenagers to riot.

OCT Clarence Birdseye, inventor of a process for deep-freezing food, dies in the US.

UN TROOPS MOVE INTO EGYPT

NOV The UN imposes a ceasefire on the Anglo-French allies and sends troops into Egypt to control the canal.

NOV Italy has the greatest number of movie theaters in Europe – more than 17,000.

NOV Work begins on an engineering marvel – the Kariba High Dam in Rhodesia.

ROCK 'N' ROLL

BILL HALEY

IN THE MID-1950S a new kind of music sprang into being in the United States. Fast, loud, and upbeat, it became known as rock 'n' roll. Rock had its roots in the styles of black Americans playing rhythm-and-blues and white musicians playing country and western. Rock 'n' roll became somewhat respectable in 1957 when Amercian Bandstand, hosted by Dick Clark, hit the television airwaves. No one had ever heard anything like it before. The exciting dance tunes with outrageous-sounding lyrics appealed to teenagers who worshiped screen rebels like James Dean and Marlon Brando. Rock 'n' roll offered a whole new approach to life, with crazy dances, hip language, and its sense of being young and modern.

Rock pioneer

With the Comets, Bill Haley hit the big time in the US with *Rock the Joint*, and became an international rock icon.

ELVIS PRESLEY

New grooves

A decade after World War II, the United States was enjoying an economic boom and young people had money to spend. Manufacturers began to target the growing teenage market – selling goods like portable record players that could be played in bedrooms, away from the family living room!

Star singles

During the 1950s, singles were released on cheaper, smaller vinyl disks that played at 45 rpm (revolutions per minute). They were a much better value than the heavier 10-in (25-cm) 78 rpm records, and teenagers bought them in the thousands.

ORIGINAL 45 OF
JAILHOUSE ROCK
BY ELVIS

CHUCK BERRY

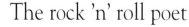

The rock 'n' roll poet

Chuck Berry developed a distinctive rock 'n' roll style from his rhythm-and-blues roots. He merged hard-driving, chiming guitar sounds with lyrics that spoke about the joys and trials of being young in the 1950s. Songs like *Sweet Little Sixteen* and *Johnny B. Goode* influenced many later musicians.

The King

The sheer excitement of Elvis Presley's mid-1950s hits – *Heartbreak Hotel, Jailhouse Rock, Teddy Bear,* and *All Shook Up* – was matched only by the sensational way he performed them live. He was unlike any other white American singer because he "sang black" with emotion and verve. Elvis swung his hips and curled his lip in a way that captured the hearts of millions of teenage girls, but outraged their parents.

Rock 'n' roll style

Rock 'n' roll was about style as well as music. You had to look good if you played, or even if you were simply listening. The coolest men wore their hair brushed up away from their foreheads and held it in place with greasy haircream.

WURLITZER JUKEBOX

Jumping jukeboxes

During the 1930s in the United States live music in roadhouses known as "juke joints" gave way to coin-operated machines offering a wide choice of records to play. By the 1950s these "jukeboxes" were hugely popular, particularly with teenagers. *Billboard* magazine's Hot 100 singles chart, launched in 1958, was based on both record sales and the number of jukebox plays.

LITTLE RICHARD

The wild man

"Awopbopaloobopawopbamboom!" shrieked Little Richard in his first big hit *Tutti Frutti,* in 1956. His acrobatic antics at the piano thrilled his audiences, and more frenzied hits followed such as *Long Tall Sally* and *Good Golly Miss Molly.* But, in 1957 Little Richard suddenly gave up rock 'n' roll music to become a church minister. He later returned to the stage to sing gospel.

ELECTRIC GRETSCH GUITAR 1959

"Pickups" amplify vibrations from the strings

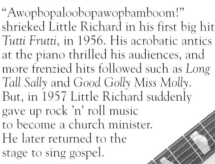

Volume control

BUDDY HOLLY

Electric guitar

Rock 'n' roll music depended heavily on the electric guitar. With its unlimited volume and its power to produce a whole range of new sounds, it revolutionized popular music.

Hit writer

Buddy Holly was one of the greatest rock 'n' roll songwriters. Between 1957 and 1959, he had seven hit singles, some with his group the Crickets and some as a solo performer. Songs like *Peggy Sue* became instant classics. The world was stunned when he died in a plane crash in 1959, at the age of 22.

Tremolo arm to vary pitch

1957

An ace for Althea

JULY 6

US tennis player Althea Gibson wrote herself into the record books this week by becoming the first black woman to win the most coveted prize in tennis – the singles title at Wimbledon, England. In the final she beat Darlene Hard 6–3, 6–2 and has played the whole tournament without dropping a single set. Thirty-year-old Gibson began her tennis career playing paddle tennis on the streets of Harlem, New York, in the United States. She is the first black player to win a major tennis tournament.

*Wimbledon winner
Althea Gibson*

Composer Leonard Bernstein

West Side hit

SEPTEMBER 26

West Side Story, an exciting new musical by US composer Leonard Bernstein and the lyricist Stephen Sondheim, opened today on Broadway in New York. An updated version of the very popular Shakespeare play *Romeo and Juliet*, it is a moving love story set in New York's rough gangland.

A WAY WITH WORDS

US writer Dr. Seuss has found a brilliant way to interest children in reading. His new book, *The Cat in the Hat*, uses only 175 simple words, but is written in comic verse. It tells of an anarchic cat who tries to persuade two children that they want to have "lots of good fun that is funny."

Five-time champion

AUGUST 4

Argentinian race driver Juan Manuel Fangio has done it again. In West Germany, the 46-year-old, nicknamed "Cheuco" ("bandy legs"), has won his 24th grand prix race, picking up his fifth world championship in seven years.

Driving for Maserati, he broke the lap record by a staggering 11 seconds at the Nurburgring race track. Fangio thrilled the 200,000 spectators by coming from behind to win. He is the most successful Formula 1 driver there has ever been.

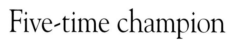

JANUARY–DECEMBER

World Events

JAN In the UK, Harold Macmillan becomes prime minister when Sir Anthony Eden resigns.

MAR Six nations – France, West Germany, Italy, Belgium, Holland, and Luxembourg – set up the European Common Market.

AUG After 170 years of UK rule, Malaya achieves its independence and elects its first president, Abdul Rahman.

SEP Dr. François Duvalier, popularly called "Papa Doc" by the people of Haiti, is elected president of that country.

Entertainment

JAN US film star Humphrey Bogart, tough but cool hero of over 50 movies, dies at 57.

MAY US star Burt Lancaster is legendary lawman Wyatt Earp in the film *Gunfight at the OK Corral*.

AUG US comedian Oliver Hardy, the plump half of the comedy duo Laurel and Hardy, dies at age 65.

SEP Finnish composer Jean Sibelius, probably most famous for his Seventh Symphony, dies at age 91.

Innovations

JAN Danish architect Joern Utzon is chosen to design the Sydney Opera House, Australia.

HAROLD MACMILLAN

AUG The "Drunkometer," which measures the amount of alcohol on the breath, is tested in the US.

OCT The USSR launches *Sputnik 1*, the first artificial satellite to go into space.

"PAPA DOC" TAKES OVER HAITI

NOV A dog called Laika is the first animal to be sent into space aboard the Soviet spacecraft *Sputnik II*.

1958

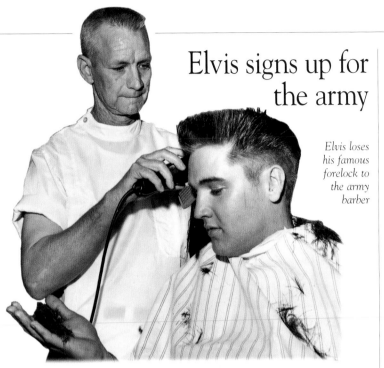

Elvis signs up for the army

Elvis loses his famous forelock to the army barber

MARCH 24

Elvis Presley was today drafted into the US Army for his national service. His call-up was postponed so that he could finish filming *King Creole*. The 23-year-old singer will serve for two years, and see his monthly earnings of $100,000 drop to just $83.20!

President de Gaulle

DECEMBER 21

The former wartime leader General Charles de Gaulle was today elected president of France by an overwhelming majority. The French hope that de Gaulle's talents as a politician will again steer France through a difficult period – this time the country seems to be on the brink of civil war over the fraught question of Algerian independence. French settlers in Algeria are determined to keep the colony under their control, but de Gaulle is hoping for a compromise with the Algerian nationalists. He will be president of France for the next seven years.

Brazilian magic

JUNE 29

The Brazilian soccer team has won the sixth World Cup, beating the host nation, Sweden, 5–2 in the final. The Brazilians played dazzling soccer throughout the whole competition, particularly 17-year-old prodigy Pelé, whose sensational goal-scoring seemed unstoppable.

17-year-old soccer star Pelé

MAY In Algeria, 40,000 French settlers riot against the French government's deal with the Algerian Nationalists.

JAN In France the first collection of 23-year-old couturier Yves St. Laurent is a great sucess.

JAN The US launches its first satellite, *Explorer I*, from the launch pad at Cape Canaveral in Florida.

THE GERMAN PLANE CRASH

JUN Greek-Cypriot leader Makarios rejects the UK peace plan for Cyprus; clashes with the Turkish-Cypriots on the island continue.

FEB Eight of the UK Manchester United soccer team are killed in a plane crash in Germany.

AUG US nuclear submarine *Nautilus* makes the first undersea voyage beneath the North Pole.

JUL King Faisal II, the crown prince, and Iraq's prime minister are murdered in an army coup and a republic is established.

MAR West Indian cricketer Gary Sobers scores a record 365 runs playing against Pakistan.

OCT The USSR agrees to lend money to President Nasser of Egypt to build the Aswan Dam.

CRICKETER GARY SOBERS

JUN Two years after the Hungarian uprising, Former Hungarian Prime Minister Imre Nagy is executed, causing much anger.

AUG Australian runner Herb Elliot breaks two world records for the mile and 1,500 meters.

DEC The world's largest oil tanker, able to carry 1,021,000 barrels, is launched in Japan.

1959

New leader for Cuba

JANUARY 2
Following a coup on the Caribbean island of Cuba, President Fulgencio Batista has fled to the Dominican Republic. Since 1952 Batista has run Cuba as a police state, favoring the interests of the wealthy elite at the expense of ordinary citizens. In 1956 his opponents began to make guerrilla attacks from the mountains. Known as "los barbudos" ("the bearded ones"), they were led by a young lawyer named Fidel Castro and his second-in-command, Ernesto "Ché" Guevara. Now the small band of guerrillas has become a national movement. In yesterday's coup, Castro rode triumphantly into the capital, Havana. The new regime is to have a president, Dr. Manuel Urrutia, but it seems that Castro will be Cuba's premier. Hopes are high that this revolution will transform life for ordinary Cubans.

Fidel Castro, the new revolutionary leader of Cuba

CUDDLY TEDDIES?
Many teenagers have a new and distinctive style. The notorious "Teddy Boys," who have a reputation for gang fights, are named for their long, Edwardian-style drape jackets, stovepipe pants, crêpe-soled shoes, and slicked-back hair.

The Dalai Lama flees Tibet

APRIL 19
The Dalai Lama, Tibet's Buddhist spiritual leader, is safe at last. Since 1950 the Chinese have ruled Tibet, and have dealt brutally with recent Tibetan attempts to regain independence. The Dalai Lama was smuggled out of Lhasa, Tibet's capital, at the end of March. He traveled over the mountains by yak, avoiding Chinese patrols, and has found sanctuary in India. Today 7,000 Tibetans gave him a rousing welcome at the West Bengali town of Siliguri before he set off to meet the Indian prime minister, Mr. Nehru.

The Dalai Lama, a fugitive in India

JANUARY–JUNE

World Events

JAN Alaska becomes the 49th, the largest, and the most northerly state of the United States.

MAR More than 3,000 people are reported dead after a hurricane hits the island of Madagascar off the east coast of Africa.

APR Cuban Revolutionary leader Fidel Castro says the US can keep its naval base at Guantanamo Bay.

JUN In Dublin, 76-year-old Eamon de Valera, three times prime minister of the Republic of Ireland, becomes president.

Entertainment

JAN Cecil B. de Mille, famous for his Hollywood biblical epics, dies at age 77.

CECIL B DE MILLE

FEB US rock 'n' roll singer Buddy Holly dies at age 22, in a plane crash in Iowa, traveling to a performance.

MAR Marilyn Monroe, Jack Lemmon, and Tony Curtis star in the US film *Some Like It Hot*.

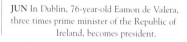

SOME LIKE IT HOT

MAR US writer Raymond Chandler, creator of detective Philip Marlowe, dies at age 70.

Innovations

JAN The Soviet *Lunik I* spacecraft flies past the Moon into orbit around the Sun.

APR The St. Lawrence Seaway linking the Great Lakes to the Atlantic Ocean opens in the US.

APR US architect Frank Lloyd Wright, master of innovative building design, dies at age 89.

MAY The UK's Jodrell Bank radio telescope transmits radio messages to the US via the Moon.

1959

New miniature car is launched

AUGUST 18

In the United Kingdom, the British Motor Corporation is launching a very innovative small car. The new Morris Mini looks just like a box on wheels, but in fact it has been carefully designed by Alec Issigonis to be both practical and cost-effective. By placing the four small wheels at the corners and mounting the engine sideways, Issigonis has created a surprising amount of space inside. The car also sits very low on the road.

The great quiz show scandal

Van Doren apparently pondering on air

NOVEMBER 2

The hugely popular US TV quiz show *Twenty-One* is today at the center of a national scandal. The current champion of the quiz show, Professor Charles Van Doren, has admitted that he had won $129,000 dishonestly – he had been shown the answers in advance. The former champion Herbert Stempel was so upset at being ousted in favor of Van Doren that he spilled the beans.

Antarctica is saved

DECEMBER 1

Only last year "the last great journey in the world" was completed when a small expedition led by the English explorer Vivian Fuchs traveled across the frozen continent of Antarctica. Now the South Polar region is in the news again as 12 countries, including the United States and the Soviet Union, sign a historic international agreement not to claim any part of it for themselves. Military bases there are to be banned, as are nuclear experiments and the dumping of nuclear waste. But the scientists of all nations will be allowed free access to the frozen continent to carry out research into the climate and geology, as well as the wildlife of one of the world's last wildernesses.

An Antarctic king penguin

JULY–DECEMBER

AUG The volcanic islands of Hawaii in the central Pacific Ocean become the 50th state of the US.

JUL US singer Billie Holiday, one of the greatest voices of jazz, dies at age 44.

JUL Australian airline Quantas makes its first flight across the Pacific from Sydney to the US.

HAWAII BECOMES THE 50TH US STATE

SEP Ceylon's prime minister, Solomon Bandaranaike, dies from wounds after being shot by a Buddhist monk.

AUG US sculptor Sir Jacob Epstein, who lived most of his life in London, UK, dies at 79.

JUL In the UK, the hovercraft makes its first sea crossing between England and France.

NOV In Havana, Cuba, Major Ernesto "Ché" Guevara, Castro's right-hand man, becomes head of the Cuban national bank.

SEP Soviet leader Khruschev is angry when, for security reasons, he cannot visit Disneyland on his US tour.

SEP The USSR's space probe, *Sputnik II*, scores the first direct hit on the surface of the Moon.

PRESIDENT MAKARIOS

DEC Archbishop Makarios, leader of the Greek Orthodox church, becomes first president of the new republic of Cyprus.

OCT UK actor Errol Flynn, famous for his swashbuckling roles in adventure movies, dies at age 50.

OCT The Soviet *Sputnik III* sends back the first-ever photographs of the dark side of the Moon.

THE LEISURE BOOM

By the mid-1950s many countries were finally recovering from the effects of World War II. Improved methods of mass production meant that luxury goods could be cheaply produced and more people than ever before could afford labor-saving devices such as vacuum cleaners and washing machines. This left extra time for recreational activities and the leisure industry boomed. As national economies prospered, people also found that they had more money to spend. A wide range of goods and services, from glossy magazines and portable record players to plastic toys and vacation packages, flooded the growing market of prosperous consumers.

Watersports

As more people spent time at the seaside, watersports took off. It was possible for many to take up exciting hobbies such as waterskiing.

Family vacations

Vacation camps were not new in the 1950s, but they became increasingly popular worldwide as more people could afford to take an annual vacation. Families stayed in cabins and took part in communal games, sports, and competitions.

Hairdryer hood

Home magazine

Taking five

By using labor-saving household appliances, 1950s housewives were able to take a breather more often. Shopping in the new supermarkets also helped them save time because they could make all their purchases under one roof. As a result, consumer goods such as magazines aimed specifically at women grew in number.

TWO WOMEN RELAX AT THE HAIRDRESSER'S

Leisurewear

Before the 1950s, there was no such thing as leisurewear. People wore the same kinds of clothes for both work and recreation. But, in the 1950s, people began to adopt more casual clothes for leisure pursuits. Blue denim jeans in particular became hugely popular throughout the world.

1955 DISNEYLAND THEME PARK
OPENS IN SOUTHERN CALIF.

1958 FIRST PASSENGER JETS SPEED
UP INTERNATIONAL TRAVEL

1958 WOMEN'S MAGAZINES
MULTIPLY AS READERSHIP GROWS

Sunshine holidays

In the 1950s, tourism became big business. Air travel was still expensive, but travel companies began to offer cheaper charter flights to overseas destinations. The Mediterranean coasts of France, Italy, and Spain attracted thousands of vacationers looking for cut-price vacations in the sun, and new resorts sprang up to cater to the growing numbers of tourists.

Sunglasses were a vital fashion accessory

Carefully groomed hair

On the beach

In glamorous resorts along the French Riviera, looking good on the beach was very important. A beach vacation often meant buying a whole new wardrobe of clothes. Boned-stiffened bathing costumes like this one were stylish without being too revealing.

Casual jacket

It's a strike!

Like movie theaters, dance halls, and bingo clubs, bowling alleys drew large numbers of people with time and money to spend. Bowling alleys encouraged families to visit by providing soft drinks and fast food, and from 1952, many alleys became mechanized, with machines replacing the pin-boys to reset the downed pins.

Soft-soled bowling shoes

Short skirt with rows of frills

BOWLING BALL

Chiffon scarf

Painted toenails

PINS

1960

Sharpeville massacre

The terrible scene at Sharpeville

MARCH 21

Today in South Africa, 69 people were killed and 186 left wounded in a deadly confrontation that will surely deepen the existing crisis there. The country's troubles stem from the South African government's racial policy, know as apartheid. This policy is intended to separate the black and white races and ensure the domination of the black majority by their white rulers. South Africa's white minority government has introduced laws that deny the black population many of their basic rights, and since 1956 only whites have been allowed to vote. Today's tragedy occurred in the black township of Sharpeville, in the Transvaal, when 15,000 blacks staged a demonstration against the "Pass Laws." These laws demand that blacks stay in their own areas, not traveling out of them without permission. When they saw the crowd approaching, local white police officers opened fire. Within minutes the scene looked like a battlefield, with bodies sprawled everywhere. Police commander Colonel D. H. Pienaar commented afterward, "If the natives do these things, they must learn their lesson the hard way."

CAPITAL OF HOPE
In April, the futuristic city of Brasilia became Brazil's new capital. Brasilia's apartment buildings have all been built in the same modern style to avoid any class distinction, and the congress is housed in impressive twin towers.

Champions of Europe – again!

MAY 18

It seems that wonder-team Real Madrid is unbeatable. The Spanish soccer stars have won the European Cup for the fifth year running. This time they beat West Germany's team Eintracht Frankfurt 7–3 in front of a spellbound crowd at Hampden Park in Glasgow, Scotland. Three of their goals were scored by Argentine star Alfredo Di Stefano. All the others were scored by the Hungarian Ferenc Puskas, nicknamed the "Galloping Major" by his teammates. It is said that Puskas uses his left foot to juggle the soap in the shower.

European Cup winners Real Madrid

Historic votes cast in Ceylon

JULY 21
The world has its first woman prime minister today. She is Ceylon's Sirimavo Bandaranaike, leader of the Sri Lanka Freedom Party, who won the country's general election yesterday with 75 seats out of a possible 150. Her rise to power has been swift. She entered politics last year after her husband, Solomon, the prime minister, was assassinated.

JANUARY–JUNE

World Events

JAN In Egypt, President Nasser lays the foundation stone of the Aswan High Dam as work begins.

MAR An earthquake, followed by a tidal wave and widespread fire, kills over 12,000 in the Moroccan resort of Agadir.

MAY Adolph Eichmann, the German SS officer who masterminded Hitler's "Final Solution," is captured by the Israelis.

JUN The UK- and Italian-ruled Somaliland territories gain their independence, uniting to form Somalia on July 1.

Entertainment

JAN Algerian-born French writer Albert Camus, author of *The Outsider*, dies at age 46.

FEB The eighth Winter Olympics opens in Squaw Valley, Calif., with a ceremony staged by Walt Disney.

MAR Joy Adamson's *Born Free*, the true story of Elsa, an African lioness, is published.

APR In the US, William Wyler's film *Ben Hur* wins a record eleven Oscars.

ALBERT CAMUS

Innovations

FEB Israeli archaeologists unearth 1,700-year-old biblical parchment scrolls.

MAR The Jodrell Bank Telescope in the UK contacts a US satellite 409,375 miles (655,000 km) away.

APR The first weather satellite, *Tiros 1*, sends pictures of the US from a height of 453 miles (724 km).

ELSA THE LIONESS

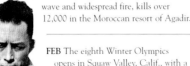

MAY The world's longest liner, the SS *France*, is launched in France by Mme. de Gaulle.

1960

The master of suspense

AUGUST 10

British film director Alfred Hitchcock certainly knows how to keep an audience on the edge of its seat. He believes that the greatest feeling of suspense comes when people know exactly what to expect – because then waiting for it to happen can drive them almost crazy. In his latest film *Psycho* trouble is plainly in store when Janet Leigh, playing a young secretary on the run with stolen money, checks into a strange, deserted motel. She eats dinner with the owner's son, twitchy Norman Bates (played by Anthony Perkins), then decides to take a shower before bed.... But to find out what happens you must wait in suspense until you see this chilling film yourself.

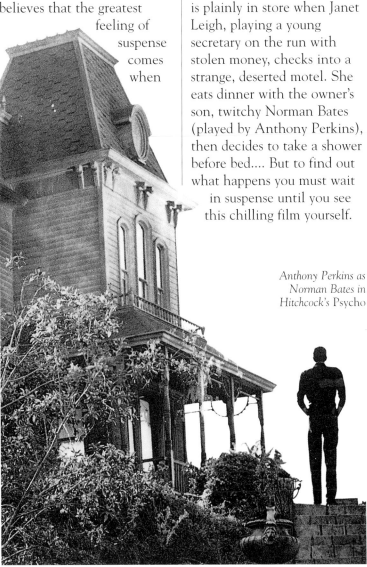

Anthony Perkins as Norman Bates in Hitchcock's Psycho

African man's marathon feat!

Abebe Bikila of Ethiopia

SEPTEMBER 10

Until now, no African athlete has ever won an Olympic gold medal in a track or field event. Today in Rome, the barefoot Ethiopian runner Abebe Bikila won the marathon in 2 hours 15 mins 16.2 secs.

Presidential debate live on TV

SEPTEMBER 26

In November this year the people of the United States will go to the polls to elect a new president. Tonight they were given an early chance to decide which way to vote – they were able to tune in to a special live debate between the Republican candidate Richard Nixon and his Democrat rival John F. Kennedy. The clash was fairly gentle but, while TV viewers were impressed by Kennedy's good looks and relaxed manner, listeners who heard the debate on the radio felt Nixon came out on top.

Kennedy and Nixon prepare to do battle

JULY–DECEMBER

JUL In the Congo, Africa, Colonel Mobutu leads the Congolese army into mutiny against incumbent President Lumumba.

JUL UK record-breaking driver, Donald Campbell, takes his new £1 million *Bluebird* car for its first test run.

JUL US submarine *George Washington* launches Polaris nuclear missiles for the first time.

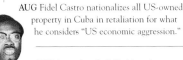

PATRICE LUMUMBA

AUG Fidel Castro nationalizes all US-owned property in Cuba in retaliation for what he considers "US economic aggression."

AUG Australian Jack Brabham becomes the new Formula 1 champion after winning the Portuguese grand prix.

AUG The US puts the world's first communications satellite *Echo 1* into orbit around the Earth.

OCT The UK's largest colony, Nigeria, gains its independence under Prime Minister Balewa, and joins the Commonwealth.

SEP US sprinter Wilma Rudolph, once a polio victim, wins an amazing three Olympic golds.

SEP Ten skeletons are discovered by archaeologists in 3,800-year-old graves at Stonehenge in the UK.

US ATHLETE WILMA RUDOLPH

OCT Thousands of people die in eastern Pakistan as the country is battered by a tidal wave and hurricane.

NOV A UK jury rules *Lady Chatterley's Lover*, a novel by D. H. Lawrence, not obscene.

OCT In the UK, Hawker Siddeley's *P.1227* vertical takeoff aircraft is tested.

1961

Youngest US president sworn in

JANUARY 20

In Washington today John Fitzgerald Kennedy was sworn in as the new president of the United States. At 43, he is the youngest man elected to the office, and he is also the first Roman Catholic. In his rousing ten-minute inaugural speech

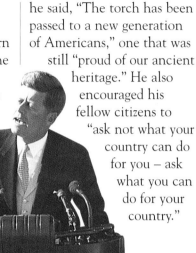

President Kennedy

he said, "The torch has been passed to a new generation of Americans," one that was still "proud of our ancient heritage." He also encouraged his fellow citizens to "ask not what your country can do for you – ask what you can do for your country."

Ham is the first chimp in space

JANUARY 31

In 1957 the Soviet Union put a dog into space and today the United States has sent up a monkey named Ham. The

Ham receives a well-earned apple

chimpanzee was blasted 150 miles (241 km) into space in a *Mercury* capsule for an 18-minute flight. After he had safely splashed down and was on board the recovery ship, Ham was given an apple as a reward for his successful performance in the operation. He is now heading back to Cape Canaveral in Florida, where experts from the space program are waiting to "debrief" him on his mission.

Bay of Pigs invasion

APRIL 19

The United States is suffering a serious blow to its pride over the prickly issue of Cuba. Relations between the small Caribbean island and its mighty neighbor have steadily worsened since Fidel Castro's revolutionaries seized power in 1959. Castro soon began moving smoothly toward a communist system of government, backed by the Soviet Union. Only two days ago, 1,500 Cuban exiles returned to the island to mount an invasion, which

they hoped would start an uprising against Castro. No US forces were involved, but they clearly supported the landing at the Bay of Pigs, an inlet on Cuba's coast 91 miles (145 km) southwest of the port of Havana. Now the invasion has failed, and US President Kennedy and Soviet premier Khrushchev have given each other blunt warnings not to interfere in Cuba's internal affairs. It seems almost inevitable that this island will cause trouble between the two powers.

Cuban anti-communist troops plan their attack

JANUARY–JUNE

World Events	**JAN** In New Delhi, India, the Russian Orthodox Church is elected to the World Council of Churches.	**MAR** The US government announces it is increasing aid to the Laos government in its fight against the Pathet Lao communists.	**APR** In New York, the UN votes 83–0 in favor of censuring South Africa for its racial policy of apartheid.	**JUN** Iraq lays claim to Kuwait after the UK officially ends its protectorate over the small oil-rich sheikdom in the Middle East.
Entertainment	**JAN** US novelist Dashiell Hammett, author of *The Maltese Falcon*, dies at age 66.	**MAR** UK conductor Sir Thomas Beecham, founder of the Royal Philharmonic Orchestra, dies.	**APR** South African golfer Gary Player wins the US masters championship by a single stroke.	**JUN** The leading male dancer with the Soviet Kirov Ballet, Rudolf Nureyev, defects in Paris, France.
Innovations	**JAN** In the UK, the one-millionth Morris Minor rolls off the production line. **DR. LEAKEY AND HIS DISCOVERIES**	**FEB** UK anthropologist Dr. Louis Leakey finds human fossils possibly one million years old in the US.	**APR** The USSR's Yuri Gagarin orbits the Earth, becoming the first man in space. **YURI GAGARIN, COSMONAUT**	**MAY** The US puts a man in space, and Kennedy claims that the US will be first to the Moon.

1961

A new wall divides Berlin

East Germans at work on the Berlin Wall

AUGUST 31

At the end of World War II British prime minister Winston Churchill spoke of an "Iron Curtain" dividing Europe. Today, a real-life network of concrete blocks and electric fences divides the city of Berlin. On August 13, the East German authorities began to build a huge wall separating East and West Berlin, to the anger of people living on both sides. Since Germany's postwar partitioning, two million Germans have fled from the hardships and political repression of communist East Germany into the West, mainly through Berlin. Now this route has been closed. But, even as the wall-builders block all the possible exit points that they can find, some refugees are still finding secret ways out. Two families have even swum across Berlin's canals to reach the West.

An East German soldier leaps through one of the last gaps in the Berlin Wall in a desperate bid for freedom

ELEGANT E-TYPE

Jaguar has unveiled its elegant and relatively inexpensive new E-type sports car to wide acclaim. The rapturous press reported that "E stands for exhilaration, excitement, [and] ecstasy."

WWF founded

The giant panda is the new emblem of the World Wildlife Fund

SEPTEMBER 11

The World Wildlife Fund was officially formed and registered as a charity today, with its headquarters on the northern shores of Lake Geneva in Switzerland. Its goal is to reverse and halt the destruction of the Earth's natural environment, and to help its human inhabitants live in greater harmony with nature. British ornithologist Max Nicholson and biologist Sir Julian Huxley have played major roles in bringing the fund into being. Its logo is a panda, a choice inspired by the recent arrival of the panda Chi-Chi at a British zoo.

JULY–DECEMBER

JUL Jomo Kenyatta is released after nine years of detention for his involvement with the Kenyan Mau Mau organization.

JUL US author Ernest Hemingway dies at the age of 61 from a self-inflicted shotgun wound.

JUL France launches a bathyscape to explore the 34,000-ft (10,363-m) Kurile Pit, an ocean chasm off Japan.

DAG HAMMARSKJÖLD

SEP Swedes take to the streets to mourn Dag Hammarskjöld, secretary-general of the UN, who died in a plane crash.

SEP Twenty-year-old US folk singer Bob Dylan inspires audiences in New York's famous Greenwich Village.

AUG The earliest surviving Roman mosaics in the UK are found at Fishbourne in southern England.

NOV In the USSR's de-Stalinization campaign, Lenin's mausoleum is reopened after Stalin's body is removed.

OCT Leonard Bernstein's 1957 Broadway musical *West Side Story* is made into a film in the US.

SEP US and UK governments call for a ban on all nuclear testing inside the Earth's atmosphere.

WEST SIDE STORY ON SCREEN

DEC In South Vietnam, James Davies has the dubious honor of being the first US soldier to be killed by Vietcong.

NOV James Thurber, the well-known US comic writer and illustrator, dies at the age of 66.

DEC US Lt. Col. Robinson flies a *Phantom II* at a record speed of 1,605.51 mph (2,583.75 km/h).

1962

Algeria independent

JULY 3

Today in a brief declaration, French president Charles de Gaulle "solemnly recognized" the independence of Algeria, bringing to an end a complex and bitter struggle that has been raging since 1954. The North African country began to come under French control in 1830. Subsequently many French colonists settled there, and after World War II any attempts to integrate Algeria more closely with France were resisted by the Algerians and French settlers alike. Recent terrorist activity

Algerians celebrate their independence

by both groups has made a peaceful solution unlikely, if not impossible. Now, after 132 years of French rule, the new republic of Algeria must work out its own destiny.

Marilyn Monroe found dead

Sad star Marilyn in her last film, The Misfits

AUGUST 5

Marilyn Monroe was found dead today by her housekeeper. She lay in bed with an empty bottle of sleeping pills nearby. The 36-year-old actress had recently been fired from the film she was working on for Twentieth Century Fox. In an article in this week's *Life* magazine, she said, "Everybody is always tugging at you. They would all like a sort of chunk of you."

POP ART

A startling new artistic style has emerged in New York City. "Pop art" borrows images from everyday life to make the viewer see them with a fresh eye. Andy Warhol's paintings of soup cans and Roy Lichtenstein's giant comic-strip cartoon frames are the new masterpieces of the genre.

A world where no birds sing

AUGUST 16

A new book by US marine biologist Rachel Carson could have a profound effect on the way we now live.

In *Silent Spring*, published today, she describes the side effects of the artificial pesticides that are commonly used on our farms and in our homes. Unless the use of these dangerous chemicals is strictly controlled, she warns, they will have a catastrophic effect on our environment. She asks us to imagine a time when no birds sing and the trees bear no fruit, and to change the way we live to prevent this from happening.

Scientist Rachel Carson

JANUARY–JUNE

World Events	**JAN** UK and US representatives walk out of talks about nuclear test ban treaties with the Soviet Union.	**FEB** As US fears mount about the stockpiling of missiles, President Kennedy imposes an embargo on the importation of Cuban goods.	**FEB** The OAS Secret Army of French settlers steps up its terror campaign in Algeria to prevent independence.	**MAY** Nazi war criminal Adolf Eichmann, former SS colonel, is executed 24 months after his capture by Israeli agents.
Entertainment	**JAN** New Zealander Peter Snell breaks the world mile record in 3 mins 54.4 secs.	**APR** In Hollywood, the film version of the hit musical *West Side Story* wins ten Oscars.	**JUN** In Chile, Brazil retains the soccer World Cup, beating Czechoslovakia 3–1.	**JUN** US singer Stevie Wonder, who is only 12 years old, hits the top of the charts in the US.
Innovations	**FEB** Astronaut John Glenn becomes the first American citizen to orbit the Earth.	**TELSTAR LAUNCHED**	**JUN** The first communications satellite, the US *Telstar I*, relays TV signals from space.	**JUN** In Paris, France, 130 men, women, and children die when an Air France Boeing 707 crashes.	**12-YEAR-OLD STEVIE WONDER**	**JUN** The European Space Research Organization is established in Paris, France.

1962

Licensed to kill

Scotsman Sean Connery as Bond

OCTOBER 1

A suave screen hero makes his debut today in *Dr. No*. Agent James Bond, code-named 007, is licensed to kill for the British secret service. Bond, played by Sean Connery, is based on the character created by Ian Fleming.

Khrushchev and Cuban leader Castro

Back from the brink of world war

OCTOBER 28

The world breathed a huge sigh of relief today as one of the most nerve-wracking weeks in history ended. Six days ago, US president John F. Kennedy announced that a US spy plane had spotted Soviet nuclear missile bases on the Caribbean island of Cuba, just 91 miles (145 km) from the coast of the United States. Since World War II the two superpowers have been competing for supremacy. When Castro's Cuba recently became a communist state, the Soviet Union took the opportunity to install nuclear weapons there – too close for comfort for President Kennedy. He immediately ordered a naval

Kennedy speaks to the press

blockade of the island and directed his armed forces "to prepare for any eventuality." The possibility of the world's first nuclear war loomed unless the Soviets agreed to remove the weapons. As the tension mounted, messages flowed between Kennedy and the Soviet premier Nikita Khrushchev. A US pilot flying over Cuba was shot down and killed. In nearby Florida 200,000 US troops stood ready. Finally, today, Kennedy promised to lift the blockade and not invade Cuba and, in return, Khrushchev agreed to remove the weapons.

Toy model of 007's Aston Martin with ejector seat

JULY–DECEMBER

SEP After a brief civil war and elections, ruling council president Ahmed Ben Bella proclaims Algeria a socialist republic.

OCT Amnesty International, an organization set up to investigate the abuses of human rights all around the world, is formed.

OCT US president John F. Kennedy states that the Soviet Union has missile bases on Cuba and imposes an arms blockade.

DEC President Kennedy lifts the Cuban arms blockade and says he favors an emergency phone link with the Kremlin.

AUG Nobel Prize-winning Swiss author Hermann Hesse, who wrote *Steppenwolf*, dies at age 85.

NOV *How the West Was Won*, a US film featuring a buffalo stampede and Indian attack, is filmed in Cinerama.

DEC John Steinbeck, US author of *Of Mice and Men*, wins Nobel literature prize.

DEC Gregory Peck stars in film *To Kill a Mockingbird*, about racism in the US.

AUG The tunnel linking France and Italy under Mont Blanc in the Pyrenees is completed.

SYMBOL OF AMNESTY INTERNATIONAL

AUG In the United States, the *Mariner II* space probe is launched toward Venus.

SEP In the UK, the world's first passenger hovercraft service completes a successful 3-month run.

HOVERCRAFT

DEC US space probe *Mariner II* sends back the first close-up pictures of the planet Venus.

1963

Soviets put first woman in space

JUNE 16

Valentina Tereshkova from the Soviet Union became the first woman to go into space today, at the age of just 26. Lieutenant Tereshkova orbited the Earth in the spacecraft *Vostok* 6 and, during the flight, spoke with the Soviet leader Nikita Khrushchev. He called her "Valya" and expressed his "fatherly pride" in her extraordinary achievement. The young cosmonaut grew up on a farm and worked in a tire factory and a textile mill before joining the Soviet space program. She is also an amateur parachute jumper in her spare time. In 1962, she was picked for the space training because of her dedication and obvious lack of fear.

Valentina Tereshkova ready for liftoff

THE WILD THINGS

Where the Wild Things Are is a new classic in the making from US children's author Maurice Sendak. The book's hero is plucky boy-rebel Max, whose brilliantly illustrated adventures with the "wild things" explore every child's anxieties and fantasies.

America dreams

AUGUST 28

Over 200,000 demonstrators marched through Washington, D.C. today to campaign for an end to discrimination against black people. Civil rights leader Dr. Martin Luther King, Jr., inspired the huge crowd with a speech advocating justice and equality through non-violent means. He declared, "I have a dream that one day this nation will rise up and live out the true meaning of its creed: 'We hold these truths to be self-evident: that all men are created equal.'"

Black civil rights leader Dr. Martin Luther King

JANUARY–JUNE

World Events

FEB Willy Brandt is reelected as mayor of West Berlin, Germany, with an overwhelming majority.

MAR John Profumo, the UK's secretary of war, claims "no impropriety" in his relationship with 21-year-old Christine Keeler.

MAY Jomo Kenyatta is elected Kenya's premier in the country's first general election, in the lead-up to independence.

JUN Pope John XXIII dies at age 81. Giovanni Battista Montini is elected as his successor, to be called Pope Paul VI.

Entertainment

FEB A tennis racket made of steel has been patented by Lacoste in France.

BEATLES SCORE A MASSIVE HIT

FEB UK group The Beatles releases its first album, named after the hit single *Please Please Me*.

APR David Lean's 1962 epic film *Lawrence of Arabia* wins seven Oscars, including Best Picture.

WORLD'S MOST EXPENSIVE FILM

JUN After cast and director changes, the most expensive film to date, *Cleopatra*, comes to the big screen.

Innovations

FEB In the UK, surgeons at Leeds Infirmary announce a successful kidney transplant.

MAR The first automatically controlled underground trains are introduced in London, UK.

MAY US astronaut Major Cooper lands in the Pacific after 22 orbits of the Earth in his *Mercury* capsule.

JUN A telephone hotline is set up for the first time between the White House and the Kremlin.

1963

Kennedy assassinated in Dallas

A nation mourns

NOVEMBER 25

Twenty-four hours after John F. Kennedy's suspected killer, Lee Harvey Oswald, was shot dead during a jail transfer, the United States president was buried at Arlington National Cemetery. Representatives of 93 nations came to pay their respects with the Kennedy family. After the service, John Jr., only three years old, saluted his father's coffin.

President Kennedy in the motorcade, moments before his death

Jackie Kennedy with the children at the funeral

NOVEMBER 22

"President Kennedy is dead." Those four bleak words are now echoing across a shocked world. John F. Kennedy, the 35th president of the United States, was shot in the head today as he was driven in a black convertible through Dallas, Texas. In a flurry of shots, the president slumped down in the car as his wife Jackie tried to help, cradling his head. He died in the nearby Parkland Memorial Hospital, only 25 minutes after receiving a terrible head wound. He was 46 years old. John Connally, the governor of Texas, was also wounded in the shooting, which turned a sunny day into the worst of nightmares. Connally's condition tonight is described as "serious." In the confusion following the shooting, police arrested Lee Harvey Oswald, a former US marine with recent Soviet contacts. Oswald strongly denies killing the president, but he is being treated as the prime suspect.

JULY–DECEMBER

AUG In the UK's greatest train robbery ever, £2.6 million in used banknotes is stolen from the Glasgow-to-London mail train.

SEP Scottish driver Jim Clark becomes the youngest Formula 1 auto champion.

JUL The first English Channel crossing by hydrofoil is made, between Ostend and London, UK.

**FRENCH SINGER
EDITH PIAF**

SEP Four young black girls are killed and 23 people injured when a bomb explodes in a church service in Alabama.

OCT French singer Edith Piaf, whose anthem was her song *Je Ne Regrette Rien*, dies at 74.

SEP In New Zealand, doctors give the world's first blood transfusion to an unborn child.

NOV A volcano erupts on the ocean floor, producing the new island of Surtsey off the south coast of Iceland.

OCT Jean Cocteau, the French playwright, artist, poet, and novelist, dies at age 74.

OCT In the UK, a model of the Anglo-French *Concorde* supersonic plane is displayed.

**SURTSEY, ICELAND'S
NEW ISLAND**

DEC In the northern Atlantic, 919 are saved from the blazing Greek liner *Lakonia*, but 117 are feared dead.

NOV UK author Aldous Huxley, who wrote *Brave New World*, dies at age 69.

NOV Viking remains found in Canada are dated 500 years before Columbus.

1964

Boxing baby beats champ

FEBRUARY 25

In one of sport's great upsets, 22-year-old US boxer Cassius Clay has beaten the champion Sonny Liston to win the world heavyweight title. Before the fight, 43 of 46 sports journalists predicted that Liston could not lose because Clay had fought professionally only 20 times. But Clay's confidence was sky-high. Claiming that Liston was "too ugly to be a world champion," he proved too quick and skillful for the older man, beating him in six rounds at Miami Beach.

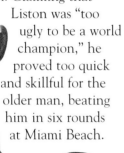

Cassius Clay, "The Louisville Lip"

Nelson Mandela

Life in prison for Mandela

JUNE 14

Three days ago, South African lawyer Nelson Mandela was sentenced to life imprisonment for sabotage and plotting to overthrow the government. Today he was taken from Cape Town to prison on Robben Island. Mandela is the leader of the banned ANC (African National Congress), which opposes the white South African government's racial policy of apartheid. His struggle to gain equality for the black population has won support the world over, and many condemn the sentence.

Equal rights at last

JULY 3

President Lyndon B. Johnson today signed the Civil Rights Act, the most far-reaching civil rights law in United States history. Black campaigners for racial equality, led by Dr. Martin Luther King, Jr., are at last achieving their goals. From now on, racial discrimination in workplaces, places of public accommodation, publicly owned facilities, and in union membership will be illegal. President Johnson, who comes from the South, where racial tension is high, has asked his people to "close the springs of racial poison."

President Johnson shakes hands with King after signing the bill

ALL-GIRL MAGIC

In two months the hottest girl group in the United States, The Supremes, has had two number-one hits there – *Where Did Our Love Go* and *Baby Love*. Diana Ross, Florence Ballard, and Mary Wilson used to sing together in church choirs in Detroit, but they are now recording with hot label Motown.

JANUARY–JUNE

World Events	**MAR** UN troops fly into Cyprus to attempt to keep the warring Greek and Turkish Cypriots apart.	**APR** Ian Smith becomes prime minister of Southern Rhodesia. He favors a unilateral declaration of independence against the UK.	**MAY** Jawaharlal Nehru, beloved prime minister of India since the country became independent in 1947, dies at age 74.	**JUN** Lal Bahadur Shastri, the former minister for home affairs, is sworn in as India's new prime minister in Delhi.
Entertainment	**FEB** The Beatles fly into Kennedy Airport, New York, to an ecstatic reception.	**APR** Sydney Poitier is the first black American actor to win an Oscar, for his performance in the film *Lilies of the Field*.	**APR** Rock group The Rolling Stones shocks the French Montreux festival with its "disheveled" look.	**JUN** Canadian-born tycoon and powerful newspaper magnate Lord Beaverbrook dies at age 85.
Innovations	**FEB** The UK and France agree to build a tunnel under the Channel between them. **SYDNEY POITIER**	**APR** West German pilot Geraldine Mock is the first woman to complete a solo round-the-world flight.	**MAY** In Egypt, the course of the Nile is diverted so the next stage of the Aswan Dam can start. **INDIAN PM NEHRU DIES**	**MAY** Soviet leader Khrushchev admits that Russia uses its satellites to spy on other countries' activities.

1964

Clint Eastwood in A Fistful of Dollars

Japanese trains fly like a bullet

OCTOBER 1

Ten days before the Tokyo Olympic Games are due to begin, a new high-speed passenger rail service has opened today in Japan. The "bullet trains" will operate on a specially built trunk line along the busy 300-mile (480-km) route between the cities of Tokyo and Osaka. The new trains make the trip in just two-and-a-half hours, cutting the previous journey time by an amazing four hours.

Cool cowboy in novel western

NOVEMBER 10

A new western with a difference is released today. A *Fistful of Dollars* is set in the United States, but filmed in Italy and Spain by an Italian director, Sergio Leone. Clint Eastwood stars as the mysterious "man with no name," a gunslinger who rides into town and plays off two rival gangs. The stark atmosphere created by Ennio Morricone's wailing musical score and Leone's camerawork makes this film unique.

The aptly named "bullet trains" lined up and ready to go

Kenya becomes a republic

DECEMBER 12

The former British colony of Kenya in East Africa became a republic today. Its first president is Jomo Kenyatta, who has been prime minister since the country was granted self-government last year. At the independence ceremony in the capital Nairobi, the

Kenya's President Kenyatta (right)

British high commissioner described Kenyatta as "the wisest old bird in Africa." But he has a controversial past. In 1953 the British sentenced him to seven years in prison for his involvement with the violent Mau Mau terrorists.

JULY–DECEMBER

AUG President Johnson says the US will take "all necessary action" against the communist regime in North Vietnam.

AUG South Africa is banned by the Olympic Committee from the Tokyo Olympics for its apartheid policies.

JUL US satellite *Ranger VII* sends the first close-up pictures of the surface of the Moon back to Earth.

NIKITA KHRUSHCHEV

OCT At the age of 70, Soviet leader Nikita Khrushchev is deposed in favor of Leonid Brezhnev and Alexei Kosygin.

AUG UK writer Ian Fleming, creator of the hit series of books about fictional spy James Bond, dies at age 56.

SEP Europe's longest suspension bridge, the Forth Road Bridge, is opened in Scotland, UK.

OCT US campaigner for black civil rights Dr. Martin Luther King Jr., who favors non-violent protest, is awarded the Nobel Peace Prize.

OCT In the Olympics, Australian swimmer Dawn Fraser, aged 27, retains her 100-m freestyle title.

NOV The world's longest suspension bridge, the Verrazano-Narrows Bridge, opens in New York City.

VERRAZANO-NARROWS BRIDGE

OCT China explodes its first A-bomb, becoming the fifth nuclear power along, with the US, USSR, UK, and France.

OCT US composer and lyricist of musical comedies Cole Porter dies at age 67.

DEC Donald Campbell sets a new world water speed record of 276.33 mph in the UK.

THE RACE TO THE MOON

IN 1961, US PRESIDENT JOHN F. KENNEDY challenged the Soviet Union to place a man on the Moon before the end of the 1960s. The idea of humans walking on the Moon had fired people's imaginations for centuries, but it remained a dream until rockets that were powerful enough had been invented. The Space Age began in 1957 when the Soviets launched *Sputnik 1*, the first satellite to orbit the Earth. It was closely followed by the US satellite *Explorer 1*. The Soviets led the race until 1965, putting the first man into space and carrying out the first space walk. But in 1969 the United States made the first manned Moon landing.

Space dog

In 1957, the Soviets sent a dog, Laika, into space to see how animals responded to weightlessness. Her condition was closely monitored and the information used for later manned expeditions.

Television camera

Extendable antenna

Radio antenna

Gagarin's reentry module

Petallike hinged panels

LUNA 9

Lunar probe

In 1966, the Soviet lunar probe *Luna 9* was the first of its kind to achieve a "soft landing" on the Moon. The probe's innovative design enabled it to bounce across the Moon's surface before coming to a gentle halt. Its "petals" and antennae then opened, and a TV camera sent back to Earth the first-ever pictures of the Moon's surface.

Radio command link antenna

Vostok 1

Soviet cosmonaut Yuri Gagarin orbited the Earth in the tiny *Vostok* capsule, which measured only 8.2 ft (2.5 m) in diameter. Despite its minute size, the capsule required a huge disposable rocket to launch it into space.

Radiator

Gas pressure bottles for life-support system

YURI GAGARIN

First in space

In 1961 Soviet leaders were triumphant when 27-year-old Major Yuri Gagarin became the first person ever to fly in space. He orbited the Earth in the *Vostok* spaceship, listening to music by Tchaikovsky during the 108-minute flight. Although Gagarin's space capsule was controlled from the ground, the cosmonaut carried a secret code that would unlock the controls in the event that he lost contact with Earth.

VOSTOK 1 SPACE CAPSULE

Final stage engine

Engine to stabilize rolling movement

1965 ALEXEI LEONEV, FIRST
TO WALK IN SPACE, USSR

1965 GEMINIS 6 AND 7, FIRST TO
RENDEZVOUS IN SPACE, US

1969 APOLLO 11, FIRST MANNED
MOON LANDING, US

APOLLO 11
COMMAND MODULE

Apollo command module

On July 21, 1969, the United States won the race when the *Apollo 11* command module reached the Moon. Two astronauts, Neil Armstrong and "Buzz" Aldrin, landed on the surface, while the third member of the crew, Michael Collins, remained in lonely orbit in the 10-ft (3-m) high command module, in which all three crew members later returned to Earth.

Saturn V

In 1969 the giant US *Saturn V* rocket launched the *Apollo 11* manned mission to the Moon. The rocket stood 364 ft (111 m) high and, with fuel, weighed almost 3,300 tons. Each of the rocket's three stages was jettisoned after it had burned up its fuel. After the third-stage engine had fired, the combined command and service module section had enough momentum to coast across into the Moon's orbit.

BUZZ ALDRIN
STANDING ON THE
SURFACE OF THE MOON

SATURN V
ROCKET

One small step

As Neil Armstrong stepped from the lunar excursion module, he uttered the now historic words, "That's one small step for man, one giant leap for mankind." The astronauts spent just over a day on the Moon, collecting samples of dust and rock, taking photographs, and making "kangaroo hops" in the Moon's low gravity. They planted an American flag before returning in the excursion module to dock with the command module and return home.

Docking radar

Tracking light

Small thruster engine to control flight

Crew hatch

Folding landing leg

Space program

Ten more US astronauts explored the Moon before the *Apollo* program ended in 1972. Since then, both US and Soviet space probes have visited almost all of the planets in our Solar System.

Footpad keeps leg from sinking into Moon dust

MODEL OF APOLLO 11
LUNAR EXCURSION MODULE

1965

Flyaway eagle Goldie escapes into the park

FEBRUARY 21

London has a new tourist attraction. For ten days now, an escaped golden eagle from London Zoo has been living in nearby Regent's Park, attracting thousands of interested fans. Known as Goldie, the seven-year-old is enjoying stretching his wings properly for the first time in five years. So far he has resisted all efforts to recapture him and seems quite happy hopping from tree to tree.

Goldie the Golden Eagle

US enters conflict

Confidence is high as the first US troops arrive in Vietnam

MARCH 31

US President Johnson has sent 3,500 marines to give protection to the South Vietnamese air base at Da Nang from attacks by the communist Vietcong. Eleven years ago, in 1954, the former French territory of Vietnam was divided along the 17th parallel of latitude. Since that time, Vietcong guerrillas have gained ground in the South with the help of communist-controlled North Vietnam and China, while military advisers from the US have sought to strengthen the South's resistance. Last year, in the "Tonkin Gulf Incident," two US destroyers reported being fired upon by North Vietnamese torpedos, and US intervention has seemed inevitable. By sending in two battalions of front-line troops, they have shown that they are now prepared to become involved.

Oscar-winning magic musical

APRIL 6

The lady herself would have the perfect word for it: "Supercalifragilisticexpeali-docious"! Walt Disney's film *Mary Poppins* has just won five Oscars in Hollywood. A musical comedy, it features a "practically perfect" nanny who amuses her young charges with all kinds of magical tricks. Disney combines live action with animation in amazing sequences.

Julie Andrews as Mary Poppins

JANUARY–JUNE

World Events	JAN UK statesman and inspirational wartime prime minister Sir Winston Churchill dies at age 90.	FEB Franco's blockade of Gibraltar, designed to force the UK to give "the Rock" back to Spain, begins to take effect.	APR The Shah of Persia survives an assassination attempt in Tehran, but three of his entourage are killed.	MAY Queen Elizabeth II dedicates an acre of ground in the UK to the memory of assassinated US President Kennedy.
Entertainment	FEB Australian runner Ron Clarke breaks the 3 mile (5,000 m) world record.	MAR Zookeepers in London, UK, capture Goldie the Eagle after his two weeks of freedom.	MAR Rodgers and Hammerstein's hit musical *The Sound of Music* is made into a captivating film.	APR The oldest soccer player in Europe, the UK's Sir Stanley Matthews, retires at age 50.
Innovations	FEB In the UK, the one-millionth Mini comes off the production line.	MAR Soviet cosmonaut Colonel Alexei Leonev becomes the first man to walk in space.	APR Two new communications satellites are launched; the US *Early Bird* and Soviet *Molyna-1*.	MAY In Canada, the de Havilland DHC-6 Twin Otter STOL makes its maiden flight.

WINSTON CHURCHILL DIES

STANLEY MATTHEWS IS TACKLED

1965

British Empire honors Beatles

OCTOBER 26

Today British pop group The Beatles became the latest Members of the Order of the British Empire, or MBEs. Their medals were presented by Queen Elizabeth II at Buckingham Palace, where a crowd of fans had gathered to catch a glimpse of their heroes. Some older MBEs have returned their medals in protest.

Paul, George, John, and Ringo show off their MBEs

UNICEF wins peace prize

UNICEF project helps children in Africa

DECEMBER 10

The United Nations Children's Fund was today awarded the Nobel Peace Prize in Oslo, Norway. Founded in 1946 as UNICEF (which stands for the United Nations International Children's Emergency Fund), the society was set up to assist children in any country that was devastated by World War II. Since 1950, UNICEF has worked on long-term projects to improve the welfare of children, particularly in the developing countries. The organization helps set up health services and nutrition programs, but still gives direct aid to children in crisis situations, wherever they are. UNICEF is financed by voluntary contributions from governments, organizations, and private individuals.

THE MODERNISTS

In Britain, Italian scooters like the *Vespa* are currently the height of chic with a youth cult called the Mods. Mods also favor snappy Italian-style clothes and music by The Who.

JULY–DECEMBER

JUL China signs agreements with North Vietnam on economic and technical matters.

JUL In the Swiss Alps, Mme. Vaucher is the first woman to climb the mighty Matterhorn.

JUL *Mariner IV*, launched from the US last November, sends back pictures of Mars.

THE MATTERHORN

AUG In the US, race riots flare in an area of Los Angeles, with 28 people reported dead and 676 injured.

AUG UK photographer David Bailey marries French film star Catherine Deneuve.

AUG The Swiss-born architect Le Corbusier, known for his avant-garde style buildings, dies at age 77.

SEP The Argentine foreign minister restates his country's claim on the Falkland Islands to the United Nations in New York.

NOV US filmmaker Walt Disney announces plans for a second Disneyland in Florida.

OCT A 1440 Viking map is published. It apparently shows the US 50 years before Columbus sailed there.

FERDINAND AND IMELDA MARCOS

DEC In Manila, with his wife by his side, Ferdinand Marcos is sworn in as sixth president of the Philippines.

DEC Mikhail Sholokhov, Soviet author of *Quiet Flows the Don*, wins the Nobel Prize for literature.

DEC Two manned US *Gemini* spacecraft achieve the first rendezvous in space.

THE SWINGING SIXTIES

IN THE 1960s, skirts got shorter, hair got longer, and for the first time in the 20th century, pop music became a driving force in society. This was especially true in Britain, home of The Beatles, whose songs provided a soundtrack to the era. "In this century," said *Time* magazine in April 1966, "every decade has its city...and for the Sixties that city is London." England's capital teemed with artists, models, pop stars, photographers, fashion designers, and hairdressers, all dedicated to the creation of new styles for the young. The fashions they set caught on all over the world. So, too, did their message that life could be a party – "If you can remember the Swinging Sixties," someone joked later, "you weren't really there!"

French chic

In the 1960s London was swinging but France was the home of *chic*. Glamorous French singer Françoise Hardy helped set a global trend by wearing her hair long and straight.

Let's Twist!
US singer Chubby Checker's 1960 hit *Let's Twist Again* launched the ultimate Sixties dance craze. "You move your hips like you're drying yourself with a towel," said Checker.

POLICE STRUGGLE TO HOLD BACK BEATLES' FANS

Beatlemania

By 1963 The Beatles had become so popular that their concerts were pandemonium. Their girl fans screamed so loudly that it was almost impossible to hear the band playing. "Beatlemania" soon spread across Europe, and then the United States.

The Fab Four

The Beatles burst onto the popular music scene in 1962 with their first single *Love Me Do* and went on to become the most successful pop group of all time. Their music epitomized the 1960s. The songs they wrote had wit and intelligence and reflected the changing mood of the times. "If you want to know about the Sixties," said US composer Aaron Copland, "play the music of The Beatles."

GEORGE HARRISON

JOHN LENNON

RINGO STARR

Sensational long hair

PAUL McCARTNEY

"Stove-pipe" pants

Chelsea boots

1965 UK DESIGNER MARY QUANT
INTRODUCES THE MINISKIRT

1965 THE ROLLING STONES
RELEASE *SATISFACTION*

1966 HEYDAY OF POP-PLAYING
PIRATE RADIO STATIONS

MICK
JAGGER

MARIANNE
FAITHFUL

*Pearly
nail polish*

*Pale lipstick was
vital for the
Sixties look*

*Black eyeliner for
outlining eyes*

Less is more

In the 1960s there was a fashion revolution. The biggest sensation was caused by the outrageously short miniskirt. Pioneered by English designer Mary Quant and French couturier André Courrèges, it was made popular by hip models like Twiggy. Within a very short time, the mini had been adopted by young women all over the world.

*Vidal Sassoon
hairstyle*

*False
eyelashes*

Stepping out

High-heeled, knee- or thigh-length boots looked just right with short mini skirts. Made of leather or plastic, the boots rapidly became essential Sixties fashion accessories.

TWIGGY

*Floral design woven
in gold thread*

Mick and Marianne

With their long hair and rebellious attitudes, Mick Jagger of The Rolling Stones and his girlfriend, solo singer Marianne Faithful, embodied the renegade spirit of swinging London.

*Some minis were a
good 6 in (15 cm)
above the knee*

PAISLEY-PATTERNED
MORRIS MINI MINOR

The Mini

Small was beautiful in the swinging Sixties, whether it meant the miniskirt, the VW Bug, or the BMC "Mini" car. In February 1965 the one-millionth BMC Mini rolled off the production line. Stylish and compact, it was perfect for London's trendies to dash around in.

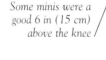

*Flat bar
shoes*

1966

India elects a new prime minister

JANUARY 19
Following the death eight days ago of Indian prime minister Lal Bahadur Shastri from a heart attack, his successor has now been elected. The new premier is Indira Gandhi, 48-year-old daughter of Jawaharlal Nehru, who was independent India's first prime minister in 1947. Mrs. Gandhi, whose husband died in 1960, is the second widow to lead her country on the Indian subcontinent – Mrs. Bandaranaike of Ceylon was the first in 1960. Indira Gandhi's victory over her rival candidate Morarji Desai, the former finance minister, has pleased the Indian people, and tonight she pledged that she would "strive to create what my father used to call a climate of peace." She also intends to honor the peace agreement with Pakistan recently signed by Mr. Shastri.

India's new prime minister, Indira Gandhi

Brezhnev emerges as new Soviet leader

APRIL 8
Since Nikita Khrushchev was ousted in 1964, the Soviet Union has lacked a clear leader. Today, however, following a typically secretive reshuffle at the Kremlin, Communist Party leader Leonid Brezhnev has taken the new title of general secretary. It appears that he now outranks Prime Minister Kosygin, President Podgory, and influential thinker Suslov. Brezhnev played a leading role in the coup of 1964, so there are fears that many of Khrushchev's reforms will now be reversed.

Leonid Brezhnev, the USSR's new general secretary

Musical wins best movie

Julie Andrews as a singing nanny – again

APRIL 18
The Sound of Music has won the Oscar for Best Film in Hollywood. This lively musical is set in pre-war Austria and follows the fortunes of the von Trapp family, whose father marries the governess of his seven children. The governess, Maria, is played by Julie Andrews, still fresh from her recent success in *Mary Poppins*. Many of the songs by Rodgers and Hammerstein are already well known from the Broadway stage version. Now, tunes like *Edelweiss*, *Do-re-mi*, and *My Favorite Things* will become the favorite songs of millions of movie fans.

JANUARY–JULY

World Events

JAN In Accra, over 1,000 political prisoners are freed as an army coup topples Ghana's president, Nkrumah.

JUN Éamon de Valera, known as "Dev," is elected president of Ireland for the second time, at the age of 83.

JUN James Meredith, the first black student admitted to the University of Mississippi, in 1962, is shot on a civil rights march.

JUN US bombers hit fuel tanks in a raid over Hanoi, the first time that they have directly attacked the North Vietnamese capital.

Entertainment

FEB US actor Buster Keaton, the stone-faced comedy star of silent movies, dies at age 70.

FEB USSR novelists Andrey Sinyavsky and Yuri Daniel are imprisoned for "slandering the state."

JUN Legendary US folk singer Bob Dylan shocks audiences in London, UK, by playing the electric guitar.

JUL England beats West Germany 4–2 in the soccer World Cup final, played in the UK.

Innovations

FEB Pictures from the Soviet spacecraft *Luna 9* show the Moon's surface to be solid.

IRISH PM DE VALERA

MAR US astronauts Neil Armstrong and David Scott achieve the first successful space docking in *Gemini 8*.

MAY A missing US H-bomb, lost after a midair collision, is found in the Atlantic off the Spanish coast.

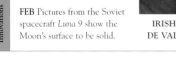
ENGLAND WINS WORLD CUP

JUN The US unmanned *Surveyor* spacecraft is the first craft to land on the Moon.

1966

Cultural revolution in China

AUGUST 13

Mao Zedong, the leader of communist China, has started "a great proletarian cultural revolution." He claims it will create the ideal state in China that he dreamed of as a young man. Launched at a mass rally in Peking, the new movement is being led by huge numbers of students organized into bands of "Red Guards." They are traveling around China with little red books, quoting Mao's thoughts

to remind people of the spirit of the great revolution of 1949. Party officials and "non-revolutionary" academics and artists are being targeted. Schools are being shut, and teachers and other intellectuals humiliated in the streets. A statement from Mao in 1927 is now appearing everywhere: "Revolution is not writing an essay, or painting a picture... revolution is an act of violence when one class overthrows another."

School buried

The slag heap engulfs the school

OCTOBER 21

A terrible tragedy has wiped out a whole generation of children today in Wales. The Aberfan coal mine's slag heap slipped suddenly, burying the village school. Local people are still working to find survivors, but 116 children and 28 adults have died.

First vertical takeoff and landing aircraft

AUGUST 13

An astonishing new British plane has been unveiled at the Farnborough air show. Known as the Hawker Siddeley Harrier, it is the world's first vertical takeoff and landing (VTOL) aircraft. A cross between a helicopter

and an airplane, it is a far cry from the wingless "flying bedstead" pioneered by Rolls-Royce in 1953. Its single engine has four nozzles, which are rotated downward for takeoff and landing, and backward for flight.

STATUES MOVED

Since c.1200 BC, eight 66-ft (20-m) statues of Rameses II have guarded the temples of Abu Simbel in Egypt. Now that the Aswan High Dam is very nearly completed, they are being moved to higher ground to avoid the rising water.

AUGUST–DECEMBER

SEP Dr. Hendrik Verwoerd, prime minister of South Africa, is assassinated by a parliamentary messenger in the House of Assembly.

NOV After the worst storms in Italy in over 1,000 years, the death toll is rising and there is "incalculable" loss to the nation's art heritage.

NOV In China, the Red Guard demands the dismissal of the Chinese heads of state Lui Shaopi and Deng Xiaoping.

DEC UK PM Harold Wilson and Ian Smith, leader of the rebel Rhodesian regime, meet for discussions.

AUG US runner Jim Ryun smashes the world mile record by 2.3 secs, running it in 3 mins 51.3 secs.

SEP Australian Jack Brabham is the first to win the world drivers' championship in his own car.

DEC Walt Disney, whose films and characters are loved by children around the world, dies at age 65.

DEC The Davis Cup for tennis remains with Australia for the third year after they beat India in the final.

AUG Soviet spacecraft *Luna 11* goes into orbit around the Moon and sends data back to Earth.

FLOODED FLORENCE, ITALY

AUG US *Lunar Orbiter 1* goes into orbit around the Moon and sends back pictures of the dark side.

NOV US *Gemini 12*, the last *Gemini* two-person mission, is crewed by Buzz Aldrin and James Lovell.

WALT DISNEY

DEC Soviet probe *Luna 13* lands on the Moon and sends back data about the soil.

1967

Bluebird takes final dive

The last moments of Donald Campbell and his Bluebird

JANUARY 4

Donald Campbell, the British world water-speed hero, has paid the ultimate price for attempting to smash his own world record. On Coniston Water in England's Lake District, he came within a fraction of a second of beating his record of 276.33 mph (444.70 km/h) when disaster struck. The jet-powered *Bluebird* leaped into the air, somersaulted, then plunged into the depths. His helmet, shoes, oxygen mask, and teddy bear mascot were found floating where the boat went down, but so far his body has not been recovered.

Ali refuses draft

APRIL 30

World heavyweight boxing champion Muhammad Ali, known as Cassius Clay before he changed his name and religion, has said that his Muslim faith will not allow him to fight as a soldier for the United States in Vietnam. Ali could face a minimum jail sentence of five years.

Football showdown

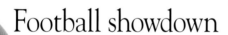

JANUARY 15

Today, in football's first championship game between the two major leagues, the Green Bay Packers of the National Football League beat the Kansas City Chiefs of the American League 35–10 at the Los Angeles Coliseum. Green Bay coach Vince Lombardi, whose motto is "Winning isn't everything, it's the only thing," welcomed the victory.

DISNEY JUNGLE BEAT

Walt Disney's enchanting new cartoon film *The Jungle Book* is based on the novel of that name by English author and poet Rudyard Kipling. It tells the story of Mowgli, an Indian boy raised by wolves in the jungle. The soundtrack features some fine upbeat songs, including *Bear Necessities*.

JANUARY–JUNE

World Events	FEB The US launches Operation Junction City, its biggest assault against the Vietcong in Vietnam.	MAR Svetlana Alliluyeva, daughter of the late Soviet dictator Joseph Stalin, defects from the USSR to the West.	APR In a military coup in Greece, Colonel Papadopoulos seizes power from the democratic government.	MAY Colonel Ojukwu of the Ibo people proclaims the eastern region of Nigeria as the independent republic of Biafra.
Entertainment	FEB In the UK, fans run wild as US made-for-TV pop group The Monkees arrives on tour.	MAR US film star Judy Garland announces her return to the screen in *The Valley of the Dolls*.	APR Barefoot UK singer Sandie Shaw wins the Eurovision Song Contest with *Puppet on a String*.	JUN US film star Spencer Tracy, who has just completed *Guess Who's Coming to Dinner*, dies at age 67.
Innovations	JAN US astronauts Ed White, Gus Grissom, and Roger Chaffe die in a ground test fire.	FEB US nuclear scientist Robert Oppenheimer, head of the team that created the atom bomb, dies at age 62.	MAR In France, President de Gaulle launches the first French nuclear submarine.	JUN China detonates its first H-Bomb in Xiang Jang, a remote area of southwestern China.

SVETLANA DEFECTS

COLONEL OJUKWU OF BIAFRA

1967

The Six-Day War

JUNE 10

For the third time in 21 years, the constant tension between the state of Israel and its Arab neighbors has erupted into full-scale warfare. It began six days ago, when the Israelis launched surprise strikes from land and air. As Israeli troops swept across Egyptian and Jordanian land, the UN security council called for an immediate ceasefire. Two days later, Jordan and Egypt had agreed to this, but Israel fought on, attacking Syria. Finally, on the sixth day, the Israelis have halted their advance and observed the UN ceasefire. They have taken over Arab territories that are many times larger than Israel itself, but the cost of the advance has been great – more than 100,000 people are feared dead.

Israeli soldiers at the Wailing Wall

Israel's General Dayan

Surrealist master Magritte dies

Ceci n'est pas une pipe.

AUGUST 15

Belgian artist René Magritte died today at age 69. He belonged to the Surrealist school of painters, whose art challenges our ideas about reality. His work explored the gap between actual objects and their images. The message under this painting reads, "This is not a pipe," because it is only the *image* of a pipe!

Revolutionary hero killed

OCTOBER 10

Ernesto "Ché" Guevara, the revolutionary hero of Cuba who helped Fidel Castro overthrow the Batista regime, has been shot by the Bolivian army. He left Cuba two years ago to spread the revolution to other parts of the world. In Bolivia, Ché planned a peasant uprising but the army cornered and killed him as well as his band of guerrillas in the jungle yesterday.

JULY–DECEMBER

JUL In Africa, European and US citizens flee Biafra as Nigerian troops step up their attack on the breakaway eastern region.

JUL The latest Beatles album, *Sergeant Pepper's Lonely Hearts Club Band*, is a huge hit.

SEP A lightweight aluminum baby stroller is designed in the UK by Owen Finlay Maclaren.

BEATLES ALBUM SERGEANT PEPPER

JUL Race riots break out in dozens of US cities: Two people have died and thousands have been reported injured.

AUG The Beatles' manager Brian Epstein is found dead after taking an overdose.

SEP UK, France, and West Germany sign an agreement to cooperate on an "Airbus" airliner.

AUG 175,000 Arab refugees are repatriated to occupied land in the Middle East in a scheme agreed by Israel and Jordan.

JUL US singer for peace Joan Baez is arrested at an anti-Vietnam war protest in California.

OCT US biochemist Casimir Funk, the inventor of the now widely used term "vitamin," dies at age 83.

DEC Australia's prime minister, Harold Holt, drowns while swimming near his vacation home in Portsea, Victoria.

DEC US actor Dustin Hoffman stars in the film *The Graduate*, about a young man alienated from society.

CHRISTIAAN BARNARD

DEC The first heart transplant is successfully performed by Dr. Christiaan Barnard in South Africa.

THE TELEVISION AGE

PEYTON PLACE

"IF YOU LET A TV through your door," warned a British newspaper in 1950, "life will never be the same." By that year, there were around 7.5 million TV sets in homes alone. But the advent of television changed things in ways that few could have foreseen. In 1962, during the Cuban Missile Crisis, US president John F. Kennedy broadcast an ultimatum to the USSR on TV. That same year, the first TV space satellite was launched. Marshall McLuhan, whose writing on mass communications caused extensive debate, wrote that the new electronic communications were turning the world into a kind of "global village." Television offered new possibilities for education and entertainment. Soap operas, situation comedies, and talk shows increased viewing numbers.

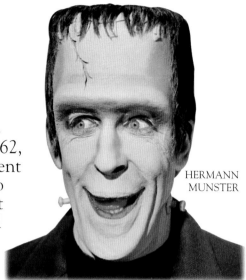

HERMANN MUNSTER

Soap operas

"Soaps" were long-running domestic TV serials, usually shown during the daytime and often sponsored by soap manufacturers. Some soaps were so popular that viewers thought of the characters as real people, identifying with their fictional problems.

For the whole family

Two very successful comedy horror shows originated in the United States in the 1960s. *The Addams Family* and *The Munsters* were the adventures of two very strange families.

World wildlife

TV brought the world into the living room, and few subjects lent themselves better to this treatment than wildlife. One of the most fascinating series of the 1960s was *The Undersea World of Jacques Cousteau*, in which the French marine expert revealed the mysteries of the oceans.

JACQUES COUSTEAU

Television style

MAHOGANY TABLE SET, 1939

FREE-STANDING CABINET MODEL, 1956

PLASTIC PORTABLE TELEVISION, 1966

SPACE-AGE GLOBE SET, 1970

JOHNNY CARSON HOSTS *THE TONIGHT SHOW*

Talk shows

Talk shows, on which a regular host interviewed a selection of celebrity guests, became popular the world over. Few hosts were as successful as the *Tonight Show's* Johnny Carson. Carson took over the show in 1962 from Jack Paar, and moved it to Hollywood in 1971 to be nearer even more glamorous guests. Carson himself was always introduced by the memorable catch phrase "Heeeeeeeeere's Johnny."

1966 SOCCER WORLD CUP FINAL IN UK
IS WATCHED BY 600 MILLION

1969 FOUR NATIONS TIE FOR TOP SPOT IN
POPULAR EUROVISION SONG CONTEST

1969 US MOON LANDING IS SEEN
LIVE ON TV ALL OVER THE WORLD

Televised sports

Television could be used to communicate images and information much faster than movie newsreels. When the Olympic Games were broadcast live from Tokyo in 1964, television viewers all over the world were able to experience the excitement of the events first hand.

TOKYO OLYMPICS 1964

BIG BIRD

Outstanding award for outstanding cartoon

In 1959 US animators Bill Hanna and Joseph Barbera won the first ever Emmy Award for Outstanding Achievement in Children's Programming. The sought-after statuette was awarded for their *Huckleberry Hound Show* (1958–62). One of the show's characters was Yogi Bear, a lovable character who always got into trouble with the park ranger for stealing picnics from visitors to the fictional Jellystone Park.

CAPTAIN KIRK

MR. SPOCK

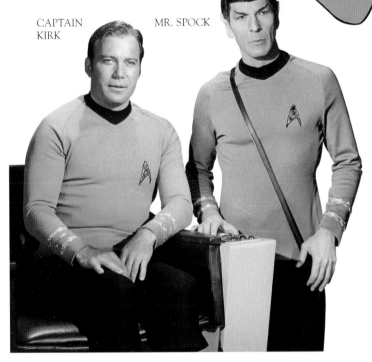

Where no man has gone before...

"Space: the final frontier...." The first series of *Star Trek* was created by former pilot and policeman Gene Roddenberry. Launched in 1966, the Starship *Enterprise* was staffed by interplanetary characters led by Captain James Kirk and his semi-alien first officer Mr. Spock. Devoted fans called Trekkies helped turn *Star Trek* into one of the most popular TV shows.

Sesame Street

Funded by the nonprofit Children's Television Workshop, *Sesame Street* was launched in 1969. The goal of the daily hour-long show was to educate preschool children in deprived areas. The show's stars were a mixture of humans and animallike characters such as Big Bird, a 7-ft (2-m) high canary, Kermit the Frog, and Cookie Monster. The show helped children with their letters, numbers, and social skills.

1968

A scene from Stanley Kubrick's 2001: A Space Odyssey

Trudeau is new Canadian leader

APRIL 21

Liberal Party politician Pierre Trudeau today succeeded Lester Pearson as Canada's prime minister. Trudeau, a 48-year-old bachelor, grew up in Montreal and speaks French and English, Canada's two native languages. He will now have to deal with the demands of many French speakers to turn their province of Quebec into an independent country.

A journey into deep space

APRIL 4

US director Stanley Kubrick has released a remarkable science fiction movie, *2001: A Space Odyssey*. Visually stunning, the film features vast spaceships floating on dreamlike journeys through deep space. It explores both the origins and the future of humankind through the eyes of an astronaut searching for the secrets of the Universe. But film audiences must be prepared to be mystified. "The feel of the experience is the important thing," says Kubrick. "Those who won't believe their eyes won't be able to appreciate this film."

King dies, but dream lives on

APRIL 9

Five days ago, US black civil rights hero Dr. Martin Luther King, Jr. was shot dead by an unknown assassin in Memphis. More than 150,000 people attended the funeral of this brilliant speaker in his hometown of Atlanta, Georgia, today. In his famous Washington speech of 1963, King declared that he had a dream that one day all Americans would live as equals. This has started to come true.

Mourners at the funeral of Martin Luther King, Jr.

JANUARY–APRIL

World Events

JAN The Czechoslovak Communist Party chooses a new "liberal" leader in 46-year-old Alexander Dubcek.

FEB The North Koreans refuse to release the US spy ship *Pueblo*, captured last month within their boundaries.

MAR Soviet cosmonaut and first man in space, Yuri Gagarin is killed in a jet airplane crash outside Moscow at the age of 34.

APR Thousands riot in West Germany following the attempted murder of left-wing student leader Rudi Dutschke.

Entertainment

JAN In London, UK, fans flock to The Beatles' new venture – an Apple clothes boutique.

FEB French skier Jean-Claude Killy wins three golds at the Winter Olympics in Grenoble.

APR The Academy Award ceremony is postponed for 48 hours in memory of Martin Luther King, Jr.

APR US millionaire oil tycoon Robert McCullough buys London Bridge for a bargain $2.4 million.

Innovations

JAN In South Africa, Dr. Christiaan Barnard performs a second heart transplant.

SKIER JEAN-CLAUDE KILLY

FEB The UK Royal Navy's first *Polaris* missile is tested successfully in the Atlantic.

MAR In the US, Lockheed presents the world's largest aircraft to date, the *Galaxy*.

LONDON BRIDGE IN ARIZONA

APR Five and ten pence coins are introduced to the UK in preparation for decimalization.

1968

Paris students riot

Student demonstrations bring Paris to a complete halt

MAY 7

For two days the streets of Paris, France, have been the scene of violent clashes between up to 30,000 students and riot police. Trouble has been brewing since the end of March, when six students were arrested after a large demonstration against the US involvement in the Vietnam War. Yesterday nearly 1,000 men and women were injured as the protesters fought with bricks and paving stones. Today, at the Arc de Triomphe, a huge crowd sang the communist anthem, the *Internationale*, and the riots seem likely to continue.

Student leader Daniel Cohn-Bendit

Another Kennedy gunned down

JUNE 6

The world was stunned today as a second member of the Kennedy family was gunned down in the United States. Senator Robert Kennedy, younger brother of President John F. Kennedy, who was assassinated in 1963, had recently joined the race for the presidency. Last night he was at the Ambassador Hotel in Los Angeles in order to thank campaigners for his recent victory in the California primary election. As he was leaving, an Arab gunman fired five shots at him. Senator Kennedy died from his wounds this morning, only 25 hours after being shot. He would probably have been elected as the next United States president.

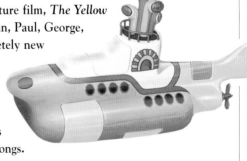

Bobby Kennedy on the campaign trail

BEATLES' YELLOW SUBMARINE

The third Beatles' feature film, *The Yellow Submarine*, shows John, Paul, George, and Ringo in a completely new way – as cartoons! This colorful and innovative fantasy about the amazing "Pepperland" includes several new Beatles' songs.

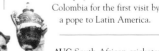

MAY–AUGUST

MAY US and North Vietnamese diplomats meet in Paris, France, to discuss the setting-up of talks to end the war in Vietnam.

JUN Helen Keller, US author and worldwide campaigner for handicapped people, dies at age 88.

MAY The UK's first successful heart transplant operation is performed at a hospital in London.

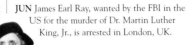

PIONEER HELEN KELLER

JUN James Earl Ray, wanted by the FBI in the US for the murder of Dr. Martin Luther King, Jr., is arrested in London, UK.

JUN In New York, US "pop" artist Andy Warhol is shot and seriously injured by writer Valerie Solanas.

JUN In the US, Roy Jacuzzi markets the first whirlpool baths, called Jacuzzi Roman Baths.

JUL In three capitals – London, Moscow, and Washington – 36 nations sign a nuclear nonproliferation treaty.

JUL Australian Rod Laver wins the first Wimbledon open championships, collecting his third Wimbledon title.

JUL German nuclear physicist and winner of the Nobel Prize for physics Otto Hahn dies at age 89.

TENNIS STAR ROD LAVER

AUG Pope John Paul arrives in Colombia for the first visit by a pope to Latin America.

AUG South African cricketer Colin Bland is refused UK entry because of his Rhodesian passport.

AUG A Channel hovercraft service opens between Dover in the UK and Boulogne in France.

1968

Czechs under siege

Czech prime minister Alexander Dubcek

AUGUST 22

The "Prague Spring" of freedom is abruptly turning into a dark, troubled winter as 600,000 Warsaw Pact troops pour into Czechoslovakia. Under Alexander Dubcek, the government has been trying to gain independence within Soviet-dominated eastern Europe. Dubcek's goal is to run the country on the principle of "socialism with a human face," rather than the oppressive form of communism imposed by the Soviet Union. This would mean greater freedom of speech and a more liberal government than in other parts of the Soviet empire. The Dubcek government had believed that the Soviets would not use force to stop the changes. Now they know better, as unarmed Czech youths try to resist the tanks.

Bob Beamon making his record-breaking jump at the Mexico Olympics

Beamon leaps into record books

OCTOBER 17

Experts have long been debating whether the thin air in Mexico City, which lies about 7,000 ft (2,134 m) above sea level, would affect performances at this year's Olympics. Now the debate will get even hotter. Despite the location, Bob Beamon of the United States has just won the gold medal in the long jump with an amazing leap of 29.2 ft (8.9 m). This jump beats the world record by almost 2 ft (0.6 m).

Tanks roll through the streets of Prague

SEPTEMBER–DECEMBER

World Events	SEP In Iran, at least 11,000 people are reported to have died in a series of earthquakes lasting two days.	OCT Jackie Kennedy, widow of assassinated US president John F. Kennedy, marries Greek business executive Aristotle Onassis.	OCT During their medal ceremony at the Mexico Olympics, US athletes Tommy Smith and John Carlos give the "Black Power" salute.	NOV Republican Richard Nixon narrowly beats Democrat Hubert Humphrey in the US elections to become the 37th president.
Entertainment	SEP The cast of the musical *Hair* is the first to appear naked on a stage in the UK.	OCT At the Olympic Games in Mexico, US athlete Al Oerter wins his fourth gold in the discus event.	NOV UK writer Enid Blyton, creator of the children's characters the "Famous Five," dies at age 71.	DEC US writer John Steinbeck, winner of the Nobel Prize for literature in 1962, dies at age 66.
Innovations	SEP Over 500 UK women have tried the new epidural anesthesia in childbirth.	OCT The US launches *Apollo 7*, the first manned *Apollo* craft, to prepare for a Moon landing.	NOV The UK's *Queen Elizabeth*, the world's largest ocean liner, completes her final passenger voyage.	DEC US spacecraft *Apollo 8* is launched in the US, en route for a manned lunar orbit.

JACKIE KENNEDY
MARRIES ONASSIS

NIXON IS ELECTED
US PRESIDENT

1969

John Lennon and Yoko Ono during their "Bed-In"

Israel's new PM

Israel's first woman prime minister

MARCH 7

The Israeli Labor Party has elected Golda Meir as the new prime minister to succeed Levi Eshkol. Golda Meir, now 70, was born in the Ukraine. She worked as a teacher in the United States before emigrating to Palestine in 1921. In 1948, on the eve of Israel's independence, she raised $50 million in the US for defense funds.

Lennon and Yoko Ono protest in comfort

MARCH 25

Five days ago in Gibraltar, John Lennon of The Beatles married Yoko Ono. For their honeymoon, this unconventional pair have taken up residence in a large double bed in the presidential suite of the Hilton Hotel, Amsterdam. They plan to stay there for seven full days as a protest against war. The world's media has immediately converged on the "Bed-In," where John and Yoko sit in their pajamas surrounded by placards reading "Bed Peace" and "Hair Peace." One cynical reporter has called it "the most self-indulgent demonstration of all time."

Supersonic *Concorde* takes off

APRIL 9

In 1962 Britain and France agreed to develop the supersonic airliner *Concorde*.

Earlier this year, prototype 001 of the aircraft took off in France, and today *Concorde* 002 took to the air from the UK for a maiden flight of 21 minutes. Around

£360 million has already been invested in this project, but there is still a long way to go. Today the plane reached only 203 mph (325 km/h), and it will not be in service until 1974 at the earliest. The two countries hope eventually to sell over 400 of them, making £4 billion by the 1980s.

JANUARY–APRIL

JAN Violence erupts in Derry, Northern Ireland, between Catholic and Protestant communities.

JAN Sir Learie Constantine, the West Indies cricketer, becomes the UK's first black life peer.

JAN In the US, NASA chooses Neil Armstrong and Edwin "Buzz" Aldrin for the first Moon landing.

NORTHERN IRISH DEMONSTRATIONS

JAN In Prague, Jan Palach dies after setting fire to himself in protest against the Soviet invasion.

MAR Paul McCartney of UK pop group The Beatles marries US photographer Linda Eastman.

FEB Human eggs are fertilized in a test tube for the first time at Cambridge University, UK.

FEB In Cairo, Yassir Arafat, a dynamic resistance leader, is appointed head of the Palestine Liberation Organization (PLO).

APR US actress Katherine Hepburn wins a record third Best Actress Oscar for her role in *The Lion in Winter*.

MAR US spacecraft *Apollo 9* splashes down safely in the Pacific after the first test of the lunar module.

PLO LEADER YASSIR ARAFAT

APR French president Charles de Gaulle resigns at the age of 78, after losing a constitutional referendum.

APR UK sailor Robin Knox-Johnston, wins the single-handed round-the-world yacht race.

APR UK engineers Booker and McConnell set up a prize fund for UK fiction.

215

1965 US WRITER ALLEN GINSBERG
COINS THE PHRASE "FLOWER POWER"

1967 US BOXER MUHAMMAD ALI
REFUSES TO FIGHT IN VIETNAM WAR

1968 PARIS STUDENTS MARCH FOR
EDUCATIONAL AND SOCIAL REFORMS

PEACE AND PROTEST

"SOMETHING'S HAPPENING HERE," sang US rock group Buffalo Springfield in 1967, "what it is ain't exactly clear...." As the swinging Sixties wore on, something *was* happening among the young people of the United States and Europe. They were losing faith in how the older generation was running the world. In particular, they were unhappy with the United States's involvement in the Vietnam War. Thousands joined protest marches and demonstrations chanting the slogan "make love, not war." Others decided to opt out of society altogether by living in communes where less value was given to money and possessions. Many pop stars shared these ideals. Two songs by John Lennon of The Beatles summed up the message: *All You Need Is Love* (1967) and *Give Peace a Chance* (1969).

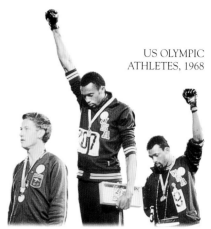

US OLYMPIC
ATHLETES, 1968

Flower power

Mid-sixties California was the birthplace of the "Flower Children," who believed the key to life was in nature. When the Soviets invaded Czechoslovakia in 1968, Prague students put flowers in their gun barrels as a peaceful protest.

Black power

Black Americans were unhappy with the unequal treatment they received in society. Two young US athletes, Tommie Smith and John Carlos, shocked the world in 1968 by giving the "black power" salute at the Mexico Olympics as a sign of black pride.

Woodstock music festival

The biggest event of the Flower Power era was the Woodstock Music and Arts Fair. Held on farmland outside New York City in August 1969, the music festival drew an audience of nearly half a million young people, united in their love of music and their desire for world peace.

STUDENTS RIOT IN PARIS

BOB
DYLAN

Songs of protest

Music was at the forefront of the protest movements around the world. In the United States singer-songwriters like Bob Dylan and Joan Baez wrote powerful antiwar songs. Dylan's *Blowin' in the Wind* combined the spiritual and political ideas of the peace movement and became an anthem for the antiwar generation.

At the barricades

In May 1968 French students rioted on the streets of Paris when their demonstrations for educational and social reforms ended in violent clashes with the police. Days of street-fighting followed between the authorities and the revolutionary students. About ten million French workers went out on strike to support the students, virtually bringing France to a standstill. Eventually French president General De Gaulle was forced to grant the students reforms and to promise the workers better wages.

1969 US FILM *EASY RIDER* SYMBOLIZES
ALTERNATIVE YOUTH CULTURE

1969 HUGE PEACE AND MUSIC
FESTIVAL AT WOODSTOCK, NY

1969 BIGGEST EVER ANTI-VIETNAM
WAR DEMO IN WASHINGTON, D.C.

Psychedelic art

The hippy drug culture inspired a whole new style of art described as psychedelic. The artists used bright, swirling patterns and vivid colors. Innovative musicians like Jimi Hendix and Joni Mitchell promoted the art form by using psychedelic images and hand-drawn graphics on their album covers, and hundreds of posters, T-shirts, and underground magazines also featured this new kind of "way-out" hippy expression.

THE BEATLES
WITH THE
MAHARISHI

The lure of the East

Many young people looked to the East and the religions of Hinduism and Buddhism, which renounce worldly goods, to make sense of the world. Many set off on the "hippy trail" across India to Katmandu in search of enlightenment. Even The Beatles visited India to find a guru.

Long "Afro" hair

Afghan coat

Strings of beads

Long, loose tunic

Flared pants, called bellbottoms

Embroidered shoulder bag

Sandals

Hippies

The first hippies made their home in San Francisco. They were easygoing, longhaired, and brightly dressed. According to the US hippy guru Dr. Timothy Leary, their goal was to turn on (take mind-expanding drugs), tune in (to the life energies they found inside themselves), and drop out (of the rat race of everyday life).

1969

Man on the Moon

JULY 21

Today, a man walked on the Moon for the very first time. With the words, "That's one small step for man, one giant leap for mankind," US astronaut Neil Armstrong stepped onto the Moon and into history. As he left the lunar module, he was watched on television by nearly 600 million people

around the world. Armstrong was joined by "Buzz" Aldrin, and the two delighted their TV audience by making big kangaroo bounds in the Moon's low gravity. They carried out experiments for two hours before returning to *Apollo 11*'s landing craft.

Buzz Aldrin steps onto the Moon

British troops in Derry

Troops into Ireland

AUGUST 15

After a week of furious street-fighting between groups of Protestants and Catholics, the British government has sent troops into Derry, Northern Ireland. More troops will almost certainly be deployed in trouble-torn Belfast as well. While many people greeted the move with relief, the Irish government and many Catholics in the

north have condemned it. The army chief in Northern Ireland has been instructed to "take all necessary steps, acting impartially between citizen and citizen." The British government hopes to limit their intervention and withdraw the troops when law and order is restored.

LONG AND SHORT OF IT

At the end of a decade that has seen ever-rising hemlines, the mini has been replaced on the catwalks. The latest new trend in the boutiques is the maxiskirt, which reaches right down to the floor. And for women who do not want their hemlines to plunge too low, there is also the fashionable midiskirt, which hovers just below the knee.

MAY–AUGUST

World Events	**JUN** Over 1,000 civilians are detained in Czechoslovakia following two days of arrests.	**JUN** US President Nixon suggests that US, Allied, and North Vietnamese troops withdraw from South Vietnam.	**JUN** In Spain, General Franco closes the land frontier with Gibraltar in an attempt to cripple the UK colony.	**JUN** In the UK, Conservative politician Enoch Powell calls for the repatriation of black immigrants.
Entertainment	**MAY** The UK's Graham Hill wins the Monaco grand prix for a record fifth time.	**JUN** US actress and singer Judy Garland, who played Dorothy in *The Wizard of Oz*, dies at age 47.	**JUN** Brazilian soccer star Pelé, considered the greatest player of the age, scores his 1,000th goal.	**JUL** The Rolling Stones play a free concert in London, UK, in memory of drowned guitarist Brian Jones.
Innovations	**MAY** Soviet probe *Venera 5* sends back data about Venus before crashing on the planet.	**MAY** The manned US *Apollo 10* orbits the Moon, as a rehearsal for the planned Moon landing in July.	**JUN** High-grade crude oil is found on the borders of the UK and Norwegian sectors of the North Sea.	**JUL** The US space probe *Mariner 6* sends back the first close-up pictures of the surface of the planet Mars.

GARLAND AND HER DAUGHTER

SOCCER STAR PELÉ

1969

Woodstock festival attracts thousands

AUGUST 17

In the United States, the world's biggest peace and rock festival has just ended near the village of Woodstock in upstate New York. Nearly 500,000 fans braved the rain to enjoy three days of inspired music from Jimi Hendrix, Janis Joplin, Joan Baez, Joe Cocker, Santana, The Who, and many more. The poor sanitation and overstretched catering facilities did not deter the happy masses, and the atmosphere remained

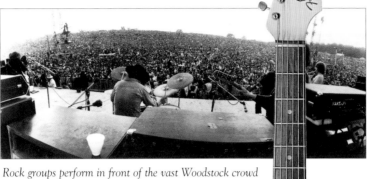

Rock groups perform in front of the vast Woodstock crowd

positive and peaceful. Many are seeing the warm spirit of cooperation at Woodstock as a vibrant symbol of the antiwar generation. It marks a fitting end to a decade of protest, peace, and love.

No Red Cross help for Biafra

OCTOBER 21

While civil war rages in Nigeria, 300,000 innocent refugees in the rebel republic of Biafra are facing starvation. In August, the Nigerian government stopped Red Cross night flights carrying relief aid, claiming that the Biafran rebels used them as a cover to deliver arms. A US adviser warns, "We have to face it that many people are going to die."

Famished children in Biafra

Old guns Newman and Redford

Robert Redford as the Kid

Paul Newman as Butch Cassidy

SEPTEMBER 23

Two of Hollywood's biggest stars, Paul Newman and Robert Redford, have teamed up in a new film. They play the title roles in *Butch Cassidy and the Sundance Kid*, a comical Western based on the lives of a pair of legendary, laid-back outlaws who led the "Hole in the Wall Gang" in the last days of the old West.

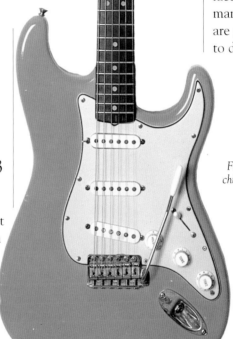

SEPTEMBER–DECEMBER

SEP In Czechoslovakia, the Communist Party expels former leader Alexander Dubcek from its praesidium, or ruling body.

OCT Jack Kerouac, the US novelist, Beat poet, and author of *On the Road*, dies at the age of 47.

OCT In the UK, the P&O ferry line announces that after 130 years it will cease passenger services to India.

GEORGES POMPIDOU

SEP North Vietnamese president Ho Chi Minh dies at age 79, while the war against the US and South Vietnam continues.

NOV South African rugby team the Springboks begin a UK tour, sparking antiapartheid protests.

OCT Supersonic *Concorde 001* breaks the sound barrier, to the joy of new French President Pompidou.

SEP In Libya, a group of revolutionary army officers, led by Muammar Gaddafi, seize power while King Idris is in Turkey.

DEC US actress Barbra Streisand stars in the smash hit musical *Hello, Dolly*, directed by Gene Kelly.

NOV In Australia, the world's longest straight-track railroad is opened, from Ooldea to Nurina.

CHANCELLOR BRANDT

OCT In Germany, Willy Brandt becomes chancellor, the first Social Democrat to be elected in 39 years.

DEC The Nobel Prize for literature is awarded to Irish poet and playwright Samuel Beckett.

DEC An Asian influenza epidemic sweeps the UK, and hundreds of people die.

1970

First jumbo jet lands at Heathrow

JANUARY 22
A new era in jet travel dawned today when a giant Boeing 747 arrived at Heathrow Airport on the outskirts of London, Britain, from New York. Weighing 392 tons (356 tonnes) and carrying 362 passengers, the Boeing 747 has rapidly acquired the nickname "jumbo." The world's biggest airliner arrived at Heathrow three hours late however, after experiencing engine problems in New York.

Apollo 13 splashes down in Pacific

APRIL 17
After a 90-hour ordeal in space, the astronauts on the *Apollo 13* spacecraft have safely returned to Earth. *Apollo 13* was crippled by an explosion in its service module early in its mission. The three astronauts on board are reported to be fit and well.

Hussein and Arafat sign truce

King Hussein and Yassir Arafat shake hands

Apollo 13 being retrieved from the ocean

SEPTEMBER 27
King Hussein of Jordan and Yassir Arafat, leader of the Palestinian Liberation Organization (PLO), have signed a truce to end the war in Jordan. The Palestinian guerrillas had earlier seized control of the north of Jordan and the approaches to the capital, Amman. But after ten days of fierce fighting with the Jordanian army, the Palestinians were driven out of their strongholds. Recent mass hijackings of Western airliners by Palestinian terrorists ended earlier this month with three aircraft being blown up at Dawson's Field in the Jordanian desert.

JANUARY–DECEMBER

World Events	**MAY** National Guardsmen shoot dead four antiwar demonstrators at Kent State University.	**OCT** Anwar Sadat becomes president of Egypt after the death of Gamal Abdel Nasser. Sadat is expected to take a more moderate line.	**NOV** Charles de Gaulle, leader of the Free French in World War II and president of France 1958–69, dies at age 79.	**NOV** 150,000 people are feared dead after a typhoon and tidal wave devastate East Pakistan. Other countries send aid.
Entertainment	**APR** Paul McCartney issues a writ in the UK to dissolve "the business...The Beatles and Co."	**SEP** Superstar guitarist Jimi Hendrix dies from a drug overdose at the age of 27, a few days after performing at a festival.	**SEP** Australian Margaret Court earns a "Grand Slam," winning all four major world tennis tournaments.	**NOV** Movie theaters in Paris, France, close for one day as a sign of respect for General Charles de Gaulle.
Innovations	**JUL** The first pacemaker driven by a nuclear battery is used at the National Heart Hospital, UK. **JIMI HENDRIX**	**OCT** UK company British Petroleum announces the first major oil find in the UK sector of the North Sea.	**NOV** The supersonic airliner *Concorde* travels at twice the speed of sound for the first time. **CHARLES DE GAULLE**	**DEC** Soviet space probe *Venera 7* becomes the first ever spacecraft to land on the planet Venus.

1971

HOT PANTS

Legs are bared again this summer as hot pants hit the streets. The tight-fitting shorts are often worn with platform shoes or boots and come in a variety of materials. However, not everyone approves of the new style – hot pants have even been blamed for several traffic accidents!

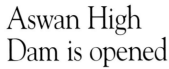

Idi Amin takes president's oath

FEBRUARY 20

Idi Amin, the former army boxing champion who seized power in Uganda less than a month ago, has declared himself president. Amin, who has the full support of the army, has banned all political activities and elections for five years.

Aswan High Dam is opened

JANUARY 15

Soviet President Podgorny joined President Sadat of Egypt at today's official opening of the Aswan High Dam on the northern shore of the Nasser Lake. The project has taken 11 years and about $1 billion to complete, with the Soviet Union providing substantial loans. The huge dam will provide Egypt with a year-round supply of water for irrigation and electricity.

Idi Amin, president of Uganda

New Disney magic

OCTOBER 1

Almost 10,000 visitors converged on Orlando, Florida, today as the gates of the Magic Kingdom at Walt Disney World opened for the first time. Walt Disney picked the site and unveiled the plans shortly before he died in 1966. He had been encouraged to build another Magic Kingdom after the success of Disneyland, California. There are seven different lands inside the Florida park, all based on favorite Disney themes. Each ride and show has been specially designed by the Disney "imagineers" and has its own storyline. Construction of the site began in 1969, and altogether it has taken 9,000 workers and more than $400 million to build the Magic Kingdom, the Seven Seas Lagoon, two golf courses, and two resorts. The formal dedication of Disney World will take place on October 25 with Walt Disney's brother, Roy, officiating.

Fairy castle in Disney World

JANUARY–DECEMBER

FEB It is good-bye to pounds, shillings, and pence as the UK introduces decimal currency, confusing many people.

APR Nineteen-year-old Jean-Claude "Baby Doc" Duvalier succeeds his father "Papa Doc" as president of Haiti.

JUN The *New York Times* prints secret Pentagon papers that reveal US government deception in the Vietnam War.

DEC Pakistan surrenders to India after a two-week war. East Pakistan becomes the state of Bangladesh.

MAY Rolling Stone Mick Jagger marries Bianca Perez Morena de Macias in France.

JUL US singer and trumpeter Louis Armstrong, famous for his jazz solos, dies at age 71.

AUG UK yachtsman Chay Blythe completes the first solo voyage around the world in a westerly direction.

OCT Scottish singer Rod Stewart tops the albums and singles charts in both the US and UK.

APR Three USSR cosmonauts are found dead in their spacecraft after visiting *Salyut 1* space station.

LUNAR ROVING VEHICLE – THE "MOON BUGGY"

JUL David Scott and James Irwin are the first astronauts to drive on the Moon.

JUL The first combined heart and lung transplant is performed in a South African hospital.

ROD STEWART

NOV US space probe *Mariner 9* transmits photos of the planet Mars back to Earth.

1957 VIETCONG REBEL AGAINST
SOUTH VIETNAMESE GOVERNMENT

1965 US SENDS IN FIRST GROUND
COMBAT TROOPS AS WAR ESCALATES

1968 VIETCONG LAUNCH
MAJOR NEW YEAR OFFENSIVE

WAR IN VIETNAM

FOLLOWING THE DIVIDE OF VIETNAM in 1954, communists in the south began to rebel against a noncommunist government. North Vietnam, intent on reunifying the country, provided backup and supplies to the communist rebels in the south, known as the Vietcong. The United States supported South Vietnam by sending money and military advisers. In 1965 the first US combat troops arrived in South Vietnam to be joined by soldiers from Australia, New Zealand, South Korea, Thailand, and the Philippines. For the United States it proved a costly and futile war. The last US troops left in 1973, but fighting continued until South Vietnam's defeat in 1975.

Ho Chi Minh

Communist leader Ho Chi Minh became North Vietnam's first president in 1954. He led the fight against South Vietnam until his death in 1969.

IDENTITY TAGS OF
US SOLDIERS

Voices of protest

The conflict in Vietnam escalated into full-scale war in 1965 and thousands of US soldiers were sent to fight. Anyone who refused to enlist was labeled a "draft dodger" and, by 1969, there were more than 543,000 US troops in Vietnam. As fighting intensified and casualties rose, antiwar feeling grew and thousands of people took part in peace rallies, protesting against the US's involvement in the war. One peaceful demonstration at the Pentagon ended in clashes between protesters and armed soldiers, and more than 250 arrests.

US MARCH FOR
PEACE IN VIETNAM

Capturing prisoners

As fighting in Vietnam spread, there were many casualties and prisoners taken on both sides. Despite the huge firepower and technological might of the United States, victory proved elusive. The Vietcong had a genius for guerrilla warfare and could disappear for days on end in the jungle.

Air attacks

In 1966 the United States launched a massive bombing campaign against North Vietnam with an air attack. Fleets of helicopter gunships continued the fight, waging war against the Vietcong, and spraying the countryside with machine gun fire. Troops were landed in remote corners of the jungle to search out the enemy.

1973 CEASEFIRE AGREEMENT
SIGNED IN PARIS

1973 LAST US TROOPS
WITHDRAW FROM VIETNAM

1975 WAR ENDS AS SOUTH
VIETNAM SURRENDERS

Vietcong with white flag

In January 1968 at the start of Tet, the Vietnamese New Year, the Vietcong launched a series of attacks on Saigon and other cities in South Vietnam. The US and South Vietnamese forces were taken completely by surprise as they thought the end of the war was in sight. Fierce and bloody street fighting followed, leaving huge numbers of casualties and terrified civilians fleeing their homes in search of safety. The offensive was finally quashed, but it proved that the war was far from over.

DESTRUCTION IN SAIGON

Vietnam on film

Over the years many films have been made about the Vietnam War. One of the most memorable of these is *Platoon*, which was written and directed by US Vietnam veteran Oliver Stone in 1986.

Coming home

From July 1969 onward US troops were gradually withdrawn from Vietnam by order of the new president, Richard Nixon. He initiated a policy called Vietnamization, which meant leaving the South Vietnamese to do their own fighting. The last US ground troops left for home in April 1973, after the signing of a ceasefire agreement in Paris earlier in the year. It was not the end of the war, however, and fighting soon resumed.

Effects of war

The long-term effects of the war on the South Vietnamese were incalculable. Huge numbers were killed in the fighting and bombing, and about half of the population (ten million people) became refugees. The economy, which depended on the export of timber, rubber, and rice was ruined after the devastation of the countryside by the widespread spraying of toxic herbicides such as Agent Orange.

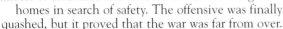

1972

Bloody Sunday in Ireland

JANUARY 30

The long and troubled history of Northern Ireland entered a new phase today as 10,000 demonstrators, defying a government ban on marches, paraded through the streets of Derry. The demonstrators were protesting against the policy of internment without trial. An estimated 600 suspected IRA members are being held by the British government in special internment camps. The marchers were confronted by British troops behind army barricades and violence erupted, with rioters hurling stones over the barbed wire. The troops retaliated with rubber bullets, tear gas, and water cannons before opening fire on the crowd. Thirteen unarmed Catholic men and youths were killed, and 17 others were wounded.

The road to peace

FEBRUARY 21

US president Richard Nixon has arrived in China for a series of historic meetings with Chairman Mao Zedong and Prime Minister Zhou Enlai. For 20 years relations between the two countries have been icy, with the United States refusing to acknowledge the communist People's Republic of China, recognizing instead Chiang Kai-shek's nationalist regime of Taiwan as China's true government. China, in turn, claimed that the United States was "the most ferocious enemy of the people throughout the world." If the talks go well, they could eventually lead to trade agreements between the two countries. Nixon is urging China to join the United States in a "long march together" on different roads to achieve world peace.

Donny's a big hit

JUNE 17

"Osmania" has swept the US and is now taking Britain as Donny Osmond tops the charts with *Puppy Love*, his eighth hit single. Donny already has four gold albums.

Richard Nixon on the Great Wall of China

JANUARY–JUNE

World Events	MAR Direct rule of Northern Ireland from Westminster is imposed by UK government.	APR President Nixon steps up the US bombing of Hanoi after communist troops invade South Vietnam.	MAY Richard Nixon makes the first visit to Moscow by a US president and attends a weeklong summit.	JUN The Duke of Windsor, who abdicated from the UK throne in 1936, is buried at Frogmore, UK.
Entertainment	FEB The musical *Cabaret*, starring Liza Minnelli, wins seven Academy Awards.	MAR Marlon Brando stars in *The Godfather*, Francis Ford Coppola's film about the Mafia.	APR The Tate Gallery in London, UK, buys Carl Andre's "Bricks" sculpture, *Equivalent 8*.	MAY The British Jockey Club allows women jockeys to compete in horse racing for the first time.
Innovations	JAN The first kidney and pancreatic tissue transplant is carried out in London, UK.	MAR The US *Pioneer 10* spacecraft blasts off for Jupiter, powered by four nuclear generators.	MAR The first video cassette recorder for professional use is introduced in Japan by Sony.	APRIL US *Apollo 16* astronauts go for a ride on the Moon in a special Lunar Roving Vehicle.

LIZA MINNELLI

THE DUKE OF WINDSOR'S FUNERAL

1972

Ground troops leave Vietnam

AUGUST 12

The last American ground combat unit has packed up and left the giant air base at Da Nang, more than eight years after the first US marines landed in South Vietnam. The United States' role in the ground war is now at an end. It is the final stage of President Nixon's policy of "Vietnamization" – bringing the troops home and leaving South Vietnam to fight the communists of North Vietnam itself. America's role in the war continues, however, with giant B-52 bombers carrying out the heaviest raids of the war on communist supply routes, as the North Vietnam army steadily advances toward Saigon in the south.

Olympic nightmare

SEPTEMBER 5

At dawn today the Munich Olympics fell victim to one of the worst terrorist attacks in the history of the modern Olympic movement. A group of Palestinian guerrillas scaled the fence surrounding the Olympic village and stormed the building housing the Israeli team, killing two Israeli team members and taking nine hostages. Twelve thousand police officers surrounded the village as the terrorists demanded the release of 200 Palestinians held in Israeli jails and their own safe passage out of Germany. Negotiations followed, with West German chancellor Willy Brandt flying in to take charge. Finally, agreement was reached to fly the terrorists with their hostages to Cairo, and they were lifted by helicopter from the village to a military airport. As the first terrorists crossed the tarmac, police marksmen opened fire in a rescue attempt that went tragically wrong. In the gun battle that followed, all nine hostages died as well as five terrorists, and one policeman.

STEPPING OUT

With outrageous soles and skyscraper heels, platform shoes are the height of fashion this year. The shoes are all the rage among the young, who are following in the footsteps of glamorous rock idols such as David Bowie and Gary Glitter.

Hooded terrorist looks out from the living quarters of the Israeli team

JULY–DECEMBER

AUG Uganda's dictator Idi Amin announces that 50,000 Asians with UK passports are to be expelled.

OCT The US and the USSR sign a Strategic Arms Limitation Treaty (SALT) to reduce the number of missiles.

NOV Republican candidate Richard Nixon wins a second term as president of the United States in a landslide election victory.

NOV Richard Leakey displays a 2.6 million-year-old human skull, found near Lake Rudolf, Kenya.

JUL Eddie Merckx of Belgium wins his fourth Tour de France cycling race.

SEP US swimmer Mark Spitz wins a record seven gold medals at the Olympics.

SEP Bobby Fischer beats Boris Spassky from the USSR to become the first World Chess Champion from the US.

SEP Russian gymnast Olga Korbut captivates crowds at the Munich Olympics.

JUL The first cable television program is aired in Britain by Greenwich Cablevision.

MARK SPITZ WINS GOLD

JUL The first female FBI agents, a former US marine and former nun, are sworn in.

OCT Credit cards are introduced in Britain for the first time.

LEAKEY DICOVERS THE OLDEST HUMAN SKULL

NOV *Pong*, the world's first computer game, is launched in a bar in the US.

1973

Vietnam peace treaty signed

JANUARY 27

A peace treaty to end the war in Vietnam has, at last, been agreed on in Paris. Once a ceasefire is declared, and the fighting stops, a multinational force will be drafted in to monitor the truce. Within two months all military prisoners will be released and all United States troops and advisers removed. President Nixon told the American people that the treaty will "bring peace with honor." The chief negotiator for North Vietnam, Le Duc Tho, declared that "right has triumphed over wrong."

Vietnam peace talks

Picasso dies at Mougins

APRIL 8

Pablo Picasso died today, at age 91, after suffering a heart attack at his château in Mougins, France. Born in Malaga, Spain, he moved to Paris as a young man and spent most of his life in France. Regarded by many as the greatest artist of the 20th century, he helped to change the course of modern art through his endless experiments with different styles, including Cubism, neo-Classicism, and Surrealism. His energy for work was legendary. It is estimated that during his long life he produced about 140,000 paintings and drawings, and 100,000 engravings. Other work by him included collages and ceramics.

Ceasefire at Wounded Knee

MAY 8

After 70 days, the Battle of Wounded Knee, in South Dakota, has ended, with Native American activists reaching agreement with the government. The conflict began when 200 members of the militant American Indian Movement seized Wounded Knee on the Sioux Oglala Reservation. Fighting resulted in two deaths, several injuries, and about 300 arrests. The Sioux Indians were protesting against broken treaties.

New tower

Sears Tower

MAY 4

The Sears Tower in Chicago, Illinois, today officially became the tallest skyscaper in the world. At a height of 1,453 ft (443 m), its 110 stories will provide office space for more than 16,500 people. The building has been specially designed to withstand strong winds.

Sioux Indian at Wounded Knee

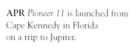

1973

MOUNTAIN BIKE

A Californian cycling club has adapted standard road bikes for riding canyon slopes. With extra gears, thicker tires, and a lightweight frame, the new mountain bikes can deal with all types of difficult terrain.

Actor Bruce Lee dies

JULY 20

Bruce Lee, actor and martial arts expert, has died in Hong Kong from cerebral edema at the age of 32. Lee, who first became a cult figure in the 1960s when he appeared in an American TV series *The Green Hornet*, later shot to international fame in the kung fu film *Fists of Fury* in 1971. Lee's latest film, *Enter the Dragon*, has sparked worldwide interest in martial arts. During one fight scene, he performed a flying kick so fast that it had to be shot in slow motion.

Bruce Lee in the film Enter the Dragon

Military coup in Chile

SEPTEMBER 11

Right-wing opponents have assassinated President Allende of Chile and overthrown the socialist government in a military coup. Led by General Augusto Pinochet, the military attacked the presidential palace with rockets, bombs, and tanks. The president held out for over two hours, supported by the presidential guard and civilian police. More than 2,500 people have been killed in the fierce fighting. Right-wing opposition to Allende has been gathering strength since he took office in 1970.

War in Middle East

OCTOBER 17

The Middle East is witnessing some of the fiercest battles between the Arabs and the Israelis since World War II.

The conflict began eleven days ago on Yom Kippur, the holiest day in the Jewish calendar, when Egyptian troops launched a surprise attack on Israel across the Suez Canal. At the same time, Syria invaded the Israeli-occupied Golan Heights, rapidly capturing Mount Hebron. Israel, at first caught unprepared, fought back, regained territory, then advanced into Syria and across the Suez Canal into Egypt. The world superpowers have stepped in, with the Soviet Union providing arms for the Arabs and the United States backing Israel.

The military attacks the presidential palace

JULY–DECEMBER

JUL Paul Getty III, the teenage grandson of oil tycoon Paul Getty, is kidnapped in the US. The kidnappers demand a ransom.

JUL England beats Australia in the final of the first ever women's cricket World Cup, scoring 279 runs for 3.

SEP The world's largest airport, covering 17,500 acres (7,082 hectares), opens in Texas.

OCT War in the Middle East stops after Egypt, Israel, and Syria accept a UN call for a ceasefire.

SEP Singer and songwriter Elton John has a number one hit single with *Goodbye Yellow Brick Road*.

ELTON JOHN

OCT The Bosphorus suspension bridge, linking Europe and Asia, is opened.

DEC Paul Getty III is freed in Italy. Earlier, his right ear was sent through the mail with a ransom demand.

SEP UK race car driver Jackie Stewart retires with a record 27 Grand Prix wins.

OCT The Sydney Opera House is officially opened in Australia.

SYDNEY OPERA HOUSE

DEC Britain goes on a "three-day week" as industry grinds to a halt, paralyzed by rail, mine, and power station disputes.

OCT The first UK legal commercial radio station, LBC, is launched.

DEC Two US *Skylab* astronauts make a record seven-hour space walk.

1974

Happy days mania

Henry Winkler as the Fonz

JANUARY 11

A new sitcom, *Happy Days*, starts tonight on ABC TV in the United States. Following the fortunes of a group of 1950s high-school kids in Milwaukee, the show's star is a character called Arthur Fonzarelli, played by Henry Winkler. "The Fonz" wears a black leather jacket and is always surrounded by girls. He is so cool that he can even turn on a jukebox by simply snapping his fingers! Television critics are predicting a big hit.

NIKE SNEAKER

The latest athletic shoes are light and comfortable and are selling like hotcakes. Some of the most exciting designs come from a new American company called Nike. This Waffle Trainer, an instant bestseller, has a revolutionary sole that was developed by pouring rubber into a kitchen waffle iron.

Hank Aaron sets new record

APRIL 8

In a match against the Los Angeles Dodgers today, Henry Louis "Hank" Aaron hit his 715th home run, breaking the record held for 39 years by the legendary Babe Ruth. Born in Alabama, Aaron was one of the first black players to enter major league baseball. Nicknamed "the Hammer," he began playing for the Atlanta Braves in 1954. Some commentators have described him as the greatest natural right-handed hitter of all time. Governor Jimmy Carter presented Aaron with a license plate marked "HLA715" to commemorate his score.

Skylab splashes down

FEBRUARY 8

United States astronauts Lt. Col. Gerald Carr, Lt. Col. William Pogue, and Dr. Edward Gibson have splashed down safely in the Pacific Ocean after setting a new record in the history of manned space flight. They have spent 84 days in orbit on board the US's first space station, *Skylab*, which was launched in May 1973. After being occupied by three different crews, who conducted a variety of medical and scientific experiments, *Skylab* is now empty, but will continue orbiting the Earth.

JANUARY–JUNE

World Events

FEB UK train robber Ronnie Biggs is arrested in Brazil, after eight-and-a-half years on the run.

FEB Soviet author Alexander Solzhenitsyn is exiled after publication of *The Gulag Archipelago*, which is critical of the USSR.

FEB Prime Minister Edward Heath calls a general election in the UK after coalminers vote for an all-out national strike.

MAY India carries out its first underground nuclear test, becoming the sixth nation to possess an atom bomb.

Entertainment

JAN In the UK, professional soccer matches are played on Sundays for the first time.

APR The film *The Sting*, starring Paul Newman and Robert Redford, wins seven Academy Awards.

MAY Shedding clothes is the latest craze as "streakers" run naked on campuses, at sports events, and even at the Oscars!

JUN 26-year-old Soviet dancer Mikhail Baryshnikov defects from the Bolshoi Ballet Company while on tour in Canada.

Innovations

JAN A company in the US develops the airbag, a new safety device for cars.

ALEXANDER SOLZHENITSYN

MAR US space probe *Mariner 10* takes the first close-up pictures of the surface of the planet Mercury.

JUN The first bar codes are introduced on products for sale at the Marsh Supermarket in Troy, Ohio.

A STREAKER

JUN Scientists warn that the chlorofluorocarbons used in aerosols may be damaging the ozone layer.

1974

Patty Hearst joins captors

APRIL 15

United States newspaper heiress Patty Hearst, who was kidnapped in February by an extremist left-wing group called the Symbionese Liberation Army, has been involved in an armed bank raid in San Francisco with her captors. The FBI has issued a warrant for the arrest of the gang, including Hearst. Hearst's parents met a ransom demand, but, instead of getting their daughter back, they received a taped message saying she had "chosen to stay and fight."

Nixon first president to resign

AUGUST 8

Richard Nixon, facing impeachment by Congress after refusing to hand over taped conversations with his aides, has announced his resignation. It is the first time in the history of the United States that a president has relinquished office. It is also the final chapter of the "Watergate" scandal, which began on June 17, 1972, when five burglars were caught planting bugging devices in the Democrats' election campaign headquarters in the Watergate complex in Washington, D.C. The scandal has rocked the Republican party to its roots, revealing a saga of dirty tricks, corruption, and cover-ups that has implicated the president himself.

Pandas get new home

SEPTEMBER 14

Two giant pandas, given to former conservative prime minister Edward Heath on his visit to the People's Republic of China, arrived today at their new home at Britain's London Zoo in Regent's Park. Ching Ching, meaning "Crystal Bright," and Chia Chia, "Most Excellent," were both born in 1972. In return for the two giant pandas, London Zoo has sent two white rhinoceroses, Nykasi and Mungo, to China.

JULY–DECEMBER

JUL Isabelita Perón becomes president of Argentina after the death of her husband, Juan Domingo Perón.

JUL US tennis players Chris Evert and Jimmy Connors win the Wimbledon singles titles in the UK.

SEP A US astronomer discovers the 13th moon of Jupiter, and names it *Leda*.

FIRST BLACK MODEL ON *VOGUE* COVER

SEP Emperor of Ethiopia Haile Selassie is overthrown and Ethiopia is declared a socialist state.

AUG Beverly Johnson becomes the first black model to appear on the front cover of *Vogue* magazine.

SEP First transmission of Ceefax Teletext, an information service, takes place on BBC TV in the UK.

NOV UK police hunt for Lord Lucan, who disappeared after his children's nanny was found battered to death.

AUG 13-year-old Egyptian school girl Abla Khairi becomes the youngest person to swim the English Channel.

OCT David Kunst, from the US, becomes the first man to have walked around the world.

BAY CITY ROLLERS

NOV IRA terrorists blow up two Birmingham pubs, in the UK, killing 17 people and injuring 120.

NOV Teen group the Bay City Rollers are the latest pop sensation in the UK.

DEC The Altair 880, the first personal computer (PC), is launched in the US.

THE FEMINIST FIGHT

AT THE BEGINNING OF the 20th century, early feminists made giant strides along the road to equality. In many countries they won the right to vote and succeeded in opening up employment opportunities, improving education for girls, and reforming certain laws. During the late 1960s and 1970s, however, a new women's liberation movement emerged. It was inspired by student protests all around the world and by the civil rights campaigns in the United States. More than a century after the first women's rights meetings, a newly politicized generation of women began to wonder how much progress had, in fact, been made. Women felt they were still fighting discrimination in a male-dominated world, where men continued to hold most of the positions of power, while women provided most of the labor.

Spreading the news

New magazines produced by women for women, such as *Spare Rib* in the UK and *Ms.* magazine in the US, were launched in the early 1970s. These magazines broke new ground with regular columns on law, sex, health, work, and the arts, instead of the traditional diet of knitting patterns and recipes. They were professionally produced, and tried to reach women in every walk of life.

Leading the movement

US writer Betty Friedan is often regarded as the mother of the modern women's movement. In 1963 she wrote *The Feminine Mystique*, in which she argued that women were discouraged from seeking careers outside of the home. In 1969 she founded the National Organization of Women (NOW). The group campaigned for equal rights for women, including legalized abortion, 24-hour childcare centers, and equal opportunities in employment and education.

PROTESTERS CARRYING SYMBOLIC CROSS

First voices of feminism

During World War II women worked in industry and agriculture. But when the men came home at the end of the war, women had to give up their jobs and return to their traditional roles as wives and mothers. Against this background, in 1949, French philosopher and feminist Simone de Beauvoir wrote her groundbreaking book *The Second Sex*. Causing shock and outrage in many quarters, de Beauvoir argued that women had been conditioned by social tradition to occupy a secondary place in relation to men.

Simone de Beauvoir
Le deuxième sexe 1

SIMONE DE BEAUVOIR

Too much to bear

On International Women's Day in 1971 a huge Women's Liberation March took place in London, England. It was the biggest women's rally in Britain since the "suffragettes" won the vote for women at the beginning of the century. Some of the marchers carried a cross made out of a female tailor's dummy draped in chains. Symbols of women's domestic enslavement – washing, a shopping bag, and an apron – dangled from the crossbar. A petition was presented to the prime minister demanding equal education, job opportunities, and equal pay, as well as free childcare, contraception, and legalized abortion.

Women in an age of change

Women's liberation in the United States grew out of the campaigns of the 1960s when thousands of students protested against the war in Vietnam and joined the fight for civil rights and racial equality. Many women realized that there was another struggle closer at hand – to liberate themselves from oppression by men. Women's groups sprang up all over the country, generating a tide of sisterly solidarity. At the 1968 Miss America Pageant in Atlantic City, feminists staged their first public protest and dumped bras and girdles into a "freedom trash bucket." The media described the event as demonstrators "burning their bras." This misleading catchphrase was used repeatedly to stereotype feminists and dismiss their campaigns.

Statue of Liberty

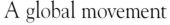

YOUNG FEMINIST
CAMPAIGNS FOR
EQUAL RIGHTS

A global movement

The women's movement has flourished in many countries all over the world for more than 150 years. New Zealand became the first country to grant national women's suffrage in 1893, while women in Switzerland had to wait another 78 years until they were granted the vote in 1971. More recently, feminists have campaigned on issues like childcare, equal education, and pay and job opportunities, aiming to change people's attitudes as well as the law.

Freedom of dress

When Ayatollah Khomeini returned to Iran in 1979, he imposed strict laws in the name of Islam that often affected the lives of women. For example, western-style dress was forbidden and women were forced to wear a head-to-toe robe called a "chador." Many Iranian women objected to this legislation and marched through the streets of Tehran chanting "freedom, not the chador," demanding the right to dress as they pleased.

Toward greater equality

Women's groups have helped reassess and redefine the traditional roles of men and women in the 20th century. Despite the achievements of the women's liberation movement of the 1970s, there is still a long way to go, with few women in top jobs or positions of power. The burden of childcare has remained largely on female shoulders, with many working mothers forced to opt for low-paying part-time jobs.

1975

Saigon falls as Americans withdraw

APRIL 30

The war in Vietnam finally ended today, two years after US forces left the area. South Vietnam surrendered as the communist North Vietnamese troops and tanks took control of the capital, Saigon, which has already been renamed Ho Chi Minh City. The last of the United States troops have left the country, airlifted to safety by helicopters. They left behind them scenes of panic as thousands of the South Vietnamese, fearful of the new communist regime, try to escape by boat and plane.

The killing fields

Khmer Rouge soldiers

JUNE 15

Cambodia, already devastated by a war that killed a quarter of a million people, is now facing another terrible human tragedy. According to reports from refugees who have managed to slip across the border into Thailand, the new communist Khmer Rouge government, led by Pol Pot, has embarked on a regime of unparalleled brutality. Since the Khmer Rouge took control only two months ago, thousands of people have been executed or worked to death. Everyone has to dress alike, and the government has forbidden the practice of any religion. Cambodians are being driven out into the countryside to till the soil with their bare hands, or to take the place of water buffalo pulling plows. They are starving, with only a daily cup of rice to eat.

SOLAR POWER BOAT

Alternative sources of energy, such as solar power, are constantly being put to new uses. This boat, *Solar Craft 1*, built by A. T. Freeman in Britain, was first put through its paces in February.

Arthur Ashe

Ashe is champ

JULY 5

Arthur Ashe, who started his amazing tennis career playing in the segregated parks of Richmond, Virginia, today became the first black men's champion at the Wimbledon lawn tennis tournament in London, UK. He beat the favorite, fellow American Jimmy Connors, in a thrilling four-set final.

JANUARY–APRIL

World Events	**FEB** Turkish Cypriot leader Rauf Denktash declares Turkish Cyprus independent.	**FEB** Margaret Thatcher wins leadership of the Conservative Party and is the first woman to lead a political party in the UK.	**FEB** In Katmandu, Nepal, 29-year-old King Birendra is crowned as the world's only Hindu and absolute monarch.	**MAR** In Riyadh, Saudi Arabia, King Faisal is assassinated by his mentally deranged nephew, who is later beheaded.
Entertainment	**MAR** In the UK, 85-year-old actor Charlie Chaplin is knighted by Queen Elizabeth.	**APR** Anatoly Karpov of the USSR becomes the youngest world chess champion at age 23.	**APR** The musical *A Chorus Line*, by Kleban and Hamlish, is first performed in the US.	**APR** US born music-hall singer and star of the Folies Bergères, Josephine Baker, dies at age 69.
Innovations	**JAN** The UK abandons the project to connect England and France with a sea tunnel.	**FEB** UK Sir John Huxley, who made important contributions to biology, especially genetics, dies at age 87.	**FEB** The UK government approves a plan for two new nuclear power stations.	**APR** Nineteen-year-old Bill Gates forms Microsoft with his friend Paul Allen in the US.

ANATOLY KARPOV

A CHORUS LINE

1975

Clay army found

JULY 11

A huge army of 6,000 life-sized terra-cotta warriors has been unearthed by Chinese archaeologists near the ancient capital of Xian. The army was first discovered by peasants digging for water. With their chariots, spears, and horses, the figures are drawn up rank by rank in battle formation. After more than 2,000 years they are still guarding the tomb of the first Qin emperor, who died in 206 BC. Qin Shi Huangdi unified the country and the name "China" is taken from his name. Under his rule, thousands of people died building the Great Wall of China. Workers who helped build his tomb were walled up inside to keep it secret.

Astronauts meet cosmonauts

JULY 17

While United States and Soviet missiles remain poised for mutual self-destruction on Earth, a historic encounter between the two superpowers has taken place in space. The US *Apollo* and the Soviet *Soyuz* spacecraft docked 140 miles (225 km) above the Atlantic ocean. Astronaut Tom Stafford and cosmonaut Alexei Leono shook hands through the hatches in the first international meeting to be held in space.

Hunting the Jackal

JULY 29

As the hunt continues for the international terrorist and hit man Ilich Ramirex Sanchez evidence is mounting that the Soviet Union's KGB has been involved in his activities. Sanchez is better known by his nickname, Carlos the Jackal. This comes from his ability to carry out successful hits and then vanish into the shadows.

MAY–AUGUST

JUN In Uganda, a tribunal finds UK author Dennis Hills guilty of "treason" for criticizing the dictator Idi Amin.

JUN In Egypt, the Suez Canal reopens to international maritime traffic for the first time in eight years.

JUN Indian prime minister Mrs. Indira Gandhi is barred from public office for six years after revelations of electoral corruption.

JUL Yitzhak Rabin arrives in Bonn on the first ever visit by an Israeli premier to West Germany.

MAY US singer Frank Sinatra wins damages from the UK's BBC over a program linking him to the Mafia.

MAY The UK's leading woman sculptor, Barbara Hepworth, dies in a fire at her studio at St. Ives, in Cornwall.

JUN Brazilian soccer hero Pelé signs a $7 million three-year contract with the New York Cosmos in the US.

JUN New Zealand athlete John Walker runs the mile in a record-breaking 3 minutes 49.4 seconds.

MAY Japanese climber Junko Tabei becomes the first woman to scale Mount Everest in the Himalayas.

JUNKO TABEI

JUN In London, UK, a session of the House of Commons is broadcast live on the radio for the first time.

JUN The UK's first North Sea oil is piped to British Petroleum's Isle of Grain refinery in Kent.

JOHN WALKER

OCT Soviet probes *Venera 9* and *Venera 10* transmit the first pictures from the surface of the planet Venus.

1975

King Juan Carlos sworn in

NOVEMBER 22

Don Juan Carlos Borbon y Borbon today became the first king of Spain since his grandfather Alfonso XIII went into exile in 1931. He succeeds General Franco, who ruled Spain with a rod of iron from the end of the civil war in 1939 until his death two days ago.

Civil war in Angola

NOVEMBER 24

Only two weeks after Angola gained independence from Portugal it is being torn apart by a civil war. At least 40,000 people are dead and a million have been made homeless. Several groups are vying for control of the country, each receiving support from major world powers. The Marxist Popular Movement for the Liberation of Angola (MPLA) is receiving military aid from the Soviet Union and Cuba, while the United States is supporting two non-Marxist movements. South Africa is backing yet another faction.

PTERODACTYL BONES

Quetzalcoatlus northropi
The TEXAS PTEROSAUR

The fossilized remains of a gigantic pterodactyl, or pterosaur, extinct for 60 million years, have been found in Big Bend National Park in Texas. With a wingspan of 51 ft (15.5 m), the pterodactyl is the largest flying creature ever discovered.

First pop video by Queen for single *Bohemian Rhapsody*

DECEMBER 20

It took six months for British pop group Queen to perfect its new album *A Night at the Opera* in one of the most expensive recording sessions in the history of rock 'n' roll. The result is that *Bohemian Rhapsody*, the seven-minute single from the album, shot to the top of the UK charts and is still riding high three weeks later. It is split into two parts – or movements – and uses state-of-the-art technology as well as snatches of classical opera. Queen has also made a special video to promote *Bohemian Rhapsody*, and this is no doubt helping boost sales.

SEPTEMBER–DECEMBER

World Events	SEP Fighting between Christians and Muslims is tearing apart the Lebanese capital of Beirut.	OCT Soviet dissident and human rights campaigner Dr. Andrei Sakharov is awarded the Nobel Peace Prize.	NOV The Australian left-wing Labour prime minister Gough Whitlam is dismissed, causing a national constitutional crisis.	DEC Armed South Moluccan terrorists surrender after a 15-day siege of the Indonesian Consulate in Amsterdam.
Entertainment	SEP Czech tennis player Martina Navratilova defects to the US.	OCT UK climbers Douglas Haston and Doug Scott conquer the southwest face of Everest.	OCT Austrian race car driver Niki Lauda becomes the world auto racing champion.	DEC Rod Stewart, lead singer of UK group The Faces, announces he is leaving the group to form his own band.
Innovations	OCT Human remains 3.75 million years old are discovered in Tanzania.	NOV UK director Ken Russell's *Lisztomania* is the first feature film in Dolby stereo.	NOV The UK's first underwater pipeline for North Sea oil is opened.	DEC UK pilot Yvonne Pope becomes the first woman to captain a jet airline.

ANDREI SAKHAROV

NIKI LAUDA

1976

Concorde flies from Paris to Rio

JANUARY 21
A regular supersonic passenger service across the Atlantic Ocean was launched today when an Air France *Concorde* airliner made its first commercial flight from Paris, France, to Rio de Janeiro in Brazil. With a cruising speed of 1,461 mph (2,338 km/h) the supersonic turbojet can cross the Atlantic in just three hours.

100 hostages rescued from Entebbe airport in intrepid raid

Some of the freed hostages

JULY 4
Israeli commandos carried out a daring rescue mission at Entebbe airport in Uganda last night, freeing more than 100 hostages held by pro-Palestinian terrorists. In a 35-minute battle, 20 Ugandan soldiers, all seven hijackers, three hostages, and one Israeli soldier were killed.

Soweto uprising

JUNE 16
The black township of Soweto, a sprawling suburb of Johannesburg, South Africa, is today witnessing scenes of horrifying violence. There is serious rioting and looting, and at least 50 people have been killed and hundreds more wounded. The violent and bloody scenes came after white riot police fired live ammunition into a 10,000-strong march of school children protesting the segregated education system. Last year the South African government issued a decree proclaiming that black secondary school academic subjects must be taught in the Afrikaans language. This sparked a wave of strikes, marches, and demonstrations culminating in today's events. For most black people, Afrikaans, a form of Dutch, is the hated language of white oppression.

A bus set on fire during the riot

JANUARY–JUNE

JAN Chou En-Lai, prime minister of China and second-in-command to Chairman Mao since 1949, dies in Peking at age 78.

JAN The UK's richest author and "queen of crime fiction," Agatha Christie, dies at age 85.

FEB Soviet officials admit to transmitting microwaves at the US embassy in Moscow.

KONICA AUTO-FOCUS CAMERA

MAR US newspaper heiress Patty Hearst is found guilty of assisting in an armed robbery with her radical leftist kidnappers.

APR German-born artist Max Ernst, leading member of the Surrealist group, dies at age 85.

MAR Japanese company Konica launches the first auto-focus camera.

MAR Isabel Perón, president of Argentina since her husband's death in 1974, is deposed in a bloodless coup by military leaders.

MAY Boxer Muhammad Ali knocks out Richard Dunn in Germany to retain his world heavyweight title.

APR Australian scientist Dr. Gerald Shannon develops a bionic artificial arm with a strong hand grip.

HOWARD HUGHES

APR The US billionaire recluse Howard Hughes dies after suffering a stroke in his private jet.

JUN Jockey Lester Piggott wins the Derby at Epsom, England, for a record seventh time.

JUN In Colorado the first women enter the formerly male-only Air Force Academy.

1976

Nadia leaps into record books

JULY 31

A tiny gymnast from Romania has stolen the show at the Olympic Games in Montreal after scoring the first perfect "10" in gymnastic history. Her name is Nadia Comaneci and she is only 14 years old. She was awarded maximum points for her dazzling vaults, leaps, and twists on the uneven bars in the team competition. She repeated the feat seven times, winning three gold medals.

Nadia Comaneci wins three golds

Probe sends pictures of planet Mars

JULY 20

Is there really life on Mars – and if so what does it look like? We might just find out – the US *Viking 1* spacecraft made a perfect landing on the Martian sand dunes today, sending back the first close-up pictures of a barren surface littered with rocks and boulders. The $500 million probe, which soon will be joined by *Viking 2*, will also report on the planet's weather conditions. More importantly, it will carry out specially designed experiments on the soil that are aimed at discovering any signs of plant or animal life.

China mourns Chairman Mao

SEPTEMBER 9

Chairman Mao Zedong, leader of the People's Republic of China and its 800 million people since 1949, has died at age 82, after suffering a series of strokes. Wreaths have already been placed on the Revolutionary Martyrs Monument in the Square of Heavenly Peace, Beijing. Many thousands of mourners are expected to file past his body, which will be preserved and is to lie in state in a transparent crystal sarcophagus. Who will succeed him is not so clear. A power struggle between rival factions within the Chinese Communist Party seems unavoidable. The party has already split into two main groups – on the left, the "radical Maoists," led by the late leader's widow Chiang Chin, and, on the right, the "moderate communists," led by Deng Xiaoping.

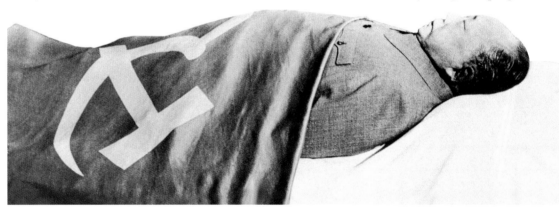

JULY–DECEMBER

World Events	**JUL** An accident at a chemical plant near Milan, Italy, releases a huge cloud of poisonous gas.	**AUG** A women's peace movement is launched in Northern Ireland at a rally of 20,000 Protestants and Roman Catholics.	**OCT** In China, Mao's widow and three other people are arrested for plotting to overthrow the government.	**NOV** A major earthquake strikes eastern Turkey, devastating 80 villages and killing 3,000 people.
Entertainment	**JUL** In the UK, 20-year-old Swedish tennis player Björn Borg becomes Wimbledon champion.	**AUG** Austrian-born film director Fritz Lang, who made *Metropolis*, *M*, and *The Big Heat*, dies at age 86.	**NOV** *Rocky*, a film about a boxer, written by and starring Sylvester Stallone, is a big hit in the US.	**DEC** UK composer Benjamin Britten, the first musician to be made a noble for life, dies at 65.
Innovations	**AUG** Left-handed check books are issued for the first time by a bank in the UK.	**AUG** After nine years' work, biologists in the US have sucessfully created the first artificial functioning gene.	**SEP** Percy Shaw, the UK inventor of "cat's-eyes," reflectors that transformed road safety, dies at 86.	**OCT** The £16 million National Theater in London, in the UK, is officially opened, three years late.

BJÖRN BORG

ROCKY

1977

Arts center opens

JANUARY 31

France acquired a new landmark and tourist attraction today – the high-tech Pompidou National Center for Art and Culture in the Beaubourg district of Paris. Designed by Italian and British architects Renzo Piano and Richard Rogers, the six-story glass building proudly displays its structural supports on the outside as well as its brightly painted ducts, tubes, water pipes, and escalators. Reactions to the unorthodox new building are predictably mixed.

Collision leads to disaster on runway

MARCH 27

Two jumbo jets collided on the runway at Tenerife airport in the Canary Islands tonight, killing 574 people, most of them vacationers from the United States and Europe. It is the worst disaster in the history of aviation. The accident happened when a Pan Am jet turned onto the runway just as another plane, belonging to the Dutch airline KLM, was about to take off. Both the aircrafts had been diverted from La Palma airport because of a bomb explosion there. As they collided, the two giant jets burst into flames and all 348 passengers on board the KLM plane died. Miraculously, there are at least 70 survivors who managed to escape from the burning wreckage of the Pan Am jet, and they are being treated for severe burns. Radio and television stations are broadcasting emergency appeals for more medical staff in order to cope with the crisis. What caused the accident is not yet known.

MORE THAN A PUPPET

Jim Henson's favorite puppets have swept to international stardom with their own TV series, *The Muppet Show*. Real-life celebrities are clamoring to be invited on the show, which has won top television awards in many countries around the world.

JANUARY–APRIL

JAN Convicted killer Gary Gilmore becomes the first person to be sentenced to be executed in the US in ten years.

JAN Charter 77, calling for civil rights for all citizens, is signed by more than 240 scholars in communist Czechoslovakia.

JAN Georgia-born ex-peanut farmer Jimmy Carter, the Democrat candidate, is inaugurated as the new president of the US.

FEB Ugandan archbishop Janani Luwum is murdered in the latest wave of killings by President Idi Amin's troops.

JAN TV series *Roots*, by black American Alex Haley, attracts record audiences in the US.

POPULAR TV SERIES ROOTS

FEB UK punk rock group the Sex Pistols is fired by its record company, EMI.

FEB In the US, the space shuttle makes its maiden flight on top of a Boeing 747.

APR Red Rum is the first horse to win the UK's Grand National race three times.

APR US company Polaroid demonstrates a new home movie system, *Polavision*.

THE INAUGURATION OF PRESIDENT CARTER

MAY Punk music is the latest youth sensation around the world.

APR Quadrophonic broadcasts are started on BBC radio in the UK.

JAN UK inventor Clive Sinclair introduces a £175 2-in (5-cm) screen television.

1977

Star Wars is box office blockbuster

MAY 25

Star Wars, a new science fiction film directed by George Lucas, is an epic tale of good versus evil. Using state-of-the-art technology, including a new computer-assisted camera system, the film is full of spectacular visual and sound effects and is already being billed as this summer's box office hit. Like all good fairy stories, *Star Wars* has a handsome hero, a princess in distress, an evil emperor, and courageous knights. It also stars two comic robots called R2D2 and C-3PO.

The robot R2D2

HYDROTHERMAL VENTS

Scientists were amazed to find the first hydrothermal vents on the seabed of the Pacific. The vents spew mineral-rich, warm water that allows animal life, such as bacteria and clams, to flourish.

Maiden voyage

AUGUST 12

The first manned free-flight test of the space shuttle orbiter *Enterprise* took place successfully today at Edwards Air Force Base in California. After the shuttle orbiter had separated from the Boeing 747 "taxi" jet at a height of 22,802 ft (6,950 m), astronauts Fred Haise and C. Gordon Fullerton flew the 84-ton glider around a U-shaped course before making a perfect landing on the dry lake runway. During the flight, which lasted 5 minutes 23 seconds, the orbiter performed as well as wind tunnel tests had predicted. The crew commented on its surprisingly quick responses and said that it handled like a fighter aircraft. The test series is designed to assess the craft's performance in the lower atmosphere. It will be concluded with four more free-flight tests before the orbiter is taken to the Marshall Space Flight Center at Huntsville, Alabama for structural tests.

The Orbiter Enterprise about to split from the Boeing 747

MAY–AUGUST

World Events	MAY Menachem Begin, former leader of a Jewish terror group, is elected Israeli prime minster.	MAY Yomo Kenyatta, president of Kenya, bans big game hunting in an effort to conserve the country's wildlife.	JUN Silver Jubilee celebrations are held all over the UK to mark Queen Elizabeth II's accession to the throne.	JUN In Spain's first election in 41 years, A. Suarez is elected president. Elections had been banned by General Franco.
Entertainment	MAY The Paris to Istanbul *Orient Express* makes its final journey after 94 years service.	MAY Eleven-year-old Nigel Short of the UK is the youngest competitor in a national chess championship.	AUG English cricket player Geoff Boycott scores his one hundredth century.	AUG US comic actor Groucho Marx, famous for his crouching walk, waggling eyebrows, and cigar, dies at age 86.
Innovations	MAY The world's largest particle accelerator is opened at CERN in Geneva.	JUN The 808-mile (1,300-km) Transalaska Pipeline System begins transporting oil across Alaska.	AUG The Soviet ship *Arktika* is the first surface vessel ever to reach the north pole.	AUG Space probes *Voyager 1* and 2 are launched on journeys to Jupiter and Saturn.

LAST JOURNEY FOR ORIENT EXPRESS

ALDOLFO SUAREZ

1977

"The King" is dead

Elvis Presley dies in Memphis

AUGUST 16

Elvis Presley, the king of rock 'n' roll, has died at Memphis Baptist Memorial Hospital, at age 42. His health had been deteriorating for some years and he was vastly overweight. There have also been persistent rumors of drug abuse. Thousands of distraught fans have gathered outside the star's mansion, Graceland, to pay their last respects. Elvis first gyrated his way to the top with *Heartbreak Hotel* in 1956. He went on to sell more than 500 million records during his long career.

Biko dies

SEPTEMBER 12

Steve Biko, the South African black leader, has died of brain injuries in a prison hospital in Pretoria. After being arrested last month, Biko was held in a police cell in Port Elizabeth. For five days he was kept naked in leg irons and handcuffs and interrogated. A struggle allegedly took place when his manacles were removed and Biko was later found dying in his cell.

Bokassa on his golden coronation throne

Boat people flee Vietnam

DECEMBER 3

Thousands of desperate refugees are fleeing to escape the communist regime that has taken over in South Vietnam. They are taking to the open sea in small, unsafe boats in the hope of reaching a country where they can live.

Coronation of Bokassa

DECEMBER 4

Jean Bedel Bokassa, president of the Central African Republic, today realized his ambitions when he was crowned emperor to the sound of tribal drums and Mozart. The former sergeant in France's colonial army, who took office in 1966, spared no expense for the ceremony. Altogether, the celebrations cost about $30 million, and were paid for by French president Giscard d'Estaing. The new emperor was wearing an elaborately embroidered coronation uniform, and his coach was pulled by specially imported horses.

SEPTEMBER–DECEMBER

SEP The US and Panama sign the Panama Canal Treaty, returning the canal zone to Panama in 1999.

SEP Japanese baseball player Sadaharu Oh beats Hank Aaron's major league record of 715 home runs.

SEP Freddie Laker's low-priced *Skytrain* service from London to New York is launched.

JOHN TRAVOLTA DOLL

OCT Hostages are rescued by German commandos from a jet hijacked by Palestinian terrorists at Mogadishu airport in Somalia.

DEC John Travolta stars in the film *Saturday Night Fever* and disco mania takes off. John Travolta dolls are a big seller.

OCT The supersonic airliner *Concorde* makes its first flight from Toulouse, France, to New York.

NOV President Sadat of Egypt visits Israel and addresses the Knesset, the Israeli parliament.

DEC Paul McCartney's new group Wings tops the charts with hit single *Mull of Kintyre*.

DEC Soviet spacecraft *Soyuz 26* docks with *Salyut 6*, the orbiting research space station.

CHARLIE CHAPLIN

DEC Israeli leader Menachem Begin declares that Israel is ready to return Sinai to Egypt.

DEC UK comic genius Charlie Chaplin dies at his home in Switzerland, at age 88.

DEC Heathrow Airport in the UK is the first airport to be connected to a city rail system.

SOUNDS OF THE SEVENTIES

WHILE HEAVY METAL AND BIG-DRAW STADIUM BANDS took off in the United States, elsewhere pop music exploded in many different directions. Glitter, or glam, rock provided welcome relief from serious progressive rock and set the scene for the New Romantics of the Eighties. Punk stuck its nose up at disco and produced a generation of successful new-wave bands that made pop music with attitude. Records were beginning to sell in the millions on both sides of the Atlantic. Some rock stars became super-rich, and a new wealthy pop aristocracy was born.

Abba wins Eurovision

Abba won the Eurovision Song Contest for Sweden in 1974. The song *Waterloo* became the first of many to sell a million copies. The music was streamlined yet catchy, as was the group's name, an acronym of the band members' initials – Agnetha, Benny, Bjorn, and Anni-Frid.

First family of pop

The Jackson Five shot to stardom in 1970, having been spotted and signed by a record company the year before at a concert in their home-town of Gary, Indiana. The Jacksons were all brothers – Michael, age 11, Marlon, 13, Jermaine, 16, Toriano, 17, and Sigmund, 19. They were managed by their father, Joe. In 1970 they released three albums that all entered the US top ten. The Jackson Five's fame lasted throughout the Seventies with a string of successful singles, albums, and concerts. They were even turned into a cartoon series!

THE JACKSON FIVE

BOB MARLEY

Reggae superstar

With the ground-breaking 1972 album *Catch a Fire*, Bob Marley and the Wailers brought reggae out of the ghettos and introduced it to a worldwide audience. Formed in 1964, the Wailin' Wailers was made up of Marley, Peter Tosh, and Bunny Livingston. The group signed with Island Records in 1972 and was renamed Bob Marley and the Wailers. After the group split up Bob Marley went on to achieve a dazzling solo career. Sadly, this was cut short in 1981, when he died of cancer. As a tribute to the superstar, his birthday was made a national holiday in Jamaica.

Rock and rollers

Tartan scarves acquired a new street popularity during the mid-1970s thanks to a Scottish group called the Bay City Rollers. Wearing head-to-toe tartan and calf-length pants, their carefully calculated image caused mass hysteria among teenagers on both sides of the Atlantic.

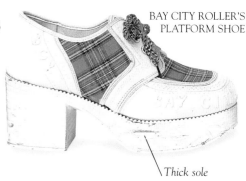

BAY CITY ROLLER'S PLATFORM SHOE

Thick sole

King of glam

Glam rock, also called glitter rock, swept the British pop scene in the early Seventies, paving the way for superstars like Queen and Elton John. Unlike progressive rock, the music was accessible and uncomplicated. The outfits, however, were extraordinary, with platform shoes, outrageous bellbottoms, and glitter galore. David Bowie put on makeup, dyed his hair, and reinvented himself as the hero of his 1972 *Ziggy Stardust* album.

DAVID BOWIE AS ZIGGY STARDUST

Pioneers of electronic pop

Kraftwerk was an avant-garde German group that experimented with synthetic electronic sounds to produce international hits like *Autobahn* in 1975, and *Man Machine* in 1978. The group had a huge influence on the birth of techno and house music in Britain. The single *Computer World* (1981) concentrated on microtechnology, using sounds from a pocket calculator and bleeps from a home computer game.

JOHN TRAVOLTA IN *SATURDAY NIGHT FEVER*

Trademark golden medallion

The disco era

An actor named John Travolta put on his dancing shoes in 1977 and leaped into the lead of *Saturday Night Fever*, a movie about a New York disco. With a throbbing soundtrack by the Bee Gees, it set feet tapping all around the world. A new disco craze was born, and teenagers everywhere copied the steps, leaps, and twirls they saw on the screen. The movie became a box-office smash and one of the most successful films about popular music ever made. The movie sold over 30 million copies worldwide, making it the best-selling soundtrack ever. Seven of the songs topped the singles charts – an all-time record!

COLLECTOR'S PUNK RECORD

Johnny Rotten

Punk rock

The Sex Pistols' lead singer Johnny Rotten could not sing, but he was very good at swearing and hurling abuse at his fans. Strangely enough, audiences loved it and the group became an instant role model for a new generation of British teenagers hungry for rebellion and something new. The first single, *Anarchy in the UK*, entered the UK top 50 at the end of 1976. The sleeve of *God Save the Queen*, the group's 1977 best-selling single, showed the Queen with a safety pin through her nose.

Punk badges

White satin flared pants

Walkin' tunes

Music was available at the flick of a wrist during the 1970s with this circular wrist radio from Japan. Known as a "toot-a-loop" or a "sing-o-ring," this radio could be placed on a table, stuck on a wall, or made into a bracelet. This forerunner to the personal walkman was all the rage among teenagers, particularly in the United States.

New wave

Post-punk groups, like the Jam, the Police, and U2, moved into the mainstream. Blondie, a successful punk group in the mid-1970s, shot to international fame in 1978 with the album *Parallel Lines*, which mixed pop and disco.

1978

Cleaning the oil-polluted coastlines of Brittany

Sea turns black

MARCH 16

The world's worst oil spill to date occurred today when the supertanker *Amoco Cadiz*, carrying 1.3 million barrels of crude oil, ran aground on rocks off the coast of Brittany in France, causing untold damage. Battered by Atlantic waves, the ship broke in two, spewing its entire cargo into the ocean. Using chemical antipollution sprays, a fleet of vessels has been fighting to control a huge oil slick that is slithering toward the Channel Islands. The spill has already blanketed 70 miles (113 km) of French coastline with a thick, black slime. This catastrophe will cause incalculable harm to local birds and other wildlife in what is France's largest bird sanctuary. It is also likely to have a devastating effect on the local fishing industry and on tourism in the region.

GARFIELD

A comic strip by Jim Davis about a fat orange cat called Garfield has gained an enormous following this year. It was launched in June and the strip now runs in more than 40 newspapers in the United States.

Test-tube baby

JULY 26

The world's first "test-tube" baby, Louise Brown, was delivered today by cesarean section at Oldham Hospital in Britain. She was conceived by the use of a revolutionary new technique called "in vitro," which is Latin for "in glass." One of her mother's eggs was fertilized in a test tube. The embryo was planted back in the womb to grow normally.

Louise, the first test-tube baby

A lot of hot air

AUGUST 17

Intrepid travelers Ben Abruzzo, Larry Newman, and Max Anderson have successfully arrived in Normandy, France. The three left US soil six days ago in their attempt to cross the Atlantic in a specially designed hot-air balloon.

JANUARY–JUNE

World Events	JAN Newspaper editor Donald Woods escapes from South Africa by swimming across the Tele River.	JAN Sweden becomes the first country in the world to ban aerosol sprays because of the damage they cause to the environment.	MAR Israeli troops attack Palestinian camps in southern Lebanon as an act of revenge for a terrorist attack.	MAY The ex-prime minister of Italy, Aldo Moro, is murdered by Red Brigade kidnappers in Rome.
Entertainment	JAN The Bee Gees' soundtrack to hit film *Saturday Night Fever* tops the charts worldwide.	MAY After being stolen, Charlie Chaplin's coffin is found buried 10 miles (16 km) from its original grave in Switzerland.	JUN Yachtswoman Naomi James completes a solo world voyage in a record-breaking 117 days.	JUN John Travolta and Olivia Newton-John star in the film of the 1950s musical *Grease*.
Innovations	FEB Humanlike footprints made 3.6 million years ago are found in Tanzania.	AEROSOL CAN APR A Swiss manufacturer invents and produces a magnetic phonecard for use in a hotel in Paris, France.	MAY A Japanese explorer completes the first ever solo trek to the north pole.	ALDO MORO JUL The first solar-powered car is invented and tested by Alan Freeman of the UK.

1978

Year of three Popes

Pope John Paul II is the youngest Pope this century

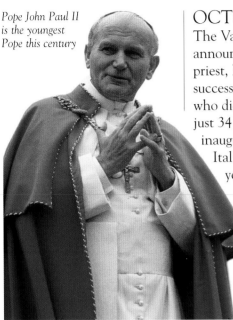

OCTOBER 16
The Vatican today announced that a Polish priest, Karol Wojtyla, is the successor to Pope John Paul I, who died of a heart attack just 34 days after his inauguration. The first non-Italian Pope for over 400 years, Karol Wojtyla is to take on the name John Paul II as a mark of respect. John Paul II is the third Pope in what has been an eventful year for the Roman Catholic church.

Little red book

OCTOBER 29
The *People's Daily*, the official Chinese Communist Party paper, has denounced the late Chairman Mao's "Little Red Book." This "Bible of Chinese communism" contains Mao Zedong's thoughts on a range of subjects. For many years it has been obligatory for everyone in China to carry a copy. Mao's "Little Red Book" has been translated into 80 different languages and has become one of the world's best-selling titles.

Cyanide surprise at Jonestown

NOVEMBER 29

The deadly cocktail

One of the strangest and saddest instances of mass suicide has taken place deep in the jungles of Guyana in a commune known as Jonestown. The bodies of more than 900 members of the People's Temple, an American religious cult, have been found following a bizarre suicide ritual to prove their "loyalty" to the cult's leader, the Reverend Jim Jones. The cult members had all drunk a fruit drink laced with cyanide, some willingly, some at gunpoint. Parents fed the poison to their children before drinking it themselves. The Reverend Jim Jones witnessed the carnage before shooting himself.

Super movie!

DECEMBER 15
Superman, alias Clark Kent, zooms onto the silver screen with spectacular special effects this winter in one of the most expensive movies ever made. The superhero from the planet Krypton embarks on an endless fight against the forces of evil in Metropolis. Directed by Richard Donner, the all-star cast includes Christopher Reeves.

JULY–DECEMBER

SEP President Sadat of Egypt and Prime Minister Begin of Israel sign a peace treaty at Camp David, Maryland.

JUL Swedish tennis player Björn Borg wins his third consecutive men's singles title at Wimbledon, UK.

OCT The World Health Organization (WHO) announces that smallpox has finally been eradicated worldwide.

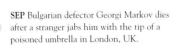

BJÖRN BORG

SEP Bulgarian defector Georgi Markov dies after a stranger jabs him with the tip of a poisoned umbrella in London, UK.

JUL Blue cartoon characters called the Smurfs top the European pop charts with their single *The Smurf Song*.

NOV Two Soviet cosmonauts spend 140 days and 14 hours in space, setting a space endurance record.

DEC Golda Meir, the first woman prime minister of Israel, dies at age 80 after suffering from leukemia for 12 years.

SEP An eclipse of the Moon is seen by 3,000 Grateful Dead rock fans at the pyramids of Giza in Egypt.

NOV Public toilets for dogs open in Paris, France, complete with posts for dogs to lift their legs against.

GOLDA MEIR

DEC Mass protests in Iran call for the abdication of the Shah and an end to the military government.

OCT Sid Vicious of the Sex Pistols is charged with murdering his girlfriend, Nancy Spungen.

DEC Laser-activated videodiscs are launched by Philips/MCA in Atlanta, Georgia.

1979

Shah of Iran is sent into exile

JANUARY 16

There was celebration in the streets and dancing on the rooftops in Tehran today as news spread that the Shah of Iran had finally fled the country. His departure comes after months of mass demonstrations against his regime and its modernizing program, which many saw as an attempt to "Westernize" the country. Opposition has been spearheaded by supporters of Ayatollah Khomeini, the fundamentalist religious leader who is living in exile in Paris. There have been many deaths and bloody clashes since the Shah sought to regain control by imposing martial law just over four months ago. Today, as cars hooted and soldiers waved flowers instead of guns, the mob toppled and smashed statues of the Shah and his father, who seized the throne in 1925.

Subway angels

FEBRUARY 13

A 250-strong flock of civilian "Guardian Angel" vigilantes is currently patrolling the New York City subway in an effort to combat soaring crime. Police officials are taking a strictly neutral stance. The organization's founder, Curtis Sliwa, hopes to extend the project outside the city.

Egypt and Israel sign peace treaty

MARCH 26

After last year's Camp David agreements, which set the scene for a settlement in the Middle East, President Sadat of Egypt and Prime Minister Begin of Israel this evening signed a peace treaty at the White House in Washington, D.C. But while a beaming US President Jimmy Carter announced "peace has come," Arab protestors could be heard denouncing Sadat as a traitor.

The accord is widely regarded in the Arab world as a sellout on the question of Palestinian autonomy. It seems likely that Egypt will be expelled from the Arab League in retaliation for signing the treaty, which indeed leaves many issues unsettled. Problems like the status of Jerusalem, the Sinai Peninsula, and the future of the Israeli-occupied West Bank are not resolved by the peace accord.

JANUARY–MARCH

World Events	JAN Pol Pot's Khmer Rouge regime in Cambodia is overthrown as Vietnamese troops invade.	JAN The UK endures a winter of discontent as strikes against a government-imposed 5% pay limit cause industrial chaos.	FEB The Ayatollah Khomeini victoriously returns to Iran from Paris, France, after 14 years in exile.	MAR Idi Amin flees Kampala in the face of the forces of the Tanzanian-backed Uganda Liberation Front.
Entertainment	FEB Ex-Sex Pistols member Sid Vicious dies of a heroin overdose in New York City.	FEB Neil Armstrong breaks five world records by soaring to 50,000 ft (15,240 m) in 12 mins in a Learjet.	FEB Jean Renoir, French film director and son of the artist, dies at age 86 in Beverley Hills, Calif.	MAR US film star Lee Marvin's ex-girlfriend sues him in a palimony suit for over $1 million.
Innovations	JAN The first digital recording is made in Austria by the Vienna Philharmonic.	FEB A system for transmitting text between computers called teletext is introduced in the US by IBM.	MAR US spacecraft *Voyager 1* sends back pictures showing that the planet Jupiter has rings.	MAR A gardening program is the first made-for-video pre-recorded tape in the UK.

SID VICIOUS

JUPITER

1979

Technicians wear protective clothing

US atomic leak scare

MARCH 30

Two days after the worst nuclear accident in the history of the United States, a new threat hangs over the Three Mile Island power plant in Pennsylvania. It is feared that a bubble of radioactive hydrogen inside the crippled reactor might explode, releasing large amounts of radiation into the atmosphere. It is also still possible that a complete meltdown might occur. Experts are claiming that the situation is being brought under control and that only a small amount of radiation has escaped so far. However, the inside of the reactor is highly contaminated and is still too hot to approach. A general evacuation of the area is not thought necessary at present, although state governor Richard Thornburgh has advised children and pregnant women to leave. The cause of the accident is not clear, but the finger of suspicion points to a fatal combination of faulty equipment and human error. It seems that an automatic valve controlling the flow of cooling water in the core of the plant's Unit 2 reactor failed to function correctly. A series of mistakes compounded the fault and by the time technicians realized what was happening, the fuel rods were beginning to melt, releasing harmful radioactive gases.

Mass graves

APRIL 2

Chilling evidence just discovered in the northeast of Cambodia points to mass murders carried out by the former Khmer Rouge regime of Pol Pot. A lake has been found to contain 2,000 skeletons, and bones and skulls have also been discovered in shallow graves.

Britain gets first woman PM

MAY 4

A triumphant 53-year-old Margaret Thatcher promised a complete transformation of the British economic and industrial climate after becoming the country's first female prime minister today. The Conservatives swept to victory with 44 percent of the vote and a 43-seat majority.

APRIL–JUNE

APR Following a referendum, Iran is declared an Islamic republic by the Ayatollah Khomeini.

APR Zulfikar Ali Bhutto, the deposed premier of Pakistan, is hanged for conspiracy to murder a political opponent.

JUN Black leader Bishop Abel Muzorewa is appointed prime minister of Zimbabwe, the renamed country of Rhodesia.

JUN US president Jimmy Carter and Soviet premier Leonid Brezhnev sign SALT II treaty limiting nuclear weapons.

APR US release of Woody Allen's film *Manhattan*, starring Allen and his ex-lover actress Diane Keaton.

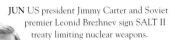

MAY The film *Alien* opens in the US with the slogan, "In space, no one can hear you scream."

JUN US movie star John Wayne (real name Marion Morrison, nicknamed "Duke") dies at age 72.

JUN World heavyweight boxing champion Muhammad Ali announces he will retire.

APR British Rail opens the first Intercity 125 high-speed train service from London to Bristol.

ALIEN

MAY UK singer Elton John becomes the first rock star from the West to tour the USSR.

MAY The worst air crash in US history occurs when 273 people die in a DC-10 in Chicago.

JOHN WAYNE

JUN The first MPs for the new European parliament are elected in Strasbourg, Luxembourg.

1979

Music to your ears, anywhere!

JULY 1

A tiny but revolutionary new stereo system has just been launched in Japan. It is called the Sony Walkman and costs $165 (Y33,000). With the help of lightweight plastic earphones, the Walkman enables you to listen to music wherever you are and whatever you are doing, even when out walking. There are plans to introduce it in the the rest of the world, using the names "Soundabout" and "Stowaway." Sony's competitors, however, doubt whether the "personal stereo" will ever catch on.

Nicaraguan victory

JULY 20

Nicaraguan dictator General Anastasio Somoza Debayle finally gave in to Sandinista rebels today and fled to the United States. True to style, he took with him an estimated $20 million from the treasury. It is the end of a cruel and corrupt dynasty that has lined its pockets and murdered political opponents since it came to power in 1933. The regime received strong backing from the United States, with $14 million in military aid being supplied between 1975 and 1978. The Sandinista rebels, named after General Augusto Sandino, the revolutionary leader killed in 1934, are forming a provisional coalition government. The new government faces enormous problems, however, in a country crippled by the devastation of civil war and bankrupted by foreign debt.

Nicaraguan victory poster

Mountbatten murdered

AUGUST 27

Lord Mountbatten, cousin of Queen Elizabeth II of Britain and the last viceroy of India, has been killed by an IRA bomb. The latest victim of the IRA's campaign to drive Britain out of Northern Ireland, Mountbatten was on vacation in a small fishing village on the west coast of Ireland, where he spent every summer. As he set out from the harbor for a day's fishing, a huge explosion ripped through his boat. His grandson and a friend were also killed.

JULY–SEPTEMBER

World Events	**JUL** Ahmed Ben Bella, hero of Algerian independence, is freed after 14 years of imprisonment.	**JUL** Islamic leader Ayatollah Khomeini bans the broadcast of pop music in Iran, arguing that it corrupts young people.	**JUL** Although he has effectively been in power since 1968, Saddam Hussein officially becomes president of Iraq.	**AUG** Khmer Rouge leader Pol Pot is sentenced to death for the genocide of the Cambodian people.
Entertainment	**JUL** Spinach-eating cartoon character Popeye the Sailorman celebrates his 50th birthday.	**JUL** UK runner Sebastian Coe sets two new world records for the 800 m and the mile in Oslo, Norway.	**AUG** Eighteen sailors die as Atlantic storms sink 25 Fastnet international race yachts off the coast of Ireland.	**AUG** UK runner Sebastian Coe sets another world record, winning the 1,500 m in 3 min 32.1 secs.
Innovations	**JUL** The first air-cushioned sneaker is developed, based on the landing gear of lunar modules. **POPEYE**	**AUG** Two Soviet cosmonauts return to Earth after spending a record 175 days in space orbiting the planet.	**SEP** A national information service is inaugurated by the UK postal service.	**SEP** Two families cross from East to West Germany in a hot-air balloon made out of curtains and sheets.

SADDAM HUSSEIN

1979

US hostages held at embassy

NOVEMBER 4

The US embassy in Tehran, the capital of Iran, has been stormed and is now being occupied by followers of the Ayatollah Khomeini. Nearly 100 embassy staff members and US marines have been taken hostage. Thousands of demonstrators have gathered outside, chanting anti-American slogans and waving placards.

Blindfolded American hostages

DURAN DURAN

With their theatrical outfits and made-up faces, New Romantic bands such as Duran Duran are setting a new trend for glamour and glitz in the UK underground music scene. Critics doubt whether they will have any commercial success.

USSR invades Afghanistan

DECEMBER 27

The Soviet Union is today maintaining that it was asked to send "urgent political, moral, military, and economic assistance" to neighboring Afghanistan as months of civil war in the country intensified. Yesterday they began airlifting troops, while motorized rifle divisions moved in from the north, accompanied by squadrons of Soviet fighters. In the capital, Kabul, Soviet forces have already overthrown President Amin and installed a puppet government. Most of the country, however, still remains in the hands of fundamentalist Muslim guerrillas, the Mujahideen, who have been waging a holy war against the Kabul government.

Mother Teresa wins Nobel Peace Prize

DECEMBER 10

This year's Nobel Peace Prize has been awarded to Mother Teresa, the 69-year-old Catholic nun who has worked tirelessly with the suffering and dying. "Personally I am unworthy," she said. "I accept in the name of the poor." She founded the Order of the Missionaries of Charity in India in 1950. It now has 700 shelters and clinics worldwide, including children's homes and soup kitchens.

OCTOBER–DECEMBER

NOV It is revealed in the UK that the queen's art adviser Sir Anthony Blunt had been a spy for the USSR.

OCT Greta Waitz of Norway wins the New York marathon in the US and sets a new women's record.

OCT The Nobel Prize for medicine is awarded to Godfrey Hounsfield, UK inventor of the CAT body scanner.

ANTHONY BLUNT

NOV Anti-US demonstrators storm the US embassy and raid other US buildings in Islamabad, Pakistan.

NOV Cameras are used to prove that Australian cricket player Jeff Thomson is the fastest test bowler.

OCT Sir Barnes Neville Wallis, UK inventor of World War II "bouncing bombs," dies at age 92.

NOV Saudi Arabian troops storm the Great Mosque at Mecca, which had been occupied by Shi'ite Muslims.

NOV Cult television series *Star Trek* moves to the big screen in hit film *Star Trek – The Movie*.

NOV UK engineers invent a catalytic convertor to reduce pollution caused by car exhaust fumes.

DEC An agreement signed in the UK ends white minority rule in Rhodesia, which becomes Zimbabwe.

DEC Box office hit *Kramer vs Kramer*, starring Dustin Hoffman, brings divorce to the screen.

KRAMER VS KRAMER

DEC The first ever flat-screened pocket television is patented by Japanese company Matsushita.

THE MICROCHIP AGE

IN 1971 THE WORLD'S FIRST MICROPROCESSOR was developed. Microprocessors contain all the main components of a computer on a single chip. This meant that electronic equipment became smaller and cheaper. Early computers filled entire rooms and were used almost exclusively by large corporations. The microchip meant that computers could fit neatly onto desktops, in the office or at home. Machines and factories became automated, with powerful microprocessors providing the brains. Robots produced cars, trains could drive themselves, and automatic washing machines offered separate programs for woolens or whites. Cheap, mass-produced electronic gadgets transformed everyday life, too. Calculators, for example, became ever smaller, finally shrinking to the size of a credit card.

MICROCHIP ON A THUMBNAIL

Magic microchip

Microchips are made of tiny pieces of silicon, often no bigger than a baby's fingernail. Each chip contains thousands of electronic components that are built up, layer by layer, to form an integrated circuit.

Circuit board

Electronic equipment contains a number of different microchips. The chips perform specific functions to do with storing, organizing, or processing data. Each chip is sealed into its own protective case with metal "legs," or contacts, that slot into a flat plastic plate called a circuit board. This is printed with metal lines that connect all the electronic components together to make the equipment work.

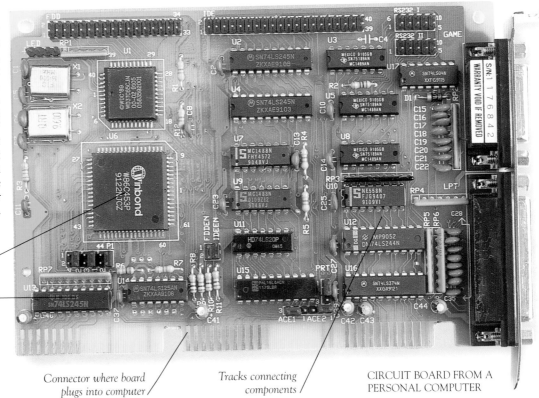

Communications chip

Logic chip

Connector where board plugs into computer

Tracks connecting components

CIRCUIT BOARD FROM A PERSONAL COMPUTER

Home computing

IBM (International Business Machines) launched its first personal computer in 1981. Built around the latest Intel microprocessor, it was operated by a brand new system called MS-DOS, which was soon used by most personal computers. The more expensive model was twice as fast as its rivals and could store much more data.

Inventing the Apple

The Apple Computer Company, founded in Silicon Valley, California, by Steve Jobs and Steve Wozniak, made history by introducing people with no special knowledge of programming or electronics to personal computing. The Apple II, launched in 1977, was the first "user-friendly" computer made specifically for the mass market. Other early microcomputers were often sold in kit form, but this came fully assembled with built-in keyboard, sound, color graphics, and optional floppy disk drive at a cost of $1,298.

1975 ALTAIR IS THE FIRST
SMALL HOME COMPUTER

1980 NEW STANDARDS ALLOW
FAST FAXES – A PAGE A MINUTE

1982 FRENCH TELECOM MINITEL
IS THE FIRST ON-LINE SERVICE

Portable video

Home movies were transformed during the 1980s by the camcorder, a portable video camera that recorded pictures and sounds electronically on magnetic tape. You could watch the results immediately on television. Camcorders gradually became cheaper, easier to use, and smaller.

Moving pictures

The introduction of sound cards, color graphics, and a new system of storing digital data on compact disc revolutionized the personal computer's capabilities during the 1980s. With the latest generation of microprocessor chips supplying the power, you could now choose images, text, and sounds to create your own stories, games, and cartoons, and to interact with what was happening on screen.

SINCLAIR EXECUTIVE
CALCULATOR

*Light-emitting diode
(LED) display*

Pocket power

Simple pocket calculators were launched in the early 1970s and could be used to add, subtract, multiply, and divide. More complex calculators followed, with lots of extra functions for carrying out complicated scientific calculations, such as sines and cosines.

Control keys

Card calculator

The smallest electronic calculators needed very little power. They used small, round, long-lasting batteries. Some calculators needed no batteries at all, like the solar-powered calculator, above, that is no bigger than a credit card. It has special light-sensitive cells that turn light into electricity.

Video games take off

Atari's *Space Invaders* (above) was one of the first TV-based video games to bring the thrills of the arcade into the home. Developments in chip technology during the 1980s led to increasingly sophisticated high-speed games. With one tiny integrated circuit, the games became smaller, cheaper, and more exciting – Nintendo's Gameboy™ (below) provided full-sized fun in a pocket-sized package.

Add it up

Unlike the first electronic calculator, which was as big as a cash register, the Sinclair Executive calculator fit easily into a shirt pocket. It was only 0.39 in (1 cm) thick and 4.7 in (12 cm) long, had a 7,000 transistor integrated circuit, and a wafer-thin battery. Launched in the 1970s, at a price of $155.40 it was very expensive. However, it was one of the first everyday gadgets to make use of chip technology.

Wrist organizer

The arrival of the wristwatch calculator in the late 1970s meant that organizing life had never been easier. This super-efficient personal organizer can be used as a diary to store appointments, memos, and messages in its memory. It can also automatically sort telephone and fax numbers into alphabetical order, and is even able to tell the time around the world.

1980

Gold rush in Brazil

JANUARY 28

Within weeks of finding a gold nugget deep in the Amazon jungle of Brazil, 10,000 gold-diggers have started to arrive, armed with picks and shovels, moving mountains of earth. What will happen to the ecosystem of the rain forest remains to be seen.

Rescue bid fails

APRIL 25

An attempt to rescue the 53 diplomatic hostages from the United States being held by Iranians in the American Embassy in Tehran, Iran, ended in tragedy early this morning. Eight members of the US's military expedition, code-named "Operation Eagle Claw," died when a helicopter collided with a tanker aircraft on the ground in the remote Iranian desert. Ironically, when the accident occurred the rescue bid had already been called off due to equipment failure, and the military expedition was actually withdrawing. President Carter appeared grim-faced on morning television to tell a shocked nation, "The responsibility is purely my own." Meanwhile, the Iranians are celebrating the failure of the rescue bid with a rally in front of the occupied American Embassy.

Molten lava spews from the volcano's mouth

Mount St. Helens erupts

MAY 18

After lying dormant for more than 120 years, the Mount St. Helens volcano, in Washington state, erupted in spectacular fashion this morning. It had been rumbling ominously for two months and emitting ash and smoke for two weeks. The explosion, which measured 4.1 on the Richter Scale, blew the top off the 9,675-ft (2,949-m) peak. Spewing earth and ash into the air the eruption turned day into night for most of the area and caused several floods and mudslides. At least eight people are feared dead, and property damage is estimated to be as much as $2.7 billion.

JANUARY–JUNE

World Events	Entertainment	Innovations
JAN Dr. Andrei Sakharov, the Soviet Union's most prominent dissident, is arrested and exiled.	**JAN** The Islamic Conference, meeting in Islamabad, condemns the Soviet invasion of Afghanistan.	**MAR** More than 100 people die when a North Sea oil platform used as a floating hotel collapses in stormy weather.

JAN Pink Floyd's album *The Wall* tops the UK and US charts.

PINK FLOYD'S THE WALL

JAN 14-year-old Nigel Short from the UK becomes the youngest world chess master.

APR French philosopher Jean-Paul Sartre, who refused the Nobel Prize for literature, dies at age 74.

MAR In El Salvador, 20 people are killed and 200 wounded at a mass for assassinated archbishop Oscar Romero.

APR Sir Alfred Hitchcock, UK film director of *The Birds* and *Psycho*, dies at age 80.

FEB *Solar Max*, the first satellite to study solar flares, is launched.

APR Cosmonauts Leonid Popov and Valery Ryumin reach *Salyut-6* space station.

JUN The *Pioneer Venus 1* space probe finds mountains higher than Everest on Venus.

ALFRED HITCHCOCK

JUN An electronic "eye" is first used in tennis at the UK Wimbledon championships.

1980

Abadan on fire as war heats up

SEPTEMBER 23
At dawn today, after months of tense border clashes, Iraqi troops launched an all-out attack against western Iran. Iraqi president Saddam Hussein's sights appear to be set on the oil-rich province of Khuzistan and the Shatt al-Arab waterway. The largest oil refinery in the world, at Abadan, is blazing after being bombarded by Iraqi artillery and bombs. Other targets, farther north, have also been attacked by the Iraqi army. The rest of the world is watching with concern as the Iran-Iraq war heats up, although the United States and the Soviet Union made it clear last night that they intend to remain strictly neutral. There appears to be no prospect of oil shortages at the moment as stocks in the West are high.

Reagan elected as US president

NOVEMBER 4
The Republican candidate Ronald Wilson Reagan today won a landslide victory to become the president of the United States. At the age of 69 Reagan is the oldest person ever elected to the nation's highest office. The former wartime movie star will replace the Democrat incumbent, peanut farmer Jimmy Carter. Reagan was first elected to public office in 1966 as governor of the state of California.

IN-LINE SKATING
A new craze is sweeping across the United States this year. The latest in-line skates, Rollerblades™, were developed by US ice hockey players Scott and Brennan Olson. Based on a classic ice hockey design, they are smooth and lightweight, which makes them fast.

Who shot J.R.?

NOVEMBER 19
After eight nail-biting months, the suspense is over. Tonight's episode finally reveals who shot J. R. Ewing, the baddie everybody loves to hate in the top television soap *Dallas*.

JULY–DECEMBER

AUG Eighty-four people are killed and hundreds injured by a bomb blast in a railroad station in Bologna, Italy.

JUL Swedish tennis player Bjorn Borg wins his fifth consecutive Wimbledon singles title.

SEP The world's longest tunnel is opened, through the St. Gotthard, a mountain in the Swiss Alps.

REINHOLD MESSNER

SEP Polish workers, having won the right to organize trade unions, set up a central organization, Solidarity.

AUG Italian Reinhold Messner climbs the 29,027-ft (8,847.7-m) high Mount Everest solo.

SEP Japanese newspaper *Asahi Shimbun* uses new computer technology to create its pages.

SEP Deposed dictator of Nicaragua Anastasio Somoza Debayle is assassinated on the streets of Asuncion, Paraguay.

SEP *Les Misérables*, the musical, is first performed at the Palais des Sports in Paris.

OCT Cosmonauts Popov and Ryumin set a new space endurance record on *Salyut-6*.

FANS MOURN JOHN LENNON

OCT Two big earthquakes, measuring 7.3 on the Richter Scale, destroy the city of El Asnam in Algeria.

DEC Ex-Beatle John Lennon is shot dead in New York City.

NOV *Voyager 1* sends back pictures that show Saturn has at least 100 rings.

1981

Yellow ribbons for US hostages

JANUARY 20

The United States is today celebrating the release of the last 52 hostages held in Iran by followers of Ayatollah Khomeini. Yellow ribbons, the American symbol of returning home, are being worn by people throughout the country. The freed hostages spent a total of 444 days in captivity. As a final snub to President Carter, who tried and failed to rescue the hostages, their release was timed to coincide with Ronald Reagan's inauguration.

Pope wounded

MAY 13

Pope John Paul II has been rushed to the hospital after being shot and seriously wounded as he blessed a crowd of 20,000 from an open-topped vehicle in St. Peter's Square, Rome. A lone gunman opened fire, hitting the Pope four times and injuring two women. The would-be assassin, 23-year-old Turkish national Mehmet Agca, was arrested immediately. He was already wanted by Turkish police after escaping from a jail where he was being held for the murder of a newspaper editor. Agca is claiming that he planned to murder the Pope in protest of Soviet action in Afghanistan and the Soviet Union's involvement in El Salvador. Some people, however, think there was another motive involving eastern European communist governments angry at papal support for the Solidarity trade union in Poland. Surgeons have already operated on the Pope, removing all four bullets. They are predicting that the Pope will make a full recovery.

Mitterrand is French president

MAY 10

Red flags are fluttering and crowds are dancing throughout France to celebrate socialist leader François Mitterrand's election victory. The new president won 52 percent of the vote, ending 23 years of right-wing government. He promises a program of nationalization, taxes on wealth, and an end to unemployment.

JANUARY–JUNE

World Events	**FEB** Gro Harlem Brundtland becomes Norway's first woman prime minister.	**MAR** Solidarity trade union stages a national strike in Poland in protest of police treatment of union activists.	**MAR** 70-year-old US president Ronald Reagan is wounded in an assassination attempt in Washington D.C.	**APR** IRA prisoner Bobby Sands, who has been on hunger strike for 42 days, wins a Northern Ireland by-election.
Entertainment	**MAR** Eighty percent of the 6,700 runners finish the UK's first London Marathon.	**MAY** Jamaican reggae superstar Bob Marley dies of cancer in Miami, Florida. He was 36 years old.	**MAY** UK group Adam and the Ants tops the charts with hit single *Stand and Deliver*.	**MAY** A new musical by Andrew Lloyd Webber called *Cats* opens in London, UK.
Innovations	**JAN** US astronomers discover a new star 100 times brighter than the Sun.	**REUSABLE SPACE SHUTTLE TAKES OFF**  **APR** The US space shuttle *Columbia*, the world's first reusable spacecraft, blasts off.	**JUN** The stealth fighter plane the Lockheed F-117 makes its first maiden flight in the US.	**ADAM AND THE ANTS** **JUN** The world's first test tube twins are born in Melbourne, Australia.

1981

The Prince and Princess of Wales leave St. Paul's in a horse-drawn carriage

Fairy-tale royal wedding

JULY 29

By royal proclamation, today was a special national holiday in Britain. London came to a standstill and street parties were held across the country as Prince Charles, the queen's eldest son, married 20-year-old Lady Diana Spencer in St. Paul's Cathedral. A total of 2,500 guests attended the ceremony, including heads of state from all over the world. Cheering crowds lined the streets to catch a glimpse of the couple as they drove back to Buckingham Palace. The bride's exquisite dress, designed by the Emmanuels of London, was made of pure silk ivory taffeta and old lace. It was embroidered with tiny mother-of-pearl sequins and had a spectacular 25-ft (7.6-m) train. It is estimated that about 700 million people worldwide watched the wedding on television.

Sadat shot in raid

OCTOBER 6

President Anwar Sadat of Egypt was today shot dead during a military parade in Cairo. The assassination of the Nobel Peace Prize winner happened as all eyes were fixed on a flyby of air force jets overhead. Four men dressed in army uniforms jumped out of an armored

vehicle, hurling grenades and spraying automatic gunfire at the platform on which the president was sitting. Sadat was hit by five bullets and collapsed in a pool of blood. In the fierce gun battle that followed, one of the assassins was shot dead. The rest of the conspirators were finally arrested. Five other people attending the parade also lost their lives in the shoot-out, and a number of other bystanders were wounded. Vice-President Hosni Mubarak has acted swiftly to take control of the country. A state of emergency has been declared and troops and riot police are out in force on the streets of Cairo. Those who are responsible for ordering the murder are not yet known. Sadat had many enemies in the Arab world after signing a peace accord with Israel and it seems likely that he was killed by members of an extremist Islamic group, such as the Muslim Brotherhood. World leaders have tonight been paying tribute to the Egyptian leader who worked so hard for peace in the Middle East.

TGV TRAIN IN FRANCE

The first "Trains à Grande Vitesse" (high-speed trains) have gone into service between Paris and Lyons in France. The TGV requires specially built tracks with steeply banked curves to reach maximum speeds of up to 186 mph (300 km/h).

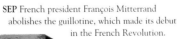

JULY–DECEMBER

AUG Iran goes into mourning after both the president and prime minister are assassinated in a bomb blast.

SEP French president François Mitterrand abolishes the guillotine, which made its debut in the French Revolution.

NOV Egypt's parliament selects Hosni Mubarak to be president after the assassination of Anwar Sadat.

DEC At least 14,000 trade union activists are arrested after martial law is imposed in Poland. Strikes continue in spite of this.

AUG Music Television (MTV) begins broadcasting to people across the US.

MTV MUSIC CHANNEL

AUG UK runner Steve Ovett clips 0.13 seconds off the world mile record.

AUG UK runner Sebastian Coe reclaims the world mile record with a time of 3 min 47.53 secs.

DEC English batsman Geoff Boycott beats Sir Gary Sobers's record of 8,032 runs in test championship cricket.

AUG US space probe *Voyager 2* arrives at Saturn after a four-year journey.

AUG US company IBM launches its new "Personal Computer" (PC).

SEP Sandra Day O'Connor is the first woman judge on the US Supreme Court.

HOSNI MUBARAK

NOV US space shuttle *Columbia* is the first shuttle to be launched twice.

DECADE OF DESIGN

THE EIGHTIES SAW AN EXPLOSION of interest in style and design. Architects and designers belonging to the post-modernist movement rejected the order of previous decades and introduced a kaleidoscope of colors, ornaments, and styles dating back to different periods in history. Others went back to basics, using industrial materials like steel scaffolding and factory flooring to produce revolutionary buildings and interiors. A new generation of upwardly mobile professionals, often known as "yuppies," adopted the latest styles. Mobile phones, bottled mineral water, and designer labels became status symbols in a money-obsessed decade.

Bags of style

Famous French names had dominated the exclusive world of haute couture for decades. They now began appearing on high fashion ready-to-wear clothes, perfume, and accessories that were sold worldwide.

Swatch watch

The cheap, plastic Swatch watch, launched in 1983, came in a wide range of designs that made it an instant fashion accessory. This transparent Swatch has become a collector's item.

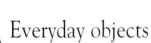

Everyday objects

The design of everyday useful objects such as lamps, flashlights, and calculators acquired a new importance during the Eighties. It was no longer enough that objects were functional – they also had to look good. The bulb of this pocket light, designed by BIB Consultants for Duracell in 1982, lights up when the top is swiveled open.

Heat-proof foam handle

Whistling bird spout

Alessi kettle

Tableware and household design became more decorative and ornamental during the Eighties, after the plain practicality of previous decades. This was due partly to new developments in computer-controlled machines that could now produce the kind of detail that had only been possible by hand in the past. Architect Michael Graves designed this steam kettle for Alessi in 1986.

Ornamental studs

High-tech skyscraper

One of the most famous examples of high-tech architecture, the Hong Kong and Shanghai Bank, was completed in 1986. Designed as a pre-fabricated kit by the British architect Sir Norman Foster, the 47-story building is supported from the outside by a huge skeleton of steel columns and trusses. Its parts were made in 80 different countries and assembled together on site.

Battery

Radio in a bag

Designed by Daniel Weil in 1981, this Bag Radio questioned the idea that electronic components should be hidden away neatly. Like many of the most exciting designs of the decade, it made people look at ordinary objects in new ways.

Speaker

Graphic design

Graphic design grew up during the Eighties due largely to advances in microchip technology. Dazzling new tricks with images and text became possible as pages began to be designed on computer screens. *The Face* magazine broke new ground with its innovative layout and style. Launched in 1980 as a music monthly, it reflected the mood of the times and appealed to a wide readership.

Japanese designer

Parisian fashion houses were stormed during the early Eighties by Japanese designers using new fabrics, textures, and shapes to challenge the traditional concepts of western haute couture. Color was played down, with designer Kei Kawakubo saying she used "shades of black." A label on some of Yohji Yamamoto's designs stated "There is nothing so boring as a neat and tidy look."

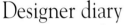

Designer diary

The Filofax™ was based on a classic design that dated back to World War I. During the Eighties it got a new lease of life and became the essential accessory for people who wanted to organize their lives efficiently. In fact, it became known as the "personal organizer." The design was simple – a small ring-binder with wallet compartments inside the covers and loose-leaf diary pages that could be changed every year. The organizer also contained blank pages for notes and memos.

Memphis style

Although it was based in Milan, Italy, the Memphis Group, founded in 1981 by architect and designer Ettore Sottsass, was named after the home of rock 'n' roll, Memphis, Tennessee. Like rock 'n' roll, it challenged convention and broke the rules, taking different elements from different cultures to invent something new. The group produced avant-garde furniture, fabric, and ceramics that helped change the face of design in the Eighties.

CARLTON ROOM DIVIDER

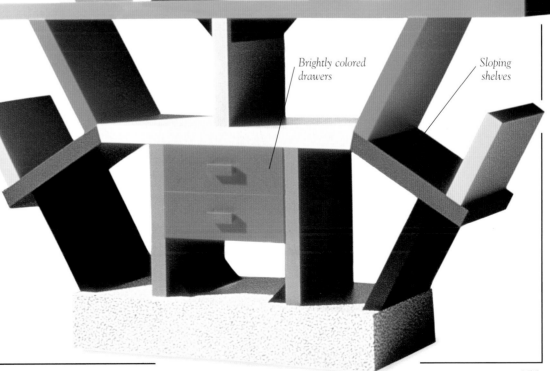

Unconventional angles

Brightly colored drawers

Sloping shelves

Royalton Hotel interior

French designer Philippe Starck was very popular in the 1980s. He reinvented the shapes of everyday objects, such as ashtrays, juicers, toothbrushes, and furniture. He also designed café and hotel interiors, including the Royalton Hotel in New York, shown above.

1982

Fight over Falklands

JUNE 14

After almost two-and-a-half months of fierce fighting, the Argentine forces that invaded the Falkland Islands in the South Pacific have today surrendered to British troops. The white flag was raised in the capital, Port Stanley, after fierce fighting at Tumbledown Mountain, Wireless Ridge, and Mount Londgon. The commander of the British land forces, Major-General Jeremy Moore, announced that "the Falkland Islands are once more under the government desired by the inhabitants." The Falkland Islands have been controlled by Britain since 1833 but have long been claimed by the Argentines, who call the islands the Malvinas. While crowds in London cheer a jubilant British prime minister, Margaret Thatcher, it seems likely that Argentine president General Leopoldo Galtieri will be forced to resign. At least 255 Britons and 700 Argentines were killed in the fighting. Many were victims of the deadly long-range Exocet missile, which has opened a new chapter in maritime warfare.

Israel drives PLO out of Beirut

AUGUST 30

After more than 12 years, the Palestinian Liberation Organization (PLO) has been forced to abandon its powerbase in Beirut, driven out by a massive Israeli bombardment that started in early June. PLO guerrilla bases in Lebanon were bombed before a force of 20,000 Israeli soldiers advanced across the border toward the city of Beirut. An international peacekeeping force has arrived to ensure the safe evacuation of PLO fighters to Arab countries. Today their leader, Yassir Arafat, left the shattered Lebanese capital to set up a new PLO headquarters in Tunisia.

TRIVIAL PURSUIT

A new brain-teasing board game has turned trivia into serious business. *Trivial Pursuit* was invented by three young Canadians and is expected to be a big hit. Players chase each other around the board answering questions divided into different categories.

Argentine soldiers

JANUARY–JUNE			
World Events — **JAN** Seventy-eight people die when a Boeing 737 crashes into a bridge in Washington, D.C.	**MAR** Nicaragua's Sandinista government declares a state of emergency because of fears of a US-inspired attack.	**JUN** King Khaled of Saudi Arabia dies at age 69. He will be succeeded by his brother Prince Fahd.	**JUN** General Galtieri is ousted as president of Argentina and stripped of his post of commander-in-chief of the army.
Entertainment — **FEB** Thelonius Monk, a popular jazz pianist from the US, dies at age 64.	**MAR** Fifteen English cricketers are condemned for embarking on a rebel tour of South Africa.	**MAR** UK film *Chariots of Fire*, directed by David Puttnam, wins an Academy Award for best film.	**MAY** Argentine soccer player Diego Maradona is contracted by Barcelona for a record $8.8 million.
Innovations — **FEB** Kodak launches worldwide a new camera that uses disk film.	**NEW DISK FILM AND CAMERA** — **MAR** Unmanned Soviet space probe *Venera 13* lands on Venus after a four-month flight.	**MAR** US space shuttle *Columbia* is launched on its third mission from Cape Canaveral, Florida.	**CHARIOTS OF FIRE WINS OSCAR** — **MAR** US company Proctor & Gamble develops the first liquid detergent for washing-machines.

NEW DISK FILM AND CAMERA

CHARIOTS OF FIRE WINS OSCAR

1982

Ancient wreck raised from ocean

OCTOBER 11

A piece of English history was raised from the seabed today when the wreck of the *Mary Rose* was slowly freed from the thick mud off the coast of Portsmouth. King Henry VIII's 770-ton flagship sank in The Solent channel in 1545 on her way to a sea battle with the French. Many relics of Tudor England have

The Mary Rose

already been recovered from the wreck, including the bones of 120 of the 715 men who drowned when the ship sank.

First artificial heart

DECEMBER 2

The first operation to implant an artificial heart in a human being has been successfully carried out at the University of Utah Medical Center in the United States. The lucky recipient was 61-year-old Barney Clark, a retired dentist from Seattle, who had been suffering from heart failure and was close to death. His new mechanical heart is made of plastic and metal and is called Jarvik-7 after its inventor, Robert Jarvik. The operation took seven-and-a-half hours and the patient is said to be doing well.

The Jarvik-7 artificial heart

Vietnam victims remembered

NOVEMBER 13

In a moving ceremony, the Vietnam Veterans Memorial in Washington, D.C. was today dedicated as a permanent tribute to the Americans who lost their lives in the Vietnam War. Made of gray granite and designed by Yale University architecture student Maya Yang Lin, the monument is inscribed with the names of more than 58,000 dead.

JULY–DECEMBER

JUL The Reverend Sun Myung Moon presides over the simultaneous marriage of 2,075 couples in New York.

JUL Italy wins the soccer World Cup in Madrid, beating West Germany in the final.

AUG The Coca Cola Company launches its new Diet Coke drink in the US.

MOONIES' MASS WEDDING

SEP Palestinian refugees are massacred by Lebanese Christian militia in refugee camps in Beirut, Lebanon.

AUG At 65, US's Ashby Harper becomes the oldest person to swim the Channel.

OCT Japanese company Sony launches the *Watchman*, a TV with a 2-in (5-cm) screen.

OCT Spain's socialist party sweeps to victory in the general election and 40-year-old Felipe Gonzales becomes prime minister.

DEC Michael Jackson releases his critically acclaimed album *Thriller*, which tops the US and UK charts.

OCT The Experimental Prototype Community of Tomorrow center (EPCOT) opens in Florida.

EPCOT CENTER OPENS

NOV Soviet premier Leonid Brezhnev dies after a heart attack, at age 75, and is succeeded by Yuri Andropov.

DEC Steven Spielberg's latest movie, *ET*, is a massive box-office hit around the world.

DEC *Time* magazine in the US votes Pac-Man, a computer character, its "Man of the Year."

1983

"Star Wars"

MARCH 23

In a speech televised across the United States, President Reagan tonight proposed a revolutionary new defense system dubbed "Star Wars." Using the most sophisticated technology, and based both on land and in space, it will protect America from Soviet attack.

Diversion at Mount Etna

KING KONG IS 50

Residents of the US's most famous city were taken by surprise when a strange figure appeared on top of New York's Empire State Building this year. King Kong is back, in the shape of a giant 82-ft (25-m) tall gorilla balloon, to celebrate the 50th anniversary of his first film.

MAY 14

People in the Sicilian towns of Nicolosi and Belpasso are today heaving a huge sigh of relief. Their homes have been saved from being engulfed in a torrent of molten lava from Mount Etna. The volcano has been erupting for the last few weeks, sending a steady stream of red-hot debris down the mountain. Experts have managed to divert the flow by using a massive explosive charge that created an artificial avalanche. This is sending the lava flow into a special channel dug by bulldozers. Rising 11,122 ft (3,390 m) over Sicily, Mount Etna is the highest and most active volcano in all of Europe, with 135 recorded eruptions to date.

JANUARY–JUNE

World Events

FEB Sixty-eight people die in Australia's worst ever bush fires. The police suspect arson.

MAY US President Reagan backs the Contra rebels fighting to overthrow the Marxist Sandinista government in Nicaragua.

MAY Diaries allegedly written by Adolf Hitler are discovered to be fakes by experts in Germany.

JUN Thousands of people in Chile take part in nationwide protests against the rule of dictator General Pinochet.

Entertainment

FEB An unknown Mozart symphony is discovered in Denmark.

FEB The $240 million race horse Shergar is kidnapped from a stud farm in Ireland.

APR The film ET wins four Oscars in Los Angeles after breaking all box-office records.

MAY Veteran UK pop star Cliff Richard celebrates his 25th anniversary in show business.

Innovations

JAN A newly discovered dinosaur, found in the UK, is named *Baryonyx walkeri*.

PRESERVED BARYONYX

FEB The Thames Flood Barrier in London, UK, is raised for the first time to protect the city from flooding.

MAR The first compact disc players go on sale in UK, France, West Germany, and Holland.

DR. SALLY RIDE

JUN Dr. Sally Ride becomes the first US woman in space on the shuttle *Challenger*.

1983

In the pink

MAY 21

American artists Christo and Jeanne-Claude have begun to dismantle their latest installation, *Surrounded Islands*. There have been mixed reactions to this version of Monet's *Water Lilies*. Eleven islands in Biscayne Bay, Florida, were surrounded with 6,500,000 ft² (603,850 m²) of shiny, pink fabric.

Soviets shoot down Flight 007

AUGUST 31

All 269 people on board a routine Korean Air Lines flight from New York to Seoul in South Korea, have died after the plane was shot down by a Soviet fighter plane off the coast of Siberia. How the aircraft strayed into restricted Soviet airspace is, at the moment, a tragic mystery. Soviet authorities are claiming that the airliner was on a US spying mission.

US invades Grenada

OCTOBER 25

The Cold War came to the Caribbean today as the United States flexed its muscles and invaded Grenada, which for the past four years has been supported by the Soviet Union. The action is being widely deplored as a violation of international law. President Reagan has justified the invasion on the grounds of protecting US citizens living in Grenada. Unrest had swept the island after the prime minister, Maurice Bishop, was murdered in a Marxist coup.

Solidarity and peace

DECEMBER 10

Lech Walesa, leader of Poland's outlawed trade union Solidarity, was today awarded the Nobel Peace Prize. He received the award for his "massive personal effort" in trying to get Polish workers the right to a free trade union – often in the face of brutal and violent opposition by the communist authorities.

JULY–DECEMBER

JUL General Jaruzelski lifts martial law in Poland after 19 months, although anti-socialist activity will still be crushed.

AUG Wham! storms the album charts with *Fantastic*. The group already has three UK hit singles.

AUG US space shuttle *Challenger* is launched again. The crew includes the first US black astronaut.

JUL In Sri Lanka more than 100 people are killed in racial violence between the Sinhalese and Tamils.

AUG Athletes from 159 nations take part in the first Athletics World Championships in Finland.

OCT Astronomers use the world's largest telescope, in the Caucasus Mountains, to spot Halley's Comet.

AUG Philippines opposition leader Benigno Aquino is assassinated as he returns home from three years' exile in the US.

SEP Alan Bond's *Australia II* wins the America's Cup yachting trophy. The US has held the trophy for 132 years.

NOV Two Soviet cosmonauts arrive home after five months on board the *Salyut-7* space station.

DEC Raul Alfonsin is inaugurated as president of Argentina, restoring democracy after eight years of military rule.

OCT UK race car driver Richard Noble sets a land speed record of 630 mph (1,013 km/h) in his jet car *Thrust 2*.

NOV An Australian woman becomes the first to give birth after receiving a donated egg.

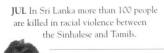
WHAM!

AUSTRALIA II

1984

Killer virus identified

APRIL 23

The discovery of the virus that causes AIDS (Acquired Immune Deficiency Syndrome) has just been announced in Washington, D.C. by the US health and human services secretary, Margaret Heckler. A team of scientists – led by Dr. Robert Gallo of the National Cancer Institute – have identified the virus as HTLV-3 (human T-cell lymphotropic virus). The announcement is, however, being bitterly contested by French scientists who claim they discovered the virus last year. Despite the scientific debate, it is clear that the rate of infection of the disease is of epidemic proportion.

India's Golden Temple attacked

JUNE 6

The Golden Temple at Amritsar, the holiest of Sikh shrines, was today stormed by Indian troops in an assault code-named "Operation Blue Star." This comes four days after the famous temple in the Punjab was seized and occupied by militant Sikh extremists demanding their own state of Khalistan. Resistance to the attack was ferocious, with the Sikhs, who are a warrior sect, well prepared. They fought from strong fortifications and a network of tunnels and manholes. As the battle raged on, the Indian authorities sent in tanks and commandos, with strict instructions not to damage the golden-domed temple. Altogether, 90 soldiers and 712 extremists have died, including Sikh leader Sant Jarnail Singh Bhindranwale.

The sacred temple

GEORGE IS THE BOY
Britain's latest pop idol is Boy George, the lead singer of Culture Club. His makeup and dresses have not hindered the group's success.

JANUARY–JUNE

World Events	**FEB** International peacekeeping force withdraws from Lebanon, leaving Beirut to the local militias.	**FEB** In the USSR Konstantin Chernenko is named new Soviet party chief after the death of Yuri Andropov.	**MAR** As many as 1,000 people are feared dead after a week of religious rioting in northern Nigeria.	**MAY** The USSR announces that it will boycott the Los Angeles Olympics due to security concerns.
Entertainment	**JAN** Johnny Weissmuller, swimming champion and star of Tarzan movies, dies at age 79.	**FEB** "Gender-bending" is the latest trend as stars dress in the fashions of the opposite sex.	**FEB** UK ice skaters Jayne Torvill and Christopher Dean win an Olympic gold medal in Yugoslavia.	**APR** South African runner Zola Budd is granted UK citizenship so that she can compete in the Olympics.
Innovations	**FEB** US astronaut Brian McCandless makes the first untethered space walk. **US ASTRONAUT**	**APR** US astronauts from the space shuttle *Challenger* successfully replace a control box in a satellite.	**APR** The first baby to have started life as a frozen embryo is born in Melbourne, Australia. **TORVILL AND DEAN**	**MAY** The first domestic robot is manufactured in the US and advertised in a New York paper.

1984

John Torrington, naval petty officer

Ice-men found

SEPTEMBER 26
The bodies of three English sailors have been discovered on Canada's Beechey Island, perfectly preserved by Arctic permafrost for 139 years. Scientists have even been able to carry out autopsies on the sailors' internal organs. The sailors died on an ill-fated expedition led by Sir John Franklin in 1845 to find the Northwest Passage from the Atlantic to the Pacific.

Indira Gandhi killed

OCTOBER 31
Mrs. Indira Gandhi, 66-year-old prime minister of India, was today ambushed and assassinated by two of her own Sikh bodyguards as she walked in the garden of her New Delhi home. She was shot ten times. It is clear that the murder was carried out in revenge for the storming of the Sikhs' holiest shrine, the Golden Temple at Amritsar, earlier in the year. Mrs. Gandhi's 40-year-old son Rajiv has already been sworn in as the new prime minister.

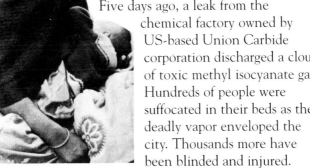

Bhopal nightmare

DECEMBER 8
At least 2,000 people have died in the Indian city of Bhopal after the worst industrial disaster in history. Five days ago, a leak from the chemical factory owned by US-based Union Carbide corporation discharged a cloud of toxic methyl isocyanate gas. Hundreds of people were suffocated in their beds as the deadly vapor enveloped the city. Thousands more have been blinded and injured.

Bishop Tutu wins Nobel Peace Prize

DECEMBER 10
Anglican Bishop of Johannesburg Desmond Tutu today accepted the Nobel Peace Prize for his nonviolent struggle against apartheid. "I have just got to believe God is around," he said. "If He is not, we in South Africa have had it."

Desmond Tutu

JULY–DECEMBER

JUL A former Nigerian transportation minister is found kidnapped in a crate at Stanstead Airport, UK.

JUL This summer's box-office hit in the US is the special effects extravaganza *Ghostbusters*.

JUL In the UK's City of London the high-tech Lloyds building, designed by Richard Rogers, is completed.

GHOSTBUSTERS

SEP After two years of negotiations, agreement is reached for the UK to return Hong Kong to China in 1997.

JUL James F. Fixx, the US man who popularized jogging, dies of a heart attack while out jogging.

JUL Soviet cosmonaut Svetlana Savitskaya becomes the first woman to walk in space.

OCT Four people die when an IRA bomb explodes during the Conservative Party conference, UK.

AUG US athlete Carl Lewis wins gold medals in two sprints, the sprint relay, and the long jump at the Olympics.

SEP The British Museum examines the body of a prehistoric man discovered in a peat bog in Cheshire, UK.

CARL LEWIS

NOV Republican Ronald Reagan wins a second term in the US presidential election.

DEC The Band Aid single *Do They Know It's Christmas?* raises $10.4 million in the UK for famine relief in Africa.

OCT Three Soviet cosmonauts return to Earth after setting a new space endurance record of 238 days.

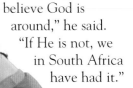

FEED THE WORLD

Live from London

At midday on Saturday, July 13, 1985, Status Quo sang *Rocking All Over the World* to a crowd of 72,000 at Wembley Stadium in London, Britain. It was the launch of Live Aid, a nonstop rock marathon, held simultaneously in London in the UK and Philadelphia in the US, and viewed worldwide by 1.5 billion people. The superstars included Queen, Elton John, and Paul McCartney.

IN OCTOBER 1984, harrowing pictures of the Ethiopian famine were shown on British television. Bob Geldof, lead singer of The Boomtown Rats band, could not get the images of starving people out of his mind and decided to do something about it. Band Aid was born. Geldof persuaded more than 40 musicians and a recording company to donate their services in recording a charity single, *Do They Know It's Christmas?/Feed the World*. It raised $10.4 million and became Britain's biggest-selling single ever. Rock stars in the United States followed suit, forming USA For Africa. Their record, *We Are the World*, was a huge hit worldwide. Geldof, and other musicians, still felt more could be done and set about organizing a huge transatlantic fundraising concert called Live Aid.

THE BEST-SELLING BAND AID SINGLE

Famine in Ethiopia

Years of drought in Ethiopia and Sudan had left more than 150 million people facing starvation. Rain had not fallen since 1981 and crops had failed. Millions of people were forced to leave their homes in search of food. The UN called it "the greatest natural disaster faced by man."

BOB GELDOF IN ETHIOPIA

Geldof's visit

Bob Geldof flew to Ethiopia in January 1985 to find out how to best use the money raised by Band Aid. He visited feeding camps in Tigre, and refugee camps in Sudan. He was horrified by what he saw. Starving people walked hundreds of miles for the chance of receiving some meagre emergency relief. At one camp he counted fifteen bags of flour that had to be shared between 27,000 people. Starving babies with swollen stomachs were too hungry to cry, and dying people curled up like stones on the hard ground.

1985 *WE ARE THE WORLD*
RELEASED BY USA FOR AFRICA

1985 LIVE AID CONCERTS
BEAMED TO 1.5 BILLION PEOPLE

1985 CONCERTS RAISE $52
MILLION FOR RELIEF EFFORT

Bob takes a bow

Live Aid was such a success that no one left Wembley Stadium before the end of the concert. For the finale, the entire cast lined up on stage to sing *Do They Know It's Christmas?*, led by Bob Geldof. The audience joined in, filling the stadium with sound.

LIVE AID
CONCERT TICKETS

Live from Philadelphia

A crowd of 90,000 people roared as the Live Aid concert began at noon in the JFK Stadium in Philadelphia. Across the Atlantic, at Wembley Stadium, the stars had already been on stage for five hours. Live pictures beamed via satellite were shown on huge screens to link the two concerts taking place simultaneously, 3,000 miles apart. The performers in Philadelphia included Bob Dylan, Mick Jagger, Madonna, Eric Clapton, and Tina Turner. The longest concert in the history of rock n' roll lasted for 16 hours. As the finale was reached in Philadelphia, it was already the next day at Wembley.

Special delivery

Thousands of tons of food were transported by Band Aid on specially chartered ships and planes from the United Kingdom to Africa, but that was not the end of the story. There was no point in sending desperately needed famine relief halfway across the world if the sacks of food then lay rotting at the dockside while people starved. Band Aid solved this problem by buying its own fleet of vehicles that could take food directly from the ports to the refugee camps.

Life-saving cookies

Famine relief usually consisted of grain and basic food stuffs, but the Band Aid team discovered that there was an urgent need for something more nutritious if children's lives were to be saved. As a result, tons of high-energy cookies and milk powder were shipped over to Ethiopia.

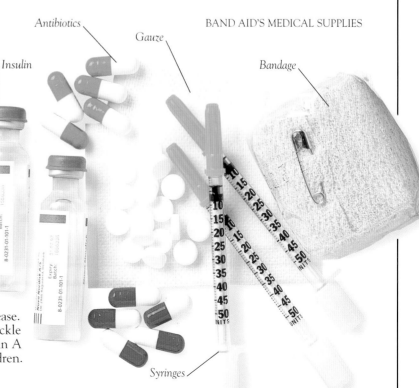

BAND AID'S MEDICAL SUPPLIES

Antibiotics

Gauze

Insulin

Bandage

Syringes

Medical aid

In addition to food and long-term aid, such as seeds, tools, and tractors, urgent medical help was vital if lives were to be saved in the appalling conditions of the refugee camps in Ethiopia and Sudan. People were dying in the thousands, not only from hunger, but also from disease. Band Aid sent tons of medical supplies, including vitamins, to tackle the crisis. One particular shipment contained 40,000 vitamin A tablets, which helped prevent blindness in the starving children.

1985

New way to get around

JANUARY 10

Electronics genius Sir Clive Sinclair has unveiled his answer to Britain's traffic problems. Known as the C5, it is a lightweight, single-seat, battery and pedal-powered tricycle. It can travel up to 20 miles (32 km) before the battery needs recharging. Sir Clive predicts that by the end of the century "the petrol engine will be a thing of the past." Critics are describing the C5 as little more than an expensive toy.

Clive Sinclair in his C5

Pandemonium at Heysel Stadium

MAY 29

The soccer world is in shock tonight after tragedy struck a European Cup Final match at Belgium's Heysel Stadium. Forty Italian and Belgium supporters died, and a further 350 were injured as British soccer fans went on a rampage. A wall and safety fence collapsed as Liverpool fans charged toward supporters of the Juventus team. In the ensuing panic, many victims were trampled or crushed to death. As a priest gave the last rites to the dying, the fighting continued with rocks and other objects being hurled through the air. Rowdy British soccer fans have recently become a growing concern and there are calls for British teams to be banned from playing in Europe.

Armed hijackers at Beirut airport

JUNE 30

Seventeen days after their TWA flight from Athens, Greece, to Rome, Italy, was hijacked by Islamic Jihad terrorists, 39 tired US hostages were released today in Beirut, Lebanon. The hijackers, who flown to a US base in West Germany where they will be reunited with their families. Meanwhile, the hijackers are still guarding the TWA jet at Beirut Airport. One of the hijackers has bragged to the waiting journalists of "the

Hijackers in the cockpit

were demanding the release of Palestinians from Israeli jails, beat up some of their hostages. One passenger, US navy diver Robert Stethem, was brutally murdered. The freed hostages were driven in a Red Cross convoy to Damascus, Syria, before being ability of the oppressed to control America." Although both the United States and Israel are insisting that no deal has been struck with the terrorists, it appears that their demands have been met, and tomorrow 700 prisoners will be released in Israel.

JANUARY–JUNE

World Events	**FEB** Gibraltar's frontier with Spain reopens after 16 years. Spain had tried to force Britain to transfer sovereignty.	**MAR** The National Union of Miners ends its year-long strike in the UK. The prime minister claims a victory.	**MAR** Fifty-four-year-old Mikhail Gorbachev succeeds as leader of the USSR after the death of Konstantin Chernenko.	**MAY** Thousands of people die after a cyclone and tidal wave batter the coast of Bangladesh. Other countries send aid.
Entertainment	**MAR** South African-born British runner Zola Budd wins a cross-country race in Lisbon, barefoot.	**APR** Australian media tycoon Rupert Murdoch buys 50% of the Twentieth Century Fox Film Corporation.	**APR** UK pop group Wham! performs in front of an audience of 10,000 in China.	**JUN** UK boxer Barry McGuigan becomes the WBA world featherweight champion.
Innovations	**JAN** The first UK mobile telephones are introduced by Racal-Vodaphone and Cellnet. **MOBILE PHONE**	**FEB** The *Concorde's* first commercial flight from London, UK, to Sydney, Australia, takes 17 hrs 3 mins 45 secs.	**JUN** US space shuttle *Discovery* blasts off with the first Arab astronaut on board. **PRINCE SULTAN – FIRST ARAB IN SPACE**	**JUN** The Sir Isaac Newton telescope, located on the Canary Islands, is inaugurated.

1985

Wreck of *Titanic* found

SEPTEMBER 3

The wreck of the *Titanic*, the luxury liner that sank on its maiden voyage in April 1912, has finally been found. It was located 400 miles (640 km) south of Newfoundland by a joint French-American expedition.

Town drowns in Colombian mud

NOVEMBER 13

A large area of Colombia has been declared a disaster zone tonight after a long-dormant volcano 81 miles (129 km) west of Bogotá erupted violently for the first time since 1845. The Nevado del Ruiz volcano spewed huge quantities of rocks, ash, mud, and water over nearby towns, and it is thought that up to 20,000 people may have died. Worst hit is the town of Armero, which has virtually disappeared under a stream of hot mud. Clouds of ash and smoke from the volcano are being carried by the wind up to 300 miles (480 km) away. It is being described as one of the most destructive volcanic eruptions in history.

Geneva summit

NOVEMBER 21

United States president Ronald Reagan flew home today after a highly successful series of summit meetings in Geneva with Soviet premier Mikhail Gorbachev. The two leaders spent a record six hours together in private sessions, with only interpreters present. Despite differences about the United States "Star Wars" space defense program, agreement was reached to begin negotiations on strategic nuclear arms control and human rights. Both men appeared to be delighted with the progress of the talks, and the course now seems set for a new era of cooperation between the world's two giant superpowers.

Gorbachev and Reagan reach agreement at talks

NEW POP SENSATION

Madonna Louise Veronica Ciccone has had a string of hit singles this year, on both sides of the Atlantic. In April she embarked on her first tour, playing to 355,000 fans in 27 US cities. Madonna has also received favorable reviews for her first acting role in the film *Desperately Seeking Susan*, as well as appearing on the cover of *Time* magazine.

JULY–DECEMBER

JUL Greenpeace peace protest ship *Rainbow Warrior* is sunk by two explosions in Auckland Harbor, New Zealand.

JUL "We Are the World" concerts are held at Wembley Stadium in the UK and JFK Stadium in US, for Ethiopia.

JUL European Space Agency's *Giotto* spacecraft, which aims to intercept Halley's Comet, is launched.

BORIS BECKER WINS WIMBLEDON

JUL South African president P. W. Botha imposes a state of emergency in black townships after unrest leaves 500 dead.

JUL Seventeen-year-old unseeded West German tennis player Boris Becker wins Wimbledon men's title.

JUL *Challenger*, the US's 50th manned space flight and the 19th space shuttle, is launched.

SEP An earthquake that measures 8.1 on the Richter Scale devastates Mexico City, killing nearly 2,000 people.

JUL UK runner Steve Cram wins the "Dream Mile" in Oslo, Norway, taking more than a second off the world record.

SEP Switzerland becomes the first country to make lead-free catalytic convertors compulsory.

ROCK HUDSON DIES

OCT The Australian government gives back Ayers Rock (Uluru) in the Northern Territory to the Aboriginals.

OCT Film star Rock Hudson dies in the US after a year-long battle against AIDS. He was 59.

NOV Halley's Comet reappears in the skies for the first time in 75 years.

1986

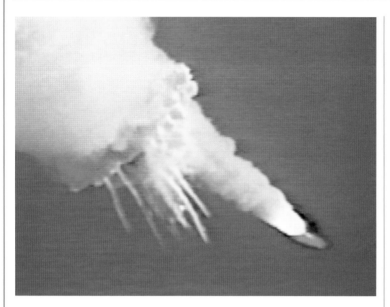

Disaster in space

DISPOSABLE CAMERA

The disposable camera, the ultimate vacation accessory, was launched by Japanese company Fuji this year. The camera consists of a 24-shot color film in a cardboard box with lens and shutter. When finished, the whole camera is sent for processing.

JANUARY 28

The United States is in shock today after the worst accident in space history. As thousands of spectators gathered at Cape Canaveral, and millions more watched on television, the space shuttle *Challenger* exploded into a massive fireball, killing all seven astronauts on board. After several delays because of bad weather, the launch seemed routine until disaster struck just 73 seconds after liftoff. Among the dead is Christa McAuliffe, a schoolteacher from New Hampshire, who had been chosen to be the first "citizen in space."

Aquino triumphs in Philippines

FEBRUARY 25

Philippines dictator Ferdinand Marcos has been ousted from power by Corazon Aquino. The coup comes after a campaign of disobedience. As Aquino supporters stormed the presidential palace, the president and his family escaped to safety in the United States. They leave behind them the trappings of a lavish lifestyle, including 1,060 pairs of shoes owned by the president's wife.

Corazon Aquino

The return of Halley's Comet

MARCH 14

A swarm of spacecraft from around the world has been heading for Halley's Comet, which is visible only once every 75 years. However, it was revealed today that *Giotto*, launched by the European Space Agency, has had the closest encounter. Named after the famous Italian artist who painted Halley's Comet as the Star of Bethlehem, the *Giotto* is traveling at 42 miles (68 km) per second. It has passed within 338 miles (544 km) of the comet. Data sent back to Earth suggests that the nucleus of the comet, which is streaking through the skies in its orbit of the Sun, is one of the darkest bodies of the Solar System.

JANUARY–JUNE

World Events	JAN Spain and Portugal become the eleventh and twelfth members of the European Community.	FEB After 29 years the Duvalier dictatorship in Haiti ends as "Baby Doc," the son of "Papa Doc," flees to France.	APR The US launches a series of air strikes against Libya in retaliation for acts of terrorism aimed at US citizens.	JUN One thousand black activists are arrested in South Africa after President Botha announces a state of emergency.
Entertainment	MAR US film star and tough guy James Cagney dies at the age of 86.	APR US actor Clint Eastwood wins landslide victory as new mayor of Carmel, California.	MAY *Top Gun*, directed by Tony Scott, is a box-office hit with Tom Cruise starring as a gung-ho pilot.	JUN For the first time yellow balls are used at the UK's Wimbledon Lawn Tennis Championships.
Innovations	JAN US spacecraft *Voyager 2* has found that Uranus has 15 moons.	FEB The USSR launches a new orbiting space station called *Mir*, which means "peace."	MAY All new telephones in the UK work by push buttons instead of old-fashioned dials.	JUN The "Mexican wave" is invented in the opening game of the World Cup when Mexico beats Belgium 2–1.

"BABY DOC" THROWN OUT OF HAITI

TOM CRUISE

1986

Nuclear disaster at Chernobyl

APRIL 30

The Soviet Union today revealed that a major nuclear accident has taken place at the Chernobyl power plant in the Ukraine. It could well be the worst civil nuclear catastrophe ever. An explosion ripped through one of the reactors four days ago, releasing huge amounts of radiation into the atmosphere. Poor safety controls, human error, and lack of containment buildings turned the accident into

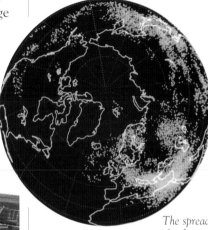

The spread of radiation

a disaster of gigantic proportions. One of the reactors is still blazing, making any attempt to plug the leak and stem the damage impossible. The other three reactors at Chernobyl have been shut down. Thirty-one people have died so far, and about 15,000 people have been evacuated from the immediate vicinity, which is already highly contaminated. At present, the global implications of the toxic meltdown and radiation leak can only be guessed at.

A handy victory for Argentina

JUNE 29

A victorious Argentinian team claimed the World Cup in Mexico today after beating West Germany 3–2 in a bad-tempered final. Argentina's triumphant captain, Diego Maradona, will be remembered for the fisted goal that helped beat England in

Diego Maradona

the quarterfinal. He later called it "the hand of God." Superstar Maradona also scored the two goals that beat Belgium in the semifinal match.

JULY–DECEMBER

JUL The US holds lavish celebrations for the Statue of Liberty's 100th birthday, after a $70 million restoration.

JUL Greg LeMond is the first cyclist from the US to win the 2,514-mile (4,023-km) Tour de France race.

JUL An underwater robot takes pictures of the inside of the wreck of the *Titanic*, which sank in 1912.

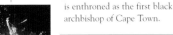

STATUE OF LIBERTY

SEP The Right Reverend Desmond Tutu is enthroned as the first black archbishop of Cape Town.

OCT *Phantom of the Opera*, the musical by Andrew Lloyd-Webber and Charles Hart, opens in the UK.

SEP Japanese car manufacturer Nissan opens a new assembly plant in northeastern England, UK.

OCT President Shimon Peres hands over the premiership of Israel to his coalition partner Yitzhak Shamir.

NOV 20-year-old Mike Tyson from the US becomes the youngest-ever world heavyweight boxing champion.

DEC Surgeons in the UK perform the world's first triple heart, lungs, and liver transplant.

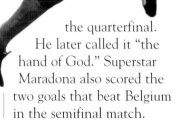

OPRAH WINFREY

NOV The Rhine River in Europe is polluted with toxic liquid pesticides after a blaze at a chemical plant in Basle, Switzerland.

DEC Oprah Winfrey becomes ratings champion of daytime television with her US talk show.

DEC Experimental aircraft *Voyager* 4 completes the first flight around the world without refueling.

THE FIGHT FOR THE PLANET

AS THE THREAT OF NUCLEAR WAR waned in the late Eighties, a new battle to save the earth began. Long-term exploitation of the planet by a fast-growing human population had carried on unchecked for generations. As a result, many precious natural resources, such as tropical rain forests, had already been destroyed, and many more, such as the ozone layer, which protects living things from ultraviolet radiation, were at risk. The climate itself was threatened because the indiscriminate burning of oil and fossils, mainly by automobiles and industry, had dramatically increased levels of carbon dioxide and other poisonous gases in the air, causing the "greenhouse effect." Global warming was the inevitable result. Most scientists believed that the average world temperature would rise by 7.2°F (4°C) by the end of the 21st century.

Smoke-filled skies

Most air pollution comes from the chimneys of coal-fired power stations and factories that emit sulfur dioxide and nitrogen oxides. These pollutants combine with elements in the atmosphere to create acid rain, which damages plants and crops and contaminates lakes and rivers.

Rain forest destruction

About half of the world's original tropical rain forest has been destroyed and, with it, countless unique species of insects and plants. During the Eighties, the rate of destruction almost doubled. An estimated 62,000 sq miles (160,000 sq km) of rain forest disappeared each year because of slash-and-burn methods of farming, logging, and mining. Vast tracts of Central and South America were also cleared and burned for cattle ranching.

Forest devastation caused by slash-and-burn farming techniques

AMAZON WASTELAND

ANTINUCLEAR DISPOSAL SIGNS

Nuclear testing

The nuclear arms race involved the constant development of deadly atomic and thermonuclear weapons. Test explosions were carried out in remote areas, under the ground, or under the sea. With the end of the Cold War, the superpowers agreed to dismantle nuclear stockpiles and to ban nuclear testing.

Calibrated sight

Trigger

Nuclear protest

Antinuclear protestors and activist groups such as Greenpeace helped focus world attention on the threat posed by nuclear weapons and the dangers of the nuclear power industry, with its highly toxic waste. The protestors' fears were confirmed in 1986 when a massive explosion at the Chernobyl power plant, in the Soviet Union, resulted in the worst nuclear accident ever, causing the contamination of vast areas of Eastern Europe and Scandinavia.

Weapon of death

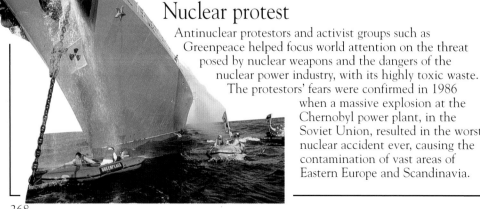

For 300 years whales have been hunted for food or to provide oil. The right whale was almost hunted to extinction in the late 1800s, and the number of sperm whales has been severely affected. But it was not until 1860, when the harpoon gun was invented, that it became easier to catch some of the faster whales. In the 1920s, the Norwegians revolutionized whaling by introducing a modern harpoon with a deadly explosive tip.

Ivory trade

During the Seventies, the number of elephants in Africa dwindled from 1.3 million to 609,000. Most of the elephants were slaughtered and left to rot by poachers in search of the "white gold," or ivory, of their tusks. When, in 1989, the African elephant was listed in the Convention on International Trade in Endangered Species (CITES), more than 115 countries agreed to stop trading in ivory.

Recycling

During the Eighties there was a newfound concern about the planet's fragile state and its dwindling resources, particularly in the rich industrialized nations. People realized that caring for the environment began at home and started to recycle wastepaper, bottles, and cans. As consumers, they also began to realize the power of their purses, opting for new planet-friendly goods that did not damage the environment, such as nontoxic laundry detergent.

Hole in the ozone layer

Each spring since the 1970s, a hole in the ozone layer has opened over Antarctica, allowing in harmful ultraviolet rays from the sun. Elsewhere, this protective layer is thinning as it is eroded by manufactured gases called chlorofluorocarbons (CFCs), which are used in aerosols and refrigerators. CFCs take about eight years to reach the stratosphere, where they can survive for a century. The Montreal Protocol to protect the ozone layer was signed in 1987 and aims to cut CFC production by 50 percent by 1999.

Violet and pink areas show the severe depletion in the ozone layer

Taking action

In October 1983, six hundred Greenpeace activists clad in "death" suits lay down as if dead in London, Britain, to protest against the Sellafield nuclear reprocessing plant, THORP, in Cumbria, and the radioactive discharges it would cause.

HARPOON GUN

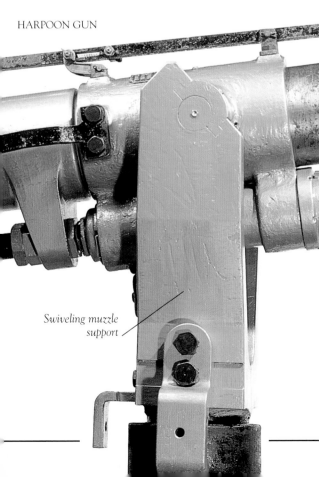

Swiveling muzzle support

Muzzle

Barbs open on impact to anchor the harpoon in the whale's flesh

Grenade-loaded tip explodes inside the whale

Fast and deadly

By the beginning of this century, steam-powered ships enabled whalers to hunt the fin whale and the blue whale in the most remote waters in the world. There were about 250,000 blue whales in the Antarctic when the first whaling fleets arrived. Now there are probably only a few hundred left. Huge modern factory ships were built that could process the dead whales at sea, rather than towing them back to shore. Whale populations plummeted, and in 1986, the International Whaling Commission (IWC) introduced a temporary ban on commercial whaling.

1987

Pilot meets red-faced Russians!

MAY 28
Strollers in Moscow's Red Square were amazed when a small Cessna four-seater light aircraft appeared from

Rust lands in Red Square

nowhere, swooped over the Kremlin and St. Basil's Cathedral, and landed on an upward slope near the huge Kremlin Wall. A young man stepped out of the cockpit and proceeded to sign autographs. Nineteen-year-old West German Mathias Rust had succeeded in dodging the combined might of the Soviet military authorities, flying solo through heavily defended airspace. Previously, he had only 24 hours of flying time to his credit.

Iran-Contra scandal

JULY 7
"God Bless Ollie" T-shirts are selling like hot cakes and telegrams of support are pouring in after Lt. Col. Oliver North defended himself to the US Congress over his part in the "Irangate" arms for hostages scandal. The much-decorated marine officer, nicknamed the president's "Swashbuckler-in-Chief," was dismissed from the National Security Council at the end of last year. The scandal concerns the $30-million profit made from the sale of arms to Iran in exchange for US hostages. The money was transferred to Contra rebels fighting the left-wing Sandinista government in Nicaragua.

JANUARY–JUNE

World Events	Entertainment	Innovations
JAN The Archbishop of Canterbury's envoy and negotiator Terry Waite is kidnapped in Lebanon.	**FEB** US pop artist Andy Warhol dies during an operation, at age 55.	**FEB** Supernova 1987A, the first exploding star visible to the naked eye, is spotted.

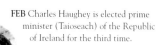

TERRY WAITE

FEB Charles Haughey is elected prime minister (Taoiseach) of the Republic of Ireland for the third time.	**APR** The Duchess of Windsor's jewels are sold in Geneva, Switzerland, for £31,380,197.
	FEB The new *European Airbus 320*, built jointly by France, Germany, Spain, and the UK, is launched.

MAR 189 people die when the 8,888-ton car ferry *Herald of Free Enterprise* sinks off the coast of Zeebrugge, Belgium.	**JUN** US actor and dancer Fred Astaire (born Frederick Austerlitz) dies in his Hollywood home at the age of 88.
MAR The DAT (Digital Audio Tape) recorder is launched by Sony in Japan for professional use only.	

ZEEBRUGGE DISASTER

JUN Fifteen people die when a car bomb planted by Basque separatist group ETA explodes in Barcelona, Spain.
JUN New Zealand's All Blacks wins the first rugby world cup, beating France 29–9 in the final.
MAR "Ecu" coins are struck in Belgium on the 30th anniversary of the European Community.

1987

Stock markets crash

OCTOBER 19

Dealers are dubbing it "Black Monday" as stock market shares plummet all around the world. Wall Street has had its worst day ever, with the Dow Jones Industrial Average plunging 508 points from 2,246.73 to 1,738.41. It is the end of the "bull market" of the last five years, which has seen a 350 percent rise in average share prices. Analysts are pointing to the appalling state of the US economy as one of the major factors. The economic boom of the 1980s appears to be at an end.

FIRST SOLAR-POWERED CAR RACE

It took General Motors' *Sunraycer* six days to win the first solar-powered car race, held in Australia this November. There were 22 entries in the 2,011-mile (3,218-km) Pentax World Solar Challenge.

Flowers sell for $53.9 million

NOVEMBER 11

The 1980s have seen the prices of Impressionist and Post-Impressionist paintings go through the roof, and a new record was set today in New York. Australian tycoon Alan Bond has bought Van Gogh's *Irises* for a staggering $53.9 million at Sotheby's United States auction house. Earlier in the year Yasuda Fire and Marine, a Japanese insurance firm, bought one of Van Gogh's most famous paintings, *Sunflowers*, at an auction held in Britain for a breathtaking £24.75 million.

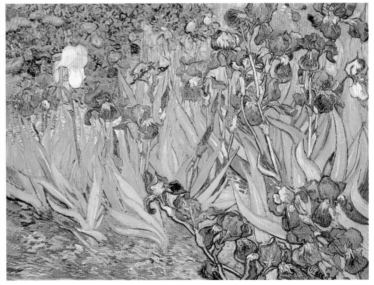

Irises by Vincent Van Gogh

Mafia on trial

DECEMBER 16

After two years the marathon trial of Sicily's Mafia, held in a special bomb-proof courthouse, reached its climax today. The 338 Mafiosi were sentenced to a total of 2,665 years in prison for crimes including extortion and murder.

JULY–DECEMBER

JUL Former Nazi SS officer Klaus Barbie, the "Butcher of Lyons," is found guilty of wartime atrocities and is imprisoned for life.

JUL The UK's Richard Branson and Norwegian Per Lindstrand cross the Atlantic Ocean in a hot-air balloon.

JUL The Soviet Union launches into Earth orbit a 20-ton space platform called *Cosmos 1870*.

JUL The Greek government declares a national state of emergency when a heatwave claims over 700 lives.

AUG Whitney Houston's album *I Wanna Dance with Somebody* enters the US charts at number one.

WHITNEY HOUSTON

NOV Construction work is started on the Channel Tunnel between France and the UK.

OCT The "Great Storm" sweeps across the Atlantic and destructive hurricane-force winds hit the UK.

AUG Tom McLean from the UK rows across the Atlantic ocean in a record-breaking 54 days 23 hours.

NOV A talking watch, which answers when asked the time, is launched by Citizen in Japan.

STORM DAMAGE IN THE UK

NOV An IRA bomb explodes at a parade in Enniskillen, Northern Ireland, killing 11 people.

AUG Lynne Cox from the US swims across the Bering Straits from the US to the Soviet Union.

DEC Soviet cosmonaut Yuri Romananko returns to Earth after a record 326 days in space.

1988

Happy birthday, Australia

JANUARY 26

Sydney Harbour is teeming today as Australia celebrates the 200th anniversary of the arrival of the first settlers from Britain. Sailing ships from all over the world are joining in, and a special fleet of 160 tall ships has

Sydney Harbour

reenacted the anchoring of the First Fleet in 1788. Other birthday events include the arrival in Adelaide of ten camels, which have trekked 2,129 miles (3,426 km) across Australia from Darwin to commemorate the part that their ancestors played in opening up the heart of the continent. Britain presented the country with a sailing ship. Aboriginal people, however, have declared it a "year of mourning," throwing wreaths into Botany Bay, where Captain Cook, the first European to discover the continent, landed in 1770.

Longest tunnel in the world

MARCH 13

The Seikan tunnel, linking the islands of Honshu and Hokkaido in Japan, was officially opened today by the Japanese minister of transportation, who described the tunnel as "a technical achievement without parallel in the world." It is the last stage in a project to link the four islands of Japan by train, something that has inspired Japanese engineers for decades. Covering a distance of 33.46 miles (53.85 km), it is not only the longest tunnel in the world, it is also the most expensive. The total cost spiraled from an original estimate of $783 million in 1971 to $6.5 billion, largely because of the extreme difficulty of tunneling through unstable and porous rock. It was drilled more than 300 ft (91.4 m) under the seabed, reaching a maximum depth of 787 ft (240 m).

The Seikan tunnel

Hannibal's trek

APRIL 19

Two elephants have just arrived in Turin, Italy, after retracing Hannibal's famous journey across the Alps from France. It took them 21 days to complete the 500-mile (805-km) trek. The trip was organized by English cricketer and fund-raiser Ian Botham.

STEALTH BOMBER

The Pentagon has released the first pictures of the F-117A *Stealth* jet fighter, the revolutionary aircraft that has been operational since 1983 and that is invisible to radar. The prototype of the B-2 *Stealth* bomber, which is designed to absorb radar, was also unveiled.

JANUARY–APRIL

World Events	**JAN** Defiant Palestinians take part in an intifada, or uprising, against occupying Israeli forces in Gaza.	**FEB** Archbishop Desmond Tutu is arrested in South Africa for defying a law banning protests outside parliament.	**MAR** Three members of the Irish Republican Army are shot dead by UK soldiers in Gibraltar. The act is widely condemned.	**APR** The National People's Congress in China votes to allow capitalist-style enterprise to set up in the communist country.
Entertainment	**FEB** Comic Relief Day in the UK raises £7 million for charity.	**FEB** UK ski jumper Eddie "The Eagle" Edwards comes last at the Calgary Olympics.	**FEB** At the winter Olympics, Pirmin Zurbriggen of Switzerland wins the men's downhill ski event.	**APR** Bernardo Bertolucci's film *The Last Emperor* wins nine Oscars, the most won by a single film in 27 years.
Innovations	**JAN** A $10 plastic polymer banknote is issued by the Reserve Bank of Australia.	**JAN** Japan's new magnetic levitation train, the *Maglev*, reaches 160.92 mph (257.48 km/h) in 30 seconds.	**FEB** UK archaeologists discover the grave of Boadicea, warrior queen of ancient Britain, under a train station.	**APR** The 8-mile (12.87-km) Great Seto Bridge, connecting two of Japan's islands, is opened.

EDDIE "THE EAGLE"

THE LAST EMPEROR

1988

160 die on *Piper Alpha*

JULY 6

At least 160 people have been killed and dozens more injured after a huge explosion at the 38,000-ton North Sea oil platform *Piper Alpha* off the coast of Scotland. Those who survived the original blast were forced to jump 200 ft (61 m) into the sea, which was covered with burning oil, in a desperate attempt to escape. Emergency services are fighting the inferno, and helicopters are scanning the area for survivors. First reports suggest the disaster was caused by a faulty safety valve that allowed the buildup of flammable gas.

Fatal flooding in Bangladesh

SEPTEMBER 4

Bangladesh has once again been hit by a catastrophic natural disaster as floods sweep two-thirds of the country. The capital, Dacca, is under water, 25 million people have been left homeless, and at least 1,000 people have lost their lives. A quarter of the year's crops have been destroyed, which will surely mean desperate food shortages. The international airport has been closed and roads and railroads

are submerged, making rescue work difficult and preventing a coordinated relief program.

Bangladesh's information minister, Mahabur Rahmanthe, has appealed for helicopters to provide emergency aid. He said, "No other country in the region has suffered so much damage from natural calamity." The tragedy comes less than a month after 700 people died when the country was hit by a monsoon.

Turin Shroud declared fake

OCTOBER 13

The famous Turin Shroud, believed to have been used to wrap the body of Christ and revered by Catholics for centuries as one of the most sacred holy relics, has been declared a fake. Extensive carbon-dating tests carried out at Oxford University in Britain and elsewhere, have proved that the linen actually dates from between 1260 and 1390. However, scientists cannot understand how a length of material more than 600 years old came to be imprinted with the blood-stained image of a crucified man.

MAY-AUGUST

MAY Socialist leader François Mitterrand is re-elected President of France for a second term, taking 54% of the popular vote.

MAY US president Ronald Reagan pays his first visit to the USSR for talks with Soviet premier Mikhail Gorbachev.

AUG In Rangoon, Burma, the president Sein Lwin resigns after huge antigovernment demonstrations and rioting.

AUG Pakistan's military ruler, President Zia ul-Haq, is killed when his plane explodes in midair.

JUN *Who Framed Roger Rabbit?*, a film mixing live action and animation, is a box-office hit.

NELSON MANDELA CONCERT

JUN 80,000 people celebrate Nelson Mandela's 70th birthday at a huge concert in the UK.

JUL Top-earning pop star Michael Jackson "moonwalks" his way to Europe at the start of a world tour.

FERRARI LOGO

AUG Legendary Italian race car magnate Enzo Ferrari, dies at age 90. He had retired in 1977.

JUN Personal TV sets for airline passengers are introduced by Northwest Airlines in the US.

JUL In the UK, automatic cameras are introduced to catch motorists running red lights.

AUG In Japan Sony launches the first video walkman, combining a color TV and VCR.

AUG An Afghan-Soviet space mission blasts off for the orbiting Russian space station *Mir*.

1988

First female Islamic PM

DECEMBER 1

Benazir Bhutto today became prime minister of Pakistan. Two weeks ago her People's Party won the country's first democratic election in 11 years. She is the first woman prime minister in an Islamic country.

BUNGEE JUMPING

People have been flocking to jump off the Kawarau Suspension Bridge. This first permanent bungee jumping site in Queenstown, New Zealand, was opened this year. Bungee jumping is now one of the most popular dangerous sports.

Devastation strikes Armenia

DECEMBER 7

A huge international relief effort is being mounted after a major earthquake struck Armenia, in the southern part of the Soviet Union, earlier today, killing an estimated 100,000 people. Nearly half a million people have been left homeless, with temperatures dropping below the freezing point and rescue work proving difficult in the mountainous and isolated countryside. The epicenter of the earthquake, near the Turkish border, measured 6.9 on the Richter Scale. It is by far the worst quake the region has ever known, with the town of Spitak, which had a population of 50,000, being completely destroyed. More than three-quarters of the apartment buildings in the city of Leninakan, which has a population of more than 300,000, collapsed, burying many alive in the rubble. Soviet premier Mikhail Gorbachev has cut short his trip to the United States to visit the devastated area.

Jet explodes over Lockerbie

DECEMBER 22

The Scottish town of Lockerbie is this morning coming to terms with the tragic events of last night. A Pan Am jumbo jet exploded over the town, killing all 259 passengers on board and at least 11 people on the ground. The airliner was on its way from Frankfurt, Germany, to New York City when it suddenly broke up in midair, scattering wreckage far and wide. It has now come out that several United States embassies around the world received a warning that a Pan Am flight would be a terrorist target for a bomb.

SEPTEMBER–DECEMBER

World Events	SEP Hundreds of thousands are left homeless in Mexico after a hurricane strikes.	NOV George Bush, the current US vice-president, wins the presidential election for the Republican Party.	DEC Thirty-six people die and 100 are injured when a packed commuter train crashes into another train in the UK.	DEC Palestine Liberation Organization chairman Yassir Arafat renounces terrorism and recognizes Israeli rights.
Entertainment	SEP US sprinter Florence Griffith-Joyner (nicknamed Flo-Jo) wins three gold medals at the Seoul Olympics.	SEP Canadian sprinter Ben Johnson is stripped of the 100 m Olympic gold medal he won at Seoul after failing a drug test.	DEC UK academic Dr. Stephen Hawking has an unlikely bestseller with his book *A Brief History of Time*.	DEC US rock star Roy Orbison, nicknamed the "Big O," dies after suffering a heart attack at age 52.
Innovations	SEP The Australian Telescope, the largest in the southern hemisphere, is inaugurated.	NOV The first unmanned Soviet space shuttle, *Buran* (Snowstorm), orbits the Earth twice in a 3 hr 25 min flight.	DEC Transatlantic optical fiber capable of carrying 40,000 simultaneous telephone calls becomes operational.	DEC Soviet cosmonauts Vladimir Titov and Musa Manarov set a new space endurance record of over a year.

GEORGE BUSH

YASSIR ARAFAT

1989

Emperor Hirohito dies

JANUARY 7

Michinomiya Hirohito, emperor of Japan for 62 years, has died. At 87 years old, he was the oldest reigning monarch in the world. His death brings to an end the era in Japan known as Showa, which means "enlightened peace." His long reign saw Japan develop into one of the most powerful economies in the world, after surviving defeat in World War II. In 1945 Hirohito admitted to his shattered nation that the emperor is not a god incarnate. Crown Prince Akihito, Hirohito's 55-year-old son, automatically became emperor at the moment his father died.

Mass demonstrations in Tiananmen Square

JUNE 9

Hundreds of demonstrators have been killed and thousands badly injured after the Chinese People's Liberation Army mounted a sudden and savage crackdown in Beijing this week. Troops advanced on Tiananmen Square, where almost half a million students and pro-democracy activists were denouncing the communist regime and demanding freedom of speech and other basic human rights. Some of the demonstrators have been on hunger strike since May 13. A "Statue of Democracy and Freedom," modeled on the Statue of Liberty, had been unveiled. As the huge armored tanks moved in, one demonstrator single-handedly stopped the advance before being pulled away. In the massacre that followed, soldiers fired indiscriminately as the protestors fought back. A similar crackdown is now taking place all over China, with hundreds of so-called "counter-revolutionaries" being rounded up and put on trial in people's courts. World leaders are condemning the horrific actions of the Chinese government.

Protestors in Tiananmen Square

A lone protestor stops the tanks from advancing. His bravery is admired throughout the world

JANUARY–APRIL

FEB After a ten-year occupation, the last Soviet troops withdraw from Afghanistan in central Asia.

JAN The world famous surrealist painter Salvador Dali dies at the age of 84 in Figueras, Spain.

JAN The world's first holographic postage stamps are issued by the Austrian postal service.

SALMAN RUSHDIE

FEB The Iranian Ayatollah Khomeini calls for the death of UK writer Salman Rushdie for blaspheming Islam.

FEB US boxer Mike Tyson retains the world heavyweight title after beating UK boxer Frank Bruno.

FEB Rupert Murdoch's £25 million *Sky* television satellite network is launched across Europe.

MAR Oil tanker *Exxon Valdez* runs aground in Alaska, spilling 11 million gallons of crude oil into Prince William Sound.

FEB *The Joshua Tree* by Irish rock group U2 is the first CD to sell one million copies.

FEB Soviet space probe *Phobos* orbits Mars and sends back pictures of its moon.

EXXON VALDEZ

APR Ninety-four people are crushed to death and 170 are injured at Hillsborough Stadium in Sheffield, UK, during a soccer match.

MAR Dustin Hoffman wins an Oscar for his portrayal of autism in hit film *Rain Man*.

APR Researchers in Toronto, Canada, identify the gene responsible for cystic fibrosis.

1989

Revolution remembered

JULY 14

Celebrations to mark the 200th anniversary of the French revolution reached a climax in Paris today. More than 5,000 soldiers and 300 armored vehicles took part in a huge Bastille Day parade down the Champs Elysée, with a flyover by 250 planes and helicopters. It was followed by a spectacular international pageant.

Dictator dies in disgrace

SEPTEMBER 28

Former dictator of the Philippines Ferdinand Marcos has died in Hawaii at age 72.

He spent the last three years of his life in exile, fighting charges of embezzlement, after fleeing the country he had defrauded of billions of dollars in 1986. He is survived by his wife, Imelda, a former beauty queen, whose 1,060 pairs of shoes became a symbol of their lavish and corrupt regime.

THE LOUVRE PYRAMID

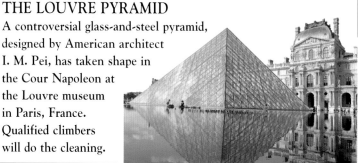

A controversial glass-and-steel pyramid, designed by American architect I. M. Pei, has taken shape in the Cour Napoleon at the Louvre museum in Paris, France. Qualified climbers will do the cleaning.

The earth moves in San Francisco

OCTOBER 17

A devastating earthquake today struck San Francisco, killing an estimated 90 people and causing billions of dollars worth of damage. The tremor, which erupted along the San Andreas Fault, lasted 15 seconds and measured 6.9 on the Richter Scale. Badly hit by the quake was the double-decker Highway 880, which collapsed, crushing many vehicles traveling on the lower road.

MAY–AUGUST

World Events	**MAY** The Czechoslovakian dissident Vaclav Havel is freed after four months in jail for inciting unrest.	**JUN** Iranian fundamentalist religious leader Ayatollah Khomeini dies in the capital, Tehran, at age 87.	**JUN** Solidarity trade union achieves a landslide victory in elections to the parliament in Poland.	**JUL** South African president P. W. Botha makes a historic visit to Nelson Mandela, the jailed leader of the ANC.
Entertainment	**JUN** UK rock group Pink Floyd stages a spectacular $3 million show in the Soviet Union.	**JUL** Prince's soundtrack album for the hit film *Batman* tops the music charts all around the world.	**JUL** The legendary UK actor Lord Laurence Olivier dies at age 82. London theaters dim their lights.	**JUL** US cyclist Greg Lemond wins the Tour de France in Paris, with an average speed of 34 mph (54.4 km/h).
Innovations	**MAY** NASA's *Magellan* space probe blasts off from the US on its way to Venus.	**JUL** The large electron positron collider (LEP) is inaugurated at the CERN research center in Switzerland.	**AUG** NASA's *Voyager 2* space probe sends back stunning pictures of Neptune's moon, Triton.	**AUG** The first newspapers to be printed with nonrubbing ink are distributed by Associated Newspapers in the UK.

MOURNING THE AYATOLLAH

LAURENCE OLIVIER

1989

Gateway to the West is opened

NOVEMBER 10 Hundreds of thousands of East Berliners are flooding to the West after the hated Berlin Wall, which has divided the city for 28 years and has come to symbolize the Cold War, was finally opened. At the stroke of midnight, checkpoints were opened and swarms of people climbed up and over the wall, while others danced and celebrated on top. East German bulldozers are today opening new crossing points.

Batman's sinister new look

DECEMBER 31 Comic book hero Batman celebrates his 50th birthday this year but he is still waging war on that archcriminal the Joker. His latest film, released by Warner Bros., puts a sinister new spin on the familiar story of good versus evil and has been an instant box-office hit. Starring Michael Keaton and Jack Nicholson, *Batman* has broken all box- office records in the United States. A sequel is planned.

Tyranny and terror end in Romania

DECEMBER 31 Romanians are tonight celebrating not only New Year's Eve, but the sudden end of Nicolae Ceausescu's 24-year tyranny and rule of terror. A small protest in Timisoara two weeks ago escalated into full-scale and bloody civil war, with the army giving crucial support to the protesters. The dictator and his wife, Elena, were executed by firing squad on Christmas day after being found guilty of "crimes against the people" and an alleged 60,000 deaths. The Communist Party was abolished yesterday and free elections are planned.

Romanians celebrate a bright future

SEPTEMBER–DECEMBER

OCT In South Africa eight jailed nationalists, including antiapartheid campaigner Walter Sisulu, are freed.

SEP Famous US songwriter Irving Berlin, whose songs include *White Christmas*, dies at age 101.

OCT Archaeologists discover the remains of Shakespeare's Globe Theatre in London, UK.

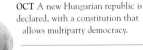

OCT A new Hungarian republic is declared, with a constitution that allows multiparty democracy.

OCT The Nobel Peace Prize is awarded to the Dalai Lama, the exiled spiritual leader of Tibet.

OCT A worldwide ban on trading in ivory is signed at a convention in Switzerland.

OCT East German leader Erich Honecker is ousted by his own Communist Party and is replaced by Egon Krenz.

NOV Rudolf Nureyev dances with the Russian Kirov Ballet for the first time since he defected to the West in 1961.

OCT NASA's space probe *Galileo* blasts off from Cape Canaveral, Florida, at the start of a six-year journey to Jupiter.

DEC Czechoslovakia's Vaclav Havel is elected as the country's first noncommunist president for 41 years.

NOV Romanian gymnast and Olympic gold medalist Nadia Comaneci seeks political asylum in Hungary.

DEC The 10,188-mile (16,300-km) national highway around the coast of Australia is completed after 15 years.

1987 REAGAN AND GORBACHEV SIGN
TREATY TO CUT NUCLEAR ARSENAL

1988 SOVIET TROOPS BEGIN THEIR
WITHDRAWAL FROM AFGHANISTAN

1989 COMMUNIST GOVERNMENTS
OVERTHROWN IN EASTERN EUROPE

THE END OF THE COLD WAR

AFTER THE SOVIET UNION EXPLODED ITS FIRST ATOM BOMB in 1949, the two world superpowers, the Soviet Union and the United States, began a nuclear arms race, known as the Cold War, that continued for over 40 years. Relations between the superpowers only began to improve when Mikhail Gorbachev came to power in the Soviet Union. In 1987 he and US president Ronald Reagan agreed to dismantle their missiles. By the end of the decade, the Soviet Union had withdrawn its troops from Afghanistan and had begun to reduce its military force in eastern Europe. At home, Gorbachev and his policies of reform were not so popular and led, ultimately, to the breakup of the Soviet Union.

Soviet propaganda

During the Cold War both the Soviet Union and the United States used propaganda including films, books, magazines, and posters to discredit one another and to fuel public fear. This 1952 anti-US cartoon appeared in a Soviet magazine and satirized the US's use of nerve gas. It shows huge rockets firing diseases such as typhus and cholera.

The arms race

By the end of the Cold War each side had enough nuclear weapons to destroy the world many times over. The first hydrogen bomb, tested in 1952, was as powerful as all the bombs dropped on Germany and Japan during World War II. During the following decades, nuclear bombs dropped by aircraft were joined by unmanned intercontinental ballistic missiles (ICBMs), multiple warhead missiles (MIRVs), and ground-hugging cruise missiles.

The fall of the Berlin Wall

In 1989, as Hungary transformed itself from a communist state into a multiparty democracy and opened its borders, the first flood of East Germans escaped from communist oppression to a new life in the West. Meanwhile, there were mass demonstrations in cities all over East Germany and the hard-line communist government resigned. An estimated one million protestors marched through the streets of East Berlin. In November, bulldozers moved in and the Berlin Wall was torn down. For the first time since 1961, when the Wall was built, East Berliners could pass freely into West Berlin. In the following weeks hundreds of thousands of people poured across the border.

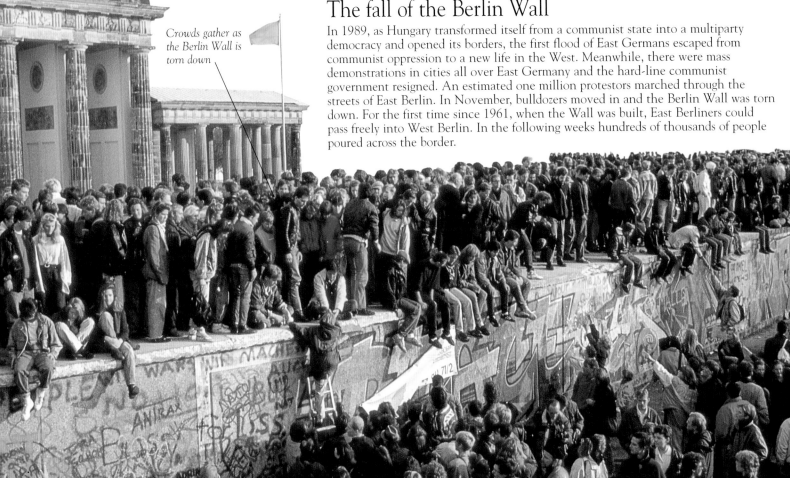

Crowds gather as the Berlin Wall is torn down

Toppling communism

In 1989 the Iron Curtain that divided Europe for more than forty years was lifted. National, ethnic, and religious unrest, suppressed for decades, erupted in the Soviet Union. People took to the streets, demanding freedom. The Baltic republics of Lithuania, Latvia, and Estonia led the way, declaring independence from Moscow. Pro-freedom movements also gathered force in the Soviet satellite states in eastern Europe. By the end of the year communism had been toppled in Hungary, Czechoslovakia, East Germany, Bulgaria, and Romania.

DISMANTLING LENIN'S MONUMENT

Lenin's statue is removed from the city center of Riga, Soviet Union

Dr. Strangelove

Stanley Kubrick made *Dr. Strangelove* as early as 1963, a year after Soviet missile bases had been installed in Cuba and the world had teetered on the brink of nuclear war. The film satirizes the insane logic of the nuclear arms race and the doctrine of deterrence known as Mutually Assured Destruction (MAD).

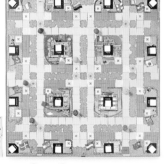

Spy Ring game

Suspicion thrived during the nuclear arms race, with espionage playing a vital role. Spies were used to find out what the other side was doing – and to catch enemy agents at home. If caught, they were often executed or jailed. This *Spy Ring* game (1965) is set in the fictional city of Espiona, and players must gather as many secrets as they can.

Soviet reformer

Mikhail Gorbachev was 54 when he became Secretary General of the Soviet Communist Party in 1985. His task was daunting – an economy bankrupted by the nuclear arms race and a government riddled with corruption. He embarked on a program of reforms, launching a new era of freedom in the Soviet Union. He promised "perestroika," a major reconstruction of the Soviet state, and "glasnost," a new policy of openness. Within months of taking office, he was proposing drastic reductions in nuclear arms.

Food lines

Although Gorbachev won instant popularity in the West for his nuclear arms agreement, domestic politics proved more problematic. His program of economic reforms made the price of bread, meat, and some other products rocket. There was an immediate increase in food shortages and a fall in living standards.

March for peace

Growing revolt against the communist government in Poland gave birth to the independent trade union Solidarity in 1980. Led by Lech Walesa, an electrician, it had huge popular support, organizing a series of workers' strikes, and bringing the country to a standstill. In 1981, the government banned Solidarity, which led to a decade of confrontation until 1989, when the ban was lifted. As the Soviet Union disintegrated, Solidarity swept to power, and in 1990 Lech Walesa was elected president.

1990

Mandela's first taste of freedom

FEBRUARY 11
After 27 years in prison, South African black leader Nelson Mandela is at last a free man. His release comes just one week after President F. W. de Klerk lifted the ban on the African National Congress (ANC), an organization that has led the black struggle against apartheid. A jubilant crowd of 2,000 supporters greeted Mandela as he left Victor Verster prison, and another 50,000 waited to welcome him in Cape Town. The campaign to free Nelson Mandela has been very much at the center of the antiapartheid movement, and Mandela paid tribute to everyone involved in the campaign. He also made clear his continued support for the ANC and his commitment to the fight against apartheid in South Africa.

A jubilant Nelson Mandela

MUTANT TURTLES
Turtle-mania has taken off with the arrival of a film starring the *Teenage Mutant Ninja Turtles* cartoon heroes. The four turtles enjoy eating pizza and fighting crime.

NASA keeps an eye on the stars

Hubble Space Telescope

APRIL 24
NASA's long-awaited $1.5 million, 13.75-ton *Hubble Space Telescope* finally blasted off today from Cape Canaveral in the United States on board the space shuttle *Discovery*. Tomorrow, with the help of a 49-ft (15-m) mechanical arm, it will be put into orbit 370 miles (595 km) above the Earth. Named after US astronomer Edwin Hubble, the telescope will probe the farthest reaches of the Universe and has been described as the greatest single advance in astronomy since the work of Galileo.

JANUARY–APRIL

World Events	**JAN** In Panama, General Noriega surrenders to US authorities and is charged with drug trafficking.	**FEB** The central committee of the USSR Communist Party votes to end the party's monopoly on power.	**FEB** The Sandinista government in Nicaragua concedes victory in an election to a US-backed coalition.	**MAR** In the Australian general election, the ruling Labor Party, which is led by Bob Hawke, is returned for a fourth term.
Entertainment	**JAN** Teen band New Kids on the Block tops the pop charts on both sides of the Atlantic.	**JAN** US tennis player John McEnroe is kicked out of the Australian Open tournament for bad behavior.	**JAN** A UK man is fined for refusing to remove a 26-ft (8-m) high fiberglass shark from the roof of his house.	**FEB** New Zealander Richard Hadlee becomes the first cricketer to take an incredible 400 test wickets.
Innovations	**JAN** US shuttle astronauts rescue a damaged space lab and bring it to Earth.	**JAN** A worldwide ban on ivory trading comes into effect to protect elephants from extinction.	**JAN** Japan launches the first space probe to be sent to the Moon for 14 years.	**APR** Four asteroids discovered in 1982 and 1983 are named after Sixties' pop group The Beatles.

GENERAL NORIEGA

SHARK ADDITION TO HOUSE IN THE UK

1990

Double murder shocks the world

MAY 28

The Irish Republican Army (IRA) has admitted responsibility for the murder of two Australian lawyers in the Dutch town of Roermond. The two men were mistaken for British servicemen and were gunned down in the main square as they got out of their British-registered cars to take photographs.

BSE leads to worldwide beef ban

MAY 31

France has today followed Austria, West Germany, the Soviet Union, and 14 other nations in banning all imports of beef and live cattle from Britain. This

follows public fears that BSE (bovine spongiform encephalopathy), or "mad cow disease," which has spread rapidly through British cattle, can be passed on in a deadly form to humans.

Saddam's sick show

Saddam Hussein with a young hostage

Hussein offered a formal peace treaty to Iraq's archenemy, Iran, in order to concentrate his forces against the international troops that are gathering in Saudi Arabia, which borders Kuwait.

AUGUST 23

Iraqi leader Saddam Hussein continues to thumb his nose at Western powers after invading and annexing the tiny oil-rich Gulf state of Kuwait earlier this month. Today he paraded American and British hostages on television in a grotesque attempt to reassure the world of their well-being. Hundreds of Westerners were taken from Kuwait and detained in Baghdad, the Iraqi capital, after the invasion. They are being held as pawns, their lives in immediate danger if the West takes any military action against Iraq in retaliation for the invasion of Kuwait. Last week, after ten years of conflict, Saddam

Iraqi man shows his support for Saddam Hussein

MAY–AUGUST

MAY Anticommunist demonstrations disrupt the USSR's May Day parade, which is held each year in Moscow.

MAY Ion Iliescu and the National Salvation Front triumph in the first free elections to be held in Romania since 1937.

JUN In Algeria, the fundamentalist Islamic Salvation Front wins control of municipal and provincial assemblies.

AUG After holding them for seven days, Saddam Hussein of Iraq frees all Western women and children hostages.

JUL Czech-born US tennis player Martina Navratilova wins a record ninth Wimbledon singles title.

JUL In the soccer World Cup West Germany beats Argentina 1–0 in the final in Italy.

JUL Opera tenors José Carreras, Placido Domingo, and Luciano Pavarotti sing together in Italy.

JUL UK rock group Pink Floyd performs a free, open-air version of *The Wall* in Berlin, Germany.

MAY Robert Maxwell's new newspaper *The European* is launched throughout Europe.

WEST GERMANY WINS THE WORLD CUP

MAY UK-produced beef is banned in UK schools as concern over BSE grows.

JUN Disney's *Dick Tracy*, the first film to be made in digital sound, is released in the US.

PERFORMANCE OF THE WALL IN BERLIN

JUL Japanese company Sony produces the revolutionary *Data Discman*, an electronic book.

1990

Germany reunited

OCTOBER 3

Bells are pealing and flags are flying as the people of East and West Germany are reunited after forty-five years of division. Germany was divided in two in 1949. Although reunification seemed inevitable after the collapse of the Soviet Union, the pace of change has been amazing. An economic integration between the two countries has already taken place and NATO membership for a unified Germany is guaranteed. However, whether a relatively wealthy West Germany will be able to afford to absorb the bankrupt East Germany remains to be seen.

New Irish president

NOVEMBER 7

Leaders of the main political parties in the Republic of Ireland are in a state of shock after 46-year-old Mary Robinson, standing as an independent candidate, was elected president. A lawyer and civil rights campaigner, she is the first woman to hold the office. She says she will speak up for society's disadvantaged.

Akihito tries out heavenly throne

NOVEMBER 12

Emperor Akihito, age 56, took his place on the "August Heavenly Throne" today in the first part of his official enthronement ceremony at the Imperial Palace in Tokyo. He is Japan's 125th emperor and succeeds his father, Hirohito, who died last year. The next, secret part of the ceremony will take place in ten days' time, when Akihito will become a living god.

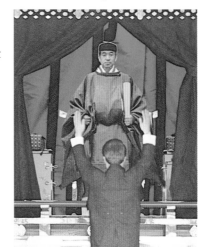

Poles finally go to the polls

DECEMBER 9

In the wake of the collapse of communism in Eastern bloc countries, shipyard worker Lech Walesa today won a historic landslide presidential election victory in Poland.

Ten years ago he spearheaded resistance to the communist regime by forming Solidarity, a free trade union, in Gdansk. He gained a huge following and has long been regarded as the country's natural leader.

SEPTEMBER–DECEMBER

World Events

NOV John Major becomes the new UK prime minister after Margaret Thatcher is forced to resign.

NOV The United Nations sets a deadline for Iraq to withdraw its troops from Kuwait, before force is used.

DEC UK and French tunnelers break through and shake hands 98 ft (30 m) under the Channel after three years of digging.

DEC Socialist Party leader Slobodan Milosovic is elected president in Serbia's first free elections for 50 years.

Entertainment

NOV Record-breaking UK cricketer Sir Leonard Hutton dies at age 74.

NOV Child actor Macaulay Culkin stars in US box-office smash hit comedy film *Home Alone*.

NOV Best-selling UK author Roald Dahl, famous for his children's stories, dies at age 74.

DEC Mexican writer Octavio Paz is named winner of the Nobel Prize for literature.

Innovations

SEP The Pope consecrates the world's biggest church at Yamoussoukro, Ivory Coast.

MACAULAY CULKIN IN HOME ALONE

OCT European space probe *Ulysses* blasts off from the US on a five-year journey to the Sun.

NOV Swiss solar car *Spirit of Biel* wins the World Solar Challenge in Australia.

CHANNEL TUNNEL BREAKTHROUGH

DEC Toyohiro Akiyama from Japan is the first fare-paying passenger in space.

1991

Dust settles in desert

FEBRUARY 28

The war in the Gulf is today at an end and Kuwait has been liberated. After a month of intensive air attacks against Iraq, the huge international forces that had gathered in Saudi Arabia crossed the border into Iraq and Kuwait to begin a four-day land battle to force the Iraqi army to flee the small Gulf kingdom. The people of Kuwait are now celebrating their liberation after nearly seven months of brutal Iraqi occupation. The capital, Kuwait City, is left without power, however, and the sun is blotted out by thick black smoke pouring from burning oil wells set on fire by Iraqi soldiers as they were forced to retreat.

Kuwaiti children greet their liberators

Famine hits and Sudan starves

MARCH 30

Relief workers are working around the clock as famine sweeps a huge area of the Sudan, putting an estimated seven million lives at risk.

Nobody knows how many people have died since the harvest failed last November. Tragically, the catastrophe was foreseen by aid agencies but Sudan's military regime rejected offers of help.

KARAOKE FOR KIDS

Tape recorders are now being designed specially for children. This one comes complete with a microphone so that children can have a crack at karaoke.

JANUARY–APRIL

JAN Abu Iyad (Salah Khalaf), the deputy leader of the Palestinian Liberation Organization, is assassinated.	**FEB** US generals Powell and Schwarzkopf lead troops in Operation *Desert Storm* to liberate Kuwait from Iraq.	**MAR** Prime Minister Guilio Andreotti announces that Italy's 49th post-war government is to resign.	**APR** European Community foreign ministers meet in Strasbourg, France, and agree to end sanctions against South Africa.
JAN Richard Branson and Per Lindstrand cross the Pacific in a hot-air balloon.	**FEB** Top UK ballerina Dame Margot Fonteyn dies in Panama at age 71.	**MAR** Kevin Costner's US movie *Dances with Wolves* wins seven Academy Awards.	**APR** The US wins the first Women's Rugby World Cup in the UK.
FEB Soviet space station *Salyut 7* reenters the Earth's atmosphere and crash lands.	**FEB** Helen Sharman is chosen to be the first UK citizen to go into space.	**MAR** US fast-food chain McDonald's launches a new low-fat hamburger called the *McLean*.	**MAR** Soviet space station *Mir* comes within 12 miles (19 km) of colliding with a cargo craft.

POWELL AND SCHWARZKOPF MASTERMIND *DESERT STORM*

FIRST WOMEN'S RUGBY WORLD CUP

1991

Cyclone devastates Bangladesh

MAY 3

At least 125,000 people have died and ten million are homeless after a 145 mph (233 km/h) cyclone hit Bangladesh three days ago. The low-lying area around the delta of the Ganges River, home to millions of subsistence farmers, has been completely devastated by the disaster. Each day more corpses are washed ashore and the beaches of Chittagong, the main port in the Bay of Bengal, are littered with swollen and decomposing bodies.

SUPERFAST SONIC

A high-tech hedgehog named Sonic has taken the world by storm this year. Star of Sega's top-selling computer game *Sonic the Hedgehog*, he is supersmart and superfast and has streaked into the lead in front of his rivals, Nintendo's *Mario Brothers*.

Yeltsin to the rescue

AUGUST 21

A dramatic coup mounted in Moscow by communist hardliners two days ago has failed. It was a last desperate attempt to reassert the power of the Communist Party and to topple Soviet premier Mikhail Gorbachev, who was placed under house arrest in the Crimea. Hero of the day was the president of the Russian Republic, Boris Yeltsin, who rallied huge popular support after climbing on a tank near the Russian parliament to denounce the coup.

A Soviet army lieutenant holds the white flag of surrender

Hostage released after 1,934 days

AUGUST 8

British journalist John McCarthy received an ecstatic welcome when he arrived home today after being held hostage in Lebanon by Islamic Jihad for five years and three months. With him he brings a letter from his captors to UN secretary general Javier Pérez de Cuellar, and the news that fellow American and British hostages are in good shape.

MAY–AUGUST

World Events	MAY More than 60 people die in street battles in South Africa's black townships.	MAY Indian prime minister Rajiv Gandhi is assassinated by a suicide bomber during a national election rally near Madras.	JUN Slovenia and Croatia declare independence from the communist Yugoslavian federation of republics.	JUN Sixty-year-old Boris Yeltsin wins Russia's first free elections, defeating official communist candidates.
Entertainment	MAY Sweden wins the Eurovision Song Contest in Rome, Italy.	MAY A pop concert in the UK raises £57 million in aid of Kurdish refugees.	JUN *Terminator 2: Judgment Day*, starring Arnold Schwarzenegger and with new special effects, is a smash hit in the US.	AUG At the Tokyo track and field events in Japan, US long-jumper Mike Powell sets a new world record of 29.36 ft (8.95 m).
Innovations	MAY Sony demonstrates the digital sound of the mini disc in Japan.	RAJIV GANDHI'S FUNERAL / JUN A treaty declares Antarctica to be a "continent for peace and science."	JUL Thousands of people arrive in Hawaii to watch a total solar eclipse that lasts for four minutes.	TERMINATOR 2: JUDGMENT DAY / JUL The European Remote Sensing satellite (*ERS-1*), Europe's first environmental satellite, goes into orbit.

1991

Soviet Union crumbles

AUGUST 31

Soviet premier Mikhail Gorbachev, badly betrayed by some of his closest allies in the failed coup two weeks ago, is struggling to hold on to power in Moscow. Fourteen leading communists have been charged with treason and await trial in prison. They include his deputy, Gennady Yanayev, KGB chief Vladimir Kryuchkov, and defense minister Dmitri Yazov. Meanwhile, seven republics, including Russia and the Ukraine, have joined the three Baltic states of Lithuania, Estonia, and Latvia in declaring independence.

Yeltsin declares Russia's independence

Dubrovnik under Serb siege

OCTOBER 26

Croatian towns along the Adriatic coast are being heavily bombarded by the Serb-dominated Yugoslav army. The army moved into Croatia four months ago after the republic, together with Slovenia, declared independence from the communist Yugoslav federation. Black smoke is rising from Dubrovnik, the "pearl of the Adriatic," which has been shelled mercilessly and is now completely besieged. Designated a "world heritage site," its unique Venetian architecture and baroque churches are at risk, as are its 50,000 inhabitants, who have been without electricity or water for weeks. A naval blockade is now preventing any supplies from getting through. With ancient ethnic hatreds boiling over, it seems increasingly likely that a bitter war will engulf the whole region.

SEPTEMBER–DECEMBER

OCT Burmese opposition leader Aung Suu Kyi, who is under house arrest, is awarded the Nobel Peace Prize.

SEP Exiled Soviet Nobel Prize winner Alexander Solzhenitsyn is officially cleared of treason in the USSR.

SEP *The Big Issue*, a new magazine sold by homeless people in aid of the homeless, goes on sale in London, UK.

TYROLEAN HUNTER

NOV UK publishing tycoon Robert Maxwell falls off his yacht and drowns near the Canary Islands.

OCT Canadian singer Bryan Adams has a record-breaking hit with the song *Everything I Do, I Do It for You*.

SEP The almost-intact body of a 4,000-year-old prehistoric hunter is found in the Tyrolean Alps, Austria.

DEC European Community heads of government meet in Maastricht, Holland, to sign a treaty on closer economic union.

NOV UK rock star Freddie Mercury, the lead singer of popular group Queen, dies of AIDS in London at age 45.

SEP Eight people are sealed inside the giant *Biosphere II* greenhouse in the US for a two-year experiment.

FREDDIE MERCURY

DEC Mikhail Gorbachev resigns as premier of the USSR, which is replaced by a Russian Federation.

DEC Fifteen-year-old Judit Polgar from Hungary becomes the world's youngest ever chess grandmaster.

OCT A joint UK-Australian team makes the first flight over Mount Everest in a hot-air balloon.

1992

Croatian soldier burns Serbian flag

Independence recognized

JANUARY 15

Slovenia and Croatia, which simultaneously declared independence from Yugoslavia in June last year, have both won recognition from the European Union. The Yugoslav federation once consisted of six republics, but is now disintegrating. Macedonia also declared independence last September and it seems likely that the ethnically mixed republic of Bosnia and Herzegovina will follow suit. There has been much fighting between the Serb-dominated federal army and the breakaway republics.

Race riots rock LA

MAY 2

The city of Los Angeles is today recovering after the worst race riots this century left 58 people dead and thousands injured.

Simmering racial tensions exploded when, despite video evidence, an all-white jury acquitted four white policemen of savagely beating Rodney King, a young black motorist. The black community was stunned by the verdict and two days of violence followed, with an orgy of looting, murder, and rioting throughout the mainly black neighborhood of South Central. Several whites and Koreans have been beaten to death, and hundreds of buildings were set on fire. The police were unable to control the angry crowds, and 5,000 soldiers and marines are now on standby just outside the city. A dusk-to-dawn curfew has been introduced throughout the city.

Soldiers look on as rioters burn down shops

VATICAN ADMITS GALILEO RIGHT

After 359 years the Vatican has finally admitted formally that the great 17th-century Italian astronomer Galileo Galilei was right when he argued that the Earth orbits the Sun. In 1633, Galileo was forced to renounce his doctrine by the Inquisition.

JANUARY–JUNE

World Events	JAN Boutros Boutros Ghali of Egypt takes over the post of secretary general of the United Nations.	APR Betty Boothroyd is the first ever woman to become speaker of the UK's House of Commons.	JUN In a national referendum, Danish voters reject the Maastricht treaty by voting against closer European political union.	JUN A steel corset is tightened around the Leaning Tower of Pisa in Italy, which is slowly sinking each year.
Entertainment	JAN Paul Simon becomes the first US star to perform in sanction-free South Africa.	FEB Film star Elizabeth Taylor celebrates her 60th birthday at Sleeping Beauty's Castle in Disneyland, California.	APR Costing millions of francs, the massive Euro Disney amusement park opens on the outskirts of Paris, France.	MAY Legendary movie star Marlene Dietrich dies in her apartment in Paris, France, at age 91.
Innovations	JAN Japan launches a 310-ton ship, *Yamoto One*, run by superconducting magnets.	FEB On the 517th birthday of its namesake, the computer virus *Michelangelo* infects IBM computers.	FEB The US and the UK promise to phase out CFCs by 1995 – five years earlier than planned.	MAR Soviet cosmonaut Sergei Krikalyev returns to Earth after ten months in the *Mir* space station.

BETTY BOOTHROYD

THE LEANING TOWER OF PISA

1992

Earth summit opens

JUNE 3
Representatives of 178 governments around the world have arrived in Rio de Janeiro, Brazil, for the opening of the United Nations Conference on Environment and Development. It is the largest United Nations conference ever held, reflecting the growing concern worldwide for "green" issues. A special "Tree of Life" will be on display, covered in leaf-shaped pledges from people all around the world who have promised to take action personally.

Celebrations in Rio as the summit opens

Monetary crisis causes chaos

SEPTEMBER 16
Shock waves shot through the world's money markets today after Britain withdrew from the Exchange Rate Mechanism (ERM). The ERM links the currencies of 12 European countries. It was created to stabilize exchange rates in preparation for a European Central Bank and a single currency.

Britain's withdrawal has caused a rift with Germany, whose economic policies are being blamed.

A royal "Annus Horribilis"

DECEMBER 9
After months of mounting rumors Buckingham Palace, the home of the British royal family, today announced that the Prince and Princess of Wales are to separate after 11 years of marriage. In a year of two royal separations and a divorce, as well as a damaging fire at Windsor Castle, it is no wonder that the queen is describing 1992 as an "Annus Horribilis" for the royals.

Charles and Diana split up

Horrors of Serbian death camps

AUGUST 15
Horrifying television pictures of Serbian prison camps have caused shock and outrage. They show starving and emaciated victims of "ethnic cleansing," a policy that has been used extensively since the Yugoslav civil war erupted. Most of the death camps are in the ethnically diverse republic of Bosnia. Huge numbers of innocent civilians have been rounded up and forcibly moved from their homes as ethnic groups attempt to "cleanse" areas of people of different origin.

JULY–DECEMBER

OCT Huge demonstrations are held in Germany protesting against the extreme racist violence sweeping the country.

OCT Demonstrations are held all over Latin America to mark the 500th anniversary of the arrival of Christopher Columbus.

NOV Democratic candidate 46-year-old Bill Clinton of Arkansas becomes the 42nd president of the United States.

DEC A devastating earthquake in Indonesia kills 1,500 people and leaves many more homeless.

JUL 10,000 competitors from 172 countries take part in the Barcelona Olympics in Spain.

OCT Poet and dramatist Derek Walcott becomes the first Caribbean writer to win a Nobel Prize for literature.

OCT US country artist Garth Brooks has a record four albums in the US top 20 chart at the same time.

OCT Agatha Christie's West End hit show *The Mousetrap* celebrates its 40th anniversary in London, UK.

JUL *Columbia* lands after the longest-ever US shuttle mission, lasting a total of 14 days.

POET DEREK WALCOTT WINS NOBEL PRIZE

SEP Twelve European countries agree to an unconditional ban on dumping waste at sea.

OCT The hole in the ozone layer over Antarctica stretches over the coast of South America for the first time.

BILL CLINTON WITH HIS WIFE

DEC Virtual reality is developed by the Spectrum Holobyte company in the US as a 3-D video game.

1993

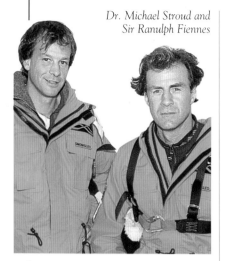

Dr. Michael Stroud and Sir Ranulph Fiennes

Ice walk ends

FEBRUARY 12

British explorers Sir Ranulph Fiennes and Dr. Michael Stroud have today completed the first unsupported crossing of the Antarctic ice shelf. The epic 1,352-mile (2,164-km) journey started last November. They used cross-country skis and sleds to carry food and equipment, sometimes walking up to 13 hours a day across the frozen wastes. The last stage of their record-breaking trek had to be abandoned, however, because Fiennes and Stroud were suffering from frostbite, infected feet, severe weight loss, and equipment failure. The Antarctic walk was undertaken to raise money for a number of charities.

Trade Center blast

FEBRUARY 26

New York ground to a halt at lunchtime today after a bomb exploded in the underground parking lot beneath the twin towers of the World Trade Center. Five people were killed and hundreds more are injured. Smoke billowed up to the 96th floor of the 110-story skyscraper as firefighters struggled for two hours to bring the blaze under control. Some people had to be rescued by helicopter from the top of the building. This is the first time there has been a terrorist bombing attack on American soil and it has shocked the whole nation. Police suspect the device was planted by Muslim fundamentalists angry at the US's policy in the Middle East. It is fortunate that so few lost their lives in the explosion. At least 55,000 people work in the Trade Center, which also attracts 80,000 visitors daily.

HAPPY BIRTHDAY, HARLEY!

It is 90 years since the first Harley-Davidson "hog" was made and as part of the celebrations, the world's biggest Harley has been built. Weighing 4.4 tons, the Harley seats six and boasts an on-board jacuzzi.

JANUARY–JUNE

World Events	**MAR** Chinese president Jiang Zemin amends the constitution to include a "socialist market economy."	**APR** Chris Hani, black rights hero and head of the Communist Party in South Africa, is assassinated outside his Johannesburg home.	**APR** Eighty-five members of a cult in the US die in a self-inflicted blaze after a 51-day siege of their Waco compound.	**APR** UN sanctions against Serbia come into force after the Bosnian-Serb parliament rejects a peace plan.
Entertainment	**APR** The UK's Grand National horse race is declared null and void after three false starts.	**APR** A record 79-day circumnavigation of the globe in a catamaran is completed by French yachtsman Bruno Peyron.	**JUN** Steven Spielberg's hit dinosaur film *Jurassic Park* takes $81.7 million at the box-office in its first week.	**JUN** Australian Damian Taylor beats seven women to win Queensland's *Miss Wintersun Queen* beauty contest.
Innovations	**JAN** Two astronauts make a record 5-hour space walk from the US space shuttle *Endeavour*.	**JAN** Norwegian Erling Kagge is the first person to complete a solo trek on foot to the south pole.	**MAR** Barbara Harmer from the UK becomes the *Concorde*'s first woman pilot on a British Airways flight.	**MAY** The first long-lasting perfume, *Shiseido* Eau de Cologne, is launched in Japan, taking 9 hours to evaporate.

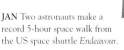

BRUNO PEYRON

JURASSIC PARK

1993

Arafat and Rabin shake hands with Clinton looking on

Yeltsin sends in the tanks

OCTOBER 4

Moscow's beseiged parliament is pock-marked with tank shells and blackened with smoke after the Russian army moved in to crush a rebellion organized by die-hard communists against President Boris Yeltsin. Fierce fighting raged inside the building before the rebellion leaders were forced to surrender.

The Russian parliament blackened by smoke

Rabin and Arafat sign peace accord

SEPTEMBER 13

Israeli prime minister Yitzhak Rabin hesitated for a split second before shaking hands with Yassir Arafat, the leader of the Palestine Liberation Organization (PLO). This historic moment in the long, troubled search for peace in the Middle East took place outside the White House in Washington, D.C. with US president Bill Clinton looking on. The handshake cements an agreement signed by Israel and the PLO that will immediately give limited self-rule to Palestinians living in Gaza, Jericho, and some parts of the West Bank. Israel will withdraw its forces from Gaza and Jericho in December and the territories will be run by a Palestinian Council to be elected next July. A permanent peace accord is, of course, the ultimate goal, but already extremists on both sides are condemning the agreement and threatening renewed violence. It seems likely that more blood will be spilled in this troubled region.

The road to peace in Ireland

DECEMBER 15

A historic declaration setting out principles for peace talks on Northern Ireland was signed today by British and Irish prime ministers John Major and Albert Reynolds.

It paves the way for Sinn Féin, the political wing of the Irish Republican Army (IRA), to join talks about the future of Northern Ireland.

Young boy on the divided streets of Belfast

JULY–DECEMBER

OCT The Nobel Peace Prize is awarded jointly to ANC president Nelson Mandela and South African president F. W. de Klerk.

OCT Benazir Bhutto, who was ousted from power three years ago, is sworn in as prime minister of Pakistan for a second term.

NOV The Maastricht Treaty finally comes into force and the European Community is renamed the European Union.

DEC Aboriginals in Australia win the right to claim land lost to European colonizers more than 200 years ago.

AUG Jacqui Mofokeng is the first black woman ever to be crowned Miss South Africa.

BIOSPHERE

SEP US rapper Snoop Doggy Dog is arrested on a murder charge at the MTV Music Awards.

SEP Nourredine Morceli from Algeria sets a new world record for running the mile.

SEP International Olympic Committee awards the year 2000 games to Australia.

AUG The Grand Hassan II Mosque in Morocco, which has a 574-ft (175-m) minaret, is dedicated.

SEP Eight US people emerge after a two-year experiment living in a "Biosphere."

DEC The first voice-operated TV/radio remote control is launched worldwide.

ABORIGINALS WIN LAND RIGHTS

DEC The first passenger trains travel through the Channel Tunnel.

THE INFORMATION AGE

TECHNOLOGY HAS REVOLUTIONIZED every aspect of life in the Nineties. Home computers, videophones, virtual reality, and robots with artificial intelligence were once science-fiction, but are now a reality. Mobile phones, fax machines, and electronic mail enable us to keep in touch wherever we are. At the cutting edge of the information revolution, the World Wide Web acts as a global encyclopedia, allowing people from all over the world to send information and tap into information resources. Huge quantities of facts and figures are shifted around the planet in seconds, turning the world into a technological "global village."

Space talk

Swarms of communication satellites circle the planet day and night, gathering information and enabling us to communicate with each other.

Electronic money

The introduction of an experimental "smartcard" may eventually lead to a cashless society. The card has a tiny microchip embedded in its plastic surface that stores money electronically, making notes and coins redundant.

£48.69

Keyring "reads" the smartcard

Computer design

Using the latest microchips, industry can accurately design and plan buildings, cars, and machine parts using computers. Computer-aided design (CAD) has become increasingly flexible and sophisticated. This screen display shows the pressures exerted on parts of a jet engine used in aviation.

Red shows high-pressure areas

SCREEN DISPLAY OF A JET ENGINE

Robot contains the latest microchip technology

Video camera

Foot contains sensors

ATTILA, THE ROBOT INSECT

Robots

The creation of artificial life has fascinated scientists for generations. Recently they have developed animallike robots called "animats." Attila, an insect animat, was developed at the Massachusetts Institute of Technology in the United States. It can perform very simple tasks and move across rough terrain by itself, negotiating small obstacles by using its own logic. The next generation of brainy robot insects will probably be used in factories to carry out checks and repairs on machinery.

1992 COLOR VIDEOPHONES
ARE INTRODUCED

1993 PORTABLE PHOTOCOPIERS
GO ON SALE WORLDWIDE

1995 US REPORT PREDICTS THAT
E-MAIL WILL OVERTAKE FAX

Computer sensitive

Scientists have developed a new electronic "NOSE" (Neotronics Olfactory Sensing Equipment) that uses tiny sensors fitted to a silicon chip to imitate the workings of a human nose. It is independent, objective, and never catches a cold. It can distinguish a good wine from a fake and might eventually replace humans in testing food, drinks, and fragrances.

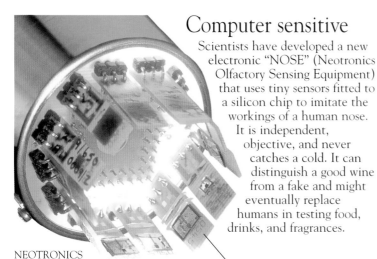

NEOTRONICS
OLFACTORY
SENSING EQUIPMENT ("NOSE")

*Polymer sensor
to detect odors*

Techno-movie

The smash hit of 1996, *Toy Story*, was the first film to be created entirely on computer. Made by Pixar Animation Studios, it used the latest technical wizardry to create amazing effects and realistic detail. Despite being computer-generated heroes, Woody and Buzz Lightyear delighted the most cynical of moviegoers, becoming the year's most sought-after Christmas toys.

VIRTUAL
REALITY
SET

*Player wears
headset*

A VIRTUAL VIEW OF THE IMAGINARY
3-D *CITY OF GIOTTO*, BASED ON
GIOTTO'S 14-CENTURY PAINTINGS

Data glove

Virtual reality

Special headsets and gloves whisk players off to another world in the latest virtual reality computer games. The headset contains two miniature television screens for 3-D stereo vision, and headphones for stereo sound. It also contains a sensor that allows the computer to calculate the direction of sight and what the player can see. The "data glove" and joystick allow the player to control the game. However, virtual reality is not only being used for exciting computer games. "Virtual tourism" will soon enable you to travel the world without leaving your home, and medical and military uses are being researched and developed.

1994

Carnage in Sarajevo central market

FEBRUARY 5

A deadly attack on the central market in Sarajevo, Bosnia, has left 68 innocent civilians dead and nearly 200 others seriously wounded. A single mortar bomb landed without warning in the middle of the busy market, crowded with weekend shoppers waiting to buy food. The UN peacekeeping forces in Bosnia, who were sent into the region in 1992 in an attempt to stop the civil war, will not say where the bomb came from. The citizens of Sarajevo, however, are in little doubt that the attack was launched by Serb troops who have taken control of the hills overlooking the city. World leaders are condemning the massacre but have not yet decided how to respond. There is still much disagreement about the role of the United Nations and NATO in the area. The United States see the Serbs as the aggressors and wants to arm the Muslims. Other nations argue that guns will only aggravate the problem.

Devastation in Sarajevo's market

Children at a refugee camp near Goma, on the border between Rwanda and Zaire

War in Rwanda

APRIL 22

The long-running ethnic conflict between Tutsi rebels and the Hutu government in the central African republic of Rwanda has erupted into violence on an unprecedented scale. The crisis was triggered two weeks ago by the death in a plane crash of the Rwandan president, Juvenal Habyarimana, who had recently reached agreement with the Tutsi-led Rwandan Patriotic Front. It is believed that his plane was shot down. Since then violent fighting between Tutsi and Hutu has turned the country into a bloodbath. According to the Red Cross, at least 100,000 people have died so far. As hundreds of thousands of people flee the fighting, makeshift refugee camps have been set up in a desperate attempt to cope with the humanitarian crisis. However, relief agencies and charities are finding it hard to get food and supplies through to the camps, and every day hundreds of refugees are dying from cholera.

JANUARY–JUNE

World Events	**FEB** India's legendary "Bandit Queen," Phoolan Devi, heroine for many low-caste Indians, is released from prison.	**MAR** Right-wing media baron Sivio Berlusconi and his Forza Italia party win the Italian general election.	**MAY** ANC leader Nelson Mandela is elected as the first black president of South Africa.	**MAY** Russian dissident novelist Alexander Solzhenitsyn returns to his homeland after 20 years spent in exile in the US.
Entertainment	**FEB** Speed skater Johann Koss sets three world records at the Winter Olympics.	**APR** Twenty-seven-year-old US rock star Kurt Cobain, of Nirvana, kills himself with a shotgun in his Seattle home.	**MAY** *Pulp Fiction*, directed by Quentin Tarantino, wins the Golden Palm Award at Cannes Film Festival.	**JUN** UK rock singer George Michael loses a lengthy legal battle with his record company, Sony.
Innovations	**FEB** Interactive television system allows US viewers to find out more about what is on. **JOHANN KOSS**	**MAR** Mercedez-Benz and Swatch unveil their new bubble car, the *Swatchmobile*, planned for 1997.	**MAR** In Germany, the new *Eurofighter 200* makes a successful first test flight. **MANDELA IS ELECTED PRESIDENT**	**MAY** The Channel Tunnel linking France and the UK is officially inaugurated.

1994

Michael ties the knot

MAY 26

It's official, Michael Jackson and Lisa Marie Presley, daughter of Elvis, did indeed get married today – despite denials from both of them. The distinctly low-key, top-secret event took place well away from the glare of the cameras in the Dominican Republic. Lacking the glitter of many of his performances, Jackson was dressed in black, wore a Band-Aid across his nose, and said "Why not?" instead of "I do."

Michael Jackson and Lisa Marie Presley

O. J. Simpson – a fallen hero

JUNE 17

Former football hero and film star Orenthal James Simpson gave himself up to police today after a dramatic car chase through Los Angeles County, watched live by millions on television. Fleets of news helicopters captured it live as "O. J.," driving a white Ford Bronco, tried to shake off the massed strength of California's highway patrol. Earlier in the day Simpson had failed to appear in court to be formally charged with the murder of his wife, Nicole Brown Simpson, and her friend Ronald Goldman, last week.

RIDE WITH A VIEW

A gigantic rollercoaster, the tallest in the world, has been unveiled in Blackpool, England. It has a record incline of 65 degrees, which churns stomachs nicely as the carriages hurtle down at 85 mph (135 km/h).

Troops sent into Chechenia

DECEMBER 11

Russian tanks and artillery today crossed the border into Chechenia after a two-week bombing campaign failed to subdue the breakaway republic, which is demanding independence from the Russian Federation. In the capital, Grozny, the Chechen leader, General Dzhokar Dudayev, remains defiant, surviving an attempt to topple him by Russian-backed opponents of his rule. His troops are fierce fighters, with a long history of guerrilla warfare. The Russian army, however, is not the force it once was and morale is low.

Russian troops enter Chechenia

JULY–DECEMBER

JUL President Kim Il Sung of North Korea, the century's longest-ruling dictator, dies after a heart attack at age 82.

JUL Brazil wins the World Cup in California after beating Italy in an exciting penalty shoot-out.

JUL Gigantic fireballs are produced in space when 21 fragments of a comet crash into the planet Jupiter.

BRAZIL WIN WORLD CUP

JUL The United Nations authorizes a US-led invasion of Haiti to drive out the military government and restore president Aristide.

AUG The World Series is canceled as Major league baseball players in the US strike over salary capping.

SEP US astronaut Col. Mark Lee makes the first untethered space walk for a decade using a jet pack.

SEP More than 900 people die when the car ferry *Estonia* sinks during heavy weather in the Baltic Sea.

NOV Boxer George Foreman, age 47, beats Michael Moorer, aged 27, to win the world heavyweight title.

SEP Kansai International Airport, built on a specially created artificial island, is opened in Japan.

KANSAI AIRPORT

AUG The IRA announces a ceasefire, paving the way for political settlement in the Northern Ireland conflict.

DEC UK writer John Osbourne, famous for the "kitchen sink" play *Look Back in Anger*, dies at age 65.

DEC Clear pictures of galaxies in their infancies taken by the *Hubble Space Telescope* are published.

1948 DR. F. MALAN INTRODUCES
THE APARTHEID SYSTEM

1950 GROUP AREAS ACT MAKES
PASS BOOKS COMPULSORY

1960 SHARPEVILLE MASSACRE
RESULTS IN 93 BLACK DEATHS

ENDING APARTHEID

IN APRIL 1994 THE NEW RAINBOW FLAG of South Africa was raised and the new anthem, "Nkosi Sikelele Afrika" ("God Bless Africa"), sung when African National Congress (ANC) leader Nelson Mandela was elected president of South Africa. The election marked the end of a long and painful struggle by black South Africans to free themselves from white rule. For more than three centuries, the country had been dominated by a white minority and, from 1948, a rigid and brutal policy had segregated the people according to race. Black people, denied the vote, had been forced to live in appalling poverty in special areas called homelands.

Apartheid

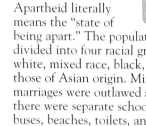

Sign indicates a "whites only" area

Apartheid literally means the "state of being apart." The population was divided into four racial groups: white, mixed race, black, and those of Asian origin. Mixed marriages were outlawed and there were separate schools, buses, beaches, toilets, and even separate park benches.

Mandela's release

Nelson Mandela was leader of the banned ANC in the Sixties, and helped found its armed wing, "Umkonto was Sizwe" ("Spear of the Nation"). In 1963 he was sentenced to life imprisonment because of his political activities. Throughout his 27 years of imprisonment, Mandela came to symbolize the struggle against apartheid and, on his release in 1990, he pledged to continue the long fight. As ANC leader in the Nineties, Mandela became South Africa's first black president.

MANDELA VISITS
HIS PRISON CELL
AFTER HIS RELEASE

Pass book

The long road to equality

In December 1991 delegates from all major South African organizations, with the exception of far-right groups, took part in the Convention for a Democratic South Africa to begin working toward a transitional multiracial government and a new constitution that would extend political rights to everyone. However, negotiations were long and difficult and political violence once again flared up in the black townships.

Fires rage in a black township

End of apartheid laws

By 1990 international pressure and social unrest compelled the government to repeal discriminatory laws. Within two years, huge progress had been made and most apartheid regulations had been abolished. Laws that classified people by race and created separate public facilities were swept away, and black people were finally able to travel freely within their own country, without carrying the hated pass book.

Economic sanctions

Worldwide concern about the abuse of human rights in South Africa grew dramatically during the 1980s as the regime suppressed political protest with increasing brutality. In 1986 economic sanctions were imposed on South Africa by the United States and the European Community. The resulting isolation caused severe damage to the economy in South Africa.

Diamonds are one of South Africa's main exports

Program of reform

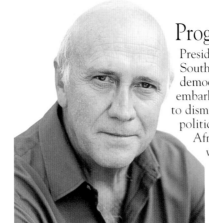

President F. W. de Klerk played a key role in South Africa's painful journey to multiparty democracy. On taking office in 1989 he embarked on an ambitious program of reform to dismantle the framework of apartheid. Banned political groups, including the ANC, the Pan African Congress, and the Communist Party, were legalized. Political prisoners were released and media restrictions were lifted. In 1994, when the ANC won a landslide election victory, de Klerk became vice-president in the new government of national unity.

A new future

Economic, sporting, and cultural sanctions were dropped after the end of apartheid, and South Africa finally emerged from international isolation. The legacy of 350 years of white domination, however, has left deep and bitter internal scars that will take years to heal. In 1996 black children were finally integrated into white schools, with armed guards employed in the beginning to secure their safety. In the same year the government set up a commission chaired by Archbishop Desmond Tutu to investigate the crimes of apartheid.

Popular opposition

Over the years popular protest against apartheid became increasingly militant. It was backed by a campaign of violence waged by banned opposition groups. Many opposition campaigners were imprisoned and tortured by the police, but this did little to deter the protesters.

BLACK AND WHITE CHILDREN STUDYING TOGETHER

South Africans line up to vote

Electoral lines

The lines stretched for miles outside polling stations as 16 million black people, together with over 9 million whites, Asians, and people of mixed race, took part in South Africa's first free election in April 1994. The voting lasted four days and was closely monitored by international observers. The ANC won a landslide victory and Nelson Mandela became the country's first black president. Posts were found in the government for leaders of the other parties to ensure that all have a say in the new South Africa.

1995

Kobe devastated

JANUARY 17
As many as 2,700 people are feared dead after a huge earthquake hit Kobe, a busy port in western Japan at the heart of an important industrial area, early this morning. It measured 7.2 on the Richter Scale and is the worst earthquake to hit Japan since Tokyo was devastated in 1923. More than 1,100 buildings, many of them supposedly earthquake-proof, crashed to the ground, and whole areas of the city have been reduced to rubble. Overhead highways and railroads collapsed, sending early-morning commuters plunging to their deaths. Fires are still raging out of control all over the city, fed by fractured gas pipes, while firefighters are facing an impossible task battling with broken water mains and blocked roads. The authorities appear to be in a state of shock after the disaster, with hundreds of thousands of people homeless in near freezing temperatures.

The federal building in Oklahoma

Blast in the heart of America

APRIL 21
Flags are flying at half mast throughout the United States after the worst terrorist outrage the nation has ever known. More than 100 people, including 15 children, were killed in Oklahoma City two days ago when a huge car bomb exploded outside a federal building, tearing a gaping hole in its side. The FBI has today arrested a key suspect, 27-year-old Timothy McVeigh, a former soldier with far-right political views and links with paramilitary "patriotic" militia groups. The nation is deeply shocked that a citizen of the United States could be responsible for such an outrage.

Peace celebrated

Peace lanterns in Hiroshima

AUGUST 6
It is exactly 50 years since the first atomic bomb was dropped on Hiroshima in Japan. Today 60,000 people commemorated the dead with a minute's silence in the Peace Park.

JANUARY– JUNE

World Events	**MAR** The Tokyo subway in Japan is paralyzed by a deadly sarin nerve gas attack that kills ten people.	**MAY** Millions of people around the world celebrate the 50th anniversary of the Allies' Victory in Europe (VE) day.	**JUN** Newly elected French president Jacques Chirac announces the resumption of nuclear testing in the Pacific.	**JUN** After massive environmental protest, Shell UK abandons plans to dump an old oil platform in the North Sea.
Entertainment	**MAR** Paul McCartney announces that The Beatles will release a new record. BEATLES' RECORD	**MAY** *Superman* star Christopher Reeve is paralyzed after falling off a horse in Virginia.	**JUN** South Africa wins the rugby world cup, beating New Zealand 15–12 in the final.	**JUN** Disney's *Pocahontas* is launched with the biggest-ever premiere in New York City.
Innovations	**JAN** Astronomers in Hawaii find a galaxy 15 billion light-years away from Earth.	**FEB** Space shuttle *Discovery* crew member Michael Foale becomes the first Briton to walk in space.	**FEB** Scientists reveal that a huge iceberg has broken away from the continent of Antarctica. SOUTH AFRICA WINS WORLD CUP	**MAR** Russian cosmonaut Valeri Polyakov lands after spending a record 438 days in space.

1995

Israeli premier assassinated

NOVEMBER 4

Israeli prime minister Yitzhak Rabin was assassinated tonight, only minutes after he addressed a "Peace Yes, Violence No" rally held in Tel Aviv. It had been called to stem the tide of right-wing resentment at the concessions made to Palestinians over self-rule. A lone gunman pushed through the security men surrounding Rabin as he left the speakers' platform and shot him twice at close range. The prime minister was taken to Ichilov hospital for emergency surgery but died one hour later. The killer, 25-year-old law student Yigal Amir, was arrested by security forces immediately. He said, "I acted alone on God's orders and I have no regrets." World leaders have been paying tribute to Rabin, who worked so hard for peace in the troubled Middle East.

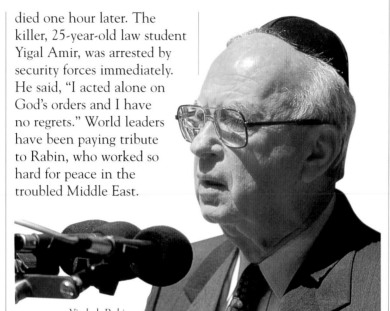
Yitzhak Rabin

Nigerian writer executed

NOVEMBER 11

Despite international appeals for clemency, the distinguished dissident writer Ken Saro-Wiwa has been executed by Nigeria's military dictatorship. Eight other environmental campaigners died with him. They had been convicted of murder at a tribunal. Saro-Wiwa led protests against the pollution of the country by oil companies.

Peace plan for Bosnia

NOVEMBER 21

After three weeks of talks in Dayton, Ohio, chaired by United States negotiator Richard Holbrook, an agreement has been struck that will hopefully bring peace to war-torn Bosnia. Slobodan Milosevic of Serbia, Franjo Tudjman of Croatia, and Alija Izetbegovic from Bosnia approved the plan, which will create a unified country divided along racial lines. NATO troops will be sent in to enforce the agreement.

JULY–DECEMBER

AUG US satellites and spy planes spot mass graves in the Bosnian town of Srebrenica, giving evidence of genocide in the war.

OCT A US jury of ten women and two men find O. J. Simpson not guilty of the murders of his wife, Nicole, and her friend.

OCT Louis Farrakhan, leader of the Nation of Islam in the US, leads 400,000 black men on a march through Washington, D.C.

DEC UK trader Nick Leeson is given a six-and-a-half year jail sentence in Singapore after the collapse of Barings Bank.

JUL Legendary Argentine race car driver Juan Manuel Fangio dies in Buenos Aires at age 84.

SEP In Hollywood, *Home Alone* star Macaulay Culkin fires his father as his manager.

OCT Seamus Heaney, a 57-year-old poet from Ireland, is awarded the Nobel Prize for literature.

NOV French film director Louis Malle, whose films include *Au Revoir Les Enfants*, dies at age 63.

O. J. SIMPSON FOUND NOT GUILTY

AUG Analysis of fossils found in Spain proves humans reached Europe earlier than was thought.

AUG Antarctic survey reveals that the fall in ozone levels is detectable in summer as well as spring.

SEP France explodes a nuclear bomb in an underground test at Mururoa Atoll in the Pacific.

NICK LEESON

NOV In Egypt, the tomb of legendary Queen Nefertiti is opened to visitors for the first time.

MUSIC IN THE NINETIES

THE MUSIC SCENE of the 1990s has exploded with a wealth of new talent. In Britain the success of new bands has generated a wave of excitement that is comparable to the mass hysteria of the "Swinging Sixties." CD sales have risen throughout the decade, and even established artists are experiencing newfound fame with the release of remixed, remastered, and unplugged versions of old favorites. The music technology revolution has brought about huge advances in high-quality digital sound with the launch of new systems such as the mini disc and the digital compact cassette.

ICE-T

Country sounds

The country music boom in the United States has become a multibillion dollar industry with *Rolling Stone* rock magazine dubbing it America's "new gold rush." Garth Brooks has spearheaded the boom with his soft, mellow rockabilly sound. His record sales have even outstripped those of global superstars such as Michael Jackson and Irish group U2.

GARTH BROOKS

Rap it up!

A truly radical musical movement, rap music has its roots in the urban street culture of young black Americans. Hard-hitting and often controversial rap artists such as Snoop Doggy Dog and Ice-T have popularized the music, establishing a global market.

Teenage idols

Certain to get teenage pulses racing, singing and dancing "boy bands" have dominated pop charts in the 1990s. When British group Take That split up in 1995, helplines were set up to console the thousands of grieving fans. Countless batches of manufactured teen idols have since found success, such as the Backstreet Boys from the United States and Irish group Boyzone. All-girl bands are also getting their share of the pop glory. Raunchy queens of pop the Spice Girls have sold over five million copies of their debut album worldwide since they first burst onto the pop scene in 1996 with their cry of "Girl power!"

Dance music

The repetitive bass-lines and drum beats of Nineties dance music have spawned a rave "club culture" with DJs elevated to the status of pop stars. The computer-generated music achieves its appeal through its wide spectrum of sounds, ranging from garage and house to techno and jungle. Ravers love to dance till they drop, take a break, and then come back for more.

TAKE THAT PERFORMS ONE OF ITS MANY TOP TEN HITS

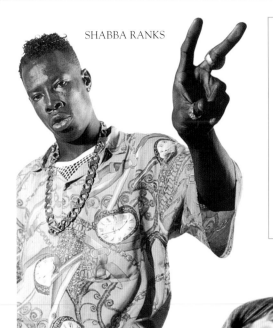

SHABBA RANKS

Independence

The diversity of popular music in the 1990s is in part due to the rise of the independent record label. Small independent labels, sometimes called "indies," are often more willing to take a chance on signing an unknown or controversial band or singer than a large multinational record company.

LIAM GALLAGHER OF OASIS

Rise of ragga

Ragga is part of the extended musical family that includes both reggae and rap. Made with digital instruments, its roots stretch back to Jamaica. Outspoken Ragga superstar Shabba Ranks has had several hit records worldwide.

BJÖRK

The invasion of Brit Pop

Pop music in Britain exploded with new vitality and talent in the Nineties. Labeled "Brit Pop" by the media, major names include Kula Shaker, Pulp, Blur, and Oasis. The British renaissance was recognized in 1996 by the magazine *Newsweek* when it described London as "the coolest city in the world."

Grunge

Firmly rooted in punk, the Grunge scene emerged in Seattle, Washington, in the early Nineties. Disaffected youth readily responded, adopting a uniform of ripped jeans, flannel shirts, and knit stocking hats. Members of Seattle's leading grunge group, Nirvana, became worldwide icons with their 1991 monster success *Nevermind*, which topped the album charts and went on to gross $50 million.

Female artists top the charts

The Nineties has witnessed a huge increase in the number of hit singles by solo female artists, from the powerful ballads of Alanis Morrisette and Sheryl Crow to the unique country sounds of kd lang. The decade has also seen the rise of Icelandic singer Björk from cult indie singer to international star.

KURT COBAIN OF NIRVANA

1996

Evil visits school

MARCH 13

Horror came to a small Scottish town yesterday morning when 16 children and their teacher were massacred in the gym of the Dunblane Primary School. Five more children and another teacher were seriously injured. The attacker, local man Thomas Hamilton, finally turned a gun on himself. A misfit, Hamilton had been sacked from the scout movement, banned from running boys' clubs, and had already been investigated by the police. Legally, however, he was allowed to own the four handguns and the 105 rounds of ammunition he used to kill his victims and himself. It took him four minutes. As the world tries to come to terms with the horrific events, demands are already being made in Britain for a complete ban on handguns. The school's head teacher has spoken bravely about the tragedy. "Evil visited us yesterday," he said, "and why we will never know."

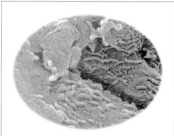

LIFE ON MARS
NASA scientists in the US have revealed evidence that a primitive life form might have existed more than three billion years ago on Mars. They have discovered possible fossil remains in a meteorite that arrived from the red planet 13,000 years ago and was found in Antarctica in 1984.

Taliban take Afghan capital

SEPTEMBER 27

After fierce fighting between rival guerrilla factions in Afghanistan's long-running civil war, Taliban Islamic fundamentalists today took control of the capital, Kabul. They have now declared Afghanistan a completely Islamic country. Taliban are enforcing strict laws wherever they seize control. All women have been ordered to wear a full veil and cover their faces in public. Breaking the dress code can lead to a beating with a stick as punishment.

An Afghan woman with face covered

JANUARY–JUNE

World Events	**JAN** The Tamil Tigers, who are fighting for a separate Tamil state within Sri Lanka, bomb the capital.	**FEB** The 17-month-old IRA ceasefire comes to an end when a massive bomb explodes in London's Docklands in the UK.	**MAR** After four decades of one-party rule, Lee Teng-Hui scores a victory in Taiwan's first democratic presidential elections.	**APR** Lone gunman Martin Bryant is arrested after massacring at least 34 people at Port Arthur on the Australian island of Tasmania.
Entertainment	**FEB** Keiki, the whale star of movie *Free Willy*, may be released into the wild.	**FEB** World chess champion Gary Kasparov beats the top chess computer Deep Blue in the US.	**FEB** Michael Jackson's performance at the UK's Brit Awards is disrupted by Jarvis Cocker of pop group Pulp.	**JUN** Germany beats the Czech Republic with a "golden goal" in extra time to win the European Cup, held in the UK.
Innovations	**FEB** A $442 million US satellite breaks away from a shuttle and is lost.	**MAR** Scottish scientists announce that they have succeeded in cloning two sheep.	**MAR** At Stonehenge, UK, carbon-dating of bone suggests that the monument may be older than previously thought.	**APR** The World Health Organization (WHO) announces the invention of a birth-control injection for men.

DOCKLANDS BOMB DAMAGE

LEE TENG-HUI

1996

The wrong cab!

OCTOBER 21

Wallace and Gromit's big adventure in New York ended happily today when they were reunited with their creator, Nick Park. The Oscar-winning British animator had accidentally left the original models of the two world-famous characters in a taxi two days ago.

Wallace and Gromit

Miss-take?

NOVEMBER 23

Irene Skliva was crowned Miss World today in the annual beauty contest, which, for the first time, took place in India. It caused widespread protest throughout the country from both women's groups and Hindu extremists. Security was tightened when a number of protesters threatened to commit suicide at the event in Bangalore.

Rwandans flee ethnic war

NOVEMBER 16

In the last two days an estimated 400,000 Hutu refugees, who fled Rwanda in 1994, have left their camps in eastern Zaire and are heading for home. The exodus comes after extremist Hutu militiamen, who had held them captive, were overrun in a surprise attack by Tutsi rebel forces, backed by the Rwandan government.

Serbs protest at fixed elections

DECEMBER 31

The Serbian capital, Belgrade, has ground to a halt as mass protest swells and threatens to destabilize Slobodan Milosevic's government. Thousands of riot police have been drafted in. Daily protests began over a month ago when opposition victories in the municipal elections were not recognized and then declared invalid by Milosevic. Last week police and government supporters attacked protestors and one man is believed to have died from the injuries he received. Morale among the protesters remains high, however, and opposition leaders look set to continue the fight well into the new year.

JULY–DECEMBER

JUL In the second round of voting Boris Yeltsin is re-elected president of Russia despite continuing ill health.

JUL Movie audiences in the US flock to see *Independence Day*, which opens, appropriately, on July 4.

INDEPENDENCE DAY

NOV French marine biologists find the remains of Alexandria, which sank beneath the Mediterranean in AD 335.

JUL A Boeing *747* jumbo jet, TWA Flight 800, explodes shortly after takeoff from New York, killing 228 people.

JUL Eleven thousand athletes from 197 nations take part in the Olympic Games in Atlanta, Georgia.

NOV The *Global Surveyor* spacecraft sets off from Cape Canaveral, Florida, on a mission to the planet Mars.

DEC US ambassador to the United Nations Madeleine Albright becomes the first woman US secretary of state.

AUG An exact replica of Shakespeare's Globe Theatre is opened on the site of the original in London, UK.

NOV The Russian *Mars-96* spacecraft falls back to Earth after two days in space, crashing in the Pacific ocean.

MADELEINE ALBRIGHT

DEC Several hundred people are taken hostage by a Marxist group at the Japanese embassy in Lima, Peru.

DEC All-female UK group the Spice Girls is the latest pop sensation, topping charts worldwide.

DEC A US satellite finds evidence of a frozen lake in a crater on the dark side of the Moon.

1973 *PIONEER 10* FIRST SPACE
PROBE TO FLY PAST JUPITER

1974 *MARINER 10* SPACE PROBE
FLIES PAST VENUS AND MERCURY

1976 *VIKING* SPACE PROBES
ORBIT AND LAND ON MARS

EXPLORING SPACE

AT THE BEGINNING of the 20th century the idea of traveling through space was just a dream. Now, humans have walked on the Moon, spent months orbiting the Earth in space stations, and sent unmanned probes to charter the planets of the solar system. The data received from probes, space telescopes, and space laboratories has increased our knowledge of space immeasurably. In the 21st century, space travel may become as familiar as air travel in the 20th century.

A man on Mars?

Sending astronauts to Mars has long been an ambition of space scientists. A manned mission would take almost a year to get there, but advances in space technology may soon make it possible.

VentureStar

The US *VentureStar* program is being developed to replace the space shuttle. The new space planes could be used as vehicles to take future space tourists into orbit.

MIR SPACE STATION

Solar panels on Soyuz craft for generating electricity

Docking port on Mir; there is room for five visiting craft at the same time

Soyuz spacecraft for ferrying crew to Earth about to dock at Mir port

Solar panels

Second Mir module for scientific experiments

Main Mir module where the crew lives

Inside Mir, living quarters are similar in shape and size to a passenger car on a train

SPACELAB ON BOARD *COLUMBIA* SPACE SHUTTLE

Spacelab

Astronauts carry out a variety of experiments in space to see how weightlessness effects living things, materials, and chemical processes. Scientists can use the knowledge they acquire to help plan future space projects. Spacelab is a laboratory carried in the US space shuttle.

Mir space station

The Russian space station *Mir* began orbiting the Earth in 1986 and astronauts from many different countries have lived and worked on board, some for months at a time, since 1987. In that time, *Mir* has grown in size. New modules have been added to the original main module, shown above, so that it is now five times bigger. There are usually three crew members on *Mir*, although it has room for six. Astronauts arrive by *Soyuz* spacecraft or shuttle orbiter. On board, they perform experiments and collect data on how humans cope with long stays in space.

Progress craft docked at aft port

1979 *VOYAGER 1* PROBE FLIES PAST
JUPITER, THEN SATURN, IN 1980

1986 *VOYAGER 2* FLIES PAST
URANUS, THEN NEPTUNE, IN 1989

1994 *ULYSSES* SPACE PROBE
FLIES OVER THE SUN'S POLES

Lonely explorers

Space probes are our eyes in space. Since the 1970s, all the planets of our solar system, except Pluto, have been visited by these unmanned spacecraft, which have sent back valuable data to Earth. The *Galileo* probe reached Jupiter in 1995 after a six-year journey.

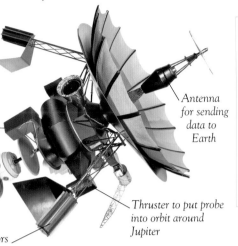

GALILEO SPACE PROBE

Antenna for sending data to Earth

One of two power generators

Thruster to put probe into orbit around Jupiter

Is there anybody there?

Although scientists have made huge advances in space exploration in recent years, they have found no signs of life in the solar system, or even discovered another planet in our galaxy that may support life. However, the Search for Extraterrestrial Intelligence, or SETI, continues.

The Hubble Telescope

The Hubble Space Telescope (HST) was launched from a US space shuttle in 1990. From Earth orbit, the view of the universe is much clearer than the view from Earth. After early problems with one of its giant mirrors, the Hubble has been able to send back remarkable images of distant stars and galaxies.

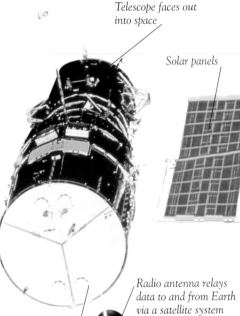

Telescope faces out into space

Solar panels

Radio antenna relays data to and from Earth via a satellite system

Back of telescope

HUBBLE TELESCOPE IN ORBIT

GIANT PILLARS OF GAS IN THE EAGLE NEBULA PHOTOGRAPHED BY THE HUBBLE TELESCOPE

The view from Hubble

The Planetary Camera on the Hubble Space Telescope has been able to photograph space phenomena from thousands of light years away with amazing clarity. For the first time, scientists can witness the dark clouds of dust and gas called nebulas, which are the birth places of stars.

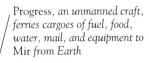

Progress, an unmanned craft, ferries cargoes of fuel, food, water, mail, and equipment to Mir from Earth

Moon base 2050

The 21st century may see the development of mining bases and space observatories on the Moon. This artist's impression shows how a lunar mining base might look. Workers would live in pressurized cylindrical modules, which would be buried under the soil.

FUTURISTIC LUNAR MINING BASE

303

1997

Dolly, the cloned sheep

Cloned sheep

FEBRUARY 23

Researchers at the Roslin Institute in Edinburgh, Scotland, have produced the first clone of an adult animal. Dolly, a Finn Dorset sheep, is now seven months old and has exactly the same genetic makeup as her mother. She was created by fusing a single cell with an unfertilized egg.

VIRTUAL PETS

Japanese electronic pets are the latest addictive craze – they need constant attention!

Tiger earns his golfing stripes

APRIL 13

Twenty-one-year-old Eldrick (Tiger) Woods made history today, becoming both the youngest and the first ever black player to win the Masters golf tournament in the United States. He finished with a score of 270, 18 under par, the lowest in the tournament's history.

Tiger Woods makes a master stroke at the US Masters golf tournament

Hong Kong handover

The official handover ceremony takes place in Hong Kong

JUNE 30

The long-awaited British handover of Hong Kong back to Communist China went according to plan, despite fears of clashes between the Chinese authorities and pro-democracy groups. In an emotional farewell speech, the last British Governor, Chris Patten, appealed for the continuation of democracy before the Union Jack flag was lowered on the stroke of midnight, after 156 years of British colonial rule. Patten is succeeded by Tung Chee-hwa, who was sworn in as the first Chinese Chief Executive of Hong Kong. The territory will now be known as the Hong Kong Special Administrative Region of China. However, much of its character and Western business practices will remain unchanged for now – China has announced there will be "one country, two systems." As the first contingents of the Chinese People's Liberation Army arrive in the former colony, the Chinese leader, Jiang Zemin, has already hailed the handover as a "victory for peace and justice."

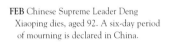

JANUARY–APRIL

World Events	Entertainments	Inventions
JAN William Jefferson Clinton, aged 50, is inaugurated for a second term as President of the United States.	**FEB** Chinese Supreme Leader Deng Xiaoping dies, aged 92. A six-day period of mourning is declared in China.	**FEB** A US civil jury orders O.J. Simpson to pay $33.5 million in damages to the families of his murdered wife and friend.	**APR** In Lima, Peru, 71 hostages are released after being held for four months by the Tupac Amaru Revolutionary Movement.

World Events — JAN William Jefferson Clinton, aged 50, is inaugurated for a second term as President of the United States. FEB Chinese Supreme Leader Deng Xiaoping dies, aged 92. A six-day period of mourning is declared in China. FEB A US civil jury orders O.J. Simpson to pay $33.5 million in damages to the families of his murdered wife and friend. APR In Lima, Peru, 71 hostages are released after being held for four months by the Tupac Amaru Revolutionary Movement.

Entertainments — JAN Steve Fosset lands in India after flying 9,672 miles from St. Louis in a hot air balloon. FEB Debbie Rowe gives birth to superstar singer Michael Jackson's baby son in Los Angeles. MAR UK film, *The English Patient*, wins nine Oscars at the US Academy Awards. MAR In the UK, ex-Beatle Paul McCartney receives a knighthood from the Queen.

Inventions — JAN Communist North Korea opens an official home page on the World Wide Web. FEB US astronauts Mark Lee and Steven Smith carry out improvements to the orbiting Hubble space telescope. MAR Comet Hale-Bopp is now at its brightest and is clearly visible to the naked eye at dawn and dusk. APR The ashes of *Star Trek* creator Gene Roddenberry are launched into space.

DENG XIAOPING

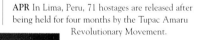

HALE-BOPP COMET

1997

Space rescue operation

AUGUST 22

Two Russian cosmonauts sent on a rescue mission to *Mir*, the accident-prone Russian space station, today carried out the first stages of vital repairs to its power system. *Mir* was badly damaged in June when it collided with a supply ship while practicing a docking maneuver; earlier this month, a computer failure caused the space station to lose its orientation. Back on Earth, there is concern in Russia and the United States about what the future holds for the 11-year-old space station.

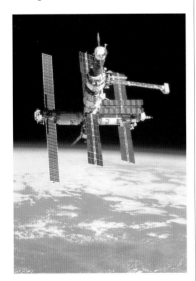

Space station Mir *orbiting the Earth*

Diana is dead

AUGUST 31

Diana, Princess of Wales, and her companion, Dodi Fayed, have been killed in a car crash in Paris. The driver also died in the accident and Diana's bodyguard was seriously injured. A whirlwind romance had been blossoming between the Princess and Dodi, son of Mohammed al Fayed, in recent weeks. The couple had dined at the Ritz Hotel, and eyewitnesses say they left the hotel in a car that was traveling at high speed. The car was reportedly being pursued by paparazzi on motorcycles when it entered an underpass and hit a concrete pillar.

A nation mourns its princess

SEPTEMBER 6

With a rare public outpouring of grief, London came to a halt today for the funeral of Diana, Princess of Wales – the "People's Princess". All week, people have been leaving flowers at the gates of Diana's home, Kensington Palace, and as the coffin left for Westminster Abbey, crowds of mourners lined the route. The Princess's sons, William and Harry, the Prince of Wales, Earl Spencer, and the Duke of Edinburgh walked behind the coffin, which was draped with the Royal Standard and covered with lilies for the last leg of its journey. The funeral service included a tribute song from Elton John and a moving speech from Diana's brother, Earl Spencer. After the service, a minute's silence was observed.

Pallbearers carry Diana's coffin into Westminster Abbey in London

MAY–AUGUST

MAY In the UK, the Labor Party wins an overwhelming victory in the General Election after 18 years of Conservative Party rule.

MAY Australian long-distance swimmer Susie Maroney swims 112 miles from Cuba to the USA in 24hrs 31mins.

MAY In New York, IBM's *Deep Blue* computer beats Russian chess grandmaster Gary Kasparov.

MARTINA HINGIS

JUN Lionel Jospin becomes France's new prime minister after a Socialist-led coalition wins parliamentary elections.

JUL In the UK, 16-year-old Swiss Martina Hingis is the youngest women's Wimbledon tennis champion since 1887.

JUN In the USA, the Ford Motor Company announced the production of 250,000 alternative fuel vehicles by 2001.

AUG Britain announces an evacuation plan for its protectorate, Montserrat, in the Caribbean after a devastating volcanic eruption.

JUL Italian fashion designer Gianni Versace is shot dead at his home in Miami.

JUL US *Pathfinder* spacecraft starts sending back pictures and data from the surface of Mars.

GIANNI VERSACE

AUG Jeanne Louise Calment, believed to be the world's oldest person, dies at the age of 122 in Arles, France.

AUG *Be Here Now* by Oasis becomes the fastest-selling album in UK history.

JUL Zeta II, a battery-powered booster for bicycles, is launched by British inventor Clive Sinclair.

1997

THE SPICE GIRLS
Girl power is here to stay as the Spice Girls, a British pop group, take the world by storm. They have topped the charts on both sides of the Atlantic and are releasing a film, *Spiceworld*.

State funeral for Mother Teresa

SEPTEMBER 13
India today held a state funeral for Mother Teresa, who died on September 5, aged 87. Mother Teresa had devoted her entire life to the poor of Calcutta. Born Agnes Gonxha Bojaxhiu, in Skopje, Albania, she entered a religious order at 21 and became a Catholic nun. She felt her calling was to work for the destitute of India and, in 1948, moved to Calcutta to work with the poorest of the poor. Here, she founded the Missionaries of Charity, which opened its first home for the destitute in 1952. Today there are over 400 such homes in nine different countries. Mother Teresa was awarded the Nobel Prize for Peace in 1979.

Indonesian fires still burning

NOVEMBER 7
The US Air Force today extended its firefighting operation in Indonesia as forest fires continue to rage, causing widespread pollution and environmental damage. Thousands of acres of forest have been destroyed on Sumatra, Borneo, and Irian Jaya, as the fires blazed out of control in the drought conditions caused by the El Niño weather pattern. Smoke from the fires is still a serious health hazard.

Firefighting in the Indonesian forests

SEPTEMBER–DECEMBER				
World Events	**SEP** In Norway, 89 countries approve a treaty to ban landmines. The US, Russia, China, and India did not sign.	**OCT** Chinese president Jiang Zemin meets US president Bill Clinton in Washington, DC, in the first US-China summit since 1989.	**NOV** A US judge overturns British au pair girl Louise Woodward's life sentence for murdering baby Matthew Eappen.	**DEC** South African president Nelson Mandela steps down as leader of the ANC. He is replaced by Thabo Mbeki.
Entertainments	**SEP** In the UK, Elton John's tribute song to Princess Diana sells 600,000 copies in one day. *ELTON JOHN CANDLE IN THE WIND*	**OCT** In Spain, racing driver Jacques Villeneuve is the first Canadian to win the Formula One Championship.	**OCT** US folksinger John Denver dies at 53, when his plane crashes in California.	**DEC** The Spice Girls, a British pop group, meet Princes William and Harry at the *Spiceworld* film premiere.
Inventions	**SEP** US space shuttle *Atlantis* picks up astronaut Michael Foale after a four-month stay on *Mir*.	**OCT** In Bilbao, Spain, the futuristic Guggenheim Museum designed by US architect Frank Geary is opened.	**OCT** Britain's supersonic *Thrust* car breaks the world land speed record in Nevada, with a speed of 763,035 mph. *THRUST*	**DEC** At the UN Global Warming Conference in Kyoto, Japan, 150 nations agree to reduce emissions of greenhouse gases.

1998

Peace for Northern Irish

APRIL 10

A historic settlement has been reached in Northern Ireland, promising peace after 30 years of violent conflict. The Unionists, who wish to remain part of Britain, and Nationalists, who believe in an independent Irish state, have agreed to form a power-sharing assembly.

Leaders of the opposing sides in Belfast, Northern Ireland

THE NEW BEETLE
The Beetle, the world's most popular car, was relaunched. It sold out right away!

Pakistan's prime minister at the test site

Nuclear tests in Pakistan

MAY 28

Despite appeals from world leaders, Pakistan exploded five nuclear devices yesterday, launching an arms race with India, who carried out similar tests earlier this month. The explosions took place beneath the Baluchistan desert. A state of emergency has been declared in Pakistan, and foreign currency bank accounts have been frozen. US president Clinton has already announced sanctions, which will cut all non-humanitarian aid to Pakistan.

World Cup victors

JULY 12

Host nation France has won the football World Cup for the first time, beating the favorite, Brazil, 3-0 in the Stade de France, Paris. More nations than ever before took part in this year's World Cup competition, and over 2.5 million fans traveled to France to watch the 64 finals games. Hero of the French team was Zinedine Zidane, who scored two goals in the first half – the third goal was scored by Emmanuel Petit. French president Chirac warmly embraced all the players as they received their medals, and by midnight, an estimated 80,000 people were celebrating in Paris – the biggest party since the end of World War II.

Top French goal-scorer Zidane raises the World Cup trophy

JANUARY–DECEMBER

APR As crisis mounts in the "Tiger" economies of Southeast Asia, Japan unveils a package of measures to stimulate its economy.

APR Pol Pot, notorious Khmer Rouge leader responsible for millions of deaths in the Killing Fields of Cambodia, dies at 72.

OCT Thousands of people are killed or left homeless as Hurricane Mitch leaves a trail of destruction across Central America.

DEC US president Bill Clinton faces impeachment over his affair with White House intern Monica Lewinsky.

FEB At the 18th Winter Olympics, snowboarding is introduced as a medal sport.

MAR The film *Titanic*, the biggest box office success of all time, wins 11 Oscars.

MAY US singer Frank Sinatra, one of the world's most popular entertainers, dies in Los Angeles at 82.

SEP The Royal Opera House in London, UK, shuts for a year as its financial crisis mounts.

JAN Australian ski-trekkers Treseder, Williams, and Brown reach the South Pole.

TITANIC

FEB Czech archaeologists open an ancient Egyptian tomb dating from 525 BC.

JUL New Hong Kong airport, designed by Briton Norman Foster, suffers growing pains.

FRANK SINATRA

OCT At 77, US astronaut John Glenn becomes the oldest man to travel in space.

2000 FIRST DAWN OF THE NEW
MILLENNIUM IS IN THE ANTARCTIC

2000 A 24-HOUR PARTY IS
HELD IN NEW YORK CITY

2000 THE UK BUILDS A
GIANT CELEBRATORY DOME

A NEW MILLENNIUM

AS THE TWENTIETH CENTURY draws to a close, millennium fever has swept the globe. In some countries, such as the Arab states, Israel, and Japan, where other calendars are used, it is, of course, something of a non-event. Iran has even banned millennium celebrations altogether. But, for much of the world, plans are on course and a bewildering array of millennium projects are being hatched. However, with an estimated population of 6.5 billion people and growing environmental awareness, scientists are already beginning to grapple with potential problems in the 21st century.

THE SITE OF CERN

Fuel of the future

Scientific fact and fiction merged at the end of 1995 when the first complete atoms of antimatter were created at Switzerland's European Laboratory for Particle Physics (known as CERN). Antimatter releases enormous bursts of energy, making it a potential fuel source.

Hotel is shaped like a sail

It's a windup!

This clockwork radio, designed by British inventor Trevor Baylis, offers a simple solution to an old problem. It does not need batteries or electricity and is therefore ideal for use in remote areas with no electricity supply in developing countries.

Aerodynamic hotel

The world's tallest hotel is taking shape in the Arab sheikdom of Dubai. It is the centerpiece of a huge new beach resort complex that will incorporate marina, waterpark, and sports and conference centers. The 1,053-ft (321-m) high hotel has 56 stories and three basements below sea level. Designed in an aerodynamic sail shape, it is located on its own artificial island, which is linked to the mainland by a road bridge.

MODEL OF
DUBAI HOTEL

Under construction

After more than 100 years, the gigantic Neo-Gothic Sagrada Familia church in Barcelona, Spain, is still a building site. Although construction began in 1882, it remains a shell. The designer, the famous Catalan architect Antonio Gaudi, who died in 1926, predicted it would take two centuries to complete. Even uncompleted, the church is a magnificent architectural achievement.

Airport on an island

A special artificial island 2.8 miles (4.5 km) long and 1.5 miles (2.5 km) wide was built in Osaka Bay to house Japan's new Kansai International Airport. It is connected to the overcrowded mainland by a six-lane highway and a railroad. The vast steel and glass terminal was designed to withstand both earthquakes and typhoons.

2000 CATHOLICS CELEBRATE THE
MILLENNIUM IN VATICAN CITY

2000 ARTISTS DECORATE THE
AVENUES IN PARIS, FRANCE

2000 AUSTRALIA STAGES
THE SUMMER OLYMPICS

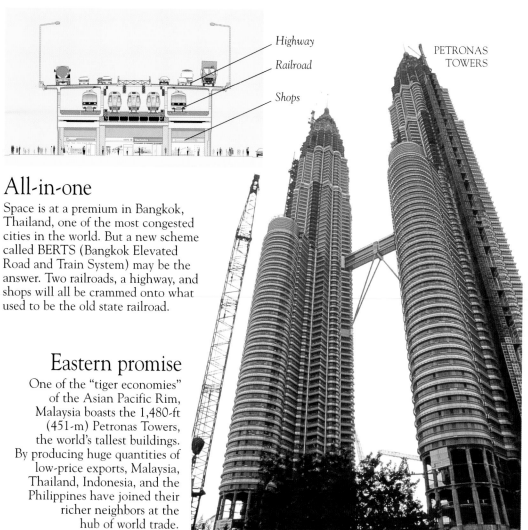

Highway

Railroad

Shops

PETRONAS
TOWERS

AN ARTIST'S
IMPRESSION
OF *ALPHA*

All-in-one

Space is at a premium in Bangkok, Thailand, one of the most congested cities in the world. But a new scheme called BERTS (Bangkok Elevated Road and Train System) may be the answer. Two railroads, a highway, and shops will all be crammed onto what used to be the old state railroad.

Eastern promise

One of the "tiger economies" of the Asian Pacific Rim, Malaysia boasts the 1,480-ft (451-m) Petronas Towers, the world's tallest buildings. By producing huge quantities of low-price exports, Malaysia, Thailand, Indonesia, and the Philippines have joined their richer neighbors at the hub of world trade.

New space age

Work is starting on an International Space Station (ISS), code-named *Alpha*, that will provide a permanent orbiting research complex in the unique, nearly zero-gravity environment of space. In a new spirit of international cooperation, the project is jointly financed and organized by Russia, Japan, Europe, and the United States. The station will take 44 assembly flights to build and is due for completion in 2002.

Car date 2096

Concept 2096, designed to celebrate 100 years of the British automotive industry, shows what cars might look like in the new millennium. It is computer-controlled and will reach speeds of 302 mph (483 km/h), with no driver, no steering wheel, and no brakes. It can also change shape and color.

CONCEPT 2096

2001 COMMON USE OF SOLAR
ENERGY FOR DOMESTIC POWER

2001 FULL PERSONAL MEDICAL
RECORDS STORED ON SMART CARDS

2007 WHOLE HUMAN DNA
BASE SEQUENCE MAPPED

LIFE IN THE 21ST CENTURY

TECHNOLOGICAL PROGRESS will dramatically change life in the 21st century. With a growing world population and dwindling natural resources, it will become more important than ever to create energy-saving living environments and more efficient ways of producing food. Homes of the future will make full use of solar power and recycling facilities, while food may be genetically modified to last longer and contain higher levels of vitamins. Global communications will also revolutionize our lives. Soon, we will be able to run a business, do all shopping, or make vacation reservations from home.

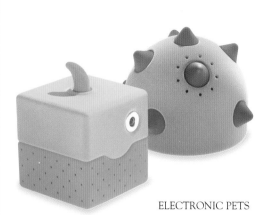

ELECTRONIC PETS

Computer companions

Designed to be companions rather than servants, electronic pets will be capable of reacting to their owner's voice commands, as well as touches or gestures. They will contain sensors, so they can become familiar with their homes just like animal pets.

Videophones

It is predicted that by the year 2020, all mobile telephones will have a video screen, so you will be able to see who you are talking to.

Soft fruit can be modified to have a longer shelf-life in stores

Sensors detect how much pressure to apply when gripping

Wire tendons operate fingers

Bananas can be modified to produce vaccines

Corn can be modified to resist corn borer pest

Tropical fruits can be modified to grow in cooler climates

FOUR-FINGERED
ROBOTIC HAND

Broccoli and cabbages can be modified to grow with a higher nutrient content

Robot servants?

Although there have been huge advances in the science of robotics, it will be a long time before we have the technology to create the kind of multi-functional robot that can perform domestic tasks. This robotic hand can grip a variety of objects but cannot remember what it has learned.

Cauliflower can be modified to be red or blue to appeal to children

GENETICALLY ENGINEERED PRODUCE

Fruit of the future

Scientists will continue to alter plants and animals by modifying their genes. It is possible to create fruit and vegetables that will grow in cold climates, resist pests, and contain more nutrients. However, such changes may have unforeseen consequences.

Internet shopping

In the 21st century it may be possible to do all your shopping from home via the internet. The electronic marketplace, or e-commerce, will revolutionize the retail industry as more stores and supermarkets go on-line. For example, music could soon be sold directly to consumers on their computers.

HOME COMPUTER

2020 SELF-DRIVE CARS
TRAVEL SMART HIGHWAYS

2025 NEW FORMS OF GENETICALLY
ENGINEERED ANIMALS AND PLANTS

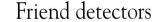

2025 EXTENSION OF HUMAN
LIFESPAN TO OVER 100

Friend detectors

A new breed of short-range communication devices could brighten up your social life. Loaded with all your personal information, "hot badges" will broadcast your profile to other nearby badge-wearers. If the profiles match, the badges will signal their wearers.

HOT BADGES

Health scanner

In the future, it may be possible to conduct your own home health checkup on a daily basis. A combined health and hygiene station will monitor your well-being while you shower. It will be linked directly to a health center that has a complete record of your family's medical history.

Tiny translators

What if you want to make friends with someone who speaks a foreign language? "Ear-ins" are tiny devices that will fit into the ear and translate from one language to another.

EAR-INS

Insulated blinds shield occupants from direct sunlight and reduce heat gain

Greenhouse provides a controlled climate around the core of the house

Solar panels heat water for domestic use, using a heat exchanger

Double-glazed windows conserve heat, but can be opened in warm weather

Blinds open and shut automatically to maximize solar energy

Main house is an insulated box inside the greenhouse; internal walls are made of concrete and clad with tiles

Exterior walls are made from lightweight, well-insulated materials

Easy living

This high-tech home has been designed to reduce dramatically the consumption of natural resources. An outer greenhouse creates a controlled climate around the inner core of the house, and solar panels are used for heating water. Inside, the energy-saving lighting, under-floor heating, and safety systems are all computer-activated and there are built-in recycling bins for different kinds of waste.

Stairs lead down to the temperature-controlled garden

Rainwater collection system has a hand pump for watering garden

Whole front wall opens up

ENERGY-EFFICIENT HOUSE

HOLLYWOOD SUPERSTARS

1900–1909	1910–1919	1920–1929	1930–1939	1940–1949

G. M. ANDERSON ("BRONCO BILLY")

An unsuccessful vaudeville actor, Anderson made his name in the first western, *The Great Train Robbery*, in 1903. He made nearly 400 films in his career.

LINDA AVISON

US actress Linda Avison was the first wife of the renowned film director D. W. Griffith, appearing in several of his "shorts" before taking early retirement.

HOBART BOSWORTH

Former producer and stage actor, Bosworth made his silent screen debut in 1909 after losing his voice. He appeared as a cowboy in *In the Sultan's Power*.

FLORENCE LAWRENCE

US leading lady of the silent screen, Lawrence made her career as the "Biograph Girl," named after the company for whom she worked.

CHARLIE CHAPLIN

A legend in his lifetime, this British-born mime artist found fame in the United States. He was best known for his role as "the Tramp," which captured the hearts of US audiences after he debuted it in 1914.

WILLIAM S. HART

A solemn-faced hero of many silent westerns, such as *Blue Blazes Rawden*, Hart became one of the key performers of the 1920s.

MARY PICKFORD

Nicknamed "the world's sweetheart" Pickford co-founded United Artists with her husband, Douglas Fairbanks, Sr., Charlie Chaplin, and D. W. Griffith.

LILLIAN GISH

Gish appeared in films from 1912. The US actress gave a memorable performance in *Broken Blossoms* in 1918.

DOUGLAS FAIRBANKS, SR.

A swashbuckling star of the silent screen, Fairbanks, Sr., produced many of his own comedy and drama films.

RUDOLPH VALENTINO

Having gained acclaim for *The Sheik* in 1921, an early and untimely death incited female suicides. His funeral was a national event.

BUSTER KEATON

Although a great clown of the silent era, Keaton was rarely seen smiling. His best-known films include *The Navigator* and *The General*.

LAUREL AND HARDY

British-born Stan Laurel teamed up with his large American partner Oliver Hardy in 1926. Arguably the finest screen comedy duo, their first success was in *The Battle of the Century*.

CLARA BOW

US leading lady Bow was the "It" girl of the 1920s, so-called after her role in the film of that name in 1927.

JAMES CAGNEY

A former vaudeville song-and-dance man, Cagney had his first screen success in 1931 with *Public Enemy*.

FRED ASTAIRE AND GINGER ROGERS

Assuredly Hollywood's most remarkable singing and dancing duo, Astaire's and Rogers's most popular films include *Top Hat*, *Swing Time*, and *Shall We Dance?*

SPENCER TRACY

A supremely cinematic actor, Tracy's rugged features initially placed him in gangster roles, but he went on to play tough but kind, intelligent men.

GRETA GARBO

Hollywood brought goddess status to this Swedish actress. In 1936 she was nominated for an Oscar for her performance in *Camille*.

CLARK GABLE

"The King of Hollywood" is best known for his part as Rhett Butler in *Gone With The Wind*, in which he costarred with Vivien Leigh.

BETTE DAVIS

Beautiful, big-eyed Davis won an Oscar for *Jezebel* in 1938 and was an Oscar nominee for *Little Foxes* and *The Letter* in the 1940s.

HUMPHREY BOGART

Bogart embodied the spirit of 1940s film noir. His classic roles were in *The Maltese Falcon*, *The Big Sleep*, and *Casablanca*.

INGRID BERGMAN

Gifted Swedish actress Bergman made her greatest films in Hollywood in the 1940s and won an Oscar for her part in *Gaslight* in 1944.

CARY GRANT

British-born Grant epitomized the debonair hero and was unsurpassed in 1940s light comedy.

KATHERINE HEPBURN

A dominant and enduring star actress, Hepburn was one of the most talented interpreters of emancipated female roles. She is unique in having won four Oscars.

312

1950–1959	1960–1969	1970–1979	1980–1989	1990–1999

MARLON BRANDO
Brando played a wide range of parts and was nominated for several Oscars. His part in *The Wild One* made him popular as a teen idol.

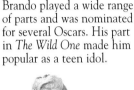

MARILYN MONROE
The number one US leading lady, Monroe's career took off in 1953 with a run of hits including *How to Marry a Millionaire* and *Gentlemen Prefer Blondes*.

JAMES DEAN
A tragic car crash ended teen idol Dean's promising career. He had already been nominated for Oscars for *East of Eden* and *Giant*.

DORIS DAY
A vivacious dance-band singer, Day was an instant success with a unique brand of innocent sex comedy. *Calamity Jane* was one of her most popular films.

PAUL NEWMAN
Newman has had a long, distinguished career. His films of the 1960s include *The Hustler* and *The Prize*.

SEAN CONNERY
Smooth Scotsman Connery shot to fame with his role as James Bond in *Dr. No* in 1962. He still plays gruff, indomitable leading men.

ELIZABETH TAYLOR
Known as much for the number of husbands she has had as for her acting, one of Taylor's most famous roles was in *Cleopatra* in 1963.

SIDNEY POITIER
A handsome and successful leading actor, Poitier won an Oscar for *Lilies of the Field* in 1963 and has helped promote racial equality.

JULIE CHRISTIE
British actress Christie won an Oscar for her role in *Darling* in 1965 and made *Dr. Zhivago* in the same year.

JANE FONDA
Former model and political activist, Fonda was first awarded an Oscar for *Klute* in 1971, and later in 1978 for the film *Coming Home*.

CLINT EASTWOOD
A success as Dirty Harry in 1971, Eastwood is also known for his spaghetti westerns, and in the 1990s was the Oscar-winning director of *The Unforgiven*.

AL PACINO
A New York-born Sicilian, Pacino made his mark in 1972 in *The Godfather*, a thrilling mafia saga of epic proportions. He starred in two *Godfather* sequels.

HARRISON FORD
After initial success with *Star Wars* in 1977, Ford has had a varied and award-studded career. He made *The Fugitive* in 1993.

JOHN TRAVOLTA
Travolta danced and sang to fame in the 1970s in *Saturday Night Fever* and *Grease*. His career resurged in the 1990s.

ROBERT REDFORD
Blond and good-looking, Redford appeared in many films during the 1970s and 1980s. Also a fine director, he won an Oscar for *Ordinary People* in 1980.

ROBERT DE NIRO
One of the century's greatest screen actors, De Niro won an Oscar for *Raging Bull* in 1980, a part for which he had to gain 55 lb (25 kg) in weight.

MERYL STREEP
US actress Streep can speak with many accents. She won an Oscar for *Sophie's Choice* in 1982 and has been nominated for others.

ARNOLD SCHWARZENEGGER
Former body-builder and winner of Mr. Universe, "Arnie" became a huge box-office star with a string of hits after *Terminator* in 1984.

TOM CRUISE
Cruise's career was launched in 1985 with *Top Gun*. He is now one of the hottest properties in Hollywood, and was an Oscar nominee for *Born on the Fourth of July*.

KEVIN COSTNER
In addition to achieving success as an actor, Costner was an Oscar-winning director in 1990 with *Dances With Wolves*, and producer of *Waterworld* in 1995.

JODIE FOSTER
A talented child actress, Foster now plays demanding roles such as the FBI agent in *Silence of the Lambs* in 1991, for which she won an Oscar, and directs.

BRAD PITT
Teen heartthrob Pitt shot to stardom in *A River Runs Through It* in 1992. He was first noticed by audiences in *Thelma and Louise*.

DENZEL WASHINGTON
US actor Washington's popular performances in the 1990s include *Philadelphia*, *Devil in a Blue Dress*, and the biographical *Malcolm X*.

TOM HANKS
After several low-key parts in the 1980s, Hanks won Oscars in 1994 and 1995 for *Philadelphia* and *Forrest Gump* and is now one of the leading US actors.

SCIENTISTS AND INVENTORS

1900–1909	1910–1919	1920–1929	1930–1939	1940–1949

WRIGHT BROTHERS

US brothers Orville and Wilbur Wright built and, in 1903, flew the first successful powered airplane. They were self-taught aeronauts, and the *Flyer* was driven by a lightweight gasoline engine, flying a distance of 2,625 ft (800 m).

GEORGE EASTMAN

Photography was difficult and time-consuming until Eastman introduced the public to the lightweight roll-film Brownie camera.

GUGLIELMO MARCONI

In 1895, Italian scientist Marconi invented radio communication. Six years later, he succeeded in sending the first radio signals across the Atlantic.

LUMIÈRE BROTHERS

The Lumière brothers invented the first practical film projector. In 1904, they marketed color plates capable of producing a color transparency.

LEO BAEKELAND

In 1909, Belgian chemist Baekeland developed the first synthetic plastic. Known as Bakelite, it was used to make all kinds of things, from pitchers to radios.

MARY PHELPS JACOB

When Jacob designed the first bra it consisted of two handkerchiefs with straps, intended to flatter the bust.

HENRY FORD

US car manufacturer Ford pioneered mass production with the invention of the moving assembly line.

MARIE CURIE

Curie pioneered research into radioactivity with the discovery of the elements polonium and radium.

ALBERT EINSTEIN

In 1916, Albert Einstein revolutionized the laws of physics with the formulation of the special and general theories of relativity.

HARRY BREARLEY

Brearley mixed steel and chromium to produce an alloy that did not rust. The result was stainless steel.

ALEXANDER FLEMING

Fleming accidentally discovered penicillin in 1928. The first samples of the antibiotic drug were used on wounded soldiers in World War II.

CLARENCE BIRDSEYE

In 1925, US entrepreneur Birdseye revolutionized the food industry with the development of a method used for quick-freezing precooked foods.

ROBERT GODDARD

In 1926, Goddard launched the first liquid-fueled rocket. Although it only rose 184 ft (56 m), it had far-reaching effects on the future of space exploration.

BALZER VON PLATEN & CARL MUNTERS

In 1922, von Platen and Munters invented the electric refrigerator in Sweden. They called it the "D fridge," and it was marketed by Electrolux.

PERCY SHAW

In 1934, Percy Shaw revolutionized road safety with the invention of road reflectors that he called "cat's-eyes." They have since saved countless lives.

CHESTER CARLSON

US lawyer Chester Carlson invented the photocopier in 1938. The first practical machines for office use went on sale in 1960.

OTTO HAHN & LISE MEITNER

Physicists Hahn and Meitner conducted research into radioactive methods, leading to the discovery of nuclear fission in 1939.

JOHN LOGIE BAIRD

The first demonstration of television was given by Baird in 1928. Eight years later, he conducted the first high-definition television broadcast in color.

WILLIAM SHOCKLEY

The invention of transistors in 1947 by Shockley and his team of scientists led to the development of microchips and compact electronic machines.

FRANK WHITTLE

Whittle built a prototype jet engine in 1937 that was first used in aircraft in 1941, becoming the forerunner of the modern jet engine.

IGOR SIKORSKY

Sikorsky developed the first practical helicopter, with a single rotor to give enough lifting power. Many modern helicopters are of this type.

ENRICO FERMI

Fermi built the first nuclear reactor while conducting research into producing controlled and self-sustaining nuclear fission.

1950–1959	1960–1969	1970–1979	1980–1989	1990–1999

ROY JACUZZI

Jacuzzi invented the first fully integrated whirlpool bath in 1968. Since then, the Jacuzzi has remained a popular form of relaxation.

EDWARD JONAS SALK

US physician Salk was the first person to develop an oral vaccine against the crippling and infectious children's disease polio.

GODFREY HOUNSFIELD

Hounsfield invented a computerized tomography (CT) scanner in 1972. It used low-intensity X rays to produce diagnostic pictures.

JOHN WARNOCK & PAUL BRAINERD

Warnock and Brainerd invented desktop publishing (DTP) software, enabling editors to create books and magazines on a computer.

TREVOR BAYLIS

Baylis invented a windup radio capable of generating its own power supply. The radio was specially designed for use in communities in Africa that lack electricity.

ALEC JEFFREYS

Jeffreys revealed that our unique DNA profiles can be used for identification purposes and therefore aid forensic scientists in the task of solving crimes.

FRANCIS T. BACON

From 1932 to the 1950s, Bacon and his team of scientists worked on creating the first practical hydrogen-oxygen fuel cell.

JANE GOODALL

Through many years of observation, UK scientist Goodall uncovered the amazing similarities between chimpanzees and humans.

CLIVE SINCLAIR

Sinclair developed miniature electronic goods, including the first pocket calculator. In 1985, he launched the C5, the world's first electric car.

DR. ROBERT WILLIAMS

Dr. Williams, director of the Space Telescope Science Institute, confirmed the existence of black holes while working with NASA's *Hubble Space Telescope*.

ROSALIND FRANKLIN

UK chemist Franklin conducted X-ray investigations of DNA, which led to the discovery of their structure in 1953.

THEODORE MAIMAN

Maiman built the first working laser beam. Today, the laser has all kinds of uses, from bar code reading to delicate surgery.

JAMES E. LOVELOCK

In his Gaia theory, Lovelock claims that the Earth and all life on it are linked as if they are a single living thing.

ERNO RUBIK

Hungarian professor Rubik launched his maddening Rubik's Cube in 1980. The puzzle looked easy, but it had to be solved by the correct combination.

DR. ALAN ROBERTS

In 1994, Dr. Roberts of the Bio-Materials Research Unit in the UK, invented a powerful superglue capable of closing severe wounds without the risk of infection.

ROLAND MORENO

In 1981, Moreno invented a credit card with its own memory by embedding it with a computer chip. Cardholders use the card to balance their bank accounts.

CHRISTOPHER COCKERELL

When Cockerell invented the hovercraft in 1955 the UK government was so impressed they placed it on the top secret list!

CHRISTIAAN BARNARD

South African cardiologist Barnard performed the first human-heart transplant on a patient with heart disease.

DENNIS GABOR

Gabor pioneered holography in 1948, but the technique was not of any practical use until the invention of the laser during the 1960s.

ABDUS SALAM

Pakistani scientist Salam was the first person from his country to win a Nobel Prize, for his theory of the electroweak force.

JOHN SANFORD

Sanford devised the gene gun in 1987. Geneticists use this instrument to introduce new genetic material into cells in order to change the structure of the cells.

DANIEL COHEN

In 1993, genetic expert Professor Cohen led a team of researchers that generated the first physical mapping of all 24 human chromosomes, known as the genome.

SPORTS STARS

1900–1909	1910–1919	1920–1929	1930–1939	1940–1949

CHARLOTTE COOPER

UK tennis player Charlotte Cooper became the first ever woman Olympic champion at the Paris Games in 1900.

RAY EWRY

The legendary US athlete Ray Ewry won an incredible ten Olympic gold medals between 1900 and 1908. He demolished all opposition in the standing long jump, the standing high jump, and the standing triple jump – events that are not contested today.

PRINCE BORGHESE

After a grueling 62 days at the wheel, Prince Borghese of Italy won the 8,000-mile (13,000-km) Peking to Paris car race in 1907.

DR. W. G. GRACE

W. G. Grace dominated English cricket for over four decades. He scored 54,211 runs and took 2,809 wickets.

JIM THORPE

An American of native American descent, Jim Thorpe won the decathlon and pentathlon at the 1912 Olympics. He was known as "the greatest athlete in the world."

SUZANNE LENGLEN

Twenty-year-old French tennis star Suzanne Lenglen was the first non-English speaking singles champion at Wimbledon, in 1919. She won the title six times in all.

HANNES KOLEHMAINEN

"Flying Finn" Kolehmainen won the Olympic 5,000-m, 10,000-m, and the 8,000-m cross country in 1912.

JACK DEMPSEY

US boxer Jack Dempsey, "The Manassa Mauler," became a national hero in 1919 after winning the heavyweight world championship.

BABE RUTH

US baseball player Babe Ruth's contract with the Red Sox was sold to the New York Yankees for $125,000 in 1920. Seven years later, he hit his record 60th home run of the season.

JOHNNY WEISSMULLER

Austrian-born American Johnny Weissmuller was the first man to swim 100 m in less than a minute. He won five Olympic medals.

DIXIE DEAN

At the age of only 21, the UK soccer player Dixie Dean, playing for Everton, scored a record sixty league goals in a total of 39 matches.

PAAVO NURMI

One of the famous "Flying Finns," Nurmi won nine Olympic golds altogether, five at the 1924 Paris Games in France. He broke the 1,500-m and 5,000-m records on the same afternoon.

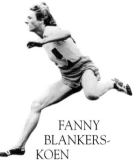

GORDON RICHARDS

Champion UK horse-racing jockey the legendary Gordon Richards galloped into the record books in 1933 with more than 246 winners in one season.

DONALD BRADMAN

The most prolific batsman ever, Australian cricketer Donald Bradman set a test match record on July 12, 1930, with a score of 334 runs in Leeds, UK.

JESSE OWENS

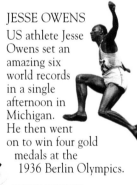

US athlete Jesse Owens set an amazing six world records in a single afternoon in Michigan. He then went on to win four gold medals at the 1936 Berlin Olympics.

FRED PERRY

Former world table tennis champion Perry, of the UK, won the US Open tennis championship in 1933, 1934, and 1936. He won the Australian Open in 1934, and Wimbledon in 1934, 1935, and 1936.

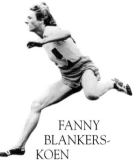

FANNY BLANKERS-KOEN

Nicknamed "The Flying Dutchwoman," Blankers-Koen won the 100 m, the 200 m, the 80-m hurdles, and the sprint relay at the 1948 Olympics in London.

MALCOLM CAMPBELL

UK racing driver Sir Malcolm Campbell broke world speed records on both land and water. He reached 300 mph (480 km) in his car *Bluebell*.

GORDIE HOWE

Canadian ice hockey professional Gordie Howe played for the Detroit Red Wings. He scored 1,071 goals in his 32-year career.

JOE LOUIS

"Brown Bomber" Joe Lewis, the first black world heavyweight champion since 1915, successfully defended his title 25 times.

1950–1959	1960–1969	1970–1979	1980–1989	1990–1999

JUAN MANUEL FANGIO

Argentine race car driver Fangio won a record five world championships in the 1950s, driving for Alfa Romeo, Ferrari, Maserati, and Mercedes-Benz.

EMIL ZÁTOPEK

Czech long-distance runner Emil Zátopek won the 5,000 m, the 10,000 m, and the marathon at the 1952 Helsinki Olympics. His wife Dana won the javelin event.

ROGER BANNISTER

In 1954, UK runner Roger Bannister was the first man to run a mile in under four minutes. He ran the distance in an incredible 3 minutes, 59.4 seconds.

LARISSA LATYNINA

One of the first great Soviet gymnasts, Larissa Latynina won a record 18 Olympic medals between 1956 and 1964 – nine gold, five silver, and four bronze.

ABEBE BIKILA

Ethiopian barefoot runner Abebe Bikila, known as "the metronome on legs," won the Olympic marathon in 1960, and again in 1964.

DAWN FRASER

Australian swimmer Dawn Fraser won the 100-m freestyle gold medal in three successive Olympics – 1956, 1960, and 1964.

MUHAMMAD ALI

World heavyweight boxing champion Cassius Clay changed his name to Muhammad Ali after converting to Islam.

BOB BEAMON

In the thin air of Mexico City, US long-jumper Bob Beamon cleared a historic 29.19 ft (8.90 m) at the 1968 Olympic Games. It was a record that remained unbeaten for more than 25 years.

EDSON ARANTES DO NASCIMENTO PELÉ

The incomparable Brazilian soccer player Pelé was only 17 years old when he played in his first World Cup.

OLGA KORBUT

The tiny Soviet gymnast Olga Korbut captivated the crowds and won two gold medals – for floor exercise and beam events – at the Munich Olympics in 1972.

LESTER PIGGOTT

Winner of some 5,200 races in Britain and overseas, this jockey has dominated racing, winning the Derby 9 times.

NIJINSKY

In 1970 Nijinsky, a three-year-old horse ridden by Lester Piggott, won the UK Triple Crown – the Derby, 2,000 Guineas, and St. Leger.

JACK NICKLAUS

US golfer Jack Nicklaus is one of the sport's greatest players. He was the first person to win five different major titles at least twice.

ZOLA BUDD

In 1985, the South African-born barefoot distance runner Zola Budd set a new 5,000 m world record of 14 mins 48.07 sec.

DIEGO MARADONA

Barcelona paid a record £5 million for Argentine soccer player Maradona in 1982. He led Argentina to World Cup victory in 1986.

JOE MONTANA

Inspirational US quarter-back Joe Montana led his team, the San Francisco 49ers, to victory in four Super Bowls in the 1980s.

JAYNE TORVIL & CHRISPHER DEAN

UK skaters Torvil and Dean won the world ice-dancing championships in four successive years. In the 1984 competition, they won an amazing 29 perfect sixes.

YAPING DENG

Chinese table tennis ace Yaping Deng became world champion in 1991. She won both the singles and doubles title at the 1992 Barcelona Olympic Games.

MARTINA NAVRATILOVA

Czech-born tennis player Navratilova, who defected to the US in 1975, won her record ninth Wimbledon singles title in 1991.

MICHAEL JOHNSON

The US superstar sprinter Michael Johnson was world champion in the 200 m in 1991 and 1993, and in the 400 m in 1993 and 1995. At the 1996 Olympics in Atlanta, he became the first person ever to win both events.

MIGUEL INDURAIN

The legendary Miguel Indurain, a cyclist from the Basque country, won the Tour de France for a record fifth time in 1995.

BRIAN LARA

In 1994, West Indian left-handed batsman Brian Lara beat Garfield Sobers's 1958 record by scoring 375 runs against England.

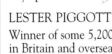

WORLD LEADERS

1900–1909	1910–1919	1920–1929	1930–1939	1940–1949

KAISER WILHELM II

Ruler of Germany between 1888 and 1918, Wilhelm II pursued a vigorous policy of expansion in central Europe. He fled to Holland following defeat in WWI.

CZAR NICHOLAS II

Nicholas II of Russia clung to power from 1894 until the 1917 revolution, when he was forced to abdicate. He was executed in 1918.

EMMELINE PANKHURST

Leading UK suffragette Mrs. Emmeline Pankhurst fought for women's voting rights, which were finally granted in 1918.

SUN YAT-SEN

The most important figure in the Chinese nationalist revolution, Sun Yat-Sen was elected president of the new republic in 1911.

LEON TROTSKY

Russian revolutionary Leon Trotsky was a leader of the 1917 Bolshevik victory. He was later exiled by Stalin.

WOODROW WILSON

US president Wilson was the leading world figure at the Versailles conference after WWI. Wilson was determined to establish a fair world peace, based on liberal principles.

VLADIMIR LENIN

Vladimir Ilyich Lenin, founder of the communist party in Russia, became the first premier of the USSR.

ROSA LUXEMBURG

Polish-born Luxemburg was a brilliant speaker and writer. She helped found the communist "Spartacists", leading an uprising in Berlin in 1919, which failed and resulted in her death.

MUSTAPHA KEMAL

Mustapha Kemal was called Ataturk, meaning "Father of the Turks," after establishing a Turkish republic in 1923.

ÉAMON DE VALERA

Irish politician de Valera was president of Sinn Féin until 1926, and a leading figure in Ireland's fight for independence from the UK.

CHIANG KAI-SHEK

General Chiang Kai-Shek was president of the Chinese Republic from 1928 to 1949, after he led the Chinese nationalist Kuomintang forces to victory over the warlords of north China.

AUGUSTO SANDINO

Nicaraguan rebel leader General Sandino waged a guerrilla war against US-backed government troops.

EMPEROR HIROHITO

Hirohito ruled as emperor of Japan for 63 years. His reign became known as *Showa* – Enlightened Peace.

MAHATMA GANDHI

Admired by all, Gandhi was at the forefront of the fight to free India from British rule by nonviolent means.

JOSEPH STALIN

Stalin's reign of terror as dictator of the USSR lasted from 1929 to 1953. Millions of peasants died, opposed to his collective farming laws.

RAS TAFARI HAILLE SELASSIE

Ras (Duke) Tafari took the name Haille Selassie, "Power of the Trinity," when he became emperor of Ethiopia in 1931.

BENITO MUSSOLINI

Italian fascist dictator Mussolini ruled Italy from 1922 for 21 years as *Il Duce* – The Leader. He tried to create an Italian empire.

GENERAL FRANCO

Franco's nationalist forces defeated the republicans in the Spanish Civil War. He ruled as dictator from 1939.

GENERAL DE GAULLE

De Gaulle fled Nazi-occupied France in 1940, and founded the Free French Movement. He was made president of France after liberation in 1944, and later became president of the Fifth Republic.

ADOLF HITLER

German dictator Adolf Hitler, known as the Führer, was responsible for the Holocaust, when millions of Jews were exterminated.

JAWAHARLAL NEHRU

After playing a key role in negotiating independence, Jawaharlal Nehru became India's first prime minister.

WINSTON CHURCHILL

A statesman and writer, Churchill was at the height of his power as UK prime minister during WWII.

1950–1959	1960–1969	1970–1979	1980–1989	1990–1999

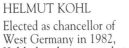

HELMUT KOHL

Elected as chancellor of West Germany in 1982, Kohl played a major role in the unification of Germany.

AUNG SAN SUU KYI

The leader of the democracy movement in Burma, she was under house arrest from 1989 to 1995.

JOHN F. KENNEDY

At 43, Kennedy became the youngest US president. He was greatly mourned after his assassination in 1963.

KONRAD ADENAUER

At 73, Adenauer became the first chancellor after WWII of the newly created West German Republic.

DALAI LAMA

Traditionally a spiritual leader, the Dalai Lama also ruled over Tibet until the 1950s. The 14th Lama, he was forced to flee Tibet after the Chinese invasion.

MARGARET THATCHER

Conservative leader Mrs. Thatcher became the UK's first woman prime minister, and held office for 11 years.

JOMO KENYATTA

Nationalist leader Kenyatta became the first president of Kenya after his country gained independence.

INDIRA GANDHI

The first woman prime minister of India, Indira Gandhi was assassinated in 1984 by her bodyguards.

MIKHAIL GORBACHEV

Soviet premier Gorbachev won the Nobel Peace Prize for his role in ending the Cold War and aiding peace.

YITZHAK RABIN

Israeli prime minister Rabin made a huge contribution to Middle East peace talks. He was assassinated in 1995.

HO CHI MINH

Communist revolutionary Ho Chi Minh became president of North Vietnam after defeating the French.

MARTIN LUTHER KING

A Nobel Peace Prize winner, King was the leading figure of the nonviolent civil rights movement in the US.

AYATOLLAH KHOMEINI

Islamic fundamentalist Khomeini inspired the 1979 revolution that created the Islamic Republic of Iran.

LECH WALESA

Lech Walesa became leader of the banned Polish trade union Solidarity. He was elected president in 1990.

VACLAV HAVEL

Czech playwright Havel set up the civil rights group Charter 77. He was elected Czech president in 1989.

YASSIR ARAFAT

PLO leader Yassir Arafat won international support for his efforts in the peace negotiations with Israel.

NELSON MANDELA

ANC leader Nelson Mandela became South Africa's first black president in 1994. He was awarded the Nobel Peace Prize for his work to end apartheid.

COLONEL NASSER

After leading the revolt against King Faruk, Nasser became prime minister of the new republic of Egypt.

GOLDA MEIR

A member of the Mapai Labor Party, 70-year-old Golda Meir became prime minister of Israel in 1969.

POPE JOHN PAUL II

Polish-born Karol Jozef Wojtyla took the name John Paul II when he became Pope in 1978.

BENAZIR BHUTTO

Benazir Bhutto was elected prime minister of Pakistan in 1988, the first woman to head an Islamic nation.

MUSIC MAKERS

1900–1909	1910–1919	1920–1929	1930–1939	1940–1949

SCOTT JOPLIN

Joplin was known as the "King of Ragtime" in the United States, particularly for his *Maple Leaf Rag*.

MARIE LLOYD

Music hall star Marie Lloyd first appeared on the UK stage at the age of only 15 and became best known for slightly saucy songs like *A Little of What You Fancy*. She was very popular with a large following.

DAME NELLIE MELBA

A hugely popular soprano, Nellie Melba took her name from her birthplace – Melbourne in Australia.

ENRICO CARUSO

The "greatest tenor of modern times," this Italian was one of the first opera singers to record extensively.

QUAKER CITY FOUR

The most famous barbershop quartet of all time, this group achieved immortality with the song *Sweet Adeline*.

DIXIELAND JAZZ BAND

This quintet of white musicians was the first jazz band to make records. Their top hits include *Tiger Rag*.

SOPHIE TUCKER

Sophie Tucker, known as "the last of the red-hot mamas," was a US ragtime singer with a raucous style.

IRVING BERLIN

One of the US's most successful popular song-writers, Berlin could neither read or compose music.

AL JOLSON

Vaudeville entertainer Al Jolson starred and sang in the first-ever talking picture, *The Jazz Singer*.

EDWARD ELGAR

One of the UK's favorite composers, Elgar won worldwide recognition with *The Enigma Variations*.

JOSEPHINE BAKER

Josephine Baker moved from the US to France, where she introduced the Charleston dance wearing only a girdle of bananas.

LOUIS ARMSTRONG

A genius at improvization, the cornet and trumpet player known as "Satchmo" became the most famous jazz musician of all times.

PAUL ROBESON

Best remembered for his version of *Ol' Man River*, Robeson was one of the most influential black performers of his decade.

TOMMY DORSEY

Trombone player Tommy Dorsey formed his own orchestra in the US. It went on to become one of the most famous swing and dance bands of all time.

ELLA FITZGERALD

One of the most technically accomplished jazz singers ever, Fitzgerald's biggest hit was *A Tisket A Tasket*.

BENNY GOODMAN

Goodman was a virtuoso clarinettist who made his name as leader of his own swing band in the US.

BING CROSBY

One of the first crooners, Crosby's recordings include *White Christmas*, which sold 30 million copies.

MAHALIA JACKSON

Jackson grew up in New Orleans and became the most popular gospel singer of her generation.

JUDY GARLAND

Garland made her stage debut at the age of three. She is best remembered for *Somewhere Over the Rainbow*.

GLEN MILLER

Known for the hit tune *In the Mood*, this famous swing band leader died during World War II.

CARMEN MIRANDA

A nightclub singer and recording star, the "Brazilian Bombshell" was famous for her towering fruit headdress.

BILLIE HOLIDAY

Nicknamed "Lady Day," American Billie Holiday was one of the greatest jazz vocalists ever.

FRANK SINATRA

The success of "ole blue eyes" as a solo artist heralded a new era of teen hysteria and idol worship.

COUNT BASIE

Given the name "Count" by a radio broadcaster, Basie ranked high among pianists and band leaders.

1950–1959	1960–1969	1970–1979	1980–1989	1990–1999

ELVIS PRESLEY

The first major rock 'n' roll star, heart-throb Elvis "The Pelvis" made fans swoon on both sides of the Atlantic with 18 US chart-toppers.

LITTLE RICHARD

With his wild piano style and sometimes manic singing style, Little Richard's first hit was *Tutti Frutti*.

DORIS DAY

Doris Day had a successful career as a singer with many international hits, including seven million-sellers.

BUDDY HOLLY

Although he died tragically young in a plane crash, rock 'n' roll giant Holly has had a huge musical influence.

RODGERS AND HAMMERSTEIN

Richard Rodgers and Oscar Hammerstein produced a string of smash-hit musicals, including *Oklahoma!* and *The Sound of Music*.

THE BEATLES

The UK's "Fab Four" were the most famous pop group of the swinging Sixties. They dominated the charts throughout the world.

THE ROLLING STONES

With a rebellious image, the live performances of this UK rock group were wild and exciting, making them a hit wherever they played.

JIMI HENDRIX

The legendary guitarist Jimi Hendrix died young but has been a huge influence on rock and jazz musicians.

ARETHA FRANKLIN

Aretha Franklin was the most important US female vocalist to emerge from the Sixties boom in soul music.

STEVIE WONDER

Blind from birth, Stevie Wonder was a child prodigy, playing piano and drums. He had his first hit when he was only 12 years old and went on to have a string of chart-toppers throughout the decade.

T-REX

Fans fainted when UK glam-rock band and teen idols T-Rex went on tour in the early Seventies.

ABBA

Swedish Eurovision Song Contest winner Abba had its first million-selling record with *Waterloo* in 1974.

BAY CITY ROLLERS

A trend for tartan took off when this new Scottish group, aimed at teenagers, burst onto the pop scene.

BOB MARLEY

Bob Marley achieved worldwide fame and helped popularize reggae, but his roots remained in Jamaica.

SEX PISTOLS

Founding fathers of punk rock, the Sex Pistols began performing live in the UK, causing outrage in 1975.

MADONNA

A genius for self-promotion, Madonna shot to fame in the mid-Eighties with hits including *Like a Virgin* and *Material Girl*.

PRINCE

One of the decade's most controversial stars, Prince's *Purple Rain* album topped the US charts for 20 weeks.

DIRE STRAITS

UK rock band Dire Straits's 1985 album *Brothers in Arms* was one of the decade's biggest sellers.

MICHAEL JACKSON

Michael Jackson achieved the status of mega-star with his 1982 album *Thriller*, which became the biggest-selling record ever.

DURAN DURAN

At the heart of the "New Romantic" backlash against punk, this UK group also appealed as teen idols.

NIRVANA

Spearheading the grunge revolution, US group Nirvana had instant success with its album *Nevermind*.

OASIS

The bad boys of Nineties rock, UK group Oasis has often been likened to the Beatles and has led the British pop revival.

TAKE THAT

Helplines for distraught teenage fans were set up when UK boy band Take That split up in 1996.

SNOOP DOGGY DOG

In 1993 US rapper Snoop Doggy Dog made history when his debut album *Doggystyle* entered the US charts at number one.

GARTH BROOKS

As a country music boom spread across the US, Garth Brooks hit the charts with his winning blend of soft rockabilly and old-style country tradition.

LAWBREAKERS

BUTCH CASSIDY
Originally named Robert LeRoy Parker, Cassidy was a cattle rustler before joining the Wild Bunch and meeting the Sundance Kid.

THE SUNDANCE KID
This outlaw, named Harry Longabaugh, teamed up with Butch Cassidy to rob banks, trains, and mines. It is believed that the pair was killed in Bolivia in 1909.

GAETANO BRESCI
The assassin of the king of Italy Umberto I, Bresci saved up his wages as a weaver in the US so he could travel to Italy to carry out the murder in 1900.

LEON CZOLGOSZ
In 1901, anarchist Leon Czolgosz shot the US president William McKinley. The president later died of his wounds.

MATA HARI
An exotic dancer, Mata Hari also tried to spy for both Germany and the Allies in WWI. She was finally betrayed by Germany and executed by the French in 1917.

ARNOLD ROTHSTEIN
Rothstein was responsible for fixing the 1919 baseball World Series by bribing members of the Chicago White Sox team.

OLD BLUEBEARD
Henri Desiré Landru, nicknamed "Old Bluebeard," seduced several French war widows and swindled them out of their life savings before murdering them.

DR. CRIPPEN
Dr. Crippen poisoned his wife, buried her in the cellar, and ran away with his mistress. He was caught on a boat bound for Canada.

AL CAPONE
The US's most famous mobster, Capone controlled the underworld in Chicago in the days of Prohibition.

JOHN DILLINGER
John Dillinger was leader of a gang of crooks famous for a series of armed bank robberies in the US. He was gunned down by FBI agents in 1934.

LEOPOLD AND LOEB
The spoiled sons of millionaires, Leopold and Loeb murdered a 14-year-old boy for fun in 1924.

SACCO AND VANZETTI
Sacco and Vanzetti killed two people in a robbery. It was thought they were convicted because they were anarchists.

PETER KÜRTEN
Nicknamed the "Vampire of Düsseldorf," Peter Kürten was finally caught and executed in Germany for nine murders and seven attempted murders. Kürten had a passion for the taste of human blood.

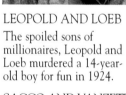

BONNIE AND CLYDE
A couple of smalltime hoods, Bonnie and Clyde became the US's most notorious criminals.

LUCKY LUCIANO
Inheriting Al Capone's position as head of the US mafia, Salvatore Luciano controlled a large number of crime rackets.

BRUNO HAUPTMANN
A German carpenter, Hauptmann was convicted of the kidnapping and murder of the toddler son of hero Charles Lindbergh.

ALBERT HOWARD FISH
One of America's worst serial killers, Fish was brought to justice in 1934. Fish cooked his victims' flesh and ate it for dinner.

GIUSEPPE ZANGARA
Zangara explained his 1933 assassination attempt on president-elect Roosevelt by saying, "I hate all officials."

JOHN GEORGE HAIGH
Haigh believed that if he destroyed his victim's body in a vat of sulfuric acid he could escape conviction in the UK, but he was wrong.

HIRASAWA
Hirasawa tricked all 16 employees of a Japanese bank into taking cyanide. When they were nearly dead, he robbed the bank.

WONG YU
In 1947 Wong Yu invented hijacking when he staged the takeover of a flying boat and demanded a ransom.

GEORGE METESKY
Metesky terrorized New York by planting bombs all around the city. However, many were duds and injuries were few.

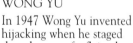

1950–1959	1960–1969	1970–1979	1980–1989	1990–1999

JOHN CHRISTIE

Eight bodies were found in Christie's home at 10 Rillington Place in London, UK. Three bodies had been stacked in a cupboard.

NANNIE DOSS

Nannie Doss admitted to killing four of her five husbands by putting liquid rat poison into their food and drink.

THE ROSENBERGS

Julius and Ethel Rosenberg were convicted of selling atomic secrets to the Russians. They were executed for espionage.

BURGESS & MACLEAN

In 1951, warned by fellow spy Kim Philby, Guy Burgess and Donald Maclean, who had been leaking secrets to Russia, fled to Moscow.

RUTH ELLIS

The last woman to be executed in the UK, Ellis shot her lover dead outside a London pub after he ended their love affair.

BOSTON STRANGLER

Albert DeSalvo strangled 13 women in Boston. He gained their confidence by claiming to be a talent scout for a model agency.

THE KRAY TWINS

Ronald and Reginald Kray controlled the underworld in the East End of London. The twins' gang was known as the "Firm."

LEE HARVEY OSWALD

Oswald was arrested for the assassination of US president John F. Kennedy. His own murder, while in custody, was caught by TV cameras.

CHARLES MANSON

Leader of a US commune called the "Family," Manson incited his disciples to carry out murders in Hollywood.

TOM KEATING

Picture restorer Tom Keating admitted to forging the works of world-famous painters. The paintings were sold as originals.

ALBERT SPAGGIARI

Spaggiari masterminded a bank robbery in Nice, France, and escaped. He got into the bank by tunneling through the town sewers.

CARLOS THE JACKAL

An international killer, Carlos worked for a variety of terrorist groups. The world's most-wanted terrorist was finally caught in 1994.

TED BUNDY

Serial killer Ted Bundy confessed to murdering 23 women over a period between 1974 and 1978. He was executed in 1989.

MICHAEL MILKEN

Milken was nicknamed "the Hannibal Lecter of American business" after he was convicted for his insider dealing and fraud.

ISSEI SAGAWA

A Japanese student, Sagawa murdered and ate a Dutch girl while living in France. He has since published his best-selling memoirs.

PABLO ESCOBAR

Escobar was a Colombian drug baron and head of the underworld. After escaping imprisonment, Escobar was gunned down in 1993.

ROBERT MAXWELL

UK press baron Maxwell drowned in 1991, escaping being charged with stealing from his company's pension fund to pay creditors.

ANDREI CHIKATILO

A Ukrainian serial killer, Chikatilo murdered 53 women and children before being caught in 1990.

NICK LEESON

Charged with fraud, Nick Leeson was responsible for the collapse of Barings, a respected UK bank.

ABIMAEL GUZMÁN

Guzmán led the "Shining Path" guerrillas in Peru and was responsible for many acts of terrorism.

THOMAS HAMILTON

Hamilton walked into a Scottish school in 1996 and shot 16 young children and their teacher dead before shooting himself.

THE US GOVERNMENT

The United States Constitution set up a federal system of government, with power shared between the national, or federal, and state governments. The federal government deals with such issues as foreign policy, health care, and defense. State governments play central roles in such areas as education and urban development, and make their own laws. The federal government is divided into three branches: the executive (the Presidency), the legislative (the Senate and House of Representatives, together known as Congress), and the judicial (the Supreme Court). Each branch has checks and balances on the others' powers. These checks and balances ensure that power is distributed so no branch becomes too powerful.

The legislative branch

This branch, called Congress, creates and passes laws. There are 100 elected senators, two from each state. States also elect representatives – the number per state is determined by the size of the state's population. Together, senators and representatives make up the legislative body known as Congress. Individuals must meet certain requirements in order to run for office. A person wishing to run for senator must be aged 30, must have been a US citizen for at least 9 years, and must be a resident of the state they wish to represent.

The executive branch

This branch enforces the laws made by Congress. The President heads this branch. The President is chosen by the electoral college, which is in turn chosen by voters. There are 14 departments in the executive branch, as well as many independent agencies. The President appoints the heads of the departments, which form his Cabinet, or advisory board. A US President serves a four-year term and may run once for reelection. Candidates must be at least 35, and have been born in the US.

The judicial branch

The judicial branch explains and interprets the laws of Congress, and decides if they are in agreement with the principles of the Constitution. This branch is headed by the Supreme Court, whose members are appointed for life by the President. There are a total of nine justices. The Supreme Court, sometimes known as "the court of last resort," is the highest court in the US and will sometimes overturn decisions made by lower courts. The Supreme Court handles cases involving two or more states.

Powers of the President

• The President is the nation's chief executive and chief of state and sees that all laws passed by Congress are carried out. He or she also has responsibility for sending Congress an annual budget of what is needed to run the federal government, and proposals for raising money.

• As Commander-in-Chief of the Armed Forces, the President gives orders to the military services. The President has the power to ask Congress to declare war and decides how the war should be conducted.

• The President can recommend laws to Congress and must either sign or veto all bills passed by Congress.

• The President appoints all Supreme Court judges and other United States court judges, cabinet members, ambassadors to foreign countries, and military and naval officers.

• The President directs US foreign policy and has the power to negotiate and make treaties with foreign countries, with the consent of the Senate.

The Democratic party

One of the two major political parties in the US, the origins of the Democratic party date back to 1792, when supporters of Thomas Jefferson established a party called the Democratic–Republican party. The Democrat–Republicans advocated a strict interpretation of the Constitution, which, in their opinion, called for giving more power to individual state governments than to a centralized government. Members of this fledgling party did not want to relinquish decision-making power to a distant, overbearing governing body because that was the sort of political environment they had opposed in the Revolutionary War. In the 1830s, the party shortened its name to the Democratic party. Democratic presidents often occupied the White House in the 60 years after the party's

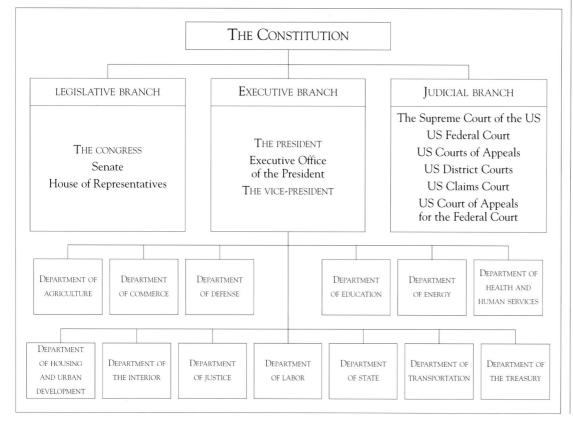

THE CONSTITUTION

LEGISLATIVE BRANCH

THE CONGRESS
Senate
House of Representatives

EXECUTIVE BRANCH

THE PRESIDENT
Executive Office of the President
THE VICE-PRESIDENT

JUDICIAL BRANCH

The Supreme Court of the US
US Federal Court
US Courts of Appeals
US District Courts
US Claims Court
US Court of Appeals for the Federal Court

DEPARTMENT OF AGRICULTURE

DEPARTMENT OF COMMERCE

DEPARTMENT OF DEFENSE

DEPARTMENT OF EDUCATION

DEPARTMENT OF ENERGY

DEPARTMENT OF HEALTH AND HUMAN SERVICES

DEPARTMENT OF HOUSING AND URBAN DEVELOPMENT

DEPARTMENT OF THE INTERIOR

DEPARTMENT OF JUSTICE

DEPARTMENT OF LABOR

DEPARTMENT OF STATE

DEPARTMENT OF TRANSPORTATION

DEPARTMENT OF THE TREASURY

founding, but dissent in the party undermined their unity and Republican presidents then dominated the White House for nearly a half century. Today a Democratic President is back in the White House as Bill Clinton serves his second term in office.

The Republican party

Nicknamed the G.O.P., or Grand Old Party, the Republican party is the other major political party of the US. Initially formed in 1854 as an antislavery party, the Republican party quickly evolved its political platform to cover a wide range of other issues. Unlike the Democrats, Republicans originally favored a strong, central government over states' rights. Abraham Lincoln won the presidential election of 1860, becoming the first Republican president. The rivalry between the Democrats and Republicans is continually revisited in presidential and congressional races, as each party endeavors to gain political dominance. The symbol of the Republican party is the elephant, while the Democratic mascot is a donkey. Cartoonists often draw humorous battles between these animals to reflect the conflicting attitudes and approaches of the Democrats and Republicans.

Other parties

Although the Democrats and Republicans are the two major political parties in the United States, third parties have surfaced throughout US history to offer a new political platform with a strategy or philosophy that did not fall into Democratic or Republican parameters. To date, none of these parties has ever gained a sufficient following to win a presidential election.

• The Prohibition party, founded in 1869, was formed to fight for the outlaw of the use of alcoholic drinks.
• An offshoot of the Republican party, the Progressive party was also known as the Bull Moose party and was founded in 1912. It called for social and economic reform. Theodore Roosevelt ran as the party's unsuccessful presidential candidate.
• The US Communist party was founded in 1919 and supported the cause of communism.
• Founded in 1948, the Dixiecrat party, or States' Rights Democratic party, broke away from the Democratic party on an anti-civil rights platform.
• In the 1992 presidential election a third-party candidate, Texas billionaire Ross Perot, won an unprecedented 19 percent of the popular vote. He ran on a platform of budget deficit reduction. His Reform party was less successful in 1996.

The 50 States of the Union

State	Capital	Year of admission
Delaware	Dover	1787
Pennsylvania	Harrisburg	1787
New Jersey	Trenton	1787
Georgia	Atlanta	1788
Connecticut	Hartford	1788
Massachusetts	Boston	1788
Maryland	Annapolis	1788
South Carolina	Columbia	1788
New Hampshire	Concord	1788
Virginia	Richmond	1788
New York	Albany	1788
North Carolina	Raleigh	1789
Rhode Island	Providence	1790
Vermont	Montpelier	1791
Kentucky	Frankfort	1792
Tennessee	Nashville	1796
Ohio	Columbus	1803
Louisiana	Baton Rouge	1812
Indiana	Indianapolis	1816
Mississippi	Jackson	1817
Illinois	Springfield	1818
Alabama	Montgomery	1819
Maine	Augusta	1820
Missouri	Jefferson City	1821
Arkansas	Little Rock	1836
Michigan	Lansing	1837
Florida	Tallahassee	1845
Texas	Austin	1845
Iowa	Des Moines	1846
Wisconsin	Madison	1848
California	Sacramento	1850
Minnesota	St. Paul	1858
Oregon	Salem	1859
Kansas	Topeka	1861
West Virginia	Charleston	1863
Nevada	Carson City	1864
Nebraska	Lincoln	1867
Colorado	Denver	1876
North Dakota	Bismarck	1889
South Dakota	Pierre	1889
Montana	Helena	1889
Washington	Olympia	1889
Idaho	Boise	1890
Wyoming	Cheyenne	1890
Utah	Salt Lake City	1896
Oklahoma	Oklahoma City	1907
New Mexico	Santa Fe	1912
Arizona	Phoenix	1912
Alaska	Juneau	1959
Hawaii	Honolulu	1959

Presidents of the 20th century

In office	President	Party, state
1897–1901	William McKinley	Republican, Ohio
1902–1909	Theodore Roosevelt	Republican, New York
1909–1913	William Howard Taft	Republican, Ohio
1913–1921	Woodrow Wilson	Democrat, New Jersey
1921–1923	Warren Harding	Republican, Ohio
1923–1929	Calvin Coolidge	Republican, Massachusetts
1929–1933	Herbert Hoover	Republican, California
1933–1945	Franklin D. Roosevelt	Democrat, New York
1945–1953	Harry S. Truman	Democrat, Missouri
1953–1961	Dwight Eisenhower	Republican, New York
1961–1963	John F. Kennedy	Democrat, Massachusetts
1963–1969	Lyndon B. Johnson	Democrat, Texas
1969–1974	Richard M. Nixon	Republican, New York
1974–1977	Gerald Ford	Republican, Michigan
1977–1981	James Earl Carter	Democrat, Georgia
1981–1989	Ronald Regan	Republican, California
1989–1993	George Bush	Republican, Texas
1993–	William J. Clinton	Democrat, Arkansas

US involvement in 20th century wars

• Although World War I started in 1914, the US did not join the fray until 1917. It fought on the side of the Allies (France, Britain, and Russia).
• World War II began in 1939 but the US joined after the Japanese bombing of Pearl Harbor in 1941. The European war ended in May 1945. The US dropped two atomic bombs on Japan in August 1945, and Japan surrendered in September.
• Between 1950–53 the US was involved in a UN-backed war supporting South Korea against communist North Korea.
• The US involvement in the Vietnam War (1965–73) was both unpopular and costly.
• The US played a major role in the 1990–91 Persian Gulf War.

CULTURE & SPORTS

The influence of US culture can be seen all over the world, from fast foods such as hamburgers, hot dogs, and soft drinks, to characters from movies and TV shows. Baseball, rock 'n' roll, the lure of the open road, the empowerment of the car, and the simple vastness of the land – all are part of the mystique of America. The selling of this mystique has become a billion-dollar industry. The US is ethnically diverse – almost all of the population is descended from immigrants, and today it is increasingly Hispanic, Asian, and African-American. Often called a "melting pot" because of all the different peoples that live in the United States, the country does owe much to the blending of cultures that has occurred.

Baseball

Baseball is America's national pastime. The first game took place in Hoboken, New Jersey, in 1846. The National League was formed in 1876, the American League in 1901, and today baseball is the most popular spectator sport in the US. It is traditional for the President to pitch the first ball at the start of each new baseball season. The season concludes with the World Series, a set of games between the top-ranking teams in the National League and American League.

Football

The popularity of football is unique to the US. The National Football League season concludes in a televised game called the Super Bowl – a day-long event including an all-star show. Television networks compete for the rights to broadcast games of both college and professional teams.

Basketball

The National Basketball Association's popularity has grown tremendously in recent years. Twenty-eight teams play 82 games over the course of one season. Sixteen teams make the playoffs based on their season records. The winner overall becomes NBA champion. Athletes who distinguish themselves in the sport are sometimes honored by having their numbers "retired." The shirt bearing the player's number is raised – like a flag – in a formal ceremony.

NBA playoff winners

1968	Boston Celtics
1969	Boston Celtics
1970	New York Knicks
1971	Milwaukee Bucks
1972	Los Angeles Lakers
1973	New York Knicks
1974	Boston Celtics
1975	Golden State Warriors
1976	Boston Celtics
1977	Portland Trail Blazers
1978	Washington Bullets
1979	Seattle Super Sonics
1980	Los Angeles Lakers
1981	Boston Celtics
1982	Los Angeles Lakers
1983	Philadelphia 76ers
1984	Boston Celtics
1985	Los Angeles Lakers
1986	Boston Celtics
1987	Los Angeles Lakers
1988	Los Angeles Lakers
1989	Detroit Pistons
1990	Detroit Pistons
1991	Chicago Bulls
1992	Chicago Bulls
1993	Chicago Bulls
1994	Houston Rockets
1995	Houston Rockets
1996	Chicago Bulls
1997	Chicago Bulls
1998	Chicago Bulls

Super Bowls

Year	Winner	Year	Winner
1976	Pittsburgh (AFC)	1988	Washington (NFC)
1977	Oakland (AFC)	1989	San Francisco (NFC)
1978	Dallas (NFC)	1990	San Francisco (NFC)
1979	Pittsburgh (AFC)	1991	Giants (NFC)
1980	Pittsburgh (AFC)	1992	Washington (NFC)
1981	Oakland (AFC)	1993	Dallas (NFC)
1982	San Francisco (NFC)	1994	Dallas (NFC)
1983	Washington (NFC)	1995	San Francisco (NFC)
1984	Los Angeles (NFC)	1996	Dallas (NFC)
1985	San Francisco (NFC)	1997	Green Bay (NFC)
1986	Chicago (NFC)	1998	Denver (AFC)
1987	Giants (NFC)	1999	Denver (AFC)

World Series winners

Year	Winner	Year	Winner	Year	Winner
1912	Boston (A.L.)	1941	New York (A.L.)	1970	Baltimore (A.L.)
1913	Philadelphia (A.L.)	1942	St. Louis (N.L.)	1971	Pittsburgh (N.L.)
1914	Boston (N.L.)	1943	New York (A.L.)	1972	Oakland (A.L.)
1915	Boston (A.L.)	1944	St. Louis (N.L.)	1973	Oakland A.L.)
1916	Boston (A.L.)	1945	Detroit (A.L.)	1974	Oakland (A.L.)
1917	Chicago (A.L.)	1946	St. Louis (N.L.)	1975	Cincinnati (N.L.)
1918	Boston (A.L.)	1947	New York (A.L.)	1976	Cincinnati (N.L.)
1919	Cincinnati (N.L.)	1948	Cleveland (A.L.)	1977	New York (A.L.)
1920	Cleveland (A.L.)	1949	New York (A.L.)	1978	New York (A.L.)
1921	New York (N.L.)	1950	New York (A.L.)	1979	Pittsburgh (N.L.)
1922	New York (N.L.)	1951	New York (A.L.)	1980	Philadelphia (N.L.)
1923	New York (A.L.)	1952	New York (A.L.)	1981	Los Angeles (N.L.)
1924	Washington (A.L.)	1953	New York (A.L.)	1982	St. Louis (N.L.)
1925	Pittsburgh (N.L.)	1954	New York (N.L.)	1983	Baltimore (A.L.)
1926	St. Louis (N.L.)	1955	Brooklyn (N.L.)	1984	Detroit (A.L.)
1927	New York (A.L.)	1956	New York (A.L.)	1985	Kansas City (A.L.)
1928	New York (A.L.)	1957	Milwaukee (N.L.)	1986	New York (N.L.)
1929	Philadelphia (A.L.)	1958	New York (A.L.)	1987	Minnesota (A.L.)
1930	Philadelphia (A.L.)	1959	Los Angeles (N.L.)	1988	Los Angeles (N.L.)
1931	St. Louis (N.L.)	1960	Pittsburgh (N.L.)	1989	Oakland (A.L.)
1932	New York (A.L.)	1961	New York (A.L.)	1990	Cincinnati (N.L.)
1933	New York (N.L.)	1962	New York (A.L.)	1991	Minnesota (A.L.)
1934	St. Louis (N.L.)	1963	Los Angeles (N.L.)	1992	Toronto (A.L.)
1935	Detroit (A.L.)	1964	St. Louis (N.L.)	1993	Toronto (A.L.)
1936	New York (A.L.)	1965	Los Angeles (N.L.)	1994	Canceled
1937	New York (A.L.)	1966	Baltimore (A.L.)	1995	Atlanta (N.L.)
1938	New York (A.L.)	1967	St. Louis (N.L.)	1996	New York (A.L.)
1939	New York (A.L.)	1968	Detroit (A.L.)	1997	Florida (N.L.)
1940	Cincinnati (N.L.)	1969	New York (N.L.)	1998	New York (A.L.)

Music

Music forms most associated with the US are jazz, country, and rock. The south-east was the birthplace of jazz and blues, originally based on the spirituals and work songs of the African-American population. Country music began as poor people's music in the southern and western states, and the soul label Motown grew up in Detroit, or Motor City. Rock music began to develop in the 1950s and is a blend of several music styles, including rhythm and blues, country, and gospel. Its rebellious, youthful dance roots have undergone many transformations – rock has gone beyond entertainment. Its messages are often political, and songs combined with videos, popularized by television networks such as MTV, have become a powerful art form.

Television

No other society has anything quite like American network TV. Television's popularity spread like wildfire in the US. Between 1945 and 1960, the number of TV sets in the US climbed from 10,000 to 60 million! Today network TV programming is available to nearly everyone, and more than 60 percent of Americans have access to private systems, which can offer viewers hundreds of channels through cable networks and satellite TV. One of the most stunning achievements in American TV was the July 20, 1969, broadcast of astronaut Neil Armstrong's first steps on the Moon.

Radio

Before the rise of TV in the 1950s, radio was the most popular form of entertainment in US households. The period from 1920 to 1940 was nicknamed "The Golden Age of Radio." During this heyday, programs like *The Lone Ranger* and *Superman* kept families glued to their radio sets for hours. In 1938, up-and-coming actor Orson Welles vividly demonstrated radio's power. His reading of H.G. Well's novel *War of the Worlds* was so convincing that millions of people believed it was a real news broadcast, and that martians had landed in New Jersey. Less dramatic, but still popular, 90 percent of today's radio stations are commercial endeavors that feature music. There are more than 9,000 radio stations currently in operation in the US. The Federal Communications Commission (FCC) monitors the stations.

Entertainment

American TV has always been one step ahead – here are a few firsts:

- The first president to appear on TV was Franklin D. Roosevelt. He was filmed opening the New York Worlds' Fair, on April 30, 1939.
- The first baseball game to be televised was between the Brooklyn Dodgers and the Cincinnati Reds, at Ebbets Field, Brooklyn, New York. It was broadcast on August 26, 1939.
- The first professional football game to be televised was between Brooklyn and Philadelphia at Ebbets Field on October 22, 1939.
- The first TV commercial was for a clock company. The commercial lasted for 20 seconds and was broadcast by WNBT New York on July 1, 1941.
- The first soap opera on TV was *A Woman to Remember*. It was first broadcast by the DuMont network on February 21, 1947.
- The longest-running TV show is *Meet the Press*. It was first broadcast by the NBC network on November 6, 1947.
- The first televised atomic bomb explosion was an "Operation Ranger" detonation at Frenchman Flats, Nevada. It took place on February 1, 1951, and was televised by KTLA, Los Angeles.
- The first coast-to-coast color TV show was the Tournament of Roses parade at Pasadena, California. Its host was Don Ameche and it was seen in color in 21 cities nationwide when it was broadcast on January 1, 1954.
- The first live presidential news conference to be televised took place on January 25, 1961. President John F. Kennedy took part in the live broadcast from the auditorium of the State Department Building in Washington, DC.

Music records

The top ten best-selling albums of all time in the US are:
1. Michael Jackson, *Thriller*
2. Eagles, *Eagles – Their Greatest Hits 1971–1975*
3. Pink Floyd, *The Wall*
4. Billy Joel, *Greatest Hits Volumes I and II*
5. Fleetwood Mac, *Rumours*
6. Led Zeppelin, *Led Zeppelin IV*
7. Boston, *Boston*
8. AC/DC, *Back in Black*
9. Hootie and Blowfish, *Cracked Rear View*
10. Alanis Morissette, *Jagged Little Pill*   (*Source: RIAA*)

The top ten best-selling singles of all time in the US are:
1. Elton John, *Candle in the Wind 1997*
2. USA for Africa, *We are the World*
3. Whitney Houston, *I Will Always Love You*
4. Tag Team, *Whoomp! (There It Is)*
5. Elvis Presley, *Hound Dog*
6. Bryan Adams, *Everything I Do (I Do It For You)*
7. Los Del Rio, *Macarena*
8. Puff Daddy and Faith Evans, *I'll Be Missing You*
9. LeAnn Rimes, *How Do I Live*
10. Madonna, *Vogue*   (*Source: RIAA*)

Theater

Since the 1920s, the US has produced great theater talent – dramatists like Eugene O'Neill, Tennessee Williams, and Arthur Miller have transported the American experience to the stage in vivid dialogue and unforgettable characters. The heart of American theater is Broadway, in New York City, where elaborate shows are produced. The Tony Awards is a televised annual ceremony celebrating outstanding performances and productions of the preceding year. Awards are given for best performances by an actor, actress, by a supporting actor, actress, best director, best musical, best play, and in a host of other categories. Many innovative, if less elaborate, productions come to Broadway from smaller "feeder" theaters, known collectively as off-Broadway, or "off-off" Broadway. But theater flourishes outside New York as well. Most large cities have resident companies, and various regional, community, college, and university groups exist. Summer stock theater, in particular, brings the form to new venues – even the great outdoors.

The longest-running shows of all time on Broadway are:

Show	Performances
1. *Cats*	6,463*
2. *A Chorus Line*	6,137
3. *Les Misérables*	4,545*
4. *The Phantom of the Opera*	4,263*
5. *42nd Street*	3,486
6. *Grease*	3,388
7. *Fiddler on the Roof*	3,242
8. *Miss Saigon*	2,910*
9. *Hello Dolly!*	2,844
10. *My Fair Lady*	2,717

(* Still running – total at March 31, 1998)

Some Tony-award winners of the 20th century include:

Year	Best musical
1950	*South Pacific*
1960	*Fiorello*
1970	*Applause*
1980	*Evita*
1990	*City of Angels*

Year	Best play
1950	*The Cocktail Party*
1960	*The Miracle Worker*
1970	*Borstal Boy*
1980	*Children of a Lesser God*
1990	*The Grapes of Wrath*

INDEX

A

D

Grieg, Edvard 29
Griffith, Arthur 72
Griffith-Joyner, Florence 274
Griffiths, D. W. 34, 52, 56, 63, 67
Grissom, Gus 208
Grivolas, Claude 10
Gropius, Walter 66, 85
Grosz, George 66
Groves, Gen Leslie R 155
Gruelle, John 49
grunge 299
Guardian Angels 244
Guernica 115
Guest, L 69
Guevara, Ché 186, 187, 209
guide dogs 54
guillotine, abolished 253
Guimard, Hector 9
guitar 99, 183, 206
The Gulag Archipelago 228
Gulbenkian, Calouste 179
Gulf War 283
Gustav, Carl 57
Guyana: mass suicide 243
Guzmán, Abimael 323

H

Haber, Fritz 65
Habyarimana, Juvenal, Pres of
   Rwanda 292
Hadlee, Richard 280
Hagen, Walter 73
Hagenbeck, Carl 28
Hahn, Otto 58, 122, 213, 314
Haig, Field Marshal Douglas 53, 56
Haigh, John George 322
Haile Selassie, Emperor of Abyssinia
   (Ethiopia) 91, 97, 107, 229, 318
Hair 214
hairstyles 81, 88, 189, 204; perm 25
Haise, Fred 238
Haiti 184, 221, 266, 293
Hale Bopp comet 304
Haley, Alex 237
Haley, Bill 170, 181, 182
Hall of Fame 8
Halley's Comet 36, 259, 265, 266
Ham (first monkey in space) 192
Hamburg: bombing 139; zoo 28
hamburger, low-fat 283
Hamid, Sultan Abdul (of Turkey) 31
Hamilton, Thomas 300, 323
Hamlet 164
Hamlisch, Marvin 232
Hammarskjold, Dag 193
Hammerstein, Oscar 89, 149, 202,
   206, 321
Hammett, Dashiell 96, 104, 192
Hampton, Lionel 149
Hani, Chris 288
Hanks, Tom 313
Hanna, William 126, 211
Hannibal, retracing steps of 272
Happy Days 228
Hard, Darlene 184
Harding, W. G., Pres of USA 69
Hardy, Françoise 204
Hardy, Oliver 91, 184, 312
Hardy, Thomas 90
Harley-Davidson motorbikes 288

Harlow, Jean 95, 99
Harmer, Barbara 288
Harper, Ashby 257
Harris, Air Marshal Sir Arthur 148
Harris, Joel Chandler 31
Harrison, George 203, 204, 213
Harrison, Wallace Kirkman 167
Harroun, Ray 38
Harry, Prince 305, 306
Hart, Charles 267
Hart, Lorenz 112
Hart, William S 312
Haston, Dougal 234
hats 81, 90
Haug, Thorleif 78
Haughey, Charles, PM of Ireland 270
Hauptmann, Bruno 322
haute couture 121, 158, 178, 185
Havel, Vaclav, Pres of Czechoslovakia
   276, 277, 319
Hawaii 187, 284
Hawke, Bob 280
Hawking, Dr Stephen 274
Hayes, John 30
Hayworth, Rita 138
Heaney, Seamus 297
Hearst, Patty 229, 235
heart: artifical 257; monitoring 17;
   operations 145, 168; transplant 209,
   212, 213, 221, 228
Heartfield, John 66
Heath, Edward, PM of UK 228, 229
Heavy Metal 240
Heckler, Margaret 260
helicopter: air-sea rescue 153; Channel
   crossing 152; combat 154; early 29
heliport 164
helium, solid 30
Hemingway, Ernest 115, 172, 175, 193
Hendrix, Jimi 217, 219, 220, 321
Henke, Kurt 118
Henson, Jim 237
Henson, Matthew 35
Hepburn, Katharine 116, 134, 215, 312
Hepworth, Barbara 233
Hepworth, Cecil 43
Herald of Free Enterprise 270
Hergé (George Remi) 92
Herman, Woody 153
Hertzog, James 102
Herzegovina 34, 286
Hess, Rudolf 130
Hesse, Herman 157, 195
Heston, Charlton 171
Heydrich, Gen Reinhard 134, 147
Heysel Stadium 264
high jump 178
hijackers 235, 239, 264
Hill, Graham 218
Hillary, Edmund 173
Hills, Dennis 233
Hillsborough Stadium 275
Hilversum Town Hall 108
Himmler, Heinrich 150, 157
Hindenburg, P von, Pres of Germany 56
Hindenburg Line 64
Hingis, Martina 305
hippies 217
Hirasawa 322
Hirohito, Emperor of Japan 85, 156,
   275, 282, 318
Hiroshima 152, 169, 296

Hitchcock, Alfred 106, 118, 131, 157,
   191, 250
Hitler, Adolf 111, 119, 123, 258, 318;
   annexation of Austria 116;
   assassination attempt 144, 145; beer-
   hall putsch 77, 78; and Czecho-
   slovakia 118, 122; diaries, fake 258;
   German chancellor 102104; and Jews
   106; invasion of Rhineland 110; *Mein
   Kampf* 83; Nazi Party 100; suicide
   149, 157; World War II 125128, 130,
   136, 138, 144
Hitler Youth 117
Ho Chi Minh 153, 219, 222, 319
Hoffman, Dustin 209, 247, 275
Hogan, Ben 173
Holbrook, Richard 297
Holiday, Billie 187, 320
Holly, Buddy 183, 186, 321
Hollywood 121, 124, 152; first film
   36; McCarthyism 159; studios 79;
   superstars 312313; *see also* Oscars
Holocaust 138, 148, 150, 158
Holst, Gustav 57
Holt, Harold, PM of Australia 209
Homage to Catalonia 115
Home Alone 282, 297
home guard (Germany) 144
home movies 237
Honecker, Erich 277
Hong Kong 152; airport 307; architec-
   ture 254, 255; China and 261, 304
Hoover, J. Edgar 95
Hoover, Herbert, Pres of USA 91, 97-99
Hoover, William 22
Hoover Building, London 109
Hope, Bob 144
Hopkins, Gerard Manley 64
Hornby, Frank 10
horse racing 237, 235, 288; women
   jockeys 224, 230
hot pants 221
Hotel, tallest 308
hovercraft 187, 195, 213
Houdini, Harry 85
The Hound of the Baskervilles 12
Hounsfield, Godfrey 247, 315
House of Commons 42, 44, 67, 233,
   242; woman speaker 286
House of Lords 35
Houston, Whitney 271
Howard, Leslie 119, 137
Howe, Gordon 316
Hubble, Edwin 76, 280
Hubble telescope 280, 293, 303, 304
Hudson, Rock 265
Huckleberry Hound Show 211
Huerta, Adolfo de la 77
Huerta, Victoriano, Pres of Mexico
   46, 47
Hughes, Howard 118, 235
Hugo, Victor 10, 106
hula hoop 176, 177
Hulton, Edward 119
Humphrey, Hubert 214
Hungary 162; fall of communism 277,
   279; uprising 181, 185; *see also*
   Austria-Hungary
huskies 40-41
Hussein, King of Jordan 169
Hussein, Saddam, Pres of Iraq 246,
   251, 281

Huston, John 131
Hutton, J. E. 29
Hutton, Sir Leonard 118, 282
Huxley, Aldous 197
Huxley, Sir John 232
Huxley, Sir Julian 193
hydrofoil 197
hydrogen bomb, *see* nuclear weapons
hydrothermal vents 238

I

I Wanna Dance with Somebody 271
IBM 156, 248, 253
Ibsen, Henrik 24
ICBM missile 278
ice cream: on stick 68
ice hockey 78
Iceland 143
Ice-men 261
Ice-T 149, 298
ice-vending machine 98
iconoscope 77
Idris, King of Libya 219
Iliescu, Ion 281
immunology 67
Imperial Airways 103
Impressionism 67, 85, 275
In the Mood 124
Incas 38
income tax: PAYE 138
India 247, 301; assassinations 162, 261,
   284; and Bandit Queen 292; Bhopal
   disaster 261; British 16, 66, 156;
   cinema 168; earthquakes 20; elections
   206; famine 8, 138; "hippie trail" 217;
   irrigation 99; last passenger liner to
   219; nuclear tests 228, 307; and
   Pakistan 221, 307; political
   corruption 233; as republic 158, 159,
   164, 166; religions 159, 192, 217;
   riots 71, 72, 79, 84, 156, 159; salt tax
   76, 97; women 45, 231
Indianapolis 500 race 38
Indonesia 234, 287, 306, 309
Indurain, Miguel 317
ink, non-rub 276
insulin 71, 72, 83
intelligence test 20
International Brigade 114, 115
International Style 108
inventors 314-315
IRA 69, 224, 280, 289; bombings 122,
   126, 229, 246, 261, 271; ceasefire
   293, 300
Iran 276; American hostage crisis 247,
   250, 252; assassinations 253; death
   sentence on writer 275; earthquake
   214; Islamic republic 245, 246;
   millennium 308; Shah of 131, 202,
   243, 244; women's dress 231; *see also*
   Persia
Iran-Iraq war 251
Iraq: Arab League 152; army coup 185;
   Gulf War 283; hostages 281; king of
   123; Kuwait 192, 281; Saddam
   Hussein 246; and World War I 55
Ireland 28; Bloody Sunday 69; death
   of Collins 72; Easter Rising 55, 56;
   and EC 226; elections 66, 186, 206,
   270; emigration 26; Home Rule 42,

Quant, Mary 205
quantum theory 31
Quebec 212
Queen 234, 240, 241, 262, 285
Queen Elizabeth, HMS 47, 126, 214
Queen Mary 32
quinine 143
quintuplets, first surviving 104
Quisling, Vidkun 146

R

Rabin, Yitzhak 233, 289, 297, 319
Rachmaninov, Sergei 35, 136
radar: airborne 124; detecting aircraft
    106, 155; radar test 104
radiation sickness 174
radio: air-to-ground 54; first broadcasts
    25, 28; car radio 72; clockwork 308;
    comedy series 116; commercial
    station 227; daily drama serial 151;
    designs 241, 254; DJs 89; election
    results 69; electric diode valve 19;
    party political broadcast 158; pirate
    stations 205; quadrophonic 237;
    sports commentary 70, 88; time signal
    78; trans-Atlantic 11, 23; wartime
    132; *War of the Worlds* 119; wireless 85
radio telephone 29
radio telescope 186, 190
radioactivity 31
radium, isolation of 37, 72
ragga 299
Rahman, Abdul 184
railways 19, 98; elevated 309; straight-
    track, longest 219; *see also* trains
Rainbow Warrior 265
rainf orest 250, 268
Rainier III, Prince of Monaco 180
Rameses II, statue of 207
Ranger satellites 199
Rank, J. Arthur 111
Ranks, Shabba 299
rap music 298
Rasputin, Grigori 57, 60
Rathbone, Basil 124
rationing 54, 132-133, 140, 160-161
Ravel, Maurice 91
raves 299
Ray, James Earl 213
Ray, Johnny 70
rayon 21
razor: disposable 11; electric 76, 98
Reader's Digest 72
Reagan, Ronald, Pres of USA:
    attempted assassination 252;
    presidential elections 251, 261; "Star
    Wars" speech 258; summit with
    Gorbachev 265; in USSR 273, 278
Rebel Without a Cause 179
record player, portable 182, 188
records: digital 244, 284; double-sided
    22; electrical recording 69; million-
    seller 13; 45-rpm 164, 182; high-
    fidelity (hi-fi) 145; independent labels
    299; long-playing vinyl 162, 167; 33-
    rpm 167; 78-rpm 63, 182; mini disc
    284; most expensive recording session
    234; singles charts 169, 183
recycling 269
The Red Balloon 170

Red Brigade 242
Red Cross 219, 264, 292
Red Guards, China 207
Red Rum 237
Redford, Robert 219, 228, 313
Redon, Odilon 56
Reed, Carol 166
Reeve, Christopher 243, 296
reggae 240
Reinhardt, Max 139
relativity theory 21, 53, 66
R.E.M. 299
Remarque, Erich Marie 93
remote control, voice-operated 289
Renner, Karl, PM of Austria 149
Renoir, Auguste 78, 244
Renoir, Jean 116, 137, 244
resistance movement 146-147
restaurants 163, 188
Reuters News Agency 73
Reynolds, Albert, PM of Ireland 289
Reza Khan, Shah of Persia 83
Rhapsody in Blue 80
Rhee, Syngham, Pres of South Korea 163
Rhineland 96, 110
Rhodes, Cecil 12
Rhodes Scholarships 12
Ribbentrop, Joachim von 126
Richard, Cliff 258
Richards, Gordon 316
Richardson, Ralph 144
Richthofen, Baron Manfred von (Red
    Baron) 63
Rickenbacker, Adolph 99
Ride, Dr. Sally 258
Riefenstahl, Leni 105
Rimsky-Korsakov, Nikolai 30
Ringling Brothers 29
Rin Tin Tin 79
Rivera, Gen Miguel Primo de 77, 96, 98
RNA (ribonucleic acid) 162
road maps 86
The Robe 170, 173
Roberts, Dr. Alan 315
Robeson, Paul 138, 320
Robinson, Edward G. 95
Robinson, Jackie 158
Robinson, Mary, Pres of Ireland 282
Robinson, Sugar Ray 157
robots: domestic 260; toy 164
Robson, Lt. Col. 193
rocket: liquid fuel-propelled 84;
    Saturn V 201; toy 177; V-2 156
rocket engine 148
rocket-powered plane 159, 173, 181
Rockettes 120
rock 'n' roll 170, 182183
Rockwell, Norman 55
Rocky 236
Roddenberry, Gene 211, 304
Rodgers, Richard 112, 202, 206, 321
Rodin, Auguste 8, 10, 59
Roentgen, Wilhelm 76
Rogers, Charles "Buddy" 92
Rogers, Ginger 102, 103, 312
Rogers, Richard 237, 254, 255, 261
Rogers, Roy 170
Rohlfs, Roland 67
rollerblades 251
rollercoaster, tallest 293
Rolling Stones 198, 205, 218, 321
Rolls, Charles 19

Rolls-Royce 19, 102
Romananko, Yuri 271
Romania: 159, 279; and Ceausescu 277;
    National Salvation Front 281; World
    War I 56, 63; World War II 136
Rome 34; fascist march on 73;
    freedom of 142
Romero, Archbishop Oscar 250
Rommel, Gen Erwin 129, 135, 145
Roosevelt, Eleanor 149
Roosevelt, Franklin D., Pres of USA
    106, 117, 129, 130, 154; fourth term
    145, 148, 149; New Deal 99, 101; first
    president to be televised 123; second
    term 111; swearing in 102; third term
    128; World War II 124, 131, 139
Roosevelt, Theodore "Teddy", Pres of
    USA 12, 17, 19, 21, 34, 52; and
    teddy bear 13; youngest president 11
Rosenberg, Julius and Ethel 323
Rosenkavalier 38
"Rosie the Riveter" 141
Ross, Diana 198
Ross, Maj Ronald 13
Rotary Club 20
Rothstein, Arnold 322
Rotten, Johnny 241
Round, Dorothy 105
round-the-world: flight without refueling
    267; walk 229; yachtsman 288
Rousseau, Henri 37
Royal Air Force 63, 129, 142
Royal Command Performance 43
Royal Navy 38, 127
Royal Opera House 125, 307
Royal Philharmonic Orchestra 192
Royal Society 84
Royce, Sir Frederick Henry 19, 102
Rubik's Cube 244, 315
Rudolph, Wilma 191
rugby 219; first international 24;
    Women's World Cup 283; World Cup
    270, 296
Rushdie, Salman 275
Russell, Jane 173
Russell, Ken 234
Russia 12, 17, 26, 39; Bloody Sunday 20,
    60; Bolsheviks 17, 59, 61, 78, 89; civil
    war 67; Duma 21, 24, 25, 28; elections
    301; independence 285; invasion of
    Chechenia 293; millennium plans 309;
    pogroms 16; Rasputin 57; riots 10, 20,
    60; Tsar 58, 60, 64; White Russians 61,
    63, 64, 67; war with Japan 18-21, 37;
    women's suffrage 44; World War I 49;
    Yeltsin 289; *see also* USSR
Russian Revolution 60-61
Rust, Mathias 270
Ruth, Babe 53, 68, 228, 316
Rutherford, Ernest 31, 66
Rwanda: civil war 292, 301
Ryumin, Valery 250, 251
Ryun, Jim 207

S

Sabu 112
Sacco and Vanzetti 71, 89, 322
Sadat, Anwar, Pres of Egypt 220, 221;
    assassination 253; and Israel 239, 243, 244
Sagawa, Issei 323

Saigon 232
Saint-Exupéry, Antoine de 136
St. Laurent, Yves 185
St. Lawrence Seaway 186
St. Louis 18-19
St. Paul's Cathedral 253
St. Petersburg 20
St. Valentine's Day massacre 92, 95
Sakharov, Dr. Andre 234, 250
Salam, Abdus 315
Salazar, António de Oliveira 103
Salinger, J. D. 167
Salk, Dr. Jonas 172, 174, 315
Samsonov, Gen 49
San Antonio Rose 127
Sanders, Colonel 128
Sandinistas 245, 256, 258, 270, 280
Sandino, Augusto 318
Sandino, Gen Cesar 246
Sands, Bobby 252
Sanford, John 315
San Francisco: earthquakes 24, 276
Sansom, Odette 146
Santana 219
Sarajevo 48, 292
Sargrove, J A 158
Saro-Wiwa, Ken 297
Sartre, Jean-Paul 143, 250
Sassoon, Vidal 204, 205
satellites: communications 191, 194,
    202, 210, 290; environmental 284;
    first (Sputnik) 184, 200; first US
    185; *Ranger* 199; scientific 250;
    spy 198; weather 190
Saturday Night Fever 239, 241, 242
Saturn: rings 226, 251; space probes
    238, 251, 253
Saturn V rocket 201
Saud, Abdul Aziz ibn 84
Saudia Arabia: 84, 232, 247
Savitskaya, Svetlana 261
The Scarlet Pimpernel 20
Schiaparelli, Elsa 120, 121
Schick, Col Jacob 76
Schlieffen, Gen von 49
Schmeling, Max 117
Schneider, Ralph 166
Schockley, William 159
Schreck, Max 72
Schuschnigg, Kurt von 117
Schwarzenegger, Arnold 284, 313
Schwarzkopf, Gen 283
Schweitzer, Albert 169
Schwitters, Karl 54
science-fiction: films 170
scientists 314-315
scooter, Vespa 203
Scopes, John 82, 83
Scott, David 206, 221
Scott, Doug 234
Scott, Capt Robert 36, 4042
Scott, Tony 266
Scrabble 162
SCUBA aqualung 137, 155
The Searchers 171
The Secret Garden 38
Segar, Elzie Crisler 93
Segrave, Maj Henry 88
Sein Lwin, Pres of Burma 273
Seipel, Ignaz, Chancellor of Austria 89
Selznick, David O 126
Sendak, Maurice 196

ACKNOWLEDGEMENTS

Dorling Kindersley would like to thank the following:

Carlton Hibbert for all his help in finishing the book
Paul Cornish at the Imperial War Museum; the Fawcett Library; Hamish MacGillivray at the London Toy and Model Museum; Nick Hill and the staff at Eden Camp Modern History Theme Museum, Malton; and the staff at Paul Smith, Covent Garden
Jacket design: Mark Haygarth
Feature illustrations and maps: David Ashby
Editorial assistance: Alison Copland, Nancy Jones, Carey Scott, Nicki Waine
Design assistance: Emma Bowden, Tony Chung, Alex Clifford, Joanne Connor, Jason Lee, Anna Martin, Iain Morris, Darren Troughton
DTP assistance: Tamsin Pender
Picture assistance: Rachel Leach, Mariana Sonnenberg
Index: Marion Dent
Specially commissioned photography: Peter Anderson, Sarah Ashun, Geoff Dann, Steve Gorton, Alex Wilson
Additional photography: M. Alexander, Geoff Brightling, Jane Burton, Martin Cameron, Peter Chadwick, Tina Chambers, Andy Crawford, Geoff Dann, Philip Dowell, Mike Dunning, Neil Fletcher, Lynton Gardiner, Philip Gatward, Steve Gorton, Peter Hayman, Colin Keates, Roland Kemp, Dave King, Liz McAulay, Robert O'Dea, Stephen Oliver, Roger Philips, Martin Plomer, Dave Rudkin, James Stevenson, Clive Streeter, Matthew Ward, Daniel Weil, Jerry Young, Michael Zabé

Picture Acknowledgements

Abbrieviations key: FJ=Front Jacket, BJ=Back Jacket, FF=Front Flap, BF=Back Flap, SP=Spine, A=Above, B=Below, C=Centre, L=Left, R-Right, T=Top and for pages 304-315: col=column

The Publisher would like to thank the following for their kind permission to reproduce the photographs:

Jacket: Allsport/Shaun Botterill: BJ/cl; Royal Pavilion, Art Gallery and Museums, Brighton: FJ/c; Casio: FJ/tcr; Jean-Loup Charmet: FJ/tcr; Corbis-Bettmann: BF/1-8, FJ/bcr, BJ/bl; Early Technology: BJ/bc; Mary Evans Picture Library: FF/b, FF/tl; Ronald Grant Archive/Columbia: BF/1-10; Kobal Collection/Warner Bros.: BJ/tr, FJ/cl; Mirror Syndication International: BJ/cr; Robert Opie Collection: FJ/tl; Rex Features: BF/1-1, FJ/cr, /© Sega Enterprises Ltd. Sp/t, FJ/tr; Science Photo Library/James King Holmes/W. Industries: BF/1-11; Frank Spooner Pictures: FJ/bc, FJ/brTeddy Bear Museum, Stratford-upon-Avon/Roland Kemp: BJ/tc; Topham Picturepoint: FJ/bl, FJ/bc

Prelims and 1900–1909: 1 Corbis-Bettmann; 2 L Science Photo Library/NASA; 3 C The Kid, Kobal Collection/First National/Charles Chaplin; 4 B National Maritime Museum; 5 BC National Motor Museum Beaulieu; 5 BCL Design Council; 5 BCR Police Academy Museum, NY; 5 BL Hulton Getty Picture Collection; 5 RBC By courtesy of BT Archives; 5 TCL Hulton Getty Picture Collection; 5 TR Liz McAulay; 6 BL Science Photo Library/Starlight; 6 LC Corbis-Bettmann; 6TL Peter Roberts Coll. c/o Neill Bruce; 6 RC Gone with the Wind, 1939, Ronald Grant Archive/Ted Turner Entertainment; 7 ABR Colorsport; 7 BC Rex Features; 7 BCL Rex Features; 7 BCR Kobal Collection; 7 BL Cleopatra, 1963, Ronald Grant Archive/Twentieth Century Fox; 7 BR Hulton Getty Picture Collection; 7 LC Rex Features; 7 RC Popperfoto; 7 TL ESA; 7 TR Brighton Museum & Art Gallery; 8 BL Sonia Halliday & Laura Lushington Photographs; 8 BR Robert Opie Collection; 8 CR Mary Evans Picture Library; 8 L Topham Picturepoint; 8 TR Mary Evans Picture Library; 9 BL Corbis-Bettmann; 9 BR Corbis-Bettmann; 9 C Mary Evans Picture Library; 9 TL Corbis-Bettmann; 9 TR Mary Evans Picture Library; 10 BL Robert Opie Collection; 10 BR Corbis-Bettmann; 10 CA The Peter Roberts Collection/c/o Neill Bruce; 10 CB The Peter Roberts Collection/c/o Neill Bruce; 10 TL Topham Picturepoint; 10 TR Corbis-Bettmann; 11 BL Visual Arts Library; 11 BR Mary Evans Picture Library; 11 TL Picasso: Harlequin & His Companion, AKG London/© Sucession Picasso/DACS 1997; 11 TR Mary Evans Picture Library; 11 CR by Jacques & Hamley Bros, UK/London Toy &Model Museum; 12 BL Mary Evans Picture Library; 12 BR Corbis-Bettmann; 12 C Hulton Getty Picture Collection; 12 TL Cooper-Hewitt, National Design Museum, Smithsonian Institution, Art Resource, NY, Gift of Margaret Carnegie Miller, 1977-111-1a/c, photo by Dave King; 12 TR Voyage dans la Lune, 1902, Kobal Collection/Melies; 13 BL Corbis-Bettmann; 13 BR Mary Evans Picture Library; 13 CL © Frederick Warne & Co., 1902, 1987; 13 CR Teddy Bear Museum, Stratford-upon-Avon/Roland Kemp; 13 TL Mary Evans Picture Library; 14 CR Hulton Getty Picture Collection; 14 TL Corbis-Bettmann; 15 CL Robert Harding Picture Library; 15 CR Corbis-Bettmann; 15 TL Robert Opie Collection; 16 BL The Granger Collection, New York; 16 BR Bridgeman Art Library London/Louvre, Paris; 16 CL Mary Evans Picture Library; 16 CR Great Train Robbery, 1903, Kobal Collection/Edison; 16 TL Hulton Getty Picture Collection; 17 BL Corbis-Bettmann; 17 CL Corbis-Bettmann; 17 CR Mary Evans Picture Library; 17 T Action Images/Presse Sportss; 18-19 CR/CL Corbis-Bettmann; 18 BL Mary Evans Picture Library; 18 BR Mary Evans Picture Library; 18 C Mary Evans Picture Library; 18 TC Mary Evans Picture Library; 18 TL Bridgeman Art Library London/Victoria & Albert Museum, London; 19 BL Mary Evans Picture Library; 19 BR Corbis-Bettmann; 19 CR Mary Evans Picture Library; 19 TR Corbis-Bettmann; 20 BL AKG London; 20 BR Mary Evans Picture Library; 20 CL Corbis-Bettmann; 20 TL Mary Evans Picture Library; 21 BL Mary Evans Picture Library; 21 BR Mary Evans Picture Library; 21 C Hulton Getty Picture Collection; 21 TL Mary Evans Picture Library; 21 TR Matisse: The Open Window, Collioure, 1905, Bridgeman Art Library London/John Hay Whitney Collection, New York/© Sucession H. Matisse/DACS 1997;
22 BC Mary Evans Picture Library; 22 CL Science & Society Picture Library; 22 TR Science & Society Picture Library; 23 BL GEC-Marconi; 23 TC Mary Evans Picture Library; 23 TL Mirror Syndication International; 23 TR British Telecommunications plc; 24 BR Mary Evans Picture Library; 24 R Corbis-Bettmann; 24 TL Topham Picturepoint; 25 BC Hulton Getty Picture Collection; 25 BL Mary Evans Picture Library; 25 CR Private Collection; 25 TC Corbis-Bettmann; 25 TL Popperfoto; 25 TR AKG London; 26 BL Corbis-Bettmann; 26 BR Hulton Getty Picture Collection; 26 CR Corbis-Bettmann; 26 TL The Granger Collection, New York; 27 BC Corbis-Bettmann; 27 BL National Park Service, Statue of Liberty National Monument; 27 CL Corbis-Bettmann; 27 TL Hulton Getty Picture Collection; 28 BR Ronald Grant Archive; 28 CR Picasso: Demoiselles d'Avignon, 1906-07, AKG London/© Succession Picasso/DACS 1997; 28 TL Popperfoto; 29 BL Popperfoto; 29 CL Hulton Getty Picture Collection; 29 CR Mary Evans Picture Library; 29 CR Mary Evans Picture Library; 29 TR Hulton Getty Picture Collection; 30 BL Mary Evans Picture Library; 30 CR Robert Opie Collection; 30 TL Hulton Getty Picture Collection; 30 TR Smithsonian Institution; 31 BL Mary Evans Picture Library; 31 BR Popperfoto; 31 CL Hulton Getty Picture Collection; 31 TL Mary Evans Picture Library; 31 TR Mary Evans Picture Library; 32-33B National Maritime Museum; 32 C Retrograph Archive Ltd; 32 CL Retrograph Archive Ltd; 32 CR Hulton Getty Picture Collection; 32 TL Mary Evans Picture Library; 32 TR Mary Evans Picture Library; 33 BR Mary Evans Picture Library; 33 CL Mary Evans Picture Library; 33 TL Robert Opie Collection; 33 TR Retrograph Archive Ltd; 34 BR Corbis-Bettmann; 34 CR Ronald Grant Archive; 34 TL Kobal Collection; 34 TR Mary Evans Picture Library; 35 BL Mary Evans Picture Library; 35 BL Mary Evans Picture Library; 35 BR Hulton Getty Picture Collection; 35 CL Corbis-Bettmann; 35 CR Tony Stone Images; 35 TR Mirror Syndication International.

1910–1919: 36 BL Hulton Getty Picture Collection; 36 BR Popperfoto; 36 CL Corbis-Bettmann; 36 TL Mary Evans Picture Library; 36 TR Corbis-Bettmann; 37 BR Corbis-Bettmann; 37 BR Mary Evans Picture Library; 37 CR Hulton Getty Picture Collection; 37 TL Hulton Getty Picture Collection; 37 TR Corbis-Bettmann; 38 BL Mary Evans Picture Library; 38 BR Corbis-Bettmann; 38 CL Mary Evans Picture Library; 38 R Tony Stone Images; 38 TL Popperfoto; 39 BL Courtesy of the Manager, National Postal Museum; 39 BR The Granger Collection, New York; 39 R Corbis-Bettmann; 39 TL AKG London/Musee du Louvre; 40 B Illustrated London News Picture Library; 40 BL Illustrated London News Picture Library; 40 CL Illustrated London News Picture Library; 41 CR Popperfoto; 41 TR Popperfoto; 42 BL Popperfoto; 42 BR Mary Evans Picture Library; 42 CL Corbis-Bettmann; 42 CR Mary Evans Picture Library; 42 TL Archive Photos; 42 TR Mary Evans Picture Library; 43 BL British Film Institute; 43 BR Illustrated London News Picture Library; 43 C Corbis-Bettmann; 43 CR Hulton Getty Picture Collection; 43 TR Hulton Getty Picture Collection; 44 B Corbis-Bettmann; 44 C Mary Evans Picture Library; 44 CL Mary Evans Picture Library; 44 TL Mary Evans Picture Library; 44 TR Mary Evans Picture Library; 45 BC Mary Evans Picture Library; 45 BR Mary Evans Picture Library; 45 C Mary Evans Picture Library; 45 CR Mary Evans Picture Library; 45 TC Mary Evans Picture Library; 45 TL Mary Evans Picture Library; 45 TR Mary Evans Picture Library; 46 BL Archive Photos; 46 CR Mary Evans Picture Library; 46 TL Mary Evans Picture Library; 46 TR Corbis-Bettmann; 47 CR Corbis-Bettmann; 47 BL Barnes Collection; 47 TL Corbis-Bettmann; 47 TR Popperfoto; 48 BR Mary Evans Picture Library; 48 CL Hulton Getty Picture Collection; 48 TR Mary Evans Picture Library; 49 BL Mary Evans Picture Library; 49 C Ronald Grant Archive; 49 CR Illustrated London News Picture Library; 49 TL David King Collection; 49 TR Mary Evans Picture Library; 51 BR Corbis-Bettmann; 51 TL Popperfoto; 52 BL Imperial War Museum, London; 52 C Topham Picturepoint; 52 CL Birth of a Nation, 1914, Ronald Grant Archive/Epic; 52 TC Mary Evans Picture Library; 53 BL Hulton Getty Picture Collection; 53 BR Mary Evans Picture Library; 53 CL Imperial War Museum; 54 BL Dada poster, 1922 by Kurt Schwitters, Vintage Magazine Co. Archive./© DACS 1997; 54 BR Ronald Grant Archive; 54 CL Hulton Getty Picture Collection; 54 TL Hulton Getty Picture Collection; 54 TR Rex Features; 55 BR Popperfoto; 55 CR Mary Evans Picture Library; 55 TR Hulton Getty Picture Collection; 56 BL AKG London; 56 BR Ronald Grant Archive; 56 CR Popperfoto; 57 BL Topham Picturepoint; 57 BR Mary Evans Picture Library; 57 CR Mary Evans Picture Library; 57 TR Hulton Getty Picture Collection; 58 CL Imperial War Museum; 58 CR Mary Evans Picture Library; 59 BL Mary Evans Picture Library; 59 BR David King Collection; 59 CR Popperfoto; 59 TL Imperial War Museum; 59 TR Hulton Getty Picture Collection; 60 BL Mary Evans Picture Library; 60 BR David King Collection; 60 CR Popperfoto; 60 TL David King Collection; 60 TR David King Collection; 61 BL David King Collection; 61 BR David King Collection; 61 C David King Collection; 61 CA David King Collection; 61 TL Jean-Loup Charmet; 62 BL AKG London; 62 BR Corbis-Bettmann; 62 CR Corbis-Bettmann; 62 TL Mary Evans Picture Library; 63 BL Tarzan, 1918, Kobal Collection; 63 BR CinePlus; 63 CR Camera Press; 63 T Illustrated London News Picture Library; 63 TR Hulton Getty Picture Collection; 64 BR Corbis-Bettmann; 64 C Corbis-Bettmann; 64 TL Mary Evans Picture Library; 65 BL Topham Picturepoint; 65 BR Carmen,Ronald Grant Archive; 65 C Paul Nash: We are making a New World, Bridgeman Art Library London/Imperial War Museum, London/Reproduced by permission of the Paul Nash Trust; 65 CR Archive Photos; 65 TL Corbis-Bettmann; 65 TR Popperfoto; 66 BL Mary Evans Picture Library; 66 BR Corbis-Bettmann; 66 CL AKG London; 66 TR Ullstein Bilderdienst; 66 TR Hulton Getty Picture Collection; 67 BL Hulton Getty Picture Collection; 67 BR Bridgeman Art Library London/National Gallery, London; 67 C Mary Evans Picture Library; 67 CL Topham Picturepoint; 67 CR Felix the Cat, Kobal Collection; 67 TR Popperfoto.

1920–1929: 68 BL Marcel Duchamps: Fountain, AKG London/© ADAGP, Paris and DACS, London 1997; 68 BL Treasure Island, 1920, Kobal Collection; 68 CR Archive Photos; 68 TL Corbis-Bettmann; 68 TR Mary Evans Picture Library; 69 BL Corbis-Bettmann; 69 BR David King Collection; 69 CR Hulton Getty Picture Collection; 70 BL Robert Opie Collection; 70 BR Mary Evans Picture Library; 70 CR Four Horsemen of the Apocalypse, 1921, Ronald Grant Archive/Metro; 70 TL The Kid, Kobal Collection/First National/Charles Chaplin; 70 TR Hulton Getty Picture Collection; 71 BL Smithsonian Institution; 71 BR Mary Evans Picture Library; 71 CL Archive Photos; 71 CR David King Collection; 71 TR Corbis-Bettmann; 72 BL Reader's Digest; 73 BR Corbis-Bettmann; 73 BR Robert Harding Picture Library; 73 C Topham Picturepoint; 73 CL Topham Picturepoint; 73 TL Nosferatu, 1922, Ronald Grant Archive/Prana-Film GMBH; 73 TL Metropolis, 1926, Kobal Collection/UFA; 73 TR Mary Evans Picture Library; 74 BL Robert Harding Picture Library; 74 BR Mary Evans Picture Library; 74 CL Popperfoto; 74 TR Griffiths Institute, Ashmolean Museum; 74 TL Mary Evans Picture Library; 75 BL Ancient Art & Architecture Collection; 75 BR Mary Evans Picture Library; 75 BR High Clere Castle; 75 CR Mary Evans Picture Library; 75 TR Robert Harding Picture Library; 75 TL Peter Clayton; 6 BL Robert Opie Collection; 76 BR National Motor Museum Beaulieu/Dave King; 76 C Topham Picturepoint; 76 CL Corbis-Bettmann; 76 CR by Meccano, UK/London Toy & Model Museum; 76 TR Archive Photos; 77 BL David King Collection; 77 BR Mary Evans Picture Library; 77 CL AKG London; 77 CR AKG London; 77 T Hulton Getty Picture Collection; 78-9 C Hulton Getty Picture Collection; 78 BR Mary Evans Picture Library; 78 TL Topham Picturepoint; 78 CL by J.A.J., Paris/London Toy & Model Museum; 78 TR Corbis-Bettmann; 78 TR Mary Evans Picture Library; 79 BL Mary Evans Picture Library; 79 BL Robert Opie Collection; 79 BR Ronald Grant Archive; 79 CR Ronald Grant Archive; 79 TL Joel Finler; 79 TR Archive Photos; 80 BC Mary Evans Picture Library; 80 C Corbis-Bettmann; 80 TL Corbis-Bettmann; 81 CL Corbis-Bettmann; 81 CR The Granger Collection, New York; 81 TC The Sheik, 1921, Ronald Grant Archive; 81 TR Hulton Getty Picture Collection; 82 BL Corbis-Bettmann; 82 BR Mary Evans Picture Library; 82 C Hulton Getty Picture Collection; 82 CL Bridgeman Art Library London/Private Collection; 82 TR Corbis-Bettmann; 83 BL Corbis-Bettmann; 83 BR Hulton Getty Picture Collection; 83 CL Corbis-Bettmann; 83 TR Corbis-Bettmann; 84 BL Corbis-Bettmann; 84 BR Topham Picturepoint; 84 C Smithsonian Institution; 84 T Hulton Getty Picture Collection; 85 BL Mary Evans Picture Library; 85 BR Bridgeman Art Library London/National Gallery, London; 85 C Mary Evans Picture Library; 85 CL Redferns/Max Jones Files; 85 TL Archive Photos; 85 TR From Winnie-the-Pooh by A.A.Milne, line illustration by E.H.Shepard copyright under the Berne Convention, reproduced by permission of Curtis Brown, London. © 1926 by E.P.Dutton, renewed 1954 by A.A.Milne. Used by permission of Dutton Children's Books, a division of Penguin Books USA Inc.; 86 BL Mary Evans Picture Library; 86 CL Corbis-Bettmann; 86 CL National Motor Museum Beaulieu; 86 CLA National Motor Museum Beaulieu; 86 CR National Motor Museum Beaulieu/Dave King; 86 TL Mary Evans Picture Library; 87 BR Mary Evans Picture Library; 87 CR Mary Evans Picture Library; 87 TL Corbis-Bettmann; 88 BL Topham Picturepoint; 88 BR Mary Evans Picture Library; 88 C Topham Picturepoint; 88 TR Illustrated London News Picture Library; 89 BL Mary Evans Picture Library; 89 BR AKG London; 89 TL Illustrated London News Picture Library; 89 TR Ronald Grant Archive; 90 BL Liz McAulay; 90 BR Knudsens Fotosenter; 90 CL Illustrated London News Picture Library; 90 CR Steamboat Willie (Mickey Mouse), 1928, Ronald Grant Archive/© Walt Disney; 90 CR Illustrated London News Picture Library; 90 T Hulton Getty Picture Collection; 91 BL Corbis-Bettmann; 91 BR Archive Photos; 91 TL Archive Photos; 91 TR Mary Evans Picture Library; 92 BL Broadway Melody , 1929, Kobal Collection; 92 BR Chien Andalou, 1929, Kobal Collection/Bunuel-Dali; 92 CL Police Academy Museum, NY; 92 CR Robert Opie Collection; 92 TC Wings, Kobal Collection/Paramount; 92 TR Oscar® A. M. P. A. S./MOMI/Photo: Dave King; 93 BR Hulton Getty Picture Collection; 93 BR Topham Picturepoint; 93 CL Popeye, Ronald Grant Archive/Paramount; 93 CR Topham Picturepoint; 93 T Mary Evans Picture Library; 94-5 BR/BL Popperfoto; 94 BL Popperfoto; 94 CL

Topham Picturepoint; 94 TR Mary Evans Picture Library; 95 TR Police Academy Museum, New York; 95 BR Popperfoto; 95 C Public Enemy, 1931, Kobal Collection/Warner Bros.

1930–1939: 96 BL Hulton Getty Picture Collection; 96 BR All Quiet on the Western Front, 1930, Ronald Grant Archive/Universal; 96 CR Anna Christie, 1930, Ronald Grant Archive/MGM; 96 TR Science Photo Library/NASA; 96 TL David King Collection; 97 BL Colorsport/Olympia; 97 BR Hulton Getty Picture Collection; 97 LC Hulton Getty Picture Collection; 97 TL Hulton Getty Picture Collection; 97 TR Corbis- Bettmann; 98 BL Popperfoto; 98 BR Jean-Loup Charmet; 98 LC Popperfoto; 98 RC Hulton Getty Picture Collection; 98 TC Jean-Loup Charmet; 98 TR Hulton Getty Picture Collection; 99 BL Popperfoto; 99 BR Robert Harding Picture Library; 99 RC Hulton Getty Picture Collection; 99 TC Hulton Getty Picture Collection; 99 TL Hulton Getty Picture Collection; 100-01 Corbis-Bettmann; 100 BL David King Collection; 100 BR Robert Harding Picture Library; 100 C Corbis-Bettmann/UPI; 100 TR AKG London; 101 CR Corbis-Bettmann; 101 TL Roger-Viollet; 101 TR Robert Harding Picture Library; 102 BL British Film Institute/Dave King; 102 BL Popperfoto; 102 LC Jean-Loup Charmet; 102 RC King Kong, 1933, Ronald Grant Archive/RKO; 102 TC Hulton Getty Picture Collection; 102 TL Hulton Getty Picture Collection; 103 BL Mander & Mitchenson; 103 BR Little Women, 1933, Ronald Grant Archive/RKO-Radio; 103 C Popperfoto; 103 CR Corbis-Bettmann/UPI; 103 TL AKG London; 103 TL Popperfoto; 104-5C Corbis -Bettmann/UPI; 104 BC Science Museum/Dave King; 104 BL Hulton Getty Picture Collection; 104 LC Hulton Getty Picture Collection; 104 RC Hulton Getty Picture Collection; 104 TC Hulton Getty Picture Collection; 105 BL Hulton Getty Picture Collection; 105 BR Roger-Viollet; 105 TR Corbis-Bettmann; 106 BL Hulton Getty Picture Collection; 106 BR Hulton Getty Picture Collection; 106 LC Corbis-Bettmann; 106 TC David King Collection; 106 CR by Chad Valley, UK/London Toy & Model Museum; 107 BL Hulton Getty Picture Collection; 107 RC R.A.F. Museum, Hendon; 107 TL E.T. Archive/Imperial War Museum; 107 TR E.T. Archive/William Sewell; 107 BR by Copp Clark under licence from Parker Bros., USA/London Toy & Model Museum; 108 TR Hulton Getty Picture Collection; 108 TL Arcaid/Dennis Gilbert; 109 BCR Robert Harding Picture Library; 109 BL Tony Stone Images/Alan Smith; 109 TR Arcaid/Alberto Piovano; 110 BL Mayerling, 1936, Ronald Grant Archive/Associated British Pathe; 110 BR Corbis-Bettmann/UPI; 110 C E.T. Archive/Bundesarchiv, Koblenz; 110 TL Modern Times, 1936, Ronald Grant Archive/Roy Export Co.; 110 TR Hulton Getty Picture Collection; 111 BL David King Collection; 111 BR Mary Evans Picture Library; 111 C Popperfoto; 111 RC Popperfoto; 111 TL Topham Picturepoint; 112 BL Elephant Boy, 1937, Ronald Grant Archive/London/United Artists; 112 C Corbis-Bettmann-UPI; 112 CR Popperfoto; 112 TL Hulton Getty Picture Collection; 113 BL Hulton Getty Picture Collection; 113 BR Corbis-Bettmann; 113 LC Pictorial Press; 113 TC Jean-Loup Charmet; 113 TL Robert Harding Picture Library; 113 TR Snow White & the Seven Dwarfs, 1937, Ronald Grant Archive/© Disney; 114 BC Jean-Loup Charmet; 114 L Corbis-Bettmann/UPI; 114 TR Hulton Getty Collection; 115 BL For Whom the Bell Tolls, 1943, Ronald Grant Archive/Paramount; 115 BR Picasso: Guernica, 1937, Bridgeman Art Library London/Museo Nacional Centro de Arte Reina Sofia, Madrid/© Sucession Picasso/DACS 1997; 115 LC AKG London; 115 TL David King Collection; 115 TR David King Collection; 116 BL Corbis-Bettmann; 116 LC La Marseillaise, 1937, Kobal Collection/Societe de Prod. d'exploitation du film; 116 TL AKG London; 117 BL E.T. Archive/Imperial War Museum; 117 BR AKG London; 117 LC Hulton Getty Picture Collection; 117 RC Corbis-Bettmann; 117 TR Hulton Getty Picture Collection; 118 BL Hulton Getty Picture Collection; 118 BR Corbis-Bettmann/UPI; 118 CR Hulton Getty Picture Collection; 118 TC Hulton Getty Picture Collection; 119 BL Bridgeman Art Library London/Private Collection; 119 BR Alexander Nevsky, 1938, Kobal Collection/Mosfilm; 119 C Corbis-Bettmann; 119 TR Popperfoto; 120-1B After the Thin Man, 1936, Kobal Collection/M.G.M.; 120 BL Mary Evans Picture Library; 120 LC Corbis-Bettmann/UPI; 120 TL Hulton Getty Picture Collection; 121 AC Wothing Museum & Art Gallery/Liz McAulay; 121 BR Roger-Viollet; 121 CR Mary Evans Picture Library/Ernst Dryden Collection; 121 TL Mary Evans Picture Library; 121 TR Worthing Museum & Art Gallery/Liz McAulay; 122 BL Hulton Getty Picture Collection; 122 BR Popperfoto; 122 CR Stagecoach, 1939, Ronald Grant Archive/United Artists; 122 TC Hulton Getty Picture Collection; 122 TL AKG London/Erich Lessing; 122 TR BM/Peter Hayman; 123 BL Hulton Getty Picture Collection; 123 BR Hulton Getty Picture Collection; 123 CR Corbis-Bettmann; 123 LC Hulton Getty Picture Collection; 123 TR Corbis-Bettmann/UPI; 124 BL AKG London; 124 C Wizard of Oz, 1939, Ronald Grant Archive/MGM; 124 TL Popperfoto; 124 TR Popperfoto; 124 BR Sonia Halliday and Laura Lushington Photos; 125 BL Gone with the Wind, 1939, Ronald Grant Archive/Ted Turner Entertainment; 125 CR Corbis-Bettmann/UPI; 125 TL Robert Harding Picture Library; 125 TR Hulton Getty Picture Collection; 126 BL Grapes of Wrath, 1940, Ronald Grant Archive/Twentieth Century Fox; 126 BR Hulton Getty Picture Collection; 126 C AKG London; 126 LC Corbis-Bettmann/UPI; 126 RC AKG London

1940–1949: 127 BL Hulton Getty Picture Collection; 127 BR Hulton Getty Picture Collection; 127 C Popperfoto;127 TR Popperfoto;128 BL Popperfoto; 128 BR Le Dictateur, Ronald Grant Archive/Roy Export Co.; 128 CL Popperfoto; 128 CR Bridgeman Art Library London/Caves of Lascaux, Dordogne; 128 T AKG London; 129 BL Hulton Getty Picture Collection; 129 BR Hulton Getty Picture Collection; 129 CR AKG London; 129 TL Robert Harding Picture Library; 130 BL Robert Harding Picture Library; 130 BR Corbis-Bettmann/UPI; 130 C National Maritime Museum/Tina Chambers; 130 TL Corbis-Bettmann/UPI; 130 TR AKG London; 131 BR Corbis-Bettmann; 131 CL AKG London; 131 CR Mirror Syndication International; 132 BL Robert Harding Picture Library; 132 CR Corbis-Bettmann/UPI; 133 BL Hulton Getty Picture Collection; 133 BR Corbis-Bettmann/UPI; 133 TL Hulton Getty Picture Collection; 134-5 Hulton Getty Picture Collection; 134 BL Christie's Images; 134 BR Hulton Getty Picture Collection; 134 LC Hulton Getty Picture Collection; 134 RC Corbis-Bettmann/UPI; 134 TC Robert Harding Picture Library; 135 BL Corbis-Bettmann; 135 BR Hulton Getty Picture Collection; 135 LC Popperfoto; 135 TL Popperfoto; 135 TR Corbis-Bettmann; 136 BL Mander & Mitchenson; 136 BR AKG London; 136 C AKG London; TL Corbis-Bettmann/UPI; 136 TR Gallimard; 137 BL Topham Picturepoint; 137 BR Ronald Grant Archive; 137 C Popperfoto; 137 TL Hulton Getty Picture Collection; 137 TR Trustees of the Imperial War Museum, London; 138 BL Corbis-Bettmann-UPI; 138 BR Hulton Getty Picture Collection; 138 CL Popperfoto; 138 TR Magnum/Dmitri Baltermauts; 139 BL Science Photo Library/Andrew McClenaghan; 139 BR Popperfoto; 139 CL Corbis-Bettmann/UPI; 139 CR Hulton Getty Picture Collection; 139 TR AKG London; 140 BR Popperfoto; 140 C Corbis-Bettmann/UPI; 140 TL AKG London; 141 BR Popperfoto; 141 L Robert Harding Picture Library (FPG); 141 TR Advertising Archives; 142 BL Popperfoto; 142 BR AKG London; 142 CL Piet Mondrian: Composition No. III with Red, Yellow , Blue, 1935 , AKG London/© 1997 ABC/Mondrian Estate/Holtzman Trust; 142 CR Trustees of the Imperial War Museum, London; 142 TL Corbis-Bettmann/UPI; 143 BL Hulton Getty Picture Collection; 143 T Corbis-Bettmann; 144 BL Corbis-Bettmann/UPI; 144 BR AKG London; 144 TL AKG London; 144 TR AKG London; 145 BL Corbis-Bettmann/UPI; 145 BR National Velvet, 1944, Ronald Grant Archive/MGM; 145 CR Hulton Getty Picture Collection; 145 TL Robert Harding Picture Library; 145 TR Robert Harding Picture Library; 146 BL Roger-Viollet/LAPI-Viollet; 146 BR Corbis-Bettmann/UPI; 146 C Robert Harding Picture Library; 146 TL R.A.F. Museum, Hendon/Dave Rudkin ; 146 TR Trustees of the Imperial War Museum, London; 147 BL Pictorial Press Ltd; 147 TL Robert Harding Picture Library; 147 CL Carl Stranle; 148 BL AKG London; 148 BR Popperfoto; 148 C AKG London; 148 CL Corbis-Bettmann; 148 TR Popperfoto; 149 BR Corbis-Bettmann/UPI; 149 BR Mander & Mitchenson; 149 CL Corbis-Bettmann; 149 CR Hulton Getty Picture Collection; 149 TL Film Poster: Kinder der Olymp (Les Enfants du Paradis), AKG London; 150 BL British Film Institute; 150 BR Popperfoto; 150 TL Hulton Getty Picture Collection; 150 TR AKG London; 151 BL Corbis-Bettmann-UPI; 151 CL Popperfoto; 151 RC Popperfoto; 151 TL Robert Harding Picture Library; 151 TR Hulton Getty Picture Collection; 152 AC AKG London; 152 BL Corbis-Bettmann/UPI; 152 BR MIldred Pierce, 1945, Ronald Grant Archive/Warner Bros.; 152 CR Hulton Getty Picture Collection; 152 TL Corbis-Bettmann; 152 TR Corbis-Bettmann/UPI; 153 BL Robert Harding Picture Library; 153 BR Corbis-Bettmann; 153 CL Robert Harding Picture Library; 153 CR AKG London; 153 T Hulton Getty Picture Collection; 154 CL Robert Harding Picture Library; 154 TR Corbis-Bettmann; 155 BC Corbis-Bettmann; 155 RC Corbis-Bettmann/UPI; 155 TL Corbis-Bettmann/UPI; 155 TR Corbis-Bettmann; 156 BL Corbis-Bettmann/UPI; 156 BR Popperfoto; 156 TL Robert Harding Picture Library; 156 TR AKG London; 157 BL La Belle et La Bete, 1946, Ronald Grant Archive/Andre Paulve Productions; 157 BR Popperfoto; 157 CL Notorious, AKG London; 157 CR Corbis-Bettmann/UPI; 157 TL Hulton Getty Picture Collection; 157 TR Pictorial Press; 158 BL Corbis-Bettmann; 158 BR AKG London; 158 RC Ancient Art & Architecture Collection; 158 TR Anne Frank House © AFF/AFS , Amsterdam , The Netherlands; 159 BL Popperfoto; 159 BR Miracle on 34th Street, 1947, Ronald Grant Archive/Twentieth Century Fox; 159 CL AKG London/AP; 159 RC Corbis-Bettmann-UPI; 159 TC Quadrant Picture Library; 160 BL Hulton Getty Picture Collection; 160 C Hulton Getty Picture Collection; 160 TL Hulton Getty Picture Collection; 161 BL Corbis-Bettmann/UPI; 161 BR Hulton Getty Picture Collection; 161 TL Corbis-Bettmann; 161 TR AKG London; 162 BL Corbis-Bettmann/UPI; 162 BL Glasgow Museums; 162 CL Hulton Getty Picture Collection; 162 CR AKG London; 162 TL Popperfoto; 163 BC Corbis-Bettmann; 163 BL AKG London; 163 CL Corbis-Bettmann; 163 CR Hulton Getty Picture Collection; 163 TR Jackson Pollock: Alchemy, AKG London/Penny Guggenheim Collection, Venice/© ARS, NY and DACS, London 1997; 164 BL Oliver Twist, 1948, Ronald Grant Archive/Rank; 164 CR London Toy & Model Museum; 164 BR Corbis-Bettmann/UPI; 164 CL Hamlet, 1948, Ronald Grant Archive/Two Cites/Rank; 164 TL AKG London; 164 TR Hulton Getty Picture Collection; 165 BL AKG London; 165 BR Quadrant Picture Library; 165 CR Hulton Getty Picture Collection; 165 TC E.T. Archive; 165 TL Popperfoto; 165 TR Hulton Getty Picture Collection

1950–1959: 166 BR Popperfoto; 166 CLB Hulton Getty Picture Collection; 166 CRB Popperfoto; 166 TC Hulton Getty Picture Collection; 167 BL Hulton Getty Picture Collection; 167 BL Popperfoto; 167 BR Image Bank; 167 CRB Archive Photos; 167 TL Corbis-BettmannUPI; 168 BL Hulton Getty Picture Collection; 168 BR Kobal Collection; 168 BR Popperfoto; 168 CLB Hulton Getty Picture Collection; 168 CRB Hulton Getty Picture Collection; 168 TR Hulton Getty Picture Collection; 169 BL Hulton Getty Picture Collection; 169 CRB Sony U.K. Ltd; 169 TL Popperfoto; 169 TR Corbis-Bettmann/UPI; 170 BL Ronald Grant Archive; 170 BR The Day the Earth Stood Still, 1951, Ronald Grant Archive/Twentieth-Century Fox; 170 CR The Red Balloon, 1956, Ronald Grant Archive/Film Montsouris; 170 TL Popperfoto; 170 TR Blackboard Jungle, 1955, Kobal Collection/MGM; 171 C The Creature from the Black Lagoon, 1954, Ronald Grant Archive/Universal Picturey; 171 TL The 7th Voyage of Sinbad, 1958 , Ronald Grant Archive/Colombia Pictures, 1958; 171 TR Ben Hur, 1959, Ronald Grant Archive/MGM; 172 BL Popperfoto; 172 BR Popperfoto; 172 CL Northampton Museums & Art Galleries; 172 CRA Hulton Getty Picture Collection; 172 CRB Camera Press; 172 TR Hulton Getty Picture Collection; 173 BL Popperfoto; 173 BR Royal Geographical Society Picture Library; 173 CL Royal Geographical Society Picture Library; 173 CR Wild One Poster, 1954, Ronald Grant Archive/Colombia; 173 TR Corbis-Bettmann/UPI; 174 BL Camera Press; 174 BR Popperfoto; 174 CA Corbis-Bettmann/UPI; 174 CR Corbis-Bettmann/UPI; 174 TL Corbis-Bettmann/UPI; 175 BL Magnum/Henri Cartier-Bresson; 175 BR Topham Picturepoint; 175 CLB SCR Photo Library; 175 CRB Popperfoto; 175 TR Corbis-Bettmann; 176 BL Mattel UK Ltd/© Barbie; 176 TL Corbis-Bettmann; 176 BR by Matchbox/London Toy & Model Museum; 177 CA Robert Opie Collection; 177 TL HASBRO/© Action Man; 178 BL Topham Picturepoint; 178 BR Topham Picturepoint; 178 CLB Hulton Getty Picture Collection/Lucien Aigner; 178 CR The Seven Year Itch, 1955, Kobal Collection/20th Century Fox, 1955; 178 TL Corbis-Bettmann/UPI; 179 BL Hulton Getty Picture Collection; 179 BR Topham Picturepoint; 179 CR Mary Evans Picture Library; 179 TL Topham Picturepoint; 179 TR Pictorial Press; 180 BR Hulton Getty Picture Collection; 180 BL see 85 TR; 180 CB Night of the Sunflowers by Emil Nolde, Bridgeman Art Library London/© The Nolde Trust, Emil Nolde; 180 CRA Hulton Getty Picture Collection; 180 TL Corbis-Bettmann/UPI; 181 BL Corbis-Bettmann; 181 BR Popperfoto; 181 CLA Topham Picturepoint; 181 CLB Corbis-Bettmann/UPI; 181 CRB And God Created Woman, 1956, Kobal Collection/Crow/Vestron; 181 TR Popperfoto; 182 BL Redferns/Michael Ochs Archive; 182 C Robert Opie Collection; 182 CB Robert Opie Collection; 182 CR Rex Features; 182 TL Redferns/Michael Ochs Archive; 183 BR Redferns/Michael Ochs Archive; 183 CL Redferns/Michael Ochs Archive; 183 TR Robert Opie Collection; 184 BL Topham Picturepoint; 184 BR Topham Picturepoint; 184 CBL Hulton Getty Picture Collection; 184 CLA Corbis-Bettmann/UPI; 184 CRA © Random House New York, 1968; 184 CRB Corbis-Bettmann/UPI; 185 BL Popperfoto; 185 BR Hulton Getty Picture Collection; 185 CB Popperfoto; 185 CBL Hulton Getty Picture Collection; 185 CRA Hulton Getty Picture Collection; 185 TL Corbis-Bettmann; 186 BL Some Like It Hot, 1959, Ronald Grant Archive/United Artists; 186 BR Popperfoto; 186 C Corbis-Bettmann; 186 CL Corbis-Bettmann; 186 TR Corbis-Bettmann; 187 BL Image Bank/Kaz Mori; 187 BR Hulton Getty Picture Collection; 187 CLB Corbis-Bettmann; 187 TL Vintage Magazine Co. Archive; 188 BL Hulton Getty Picture Collection; 188 BR Popperfoto; 188 TL Popperfoto; 188 TR Hulton Getty Picture Collection; 189 CL Corbis-Bettmann; 189 TCR Robert Opie Collection; 189 TL Robert Opie Collection.

1960–1969: 190 BL Topham Picturepoint; 190 CLB Tony Stone Images/Ary Diesendruck; 190 CRB Topham Picturepoint; 190 TL Popperfoto; 190 TR Topham Picturepoint; 191 BL Hulton Getty Picture Collection; 191 BR Corbis-Bettmann; 191 CL Psycho, 1960, Kobal Collection/Paramount Pictures; 191 CRB Corbis-Bettmann; 191 TR Hulton Getty Picture Collection; 192 BL Topham Picturepoint; 192 BR Topham Picturepoint/Syndicated File Features; 192 CLB Popperfoto; 192 CRB Corbis-Bettmann; 192 TL Corbis-Bettmann; 193 BC Topham Picturepoint; 193 BL Corbis-Bettmann; 193 BR West Side Story , 1961, Kobal Collection/Mirisch Pictures; 193 TL Popperfoto; 194 BL Corbis-Bettmann; 194 BR Archive Photos; 194 CLB Magnum/Eve Arnold; 194 CRB Corbis-Bettmann; 194 TL Magnum/Nicolas Tikhomiroff; 194 TR Warhol: Campbell's Soup Can, 1962, Bridgeman Art Library London/Saatchi Collection, London /© ARS, NY and DACS, London 1977; 195 BL Amnesty International; 195 BR Camera Press; 195 TL Archive Photos; 195 TL Corbis-Bettmann; 195 TR Archive Photos; 196 BR Popperfoto; 196 CL Novosti; 196 CRB Corbis-Bettmann; 196 TC Harper Collins; 197 BL Corbis-Bettmann; 197 BR Sygma/P.Vauthey; 197 CRB Archive Photos; 197 TR Corbis-Bettmann; 198 BL Lillies of the Field , 1964, Kobal Collection/Rainbow Productions; 198 BR Hulton Getty Picture Collection; 198 CLB Corbis-Bettmann; 198 CRA Topham Picturepoint; 198 CRB Mirror Syndication International; 198 TL Corbis-Bettmann; 199 BL Hulton Getty Picture Collection; 199 BR Image Bank/Bruce Wodder,; 199 CLB Topham Picturepoint; 199 CR Corbis-Bettmann; 199 TC Fistful of Dollars, 1964, Ronald Grant Archive; 200 C Science Photo Library/Novosti; 200 TL Camera Press; 201 BL Science Photo Library/NASA; 201 CL Corbis-Bettmann; 201 TL Science Museum/Geoff Dann; 202 BL Corbis-Bettmann; 202 BR Popperfoto; 202 CLB Mary Poppins, 1964, Ronald Grant Archive/© Walt Disney; 202 TC Archive Photos; 203 BL Topham Picturepoint; 203 BR Corbis-Bettmann; 203 CLB Topham Picturepoint; 203 TC Archive Photos; 204 B Redferns/Val Wilmer; 204 C Hulton Getty Picture Collection; 204 TL Hulton Getty Picture Collection; 204 TR Corbis-Bettmann; 205 BL Mirror Syndication International; 205 R Camera Press/John S. Clarke; 205 TL Rex Features; 206 BL Popperfoto; 206 BR Mirror Syndication International; 206 CL Topham Picturepoint; 206 CR Magnum/Semyon Raskin; 206 TL Archive Photos; 206 TR Topham Picturepoint; 207 BL Popperfoto; 207 BR Magnum/Rene Burri; 207 CR Popperfoto; 207 TR Popperfoto; 208 BL Topham Picturepoint; 208 BR Camera Press; 208 CRA Corbis-Bettmann; 208 CRB Jungle Book , 1967, Ronald Grant Archive/© Walt Disney; 208 TL Hulton Getty Picture Collection; 209 BL Topham Picturepoint ; 209 BR Hulton Getty Picture Collection; 209 CLB Rex Features; 209 CRB Magritte: The Betrayal of Images: "Ceci n'est pas une pipe", 1929, Bridgeman Art Library London/ Los Angeles County Museum of Art/ © ADAGP, Paris and DACS, London 1997; 209 TL Archive Photos; 209 TR Topham Picturepoint; 210 BL Image Bank/ Eddie Hironaka,; 210 BR Corbis-Bettmann; 210 CB Popperfoto; 210 TL 2001 A Space Oddyssey , 1968, Kobal Collection/MGM; 210 TR Hulton Getty Picture Collection; 211 BL Corbis-Bettmann; 211 BR Corbis-Bettmann; 211 CLA Magnum/Martine Franck; 211 CRA Mirror Syndication International; 211 TL Magnum/Bruno Barbey; 212 BC Early Technology; 212 BL Early Technology; 212 BR Corbis-Bettmann; 212 CB Early Technology; 212 CLB Early Technology; 212 CR Planet Earth Pictures/Flip Schulke; 212 TL Pictorial Press; 212 TR Hermann Munster, Kobal Collection/Universal; 213 BL Star Trek, Kobal Collection/Paramount TV; 213 C Corbis-Bettmann; 213 CR Corbis-Bettmann; 213 TL Corbis-Bettmann; 214 BL Corbis-Bettmann; 214 BR Popperfoto; 214 CB Hulton Getty Picture Collection; 214 TL Corbis-Bettmann; 214 TR Corbis-Bettmann; 215 BL Mirror Syndication International; 215 BR Camera Press; 215 C Popperfoto; 215 TL Hulton Getty Picture Collection; 215 TR Corbis-Bettmann; 216 BL Magnum/Bruno Barbey; 216 CL Redferns/Elliot Landy; 216 CR Redferns/Elliot Landy; 216 TR Corbis-Bettmann; 217 CLB Pictorial Press; 218 BL Corbis-Bettmann; 218 BR Topham Picturepoint; 218 CL N.A.S.A.; 218 CRB Camera Press; 218 TR Mirror Syndication International; 219 BL Popperfoto; 219 BR Mirror Syndication International; 219 CLB Popperfoto; 219 CRB Popperfoto; 219 TC London Features International.

1970–1979: 220 BL Redferns/David Refern; 220 C N.A.S.A.; 220 TL Mirror Syndication International; 220 TR Topham Picturepoint/STF Adams; 221 BL Science Photo Library/NASA; 221 BR Redferns; 221 CB Rex Features; 221 CR Spectrum Colour Library; 221 TC Topham Picturepoint; 222-23 B Corbis-Bettmann/UPI; 222 CA Corbis-Bettmann; 222 CLB Corbis-Bettmann/UPI; 222 TR Corbis-Bettmann/UPI; 223 CLA Corbis-Bettmann/UPI; 223 CR Corbis-Bettmann/UPI; 223 TC Corbis-Bettmann; 223 TR Vintage Magazine Co. Archive; 224 BL Vintage Magazine Co. Archive; 224 BR Rex Features; 224 CRB Topham Picturepoint/AP; 224 TL Popperfoto; 224 TR Pictorial Press; 225 BL Rex Features; 225 BR Rex Features; 225 CLB Royal Pavilion, Art Gallery & Museums, Brighton; 225 CRB Magnum/Raymond Depardou; 225 TL Corbis-Bettmann/UPI; 226 BL Rex Features; 226 BR Topham Picturepoint/AP; 226 CL Popperfoto; 226 CR Corbis-Bettmann/UPI; 226 TC Rex Features; 226 TR Topham Picturepoint; 227 BL Pictorial Press; 227 BR Topham Picturepoint; 227 C Enter the Dragon, 1973, Kobal Collection/Concord/Warner Bros.; 227 CL Hulton Getty Picture Collection; 227 CRB Frank Spooner Pictures; 228 BL Rex Features; 228 BR Corbis-Bettmann/UPI; 228 CA Nike; 228 CB Science Photo Library/NASA; 228 L Rex Features; 228 TR Corbis-Bettmann/UPI; 229 BL Vintage Magazine Co. Archive/Conde-Nast; 229 BR Pictorial Press; 229 CLB Rex Features; 229 TL Corbis-Bettmann/UPI; 229 TR Corbis-Bettmann/UPI; 230 BL Corbis-Bettmann/UPI; 230 BR Hulton Getty Picture Collection; 230 C Corbis-Bettmann/UPI; 230 CRB "Les trois graces" Coll. Jacques Grinejoro/ © J. Ducange-TOP; 230 TR Vintage Magazine Co. Archive; 231 B Corbis-Bettmann/UPI; 231 CR Corbis-Bettmann/UPI; 231 TL Corbis-Bettmann/UPI; 231 TR Rex Features; 232 BL Camera Press/Novosti; 232 BR Corbis-Bettmann; 232 CA Rex Features; 232 CLB Frank Spooner Pictures; 232 CR Popperfoto; 232 TR Rugby Advertiser; 233 BL Hulton Getty Picture Collection; 233 BR Allsport; 233 CL Rex Features; 233 CR Science Photo Library/NASA; 233 CRB Popperfoto; 234 BL Rex Features; 234 BR Allsport/MSI; 234 CLB Rex Features; 234 CR Retna Pictures Ltd/Michael Putlano; 234 TC Rex Features; 234 TR © Texas Memorial Museum; 235 BL Konica; 235 BR Popperfoto; 235 C Popperfoto; 235 CR Popperfoto; 235 TL Topham Picturepoint; 235 TR Rex Features; 235 TR Rex Features; 236 BL Rex Features; 236 BR Rocky, 1976, Kobal Collection/United Artists; 236 C Rex Features; 236 TL Rex Features; 236 TR Rex Features; 237 BL Corbis-Bettmann/Everett; 237 BR Woodfin Camp & Associates; 237 CLB Mirror Syndication International; 237 TL Robert Harding Picture Library; 237 TR Popperfoto; 238 BL Science & Society Picture Library; 238 BR Rex Features; 238 CB Rex Features; 238 TL by Denys Fisher, USA/London Toy & Model Museum; 239 BR Reproduced by permission of the Post Office; 239 CLB Rex Features; 239 CR Topham Picturepoint/A.P.; 239 TL Redferns/Michael Ochs Archive; 239 TR Rex Features; 240 C MTV; 240 CB London Features International; 240 CL Retna Pictures Ltd/David Corio; 240 TL Rex Features; 241 BR © EMI Records; 241 R Saturday Night Fever, 1977, Kobal Collection/Paramount; 241 TL Rex Features; 242 BL Pixi Co, Paris; 242 CB Rex Features; 242 CR Rex Features; 242 TL Rex Features; 242 TR © Paws Inc., 1978; 243 BL Allsport; 243 BR Rex Features; 243 CLB Rex Features; 243 CR Superman, 1978, Kobal Collection/Warner Bros; 243 TL Rex Features; 243 TR Corbis-BettmannUPI; 244 BL Pictorial Press; 244 BR Science Photo Library/NASA; 244 CL Corbis-Bettmann/UPI; 244 CRB Rex Features; 244 TC Rex Features; 245 BL Vintage Magazine Co. Archive; 245 BR Rex Features; 245 CB Rex Features; 245 CLB Rex Features; 245 TL Science Photo Library/Alexander Tsiaras; 246 BL Popeye, Ronald Grant Archive/Disney/Paramount; 246 BR Camera Press; 246 C South American Pictures; 246 CR Frank Spooner Pictures; 246 TI Sony United Kingdom Ltd; 247 BR Kramer vs. Kramer, 1979, Kobal Collection/Columbia; 247 CL Mirror Syndication International; 247 CR Frank Spooner Pictures; 247 TL Rex Features; 247 TR London Features International/Joe Bangay; 248 BC Woodfin Camp & Associates/Jim Wilson; 248 BL IBM; 248 TL Science Photo Library/Charles Falco; 248 TR Science Photo Library/Alfred Pasieka; 249 C Design Council/Sinclair Research; 249 CL Casio; 249 CR Atari; 249 CRB Casio; 249 TR © 1996 KA Inc All Rights Reserved.

1980–1989: 250 BL Retna Pictures Ltd/Adrian Boot; 250 BR Rex Features; 250 CLB Rex Features; 250 TL Magnum/Sebastiao Salgado; 250 TR Woodfin Camp & Associates/Roger Werth; 251 BL Rex Features; 251 BR Frank Spooner Pictures; 251 CB Image Bank/John P. Kelly; 251 CLB London Features International; 251 CR Sygma; 251 TL Frank Spooner Pictures; 252 BL N.A.S.A.; 252 BR Redferns; 252 CLB Frank Spooner Pictures; 252 CR Rex Features; 252 TL Woodfin Camp & Associates/Jim Anderson; 253 BL MTV; 253 BR Camera Press; 253 CB Rex Features; 253 CR Frank Spooner Pictures; 253 TL Rex Features; 254 Bl © Ian Lambot; 254 C Alessi spa Italy; 254 Cl Duracell UK Ltd; 254 TL Yves Saint-Laurent-Rive-Gauche; 254 TR Swatch; 255 TR Rex Features; 255 BR Memphis, Milan; 255 CLA Attenborough Associates; 255 CLB © Royalton Hotel, New York; 256 BL National Museum of Photography, Film & T.V.; 256 BR British Film Institute; 256 CL Rex Features; 256 TR Frank Spooner Pictures; 257 BL Rex Features; 257 BR Rex Features; 257 CL Magnum/Peter Marlow; 257 CR Science Photo Library/Hank Morgan; 258 BL Natural History Museum, London; 258 BR Rex Features; 258 C Rex Features; 258 CLB Frank Spooner Pictures; 258 TL Frank Spooner Pictures; 259 BL Rex Features; 259 BR Frank Spooner Pictures; 259 CL Frank Spooner Pictures; 259 CRB Rex Features; 259 TC Frank Spooner Pictures/Christo & Jeanne-Claude; 259 TR Frank Spooner Pictures; 260 BL N.A.S.A.; 260 BR Allsport/Tony Duffy; 260 C Frank Spooner Pictures; 260 CR Redferns/Ebet Roberts; 260 TL Science Photo Library/NIBSC; 261 BL Ghostbusters, 1984, Ronald Grant Archive/Columbia; 261 BR Allsport/Steve Powell; 261 CR Rex Features; 261 LB Popperfoto; 261 TC Frank Spooner Pictures; 261 TL Frank Spooner Pictures; 262 B Rex Features; 262 CL Frank Spooner Pictures; 262 TL Rex Features; 262 TR Mercury Records; 263 BL Oxfam/B. Russell; 263 CL Red Cross/L. de Toledo; 263 TL Rex Features; 263 TR Frank Spooner Pictures; 264 BL Ericsson Mobile Communications AB; 264 CLB Frank Spooner Pictures; 264 CR Frank Spooner Pictures; 264 TL Rex Features; 264 BR Rex Features; 265 BL Allsport; 265 BR Ronald Grant Archive; 265 CB Redferns/Ebet Roberts; 265 CLB Frank Spooner Pictures; 265 CRA Sygma/A. Nogues; 265 TC Frank Spooner Pictures; 266 BL Frank Spooner Pictures; 266 BR Top Gun, 1986, Ronald Grant Archive/Paramount; 266 CLB Fuji; 266 CRB Science Photo Library/Jerry Lodriguss; 266 TL Frank Spooner Pictures; 266 TR Frank Spooner Pictures; 267 BL Frank Spooner Pictures; 267 BR Ronald Grant Archive; 267 CL Science Photo Library/Novosti; 267 CRA Science Photo Library/Lawrence Livermore Laboratory; 268 BL Greenpeace Inc./Venneman; 268 C Environmental Picture Library/Herbert Girader; 268 CLB Greenpeace Inc.; 268 CR Science Photo Library/Starlight; 268 TL Science Photo Library/Simon Fraser; 269 CL Science Photo Library/NASA; 269 TL Oxford Scientific Films/Rafi Ben-Shahar; 269 NBR Greenpeace Inc./Culley; 269 CA Greenpeace Inc./Hodson; 270 BR Popperfoto; 270 TL Sygma/ © John Hillelson Agency; 270 TR © Wally McNamee; 270 BL Reuters; 271 BL Redferns; 271 BR Frank Spooner Pictures; 271 CL Science Photo Library/Peter Menzel; 271 CR Rex Features; 271 TL Woodfin Camp & Associates; 271 TR Rex Features; 272 BL Rex Features; 272 BR Frank Spooner Pictures; 272 C Rex Features; 272 CLA Rex Features; 272 CR Rex Features; 272 TR Allsport/Adrian Murrell; 273 BL Rex Features; 273 C Rex Features; 273 CLB Topham Picturepoint/A.P.; 273 CR Science Photo Library; 273 TC Topham Picturepoint/A.P.; 274 BL Rex Features; 274 BR Rex Features; 274 CLA Rex Features; 274 CLB Allsport/Thierry Martinez; 274 CRB Rex Features; 274 TR Rex Features; 275 BL Topham Picturepoint; 275 BR Rex Features; 275 CB Topham Picturepoint/A.P.; 275 TL Woodfin Camp & Associates/Mike Yamashita; 275 TR Rex Features; 276 BL Woodfin Camp & Associates; 276 BR Moviestore Collection; 276 CL Rex Features; 276 CR Science Photo Library; 276 TL Woodfin Camp & Associates/Francois Perri/Cosmos; 276 TR Robert Harding Picture Library; 277 BL Rex Features; 277 BR Hulton Getty Picture Collection; 277 C Rex Features; 277 CR Mirror Syndication International; 277 TL Rex Features; 278 B Rex Features; 278 C Rex Features; 278 TL David King Collection; 279 BC Popperfoto/Anatoly Sapronenco; 279 BR Rex Features; 279 CL © Hasbro; 279 CR Rex Features; 279 TL Dr Strangelove, 1963, Kobal Collection/Hawk Films Prod./Colombia; 279 TR Corbis-Reuter/Bettmann.

1990–1996: 280 BL Rex Features; 280 BR Rex Features; 280 C Rex Features; 280 CLB Rex Features; 280 CRA Rex Features; 281 BL Popperfoto; 281 BR Frank Spooner Pictures; 281 CLB Science Photo Library/CUL/Eurelios; 281 CRB Frank Spooner Pictures; 281 TL Rex Features; 281 TR Rex Features; 282 BL Home Alone, Kobal Collection/Twentieth Century Fox; 282 BR Rex Features; 282 CL Magnum/Bruno Barbey; 282 CLB Popperfoto; 282 CRB Rex Features; 282 TR Popperfoto; 283 CLB Magnum/Bruno Barbey; 283 BL Magnum/Misha Erwitt; 283 TR Rex Features; 284 BL Terminator 2 , Kobal Collection/Carolco; 284 BL Rex Features; 284 CL Popperfoto; 284 CLB Frank Spooner Pictures; 284 CRB Rex Features; 284 TR Rex Features/ © Sega; 285 BL Frank Spooner Pictures; 285 BR Redferns/Suzi Gibbons; 285 CLB Popperfoto; 285 TR Popperfoto; 286 BL Popperfoto; 286 TL Katz Pictures/F. Horrat; 286 BR Image Bank/Bullaty/Lomeo; 286 CRA Science Photo Library; 286 CRB Popperfoto; 287 BL Magnum/Alex Webb; 287 BR Popperfoto/Bob Pearson; 287 CL Rex Features; 287 CLA Frank Spooner Pictures; 287 CRB Popperfoto; 287 TR Frank Spooner Pictures; 288 BL Allsport/Vandystadt Agence de Presse; 288 BR Jurassic Park, Kobal Collection/Amblin/Universal; 288 CR Katz Pictures/© Haviv-Saba/R.E.A.; 288 CRA Rex Features; 288 TL Topham Picturepoint/c.UPPA; 289 BL Image Bank,/Joseph Szkodzinski; 289 BR Image Bank,/Michael Salas; 289 CRB Magnum/Paul Lowe; 289 TL Popperfoto; 289 TR Popperfoto/Eric Feterberg - AFP; 290 BL Science Photo Library/Peter Menzel; 290 CLA Rex Features; 290 CRA Science Photo Library/Rosenfeld Images; 290 TL Science Photo Library/G.E. Astro Space; 291 CB Science Photo Library/James King/W. Industries; 291 CL Science Photo Library/Plailly/Eurelios; 291 TL Science Photo Library/Geoff Tompkinson; 291 TR Frank Spooner Pictures/© Walt Disney; 292 BL Allsport/Shaun Botterill; 292 BR Rex Features; 292 CL Popperfoto; 292 CLB Frank Spooner Pictures; 292 CRB Rex Features; 292 TR Frank Spooner Pictures; 293 BL Popperfoto; 293 BR Tony Stone Images/Demetrio Carrasco; 293 CRB Frank Spooner Pictures; 293 TL Popperfoto; 293 TR Topham Picturepoint; 294 BL Topham Picturepoint; 294 BR Rex Features; 294 C Popperfoto; 294 TR Rex Features; 295 BL Rex Features; 295 CL Rex Features; 295 CR Topham Picturepoint/Associated Press; 295 TL Rex Features; 296 BL Camera Press; 296 BR Popperfoto;296 CLB Rex Features; 296 CRB Magnum/Philip Jones Griffiths; 296 TR Popperfoto; 297 BC Rex Features; 297 BL Popperfoto; 297 BR Popperfoto; 297 CA Magnum/Stuart Franklin; 297 CRB Popperfoto; 298 BC Retna Pictures Ltd/Clemns Ricken; 298 CR Redferns/Mick Hutson; 298 TL Redferns/Des Willie; 298 TR Retna Pictures Ltd/Jay Blakesberg; 299 CLB S.I.N./Gene Simon Taylor; 299 BR Redferns/Ebet Roberts; 299 TR Redferns/Marc Marnie; 299 TL Retna/David Corto; 300 BL Popperfoto/Reuters; 300 BR Frank Spooner Pictures; 300 C Science Photo Library/NASA; 300 RC Popperfoto; 300 TL Topham Picturepoint; 301 BL Independence Day, 1996, Kobal Collection/Twentieth Century Fox; 301 BR Popperfoto/Reuters; 301 CL Popperfoto/Reuters; 301 CR Popperfoto/Reuters; 301 TL Popperfoto; 301 TR Frank Spooner Pictures; 302 BL Image Bank; 302 CL The Forster Company; 302 BR Popperfoto/Reuters; 302 TR W.S.Atkins; 302 TL Science Photo Library/Cern; 303 B Rex Features; 303 C Frank Spooner Pictures; 303 TR Science Photo Library/NASA; 303 TL Graphics Group, Ove Arup & Partners.

Century at a glance: 304 col.1/a Kobal Collection; 304 col.1/b Woman of Passion, Kobal Collection/United Artists; 304 col.1/c Kobal Collection; 304 col.2/a Ronald Grant Archive; 304 col.2/b Ronald Grant Archive; 304 col.2/c Ronald Grant Archive; 304 col.3/a The Sheik, 1921, Ronald Grant Archive; 304 col.3/b Corbis-Bettmann; 304 col.3/c C orbis-Bettmann; 304 col.3/d Corbis-Bettmann; 304 col.4/a Top Hat, 1935, Ronald Grant Archive/RKO; 304 col.4/b Corbis-Bettmann; 304 col.4/c Gone with the Wind, 1939, Ronald Grant Archive/Ted Turner Entertainment; 304 col.5/a Ronald Grant Archive; 304 col.5/b Corbis-Bettmann; 304 col.5/c Ronald Grant Archive; 305 col.1/a Corbis-Everett; 305 col.1/b Robert Harding Picture Library; 305 col.1/c Giant, 1956, Ronald Grant Archive/Warner Bros.; 305 col.1/d Calamity Jane, 1953, Kobal Collection/Warner Bros.; 305 col.2/a Robert Harding Picture Library; 305 col.2/b Ro nald Grant Archive; 305 col.2/c Lilies of the Field, 1963, Ronald Grant Archive/Rainbow Productions; 305 col.3/a The Godfather, 1971, Ronald Grant Archive/Paramount; 305 col.3/b Moviestore/Lucasfilms; 305 col.3/c All the President's Men, 1976, Ronald Grant Archive/Warner Bors.; 305 col.4/a Raging Bull, 1980, Ronald Grant Archive/Raging Bull; 305 col.4/b Moviestore; 305 col.4/c Moviestore; 305 col.5/a Silence of the Lambs, 1991, Ronald Grant Archive/Orion; 305 col.5/b Moviestore; 305 col.5/c Moviestore; 306 col. 4/a Corbis-Bettmann; 306 col.1/a Popperfoto; 306 col.1/b GEC-Marconi; 306 col.1/c Ronald Grant Archive; 306 col.2/b Corbis-Bettmann; 306 col.2/b Mary Evans Picture Library; 306 col.2/c Corbis-Bettmann; 306 col.2/c Science Museum/Science & Society Picture Library; 306 col.3/b Corbis-Bettmann/UPI; 306 col.3/c Corbis-Bettmann/UPI; 306 col.3/c Hulton Getty Picture Collection; 306 col.4/b AKG London; 306 col.4/c Corbis-Bettmann; 306 col.5/a Corbis-Bettmann/UPI; 306 col.5/b Rex Features; 306 col.5/c Rex Features; 306 col.5/d Corbis-Bettmann; 307 col.1/a Rex Features; 307 col.1/b Popperfoto; 307 col.1/c Science Photo Library; 307 col.1/d Hulton Getty Picture Collection; 307 col.2/a Popperfoto; 307 col.2/b Corbis-Bettmann; 307 col.2/c Rex Features; 307 col.3/a Topham Picturepoint; 307 col.3/b Rex Features; 307 col.3/c Science Photo Library/Anthony Howath; 307 col.3/d Science Photo Library/Cern; 307 col.4/a Science Photo Library/Peter Menzel; 307 col.4/b Frank Spooner Pictures; 307 col.4/c Frank Spooner Pictures; 307 col.5/a Science Photo Library/David Parker; 307 col.5/b Private Collection; 307 col.5/c Frank Spooner Pictures; 308 col.1/a Hulton Getty Picture Collection; 308 col.1/b Hulton Getty Picture Collection; 308 col.1/c Hulton Getty Picture Collection; 308 col.1/d Mary Evans Picture Library; 308 col.2/a Hulton Getty Picture Collection; 308 col.2/b Topham Picturepoint; 308 col.2/c Corbis-Bettmann/UPI; 308 col.3/a Corbis-Bettmann; 308 col.3/b Topham Picturepoint; 308 col.3/c Hulton Getty Picture Collection; 308 col.3/d Hulton Getty Picture Collection; 308 col.4/a Hulton Getty Picture Collection; 308 col.4/b Hulton Getty Picture Collection; 308 col.4/c Popperfoto; 308 col.5/a Hulton Getty Picture Collection; 308 col.5/b Popperfoto; 308 col.5/c Corbis-Bettmann; 309 col.1/a Hulton Getty Picture Collection; 309 col.1/b Hulton Getty Picture Collection; 309 col.1/c Corbis-Bettmann/UPI; 309 col.2/a Allsport/Hulton Getty; 309 col.2/b Corbis-Bettmann; 309 col.2/c Corbis-Bettmann/UPI; 309 col.2/d Colorsport; 309 col.3/a Colorsport; 309 col.3/b Colorsport; 309 col.3/c Allsport/MSI; 309 col.4/a Allsport/Steve Powell; 309 col.4/c Colorsport; 309 col.5/a Colorsport/Stewart Fraser; 309 col.5/b Colorsport; 309 col.5/c Allsport/Ben Radford; 309col.4/b Colorsport; 310 col.1/a AKG London; 310 col.1/b David King Collection; 310 col.1/c Mary Evans Picture Library; 310 col.2/a David King Collection; 310 col.2/d AKG London; 310 col.3/b Corbis-Bettmann/UPI; 310 col.4/b Hulton Getty Picture Collection; 310 col.4/c Mary Evans Picture Library; 310 col.5/a Hulton Getty Picture Collection; 310 col.5/b Hulton Getty Picture Collection; 310 col.5/c Hulton Getty Picture Collection; 310 col.5/d Corbis-Bettmann/UPI; 310col.2/b Mary Evans Picture Library; 310col.2/c David King Collection; 310col.3/a AKG London; 310col.3/c Mary Evans Picture Library; 310col.4/a Mary Evans Picture Library; 311col.1/a Popperfoto; 311col.1/b Corbis-Bettmann; 311col.1/c Corbis-Bettmann/UPI; 311col.1/d Popperfoto; 311col.2/a Corbis-Bettmann/UPI; 311col.2/b Corbis-Bettmann/UPI; 311col.2/c Corbis-Bettmann/UPI; 311col.2/d Rex Features; 311col.3/a Rex Features; 311col.3/b Topham Picturepoint; 311col.3/c Popperfoto; 311col.3/d Rex Features; 311col.4/a Sygma/A. Nogues; 311col.4/b Rex Features; 311col.4/c Popperfoto; 311col.4/d Rex Features; 311col.5/a Popperfoto; 311col.5/b Popperfoto; 311col.5/c Rex Features; 311col.5/d Frank Spooner Pictures; 312col.1/a Corbis-Bettmann; 312col.1/b Mary Evans Picture Library; 312col.1/c Mary Evans Picture Library; 312col.1/d Mary Evans Picture Library; 312col.2/a Corbis-Bettmann; 312col.2/b Corbis-Bettmann/John Springer Collection; 312col.2/c Kobal Collection; 312col.2/d Mary Evans Picture Library; 312col.3/a Hulton Getty Picture Collection; 312col.3/b Kobal Collection; 312col.3/c Corbis-Bettmann; 312col.4/a Corbis-Bettmann; 312col.4/b Corbis-Bettmann; 312col.4/c Kobal Collection; 312col.4/d Kobal Collection; 312col.5/a Popperfoto/Archive Photos; 312col.5/b Corbis-Bettmann/UPI; 312col.5/c Corbis-Bettmann/UPI; 312col.5/d Kobal Collection; 313col.1/a Corbis-Bettmann/UPI; 313col.1/b Kobal Collection; 313col.1/c Corbis-Bettmann; 313col.2/a Redferns/Val Wilmer; 313col.2/b Pictorial Press; 313col.2/c Redferns/David Redfern; 313col.2/d Pictorial Press; 313col.3/a Rex Features; 313col.3/b Pictorial Press; 313col.3/c Retna Pictures Ltd/David Corio; 313col.3/d Redferns/Richie Aaron; 313col.4/a Redferns/Mick Hutson; 313col.4/b Redferns/Lorne Resnick; 313col.4/c Redferns/Ebet Roberts; 313col.5/a Retna Pictures Ltd/Chris Taylor; 313col.5/b Redferns/Michael Linssen; 313col.5/c Redferns/Rogan Coles; 313col.5/d Frank Spooner Pictures; 314 col.2/a Hulton Getty Picture Collection; 314col.1/a Topham Picturepoint; 314col.1/b Peter Newark's Pictures; 314col.1/c Granger Collection; 314col.2/b Topham Picturepoint; 314col.2/c Peter Newark's Pictures; 314col.3/a Corbis-Bettmann; 314col.3/b Corbis-Bettmann; 314col.3/ci Corbis-Bettmann/UPI; 314col.3/cii Corbis-Bettmann/UPI; 314col.3/d Popperfoto; 314col.4/a Corbis-Bettmann/UPI; 314col.4/b Corbis-Bettmann/UPI; 314col.4/c Topham Picturepoint; 314col.5/a Hulton Getty Picture Collection; 314col.5/b Hulton Getty Picture Collection; 314col.5/c Topham Picturepoint; 315col.1/a Corbis-Bettmann/UPI; 315col.1/b Peter Newark's Pictures; 315col.1/c Popperfoto; 315col.2/a Corbis-Bettmann/UPI; 315col.2/b Hulton Getty Picture Collection; 315col.2/c Popperfoto; 315col.2/d Topham Picturepoint; 315col.3/a Hulton Getty Picture Collection; 315col.3/b Rex Features; 315col.3/c Rex Features; 315col.4/a Topham Picturepoint; 315col.4/b Rex Features; 315col.4/c Popperfoto; 315col.5/a Popperfoto; 315col.5/b Rex Features; 315col.5/c Associated Press Picture Library; 315col.5/d Frank Spooner Pictures.

Every effort has been made to trace the copyright holders. Dorling Kindersley apologises for any unintentional omissions and would be pleased, in such cases, to add an acknowledgement in future editions.

1950s

- 1950 Pass books become compulsory in South Africa.
- 1950 North Korea invades South Korea.

- 1952 *This is Cinerama* uses wide-screen system.
- 1952 Eva Perón, wife of Argentine president, dies.
- 1952 Crown Prince Hussein becomes king of Jordan.
- 1953 UK scientists reveal the structure of DNA.
- 1953 Miniature matchbox toy cars are an instant hit.

- 1953 Blue jeans become popular as leisure wear.
- 1953 New Zealander Edmund Hillary and Sherpa Tensing climb Everest.
- 1954 In the US, a new vaccine against polio is tested.
- 1954 UK athlete Roger Bannister runs a mile in under four minutes.

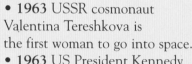

1960s

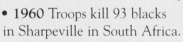

- 1960 Troops kill 93 blacks in Sharpeville in South Africa.
- 1960 Sirimavo Bandaranaike of Ceylon is the world's first woman prime minister.

- 1961 Democrat John Kennedy is sworn in as US President.
- 1961 East Germans build wall to separate east and west Berlin.
- 1962 US actress and sex symbol Marilyn Monroe is found dead.
- 1962 UK group The Beatles' first hit single is *Love Me Do*.

- 1963 USSR cosmonaut Valentina Tereshkova is the first woman to go into space.
- 1963 US President Kennedy is assassinated in Dallas.
- 1964 Vidal Sassoon creates sharp new hairstyles.
- 1964 Nelson Mandela is imprisoned in South Africa.
- 1964 Kenya is made a republic.

1970s

- 1970 King Hussein of Jordan and Yassir Arafat of the PLO sign a war truce.
- 1971 A microprocessor (chip) is developed.

- 1973 The Vietnam ceasefire is signed in Paris, but war does not end.
- 1973 Picasso dies in France.
- 1973 President Allende of Chile is assassinated.
- 1974 President Nixon resigns.
- 1974 Altair is the first small home computer manufactured.

- 1975 The Vietnam War ends as South Vietnam surrenders.
- 1975 A terra-cotta army is found by Chinese archaeologists excavating a tomb.
- 1975 Civil war breaks out in Angola after it gains independence.
- 1976 White police fire on children in Soweto, South Africa.

1980s

- 1980 Mount St. Helens volcano, in Washington, erupts.
- 1980 The Iran-Iraq war escalates.
- 1981 Nobel Peace Prize winner President Sadat of Egypt is assassinated.

- 1982 The French launch their telecom minitel on-line service.
- 1983 President Reagan of the US proposes a new defense system called "Star Wars."
- 1984 News reports of famine in Ethiopia stun people all over the world.

- 1984 Scientists warn of global warming (the greenhouse effect).
- 1984 The virus that causes AIDS is discovered.
- 1984 A chemical leak in the Indian city of Bhopal kills at least 2,000 people.
- 1985 Live Aid concert is watched by 1.5 million people.

1990s

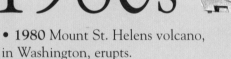

- 1990 The *Hubble Space Telescope* is launched from Cape Canaveral in the US.
- 1991 Coup in the USSR topples premier Gorbachev.

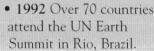

- 1992 Over 70 countries attend the UN Earth Summit in Rio, Brazil.
- 1992 Race riots rock Los Angeles, California.
- 1992 Personal color videophones are introduced.
- 1992 Film of conditions in Serbian death camps cause shock and outrage worldwide.

- 1993 Terrorists explode bomb under the World Trade Center in New York.
- 1993 Israeli prime minister Yitzhak Rabin and PLO leader Yassir Arafat sign peace accord in the US.
- 1993 Aboriginals in Australia win back land.
- 1993 Pop artist Prince changes his name to a symbol.